The Ascendance
of Israel's
Radical Right

The Ascendance of Israel's Radical Right

EHUD SPRINZAK

New York   Oxford
OXFORD UNIVERSITY PRESS
1991

Oxford University Press

Oxford   New York   Toronto
Delhi   Bombay   Calcutta   Madras   Karachi
Petaling Jaya   Singapore   Hong Kong   Tokyo
Nairobi   Dar es Salaam   Cape Town
Melbourne   Auckland
and associated companies in
Berlin   Ibadan

Published by Oxford University Press, Inc.
200 Madison Avenue, New York, New York 10016

Oxford is a registered trademark of Oxford University Press

Library of Congress Cataloging-in-Publication Data
Sprinzak, Ehud.
The ascendance of Israel's radical right / Ehud Sprinzak.
p. cm.   Includes bibliographical references and index.
ISBN 0-19-505086-X
1. Nationalism—Israel.
2. Israel—Politics and government.
3. Religious Zionism—Israel.   I. Title.
DS126.5.S64   1991
320.5'4'095694—dc20
90-26174

9 8 7 6 5 4 3 2 1

Printed in the United States of America
on acid-free paper

For Rikki

Acknowledgments

The research for this book was started in the summer of 1984 as my immediate response to two unexpected developments: the discovery in April 1984 of the "Jewish Underground" of Gush Emunim, and the July election of Rabbi Meir Kahane to the Knesset. At that time I first felt the need to think and talk about the Israeli radical right as a distinct political category, and to survey its social and cultural boundaries. I was very fortunate to have a prompt response to my ideas by the Jerusalem Van-Leer Foundation, which supported an early pilot study of the subject, and even more so to receive a generous grant from the Harry Frank Guggenheim Foundation to conduct a comprehensive study of the Jewish Underground and its cultural and political milieu. A residence fellowship for a year at the Woodrow Wilson International Center for Scholars, in Washington D.C., which was devoted to general reflection and writing on the relationship between violence and politics, was most helpful in the crystallization of this book. The actual writing of the first draft took place at the American University in Washington, D.C., where I spent the 1986/87 academic year as a Visiting Research Professor. Another fellowship from the Harry Frank Guggenheim Foundation, a small research grant by the American Jewish Committee, and the generous hospitality of the School of International Service of American University made it possible for me to completely devote myself to research and writing.

The names of the individuals whose knowledge and good judgment have helped me to rethink early conclusions, sharpen my arguments, and improve the manuscript are too numerous to be mentioned here. They include several colleagues at the Department of Political Science of the Hebrew University of Jerusalem, the high quality group of the 1985/86 Woodrow Wilson Fellows, my friends and colleagues from the Israel Study Association in the United States, who commented on an early paper I gave on the subject, my students in Jerusalem and the United States who were very challenging critics, and many more who have heard me talk on the subject in the last five years and made useful comments. I am especially grateful to Karen Colvard of the Harry Frank Guggenheim Foundation, who has demonstrated continued interest in this project and my work in general, and who has been especially patient about deadlines. Her friendship and continued support has been most important for me in hard times. Thanks go also to Yehuda Elkana and Alouf Hareven of the Jerusalem Van-Leer Foundation for their early encouragement and support, to my dear friend Shula Bahat of the American Jewish Committee and her colleague David Singer, the AJC's Director of Research, for their interest and support, and to my friends at the American University, Dean Louis Goodman and Louise Shelly for their gracious hospitality. I am especially grateful to my colleagues Charles S. Liebman, of Bar Ilan University, and Emmanuel Guttman, of the Hebrew University of Jerusalem, who spent many hours reading the entire manuscript, making useful suggestions and corrections, far beyond the call of duty. Shlomo Avineri, Itzhak Galnoor, and Abraham Diskin, friends and colleagues at my department have been very kind in reading and commenting upon a summary essay of the book. I cannot think of a kinder, more understanding, and helpful editor than Valerie Aubry of Oxford University Press. Not the least of her contributions to this book has been the recommendation to use the superb skills of David Frederickson as a line-editor. And last but not least my wife, Rikki. This book would probably have never been completed without her continued intellectual and emotional involvement. Rikki has served on occasions as my research assistant, academic consultant, and personal counsellor. But most frequently she was my harshest, though loving, critic. I owe her more than I can express.

Washington, D.C.   E.S.
January 1991

Contents

Chronological Table

70 A.D.

Jerusalem and the Second Temple are destroyed by the Romans; beginning of two millennia of Jewish exile.

1882

First Aliya to Eretz Yisrael; beginning of Zionism.

1887

August 29–31. Basel, Switzerland, First International Congress of Zionists, Theodor Herzl presiding.

1917

November 2. The Balfour Declaration; British government makes a commitment for a National Home for the Jews in Palestine
December. British conquest of Palestine.

1920

British Mandate established in Palestine.

1925

April. Vladimir Jabotinsky launches the Revisionist Movement.

1928

Brit Habirionim, an ultranationalist group, is established in Palestine.

1929

August. Arab riots start on the Temple Mount in Jerusalem; massacres of Jews in Hebron and Safed.

1933

January. Adolf Hitler becomes Chancellor of the Reich.

June. Mapai leader Chaim Arlozoroff is assassinated in Tel-Aviv; members of Brit Habirionim are arrested as suspect, but released for lack of evidence.

1936

April. Outbreak of Arab Revolt in Palestine, including massive anti-Jewish terrorism.

1937

David Raziel becomes Commander of Etzel and launches anti-Arab counterterrorism campaign.

July. The Peel Commission recommends the partition of Palestine between Jews and Arabs; first use of term "transfer."

1939

May. British White Paper repudiates partition, limits Aliya and land purchase, envisages an Independent Palestinian State.

September. Outbreak of Second World War.

1940

Spring. Abraham Stern splits Etzel, launches Lehi.

August. Jabotinsky dies in New York.

1942

February. Abraham Stern is caught by the British and shot point blank.

Summer. David Raziel is killed in Iraq while on intelligence mission for the British.

1943

Itzhak Shamir, Nathan Yelin-Mor, and Dr. Israel Sheib (Eldad) become joint commanders of Lehi.

1944

February. Menachem Begin, new Etzel Commander, declares a revolt against the British.

November. Lord Moyne, British Minister of State in the Middle East is gunned down in Cairo by Lehi members; the "Saison"—Hagana, and Palmach operation against Etzel and Lehi terrorism—starts.

1947

November. U.N. General Assembly passes Partition Resolution, which amounts to recognition of Jewish (and Arab) right for self-determination in Palestine; a civil war between Jews and Arabs breaks out in Palestine.

1948

May 14. The British leave Palestine; Ben-Gurion declares in Tel-Aviv the establishment of the State of Israel; the new state is invaded by five Arab armies.

June. The Altalena arms ship, brought by Etzel to Israel, is intercepted by the army, and finally sunk near Tel-Aviv; Etzel is dissolved, and Herut party is established by Menachem Begin.

September. Count Folke Bernadotte, the U.N. Mediator in the Middle East is assassinated in Jerusalem by Lehi members.

1949

Foundation of Chug Sulam, an extreme right-wing group, by Dr. Israel Eldad.

1956

October. Sinai Campaign; Israeli army defeats Egypt and captures Sinai; Israel evacuates Sinai in return for its demilitarization and free navigation in the Straits of Tiran.

1967

May 15. Egyptian army goes into Sinai, in violation of the 1957 understanding; the "longest month" begins.

May 23. Egypt's President Nasser unilaterally closes the Straits of Tiran to Israeli shipping; war is imminent.

June 5–11. The Six-Day War.

Summer. The Land of Israel Movement is established.

1968

Passover. Rabbi Moshe Levinger's group settles in Hebron's Park Hotel; Israeli government decides to establish a city, Kiryat Arba, adjacent to Hebron.

Summer. Rabbi Meir Kahane establishes the Jewish Defense League in New York City.

1971

September. Rabbi Kahane immigrates to Israel, establishes JDL-Israel, later to become Kach.

1973

Gariin Elon Moreh is established in Kiriyat Arba.

October 6–22. Yom Kippur War.

1974

March. Gush Emunim is officially established in Gush Etzion.

1975

The city of Yamit is established in northern Sinai.

December. Gariin Elon Moreh is allowed to stay in a military barrack in Kadum after seven previous forced evacuations.

1977

May 17. Likud wins national elections; Menachem Begin becomes prime minister.

November. President Sadat visits Jerusalem.

1978

September 17. Camp David Accords are signed between Israel, Egypt, and the United States; Banai is established in order to fight the Accords.

First meetings of the Jewish Underground; on the agenda: a plan to blow up the Dome of the Rock on the Temple Mount.

1979

September. The Tehiya party is established in Jerusalem.

1980

May 3. Six yeshiva students are murdered by a PLO squad in Beit Hadassah, Hebron.

June 2. The "Mayors Affair"; Cars of two West Bank mayors are blown up by the Jewish Underground.

The Knesset passes the Jerusalem Law, annexing Jerusalem to Israel, officially.

1981

November. The Tehiya wins three Knesset seats in national elections.

The Knesset passes the Golan Heights Law, officially annexing the Golan Heights to Israel.

1982

January–April. Struggle of the Movement to Halt the Retreat in Sinai; Yamit is evacuated as planned.

June. Israel invades Lebanon; the Tehiya joins Begin's coalition, with Yuval Ne'eman as energy and science minister.

1983

July. Members of the Jewish Underground attack Islamic College in Hebron, kill 3, wound 33.

1984

April. The Jewish Underground is caught red-handed while wiring five Arab buses. Tzfia group is established in the summer by Rabbi Israel Ariel to promote the ideas of the underground.

July. Rabbi Kahane elected to the Knesset; Tehiya-Tzomet get five seats, become third largest Israeli party, but remain in opposition to first Unity Coalition of Likud and Labor.

1985

Knesset passes anti-racism (anti-Kahane) law.

1987

Tzomet split from the Tehiya.

December. Outbreak of the *intifada.*

1988

Spring. General (res.) Rehavam Ze'evi establishes Moledet; calls for "transfer."

September. Kach is disqualified by Central Election Committee; Supreme Court upholds decision.

November. Radical right parties win seven Knesset seats, but remain in opposition; second Unity Government between Labor and Likud is formed.

December. "Algiers Statement"; Yassir Arafat recognizes U.N. 242 Resolution and agrees to a Palestinian state side by side with Israel.

1990

March—June. Unity Government breaks down; Shamir forms narrow right-wing coalition. Ne'eman, Eitan, and Cohen become members of cabinet.

October 8. Temple Mount eruption; 21 Palestinians killed.

November 5. Rabbi Meir Kahane is assassinated in New York City.

The Ascendance
of Israel's
Radical Right

Introduction

Israelis were stunned when they learned on April 27, 1984, that a plot to blow up five buses full of Arab passengers during a crowded rush hour had been only barely averted. Within days, twenty-seven suspected members of an anti-Arab terrorist network were arrested. Soon it was learned that the suspects had been responsible for an unsolved 1980 terror case in which two West Bank Arab mayors were crippled and three others saved only because of a last-minute failure to wire their cars. Several members of the group also claimed responsibility for a score of violent acts against Arabs including the murderous 1983 attack on the Islamic College in Hebron that took the lives of three students and wounded thirty-three.

The most shocking discovery was that the group had an elaborate plan to blow up the Muslim Dome of the Rock on Jerusalem's Temple Mount, the third most sacred site in Islam. The group had made a careful study of the sanctuary's construction, stolen a huge quantities of explosives from a military camp in the Golan Heights, and worked out a full attack plan. Twenty-eight precision bombs were manfactured that were meant to destroy the Dome without causing any damage to its surroundings. The architects of the operation planned to approach the place surreptitiously, but were ready to kill the guards if necessary, and therefore had bought special Uzi silencers and gas canisters. More than twenty skilled Israeli reservists were to take part in the operation. Only a last-minute split within the group kept the scheme from being attempted as planned in 1982. This is fortunate because the damage would have been enormous. A simulated war game at Harvard University concluded that conservatively it would have caused a new phase in the Middle-East conflict, a crisis broader, deeper, and longer-lasting than anything in the past. A less conservative estimation suggested the scheme could have triggered a third world war.

What surprised observers in April 1984 was not so much the existence of a terror group, as the identity of its members. They belonged to Gush Emunim ("the Bloc of the Faithful"), a fundamentalist religious group committed to establishing Jewish settlements in the West Bank (biblical Judea and Samaria). Though Gush Emunim was an aggressive (and sometimes even illegal) settlement movement, it had never openly embraced an ideology of violence. Its orthodox leaders asserted a biblically based Jewish claim to Judea and Samaria, but had never advocated deporting the Arab population.[1] Instead they professed the belief that a peaceful and productive coexistence with the Arabs, under a benevolent Israeli rule, was both possible and desirable. That any of these highly educated and responsible men, some of them high-ranking army officers and most of them heads of large families, would resort to terrorism was completely unexpected.

The exposure of "respectable" Jewish terrorism was followed, three months later, by another unexpected event: the election to the Knesset (Israel's parliament) of Rabbi Meir Kahane, an extreme religious fundamentalist and leader of the Kach ("Thus") party, which called for the expulsion of the Arabs from historic Palestine (Rabbi Kahane was murdered on November 5, 1990, in New York). Nearly 26,000 (1.3 percent) Israelis voted for Kach, including 2.5 percent of Israeli soldiers. Almost everybody remembered that it was Kahane who, since 1974, had publicly advocated T.N.T., which in his terminology stood for *Terror Neged Terror,* Jewish terrorism in reaction to Arab terrorism.[2]

Astonished Israelis did not have to wait long to discover what the new party was all about. A day after the elections, Kahane and his supporters held a victory parade to the Western Wall in old Jerusalem. Passing provocatively through the Arab section of the Old City, Kahane's excited followers smashed through the market, overturning vegetable stalls, hitting bystanders, punching the air with clenched fists, and telling the frightened residents that the end of their stay in the Holy Land was near, a kind of street brutality that has often been repeated since then, especially following anti-Jewish terror incidents. But instead of being shocked by the violence—until then seen only in old newsreels of pre-1945 central Europe or in modern scenes from Teheran—some Israelis liked what they saw. In fact, support for Kahane increased substantially. Polls conducted between the summer of 1984 and Kach's 1988 disqualification by the Supreme Court steadily gave him between 2.5 to 7 percent of the total vote. Several studies of high school students have shown an exceptional support for Kahane among the young: one found that about 40 percent said they agreed with his ideas and 11 percent said they would vote for him. A general atmosphere of forgiveness and "understanding" of the acts of the Jewish underground has also surfaced among many Israelis.[3]

The rise of religious fundamentalism, extreme nationalism, and aggressive anti-Arab sentiment in Israel since 1984 reveals a significant political and cultural process that has neither been fully recognized nor been named for what it is—the emergence of the Israeli radical right. It now appears that the broader Israeli nationalist right, which had been thriving since the Six-Day War (1967), has undergone a significant political and ideological transformation. The apparently unified political and ideological force unquestionably headed by Menachem Begin, the leader of Likud, has since 1978 become fragmented. This process of political and cultural differentiation, which was relatively unnoticed for several years, finally came into full maturation in 1984.

This book examines the significance of these developments for Israeli politics and public life. Its purpose is fourfold: to describe the conditions and events that produced Israel's radical right; to examine the theory and practice of the movements that compose it and trace their ideological origins; to gage the radical right's impact on Israel's political culture and institutions; and to assess the implications of radical right politics for Israeli democracy and national security.

The first part of the book traces the 1967–1984 evolution of the radical right. It examines the impact of the Six-Day War on the Israeli psyche and describes the early rise of the new territorial maximalism, the school which believes that Israel is entitled to all the territories it took from the Arabs, by right, and that these territories should be officially annexed. It shows that although the ideological seeds of the right-wing extremism were planted in the Israeli mind immediately following the Six-Day War, the radical right was only articulated politically in 1978, as a reaction to the Camp David Accords. Camp David was a bitter moment of truth for the burgeoning Israeli territorial maximalism. It revealed the great ideological divide between the moderate members of the nationalist camp, who were ready to make painful compromises for real peace, and the radicals who believe that no peace is more sacred than the territories.

The second part of the book focuses on the hard-core movements of the radical right: Gush Emunim (the Bloc of the Faithful), the messianic movement of the settlers in Judea and Samaria; the Tehiya (Renaissance) party, which has been trying to bridge the traditional gap between religious and secular Jews through the idea of the Greater Land of Israel; Tzomet (Crossroads), General (res.) Rafael Eitan's movement, a maximalist party with great appeal among the hard-core Labor settlement movement; Moledet (Homeland), the new party of General (res.) Rehavam Ze'evi, which demands to "transfer" all the Arabs of the West Bank to the surrounding Arab countries; and Kach, Rabbi Kahane's violent movement which was barred in 1988 by Israel's Supreme Court from running to the Knesset but whose ideas have remained popular among lower-class Israeli citizens.

The work concludes that, while the radical right does not pose an immediate threat to Israel's democratic system of government, it has made a significant contribution to the erosion of Israel's democratic culture, and may be more damaging in the future. The book's structure is as follows.

Chapter 1 identifies the radical right as a political camp and examines its main features as a distinct sociocultural phenomenon. The radical right is shown to consist of a relatively small number of true believers whose intense

dedication to their cause, penetration of all echelons of Israel's power structure, and strategic location in the occupied territories make their influence in
national politics much greater than their sheer number.

Chapter 2 traces the roots of the radical right in pre-1948 Zionist history. Four schools are examined: the ultranationalist tradition of poet Uri
Zvi Greenberg, Brit Habirionim and Lehi; the radical legacy of Vladimir
Jabotinsky and Betar; the "activist" tradition within the Labor movement;
the maximalist messianism of Rav Kook. The exploration of the old radical
right is concluded by an analysis of the decreasing historical relevance of this
school after the Holocaust and the establishment of the State of Israel.

Chapter 3 examines the impact of the Six-Day War on the Israeli mind
and describes the rise of the new territorial maximalism between 1967 and
1978, exhibited in the Land of Israel Movement, Gush Emunim, and the
Kahane movement. Also explored are several representative formulations of
the new territorial Zionism and the early confrontations of the movements
associated with this school and the Israeli government.

Chapter 4 traces the political articulation of the radical right. It shows
that the radical right emerged out of a split within the nationalist right and
was created as a reaction to the 1978 Camp David Accords which implied
significant territorial and political concessions by Israel, concessions the
radicals were unwilling to accept. The chapter describes the evolution of the
Tehiya party, the radicalization of Rabbi Meir Kahane, the emergence of
settler vigilantism in the occupied territories, the rise of of the Jewish Underground, and the struggle of the Movement to Halt the Retreat in Sinai.

Chapter 5 portrays Gush Emunim, the most vital component of the
radical right, its ideo-theology and its unique political style. It follows the
evolution of the movement's "invisible realm": the political, cultural, economic, and military structures of the West Bank settlers controlled by Gush
Emunim members, which make it a most powerful infrastructure for the
entire radical right. Also examined are the crises undergone by the movement throughout its history, the current conflicts and divisions within its
leadership, and Gush Emunim's interaction with the *intifada*, the Palestinian
uprising in the West Bank and Gaza.

Chapter 6 describes the three political parties that represent the radical
right in the Knesset: the Tehiya, Tzomet, and Moledet, which are shown to
be the product of exemplary leaders more than the creation of masses of
people and popular action. The analysis includes therefore a discussion of
the careers and political styles of the leading figures of the three parties and
an attempt to assess their personal contribution to the radical right. The
chapter describes the post-1984 legitimization of the idea of "transfer," a
Jewish-Arab population exchange that seeks to achieve the expulsion of the
Arabs of the occupied territories "in exchange" for the Jewish refugees from
Muslim countries. It also examines the relationships between the parliamentary radical right and the Likud, Israel's main right-wing party.

Chapter 7 focuses on the legacy of Rabbi Meir Kahane and the politics of his party, Kach, which was untill Kahane's assassination a one-man show of a true believer who was certain that present-day reality should be governed according to all the laws and injunctions of the Torah. Kahane's unique interpretation of Judaism, his legitimation of Jewish violence and terrorism, and his concrete plans for the expulsion of the Arabs are carefully examined. Kahane's political behavior, which combined a special blend of Jewish Social Darwinism with a penchant for violence, is portrayed as "quasi-fascist," and Kach as a loosely structured protest movement that attracts bitter people moved by fear and a deep sense of social alienation.

Chapter 8 deals with the religious individuals and groups whose ideologies and politics lie between Gush Emunim and Rabbi Kahane, but who feel uncomfortable with both. These are the "cultural radicals"; most are as radical as Kahane, but rather than joining his politics, they have focused on bringing about a cultural revolution in the nation. Exemplars are the ideologist of the Jewish Underground, Yehuda Etzion, with his grand theology of active redemption, the Tzfia (Looking Ahead) association and Rabbi Israel Ariel, critics of Gush Emunim, and Yoel Lerner and other former Kahane associates. The contribution of the cultural radicals to the intensifying struggle over the Temple Mount is also examined. The chapter's conclusion is that while the cultural radicals may not have a large following or organized political power, they do play an important role in the collective consciousness of the radical right.

Chapter 9 examines the attitude of the radical right toward Israeli democracy, attempts to place its various schools in the context of a century of Zionist history, and speculates about its future. It is shown that while most radicals accept the legitimacy of the Israeli regime, the "democracy" they see themselves part of is narrow and incomplete. An inquiry of the Zionist origins of the radical right suggests that most of its movements are rooted in classical Zionism, but that the old radical right was marginal, and played a minor role in the creation of the State of Israel. The chapter is concluded by an examination of the impact of the *intifada* on the radical right, and by two alternative scenarios regarding its future.

1

What Is the Radical Right? A Political and Cultural Profile

The Radical Right: Historical and Theoretical Perspectives

The key concept this work uses in describing the rise of the new Israeli ultranationalist camp is the "radical right," a common term that has never been satisfactorily clarified. It was first developed in the 1950s and 1960s to denote the populist and anti-Communist extreme right in America, and then expanded backwards to include the large ultranationalist camp that emerged in Europe between the two world wars. But this theoretical expansion produced two different concepts of radical right which have never been the same. In the European context the concept has been used to characterize the powerful authoritarian, militaristic, anti-socialist, and anti-democratic school whose intellectual roots go back to the 1880s, but whose political fortunes only rose after the end of World War I. This classical radical right was an equal party to the great ideological struggle between Socialism, Communism and Liberal Democracy for the "soul" of Western Civilization. The rise of fervent nationalism in newly established states following the dissolution of Imperial Russia and the Habsburg Monarchy, the crisis of the Weimar Republic in Germany, the emergence of Italian Fascism, Pilsudski's victory in Poland, the depression of 1929, Hitler's 1933 takeover and the Civil War in Spain have all contributed to a great instability in Europe and to a pervasive belief that a new civilization could be created, an alternative to democracy and socialism, based on the supremacy of the nation and the virtuous activity of political elites.[1]

The most known products of the classical European radical right had been Italian Fascism and German Nazism, but the phenomenon was intellectually and politically much wider. Not only was the new *weltanschauung* extremely hostile to the Soviet Union and its communist message, but it implied a complete delegitimation of bourgeois society and liberal democracy. Having been perceived as representing moral relativism, compromise, and unending parliamentary debate, both were portrayed as soft, sluggish, unable to meet the communist challenge and unfit to serve the national genius.[2]

The classical radical right was born out of repressed national pride, humiliating minority status, and violated geographical borders. It was just natural that its spokespersons reacted by glorifying the nation, sanctifying ancient borders, and practicing aggressive foreign policy and militarism. On occasions they displayed fervent religiosity or a "nationalized" neo-religiosity.[3]

The American scholars who discovered the radical right in the mid-1950s, very much through the unexpected popularity of Senator Joseph MacCarthy, have associated the concept with a somewhat different phenomenon. Sociologists such as Daniel Bell, Seymour Martin Lipset, Edward Shils, Talcott Parsons, David Riesman, and historian Richard Hofstadter[4] used the "radical right" to denote a wide variety of groups and small political parties that rekindled a special American tradition of right-wing radicalism. This old school of nativism, populism, and hostility to central government was said to have developed into the post-World War II combination of ultranationalism and anti-communism, Christian fundamentalism, militaristic orientation, and anti-alien sentiment.[5]

The American radical right was recognized to be made of "political groupings or ideological coalitions occupying the political terrain between (but not including) Midwestern Republicanism and American Fascism."[6] Its most recognized organization was the John Birch Society, and it further included such organizations and associations as The American Coalition of Patriotic Societies, The American Security Council, Cardinal Mindszenty Foundation, Veritas Foundation, The Christian Anti-Communism Crusade, The Minuteman, Young Americans for Freedom, and many others.

The concept of the radical right had been useful in the American context for two reasons: it was instrumental in accounting for "status politics"—the attraction of "status losers" in society to extremist xenophobic groups,[7]— and it helped to allocate a special conceptual space to a political school that could neither be put in the same category of the moderate Republican right nor be associated with revolutionary Fascism. While being truly extreme, most of the groups that were gathered under the radical right umbrella were very American. They espoused the constitution (according to their own interpretation), revered the founding fathers, and said they were the true representatives of "the American way of life" which the liberals, the communists, the Catholics, the blacks, the Jews, and the "big bureaucrats" had conspired to destroy.[8]

A comparative examination of the European "classical" radical right and the American postwar radical right reveals a very meaningful historical and conceptual disparity. While the European radical right was in the 1930s a major contender for the ideological hegemony of Western Civilization, both intellectually and politically, American right-wing extremism has always been a local and marginal phenomenon. Also, the classical radical right was perceived by most of its adherents as an *alternative* to the entire democratic order while most of the groups belonging to the latter have only been opposed to *certain elements of American democracy*. There is no question that despite some ideological and behavioral similarities between the two there is also a marked difference.[9] While the entire European radical right was close to the model of revolutionary Fascism, the American radical right has been republican, conservative, and reactionary at most. Most right-wing American extremists believe that the desired American revolution has already taken place but that it has been betrayed by modern pluralist democracy and central government.

This work follows the American model of the radical right, not the European. There is, to be sure, very little agreement between the Israeli radical right, the American extreme right, and similar present-day European extremist movements that naturally draw upon different intellectual and religious traditions. Yet the term seems useful in the Israeli context for almost the same reasons it was found useful by the American sociologists in the 1950s and 1960s. The political camp that has emerged in the last two decades does not fit the traditional features of the Israeli nationalist right, yet it is also not revolutionary or fascist. Instead it is ultranationalist, extralegal, hostile to pluralist democracy with the movements and parties of this camp earnestly believing that they are exclusively the true Israelis and the genuine Zionists. While the Israeli right-wing extremists are obviously not anti-semitic as most Christian radical right groups are, they display many xenophobic features and often express ethnic discrimination and Social Darwinism.

The Radical Right as an Israeli Paradox

To understand the political and cultural change brought about in Israel by the rise of the post-1967 radical right, we must first recall Israel's unique history. The Jewish state that reached independence in 1948 did not emerge normally out of an indigenous anti-colonial struggle against the British in Palestine. Rather, it was, and still is, one of the most "unnatural" states in modern history—a state of newcomers, the vast majority of whom arrived after the colonial power had clearly established itself. Israel gained statehood not only as a result of the political and military skill of its Zionist founders but also because, following the Holocaust, it was recognized as one of the only safe homes for a nation of victims and refugees.

Zionism, the earlier liberation movement of the Jews, was never a democratic movement in the full, constitutional, Western sense. However, by its very composition and internal logic it had to be democratic, since it was made of representatives of dispersed communities, many of them constantly repressed and humiliated. Since the end of the nineteenth century it was clear to the founders of the movement that the polity they would one day establish in Eretz Yisrael (the Land of Israel) would be open, free, egalitarian, and just. And most of these people were also strongly opposed to the traditional theocratic elements of Judaism, believing that a modern secular, democratic, Jewish state was no contradiction in terms. Israel's 1948 Declaration of Independence, which reflected a wide national consensus, spelled these ideas out very clearly:

> The State of Israel will be open to the immigration of Jews from all countries of their dispersion; will promote the development of the country for the benefit of all its inhabitants; will be based on the principles of liberty, justice, and peace as conceived by the Prophets of Israel; will uphold the full social and political equality of its citizens, without distinction of religion, race, or sex; will guarantee freedom of religion, conscience, education and culture; will safeguard the Holy Places of all religions; and will loyally uphold the principles of the United Nations[10]

The post-1948 Israel was not a perfect democracy. It was ruled for many years by one political party, Mapai (now the Labor party), which controlled most of the positions of power and influence, administered most of the nation's labor unions and economic resources, and dominated the political culture of the nation.[11] The Arab minority, which could vote and elect its representatives to the Knesset, was for many years kept under strict military government as a security precaution.[12] And there were several harsh emergency regulations, a legacy of British colonial rule, which made it possible for the government to suspend ordinary legal procedures in case of emergency.[13]

Nevertheless Israel was democratic in a great many respects. It catered to the democratic ethos and was unanimously proud of being part of the democratic West. It institutionalized a competitive party system and demonstrated a high level of political participation. While Israelis did not have a formal constitution, or a comprehensive bill of rights—nor do they yet—the state nevertheless established an elaborate court system that has always been independent and highly respected. And Israel's free press made sure that the voice of the opposition was heard and that almost no political organization was barred from the political process.[14]

It would therefore be no exaggeration to claim that in Israel's first twenty years an influential Israeli extreme right was a contradiction in terms, an un-Israeli phenomenon. This was largely because many Israelis, being refugees of the Holocaust, could not even tolerate the thought of extreme ultranationalism and autocracy, and because the vast majority of the other Israelis internalized these values without having gone through the experience. A tiny camp of right-wing extremists, former members and supporters of the small ultranationalist anti-British underground Lehi, did continue to exist. But they were never part of the national consensus and had no political power or influence. They represented, at the most, a small ideological circle that was formed before World War II and refused to die.[15]

The Radical Right as a Political Camp

Perhaps because of this history, few observers, whether Israeli or not, are willing to recognize the magnitude of the new Israeli radical right and its impact on national politics. When faced with the attitudes and activities of this camp they argue that its members are the lunatic fringe. As disturbing as these activities are, so runs the argument, the radical right has usually no say in the government and its impact on critical national decisions is minimal at best.

A numerical examination of the case tends to support this proposition. The hard-core movements and parties of the radical right are small, young, and relatively poor. Their representation in the 12th Knesset does not exceed 6 percent. They are no match for Israel's older and larger political parties, such as Labor, Likud, the National Religious Party, or even for the smaller ultra-orthodox parties of Agudat Israel and Shas. They cannot compete with the powerful Histadrut (the General Federation of Labor), or challenge the old and prestigious Kibbutz and Moshav settlement movements.

But this argument and this examination miss three elements that make the radical right a most effective agent in present Israeli politics and culture: its sophisticated penetration of the larger parties, the exceptional determination of its members, and the strategic location of its constituency.

One of the great successes of the radical right has been its ability to penetrate the Likud and the National Religious Party. Thus, aproximately a quarter of the leaders and members of the Likud look at the world today through the ideological and symbolic prism of the radical right. The most outstanding example is cabinet member Ariel Sharon, a person with great charisma and a large following, who thinks and talks like the ideologues of the extreme right, and exerts a significant influence in the party's councils.[16] The National Religious Party, an old power broker in Israeli politics, has also been a target of the radical right, especially of the young and talented activists of Gush Emunim. And indeed, between 1986 and 1988 the NRP underwent a quiet ideological reshuffle that drove it to the bosom of the radical right. Two of the top three Knesset members of the NRP are devoted radicals, and its political platform reads almost like a Gush Emunim pamphlet.

The radical leaders of the Likud and the NRP are not isolated in the Knesset; their opinions are shared by several Knesset members of the ultra-orthodox Agudat Israel and Shas, and enjoy the support of hundreds of thousands of Israelis. A proper measure of the real parliamentary power of the radical right is the "Eretz Yisrael Front" in the Knesset, a caucus of over thirty Knesset members, one-fourth of the total, who united in the beginning of 1989 to express concern about the undue moderation of the 1989 Unity Government and to block any compromise over the occupied territories.[17]

Thus, the radical right should not be seen as an isolated extremist faction that stands in diametrical opposition to both Israeli democracy and the moderate right, but rather as a very influential school that has been pushing the entire Israeli right toward greater ultranationalism, greater extralegalism, greater militarism, greater ethnocentrism, and greater religiosity. The radical right is neither separated historically nor detached politically from the larger Israeli right. It is instead the right pole of the Israeli nationalist continuum, whose left pole is the moderate right. It is a political and ideological camp of true believers whose values and ideas are sometimes shared by large number of Israelis who are usually not considered radical.

Another crucial fact about the Israeli radical right is the high intensity of its operations and the great effectiveness of its activists. Political scientists have realized in the last four decades that power and influence in a democracy are not simply a function of sheer numbers. A small but intense minority may sometimes counterbalance a large silent or ineffective majority, and have its programs carried out.[18] Israelis in general have never been silent, but some have been more vocal than others and much more effective. The hard core of the Israeli radical right is made up of true believers who are also pragmatic and politically skillful. They are totally committed to the defense of "Greater Israel," and they advance this cause in many sophisticated ways. Their leaders are good communicators, excellent lobbyists, and when needed, skillful demonstrators and extraparliamentary activists. Several illustrious generals, scientists, and mainstream Zionist public figures who were converted to the cause of Eretz Yisrael by the traumatic experience of the Six-Day War lead the radical right. They speak in the name of traditional Zionism, of which they believe they are the only remaining representatives, and manipulate national symbols such as pioneering, settlement, and defense. Their leadership and dedication are respected well beyond their immediate constituency.

But perhaps the most important asset of the Israeli radical right is the strategic location of its hard core, the settlements of the West Bank. The radical right crystallized around the demand to annex the occupied territories to Israel, and has grown in response to the political developments that have led Israeli leaders in the opposite direction. The settlers of Judea and Samaria (as they prefer to call the West Bank), and Gaza—for whom the dilemma of annexation versus evacuation is an existential issue of the first degree—have always been the most determined part of this camp. The Jewish Underground of Gush Emunim, which emerged in a reaction to the first Israeli evacuation of Sinai, agreed upon in 1978, was made up of devoted settlers; several supporters of Rabbi Kahane, who are now active in a few conspiratorial groups organized to prevent similar retreat in the West Bank, also come from settler circles.

The settlers are not very numerous—nearly 100,000 in 1990—but for many Israelis they represent the only true heirs of the Zionist pioneers who expanded the small Jewish community in Palestine and built Israel from scratch. For the entire Israeli right, about half of the nation, Gush Emunim especially, represents the idealism and self-sacrifice of the good old days. In many respects it fulfills for them the same role the tiny Kibbutz movement once fulfilled for the Labor movement.

The settlers of Judea, Samaria, and Gaza are also the ones who maintain daily contact with over 1.5 million unhappy Palestinians. In that capacity they have a significant impact on national politics, much larger than their sheer numbers. In spite of the heavy presence of the army in West Bank, the settlers, who are armed and well organized, can turn the occupied territories into hell, if they only want to. Therefore, even cabinets hostile to the radical right cannot afford to ignore its attitudes and demands. Rabbi Kahane's followers may still be beyond the pale, but not Gush Emunim, Tzomet, and Moledet. These movements and their leaders are part and parcel of the Israeli body politic, and are considered legitimate partners in the political process, casting a large shadow over the future of the Jewish state. What the radical right does or does not do is a question no Israeli, Arab, or anyone interested in the Middle East can afford to ignore.

The *intifada* is a case in point. The Palestinian uprising was directed at Israel's occupation in general, not its radical right. But the *intifada* would not have broken out without the growing Arab-Israeli friction in Judea, Samaria, and Gaza, and without the Palestinian fear that the Jews were about to take over the entire area through massive settlement.[19] The settlers and the spokespersons of the radical right have created this fear by word and deed, primarily by establishing over a hundred and thirty settlements in the occupied territories. Even moderate critics of the settlers maintain that they have created a huge time bomb for Israel, whose safe defusing is becoming harder each day the occupation continues. Without doubt, the settlements and the radical right are among the most concrete barriers to Israeli compromise with the Palestinians and the Arab world, a force to reckon with whenever a peace plan is broached.

The Radical Right as a Sociocultural Phenomenon

Another way of understanding the Israeli radical right is to look at it as a pervasive political culture that presupposes certain types of behavior and orientations. As such, the radical right crosses lines of party, social origin, economic strata, and education. Most of the hard-core members of the "pure" movements of the new camp are middle-class Ashkenazi Israelis, both religious and secular, but the movements include many Sefardi Jews from poor neighborhoods and development towns. These people add populist chauvinism and crude anti-Arab sentiment to the ideological radicalism of the hard core. And both groups have contributed to a cult that combines extreme attitudes regarding the indivisibility of the Land of Israel, bitter hostility toward Arabs and special expressions implying never-ending war against the PLO, and a constant siege mentality along with enthusiastic utterances about religious redemption. I would estimate that these attitudes are shared by about 20 to 25 percent of the Jewish citizens of Israel, in all areas: in schools, universities, military camps, markets, and synagogues.[20] Though various components of the radical right are engaged in conflicts and rivalries, they nevertheless speak almost the same language, have the same ideological enemies, and share an image of a desired Israel. The Israeli radical right is, as always, an integral part of the thriving nationalist camp, yet its distinct ideology, mentality, behavior, and symbology set it apart from the larger right-wing camp which wants the Land of Israel to remain geographically undivided.[21]

Despite the image promoted by its rivals, the Israeli radical right is not fascist. The political and social model that appeals to most of its leaders is drawn neither from foreign ideologies nor from anti-bourgeois, anti-parliamentary, and anti-democratic ideas. It is, instead, the model of a limited democracy taken from the era before the 1948 founding of the State of Israel. Though many in the radical right have an ideal Jewish utopia in mind, in practice they cherish the values and behavior of the Zionist founding fathers. Like the American radical right who constantly hark back to the founding fathers, the Constitution, rugged (pre-FDR) individualism, and "the American way of life," the Israeli radicals yearn for the old days of the yishuv—the Jewish community in Palestine—when each Zionist settlement counted, when Hagana (defense) was "a real thing," and Jews worried about Jews, not Arabs.

Rabbi Moshe Levinger, Gush Emunim's first settler, recently wrote: "In the old days Labor people worked for settlement, immigration, security, and peace with our neighbors. Today the political program of Labor has only one item, an agreement with the neighbors."[22] Other founders of Gush Emunim are similarly nostalgic. They all draw upon the background of Hapoel Hamizrahi, an old school of religious Zionists who were very close to the Labor movement in its high yishuv days; they and the Labor veterans who have moved to the radical right look back on the good old days and wonder how they were all lost.

Even the American-born Meir Kahane, who neither belonged to this tradition nor shared its nostalgia, occasionally paid lip service to the old mores. In this spirit he chose to commemorate David Ben-Gurion's anniversary by remembering the founder of Israel as the man who did not hesitate to expel many Arabs from the new state and put the rest under strict military government, citing

> his excellent work concerning the Israeli Arabs—the establishment of a military government, the *de facto* expulsion of Arabs during the War of Independence, and statements like "Expel them" in reply to Itzhak Rabin, who

wanted to know what he should do with the Arabs of Lydda and Ramia after the two cities were liberated in 1948; "What a beautiful view," on seeing the expulsion of Arabs from Haifa, and "What are they doing here?" when he arrived in Nazareth and saw that the Arabs had not been expelled.[23]

The members of the Israeli radical right, like right-wing radicals in other countries, do not really understand what happened to their people, what corrupted them and turned them so soft, so liberal, and so pluralistic. They see themselves as perfect Zionists, the true inheritors of the old settlers and the fighters of the 1948 War of Independence. Many of them also consider themselves good democrats, more precisely, good *Jewish* democrats.[24] The Zionist Yishuv, they argue, was established in a democratic way and was operated as a democracy. Nevertheless it was a limited democracy and did not include terms of universal pluralism. The Zionist founders were therefore not anti-democratic, but were not fools either. Instead of rehearsing John Stuart Mill or John Dewey all day long, they set out to build a viable polity for their own people.

The conclusion of this line of thinking is thus very clear. When the government of Israel stands in violation of the tenets of Zionism, which imply a consideration of the interests of the Jews as paramount, it must to be resisted, just as the British government was resisted in the 1930s and 1940s by the Zionist founding fathers. The "anti-Zionist" acts of the present-day government must be overruled, just as similar acts of the official organizations of the Yishuv itself were overruled by zealous pioneers.

The ideologues of the radical right, to be sure, do not really want to go back to the old, pre-sovereign days. What attracts them is the early value system, a framework of Zionist norms free of legalistic barriers and excessive democratic obsessions.

Israel's radical right contains a very prestigious fundamentalist element, expressed by Gush Emunim and its ideotheology. Rabbi Kahane's writings also contained a strong fundamentalist orientation, a demand to apply today the law of the Bible. For many Israelis, the fundamentalism of Gush Emunim is appealing because it is a partial religious system. It concentrates almost exclusively on the territorial sacredness of the "Kingdom of Israel in the making" that is the present state of Israel. Unlike the Haredim—the ultra-orthodox anti-Zionist extremists who live by almost every single rule of medieval Halakha as if the state did not exist and the world had not changed[25]—the fundamentalists of Gush Emunim are very modern, nationalist, and pragmatic. They are full of admiration for the state and the instruments of its sovereignty—the government and the military.

The fundamentalism of Gush Emunim, which is tolerant of many forms of secularization, commands them to sanctify every single acre of land that was promised to Abraham by God. It tells them that they are living in an age of redemption in which they must follow the course of the great biblical conquerors, Joshua and King David, by settling all the territories that were recovered by the Joshuas of our time. Benny Katzover, a leading figure in Gush Emunim, illuminates its special territorial fundamentalism:

> In every age and time, there is one point, a special point, through which all that is good sheds light. . . . In the beginning of the messianic age, the critical point is Eretz Israel and everything else derives from it. Without its settlement no holiness operates in the world.[26]

This new fundamentalism fits in rather nicely with the psychology of many older Israelis—some maximalists, and others who were active in settlement and defense in the pre-state era. They are charmed by the vigor and vitality of the youngsters of Gush Emunim who remind them of their own glory days. They seem to hold to a kind of secular neofundamentalism, which approves of Gush Emunim's theology from a non-orthodox angle. This neofundamentalism holds that Zionism, though secular, was never devoid of deeply seated religious beliefs embodying as it did the centuries-long aspirations of returning to Eretz Israel. According to neofundamentalist thinking, the theologians of Gush Emunim, the late Rabbis Kook (father and son), discovered the correct formula for future political Zionism. Arguing that the secular Zionists are legitimate partners in the process of redemption, they made it possible for orthodox and nonorthodox Jews to ally and strive together for national grandeur.[27]

Political protest, illicit settlement, and civic disobedience have been the tools of Israeli right-wing radicals since 1973.[28] At first, however, these actions were almost tentative. Gush Emunim, whose political theology had always expressed great respect for the government, was highly apologetic about its extralegalism. Its leaders genuinely tried to limit excesses. Their ambivalence was shared by some of their supporters. Menachem Begin, for example, the leader of the opposition, was especially equivocal. On the one hand he truly loved the youngsters of the Gush, and visited some of their illicit settlements; on the other hand he maintained a great respect for the rule of law.

But the Gush members' uncertainty about extralegal actions came to an abrupt end with the signing of the Camp David Accords of 1978. It became clear that efforts to maintain a grip on the totality of Eretz Israel would have to involve major extralegal actions, since the parliamentary nationalist right could no longer be trusted. Thus in 1982, all the Tehiya Knesset members left the House and went to "resettle" Yamit, the center of Jewish settlements in northern Sinai that was to be evacuated within three months in accord with the Israeli-Egyptian Peace Treaty. With this action, the radical right asserted that illegal extraparliamentarism was as legitimate an avenue of action as legal parliamentarism. This new doctrine has, since the retreat from Sinai, been widely applied. It had become the guideline of Kahane's actions in the streets, and it has led many other Israelis to disregard law and order.

The extralegal attitude of the radicals reached its peak in the fall of

1985. When the Council of the Settlers in Judea, Samaria and Gaza (Moetzet Yesha) learned about the prime minister's new initiative for peace (which involved possible territorial concessions), it issued the unprecedented warning that any Israeli government which would give up Jewish territories would lose its legal basis.[29] Attorney Elyakim Haetzni, who stood behind the pronouncement, did not hesitate to tell the Prime Minister, Mr. Peres, that a territorial concession would put him in the position of the French General Petain, who collaborated with the Nazis in World War II and was later tried for treason.[30]

A leading segment within the Israeli radical right is convinced that Israel's military might, which is considerable, can be translated at any given moment into political power and national achievement. This conviction goes back to the Six-Day War. The 1967 campaign, in which three Arab armies were defeated in six days, proved that Israel was a major power and that a well-coordinated military operation could change the balance of power in the area.

For the fundamentalists, Israel's immense might requires no rational explanation. In the age of redemption, in which the nation is to reclaim the Land, God is manifestly standing behind the army. For this reason Rabbi Meir Kahane believed that it is *Hillul Hashem,* a desecration of the name of God, to be fearful of the Gentiles.[31]

The secular neofundamentalists, on the other hand, do not need the religious argument. Zahal, the Israeli Defense Force, is a highly qualified and well-trained army that they feel can beat any combination of its enemies at any time. The military setbacks of the Yom Kippur War were an aberration, caused by a unique combination of surprise attack and erroneous operation of the army, yet the war was won. The same thing happened in Lebanon in 1982; had the army been led by a determined government, the war would have ended in a great victory and the possible annexation of more biblical Jewish territories.

Thus, for the militaristic school of the radical right there is only one explanation why Israel is not yet great: its life is dominated by a handful of leftists, Zionists without vision, and weak and hesitant individuals. Among the weaklings are even some Likud members who are scared of their own shadows. Israel, according to this school, has never been so strong. Had military force been used correctly, the Jewish state would not now be in trouble. Judea and Samaria would since have been annexed, and the PLO bases all around the Mediterrean destroyed. The Temple Mount's Moslem shrines would have either been demolished or kept under tight Israeli control, and the "shameful escape" from Lebanon would have been prevented.[32]

The Israeli radical right, despite its growth in power and popularity, is living a paranoiac life. Its leaders are convinced that there is an active conspiracy to betray the people of Israel and the destiny of Zionism. The grand conspiracy includes the Jewish "Ashafists" (PLO'ers) who collaborate willingly with the enemy, leftists who care more about the international left than about their homeland, President Sadat (when he was alive), who fooled Israel into a phony peace, and the evilmongers of the U.S. State Department.[33]

One might argue that since Israeli leaders constantly discuss possible territorial compromises with a Jordanian-Palestinian entity, these fears are legitimate. However, the words of radical spokespersons suggest otherwise. Most of the members of this camp seem unable to distinguish between legitimate political proposals and conspiracy. Their political epistemology is not pluralist but monistic. Their world is divided simply between the sons of light (themselves) and the sons of darkness (anyone who disagrees). Such a world has no room for legitimate opposition. Every political rival is a conspirator.

This conspiracy mentality excoriates the Israeli media as well. Most radical rightists are convinced that Israel's public television, the only channel in the country, is full of anti-Zionist leftists. These traitors project a negative image of the right, and instead of boosting public morale they devastate it by constantly presenting the case of the PLO and avoiding "constructive" national projections. The media is responsible for Israel's losing the war in Lebanon and for much of the present gloomy spirit of the nation.[34]

There are those who argue that the most important feature of the new extremism is not its "radical rightism" but its religious fundamentalism. Having correctly identified Gush Emunim as the most original and influential component of the new radicalism, they argue that its fundamentalism overshadows all other political characteristics of the radical right.[35] The growing popularity of Rabbi Kahane's ideas provides additional support for this argument, for there is no question that Kahane's fundamentalist reading of the scriptures was even more rigid than Gush Emunim's.

However, the characterization of the entire new camp as fundamentalist is untenable. As influential as the fundamentalist centers of Gush Emunim and Kach are, they are only a small part of the new phenomenon. Most of the leaders of the radical right and the vast majority of its followers are not religious fundamentalists and their support of the politics of the new extremists does not depend on their commitment to the literal texts of the Torah. The hard core of Gush Emunim members (including teenagers and children) does not exceed 15,000, and there are only a few dozens activists of Kach who can be said to act out of fundamentalist motivation. Most of the top leaders of the Tehiya, Moledet, and Tzomet, who have been playing a crucial role in spreading the new radicalism, are secular Jews who espouse the cause of the Greater Eretz Yisrael for reasons not obviously related to fundamentalist doctrines. So do the radical leaders of Likud.

Of the hundreds of thousands of Israelis who share the beliefs and orientations of the radical right, almost all are unfamiliar with the fundamentalist doctrines of Gush Emunim and Rabbi Kahane, and precious few follow their religious practice. They support their politics because they feel unsafe in a small Israel, are suspiciously hostile of the Arabs, and mistrust the nation's moderate leaders. The distinguishing feature of the new extremist camp is therefore not its fundamentalism but its radical rightism, a combination of ultranationalism, militarism, ethnocentrism, and religiosity.[36] The religious fundamentalism of Gush Emunim and Kahane, while a very important component of the new extremism, is just one part of a larger politico-cultural phenomenon.

2

The Zionist Roots
of the Radical Right

The Israeli radical right arose in reaction to a series of events that started
with the Six-Day War and ended with the Camp David accords and the
government's agreement to withdraw from some of the territories occupied
in 1967. In the process of its formation, the radical right was very successful
in tapping social and intellectual resources not traditionally associated with
the Israeli Right. But the emerging ultranationalist camp, a new Israeli socio-
political phenomenon by all standards, is not totally rootless. A long forgotten chapter in Zionist history has in it a marked ultranationalist thinking
and action. No examination of the new Israeli radical right can be complete
without a short exploration of this maximalist tradition, and in particular
the legacy of four schools that were active and influential in Mandatory
Palestine: the ultranationalist tradition of Uri Zvi Greenberg, Brit Habirionim, and Lehi; the radical legacy of Vladimir Jabotinsky and Betar; the
"activist" tradition of the Labor movement; and the messianic school of
Rabbi Avraham Itzhak Hacohen Kook.

The Ultranationalist Legacy

The school most identified in the Mandate period with the idea of a radical
right grew up within the Revisionist Movement of Vladimir Jabotinsky,
which constituted the right wing of World Zionism. It was the ultranationalist wing of Revisionism, and was articulated by organizations
such as Brit Habirionim and Lehi. The old radical right was moved by two
fundamental beliefs: that the British were oppressive rulers who had to be
expelled from Palestine by force, and that the emerging extreme right of the

time, with perhaps the exception of the Nazis, provided a viable ideology and a relevant model of political action.

The early ideologues of this camp, Uri Zvi Greenberg, Abba Achimeir, and Yehoshua Heshel Yevin, represented an impatient Zionism that concluded that the British had betrayed the Jews and abrogated the terms of the Balfour Declaration. Fascinated by other nationalist movements, especially the Italian, the Polish, the Czech, and the Irish, all of which had reached independence through military effort, they concluded that the British had to be expelled from Eretz Yisrael by force. The fact that the Jews in Palestine were a small ethnic minority of mostly new immigrants, and that a much larger native community questioned their very right to the land, was not allowed to hobble the great dream. From its inception, this ultranationalist circle was characterized by a conviction that strong will and determination constitute the most important political resource, and that they alone could change the world.[1]

This small group of ultranationalist ideologues who started to write and preach in the late 1920s was not philosophically homogeneous, for each of its members constructed his ultranationalism from different historical and philosophical sources. Profoundly influenced by the growing European radical right, they all agreed on a principled rejection of democracy and hostility toward socialism. Zionist socialism was perceived as a threat to nationalism. Only the Hebrew nation and its future instrument of power, the Jewish State, were sacred. Thus, in addition to their rejection of the policies of the *yishuv* vis-à-vis the British, the Revisionist ultranationalists were driven by a conceptual animosity toward the workers' parties.

And there was another important ingredient in their thinking: a romantic return to the Biblical past of the nation and the aspiration to reconstruct the days of the early Hebrews who took Canaan by force and extended it by military means to the large Davidic kingdom.[2] Most appealing to these revolutionaries was not the image of the self-sufficient Jewish farmer-pioneer, but rather the model of the Jewish fighter, the Hebrew national who takes his land by force.

Thus in the 1930s, when the Zionist socialists had already become an establishment in Palestine, with organizations and bureaucracy, these young extremists became the epitome of anti-establishment revolution. Their acute sense of revolt was expressed by the name they chose for their group in 1931, Brit Habirionim (the Covenant of Thugs). The ancient Birionim were the most extreme faction of the Jewish Zealots in the first century C.E., who fought against the Romans before the destruction of the Second Temple. Their devotion to Judaism was so complete that they refused to compromise for less than total religious and political autonomy. Given the huge power of the Roman empire and its complete hegemony in the East, their attitude led to national disaster. The Zealots conducted a brutal terror campaign against both the Romans and moderate Jews, and were instrumental in heightening the conflict to a point of no return. The tragic destruction of the Temple was the beginning of the process that led to a two-thousand-year national exile. It was this destructive role in the events of the Great Revolt that gave the Birionim, and the Zealots in general, a negative name in Jewish tradition and Halakhic discourse.[3]

By calling itself Brit Habirionim, the small group of Greenberg, Achimeir, and Yevin clearly communicated radicalism, anti-establishment sentiment, and defiance. And the rebellion was directed not only against the British, the Arabs, and the Labor establishment, but also against the religious orthodoxy for whom the concept Birionim was an anathema. Thus, although they read the Old Testament carefully, the Birionim's ennoblement of the Jewish past was neither halakhic nor historical. It was above all a mythological rediscovery of the glorious tales of the nation, a romantic glorification of the old days of blood, soil, heroism, and conquest.

The intellectuals of Brit Habirionim, to be sure, were not engaged in any actual rebellion. They mostly wrote and preached, and in the early 1930s were involved in several symbolic demonstrations against the British, Nazi Germany, and the Arabs.[4] Nevertheless, their politico-cultural influence was considerable. Their fervent attacks on the British and their Jewish "collaborators," the leaders of the official Zionist movement, came at a time in which a major rift in the Zionist movement was forming, the conflict between Jabotinsky's movement and the rest of organized Zionism.

Many followers of Jabotinsky, especially the young in Palestine, were deeply moved by the rhetoric and antiworker militancy of the new school.[5] A special role in this radicalism had been played by Yonathan Ratosh (Uriel Shelah), the future founder of the "Canaanite" school. Ratosh, who brought the Ultranationalist critique of official Zionism to the point of absurdity was later to demand that the new Hebrews (the Zionists in Palestine) sever all their relations with Judaism and Diaspora Jews and create, by force if need be, a huge "Canaanite" state made of all Middle Eastern minorities sharing ancient biblical roots.[6]

The Radical Legacy of Jabotinsky and Betar

Vladimir Jabotinsky, the revered leader of Zionist Revisionism, was never party to the emerging radical right of Achimeir and Greenberg, though he occasionally backed Brit Habirionim notwithstanding.[7] His admiration for Great Britain and for the virtues of democracy, liberalism, and the rule of law is widely recognized today and explains, at least partially, his complete refusal to fight the British and relieve them from the moral duty of establishing a Jewish state implied in the Balfour Declaration.[8]

Nevertheless, certain radical elements in Jabotinsky's thinking and political style made it possible for the members of Brit Habirionim and other radical groups to admire him and include him in their extremist *weltanschauung*.[9] It is through his partial legitimation of the historical radical right that Jabotinsky himself was and remains a part of their legacy to Zionism. Perhaps his most important contribution to younger radical followers was his integral nationalism, the fervent belief that the nation is the supreme foundation of legitimate political action.[10] Jabotinsky's numerous expressions of support for civil liberties, individual freedoms, and a free economy show that he was clearly open to pluralistic thinking,[11] but these expressions rarely guided the man's concrete political action. Most of his followers overlooked his somewhat esoteric and theoretical liberalism in favor of his nationalist rhetoric and mode of action that stressed monism, militarism, discipline, order, and bitter defiance of official Zionism.[12]

Jabotinsky's most cherished creation was Betar, the youth movement that became the main politicization agent of Revisionist activists, pioneers, and fighters. Betar never emphasized pluralism, openness, or debate. It was, on the contrary, a semimilitaristic entity that stressed hierarchy, discipline, obedience to superiors, rituals, and ceremonies.[13] Betar's brown shirts, which greatly resembled the Nazi uniform, were not exactly a symbol of peace and tranquillity. Military values were seen as more than a necessary instrument on the road to self-determination; they were rather a virtue, a symbol of national sovereignty, and an expression of collective national liberation. Romantic heroism was cultivated by Jabotinsky to such an extent that the movement's great heroic myths, Shimon Bar-Kochba and Joseph Trumpeldor, became national fighters who fought and gave their life for freedom. Old and new battle sites like Massada, Betar, and Tel Hai were made sacred pilgrimage sites for thousands of Betar youngsters.[14]

Jabotinsky's unconditional demand that the future State of Israel be established on both sides of the Jordan river, his penchant for militarism, his ideological commitment to monism, his economic corporatism, and his fervent anti-Labor stance were instrumental in sustaining the spirit of the radical right in Betar long after the demise of Brit Habirionim. And as Yonathan Shapiro has shown, it was highly appealing to a whole age cohort of Betar activists who grew up in Poland between the 1920s and 1930s under the spell of Joseph Pilsudski and the Polish extreme right.[15]

There was in fact, as Shlomo Avineri has shown, a built-in paradox in the thinking and politics of Jabotinsky. His integral nationalism led him, on the one hand, to stress elements of power and force as the proper foundations of political action. On the other hand, beyond the level of rhetoric, Jabotinsky was fully aware of the tremendous weakness of the Jews.[16] This was the reason why he could not support the politics of Brit Habirionim in the early 1930s and was extremely uncomfortable with the anti-British operations of Etzel, the Jewish Underground identified with the Revisionist movement, in the closing years of the decade.

But this was also the reason why Betar and Etzel started to drift away from the aging leader.[17] Neither organization, and especially Etzel, which since 1937 had been engaged in active anti-Arab terrorism, could accept Jabotinsky's paradox. Being unimpressed by his political realism regarding the powerlessness of the Jews and by his latent admiration for Western liberalism and democracy, they opted for a more radical direction expressed by an active military struggle against the British and a belief in military solutions for political problems.

In 1940, Abraham Stern (Yair) brought this radical course to its logical conclusion. Reviving the legacy of Brit Habirionim, Stern decided to free himself of Jabotinsky's paradox by challenging the entire Revisionist paradigm. He split away from Etzel, declared an open revolt against the British, and went underground in the hope of leading the entire Jewish liberation movement toward the creation of the "Kingdom of Israel" free of British and Arabs. Completely ignoring the constraints of political reality, Stern started on a suicide course that resulted in his own death in 1942 and almost completely obliterated his entire organization.[18]

The "Activist" Tradition of the Labor Movement

The pre-1948 Labor movement was extremely hostile to the political right of Jabotinsky and was hardly ready to distinguish between Revisionism in general and the radical right in particular. But this opposition was not based on a great respect for universal human rights, democratic pluralism, and tolerance. In fact, on many of these issues Labor did not significantly differ from the Revisionists. The Workers' parties of the 1930s were much more intolerant and totalitarian than is usually recognized today. Their animosity to the right was a result of two major realities of the time: the hostility of world socialism after World War I to the fascist threat of central Europe, and the struggle between Labor and Revisionism for the hegemony of Zionism. Thus, the Revisionists and the ultranationalists of the 1930s and 1940s were fought not because of their deficient liberalism but because they threatened to take over the leadership of the Zionist movement and refused to play by the rules of limited democracy it imposed.[19]

The political orientation of the Labor movement and its "civil religion" differed significantly from Revisionism in its emphasis on constructive pioneering, hard labor, and pragmatic and piecemeal politics rather than militarism, heroism, and monistic nationalism.[20] But on certain issues, such as the territories of Eretz Yisrael and the Arabs, there were some surprisingly important similarities. The question of partitioning of Eretz Yisrael, for example, was heatedly debated in Labor circles from the late 1930s onwards. Some very prominent Labor leaders such as Berl Katznelson, the ideologue of Mapai, and Itzhak Tabenkin, a prominent kibbutz leader, were strongly opposed to the idea.[21] Tabenkin's mighty Kibbutz movement later became extremely bitter over the 1947 partition and continued to cherish the idea of a return to the lost part of the homeland long after the end of the 1948 War of Independence.

As regards Arabs, not much attention was paid to their fate in the future enlarged State of Israel. In fact, the whole issue of Palestinian national rights was not seriously addressed by any of the Labor maximalists with the exception of David Ben-Gurion. They were convinced that the local Palestinians would either leave for the surrounding Arab states or be happy within a modern and benevolent Jewish polity.

It was in the context of a maximalist Jewish State that the concept of "transfer" first emerged in Labor circles. The term implied the evacuation of a significant number of Arabs from the future Jewish State to assure its homogeneity and freedom from ethnic conflicts.[22] The idea of transfer, it should be stressed, did not evolve in the abstract. It was mostly a reaction to two major developments that took place in Palestine in the 1930s, the Arab Revolt and the 1937 report of the Peel Commission recommending, among other things, the partition of Palestine and the establishment of separate Arab and Jewish states. The Labor leaders who supported the idea of transfer in the late 1930s and the beginning of the 1940s, including Ben-Gurion, were convinced that the British could enforce it in the context of an overall settlement of the Palestinian problem.[23] Having no doubt that the Jewish cause was more important than justice to the Arabs, they paid little attention to the real or potential plight of the Palestinians and approached the problem in pragmatic political terms.

The debate between Labor and Revisionism on the fate of the Arabs prior to the establishment of the State of Israel was not based on moral and normative thinking but on political and strategic considerations. It was mainly concerned with how the interests of the *yishuv* and its long-range desire for statehood would be best served. While the Revisionists, and especially the radical right, were impatient and determined to push for immediate independence irrespective of the Arab majority, the Labor leaders, and especially David Ben-Gurion, were very realistic and cautious. Fully aware of the weakness of the Jews and their dependence on Great Britain, Labor considered the right-wing radicals adventurous and dangerous fascists unfit to deal in national politics.[24]

This difference in approach came to the fore in the famous *Havlaga* (Self-Restraint) debate. Following the outbreak of the Arab Rebellion in 1936 and the intensification of terrorism against Jews in Palestine, there was a public outcry for proper response and revenge. Etzel, under the command of David Raziel, responded in kind and developed a massive counterterrorist campaign. Its underground fighters ambushed Arab civilians and planted bombs in crowded Arab markets and public places. But David Ben-Gurion and most of his colleagues urged patience and measured response. They demanded that despite Arab brutality, the Jews had to *Lehavlig* (restrain themselves) and show that, unlike the Arabs, they were civilized and humane.[25]

However, most Labor leaders were less concerned with moral considerations than with political facts. Unlike the commanders of Etzel and the intellectuals of the radical right who supported them, Ben-Gurion and his colleagues understood that unrestrained Arab violence was politically useful for the Jews. It alienated the Arabs from the British, damaged their cause internationally, and forced the Mandatory government to use military means against Arabs.[26] Thus, while Etzel was forced to go underground and to organize its troops for small hit-and-run operations, the British granted a semiofficial status to the military wing of the Histadrut, the Hagana, which was allowed to create a mass defense system that later became the foundation of the Israel army.

But perhaps the greatest contribution of the Labor movement to the old aggressive Zionism was made by the Labor *activists*. Labor activism was never a radical ideological school, and did not have a textbook of common principles of action. It was instead a matter-of-fact orientation, a belief that the borders of Zionism would not be determined by those who talk and moralize but by individuals of action. The activists within the movement were those who advocated a constant expansion of Jewish settlement in Palestine, with or without official permission.[27] Given the hostility of the Arabs and the noncooperation of the British, Labor activists soon expanded from settlement to defense, and in many cases to illegal defense. Responding to the attacks of local Arab gangs, the activists developed a very militant attitude and recommended aggressive response.[28]

While most Labor Zionist activists were followers of Itzhak Tabenkin, leader of Achdut Ha'avoda party, and identified with his general brand of Marxist-socialist Zionism, a significant number of Mapai activists shared their militancy with respect to the Arabs. What united them with Achdut Ha'avoda activists was that both tended to "see the Arab question through the rifle's sight." Leaving aside the tormented debates of the 1930s regarding the rights of the Palestinian Arabs and their national aspirations, both groups were convinced that every barrier on the road of Zionist fulfillment had to be removed. The growing Arab hostility toward the very existence of the Jews in Eretz Yisrael and their 1947 determination to wipe out the future Jewish state drove the Labor activists to the pessimistic conclusion that the struggle against the Arab local population should not be constrained.[29]

What was typical of the anti-Arab orientation of the activists of the Labor movement was a very shrewd recognition that unlike the Revisionist approach, the problem had to be acted upon in secret rather than preached about in public. The most extreme among them since the 1930s had no doubt that the Arabs constituted a mortal danger to the Jewish future and had to be evicted. Josef Weitz, the director of the Jewish National Fund, the foundation in charge of the reclamation of land in Palestine, and an arch-Labor activist, wrote in his diary in 1940:

> It must be clear that there is no room in the country for both peoples. . . . If the Arabs leave it, the country will become wide and spacious for us. . . . The only solution [after the end of World War II] is a Land of Israel, at least a

western Land of Israel [i.e., Palestine], without Arabs. There is no room for
compromises.
      . . . There is no way but to transfer the Arabs from here to the neighbor-
ing countries, to transfer all of them, save perhaps for the Arabs of Bethlehem, Nazereth, and old Jerusalem. Not one village must be left, not one
tribe. The transfer must be directed to Iraq, Syria, and even Transjordan. For
this goal funds will be found. . . . And only after this transfer will the country
be able to absorb millions of our brothers and the Jewish problem will cease
to exist. There is no other solution.[30]

During the 1948 war, Weitz was involved in the secret Jewish Transfer
Committee, which issued guidelines assuring that no Arab refugee from
Palestine was allowed to come back.[31] There was never, to be sure, an
official Labor policy of expulsion of Palestinian Arabs during the war, and
the leaders of the newly created Israeli state were careful not to mention in
public any such possibility. But many field commanders, who happened to
share the activist orientation, saw to it in 1948 that a large number of Arabs
did leave Palestine.[32] And very few of the Israeli Labor leaders regretted the
unexpected development.[33] Viewing it as one of the great miracles of the
war, they convinced themselves that unlike an intended transfer, planned
and talked about in peacetime, a *de facto* transfer that occurred during a
war started by the Arabs was legitimate and irrevocable.[34]

The Maximalist Messianism of Rav Kook

One of the most common beliefs about Gush Emunim is that it changed the
political orientation of the Zionist religious camp after 1967, moving it from
the moderate left to the maximalist right. Until 1967, so the argument runs,
the National Religious Party and the Mizrahi movement, the dominant
organizations of this camp, were very pragmatic, non-messianic, and moderate. They were not interested in major national issues, giving full endorsement to the security and foreign affairs policy of Mapai. It was only after the
great and miraculous victory of the Six-Day War that Gush Emunim came to
the fore, preaching messianism and ideologically taking over the movement.
      But this interpretation, as Eliezer Don-Yehiya has recently argued, is
only partially correct, being historically true for only the last forty years or
so. Don-Yehiya shows in fact that since its 1902 establishment, the political
orientation of the Mizrahi, the mainstream in religious Zionism, has gone
through several different phases. While most of the time the movement has
been moderate and pragmatic, there were times in which it was maximalist
and messianic.
      Rabbi Reines, for example, the movement's first spiritual leader, advo-
cated very cautious and pragmatic politics. Zionism for him was not a
messianic phenomenon, the beginning of heavenly redemption, but a pragmatic solution for the pressing problems of the persecuted Jews. One could

not consequently draw from the rise of secular Zionism far-reaching conclusions about the past and the future "Kingdom of Israel." Reines advocated therefore very cautious and pragmatic politics.

But this moderate stance, Don-Yehiya shows, changed during the 1920s and 1930s under the influence of Rabbi Avraham Itzhak Hacohen Kook. This messianic thinker, who became in 1921 the first Chief Ashkenazi rabbi of the Jews of Palestine, introduced a strong maximalist component to the thinking of the Mizrahi movement.[35] With Kook's conviction that secular Zionism indicated the beginning of redemption, the movement adopted a very ambitious approach to Eretz Yisrael and was totally hostile to the partition of Palestine. While not radical in its actions, it spoke the language of the Land of Israel in its entirety, cared little about the Arabs, and was close to the maximalist circles in the *yishuv* on many issues.[36]

The maximalist orientation of the Mizrahi started to change in the 1940s following the historical developments of the decade. The Mizrahi became enthusiastic about Ben-Gurion's 1942 Biltmore Plan, which called for the establishment of a sovereign Jewish State in any available part of Palestine.[37] And learning about the horrible disaster of European Jewry in the Holocaust, the religious Zionists came to the conclusion that a Jewish state in part of Palestine was preferable to no safe place for Jews at all. The painful renunciation of the great dream of the entire Eretz Yisrael was profoundly expressed by Rabbi Fishman, one of the leaders of the Mizrahi, who spoke at a 1947 meeting: "If God intends to leave us without Jews, then I am ready to give up Eretz Yisrael and the Messiah. I know this is heresy, but if this is the case then I am an heretic."[38]

The imposing and successful leadership of David Ben-Gurion during Israel's War of Independence and the tightening political alliance of the Mizrahi with Mapai after 1949 led to a growing compliance of the religious Zionists with the policy of Israel's major party, an orientation that only started to change after 1967. But the change was closely related to the somewhat forgotten ideotheology of Rav Kook, which was quietly kept alive in the Rabbi's own small yeshiva in Jerusalem, Merkaz Harav.

While most of organized religious Zionism went along with Labor, there were small orthodox circles that always maintained close relations with the Revisionists. In 1935, a change in Jabotinsky's attitude toward Jewish orthodoxy facilitated this connection and solidfied a long emotional alliance between secular and religious nationalists.[39] The fact that David Raziel, Etzel's commander from 1936 to 1941, was an observant Jew who had studied for a while in Yeshivat Merkaz Harav, and that Abraham Stern was full of respect for orthodox Judaism, was very significant for young orthodox maximalists who could join both undergrounds without hesitation.[40]

One of the religious circles that supported the ultranationalist right was Brit Hahashmonaim (the Hasmonean Covenant) movement. Brit Hahashmonaim was established in 1937 by several religious youngsters in order to educate youth in the Hasmonean tradition of uncompromising struggle for freedom. The most active member of the group was Rabbi Moshe Halevi Segal, a member of Etzel and a former member of Brit Habirionim, and the person who first blew the *shofar* at the Wailing Wall in 1931, in an outright defiance of the British order. While the founders of the group were profoundly influenced by Rav Kook, they were action-oriented and instructed their followers to join Etzel. In 1944, Lehi's commander Itzhak Shamir and Rabbi Segal held a series of talks, and the latter, convinced of the great similarity between the platform of Brit Hahashmonaim and the ultranationalist Eighteen Principles of Revival of Abraham Stern, asked all the members of the Brit to join Lehi. Most of them did.[41] They strengthened the underground and broadened its appeal, becoming the foundation of Lehi's religious wing. Rabbi Segal later became the first Jewish settler in the freed Jewish Quarter of Old Jerusalem after the 1967 war and was also one of the 1979 founders of the Tehiya party.

The Political and Historical Marginality of the Old Radical Right

In spite of the vocal ideological presence of the old radical right in Zionist politics in the 1930s and 1940s, it was, until 1967, a marginal political phenomenon. The main force within the *yishuv* had been Labor Zionism, powerful both politically and ideologically, dominating the Zionist venture in Palestine and the emerging state.[42] The ideas and programs of the radical right appealed to relatively few Zionists, who were not only culturally marginal in the Zionist milieu, but were also politically persecuted. The allegation that members of Brit Habirionim were responsible for the 1933 assassination of Labor leader Haim Arlozoroff, and the 1935 establishment of an alternative Zionist movement by Jabotinsky, in clear defiance of the existing movement, began a long period of intentional marginalization of the Zionist right and ultra-right. The "secession" of Jabotinsky and the later establishment of two "secessionist" undergrounds in Palestine led to a very intense delegitimization of the Zionist right.[43] To be a *Poresh* ("secessionist") in the early 1940s was not merely to belong to the Revisionist movement, Etzel or Lehi. It amounted to membership in illegitimate subversive bodies that were denoted by the official interpreters of Labor Zionism as fascist. Probably no more than 10 to 15 percent of the *yishuv* supported the right, and most of these supporters were not radical.[44]

The more successful Labor Zionism became in building toward a Zionist state, the lesser the historical role of the right and the radical right. Etzel and Lehi were highly instrumental in driving the British out of Palestine in the 1940s, more than was recognized by the official interpreters of "legitimate Zionism,"[45] but their support for the growing Jewish polity in Palestine was minimal at best. They made no contribution to the self-governing institutions of the state in the making and had no interest in building the economic infrastructures of the *yishuv*.[46] And Etzel, Lehi, and the weak Revisionist party took almost no part in the great diplomatic effort to gain legitimacy and international support for the emerging Jewish state.

Furthermore, they were badly prepared to meet the real challenge of the new state: the war with the Arabs. Fixated as it was on the British, the Israeli nationalist right became irrelevant the moment the British left Palestine.

The Second World War, the Nazi and Fascist experience, and the Holocaust had also contributed to the historical irrelevance of the radical right. In the 1930s the historical radical right was a relevant ideological school, seen by many as a viable alternative to world communism on the one hand and "decadent" liberal democracy on the other. Not only the Polish radical right but also Italian Fascism were highly attractive for the radical wing of the Revisionist movement. The Fascist appeal was partly responsible for Abraham Stern's bizarre 1941 effort to form an anti-British alliance with the Axis powers.[47] But the experience of the war and especially the Holocaust destroyed the fascination of Fascism for the vast majority of the world. The loss of the war was also an ideological disaster for world Fascism, driving it at once to the very margins of modern civilization. This was even more the case for Jews and Zionists. Very few ultranationalists remained loyal to their prewar political platforms, and many of them began to deny ever having been close to the European radical right.

The 1947 U.N. Partition Resolution, the 1948 War of Independence, and the establishment of the State of Israel made the grand vision of the radical right completely unrealistic. Even veteran Revisionists who were mostly oriented toward a glorious national war of liberation were disoriented. It was therefore natural that despite some bloody incidents between Etzel and the new Israel army, Menachem Begin's new party, Herut, became part of the Israeli parliamentary system.[48] But Herut's past radicalism, extremist rhetoric, and commitment to the dream of *"Shtei gadot layarden zo shelanu zo gam ken"* ("There are two banks to the Jordan river; this one is ours and the other too"), which implied a principled rejection of the partition of Eretz Yisrael and the aspiration for a military conquest of the Kingdom of Jordan, was continuously used by Mapai's shrewd politicians to keep Herut beyond the pale of legitimacy.[49] The majority of Lehi's veterans, who in September 1948 committed their last defiant terror act, the assassination of Count Bernadotte, the U.N. Mediator in Palestine, also gave up their underground life and in 1949 joined the new system. Organizing in the form of the Fighters Party, they implied at least a partial recognition of the newly created Israeli state and its norms.[50]

The only organized component of the radical right that remained loyal to the old ideology and continued to function after 1949 was the small ideological group, Chug Sulam (the Ladder Circle). Organized by Dr. Israel Eldad, a devotee of Uri Zvi Greenberg and a former chief ideologist of Lehi, Chug Sulam vowed to preserve the dream of the greater Kingdom of Israel. For that purpose it published a highly ideological magazine, *Sulam*, and organized educational and ideological activities for youth. Completely detached from the historical reality of the new State of Israel, *Sulam* published anti-British articles "exposing" the British intention to reoccupy Palestine via Jordan, antigovernment articles attacking the decadent party system of the truncated Jewish State, and essays on the indivisibility of Eretz Yisrael and its promised borders. In an age of prestigious democracy it called for the installation of a Jewish dictatorship and for a war of conquest against most of the new state's neighbors. A celebration of Israel's Day of Independence was occasionally ended by the call "next year in Amman."[51]

The total isolation of Chug Sulam from the nation's public life did not prevent the establishment, in the early 1950s, of two new small undergrounds that vowed to topple the regime: Brit Hakanaim (the Covenant of Zealots) and Machteret Malchut Yisrael (the Kingdom of Israel Underground). The first operated between 1949 and 1951, and was mostly interested in fighting the secular character of the new state; the second acted from 1951 to 1953, and was involved in "defending and uplifting" the national honor. Both were captured by the Shin Bet (Israel's secret service) before they caused major damage, but they left an impact nevertheless. While Brit Hakanaim burned nonkosher butcher shops and set ablaze cars driving on the Sabbath, the Kingdom of Israel Underground was involved in larger operations. Reacting to the 1952 Doctors' Trial in Moscow, it blew up the Russian Consulate in Tel Aviv, and repeated the same act in the Czech consulate in response to the Slansky-Klementis show trial in Prague. Following the intense public debate over the German reparations, the underground conducted several symbolic attacks against artists performing German music.[52]

But the arrest of the members of these radical undergrounds and the growing irrelevance of Chug Sulam to the problems faced by the State of Israel of the 1950s slowly brought about the final decline of the old radical right. The army's aggressive retaliation operations against enemy targets in Jordan and Egypt in the first half of the 1950s, the 1956 Sinai Campaign, and Ben-Gurion's and Dayan's hawkish posture became attractive to many people who had rightist tendencies and backgrounds. The illustrious operations of Commando Detachment 101, and later the Israeli paratroopers under the command of major Ariel Sharon, provided the old ultranationalists with new myths of Israeli heroism.[53]

By the early 1960s *Sulam* stopped publishing. Dr. Israel Eldad became a professor of biblical Jewish history at the Technion; his devoted student, Geula Cohen, started to write for *Ma'ariv,* and the radical right became *passé.* Neither its ideologues nor its historical adversaries expected it ever to be resurrected.

3

The Revival
of Territorial Maximalism
in Israel

The Six-Day War transformed the Israeli political psyche and changed the political thinking of the entire Middle East. The Israel of June 11, 1967, was not the anxiety-ridden nation that went to war six days earlier. Though stunned and disbelieving, the Israelis recognized the greatness of their military victory. The unification of Jerusalem, the destruction of the combined armies of Egypt, Jordan, and Syria, and the capture of the West Bank, Sinai, and the Golan Heights were possibilities only dreamed about before. The occupied territories were three times bigger than Israel proper, which the traditional siege mentality of the Israelis made seem even larger.

It is therefore not surprising that numerous Israelis developed an "imperial" conviction that their state was the strongest force in the Middle East, a world power in the class of England, France, or Italy. Many were quick to see an inner logic and historical necessity that made the war and its results inevitable. This resulted in the revival of a Zionist tradition of "territorial maximalism," which had over the previous two decades become politically obsolete. And it is this orientation that sanctifies the principle that "never again should Eretz Yisrael be divided" that has become, since 1967, a most energetic and influential tenet in modern Zionism.

The Longest Month

A full grasp of the revival of Israeli territorial maximalism, both as an ideology and political mentality, must be grounded in an understanding of the political situation that produced the Six-Day War. This is especially true of that period which writer Michael Bar-Zohar had named "the longest month," the four weeks from May 14 to June 11, 1967.[1]

May 14, 1967, Israel's nineteenth Independence Day, was the day the country's leaders learned that Gamal Abd al-Nasser, Egypt's president, had decided to move his troops across the Suez Canal into Sinai. At that time very few Israelis believed that the Egyptians were capable of a challenge of this magnitude. All intelligence reports of the army and the secret services portrayed a troubled Nasser, militarily and politically overextended in the civil war in Yemen. These conclusions were shared by the general Israeli public, leading to the portrayal of Nasser as a "paper tiger."

This illusion was shattered in the space of ten days. Not only did the "helpless" Egyptian president move his troops into Sinai, but in the following week he blatantly violated the understanding reached in 1957 with Israel following Egypt's defeat. Nasser declared the international waterway of the Straits of Tiran closed, and asked the United Nation's Emergency Force (UNEF) stationed in Sinai and the Gaza strip to leave.

Nasser's message was clear: he no longer feared Israel. Believing that Israel's military superiority was in fact an illusion, Nasser called Israel's bluff, moving to relieve Syria of Israeli pressure. The move was so successful, and Israel's loss of confidence so clear, that for the first time in fifteen years, the Egyptian leader was ready to give a serious consideration to an old commitment of his, to settle the final Arab score with Israel by military means.[2]

Nasser's sudden move stunned the entire community of nations. The Soviet Union, thrilled by its ally's success, made it clear it would veto any anti-Egyptian motion in the U.N. Security Council. United Nations Secretary-General U Thant willingly agreed to withdraw the UNEF troops from Sinai and Gaza, leaving no buffer between the Israeli and Egyptian armies.[3] An American proposal to reduce the tension by sending an international flotilla to test the Egyptians in the Straits of Tiran failed miserably; very few European nations were willing to risk any involvement.[4]

Israel was thus unprepared militarily and isolated politically—emissaries sent to mobilize support around the globe returned home empty-handed. There was a lot of sympathy and understanding, but no nation was willing to help fight Israel's war or risk an unpleasant confrontation with the Soviet Union. There was, however, a moving show of support from Jews all over the world. Non-Zionist Jews, who had never before identified with the Jewish state, rediscovered Israel. Many of them sensed a possible Holocaust and wanted to help. Nevertheless, they could do very little. The ominous shadow of Nasser and his Russian-equipped military loomed large and could not be offset by petitions, demonstrations, and emergency fund raising.

Nasser could not have picked a better time for his move. Everyone in Israel, including the political elite, was caught off guard. The mood was gloomy; an acute economic depression included an exceedingly high rate of unemployment. Many people spoke seriously about the end of the Zionist dream. Others voted with their feet and left the country. The most common joke of the time had to do with finding a fool to stay behind to turn off the lights at Lod, Israel's only international airport.

Levi Eshkol, Israel's prime minister and minister of defense, had not yet established his authority in the vital area of security. Living in the wrathful shadow of his great predecessor, David Ben-Gurion (who considered Eshkol unfit to rule), he had initiated since 1964 a very aggressive policy of military retaliation against the Arabs, and especially against Syria.[5] To his dismay, however, this hawkish posture did not help him politically in 1967. No one within the nation's ruling circles mistook Eshkol for Ben-Gurion, and very few were content to leave him alone at the helm when Israel's most serious ordeal was about to unfold.

The confusion and insecurity extended beyond the political leadership to the military. Informed Israelis learned that the army's chief of staff, Itzhak Rabin, collapsed from fatigue and hypertension on May 23, the day Nasser closed the Straits of Tiran, and offered his job to his deputy commander, Ezer Weizman.[6] If an experienced chief of staff broke down, dismayed observers could only conclude that the situation must be extremely dangerous.

Perhaps Levi Eshkol was not really frightened by Nasser's move, but in the last week of May he certainly conveyed the image of fear. Instead of acting decisively and leading with confident strength, Eshkol projected confusion and indecision. Unlike the decisive Ben-Gurion, who had reached his most critical decisions with few advisors, Eshkol immersed himself in countless deliberations and had to know what everybody else thought. He seemed to be waiting for a collective decision that would relieve him from the grave responsibility of either going to war or making painful concessions.

During a special radio address to the nation, the prime minister stuttered badly. Unable to read the illegible text that his aides had hastily prepared, Eshkol had to stop several times to consult with them. It was a catastrophe. All the fears and anxieties of his listeners, the vast majority of the nation, were confirmed. Israel was facing its biggest challenge under shaky leadership.

Much of the country wanted to have Eshkol replaced by a more reassuring and authoritative leader. The most humiliating proposal came from Shimon Peres and his small Rafi party. Their idea was to suspend the nation's ordinary democratic procedures and form a national emergency government made up of representatives of all political parties and headed by eighty-one-year-old David Ben-Gurion. The rationale was that Nasser's daring move had damaged Israel's morale and made an immediate military operation extremely risky; Israel had lost the first round and had to amass military and political support before it could regain the initiative. Only Ben-Gurion could break the bad news to the nation and keep it from falling apart.[7]

Not since 1948 had Israelis been so conscious of the enormous vulnerability of their country, a thin strip of land along the Mediterranean surrounded by sixteen Arab nations. Frightened, isolated, and deserted, they could not but hate the political arrangement of 1949 that left them open to attack from all sides. *Israel was Massada,* a small rock in the midst of a hostile wilderness. All remembered the heroic story of the last defenders of Jerusalem, who committed suicide at Massada, a mountain fort in the Judean desert, in order not fall into the hands of the Romans. The chief military rabbinate, the authority in charge of burials, was rumored at the end of May 1967 to be planning to turn public parks and recreation areas into graveyards.[8]

Israel finally went to war on June 5, 1967. The average Israeli soldier did not go to win big. He went only to survive, to make sure that his small state and his family stayed alive.

These mental and psychological conditions shaped the thinking of the new maximalists: an immense sense of national vulnerability, personal insecurity, memories of the Holocaust, and then, suddenly within a week, the destruction of all the threatening Arab armies and a return of the nation to much of its biblical territory. It was a mental revolution. Most Israelis were shocked and confused by the immensity of their victory. Not only were they and their country saved, but a twenty-year-old political paradigm had been smashed.[9]

Some of them, however, were very certain about one critical element: never again would they let their homeland be weak and vulnerable; never again would Israel become a Massada. For nearly half of Israel's citizens the outcome of the Six-Day War created a new political psychology and new identity: Israel's territorial maximalism.[10]

The Land of Israel Movement

The ideological movement that was to formulate the creed of the new Israeli territorial maximalism was called *Hatenua Lemaan Eretz Yisrael Hashlema* (the Movement for the Whole of Eretz Yisrael; in short, the Land of Israel Movement, LIM). Its highly publicized founding manifesto of September, 1967, laid the foundations of the new political gospel in very straightforward terms:

> Zahal's victory in the Six-Day War located the people and the state within a new and fateful period. The whole of Eretz Israel is now in the hands of the Jewish people, and just as we are not allowed to give up the *State of Israel,* so we are ordered to keep what we received there from its hands: *the Land of Israel.* . . .
>
> Our present borders guarantee security and peace and open up unprecedented vistas of national material and spiritual consolidation. Within these boundaries, equality and freedom, the fundamental tenets of the state of Israel, shall be shared by all citizens without discrimination.[11]

Here was an unequivocal assertion that the conquest of vast Arab territories was irreversible. The war had produced historical justice, returning the entire Eretz Yisrael to the hands of the Jews. Israel was justly entitled to secure borders within which to accomplish its two fundamental goals, absorption of immigrants and settlement.[12]

Had the document been signed solely by representatives of traditional Zionist maximalism, it would hardly have been as significant. The Six-Day War did not invent the Jewish doctrine of the indivisibility of Eretz Yisrael. An old school of territorial maximalists belonging to the Revisionist movement, founded by Vladimir Jabotinsky in the twenties, and its offshoots already existed in Israel, ready to embrace the consequences of the 1967 war with a forty-year-old ideology. These maximalists included Menachem Begin's party Herut (Freedom), old followers of Brit Habirionim and former members of the Lehi underground. Thus it was not surprising to find among the LIM signatories such names as Professor Eri Jabotinsky, Vladimir's son; Dr. Reuven Hecht, a veteran Revisionist; Uri Zvi Greenberg, the poet laureate of the extreme Zionist right since the 1930s; and Dr. Israel Eldad, a former commander of Lehi and a well-known ideologue of *Malchut Yisrael* (the Kingdom of Israel). These people had always been nostalgic about the indivisible Eretz Yisrael and hostile to the 1948 partition of Palestine. Before 1967, though, very few other Israelis took the maximalists seriously. After the 1947 U.N. Partition Resolution, the 1948 war, and the consolidation of the State of Israel in the territories it salvaged from the Arabs in 1949, the issue of the indivisibility of Palestine became academic. It had no electoral appeal and was rarely discussed in any public forum.

What made the Land of Israel Movement manifesto important were the many signers identified with the Labor movement or its fundamental tenets. The most significant and active group were people who had followed David Ben-Gurion when he left Mapai in 1965 to form Rafi. They included the famed poet Nathan Alterman; the essayist and writer Zvi Shiloah, Isser Harel, Israel's legendary first head of Mossad; and Rachel Yanait Ben-Zvi, the widow of Israel's second president, Itzhak Ben-Zvi. They were joined by notables associated with Mapai: Chaim Yahil, former director-general of the ministry of Foreign Affairs; and Uzi Feinerman, the secretary-general of the Moshav movement. These representatives of Israel's political elite were joined by a gallery of illustrious reserve generals: Major General Yaacov Dori, the army's chief of staff during the War of Independence, and Brigadier Generals Dan Tolkovsky, Eliyahu Ben-Hur, Abraham Yaffe, and Meir Zorea. Israel's future Nobel Laureate, writer S. Y. Agnon, was also present, as were many other authors, poets, and critics.

Taken altogether, the seventy-two signatories of the manifesto were probably the most distinguished group of names ever to have joined a public cause in Israel. And what was most striking was that this document united many former opponents: before 1967, the LIM would have been impossible.[13] Right from its start, therefore, it became a significant political force.

The Land of Israel Movement, it is important to stress, was neither an opposition group nor an extremist protest movement. On the contrary; its members were proud of both the government and the military for the great victory of the Six-Day War. They were alarmed by the growing voices within Israel, and the mounting pressures from outside, to trade the occupied territories for a peaceful solution with the Arabs according to some pre-1967 conceptions, and they believed the government needed their help to strengthen its political resolve. Consequently, the LIM saw itself as an "ideological interest group" in charge of defending and promoting the issue of Eretz Yisrael.[14]

Nathan Alterman, the central figure of the movement, did not want to involve active politicians, for fear that they would use the movement to advance their political careers.[15] He concentrated instead on recruiting writers and poets who could give the new movement a metapolitical quality. The roster Alterman put together overshadowed anything the Israeli intellectual left could come up with.[16]

The lack of active politicians did not, of course, preclude politics. Most of the movement's members were identified with established political parties. The dominant group within the LIM, former Rafi members, were especially pleased with the new situation. One of Rafi's leaders, Major General (res.) Moshe Dayan, was popularly seen as the architect and hero of the Six-Day War. Not only had he pulled Israel to a great victory, but he had brought this splinter party from political isolation to the center of national action. And Moshe Dayan was the man who, upon reaching the Wailing Wall on the war's fourth day, uttered the unforgettable words: "We have returned to all that is holy in our land. We have returned never to be parted again."[17] In another emotional ceremony that followed the war, the burial of the casualties of 1948 on Jerusalem's Mount of Olives, Dayan repeated the theme:

> We have not abandoned your dream and we have not forgotten your lesson. We have returned to the mountain, to the cradle of our people, to the inheritance of the Patriarchs, the land of the Judges and the fortress of the Kingdom of the House of David. We have returned to Hebron and Schem [Nablus], to Bethlehem and Anatot to Jericho and the fords of the Jordan at Adam Ha'ir[18]

This sense of fulfillment and satisfaction was shared by all the components of the new movement. Veteran Revisionists, like Eri Jabotinsky and Samuel Katz, had always been hostile to the 1948 partition of Palestine and repeatedly argued that daring policy could place the entire Eretz Yisrael in the hands of the Jews. For many years, however, they had had no political forum for their views. Personal conflicts with Menachem Begin had driven them out of Herut, the only party that still subscribed to the old Revisionist creed. The new movement not only fitted their old ideology, but made it possible for them to rejoin Israel's public life without submitting to the dictates of Begin.[19]

The most ecstatic members of the LIM were probably the former leaders of Lehi and the old Zionist extreme right, the poet Uri Zvi Greenberg and Dr. Israel Eldad. Greenberg, Eldad, and other ideological extremists had, from the 1930s through the early 1950s, developed, as will be recalled, a unique set of ideas that most Israelis considered mystical insanity, the vision of the "the Kingdom of Israel." Its main theme was that the returning nation had to conquer the entire Promised Land by force, in a process that necessarily involved blood, glory, and honor.[20] The truncation of Israel in 1948 was to them a national humiliation and disgrace. Until 1967 this group, opposed to the dominant political ethos of Labor Zionism, shunned even by the Revisionists, was considered anathema and pushed to the very fringes of society.[21]

Though the followers of Jabotinsky shared many of the same beliefs, they could not forget that Abraham Stern (Yair) had defied Jabotinsky's last command in 1940 and split the Irgun by creating his own underground movement. And they were never impressed by the mystical vision of "the Kingdom of Israel." After 1948 the Revisionists had been able, under Begin's leadership, to enter legitimate political life, but Eldad and his followers remained outside mainstream right-wing politics. Only after the Six-Day War and the establishment of the LIM were Eldad's views accepted as relevant and legitimate. At first Eldad, convinced that his ultranationalist reputation would damage the new movement, refused to join the LIM. He could not believe that former adversaries were ready to share with him a common ideological home.[22]

Another important component of the Land of Israel Movement came from the Achdut Ha'avoda party, affiliated with Hakibbutz Hameuchad (the United Kibbutz) movement. These people brought to the LIM a unique ideological legacy and a strong political orientation. They were disciples and followers of Itzhak Tabenkin, the legendary kibbutz leader who alone among the founders of Israel's Labor movement never abandoned the ideal of Eretz Yisrael.

The idea of the partition of Palestine, first broached in the late 1930s, was not easily accepted by the Labor leadership. It took David Ben-Gurion many years to convince his colleagues that this was the only chance for independence and international recognition for the Jews of Palestine.[23] The 1947 U.N. Partition Resolution and Israel's success in the war of 1948 seemed to prove Ben-Gurion right.

Nevertheless, Tabenkin, whose personal charisma was always much stronger than his eclectic political theory, believed that a true Jewish redemption could take place only in the context of communal settlement in the entire Eretz Yisrael. The religious, nationalistic, and chauvinistic aspects of redemption played no role in his convictions; instead he believed in a genuine pioneering spirit and a mystical socialist vision of redemption. This authoritative and unchallenged leader of Hakibbutz Hameuchad never ceased to think that the best way to regenerate the Jewish people in Eretz Yisrael was to turn the entire nation into one big association of kibbutzim. Only such revolutionary socialization could overcome the Diaspora mentality and create a new Jew.[24]

This vision of agricultural, communal, and pioneering socialism, worked out by Tabenkin beginning in the 1920s, was not universalistic. It was very Jewish and particularistic. It was nourished by a deep suspicion of the Arabs, the British, and the rest of the world. And it was based on Tabenkin's unshakable conviction that the great transformation could take place only in the entirety of Eretz Yisrael. Tabenkin, who had no interest in practical politics, never forgave Ben-Gurion for endorsing the partition of Palestine. The U.N. Partition Resolution was an agonizing event for many of Tabenkin's followers; they refused to rejoice with the rest of the nation, since much of the land was left in Arab hands.[25]

We cannot say that Tabenkin's followers—including his sons Moshe and Yosef, and individuals like Menachem Dorman and Benni Marshak—had been waiting impatiently since 1949 for the conquest of the West Bank, but it is clear that Hakibbutz Hameuchad never gave up the idea of greater Israel. In its February 1955 convention, Hakibbutz Hameuchad passed resolutions that made its position clear:

> Article 2: Eretz Yisrael in its natural boundaries is the historical homeland of the Jewish people and the space for immigration, settlement, and fulfillment of the Zionist endeavor
>
> Article 20: Socialist Zionism, in its full meaning and framework, cannot be fulfilled in a divided Eretz Yisrael but only in a complete Eretz Yisrael, in the Hebrew socialist state of the Jewish people . . . and the Arabs living in the land.[26]

And while the urgency of reuniting Eretz Yisrael had lost much of its momentum after the 1956 Sinai campaign, Tabenkin and his close followers never gave up on the ideal. Just a year before the 1967 war Tabenkin reiterated his commitment in a seminar held at Ef'al, the ideological center of Hakibbutz Hameuchad. Discussing the present political irrelevance of the issue, he stressed that it was nevertheless extremely important that "the son, the daughter, the student, who go to the army, see this matter as a goal," and continued, "when Jews are told about Zion, they think about the entire Eretz Yisrael." Tabenkin said that if war came (though he hoped it would not), "in every place where the war would make it possible, we would push for the restoration of the integrity of the land."[27] Curiously, Tabenkin did not sign the first LIM manifesto, though he fully endorsed the movement and its ideas.[28]

It should be noted for the record that the LIM was briefly joined by another literary-ideological circle, the Canaanites, who were never content with Israeli Zionism and democracy. Led by poet Yonathan Ratosh, the Canaanites believed that Israeli Jews should sever their relations with Diaspora Jewry, abandon Zionism, and invest their political energy in the creation of a huge "Canaanite alliance" in the Middle East, made of all the non-Muslim and anti-Arab minorities in the area. They had no objection to pursuing this goal by force and suggested that Israel establish a military dictatorship. Before long, however, they were kicked out of LIM, the excuse being their total nonacceptance of the Zionist ideology and the Israeli regime.[29]

At first the Land of Israel Movement was more of an intellectual club than a fighting mass organization—a typical elite group made up of elderly notables who gave no thought to, and were incapable of, actually leading a radical movement of protest. None of them were young, angry, or powerless. All were successful achievers who had full political and media access, and most accepted the Israeli system of government and the prevailing norms of democracy. They were convinced that *they were* the nation. They truly believed that there was no contradiction between the new Israel that had just been formed by the Six-Day War and the principles of the old Israel. Their reiteration, in their founding manifesto, of the principles of equality, freedom, and the "tenets of the state of Israel" was genuine and sincere. The movement did not aspire to be more than a single-issue ideological group, operating within a fully legitimate regime. If the new territorial maximalism carried within it the seeds of the future radical right, most of its founders were unaware of it.

Between Messianism and Fundamentalism: The Roots of Gush Emunim

Zionist religious Jews were especially stunned by the outcome of the Six-Day War. It did not square with the non-messianic, pragmatic stance most of them had maintained for years. It could only be comprehended as a miracle: The God of Israel had once again showed His might. He had come to the rescue of His people in their worst moment of fear and anxiety, and, as in the days of old, had turned an unbearable situation upside down. In one blow He placed the whole of Eretz Yisrael—the object of yearning and prayers for thousands of years—into the hands of His loyal servants.

While most religious Israelis reacted to the outcome of the Six-Day War with as much bewilderment as joy, one group had expected just such an event.

This was the group gathered around Yeshivat Merkaz Harav in Jerusalem. The head of the Yeshiva, Rabbi Zvi Yehuda Hacohen Kook, who had succeeded its founder, his revered father Rabbi Avraham Yitzhak Hacohn Kook (the first Chief Rabbi of the Jewish community in mandatory Palestine), had long been preoccupied with the incorporation of the entire Eretz Yisrael into the State of Israel.[30] His dreams were widely shared by his students before the Six-Day War, and were discussed in many courses and Halakhic deliberations (discussions of orthodox Jewish law and tradition).

Following the teaching of his father that ours is a messianic age in which the Land of Israel is to be reunited and redeemed, Rabbi Zvi Yehuda left no doubt in the minds of his students that in their lifetime they were to see the great event. Thus, unlike the rest of the Zionist religious community, the graduates of Merkaz Harav were mentally and intellectually ready to absorb the consequences of the war—but not before witnessing a unique, seemingly miraculous event. On the eve of Independence Day in May 1967, just one day before the beginning of the crisis that led to the war, graduates of Merkaz Harav met at the yeshiva for an alumni reunion. As was his custom, Rabbi Zvi Yehuda Kook delivered a festive sermon, in the midst of which his quiet voice suddenly rose and he bewailed the partition of historic Eretz Yisrael and the inability of the Jews to return to the holy cities of Hebron and Nablus. His faithful disciples were told that the situation was intolerable and must not last.[31] When just three weeks later, in June 1967, some of them reached the Wailing Wall as soldiers and found themselves citizens of an enlarged Israel, the graduates of Merkaz Harav were convinced that a genuine spirit of prophecy had come over their rabbi. Just minutes after the conquest of the Wall, a platoon commander sent a jeep to bring Rabbi Kook to the holy site. There he was met by two of his overwhelmed students, paratroopers Hanan Porat and Israel Shtieglitz (Ariel), future activists of the radical right. In front of his students and the entire battalion Rabbi Zvi Yehuda solemnly declared

> We hereby inform the people of Israel and the entire world that under heavenly command we have just returned home in the elevations of holiness and our holy city. We shall never move out of here.[32]

Thus, in one stroke a flame had been lit and the conditions made ripe for imparting a new messianic and fundamentalist ideology to a wide religious public, especially to young Zionist Jews. A totally new kind of religious spirit and literature emerged that focused on the messianic and eschatological meaning of the Six-Day War. The war was seen as a miracle embodying all the signs cited by the Prophets and the Halakhic authorities as indicating the coming of the Messiah.[33] The new orientation made it clear that the territories of Eretz Yisrael were physically and spiritually inseparable from the people of Israel.

Zvi Yehuda Kook, the unknown rabbi who spearheaded the new interpretation, was elevated to the status of a charismatic guru. His disciples became missionaries equipped with an unshakable conviction in the divine authority of their cause. In time they were to transform a passive religious community into an active and excited political constituency.

How does the messianism of the new ideology relate to its fundamentalism? Let us compare the theologies of its two spiritual fathers—Rabbi Avraham Yitzhak Hacohen Kook, the man who established Yeshivat Merkaz Harav— and his son Rabbi Zvi Yehuda Kook, who became head of the Yeshiva and lived to see the Six-Day War.

The elder Rabbi Kook, by far the more original thinker, believed that the era of redemption of the Jewish people had already begun. It was character- ized by the rise of modern Zionism, the Balfour Declaration, and the grow- ing Zionist enterprise in Palestine:

> And there is no doubt that this great movement [Zionism] is *Atchalta D'geula* (the beginning of redemption), which is about to come soon, in our own days. And for our people and the cities of our God we have to be strong.[34]

Although not unprecedented, Kook's interpretation of redemption was uncommon and daring. It deviated from the traditional Jewish belief that the messiah could come only through the single metahistorical appearance of an individual redeemer. And there were clearly some elements of heresy in the new interpretation, for it assigned a holy and redemptive status to the Zionists—the modern Jewish nationalists who wanted to establish in the Holy Land a *secular* state.[35] Kook's argument that the secular Zionists were God's unknowing emissaries subjected him to the hostility of the old reli- gious community in Palestine, especially the ultraorthodox, who considered Zionism a heresy.[36]

But the elder Kook hardly advocated political fundamentalism or "opera- tive messianism." Acting and writing in the 1920s and 1930s, he supported the political approach of the secular Zionist movement, one of slow and prudent progress toward national fulfillment. He did not establish a political movement and never called for a policymaking process based on the To- rah.[37] The theology taught in Yeshivat Merkaz Harav had no immediate policy consequences and made no political demands.[38]

Israel's victory in the Six-Day War transformed the status of the theology taught at Merkaz Harav as well as the existential reality of its students and graduates. Suddenly it became clear to these young people that they were indeed living in a messianic age and that messianism had a concrete meaning in their everyday life. Ordinary reality assumed a sacred aspect, in which every event possessed theological meaning and was part of the metahistori- cal process of redemption.[39] Though this view was shared by several authori- ties such as Rabbi Shlomo Goren, the Chief Rabbi of the army, and Rabbi Zvi Moshe Neriah, the senior rabbi of the Bnei Akiva yeshivot, it was most effectively expounded by Kook's son, Rabbi Zvi Yehuda, heretofore only an unknown interpreter of his father's writings, who now became an active ideologue and the spiritual leader of a new messianic movement.

Rabbi Kook defined the State of Israel as the Halakhic "Kingdom of Israel in the Making" and the "Kingdom of Israel as the Kingdom of Heaven on Earth." Referring to the Six-Day War and its experience he said: "We are living in the middle of redemption. The Kingdom of Israel is being rebuilt. The entire Israeli army is holy. It symbolizes the rule of the people on its land."[40] Every Jew living in Israel was, according to Rav Zvi Yehuda Kook, holy, all phenomena, even the secular, were imbued with holiness. Not only Kook's students, but all Israelis, were expected to recognize the transformation and behave accordingly. The government was to conduct its affairs according to Maimonides' "Rules of Kings" and to be judged by these rules and Torah prescriptions.[41]

As for Eretz Yisrael, the Land of Israel, the land—every grain of its soil—was declared holy in a fundamentalist sense. In that respect Kook differed from the new territorial maximalists—the occupied territories were inalienable not for political or security reasons, but because God had promised them to Abraham 4,000 years ago, shaping the identity of the nation. Rabbi Zvi Yehuda was so attached to this fundamentalist formula that in spite of his great enthusiasm for the Land of Israel Movement he refused to sign its manifesto. Its preamble proclaimed that "the whole of Eretz Yisrael is now in the hands of the Jewish people"; but this was, in a fundamentalist sense, false. Abraham's Promised Land was bigger than Palestine, it included parts of present-day Jordan, Syria, and Iraq—territories to which the Jewish nation was not allowed, in principle to forsake its claim.[42] While he never called for a new war to conquer these farther territories, Rabbi Zvi Yehuda advocated keeping the areas already occupied. In an early "call" to his students, "Lo Taguru" (Be not afraid), he said, "This land is ours; here are no Arab territories or Arab lands, but only Israeli territories—the eternal land of our forefathers, which belongs in its Biblical boundaries to the government of Israel."[43] Complete national salvation, Kook instructed his students, could only take place in the context of the Greater Israel; withdrawal from the new territories would be against God's intention (clearly demonstrated in the Six-Day War) and would mean forfeiting redemption.

While Rabbi Zvi Yehuda Kook and his followers were very clear about the requirements of the time and the path to follow, they saw no need in 1967 to establish a political movement of their own. They were, in fact, very pleased with the government, the legitimate carrier of the nation's redemptive calling, and the army. The Land of Israel Movement, which received Kook's full support, would transmit the Eretz Yisrael idea to the nation, and since God was active behind the scenes, there was no reason to worry.

Most of the immediate political activity of the would-be Gush Emunim in the post-1967 years took place within the National Religious Party. It was conducted in the context of the struggle of a new age cohort to assume leadership positions and influence within this pragmatic party that was an old ally of the ruling Labor coalition. The young generation of the NRP was extremely unhappy with the traditional passive role the party played in the government of Israel on national issues such as security and the conduct of foreign affairs. Its leaders, former Bar Illan student activists such as Zevulun Hammer and Yehuda Ben-Meir, demanded that the NRP participate actively in all the critical issues facing the nation, and the emerging Eretz Yisrael ideology was a good place to start.[44]

While the young graduates of Merkaz Harav helped form a rabbinical consensus on the sanctity of Eretz Yisrael and thus helped reformulate the political platform of the NRP, their real contribution was to launch the actual Jewish return to the West Bank. Kook's followers pushed the government to resettle Gush Etzion, a pre-1948 Jewish agricultural area that had been captured by the Jordanian Arab Legion during the War of Independence.[45]

In 1968 Rabbi Moshe Levinger, one of Rabbi Zvi Yehuda's most devoted students, led seventy-nine followers in the first Jewish return to Hebron. The operation began in illicitly moving into the Park Hotel in Hebron, to Moshe Dayan's great annoyance. This became the model for Gush Emunim's illicit operations. The unauthorized settlement, was followed by a declaration that the settlers will never leave, and finally by an agreement to be moved to a nearby military compound. It involved tremendous dedication, great political pressure, and intense lobbying. Soon the government decided to establish Kiryat Arba, a new Jewish city next to Hebron.[46]

Thus the young followers of the new theology of Eretz Yisrael found out about national politics. They learned firsthand about diplomatic pressure, political manipulation, politicians' personal ambitions, and internal rivalries. And they found out that one could not remain a pure true believer if one wanted to get things done. Even in the messianic age there was room for shrewd lobbying, cheating, and bluffing. Rabbi Moshe Levinger, leader of the new settlement of Kiryat Arba, became the role model: learned, highly observant, realistic, innovative, and manipulative.[47] Levinger and his colleagues proved astute students of Israeli politics. They quickly realized that the Israeli coalition governments, though united in times of war, were divided in peace—and that it was easy to manipulate ambitious cabinet ministers against each other.[48] To their great disappointment they found that the government, the "Kingdom of Israel in the Making," was *unaware* of its role in the process of redemption, and was not even sure about its short-range goals. In this context, young people, armed with unworldly religious excitement, unshakable conviction in their cause, existential resolve, and some political savvy could work miracles.

By 1973 they were ready for a new, more daring venture, the first Jewish penetration of Samaria, the densely populated northern part of the West Bank. The actors were a small group called Gariin (nucleus) Elon Moreh, led by students from the small yeshiva of Kiryat Arba. Impatient with the slow progress of the Jewish settlement of the West Bank and especially with the hesitation of the government on settlement in Samaria, the group, under the leadership of Benny Katzover and Menachem Felix, decided one day to lay aside the holy books—*"Sogrim et hagmarot."* This decision, which has already attained mythical status in the short history of Gush Emunim, meant that although studying Torah at the newly established Kiryat Arba was extremely significant, an even greater calling was the settlement of Samaria.[49] They believed that what was now needed was to challenge the inaction of the Israeli government, break the stalemate on settlement, and make sure the process of redemption continued. Elon Moreh was the biblical name of Nablus, and forming a Gariin—a social nucleus for a future settlement—with this name meant that Nablus, the biggest Palestinian center on the West Bank, was a target for Jewish settlement, with or without official sanction.

While the new Zionist fundamentalism blossomed after the Six-Day War, it is important to recognize that it grew out of social and political processes that had been in the making long before 1967. The disciples of Rabbi Zvi Yehuda Kook, who studied at Merkaz Harav since the early 1950s, were not isolated individuals who discovered the light through mystical revelation. They came to Merkaz Harav from the community of the so-called "knitted skullcaps," the Bnei Akiva youth movement, Hapoel Hamizrahi, and adherents of the Torah Va'avoda (Torah and Labor), the founders of the religious kibbutz movement.

Bnei Akiva, the religious parallel to several other Israeli pioneering youth movements, provided the quality manpower for many of Israel's kibbutzim. Its graduates were involved in establishing many Zionist enterprises in Palestine and were closely connected to the Labor movement and its pioneering ethos.

Religious Zionists were part of the political, economic, and cultural fabric of the country, with their own variegated semi-private educational system.[50] For many years, however, these people suffered from a major cultural drawback: as observant orthodox Jews who wore knitted skullcaps, they were outsiders. A main feature of modern Zionism had been its secularism and anti-clericalism. Most modern Zionists revolted against the Jewish *shtetls* of Eastern Europe, which represented for them all the maladies of the Diaspora. And the *shtetls* were made up, according to the Zionist caricature, primarily of orthodox Jews who, instead of protecting themselves against a hostile and antisemitic world, lived marginal and unproductive lives and prayed all day long. The Zionist maxim of *Shelilat Hagalut* (the negation of Diaspora) implied for the vast majority of Israeli Zionists the rejection of orthodox Judaism, its practitioners, and its symbols.[51] This prevalent orientation created tremendous identity problems for the religious Zionists who believed there was no contradiction between the traditional Jewish yearning to return to Zion and modern Zionism. They were part of all the exciting developments in Israel, but they were denigrated as secondary partners.

Thus, the youngsters of Bnei Akiva had internalized a profound sense of bitterness and frustration. Truly Zionist and idealistic, they had developed two hidden ambitions: to erase the shame of their parents, who had agreed to play a humiliating auxiliary role in building the Jewish state, and to outdo the secular Zionists. Witnessing the constant decline of Israel's secular pioneering and public spirit and the growth of materialism and self-interested individualism, they found it easy to imagine another kind of Zionism, more Jewish and closer to the true spiritual sources of the nation.

Long after Gush Emunim was founded, it was learned that its leaders came from a secret Gariin, formed in 1952 by teenagers from Yeshivat Kfar Haroe who vowed to work for a spiritual and cultural transformation of the nation. They called themselves *Gahelet* (embers), which also stood for *Gariin Halutzi Lomdei Torah* (a pioneering nucleus of Torah students). The Gahelet charter said, "We must kindle the flame of the future generations, to look forward to the day in which every man in Israel will sit under his vine and fig tree in full observance of the Torah of Israel."[52] When the twelve members of this secret group discovered the writings of the elder Rabbi Kook, they joined Merkaz Harav and became devoted students of the younger Rabbi Kook.

Until the 1950s Merkaz Harav was a small and unimportant religious seminary in Jerusalem. The death of Rav Kook, in 1935, had left the yeshiva without a leader. None of his successors was as charismatic and original as the founder, and few students were attracted to the place. But the orientation of Merkaz Harav, based on the unique legacy of the late Rabbi, was nevertheless different from the approaches adopted by other yeshivas. The heads of the yeshiva—Rabbis Harlap, Ra'anan, and Zvi Yehuda Kook— had never been ambivalent about the newly created State of Israel. Its secular nature had not disturbed them, for they had been convinced that in due course the Israelis would repent and return to tradition and Torah. The very attainment of national independence was seen by them as a fulfillment of the prophesies of their revered mentor. They were especially excited about the army of the new state, and unlike many rabbis, they made Yom Hatzmaut (Israel's Independence Day) a high religious holiday full of spiritual meaning.[53] Every Yom Hatzmaut, Merkaz would have an alunni get-together, at which a major sermon by the rabbi would be delivered.

This positive attitude toward the State of Israel had apparently attracted the young members of Gahelet. Here was a yeshiva that conceived itself as an integral part of the nation's Zionist regeneration and did not feel apologetic about its religious character. These were rabbis who did not think that reading and rehearsing the Torah and Halakha were antithetical to state matters: security, foreign policy, or economy.

Starting in the mid-fifties, Yeshivat Merkaz Harav slowly became the spiritual center of the new approach to religious Zionism. The new students listened attentively to the idealistic and nationalist sermons of Rabbi Zvi Yehuda and to his very Israeli interpretation of his father's books. In addition to their scholarly attraction to this person, the students developed a very emotional attachment to him. The childless rabbi gave the young students all his love and attention, and Merkaz Harav became for them a second home and a family.[54]

After they graduated, Kook's students continued to preach the Merkaz Harav gospel in and out of Bnei Akiva circles. Without being aware of their contribution, they had participated in an undeclared cultural competition between Israel's secular educational system and their own. Although there was no outright war between the two systems in the 1950s and 1960s, there was an immense tension. They represented opposing approaches to public and private life, and in the 1950s there were many indications that the religious were being overcome by the grand process of secularization.

Today we know that this never happened. The victors in this power contest were the religious educational system and the subculture of the Hapoel Hamizrahi and the "knitted skullcaps." In contrast to the other sectors of the Zionist educational system, which in the course of being nationalized lost their specific normative characters and underwent an astonishing ideological dilution, the religious Zionists developed an educational system that created norms of life and behavior of the highest order for a quarter of the school population. Thus the religious Zionist public was spared the general decline that beset the country's secular educational system and, indeed, may have even been consolidated by it.

Around that educational system, complete life patterns were created for an entire public, which reinforced its religious life not only at home and in the synagogue but also (for its children) in the neighborhood kindergarten and in the ulpanah (religious academy for girls) and yeshiva.[55] The ideological leadership of this system was partly being taken over in the 1960s by the graduates of Merkaz Harav.

This process of pre-1967 ideological discovery of Eretz Israel, in which a whole Bnei Akiva generation moved slowly in a nationalist direction, was not revolutionary. It was gradual, and consistent, and it had both educational and political aspects. The most significant development in the educational sphere was the emergence of Yeshivot Hesder (arrangement) which combined an advanced religious education with military service in the Israeli army. Hesder (arrangement) refers to agreements between the yeshivas and the Ministry of Defense. The new type of yeshivas brought religious youth into direct contact with national issues they were not aware of before. Young people of military age would now go for one year of yeshiva study, with some military exercise, and later join the army for an intense period of training. While not comprehensive or numerically large before 1967, the new arrangement was part of a larger process that helped close the gap between the secular side of the Israeli life and the religious.[56] Thus, it is possible to conclude that by the mid-1960s, a whole generation of impatient Bnei Akiva graduates and youth, with a Merkaz Harav spiritual elite, stood ready to change the course of modern Zionism if the right events should take place. And they did within one June week, 1967.

Rabbi Meir Kahane and the Birth of the Israeli Jewish Defense League

In September 1971, the growing Israeli territorial maximalism movement got an unexpected reinforcement. Rabbi Meir Kahane, the notorious head of the Jewish Defense League (JDL), an American Jewish vigilante organization, moved to Israel. Kahane, an orthodox rabbi, did not conceal his sympathy for the most extreme interpretations of the Land of Israel Movement and the growing Zionist messianism. Already at that early day he was the most radical among the maximalists, a position he never relinquished.[57]

Unlike the other territorial maximalists, Kahane had his roots in America and in the American scene of the 1960s. In 1968, he and a few other young orthodox Jews established the JDL as a self-proclaimed vigilante movement aimed at defending Jewish neighborhoods in New York City. At first the league was mostly concerned with local issues: "crime in the streets," "black anti-Semitism," "do-nothing government," and "changing neighborhoods."[58] Paradoxically, the inactivity of the Jewish establishment helped Kahane, whose penchant for violence was obvious from the start. The leadership of the American Jewish community dissociated itself from the vigilante rabbi without offering a single solution to the problems he addressed. Consequently, Kahane became attractive to lower-middle-class urban Jews, who suffered from anti-Semitism and violence in the streets. And he also found a young Jewish middle-class generation looking for an anti-establishment hero.

The ambitious rabbi from Brooklyn, a talented speaker, knew how to pluck the sensitive chords of Jewish anxiety. He spoke bluntly about American anti-Semitism, manifest and latent, and helped assuage his listeners' guilt about the Holocaust. The Jewish establishment was his prime target; he constantly reminded his audience how little the Jewish leadership had done during World War II to stop the killing of Jews in Europe and of how hesitant they now were in fighting black anti-Semitism. "Never Again" became the slogan of the JDL: never again were Jews to be defenseless.[59]

Kahane's success in activating young Jews for aggressive self-defense against anti-Semitism in America did not escape the attention of several ultranationalist Israelis who believed there was an even more important Jewish cause to fight for, the plight of Russian Jews. According to Robert Friedman, Kahane's biographer, it was Geula Cohen, former Lehi activist, and Herut Knesset member since 1969, who first introduced Kahane to the subject, and who was also instrumental in forging a secret, semi-official support group for Kahane in Israel.[60] Since 1969, the repression of Soviet Jewry and the refusal of the Soviet Union to let Jews emigrate became the major item on the agenda of the JDL. Russian diplomats were attacked, first in the United States then in Europe, Russian artists were harassed, and demonstrations were held in front and inside of Russian agencies. Kahane had apparently identified a very sensitive issue for which it was possible to mobilize considerable support. The Rabbi's extraordinary ability to dramatize this struggle by the use of symbolic and real violence, and to gain media attention, popularized the JDL and facilitated fund raising and recruitment. In the beginning of the 1970s the JDL had many thousands of activists all over the United States, branches in Europe and South Africa, and admirers in Israel.[61]

For his enthusiastic supporters, Kahane launched a new gospel of Jewish self-transformation and mutual responsibility: "The American Jew, from now on, will become a new person, proud of his origins, capable of defending himself and fully devoted to the cause of his brothers all over the world."[62] Action quickly followed. Though until 1969 most JDL activities included only *symbolic* violence permitted by law, the league soon became involved in illegal acts and actual violence. After attacking an anti-Semitic radio station, JDL members were sent to jail. In 1970 and 1971 they conducted a score of violent assaults and bombing of Russian institutions in the United States, including Aeroflot, Intourist, several Soviet cultural centers, Amtorg, Russian diplomatic missions, and the residences of Soviet officials in New York and Washington. American firms, doing business with the Soviet Union and institutions involved in Soviet-American cultural exchange were also subjected to JDL aggression.[63]

The JDL thus evolved a unique ideology and style, claiming the right to defend fellow Jews wherever there was trouble. The young rabbi from Brooklyn, as associate editor of the Brooklyn *Jewish Press,* the largest selling Anglo-Jewish newspaper in America, could use his weekly column to develop a full-fledged ideology; books based on these essays spread his influence. The key concept of the new philosophy was *Ahavat Yisroel* (Love of Jewry), a mutuality that implied the obligation to help Jews in trouble, with no reservations and conditions.

> The pain of a Jew, wherever he may be, is our pain. The joy of a Jew, wherever he may be is our joy. We are committed to going to the aid of a Jew who is in need without distinction, without asking what kind of Jew he is. . . .
>
> We do more, however, than pay lip service to the concept of love of Jewry. We act upon it. There is no limit to the lengths to which we will go when necessary to aid a fellow Jew. We must be prepared to give our efforts; we must be prepared to give our moneys; and, if need be, we must be prepared to give our lives for the Jewish people.[64]

But the new element in the JDL's message was not its readiness to help other Jews, but to do it violently, unconditionally, and with "no limit." Even then Kahane made it clear that no geographic boundaries or legal prohibitions were to stop him from "defending Jews." He also stated bluntly that "Jewish violence to protect Jewish interests is *never* bad."[65] Kahane rarely deigned to play according to rules imposed by authorities he did not recognize, and he seldom restrained himself or criticized his followers for violence.

In ideology, Kahane was greatly influenced by Vladimir Jabotinsky, the founder of Revisionist Zionism. Kahane had participated in Jabotinsky's youth movement, Betar, and was especially taken by the master's favorable attitude toward Jewish self-defense and Jewish dignity; he adopted two of Betar's most famous slogans—*hadar* (glory, self-pride) and *barzel* (iron, iron fist)—as slogans of the Jewish Defense League.[66] What Kahane ignored was Jabotinsky's comprehensive liberal outlook and great respect for legality, which had greatly restrained Betar's militancy. The JDL youngsters were instructed to be demonstrably proud of their Jewish origins and have no guilt about using the "iron fist" against the enemies of Jews. They were told, in addition, to be obedient to their leader (*Mishmaat Yisroel*—Jewish discipline and unity), and to be fully confident that God was behind them and their nation (*Bitachon*—faith in the indestructibility of the Jewish people).[67]

It is hard to identify the sources of Kahane's most notorious ideological contribution to the American JDL, the glorification of Jewish violence. Judging from his early writings, it appears that Kahane's insatiable urge to resort to exhibitionist violence has been his response to the repressions and humiliations of Jews since time immemorial, and especially during the Holocaust. All of Kahane's early writings communicate a profound internalization of the evils committed against Jews, and a deep resentment that this experience had destroyed their readiness to fight back. By legitimizing unmitigated violence against the enemies of the Jews, Kahane seems to believe he is destroying the ghetto mentality of the Jew and reconstructing genuine Jewry, "the Jews of old":

> Once upon a time, the Jew was not a member of the ADL [the American liberal Anti-Defamation League, an organization highly critical of the JDL's violence]—neither in form nor in spirit. It was not in the role of Mahatma Gandhi that the Jews fought at Massada; the men of Bar-Kochba and Judah Macabee never went to a Quaker meeting. The Jews of old—when Jews were knowledgeable about their religion, when they turned the page of the Jewish Bible instead of turning the Christian cheek—understood the concept of the Book and the Sword. It was only in the horror of the ghetto with its fears, neuroses, and insecurities that the Jew began to react in fright rather than with self-respect. That is what the ghetto does to a Jew.[68]

Meanwhile, Kahane was developing his own version of *catastrophic Zionism,* an ideology that predicted a new holocaust and called upon the Jews of Diaspora to return to Israel before it was too late. Nineteenth-century Zionism, it should be recalled, had a very strong catastrophic component. Leo Pinsker and Theodor Herzl, its most influential theoreticians, came to their conclusion that Zionism was inevitable as a result of the threat to the physical security of the Jews in Eastern Europe at the turn of the century. They convinced themselves, and many generations of young Zionists, that anti-Semitism was so severe that it was just a matter of time before the entire nation was eliminated by either physical destruction or spiritual assimilation.[69] The doctrine of *Shelilat Hagalut* (the Negation of the Diaspora) was a direct product of this catastrophic Zionism.

Catastrophic Zionism declined as the Zionist enterprise in Palestine evolved and political Zionism succeeded after 1917; Jabotinsky's warnings of growing European anti-Semitism in the 1930s were the exception. The establishment of the State of Israel, the emergence of the powerful American Jewry, and the respectable presence of Jewish communities all over the democratic West have left the thesis of catastrophic Zionism with little explanatory power.

Kahane could not care less. Since 1968 he talked about the gathering storm, the incipient disaster. Soon the enemies of the Jews would overcome their guilt about the destruction of European Jewry and start to plan the new holocaust. America of the melting pot, the dream of millions of Jewish immigrants, Kahane told his audience, was beginning to undergo in the 1960s both an economic recession and a severe moral and social crisis. Inevitably, the classical scapegoats, the Jews, would be attacked once more.[70]

Kahane's catastrophic Zionsim was the rationale behind his "program for Jewish survival," the subtitle of his book *Never Again* and his call for a comprehensive series of steps to save American Jewry from extinction. While most of the suggestions sought to reform Jewish life in America—by reforming the Jewish educational system, fighting the corrupting influence of assimilation, and defending Jewish rights, by force, if necessary—the ultimate step called for was emigration to Israel. Though Jews in the Diaspora could help themselves by returning to full Judaism and defending their rights and dignity, the Diaspora itself was doomed; there was no chance for a long-range Jewish survival outside the State of Israel.[71]

Furthermore, Kahane saw the America of the 1960s as a troubled land, a modern Sodom or Gommorah, but Israel, the land of the prophets and conquerors, was all good, the true answer to all the present Jewish miseries. The young state that freed itself *by force* from British colonialism and built a military machine capable of defeating all the Arab anti-Semites was the manifestation of Kahane's early dreams. Only Israel could produce the new Jew, a healthy and complete Hebrew national.[72]

Meir Kahane emigrated to Israel, arriving on 12 September 1971. He and his supporters have always maintained that this was the logical next step in the realization of his Zionist ideology. But less favorable interpretations point out that by 1971 Kahane had come to a dead end: in the spirit of détente the American administration was by then determined to rein in extreme anti-Soviet activity, and the FBI had made it clear to Kahane that it had sufficient evidence to send him to prison. He had in fact been given a suspended sentence of four years' probation. The critics maintain that Kahane, unable to face the consequent decline of his movement, decided to emigrate to Israel, claiming ideological grounds.[73]

In Israel, Kahane was warmly welcomed by the political right and the media. He said he did not intend to get involved with national politics or run for the Knesset; he would instead devote himself to education. He wanted to found his own *kirya* (educational center) and a kibbutz. Jerusalem would be the international center for the JDL, and prospective JDL members would come to Israel for a leadership training course. Kahane also stated his wish to replace the "internationalist" orientation of young Israelis with a healthy nationalism.[74]

However, Rabbi Kahane was not destined to pursue a career in education. He craved publicity and needed action in the streets. He also could not be content with the ideological politics pursued by most of the territorial maximalists in the early 1970s. Even the most extreme of them could not quite figure out this strange and impatient person who did not join their movements and would not submit to any period of initiation into the Israeli political style.

The Israeli public learned in 1972 that the JDL had become fully operative in Jerusalem. Surrounded by a handful of young American supporters who had followed him to Israel, and by a smaller group of young Russian *émigrés,* Kahane took to the streets. Besides demonstrating against the Soviet Union, he exploited two new issues: Christian missionary activities in Israel and the sect of American blacks in Dimona. Though in principle Israelis reject any kind of Christian missionary activity and considered it a manifestation of religious hostility, there had rarely been any serious trouble over this issue. However, never shy of publicity, Kahane was determined to apply the strictest rules of the Halakha (which prohibit the presence of Christians in the Holy Land) and evict the missionaries from the country—and to do it noisily. Similarly he and his followers aggressively demonstrated against a small black sect who recently settled in the southern development town of Dimona, and claimed to be genuinely Jewish, though it certainly was not. Small and highly isolated, it went almost unnoticed until Kahane made headlines by drawing attention to it.[75]

But it took Kahane less than a year after his arrival in Israel to focus on his prime target—the Arabs. In August 1972, JDL leaflets were distributed all over Hebron. The astonished Arab residents learned that Meir Kahane was summoning their mayor, Muhamad Ali Ja'abari, to a public show-trial for his part in the 1929 massacre of the ancient Jewish community of Hebron. The military authorities were fully aware that this was a very sensitive issue, given that treatment of the inhabitants of the occupied areas was carefully monitored by international agencies. Despite strict orders to prevent his provocative visit, on 27 August, Kahane, escorted by two of his followers, appeared in front of the mayor's office in Hebron at exactly the announced time of the public trial. He was stopped and sent back to Jerusalem, but the shock waves created by his visit were deeply felt.[76]

Of course, no public show-trial was ever held in Hebron or any of the numerous Arab towns and villages Kahane visited over the years. There have always been police or military units on hand to stop him from provoking a confrontation with the local residents. But Hebron established Kahane's reputation for expertise in provocation and headline-making in Israel. Recognizing full well the great impact of these tactics on the Arab population of Judea and Samaria, as well as on Israeli Arabs, Kahane proved resourceful and imaginative.

His message was always the same: "The Arabs do not belong here; they must leave." In this spirit, in 1972 Kahane initiated an organized operation to encourage the Arabs to emigrate.[77] Promising full compensation for property, he developed his theme that only massive Arab evacuation would solve Israel's problems: just as two people cannot sit on the same chair, so it is impossible for the two nations, Israeli and Palestinian, to coexist in the Land of Israel.

While specializing in symbolic action, Kahane did not abstain from involvement in acts of violence against Arabs. In 1972, following the terrorist massacre of the Israeli athletes at the Olympic games in Munich, he launched an attempt to sabotage the Libyan Embassy in Brussles. He secured the support of Amichai Paglin, who had been chief of operations of the Irgun underground during the British mandate. The plot was exposed at Ben-Gurion Airport when a container of arms and explosives was discovered.[78]

Prior to the Yom Kippur War of October 1973, no other territorial-maximalist group used tactics like Kahane and his JDL; they did not specialize in direct action or consider systematic extraparliamentary politics proper behavior. Neither the Land of Israel Movement nor the incipient Gush Emunim asked the Arabs to leave. Kahane's radicalism was unique. But though the extreme rabbi was isolated, he attracted considerable attention. This was probably the reason he decided to run for the Knesset and the explanation for his successful fundraising. The result was an "almost" success. Kahane polled 12,811 votes, just a few thousands short of the required number for a Knesset seat.

Livneh's *Israel and the Crisis of Western Civilization*

While most of the secular territorial maximalists avidly believed their new Eretz Yisrael gospel, they were unable to give it a coherent theoretical framework. Each of the secular schools that joined the Land of Israel Movement—from Hakibbutz Hameuchad's activists to Jabotinsky's Revisionists to smaller groups and individuals—maintained their old convictions with slight modifications.

They all agreed on three fundamental points: Israel's utmost need for secure borders, the nonexistence of a Palestinian nation, and the insignificance of the "demographic problem"—the danger that if the occupied territories were annexed, the Jews would lose their majority in Eretz Yisrael. *Zot Ha'aretz* (This Is the Land), the new ideological magazine of the LIM, continuously rehashed these topics in all possible variations. They were repeatedly published in Israel's most distinguished dailies and discussed in countless symposia and seminars. Three of the leading ideologues of the movement—Samuel Katz, Moshe Shamir, and Zvi Shiloah—published lengthy books about the post-1967 Israeli reality, but none was ideologically new. Arabs were told, one way or another, that they were wrong all along and that they could no longer trust their leaders, who had brought disaster upon them. Israelis were exhorted to recognize how mighty and wonderful their country really was.[79]

The only exception to this combination of intense tactical polemics and unsystematic thinking was a comprehensive and original book by Eliezer Livneh, *Israel and the Crisis of Western Civilization,*[80] published in 1972. Livneh, seventy, was a typical LIM elder statesman with an impressive Zionist record. After emigrating to Palestine in 1920 and joining Tabenkin's kibbutz Ein-Harod, Livneh soon rose from day laborer to labor leader. He held many public offices, including a sensitive political job for the Zionist movement in prewar Nazi Germany. Between 1940 and 1947 Livneh directed the political section of the Hagana, the semi-military organization of the *yishuv's* leadership. A prominent member of Mapai, Israel's ruling socialist party (later to become the Labor party), he served in the Knesset from 1948 to 1955 and was an editor of *Hador,* an influential Mapai newspaper. But in the 1950s Livneh started to drift away from Mapai. This learned and independent person grew critical of Mapai's monopolistic, "Bolshevik," way of running the country. In time he left the party, favoring less and less central planning and a freer market. In the 1960s and early 1970s Livneh was a distinguished columnist for Israel's most influential newspapers and magazines.

Like many of his new colleagues in the Land of Israel Movement, Livneh was profoundly transformed by the experience of the "longest month" in 1967. And very much like them he came to the conclusion that post-1967 Israel could not be secure without a massive *Aliya* ("ascent"—i.e., Jewish immigration). Nevertheless, only Livneh seemed to understand that the state of Israel they all wished for needed a totally different ideological framework. Livneh realized that the LIM was actually advocating a new kind of Zionism and Zionist justification, a set of orientations and aspirations that could not be exhausted by *tactical* arguments about the wicked Arabs, the unfriendly world, and the need for a territorial space for defense.

Therefore he set out to write an ambitious essay, a book that would update Zionist ideology and develop a new logic to legitimize the Israel of the 1970s. Such a book, of necessity, would reexamine classical Zionism in the light of more recent developments: the establishment of the State of Israel, the Holocaust, the emergence of the powerful American Jewish community, and the misery of Soviet Jewry. Further, it would review the Israeli-Arab complex in the perspective of the Six-Day War.

Livneh understood that a new Zionism had to represent Israel as the only alternative for all Jews, and must present a better argument for the existence of the state than the old and anachronistic Zionist clichés about anti-Semitism. He set out to show that after 1967 Israel had acquired a spiritual quality superior both to the older Israeli condition and to the Jewish Diaspora existence in the affluent West. The result was a new and sweeping theory:

> Ninety years have passed since the rise of the present secular return to Zion. . . . Shouldn't we recognize that the foundations of the Jewish existence have totally changed since that time? The Diaspora is not the same Diaspora, Eretz Yisrael of the 1970s is not the Eretz Yisrael expected then, and the Western Gentile environment of Diaspora Jews is completely different from the environment seen by the Zionist thinkers in their time. Western civilization has entered a new age which differs from the previous ones no less than they differed from the Middle Ages.[81]

According to Livneh, the Six-Day War was significant not only for its visible political and military achievements, but also for illuminating the new existential reality of the Jewish people. In a single moment of truth it helped identify three major historical developments: the rise of the "Judeo-Israeli civilization," the decline of the permissive and decadent Western-liberal civilization, and the demise of the viability and creativity of the Jewish Diaspora. This was indeed an ambitious theory.

> The Jewish people is not a nation that belongs to one of the great civilizations—the Christian-humanist, the Buddhist, the Hindu, or the Muslim—but is a distint human phenomenon. Yisrael determines its own modes of interaction with the natural and human environment, and demands of its daughters and sons different mores. Its experience is not limited to the spiritual, emotional or social spheres—belief, beauty, morality, mundane and social contact—but touches upon everything.[82]

The construct of the "Judeo-Israeli civilization" is essential for Livneh's theory, for it helps him to attack the "decadent" Western civilization from a position of strength. Not only should Israelis face Western civilization with pride but Diaspora Jews as well; in the State of Israel they have a cultural sanctuary, an address to return to, a civilization of their own. And when "the Diaspora as an independent and viable phenomenon has come to its end," they can come home.[83]

The Six-Day War, according to Livneh, produced a spiritual breakthrough. In one intense week, it exposed the existential weaknesses of both Israeli and Diaspora Jews, and demonstrated the relevance of four thousand years of Jewish history in the conduct of public affairs.[84] The dominant

Jewish nationalism before 1967 (Livneh's own Zionism) was mistaken because it was atheistic, detached from the genuine spiritual wellsprings of the nation. Most secular Israelis felt superior to religious Jews, but the anxiety of May 1967 brought the two groups together and bridged over all previous differences. And it produced, through its great success, the future model for Jewish living in Israel, a combination of an orthodox Jewish culture with a secular neoreligious respect for the heritage of the nation.[85]

Although Livneh does not call for a total desecularization of Israel and does not use the terminology of redemption, the affinity between his new Zionism and the ideo-theology of Merkaz Harav is clear. *Israel and the Crisis of Western Civilization* is full of references to Rabbi Avraham Itzhak Hacohen Kook and quotations from his *Orot*. Livneh's historical analysis of the modern return to Zion is reminiscent of Kook's historiosophic account. It speaks about Zionism as a teleological process of return to Eretz Yisrael, as much spiritual as concrete. It is a process of a growing religious experience, an increasing awareness of the nation's true heritage. It is a progress toward eliminating the gap that divides religious and secular Jews, forming a new normative consensus that would go beyond political issues and public culture.[86] Livneh is obsessed with the permissive West and its licentious life and discusses such issues as free sex, the purity of the family, and the sanctity of the Sabbath at great length. His chapter on "The Ecology of the Returnees to Zion" is full of neoreligious themes and the conviction that only a genuine respect of the rich tradition of Jewish orthodoxy would solve the nation's problems.[87]

Livneh's affinity with the incipient Gush Emunim shows most clearly on the issue of Eretz Yisrael. One chapter, "The Six-Day War and Its Spiritual Meaning," enthusiastically describes the Israelis who returned to Judea and Samaria, Sinai and the Golan Heights. The immense excitement felt toward the occupied territories serves him as an uncontested proof that the territorial conquests of the Six-Day War were bound to happen and were morally just.

> The territories liberated in the Six-Day War are officially called "Occupied." But more than they are occupied by Israel they have Israel under occupation.
>
> Not only had the integration of the nation with its most historic places taken place, but Israel was now once again whole in both a spiritual and physical sense. Israel was now the deep and burning Jordan valley, the snowy tops of Mount Hermon which feed the valleys with their water, the variegated mountains of Judea and Samaria and the spacious deserts of Sinai which provide a sense of security.[88]

The new Israeli empire thrilled Livneh. Security was one reason for holding onto the new territories, but not the primary one. Even more than the emerging Gush Emunim, he represented the new Eretz Yisrael mystique. This school saw in every inch of the new territories, including even parts that God had not promised to Abraham, something holy and inalienable. It was as if the process itself, the incredible response to the Egyptian challenge of May 1967, the victory in the war, had sanctified the territories. Thus, only the Israelis had any right to these lands. And no force in the world could make Israel ever give them back.

Israel and the Crisis of Western Civilization was never presented as the official creed of the Land of Israel Movement; much of it, especially Livneh's perception of the non-Jewish world, was exclusively his. But it was far from being an isolated treatise by a detached intellectual; rather it was a mature product of one of the most prolific ideologues of the LIM, an authority to everyone within the movement. Though the other luminaries of the movement had not approved the book in advance, it certainly appealed to them. It would have been hard *not* to appreciate what Livneh did for the movement by providing it with a comprehensive post-1967 ideology.

This was, then, the new ideology of the secular territorial maximalists: ultranationalist, expansionist, intellectually megalomaniac, neoreligious, self-confident, and optimistic. Together with the new theology preached from Yeshivat Merkaz Harav and its widening circle, and the polemical literature published in *Zot Ha'aretz* and other periodicals, it indicated the coming of age of a new Israeli Zionism. The new territorial maximalism was much more than a relic from the past. It was a vigorous cultural and social school, one bound to have a lasting effect on the future of Israel's culture and politics.

A careful reading of Livneh's book, as well as other less systematic literature of the new school, is important not only for what it says, but also for what it does not say: *in 1972 the secular maximalist camp had no criticism of the Israeli political process and no conscious quarrel with the democratic values of the nation.* Neither Livneh nor any of his colleagues questioned, for example, the provisions in Israel's Declaration of Independence securing the social and political rights of the Arabs. They sincerely believed that these principles were as applicable to the greater Land of Israel as they were to the pre-1967 Jewish state. Livneh was optimistic about the future relationships of Jews and Arabs in Israel. He clearly felt that "the civic-personal options" regarding their future should be left in the hands of the Arabs of Eretz Yisrael. All the Arabs (Livneh made no distinction between Israeli Arabs and those of the new territories) had the right to full Israeli citizenship, including the electoral process. They were entitled to official positions within the government and the nation's other public domains. Those who wanted to maintain dual citizenship in Israel and one of the neighboring countries were to do so. And Israel was not, of course, to stop the Arabs interested in emigration.[89] Livneh's optimism and liberalism showed very clearly in the conclusion of his chapter on Arab-Jewish relations:

> The historical processes of *Shivat Tzion* (the return to Zion) make a favor-able policy towards the Arabs necessary and possible. The Zionist thinkers

knew that the Jews were not returning to an unpopulated country. The Arabs are part of the Israeli state and belong to its nature, including its cultural nature. Israel without the Arabs would be missing an important component. Most Israeli Jews feel that in their guts, although many of them are unable to explain it.[90]

The Politics and Practices of the Territorial Maximalists

At first the new territorial maximalists (the Kahane group excepted) did not intend to organize politically, but they were soon pulled into the very heart of Israeli politics. The occupied territories were not annexed to Israel, and their rate of settlement by Jews was very slow. In addition, the government faced many external pressures to withdraw. The new maximalists also discovered that about half of the Israelis did not agree with what they considered the main lesson of the war: that no single square inch of the occupied territories should be returned to the Arabs. Politically moderate intellectuals proposed imaginative peace plans, at the core of which stood major territorial concessions. Influential ministers, including Prime Minister Levi Eshkol and Foreign Affairs Minister Abba Eban, listened attentively. A Movement for Peace and Security was established to pursue these goals.[91] Under these circumstances, the activists of the LIM and the future members of Gush Emunim had no choice but to join the political fray and start lobbying decision-makers and politicians. Later they would hit the streets.

The Land of Israel Movement's initial strategy presupposed that it was associated with the ruling Labor alignment and that its loyalists within the government made it unnecessary to organize politically. For the most part the assumption was correct, for the most outspoken leaders of the movement were old Labor hands, closely connected with either Defense Minister Moshe Dayan or Deputy Prime Minister Yigal Allon. Both Allon and Dayan had, at first, maximalist and hawkish reputations. Dayan, Israel's No. 1 soldier, was perceived as the architect of the Six-Day War and known for his emotional attachment to the Land of the Bible in its entirety.[92] Allon, an illustrious general from the war of 1948 and one of the most prominent representatives of Hakibbutz Hameuchad in politics, had long been recognized as a maximalist and a great believer in territorial-strategic depth.[93]

Nevertheless, both men proved to be, from the LIM's perspective, unpredictable and unreliable. Dayan, skeptical of the ability of the Arabs to make formal peace and stick to it, was on occasion sympathetic to the new territorial maximalism. But he was also very pragmatic and cautious. He never used the language of the Land of Israel Movement and made it clear that a *de jure* annexation of the territories was out of the question.[94] If there was to be a *de facto* annexation, it would happen only by default, because no Arab ruler agreed to talk to Israel directly. And Dayan was, in general, dubious of the notion that excited settlers might determine the security policy of Israel. He therefore only approved limited settlement in Judea and the Jordan River Valley.

But Yigal Allon was a greater disappointment. This veteran student of Tabenkin, who in 1948 had demanded that Israel's permanent borders be set on the Jordan river and in the middle of Sinai, adopted a different position after 1967. Allon, like many moderates, worried about the "demographic problem"; the plan he worked out was anathema to the LIM ideologists. The Allon Plan called for Jewish settlement of the Jordan River Valley and a few areas in the Hebron vicinity for security reasons, returning most of the other Arab-populated areas to Jordan in the context of a comprehensive peace.[95]

Thus, while Dayan and Allon could be trusted on some issues, their presence in the cabinet could not provide the iron-clad guarantees the Land of Israel Movement needed. Even the settlement of Gush Etzion and Kiryat Arba, two initiatives that were finally approved by both men, first required several LIM illicit operations.

When Dr. Israel Eldad decided to run for the Knesset in 1969 as the head of the Eretz Yisrael List, it was clear that the non-Labor members of the Land of Israel Movement had decided to become more political. Not all the movement's activists were happy about the step, but several prominent Labor-movement members—Haim Yachil, Nathan Alterman, Eliezer Livneh, and Moshe Shamir—endorsed it enthusiastically. Their support implied a call *not* to vote for the Labor alignment.[96] Eldad was not elected, but other LIM members, running on various tickets, were. Isser Harel and Yigal Horowitz were elected on the State List, Benjamin Halevy with Gahal (the Herut-Liberal Bloc), and Rabbi Neriah and Dr. Avner Shaki through the National Religious Party. By 1969 the LIM had a significant Knesset representation; no longer solely an ideological entity, it was in no one's political pocket.

The growing rift between the LIM and the Labor alignment was revealed in 1970 when Begin's Gahal left the Unity Government. The issue at stake was an American-proposed cease-fire on the Suez Canal, part of the Rogers Plan for an Israeli-Egyptian settlement. When the cabinet of Golda Meir agreed, Begin, an *old* territorial maximalist, saw the beginning of Israeli withdrawal from the occupied territories, and he angrily resigned. Alarmed by the American pressure and Israeli acquiescence, he suggested that the LIM, Gahal, and other "Eretz Yisrael patriots" join forces in a nonpartisan Committee to Prevent Withdrawal. Begin was even ready to let Itzhak Tabenkin, an old rival, head the new body.

Tabenkin was not impressed. Not only did this old revolutionary socialist refuse the offer but he decided to leave the Land of Israel Movement altogether. Unable to forget the pre-1948 rivalries with the "fascists," he mistrusted what he and a few followers understood as a move to turn the LIM into a Revisionist front.[97]

But Tabenkin's secession did not hurt the LIM. On the contrary, it helped its growing right-wing configuration. Most of the LIM leaders, including many former Laborites, were disappointed with the pragmatic and indecisive Labor alignment. Their prime concern was their territorial maximalism; they viewed everything else through this prism. By 1970 most members of the LIM felt the old territorial maximalism of Menachem Begin much more to their liking than their pre-1967 Laborite associations, and that the traditional Revisionists, whom they had fought tooth and nail in the 1930s and 1940s, were now their natural allies. Post-1967 reality was to change some of the most fundamental ideological alignments of Zionist politics.

As disappointed as the territorial maximalists were with the indecisive public position of the Labor alignment on the future of the territories, they could not ignore the fact that creeping annexation had actually been taking place since 1967. The 1967 "three no's" resolution passed at Khartoum by the leaders of the Arab nations after the war (no peace with Israel, no negotiations with Israel, and no recognition of Israel), strengthened the hand of those cabinet ministers who favored a greater Israeli presence in the territories.[98] An early, secret resolution of the government to trade Sinai and the Golan Heights for peace with Egypt and Syria, and to initiate negotiations with Jordan on much of the West Bank, was abandoned.[99]

In 1969 an "oral doctrine" was approved by the central committee of the Labor alignment. It stated that the Jordan River would remain Israel's security border and that Israel would keep the Golan Heights, the Gaza Strip, and the Straits of Tiran. The doctrine was expanded upon in the Galili Document of September 1973, which outlined a comprehensive four-year development plan in the occupied territories. Israel was to start new settlements in the Jordan Valley, the Golan Heights, and Northern Sinai. Industry, agriculture, and water resources were to be developed, and several of the early settlements were to become Jewish cities. The document, presented as a recommendation to the central committee of the Labor party, opened the way for a vast concentration of West Bank lands in the hands of Jews.[100]

The Galili Document did not completely endorse the ideological creed of the LIM, since it implied that Jewish settlement would take place only in limited security areas (for the most part those identified in the original Allon Plan), but it went a long way in the direction of the LIM. It bestowed a sense of stability on the Jewish presence in the territories. No one could ignore the massive Israeli drive into the territories—the huge expansion of Jerusalem, settlements in the Golan Heights and the Jordan Valley, and the permanent military government of Judea, Samaria, and Gaza[101] And the competition between the cabinet's two leading figures, Moshe Dayan and Yigal Allon, only helped the process; each tried to score political points by backing various settlement projects.

The transformation of the Land of Israel Movement was completed in 1973 when it decided to establish a front organization, Labor for the Whole of Eretz Yisrael, and endorse the newly created Likud (expanded from the former Gahal) for the coming general elections.[102] The old and the new territorial maximalists were now *politically* united, the result of a gradual ideological and political evolution.[103] The 1973 LIM was an ultranationalist movement whose natural location on the Israeli political map was to the right of Menachem Begin. It still maintained a warm relationship with some of its former Labor allies (Israel Galili), and said it was fully committed to the tradition of Labor Zionism. Nevertheless, its political future was now bound with Menachem Begin, the chief public protagonist of Eretz Yisrael. And the new territorial maximalists could legitimately feel that never before had their ideas been so acceptable to so many Israelis.[104]

The 1973 Yom Kippur War caught the territorial maximalists, like the rest of the nation, by surprise. But it did not change their political doctrines or ideological convictions. On the contrary, the leading ideologists of the Land of Israel Movement were certain the new borders had saved the Jewish state from extinction.[105] Since their thesis had now been tested under real fire, and in their view proven to be correct, they were strengthened in their determination never to relinquish any land.

The religious territorial maximalists were equally determined. Rabbi Yehuda Amital, a great admirer of the teachings of Rav Kook, published an important theological essay, "On the Significance of the Yom Kippur War." The war, according to Amital, did not hurt the messianic process of redemption but was, on the contrary, its reaffirmation. It was an attempt of the Gentiles to survive, and perhaps unknowingly, to stop the coming of the Messiah. But the attempt had no chance, for it went against God's own plan. The war's function for the Jews was "the purification . . . of the congregation of Israel."[106] The 1973 war was in Amital's words one step further in the "elevation of Holiness," profound with spiritual meaning.

But the Yom Kippur War created a problem the territorial maximalists were unprepared for. It paralyzed the Israeli government and weakened the morale of the Israeli people. Never before had all the top policymakers of Israel been so discredited. In the end, Israel won the military battle but lost the political war. The overconfident political and military establishment had not believed the Arabs capable of launching a serious attack; as a result, more than 2500 Israelis died in battle and 5000 were wounded. The air force, which had won the war in 1967 in eight hours, this time lost nearly 25 percent of its planes. The IDF was in total disarray—many units were destroyed; others suffered immense losses. A massive American airlift was needed to keep the army going.

A new term, *mechdal* (culpable blunder), was on everyone's lips even before the end of the war.[107] Several distinguished generals blamed each other for failures, and their feuds were vented freely in the press. So damaged was the cabinet's authority that neither Golda Meir, the prime minister, nor Moshe Dayan, her minister of defense, was either able or ready to silence the bitter generals. Less than three months after the war's end, large protest movements of civilians and soldiers called for the resignation of the ministers responsible for the *mechdal*—Dayan and Meir in particular.[108]

The Agranat Report, the first interim report of an investigative committee, was published in April 1974. It dealt exclusively with the military, but it was clear that the Meir cabinet had reached its end. The protest movements, a non-ideological cross section of the population, would not let the politicians make scapegoats of the soldiers. And thus, in April 1974, less then four months after they had won the election, Golda Meir and her top ministers, Dayan (defense), Eban (foreign affairs), and Sapir (finance) stepped down.

The new territorial maximalists watched the evolving crisis with growing unease. Like everybody else, they were appalled by the intelligence failure to anticipate the Arab attack and were disappointed with the government. Many joined the protest movements. But the collapse of the government was immensely disquieting.

The new cabinet of Itzhak Rabin did nothing to reassure the LIM leaders. They were especially troubled by the aggressive diplomacy of Henry Kissinger, the American secretary of state, who pushed Israel into a minor, but strategically significant, territorial compromise with Egypt and Syria.[109] As the government approached the disengagement agreements with Egypt and moved closer to some retreat in the Golan Heights, Kissinger became, in the eyes of the LIM ideologues, a monster, a self-hating Jew, and a very serious threat to the safety and integrity of the State of Israel. The Rabin cabinet quietly rescinded the Galili Document and assumed a defensive posture.

Rabin's concessions to Sadat were attacked in *Zot Ha'aretz*, the LIM journal, and compared to Chamberlain's 1939 concessions to Hitler at Munich.[110] The real blunder of the Meir cabinet, according to the LIM critique, was its failure to settle the occupied territories on a massive scale when it held all the cards. But even then, in mid-1974, it was not too late. The Israeli military had won the war and was still strong enough to dismiss all the threats and pressures. All that was needed was resolve and determination. Instead of making concessions, the government should have started a new settlement drive all over Eretz Yisrael, so that the world could recognize Israel's real strength.[111]

A most significant response to the crisis of the Yom Kippur War was the birth of Gush Emunim in March 1974, amid the gloom of the first territorial concessions in Sinai. The founders, all former students of Merkaz Harav, were determined to oppose further concessions and instead to help extend

Israeli sovereignty over the occupied territories.[112] At first, Gush Emunim was a faction within the National Religious Party, then a partner in the Labor coalition government; the faction included Zevulun Hammer and Yehuda Ben-Meir, two leading figures of the young generation of the NRP.[113] But the new movement soon gave up its party alignment. The members of Gariin Elon Moreh, the religious nucleus established in Kiryat Arba to spearhead the settlement of Samaria, were asked to join; they required that the Gush sever its relations with the NRP.[114] The emphasis on settlement instead of politics echoed the position of Rabbi Moshe Levinger, the unchallenged leader of Kiryat Arba. After leaving the NRP, the members of Gush Emunim refused to identify with any party, even the LIM. Strongly motivated and led by talented young rabbis and activists, they were confident in their mission, and equally confident that they genuinely represented the national interest. The Gush's manifesto, written by the thoughtful Hanan Porat, stated its intention to revive Zionism and promote a national reawakening. It found no contradiction between Zionism—traditionally a secular movement—and orthodox Judaism, since the shared objective was redemption.

> The purpose is to bring about a grand movement of reawakening within the people of Israel in order to fulfill the Zionist vision in its entirety, with the recognition that the origins of the visions are rooted in Israel's tradition and in the foundation of Judaism and its goal—the full redemption of the people of Israel and the rest of the world.[115]

It is important to stress that at first Gush Emunim, like the LIM in 1967, did not perceive itself as an extremist movement and did not foresee a serious conflict with the government or the Labor alignment. Rabbi Zvi Yehuda Kook, the head of Merkaz Harav, who maintained his spiritual authority over the movement without actually participating in its daily decisions, never retracted the full legitimacy he accorded the government of Israel, the Knesset, and the army. These institutions were to remain holy and unchallenged. The members of Gush Emunim acted out of a conviction that the people of Israel and their government *needed* their guidance in their moment of crisis.[116] This was, after all, the historical pattern of pioneering Zionism: an illicit minority action followed by a majority recognition and gratitude. Gush Emunim saw itself as the unselfish instrument of the divine process of redemption. Full of love, it could not possibly think about real conflict with the nation and its government.

While the Labor government of Itzhak Rabin was in power (1974 to 1977), Gush Emunim pursued three types of activity: it joined the Land of Israel Movement in protesting the Interim Agreements with Egypt and Syria, it staged symbolic demonstrations in Judea and Samaria to underscore the Jewish attachment to these parts of Eretz Yisrael, and it carried out settlement operations in the West Bank and Golan Heights. By far the most controversial issue pursued was the demand that Israel settle the densely

Arab populated Samaria. Basing its claim on God's promise to Abraham some 4000 years earlier and on the biblical memories of ancient Jewish cities such as Shchem and Shilo, Gush Emunim challenged the government's tacit acceptance of the Allon Plan. No number of Arabs, the Gush maintained, could possibly invalidate the Jewish right to live anywhere in their promised land.

The main effort to settle in Samaria was carried out by Gariin Elon Moreh, the most influential settlement nucleus in Gush Emunim. Seven times the Gariin members, backed by the entire Gush Emunim, tried to settle in Samaria illicitly, and seven times they were evacuated by the army. Nevertheless, after each effort the Gush was better able to outmaneuver the military in the field, mobilizing greater public support and recruiting more enthusiastic settlers. It was a battle of resolve and patience, of cunning and pressure, a political struggle between a mighty but divided government, and a weak but united Gush. By December 1975 the struggle was over. Prime Minister Itzhak Rabin ordered the settlers out of their temporary settlement but allowed them to stay in Kadum, a military compound nearby. They never left the area, and the principle that Samaria was open to Jewish settlement was, at least partially, established.[117]

There is no doubt that the territorial-maximalist camp was more bitter and radical after the Yom Kippur War than before. The excitement and enthusiasm of the early 1970s were gone, and with them the optimism of the old warriors. *Zot Ha'aretz,* the LIM magazine, was scathing about the weak government and its conduct of public affairs, noting the government's inclination to compromise the territories and pointing out the analogy of Munich, 1939.

Even Gush Emunim, which repeatedly stressed its loyalty to the institutions of the "Israeli sovereignty," developed an important theoretical proposition, the distinction between *legal* and legitimate acts. Gush leaders elaborated the distinction: the government's refusal to approve of certain settlements may have been formally legal, but substantially it was illegitimate.[118] Zionism, which according to Gush Emunim was the fundamental constitution of the land, had always called for an unconditional settlement of the entirety of Eretz Yisrael. A government acting against the settlement of its heartland was thus acting "unconstitutionally" and undermining its own legitimacy; it was placing itself in the same category as the British Mandate government, which in 1939 had barred Jewish immigration and settlement in Palestine. Settling Samaria had been declared illegal by the government, but it was as legitimate as the earlier "illegal" Jewish settlement in Palestine. Gush Emunim was determined to settle Samaria, with or without the legal approval of the authorities.

A retrospective examination of the members of the Land of Israel Movement, Gush Emunim, and Kach shows that by the mid-1970s they were different in their epistemology and political convictions from the rest of the

Israeli political community, including most of the Likud activists. They were true believers, committed to the settlement of Eretz Yisrael and the annexation of the territories. They were not interested in considerations of *real politik,* big-power diplomacy, and international law. These orientations, however, did not yet display salient political radicalism or extreme opposition to the prevailing rules of Israeli politics. While some of Gush Emunim's settlement attempts produced small-scale clashes, Gush members were in general very cautious. They felt sorry for the soldiers who had to participate in the evacuations, and not a few among them found themselves confronting friends from their own military units. There was also a standing ruling of Rabbi Zvi Yehuda Kook, who had always been a great admirer of the army and forbade any intended physical confrontation with it.[119] The early history of the settlers was thus relatively nonviolent. They did not collide with other Israelis and their contacts with Arabs were minor.

The main reason for the relative moderation of the new territorial maximalists seems to have been their conviction that they were part of a larger established parliamentary camp, the territorial maximalism of Herut and the hawkish section of the National Religious Party. Menachem Begin, whose political influence was on the rise, was the great hope of these people, and though they occasionally resorted to extraparliamentary methods, they were restrained by their belief that they would soon have a parliamentary majority in sympathy with them. Some members of Gush Emunim, it is true, were not fully sure of Begin—the "Zionist of words instead of actions"— but most of them were happy with his Eretz Yisrael rhetoric.[120] In the mid-1970s Begin's Herut gave unconditional support to the settlement efforts of Gush Emunim, and Likud Knesset members like Geula Cohen and Ariel Sharon, visited their illicit settlements. In January 1975 Herut held its convention in Kiryat Arba, and endorsed the activities of the Herut Youth who were collecting signatures on a petition against returning the West Bank to "foreign rule" and in favor of settling Judea and Samaria.[121] Avraham Yoffe, an LIM leader and former general, was himself a Likud Knesset member, the only real concern of his movement and Gush Emunim was to elect their political allies to lead the government.

Thus there was no question, in the minds of the territorial maximalists on May 17, 1977, that their long wait for full political legitimization was over. Menachem Begin, the man who had promised to support the idea of the whole of Eretz Yisrael, was surprisingly elected as the next prime minister of Israel. Perhaps no one was happier than Rabbi Meir Kahane, who responded to the event with total jubilation:

> For the first time since its establishment, the State of Israel has as its prime minister potential a man who thinks like a Jew, acts like a Jew, faces television with a yarmulka on his head, and actually speaks the "one little word" that we have waited to hear from the lips of Ben-Gurion, Sharett, Eshkol, Golda, Rabin, and Peres. Menachem Begin, the potential prime minister of Israel, faces the nation and the world and thanks G-d, the one little word that

the polysyllabic Eban finds impossible to pronounce. And he reads from Psalms and thanks the Almighty. Miracle? Miracle of Miracles.[122]

Every true believer was thrilled, when shortly after his election Begin visited Elon Moreh for the inauguration of a new synagogue and proudly declared, "We shall have many more Elon Morehs."[123]

4

The Rise
of the Radical Right,
1978–1984

The Crisis of Camp David

The Israeli radical right was born on September 17, 1978. The Camp David Accords, signed that day by Prime Minister Menachem Begin and Presidents Anwar al-Sadat of Egypt and Jimmy Carter of the Unites States, stunned the new territorial maximalists.[1] Only a year ago, Begin, had become prime minister with their active support; now he had betrayed them. Reversing years of uncompromising Eretz Yisrael rhetoric, Begin agreed to return all of Sinai to the Egyptians and to work torward Palestinian autonomy in Judea and Samaria.

To the maximalists, autonomy implied a Palestinian state in the making. And the retreat from Sinai meant the evacuation of Yamit, the newly built capital of northern Sinai, and the destruction of the flourishing Jewish *moshavim* (cooperative settlements) in the area. Never before had Jews given up Jewish settlements willingly; the Camp David Accords were a suicide operation, a crime against the nation.

The maximalists had thought themselves secure under Begin. Itzhak Rabin, his predecessor, had staunchly opposed territorial maximalism, and during his administration, the members of the Land of Israel Movement, Gush Emunim, and Kach had reason to fear the loss of Eretz Yisrael. They saw Menachem Begin's accession to power as leading to the political realization of their dreams. They had believed that Begin would annex the West Bank to Israel, or at least launch a massive settlement of all the occupied territories.[2] And Kahane thought Begin would "take care" of the Arabs.[3] Camp David destroyed all these illusions. Maximalist dreams were replaced by a reality that looked like these true believers' worst nightmare come true.

71

Already before Camp David there had been indications of a rift within the maximalist camp. Despite his famous commitment at Elon Moreh, Begin was cautious about new settlements in the West Bank. The members of Gush Emunim, who thought of themselves as his "dear children," were non-plussed when his office gave them the runaround. Soon Gush youngsters again took to the hills of Samaria, setting up strongholds in protest.[4] Begin had not come out against U.N. Resolution 242, which called upon Israel to exchange territories for peace, and he proved an ardent legalist on many issues of international law. His attitude toward the Arabs was a great deal more moderate than that of his true-believing partners or his own former rhetoric. On occasion he would remind his audience of the liberal approach to the Arabs taken by Vladimir Jabotinsky, his adopted mentor. In short, Begin, who found a common language with his new minister of foreign affairs, the pragmatic Moshe Dayan, soon proved that he did not intend to maintain his perennial image as extremist and radical.[5]

In fact Camp David should have come as no surprise. It was consistent with Begin's earlier positions on a possible settlement with the Arabs, if not with his public rhetoric. Already in 1976, under the moderating influence of Ezer Weizman, his future minister of defense, Begin agreed in principle to trade most of Sinai for peace. He also spoke about autonomy for the Arabs of the West Bank, an idea that went back to Jabotinsky.[6] The 1977 Likud platform made these points quite clear.[7]

The crisis after Camp David and the rise of the radical right took place because the young members of Gush Emunim, the followers of Rabbi Kahane, and the veterans of LIM had been mesmerized by Begin's public rhetoric and deceived themselves by ignoring the huge gap between their mystical dreams and Begin's actions. In total contrast to the **political** pragmatism of the heir of Jabotinsky, they never thought about such notions as political constraints, unavoidable compromise, or diplomacy. International law was for them a hostile invention of the Gentiles, and a commitment to the rule of law in any modern sense rarely crossed their minds. Many of the radical right had never seriously considered Arab influence in international relations and were totally blind to the existence of the Palestinian question. The rift between the radical rightists and Menachem Begin had in fact existed long before September 1978; the moment of truth at Camp David only exposed it.

The emergence of the radical right after Camp David was tortured. Many of the future radicals found it hard to confront the man who had only recently been their hero. This was especially true of those dissidents who had shared many years of political opposition with Begin, for whom he was both a personal example and political leader. To make matters worse, Camp David made Menachem Begin highly popular, both in Israel and abroad. Those who believed they had to oppose Camp David in order to defend the true interests of the nation had to go against the common sentiment and consensus.

Thus in the fall of 1978 the radical right started out as a tiny minority with very few supporters and few political assets. But the new camp had a very clear direction. It led to the establishment of the Tehiya (Renaissance) party, radicalized Kahane, and created a deep crisis within Gush Emunim. As long as the peace with Egypt was popular and Begin politically in control, the dissenters of the Tehiya, Gush Emunim, and Kach did not have a chance. They were vocal but politically insignificant.

But developments in the 1980s changed all that. Israel's deteriorating relations with Egypt, the 1981 assassination of President Sadat, the fiasco in Lebanon, the high rate of inflation, Begin's failing health and mysterious resignation, all played into the hands of the radical right. These dedicated fundamentalists greatly extended their influence and involvements; by the middle of the decade, the radical right had become a significant force in the life of the nation.

From Banai to the Tehiya

The first and most visible reaction to the Camp David Accords was the establishment on November 1, 1978, of Banai, an umbrella organization of several groups that felt betrayed by Begin. Most prominent were the Land of Israel Movement, Gush Emunim, and those who called themselves the Upholders of Herut Principles. Several smaller entities were represented: the Ein Vered Circle (Labor settlement veterans), representatives of the settlers in Judea, Samaria, and the Rafiah Salient (northern Sinai), members of the La'am party (a small nationalist component of the Likud), a small student organization called False Peace, and several members of the Ben-Gurion Circle of the Labor party also associated themselves with the new body. The Camp David Accords brought these groups together, though most had existed earlier.

President Sadat's November 1977 trip to Jerusalem did not at first alarm the future radicals. Still thrilled by the *mahapach* (extreme change) that brought Begin to power, they had no reason to suspect their leader. The visit of Egypt's president in fact validated their long-held thesis that peace between Israel and the Arab world required not territorial concessions, but a strong and confident government. Thus, the central committee of Gush Emunim was quick to congratulate the prime minister, saying that "it is the steadfast position of this government that started to pave the road."[8] Knesset member Geula Cohen, later a leading opponent, told Sadat in utmost seriousness that Israel and Egypt could "now take joint action against the red imperialism."[9]

The rejoicing did not last long. A month after the Sadat visit, Begin left for Washington to confer with President Jimmy Carter, and on December 15, 1977, he announced in Washington his first conditional outline for peace. The key features were a readiness to evacuate most of Sinai and an

Administrative Autonomy Plan for the Arabs of the West Bank, tentatively giving them an independent civic and political status, to be directed by their elected representatives. For the Eretz Yisrael devotees, the plan was completely unacceptable, but since the prime minister was abroad they decided to wait for his clarifications. Geula Cohen, though greatly alarmed, decided to moderate her criticism. Referring to Begin as a great leader, she expressed her full confidence in him: "We have a fundamental trust in Begin. . . . I do not know a better person to get for us the best possible maximum within the narrow space we have."[10]

But soon enough the territorial maximalists discovered that their fears were well founded. Back from Washington, Begin met the representatives of Gush Emunim and the LIM and told them emphatically that no peace agreement with Egypt was possible without a withdrawal from Sinai. And he wanted that peace badly.[11] By the end of 1977 it was clear that Begin was serious and that "Eretz Yisrael was in big trouble." The Likud Knesset delegation approved of Begin's plan overwhelmingly, and the act was shortly repeated by the entire House.

The dissenters soon organized a coordinating committee. The LIM and Gush Emunim would of course be part of it, but the dissenters were joined by two more bodies. The first was a Herut group from Jerusalem led by Gershon Solomon, a veteran party member and its representative in the Jerusalem municipal council. The second was a new circle that called itself the Upholders of Herut's Principles. The opposition of these groups was significant; many of their members were old comrades of Begin from the glorious days of the Irgun underground. The Upholders, who coalesced on February 1, 1978, claimed they, and not Menachem Begin, were the true representatives of Jabotinsky's ideas. Some had been active since 1976 when they established in Jerusalem the hawkish Circle for Daring Political Action.[12]

In January 1978 a crisis in the negotiations with Egypt gave the dissenters renewed hope. Then a disagreement between Menachem Begin and President Carter in March put the whole peace process in question. The crisis prompted the rise of Peace Now, a movement of reserve officers concerned about the failure of Begin to respond to the challenge of peace.[13]

Once again the radical maximalists took heart. Begin, they believed, was "coming to his senses." In view of Sadat's "intransigence" and Carter's "duplicity," he was urged to review the whole process and renounce his plan. Gush Emunim again expressed support for Begin.[14] The Land of Israel Movement organized a rally in Yamit to reassure the worried Sinai settlers.

Suspicious of Sadat, the radicals convinced themselves that the crisis in negotiations could not be resolved. Even visits of American Vice-President Walter Mondale in July and Secretary of State Cyrus Vance in August solved nothing. A final attempt scheduled for September, at Camp David, was worrisome but did not look too dangerous; Sadat wanted too much. The target of the dissenters in these months was no longer Begin but Peace Now and its demands for what was obviously a "false peace."[15]

The Camp David Accords shattered the dissenters. The Agreement was worse than they could have imagined. Begin's original peace plan was badly truncated—his public commitment to maintain the settlements in northern Sinai was abandoned, and his agreement to an autonomy for Arabs plan was seen as the first step toward a Palestinian state. Not only had Begin subscribed to U.N. resolutions 242 and 338, which established the principle of trading territory for peace, but he had acknowledged the "legitimate rights" of the Palestinians.[16] A total break between Begin and the radicals was inevitable.

When a triumphant Begin returned to Israel on September 22, 1978, he was welcomed at the city gates of Jerusalem by Mayor Teddy Kollek and the entire city council. Among the welcomers was councilman Gershon Solomon, the leader of the Upholders of Herut's Principles, who held a large black umbrella and shouted, "You are giving us peace like Chamberlain's." Any reference to the infamous 1939 agreement that handed Czechoslovakia to Hitler, has always reverberated in Israel.[17] This emotional tactic had often been used by Begin, but now the shame was laid at his door. Yuval Ne'eman, president of Tel Aviv University and Israel's most noted physicist cabled the speaker of the Knesset, Itzhak Shamir, "The surrender of Yamit, Offira (Sharem el Sheikh), and other settlements of the Sinai implies Israel's future return to the borders of 1948 and the surrender of Judea, Samaria, Gaza, the Golan Heights, and East Jerusalem."[18] Several Irgun and Lehi veterans, who joined the protesters, announced that they were unalterably opposed to the agreement and would not exclude the use of violence.

Banai was formed at this point in response to the popular acclaim for the Camp David Accords aroused both in Israel and abroad. Banai's major target, Menachem Begin, was at the height of his career, supported by friends and former foes alike. For the first time in his life, Begin was a truly national leader, seen as a man of peace, and a statesman. There was no doubt that the people of Israel were enthusiastic about the Camp David Accords, and they were overwhelmingly approved by the Knesset. The people who formed Banai ruled out ordinary means of expressing opposition to the government, namely establishing a political party. It made more sense to form protest movements to unmask the false agreement and expose its flaws to both the nationalist right and the general public. The full name of the new group, "Brit Ne'emanei Eretz Yisrael" was suggested by Naomi Shemer, one of Israel's most popular poets.[19]

Unexpectedly, Banai did very well. It kept the nascent radical right together and helped it regain its confidence. Banai had only two real courses of action: to lobby against the confirmation of the Camp David Accords within the parties of the ruling coalition, with a dismal chance of success; and to stage an extraparliamentary struggle against the Accords in an attempt to sway the Israeli public from supporting them. These two missions kept Banai's leaders busy.

Banai's Knesset members and lobbyists continuously warned other politicians, in both private and public, about the dangers of an agreement with Egypt. Sadat's pro-Nazi record was often mentioned in order to demonstrate his unreliability and support the contention that he was using the Accords only to get Sinai back before going to war with Israel again. Surrendering the oil fields in Sinai would be an economic disaster leading to the loss of economic independence. And the Accords were, of course, also presented as a mortal blow to the nation's security.[20]

As for the wider struggle, Banai held demonstrations in Israel's main cities and the settlements in areas to be returned. One of the most memorable acts took place after the Nobel Peace Prize was awarded to Menachem Begin. Banai urged everyone either to cable Begin or to telephone, asking that he not go to Oslo. Three large black paper statues were placed in front of Jerusalem's most crowded shopping center. The first commemorated the peace ("with honor") signed in Munich in 1939 between Neville Chamberlain and Adolf Hitler. The second "honored" the Nobel Prize awarded to Henry Kissinger in 1973 for bringing "peace" to Vietnam, and the third was dedicated to the newest Nobel Laureate, Menachem Begin, for his "achievement" at Camp David.[21]

But the miracle that Banai hoped would torpedo the peace process did not come. On March 29, 1979, Begin, Carter, and Sadat signed the Egyptian-Israeli Peace Treaty in Washington. Now only the Israeli voter could undermine the most fatal result of the peace process, the destruction of the settlements of northern Sinai. The final stage of the Israeli evacuation of Sinai was scheduled for April 1982, and elections for the Knesset were to take place in November 1981. It was thus theoretically possible that a direct appeal to the voter could save Yamit and its surrounding settlements.

This possibility was not missed by the true believers of the radical right. By 1979 they could count on five Knesset members, several political movements, and rich experience in direct action. The politicians among them were, nevertheless, very hesitant. Familiar with the conservatism of the Israeli voter and with the history of failures of small political parties, they were reluctant to start a new "anti-Camp David" party.

An outside initiative was needed, and it was surprisingly provided by Yuval Ne'eman, the president of Tel Aviv University. He was well known for a brilliant career as an intelligence officer in the 1950s and for his achievements in physics since the 1960s, but not for his political views. He was never a registered member of the LIM and was not an ardent supporter of Gush Emunim. In fact, until the Yom Kippur War, Ne'eman had been a dove with no shred of sympathy for the cause of Eretz Yisrael. Even after the war, when his opinions began to change, he was still willing to work for Shimon Peres, Israel's minister of defense, as a special aide on security.[22] It was the peace with Egypt that radicalized Ne'eman. A rational and soft-spoken person who never concealed his academic manners and analytical way of thinking, Ne'eman became convinced that the Camp David Accords were a death trap for the nation and that the people of Israel were being decieved by

Menachem Begin. Witnessing the hesitation of his new Banai colleagues, Ne'eman decided to step into the heat. He issued a public call for the establishment of a new party to fight the Camp David Accords. Within two weeks he had a thousand respondents—not a bad turnout for an amateur politician.

There were other developments among the disappointed radicals. A growing section of Gush Emunim had long been advocating establishing a new religious party that would be loyal to the ideal of Greater Eretz Yisrael and to the religious Zionism of Merkaz Harav. They wanted to settle the score with the "duplicitous" National Religious Party, which they felt had betrayed Eretz Yisrael just as Begin had done.[23] Ever since Gush Emunim's birth, its relationship with the NRP had been ambivalent. The NRP was the only political arm of religious Zionism in Israel, and the Gush members had grown up within Bnei Akiva, the youth branch of the World Mizrachi movement and the NRP. But the Gush was also a revolt against the timid NRP, the party that no longer "really cared about Eretz Yisrael" and sold its political services cheaply to the highest bidder.

Under the influence of Gush Emunim and a new generation of its own political professionals, the NRP became prouder in the late 1960s, more hawkish and loyal to the integrity of Eretz Yisrael; from loyalty to the Labor party it moved toward Likud. Zevulun Hammer and Yehuda Ben-Meir, the two young leaders of the renewed party, were close to the heads of Gush Emunim in age, mentality, and convictions, and the Gush had had every reason to believe its influence over the party was growing. The 1977 election strengthened this impression. Rabbi Haim Drukman, a senior Gush Emunim activist and a close student of Rabbi Zvi Yehuda Kook, was the person the Gush most wanted to see in the Knesset. His elevation on the NRP candidates' list to no. 2 for the 1977 elections indicated that the electoral influence of the Gush was greatly appreciated by the party.[24]

But in 1978 the NRP again lost its resolve: with the exception of Drukman, all its leaders supported the Camp David Accords. Once again the NRP became a docile political partner of a dominant secular party, this time the Likud. Gush Emunim activists like Hanan Porat, Gershon Shafat, and Rabbi Eliezer Waldman, citing this betrayal, proposed establishing a new party. This movement toward politicization, however, was resisted by such members of the Gush as Rabbi Moshe Levinger, who argued that it would be a grave mistake, since the Gush had attained its unique moral and political impact precisely because it kept itself above politics.[25]

A third element of Banai was also intensely preoccupied with the future, the Upholders of Herut's Principles. Geula Cohen and Moshe Shamir, the leading opponents of Camp David within the Likud Knesset delegation, were sure they could not work with Begin and the supporters of the peace. But they were less sure about the alternative. While enthusiastic about Ne'eman's initiative, both Cohen and Shamir were skeptical of the political chances of a single-issue party opposing Camp David, which was what Ne'eman proposed. Cohen and Shamir saw this approach as shortsighted.

Cohen, the Israeli version of the Spanish La Pasionaria, was never content with instrumental politics. For her politics was always confessional and moralistic. She believed that the support for Camp David was a clear symptom of malaise; dearly few Israelis realized that the time to enjoy life and live in peace had not yet come. Thus, Camp David was for Cohen more than a political mistake. It was a sign of a national weakness, weariness, an inability to face real challenges.[26]

This analysis led people like Cohen to an important conclusion. What was needed was not just a political party but a movement of national revival. Fighting Camp David made sense only in the context of a larger struggle for the rejuvenation of Zionism.

The person who brought the three strands together was Rabbi Zvi Yehuda Hacohen Kook, the mentor of Gush Emunim. Rav Zvi Yehuda, as he was called by his followers, was intimately involved in many important political developments in Israel in the 1970s. Like his followers, he was unhappy about the Camp David Accords. Inevitably he would join the soul-searching and debates that preoccupied many of the radicals in the spring of 1979. No Gush Emunim decision could be made without him.[27]

Rabbi Kook was first approached by Gush Emunim's Hanan Porat and Rabbi Eliezer Waldman, who bought Geula Cohen, intending to recommend the establishment of a new religious party. They were unsure of the rabbi's reaction since his most trusted man was Rabbi Haim Drukman of the NRP, whose high party rank in the Knesset was due to Kook's efforts and influence.[28] To the visitor's surprise Kook was enthusiastic about forming a new hawkish party. He did not even mention the NRP, and favored a party that would bring religious and secular Jews together as equal partners.

Later, Kook suggested such a party to Ne'eman and his group. He felt that the holiness of Eretz Yisrael was capable of unifying all groups. Those who believed in Eretz Yisrael, Kook proposed, believed by implication in the Torah of Yisrael and in the God of Yisrael. Agreement on the indivisibility of the Land could only lead to political unity.[29]

Kook's recommendation tipped the scales in favor of a new united movement. It also helped resolve the debate within Gush Emunim regarding the politicization of the movement. The Gush decided to lend the new party full support but to remain apolitical and independent. Gush Emunim members were therefore free to support the political party of their choice.[30]

The Tehiya movement was officially established on October 8, 1979, in Jerusalem. The name of the new movement was suggested by Hanan Porat, who had originally picked it for the religious movement he had wanted to build as an alternative to the NRP. The name appealed especially to former Lehi members like Geula Cohen and Israel Eldad, for it also commemorated Abraham Stern's long-forgotten "Tehiya Principles."[31] The official name was *Tenuat ha-Tehiya—Brit Ne'emanei Eretz Yisrael* (The Renaissance

Movement—The Covenant of the Upholders of the Land of Israel). The name conveyed the main message of the Tehiya leaders: the need for a genuine return to the good old Zionism, the Zionism of creation, of pioneering, of self-sacrifice and vision. This message was further expressed in the emblem of the movement, a photograph of a young and handsome Israeli pioneer looking ahead with burning hope in his eyes. At its founding convention in Jerusalem, the party's manifesto, *Kol Koreh* (A Call), was published. This critical document charged the government of Israel with betraying its main mission, the continuation of the great march of Zionism. The modern return to Zion was successful, including "the ingathering of the exiled, the building of the the land and its settlement, the expulsion of the foreign rulers, the establishment of the state and its solidification, the liberation of Eretz Yisrael territories—with the reunification of Jerusalem as its peak—and the emergence of a solid society." But this great process was being halted by the present regime, and there was an urgent need to revive Zionism and rekindle the dwindling flame.[32] This was the call of the Tehiya to the Israeli public; those who cared about the old values were urged to support it in the next elections.

But well before the elections of 1981, Geula Cohen and Moshe Shamir, acted in the Knesset. They seceded from the Likud in 1979 and formally established the Tehiya faction in the Israeli parliament. Fully aware that provocative Knesset behavior could get free publicity both Cohen and Shamir played their positions to the full. They took advantage of every opportunity to attack the government and argue that, in view of the large Knesset support for the peace treaty with Egypt, the Tehiya remained the only viable opposition.

Geula Cohen, passionate by any standards, did especially well. Not only did she cause the speaker of the House to censure her repeatedly, but on occasions she made sure she was kicked out of the Knesset—with photographers present. Cohen's greatest parliamentary success was the approval of a rare Basic Law in 1980 formally annexing Jerusalem and naming it the capital of Israel.[33] While preparing the carefully formulated draft bill in the Knesset, the Tehiya also collected thousands of signatures in the streets.

The new party' hopes of stopping the evacuation of Sinai through the polls were shattered in the elections of 1981. The Tehiya won only three Knesset seats. Begin's Likud received a handsome plurality, and did not need the support of Yuval Ne'eman, Geula Cohen, and Hanan Porat in forming a coalition. The continuation of the Israeli withdrawal from northern Sinai, in accordance with the treaty with Egypt, was assured.

This prompted the Tehiya's most systematic attack on the Israeli legal order. All three Tehiya Knesset members left the House and went to Yamit to participate in the illegal struggle against the withdrawal. They made it very clear that their opposition to the "illegal" act of the surrender of Israeli territories to the Egyptians was more important than their loyalty to Israel's rule of law or to the Knesset whose oath of allegiance they had taken just a few months earlier.[34]

The radicalism of the Tehiya and its commitment to the greater Eretz Yisrael had not hampered its realism and political pragmatism. Thus the party's leaders decided to join the Likud coalition in the summer of 1982. What brought Ne'eman and his colleagues to make the move was the June 1982 invasion of Lebanon.[35] Ne'eman was an early advocate of a massive Israeli operation in Lebanon, which he believed was necessary to destroy the PLO military might in the north, and thereby to eliminate the pro-PLO spirit in the West Bank.[36] He was therefore very pleased with the Begin-Sharon invasion of Lebanon. Though Sinai was lost for the present, there were other parts of Eretz Yisrael to care for, dozens of West Bank settlements craving support.

And there was a very real change in the orientation of the Likud administration. Even before the mysterious resignation of Menachem Begin in August 1983, the nationalist administration differed greatly from the cabinet responsible for the 1979 peace with Egypt. Moshe Dayan and Ezer Weizman, the major supporters of Camp David, were out. They were replaced by Moshe Arens, who had voted against the accords, and Itzhak Shamir, who had abstained. The deal offered to the Tehiya was hard to refuse: Ne'eman was to be made Israel's minister of science and energy, and he would also head the powerful government settlement committee; the settlements were to get 500 million shekels for new ventures in the West Bank.[37]

Thus, the Tehiya party that won five Knesset seats two years later in the 1984 elections was no longer a marginal political phenomenon. It was a former cabinet partner and a political organization with credible record of action. The Tehiya proved that in the Israel of 1980s it was possible to be a genuine right-wing radical and operate within the framework of the government. Neither its leadership nor its activists were ever asked to pay for their contentious behavior and illegal operations.

The Further Radicalization of Rabbi Meir Kahane and the Rise of Kach

Unlike most radical dissenters of the late 1970s, Rabbi Meir Kahane was a radical with the credentials to prove it. This man, who in America in the early 1960s infiltrated the John Birch Society as an FBI informant, and who later led the American JDL to extremism and violence, was by the early 1970s the most skillful person in Israel extraparliamentary provocations and tactics of direct action.[38] He was the epitome of the right-wing radical, an activist oriented toward street violence, crude propaganda, and smear campaigns.

Before the Yom Kippur War, Kahane was very much alone among the territorial maximalists garnering most of the publicity granted ultranationalist operations. But after the war the newly established Gush Emunim began using tactics similar to his. The period after 1973 was thus very hard for Kahane—he neither had a large following nor did he receive much attention. And Kahane, who had never been able to start constructive ventures or participate in a collective effort led by others, had a real problem. His only way to survive politically was to do something no one else had yet done.

Kahane's solution was to violently polarize the relationships between Jews and Arabs in the West Bank. Followed by several admirers, Kahane, who had just changed the movement's name to Kach (Thus!), moved in 1975 to Kiryat Arba for the purpose of exacerbating the volatile relationship between Jews and Arabs. While he himself spent much of the second half of the 1970s in America, serving a jail sentence in New York, and struggling to retain control over the decaying American JDL, his Israeli followers were involved in numerous anti-Arab operations. Many of these were conducted in the name of T.N.T. (Terror Neged Terror—the Hebrew acronym for anti-Arab Jewish terrorism).[39] And since, unlike the Gush Emunim members, Kahane never believed that the Arabs could live quietly under a benevolent Jewish rule, he was certain that in due time all the settlers of the West Bank would follow Kach's example.

Nevertheless, until 1977 Kahane had one soft spot that blocked his total radicalization and alienation from the Israeli normative system: his untold admiration for Menachem Begin. Kahane grew up within the Revisionist movement of Vladimir Jabotinsky and was an old Betar member. His father, Rabbi Charles Kahane, was very active in the American Revisionist movement. One of Kahane's most vivid memories was Jabotinksy's visit to his home in the late 1930s. In 1947, an adolescent Kahane picketed Ernest Bevin, Great Britain's minister of foreign affairs, who was responsible for Britain's pro-Arab orientation. The incident resulted in Kahane's first arrest.[40]

Kahane, who was always fascinated by the use of physical force, was captivated by Jabotinsky's idea of Barzel Yisrael (Israel's Iron)—the idea that the Jews of the Diaspora were to respond in kind to every physical assault, and that the sovereign Jewish state should have a strong army. Kahane, like Begin, referred to the Israeli military not as Zva Hahagana Le-Yisrael (Israel *Defense* Forces) but as Zva Yisrael (Israel's Army). And while Kahane alone did not endorse the Likud in the elections of 1973 and 1977 and ran on his own ticket, he nonetheless supported Begin. In an early 1973 interview he explained that his race for the Knesset had nothing to do with animosity toward Begin; on the contrary, he hoped for a stronger Begin in the Knesset. His argument in those years was that he, as an orthodox rabbi, was capable of introducing a genuine nationalist religious party, one that would support Begin instead of selling out to Labor.[41]

Inevitably, the Camp David Accords were a profound shock to Meir

Kahane. He was transformed at once. The previously admired prime minister of Israel had, instantly, become a traitor. By succumbing to the pressure of the Gentiles, Begin defamed the name of God:

> The heart of the Begin tragedy is that a man who was a symbol, for half a century, of Jewish pride and strength, surrendered Jewish rights, sovereignty, and land out of a fear of the Gentile pressure. It is in a word, *Hillul Hashem*, the humiliation and desecration of the name of G–d by substituting fear of the finite Gentile for Jewish faith in the G–d of creation and history.[42]

Kahane was henceforth relieved of his ideological allegiance to the successor of Jabotinsky. And he was now free from an additional bond, loyalty to Israel's democratic form of government. Kahane, it is clear, was never a great champion of democracy. However, if a legally elected government under Menachem Begin was capable of solving the pressing problems of Eretz Yisrael and the Arabs, he maintained some allegiance to the system. But now Begin had proven himself part of a rotten system; the whole secular framework was corrupt. Kahane never explained why he had expected Menachem Begin to act like Kahane, but in a later interview, journalists Alex Ansky and Itzhak Ben-Ner, asked if he was disappointed with Begin:

> *Answer:* "Yes, very deeply so. That night, when he was elected, it was a great moment for me. This was a man I expected to start here, really start, a revolution. He didn't do it."
>
> *Question:* "Did you expect him to start the evacuation of the Arabs from the land?"
>
> *Answer:* "Yes, but not only this."
>
> *Question:* "Did you really have a basis for the belief that Begin would evacuate them?"
>
> *Answer:* "Sure!"
>
> *Question:* "On what basis?"
>
> *Answer:* "It is not only me, they believed it too."
>
> *Question:* "They who?"
>
> *Answer:* "The Arabs. I remember. They were silent one month, two months, three months—they were afraid of him, they thought he was Begin."[43]

After 1978, Kahane grew even more extreme. His terminology became as radical as the operations of his followers. The prime target of his fulminations became Israel's Declaration of Independence. The 1948 document, which promised equal rights to all the inhabitants of the Jewish state regardless of race, religion, and nationality, was now presented by Kahane as a contradictory document.

Unlike others on the radical right who felt committed to the respected document, Kahane had never agreed that the State of Israel should be committed to general "non-Jewish" humanistic principles such as equal rights. In his 1973 book *The Challenge—The Chosen Land* he stressed the impossibility of an equal Arab existence in Israel. Profoundly hostile to all enemies of the Jews, Kahane's prognoses were based on a simplistic worst-case analysis of the Arab-Israeli conflict: if the Jews did not "take care" of the Arabs first, the Arabs were bound to wipe them out or evict them from Palestine.[44]

Before 1978, though, Kahane, as an American immigrant with no part in the heroic Zionist past, did not dare challenge Israel's most cherished document. But the Camp David Accords and the "fall" of Begin removed all his inhibitions. The leader of Kach was ready to call the "bluff" of the document: it was, according to him, the most damaging statement ever made in the history of Zionism:

> Does "free" mean that they are free to work for an Arab majority in Israel? Does that mean they are free to give birth to many babies, very many, so that in the future they will be free to establish, by means of their vote, an Arab majority in the Knesset? Does "free" means an equal right for an Arab majority in the Knesset to decide that the state be named "Palestine"? That the Law of Return which today allows Jews, not Arabs, automatic entrance and citizenship, be canceled? In short, could the Arabs of the Jewish state . . . be free and equal to move to the voting booth in silence, in relaxation, even in complacency, and democratically bring an end to Zionism and to the Jewish state?"[45]

According to Kahane, the words *freedom* and *equality* in Israel's Declaration of Independence are meaningless. It is unrealistic to believe that the Arabs can identify with the values of a Jewish state, established on what they consider by right their own land. It makes more sense to expect the Arabs not to forsake the idea of Arab Palestine and to do whatever they can to bring it about, including taking advantage of the Jews' values and generosity.[46]

The personal disenchantment of Rabbi Meir Kahane with Menachem Begin, and his consequent radicalization, did not help him a great deal with the Israeli public. In 1980 he added a new chapter to his extralegal record: when authorities discovered a plot to destroy the Dome of the Rock on the Temple Mount with a long-range missile, he was detained for nine months in an administrative arrest.[47] In the elections of 1981 he was supported by only 5128 voters, 0.3 percent of the electorate. Although this was slightly better than his support in 1977 elections (4396, or 0.2 percent), the change neither suggested a trend nor promised a future. No one took Kahane seriously. Marginal and crazy, his Kach party was seen by most Israelis as another of those unrealistic lists formed for each election in a futile attempt to attract attention.

Only in the period of 1981–1984 did a popular swing in the direction of the extremist rabbi start to take shape. This shift was caused by three parallel processes, on which Kahane personally had little influence: the decline in the authority of Menachem Begin, the fiasco of the war in Lebanon, and the emergence of the social-nationalist-religious-ethnic protest against the Arab minority in Israel.

In 1980 Menachem Begin's physical condition and political fortunes deteriorated. At times he seemed totally out of control of his cabinet; the Likud's most outspoken ministers, Ezer Weizman (defense) and Ariel Sharon (agriculture), were at each other's throats. Weizman, profoundly touched by the peace with Egypt, was moving to the left. Pushing to continue the peace process, he opposed settlement in Judea and Samaria and discounted the growing PLO influence.[48] Sharon, on the other hand, saw the peace with Egypt as an opportunity to strengthen Israel's hold on the West Bank, and did not care about continuing the peace process. The result was open conflict, intensified by the huge egos and aspirations of the two former military heroes.[49] Other cabinet ministers, like Yigal Yadin and Itzhak Modai, were embroiled in the conflict, and the press was full of detailed reports about the infighting. Begin, though formally chairing the cabinet meetings, looked feeble and remote. The entire government of Israel seemed anarchic and incompetent.[50]

Then suddenly in 1981 Begin's decline ended. Responding to a marked decrease in popularity and an almost certain loss at the next election, the prime minister surprisingly regained his strength and combative spirit. He intensified his rhetoric, sounding like the old pre-1978 Begin.[51] Just a month before the election, Begin made a most crucial decision, to bomb Iraq's nuclear reactor. When the spectacular operation ended with total success, Begin became unbeatable. He also won by portraying Labor and its allies as treacherous, disloyal, and discriminatory against the weak strata of Israeli society, the Oriental Jews.[52]

Begin's recovery did not help Kahane in the short run, for they were both appealing to the same sentiments and using the same arguments. The precise turning point in the rabbi's fortunes may well have been the Christian massacres in the Palestinian refugee camps of Sabra and Shatila, in the fall of 1982. The massacres produced the fall of Ariel Sharon, the chief architect of the Lebanon war, and finally stigmatized the war as a political failure. There was no question, after Sabra and Shatila, that Israel's Operation Peace for the Galilee was a failure.

Begin's days were numbered. In August 1983 he simply collapsed. Mental and physical exhaustion ended the political career of Herut's leader and placed Itzhak Shamir at the head of the government. Begin, Israel's most appealing orator since Ben-Gurion, the father figure of the "second Israel," the Oriental Jews, was no longer in command, and the mediocre Shamir was no substitute. There was now an emotional and political vacuum in Israeli politics. Kahane was fully prepared to fill the void. The Likud's militant rhetoric after 1981 had legitimized much of Kahane's language, and he used the situation to the fullest.[53] He was so successful that in 1984 nearly 26,000 voted for Kach, his party. Probably even more Israelis were sympathetic to his positions, but felt the man himself was unelectable. It is clear that most of the people who voted for Kach in 1984 had been strong Begin supporters in 1981.

Meanwhile another, more significant, process was reaching maturation— the rise of nationalist-religious-ethnic-anti-Arab sentiment. Without question this process greatly benefited Kahane in the 1980s. The new anti-Arab sentiment had to do with the dramatic evolution of the PLO and the Palestinian nationalism associated with it.

The Palestinian Liberation Organization was no longer a weak terror organization without status or recognition. By the end of the 1970s it had acquired the status of a recognized mini-state. The Arab success in the Yom Kippur War, and the oil embargo that followed, gave the PLO the chance to prudently turn itself into a relatively moderate political organization that expressed a struggle for the liberation of a poor people with no land. Backed by the Third World and nourished by the Western fear of the oil crisis, the PLO made its way to the U.N., receiving worldwide recognition. The PLO further established a mini-state in Lebanon, with its own government, bureaucracy, citizens, army, banks, and health services.[54]

This development buoyed up both the Palestinians of the West Bank and the Israeli Arabs. The Palestinians saw Israel's creeping annexation of the occupied territories as being counterbalanced in Lebanon. For many Israeli Arabs the PLO provided a new focus of attention and identification.

Before 1973, the PLO had played only a minor role in the collective consciousness of the Israeli Arabs. The State of Israel, the winner of the Six-Day War, was powerful and successful. Some of this image rubbed off on the Israeli Arabs; they were after all, Israelis. Even after the opening of the borders, and the first shock of meeting their relatives in the occupied territories, the Israeli Arabs did not really feel Palestinian. Their economic progress in Israel, the twenty years they had been cut off from the Arab World, and the power of their country had made it difficult for them to identify with the losing Palestinian cause.[55]

But this seems to have changed in the Yom Kippur War. Israel was no longer self-confident and invincible. The Israeli Arabs did not instantly lose their Isreali consciousness, but the PLO began to look attractive, and many of them started to relate to Palestinian nationalism.[56]

The most significant expression of the new spirit of Palestinian defiance took place on March 30, 1976, on what was called the Land Day. A general Arab strike against unjust expropriations of land in the lower Galilee evolved into violent demonstrations. Israeli police and military units were attacked by rocks and molotov cocktails. In the end six Israeli Arabs were killed and thirty-five Israeli policemen and soldiers were wounded. The Land Day was a watershed, opening a new era of fervent identification with Palestinian national symbols. Nowhere was the new extremism felt more strongly than in Israel's universities. The Arab students had been divided between the traditional radicals, members of Rakah (the New Communist

List), and a new organization, Ibna-al-Balad (the Sons of the Village). In December 1979, a group close to the Ibna-al-Balad won the elections of the Arab student union at the Hebrew University of Jerusalem. Its platform had three demands: that the Palestinian Covenant, the constitution of the PLO demanding the elimination of Israel, be adopted as the student union's official creed; that the State of Israel be replaced by a secular democratic Palestinian state; and that terrorism be recognized as a legitimate part of the Palestinian struggle for self-determination.[57] The universities of Haifa and Beer Sheba witnessed similar eruptions. There were numerous fights between Arab and Israeli students over incidents such as the desecration of the Israeli flag or the public singing of the PLO anthem Biladi-Biladi (My Homeland, My Homeland).

Rabbi Meir Kahane did not immediately reap the political dividends of these events. But by the late 1970s he knew he was on the right track. Other right-wing radicals were very vague on the Arab issue, but Kahane had predicted the rise of the new Arab extremism in his 1973 book, *The Challenge:*

> Not only the Arab in the liberated territories sees himself as a "Palestinian" and believes that the Jews stole his land. The Arabs who live in the pre-June 1967 Eretz Yisrael . . . those who have had Israeli citizenship since 1948, the Arabs "with equal rights" who enjoy freedom in the Jewish state, think in the same way. He [the Arab] does not see himself as part of the state, for he is an Arab not a Jew, a Palestinian not an Israeli. He feels no loyalty to his government—for he does not see it as his government. He is hostile and is full of hate for the Jewish majority, for in his heart he is a "Palestinian" and an Arab nationalist. . . . But since he suffers from a guilt feeling, for his Israeli citizenship, he is a much more dangerous enemy. . . .
>
> In the coming years we shall witness a growing number of Arab intellectuals whose nationalism will radicalize and become a great deal more extremist. We shall witness a growing number of Arabs who would not find spiritual and intellectual satisfaction in the professions open to them, and of many others who will not find suitable jobs for their expectations. We shall witness a society whose main blue-collar workers would be Arabs and the others Jews. This situation would produce growing frustration, tensions, demonstrations, strikes, violence, and attempts of subversion and revolution.[58]

Kahane's 1973 predictions proved, by the end of the decade, accurate. Not only was he right about the frustrated young Arab intellectuals who discovered Palestinian nationalism, but he was also correct about the growing friction between Jews and Arabs in the job market. No competition had ever existed between the two sectors in well-paid or even moderate positions, but the early 1980s produced a growing perceived competition for the lower-paying jobs. In 1980–1981 Israel's economy started to shrink, and the first to suffer were the country's outlying development towns. High inflation rates destabilized pay scales, and many workers began to demand constant pay increases. Factories and shops that were unprepared for the new situation found Arabs to be inexpensive alternatives to Jewish labor. The Arabs, especially the residents of the occupied territories, were willing to work for low pay and without labor organizations. There is in fact no hard proof of a large-scale *real* Jewish-Arab competition in the job market, but in Israel's developing towns there was a strong *perception* of such competition. The Arabs were seen as willing to work for dismal wages that no Jew would lift a finger for. The result was inevitable, a growing Jewish hostility toward the Arabs—people who "stole" jobs, hostile aliens enchanted with the new Palestinian nationalism.[59]

Had Meir Kahane been a more balanced and moderate politician, he might well have been elected to the Knesset in 1981, along with the Tehiya leaders. His analysis of the Arab situation was, from the angle of the radical right, realistic. His forecasts were correct. His solution of evicting the Arabs was far more consistent than the suggestions of many of his competitors. But the Kahane of the streets was an altogether different person from the analytic Kahane of the books—a bundle of unrestrained emotions, violent eruptions, and an insatiable thirst for publicity. Apparently those who might have voted for him needed, in addition to good analysis, a credible and legitimate communicator. The leader of Kach did not project this image in 1981, and his potential supporters voted for Begin. By 1984 the situation had changed a great deal. Begin was gone. Kahane was still an outsider, but the rhetoric of the Likud and the growing radicalism of the Tehiya and Gush Emunim made many of his opinions acceptable.[60] Thus in 1984, frustrated settlers, bitter residents of developing towns, angered young soldiers, and insecure people all over the country—25,906 of them in all—joined forces to lift a ten-year-old political ban from the head of Kach and put Kahane safely in the Knesset.

Settler Vigilantism and Violence in Judea and Samaria

In March 1981, some of Israel's most distinguished law professors wrote a letter to Itzhak Zamir, the state's attorney general, demanding an official investigation of several alleged acts of violence committed by settlers against local Arabs in the West Bank. The letter and a strong Supreme Court denunciation of the indecisive prosecution of Jews involved in anti-Arab acts persuaded Dr. Zamir to name his deputy, Judith Karp, to head an investigative committee. A year later, in May 1982, the devastating Karp Report was presented. Not only did it confirm the existence of Jewish anti-Arab vigilante activities but it showed that most of these acts went unpunished. Out of a sample of seventy cases reviewed by the committee—which involved killing, wounding, physical assaults, property damage, and the use of armed and unarmed threats—fifty-three were never prosecuted. Of these fifty-three cases, forty-three were closed for lack of suspect identification, seven for lack of an official complaint, and three because there was not enough public interest to justify prosecution.[61] Though the committee did not study each case in detail, a random examination uncovered sloppy investigation. Several cases were reopened after the committee demanded it.

Rabbi Meir Kahane had been the first to introduce Jewish violence and vigilantism into the complex of relations between Jews and Arabs in the West Bank. Vigilantism had preoccupied Kahane's Jewish Defense League in its earliest American phase, when it took to the streets, first to defend Jews against the violence of other minorities, but soon expanding to aggressive offense against Russian and Arab diplomats. Kahane's move to Israel did not change his philosophy—he was soon preaching vigilantism against Christian missions in Israel, finally making the Arabs his permanent target. Kahane believed that any Arab who was not ready to publicly vow loyalty to the idea of a Jewish state was a security risk. And since there was no question that all the Arabs of the West Bank were either actual or potential PLO accomplices, Kahane advocated vigilantism to help the security forces in the area keep the Arabs under tight control,[62] and terrorism to convince the Arabs to emigrate.

In the early days of Gush Emunim settlements in Judea and Samaria, there was a world of difference between the ideas of Kahane and the attitudes of the idealistic young settlers. Kahane was not part of their culture and did not share in their ideology; they despised the anti-Arab hooliganism he advocated. Gush Emunim believed in the possibility of coexistence with the Arabs. The Gush's young rabbis and their followers vehemently reiterated that they did not intend to uproot the Arabs of Judea and Samaria. Instead, the non-Jewish residents were to be treated as *ger toshav*, ("alien resident")—that is, like people of Canaan, whom the Torah commanded to respect and treat humanely. True, even in its most liberal stages Gush Emunim was willing to grant full political rights only to those Arabs who vowed loyalty to the Zionist idea, while the rest were to be offered residency rights only, but all in all the early rhetoric was full of understanding and consideration. Most of the Gush leaders truly believed that a fruitful coexistence on the West Bank was possible and that the local population would enjoy and benefit from their presence.[63] There was, they argued, plenty of room on the West Bank for Jews and Arabs alike, and since the Arabs had always lived under brutal and inhumane foreign domination, they would appreciate the humanity of the Jews, the real owners of the land.

The fly in the ointment was the fact that the local Arabs had never been consulted about this concept of "benevolent" coexistence. Nor did they know or care about the Torah concept of "alien resident." The West Bank Arabs considered the Israeli takeover as a forced occupation, pure and simple. By occupying the area the Israelis had expanded upon the injustice they committed in 1948, when they established the State of Israel on the ruins of Palestine. The more ideological circles among the Palestinians talked about Israel's "colonialism," while the masses simply identified with the PLO.

But conflict between the settlers and the local Arabs did not emerge immediately. As long as Jewish settlers were relatively few and they settled mostly outside the densely populated areas, Arab animosity could be contained and the myth of coexistence maintained. This was the case during the Labor administration of Itzhak Rabin, when the government strictly forbade Jewish settlement in Samaria and would not allow land to be confiscated. Most of the Jewish-Arab violence in that period had to do with PLO guerrilla and terror operations, which were taken care of by special military units or by the effective military government of Judea and Samaria.[64]

But even in those early days, one place in the West Bank caused a great deal of friction. This was Hebron; the bone of contention was the Cave of the Patriarchs (the *Machpela*), the traditional burial place of Abraham, Isaac, Jacob, and their wives—the second-holiest place for Jews. Just after the Six-Day War, the Israeli military government opened the shrine for regular prayers and visits. Since the site had for generations been a Muslim mosque, special arrangements were made to secure Jewish access without infringing on the rights of the Arabs and without desecrating the large worship halls. The general policy of Moshe Dayan, Israel's minister of defense, was to respect freedom of religion and to make as few changes as possible in the status quo.[65] The practical consequence of the policy in Hebron was that most of the Cave of the Patriarchs was left in Muslim lands while Jewish worshipers were allowed to pray only at certain hours.

This arrangement worked, briefly. But the Jewish settlers in Hebron, under the zealous leadership of Rabbi Moshe Levinger, believed that all of Hebron was Jewish land by right, and the fact that Jews had not had control of the Cave of the Patriarchs for generations was a result of historical injustice. They were consequently determined to change the status quo, and pushed incessantly for more space and longer prayer hours in the shrine.

Inevitably, this led to growing Arab hostility and conflict. Unlike other early settler demands, the Jewish aggrandizement at the Machpela was a zero-sum game: every gain by the Jews was an Arab loss. Rabbi Levinger and his followers sought to achieve their goal of controlling the shrine by stages, without causing an open conflict with the military government. They would refuse, for example, to leave on Friday in time to let Muslim worshipers come in. Or they would leave the halls but block the main entrance. When the settlers' demands on prayer were fulfilled, they started to push for *Kiddush* in the cave—the rite of taking wine after services on Sabbath and other occasions. They also demanded that the Israeli flag be flown over the shrine on Israel's Independence Day.[66]

All these encroachments were extremely insulting to the Muslims—especially the drinking of wine. Islam strictly forbids alcohol, and bringing wine into the mosque was seen as intended humiliation. This friction led directly to violence in the cave itself and in the area as a whole. In 1968, a hand grenade was thrown at a group of Jewish visitors in front of the mosque. After that, a special military guard was assigned to the area. From the summer of 1975 onward, the situation around the Machpela became extremely tense, and Jewish-Muslim skirmishes became routine.[67] A Muslim crowd erupted in 1976 when a Kiryat Arba resident stole Quarn scriptures from the mosque. Arabs stormed into the Jewish part of the building, expelled the worshipers, and set Jewish scrolls and ceremonial objects on fire.[68] Only prompt military intervention prevented a bloodbath.

The Likud victory in 1977 brought an end to the cautious settlement policy of the Labor administration. The new policy called for massive settlement of the entire West Bank. The main ideological message of the plan was that all of Eretz Yisrael was open for Jewish settlement. Its practical purpose was to create an irreversible situation in the West Bank, so much settlement that a future political compromise over the area would be impossible. The most important part of the plan was to have Arab-populated Samaria settled by Jews, so that Labor's Allon Plan became permanently invalidated. The Likud settlement program had an enormous impact on the West Bank. It profoundly polarized relations between Jews and Arabs, leading to an increase in violence.

As earlier, the focus of the new situation was in Hebron. The real objective of Rabbi Levinger and his followers had always been to settle in Hebron, King David's first capital. Biblical commandments were only one reason for the desire to settle in sacred Hebron. Another was the bitter memories of the 1929 Arab pogrom, in which the entire ancient Jewish community of the city was destroyed.[69] Sixty-seven Jews were brutally murdered, while the rest barely escaped with their lives. Rabbi Levinger made no secret of his desire to reintroduce a Jewish community in Hebron; the Kiryat Arba compromise, though seen as a great achievement in 1968, was only a temporary solution. One of Levinger's strongest legal arguments regarding the right to resettle Hebron was the existence of Jewish property in the Arab city, buildings like Beit Hadassah and Beit Romano, abandoned since 1929. Since 1976, Jewish settlers had repeatedly attempted to establish permanent residence in these buildings. The Rabin administration had repeatedly rebuffed the settlers' attempts.[70] Ezer Weizman, Begin's minister of defense and a very strong supporter of the peace process, tried to do the same, but he was outmaneuvered by Miriam Levinger, the Rabbi's wife.

In April 1979, Mrs. Levinger and several other Kiriyat Arba women occupied Beit Hadassah and refused to leave. Aware of Begin's commitment to the settlement of all of Eretz Yisrael, and equally aware of his gentlemanly manners, the settlers decided to have the women establish a Jewish presence in Hebron. The tactic of placing the ladies at the "forefront of the battle for Eretz Yisrael" worked; although the "new settlement" was not recognized officially, the women were not evacuated either.

Official recognition came only a few months later. Responding to the murder in Hebron of a young yeshiva student, Yehoshua Saloma, Begin decided to punish the local Arabs by legitimizing the Jewish return to the city: several families would be allowed to reside in Hebron and a small yeshiva would be established in Beit Hadassah.[71] The Levinger family was the first to move, with others following.

The new step alarmed the Arab citizens of Hebron. Ever since the Six-Day War they had lived in fear of an evacuation. Levinger's activities confirmed those fears. There followed a series of increasingly violent exchanges between Jews and Arabs. The murder of six Jewish yeshiva students, in Beit Hadassah in May 1980, was the peak of the cycle of violence. As we shall see, it triggered retaliation from the Jews in June.

From the beginning of the Israeli return to the area, the settlers had been allowed to carry arms. There was nothing sinister or anti-Arab in this policy, it was simply a realistic recognition that the occupied territories were a high-risk area. This was especially true in 1968–1970, when life in the West Bank was destabilized by PLO guerrilla and terror operations; all the new settlements were designated "confrontation settlements," and the military authorized settlers to shoot in self-defense. In 1978, Israel's chief of staff, General Rafael Eitan, assigned the settler community partial responsibility for securing the West Bank. Hundreds of settlers were transferred from their regular army units to units in the West Bank, where they protected their own settlements and secured cultivated fields, roads, and commercial and general community facilities. Every settlement was required to have an assigned number of fit combatants, including officers. These were to perform their active duty on a part-time basis while leading civilian lives. Regional mobile forces equipped with armored personnel carriers helped police the Palestinian population.[72]

The commanders probably saw this regional defense system as the best and cheapest way to secure the settlements against Arab attack. It was also part of the Zionist tradition: in pre-state Palestine, Jewish border settlements and kibbutzim defended themselves. Nevertheless, the growing friction between settlers and local Arabs produced many dubious uses of official arms. Some of the regional defense units, like the Judea company consisting of settlers in the Hebron Mountains, became notorious for being trigger-happy and for brutally mistreating the local Arabs.[73] The military government of the West Bank, whose officers were often ideological supporters of Gush Emunim, was neither capable of dealing with the problem nor interested in doing so.[74]

The step to vigilantism was a small one. A comprehensive account was compiled in 1983 by David Weisburd, who systematically examined the involvement of the settlers in anti-Arab vigilantism and the attitude of the entire community toward this phenomenon. He found that 28 percent of the

male settlers and 5 percent of the female settlers admitted to having participated in some type of vigilante activity.[75] Even more relevant was that 65
percent of Weisburd's five hundred respondents agreed with the statement,
"It is necessary for the settlers to respond quickly and independently to Arab
harassment of settlers and of settlements." Only 13 percent of the settlers
disapproved of vigilantism; Weisburd concluded that Gush Emunim's support of vigilantism "represents community sentiment, not the view of a
small group of radicals or trouble-makers."[76]

   It should of course be stressed that most acts of settler vigilantism were
triggered by Arab harassments, such as road stoning or individual anti-
Jewish assaults. Usually the settlers did not file complaints of such incidents
with the police before acting, feeling they were either ineffective or indiffer-
ent. Thus, by the late 1970s the settlers developed a vigilante philosophy; as
one settlement leader said,

> Our attitude has been that we cannot afford to allow any actions of hostility
> by the Arabs to go unanswered. . . . If during the day or night a rock was
> thrown by x amount of Arabs(at a car). We will go out and react. Now, what
> that reaction means really depends on the situation. We sometimes go talk to
> the mukhtar [the village head] and warn him; sometimes we try to catch the
> kids or the people, whoever it was responsible for what was done. The
> general idea, as I have said, is that we found that if we don't react, the Arabs
> will translate it as a sign of weakness. And once we are in that situation, we
> really don't have any point of strength to make sure this won't happen
> again.[77]

   Over the years the vigilante philosophy has developed another buttress,
namely the image of the Arab whose culture and values are based on primi-
tive power structures. The settlers speak about this "Arab mentality," which
explains the necessity for a constant settler vigilance. One person told
Weisburd,

> There have to be good relations with the Arabs as far as possible. But one has
> to show firmness if they make trouble. Because the mentality of the Arabs is
> such that they are used to the situation that people with power have to show
> their power. If someone throws a stone at you, you don't walk over and say
> Shalom. . . . Rather, first of all, you throw two stones at him and afterwards
> Sulhah (meeting of reconciliation).[78]

   The vigilantism has become a way of life: if force is constantly needed to
keep the Arabs in line, the settlers cannot depend on ordinary law enforce-
ment. By 1980 there were persistent rumors about a growing Jewish vigilantism vis-à-vis the unruly Arabs. A massive settler attack on Ramala on April
24, 1980, in retaliation for previous Arab rock-throwing indicated an escalation in the Jewish-Arab tension. It served in fact as a prelude to the full-scale
terrorism that followed from both sides.[79]

   Perhaps the fullest elaboration of the Gush Emunim vigilante philosophy
was made by Yehuda Etzion, in telling a court about his participation in the

attempted assassination of three Arab mayors, in retaliation for the death of six yeshiva students by Arab terrorists.

> Planning and executing the attack on the murder chieftains took only one month of my life, one month that started with the assassination night of six boys in Hebron, and ended up in conducting this operation. I insist that this operation was right. So right in fact, that to the best of my understanding . . . even the law that prevails in the State of Israel could recognize its justice or ought to have recognized it as a pure act of self-defense. . . . It is unquestionable that in our present reality . . . the reality of the sovereign state of Israel . . . the defense forces of the state had to take care of this matter, quickly, neatly, and effectively, so that nobody could have, in his right mind, questioned such an operation. Furthermore, I do not deny that it was a clear case of undue excessive force. But the situation at stake was a case in which the "policeman" responsible for the matter not only stepped aside, . . . not only ignored the gravity of the case and the fact that the murderers were allowed to act freely, . . . but developed a friendly relationship with them. . . . This situation, sirs, was a case of no choice, a condition that created a need to act in the full sense of the word, for the very sake of the preservation of life.[80]

No one familiar with the literature on vigilantism could miss the classical logic of the vigilante mind. Yehuda Etzion told the court that he took one month of his life—a life otherwise devoted to seeking redemption—to become a vigilante terrorist.

A typical vigilante movement never sees itself in conflict either with the government or with the prevailing *concept* of law. It is not revolutionary and does not try to destroy authority. Rather, what characterizes the vigilante mind is the profound conviction that the government and its agencies have failed to enforce the law or to establish order in a particular area. Backed by the fundamental norm of self-defense and speaking in the name of the law of the land, vigilantes see themselves as enforcing the law and executing justice.[81]

When Etzion responded, in May 1980, to the request of friends from Kiryat Arba to help avenge the blood of six yeshiva students murdered in Hebron, he was not thinking of messianism but of vigilantism. He took a short leave of absence from his main concern to take care of an altogether different business.[82]

David Weisburd published his results before the Jewish Underground came to light, and his work helped make it possible to understand the environment that would produce such a phenomenon. He writes,

> The vigilantism of Gush Emunim settlers is part of an organized strategy of social control calculated to maintain order in the West Bank. Though a minority of settlers actually participates in vigilante acts, they are not isolated deviant figures in this settlement movement. Rather, those vigilantes are agents of the Gush Emunim community as a whole. They carry out a strategy of control that is broadly discussed and supported.[83]

The Jewish Underground of Gush Emunim

The most extreme reaction to the Camp David Accords was disclosed in 1984, following the arrest of the group the Israeli press dubbed the Machteret Yehudit (the Jewish Underground), though the connection between the underground and the 1978 agreement was not apparent at first. The suspects were associated with several acts of anti-Arab terrorism that had taken place in Judea and Samaria since 1980: an assassination attempt on three Arab mayors, a murderous attack on the Muslim college of Hebron, and an attempt to blow up five Arab buses full of passengers. At the time these acts looked like an organized vigilante effort of the settlers to fight growing Arab terrorism, an ad hoc operation against the PLO. However, today it is clear that the Machteret was not started as a Gush Emunim counterterrorist unit aimed at avenging Jewish blood. The first meetings of the members of the group took place in 1978, long before they first used firearms. The topic on the agenda was none other than a massive operation on the Harem-esh-Sherif (the Muslim area on the Temple Mount) and the blowing up of the Dome of the Rock.

The idea of blowing up the Muslim shrine was conceived and developed by Yeshua Ben-Shoshan and Yehuda Etzion. Both—especially Etzion, one of the founders of Ofra, a major center of Gush Emunim in Samaria—had been part of the Gush Emunim spirit and milieu for years. But more than most members of the movement, they were preoccupied with the mystery of redemption and its realization.[84]

The Camp David Accords were, for both men, a disaster of cosmic magnitude. Their conviction in the imminence of redemption had no room for reversals or setbacks. Human error could not stop or postpone a divinely guided process. The explanation that Begin had erred at Camp David or succumbed to the pressure of the Gentiles did not square with their messianic comprehension. A setback of the magnitude caused by the Camp David Accords could be explained only one way: God Himself had decided to interfere in the process of redemption—either because He was angry with His people, or because He wanted to warn them of something. Ben-Shoshan, who was intensely preoccupied in studying the Kabala (mystical Jewish texts) and Etzion, who had been studying the writings of little-known ultranationalist writer, Shabtai Ben-Dov, had no difficulty in discovering the root of the trouble. It was the existence of the "abomination," the Muslim Dome of the Rock, on the Temple Mount.

Mount Moria, the most sacred place of the historical Jewish nation, the ancient location of the First and Second Temples, was not just another site in the Holy Land. It was the source of the nation, its very soul.[85] The final act of redemption for the People of Israel, the building of the Third Temple, was bound to take place on the Temple Mount. But the government of Israel had decided in 1967, immediately following the conquest of the Mount, to leave it in the hands of the Arabs. Thus the government had collaborated willingly in the desecration of the holy place and had committed an unforgivable sin.[86]

It was the catastrophe of Camp David in 1978 that changed this situation for some members of Gush Emunim. While most of the members of the Gush, who also agonized about the event, were able to follow Rabbi's Kook instruction to maintain their allegiance to the State of Israel and to react only through political protest, a few could not.[87] Menachem Livni, the "operational commander" of the underground, described to his investigators after the group's arrest how the whole bizarre plot started:

> Shortly after President's Sadat visit to Israel, I was approached by a friend who showed me the picture of the Dome of the Rock, to which I shall hereafter refer as the "abomination." My friend argued that the existence of the abomination on the Temple Mount was the root cause of all the spiritual errors of our generation and the basis of hold of Ishmael [the Arabs] in Eretz Yisrael. In this first meeting I did not clearly understand my friend, and more meetings were held in which an additional friend joined.[88]

The first friend was Yeshua Ben-Shoshan, the Kabalist. Ben-Shoshan, a quiet and mysterious Yemenite Jew, was never part of the active leadership of Gush Emunim nor a member of any of its settlements' nuclei. He had been living in Jerusalem with his large family, served with distinction as a career army officer, and was the follower of several Kabalistic rabbis who had no relationship with Gush Emunim. But Ben-Shoshan had been deeply involved in the early illicit settlements of the Gush and admired the people who were determined to pave the way to redemption through settlement in all of Eretz Yisrael. The settlers, in turn, loved this humble, soft-spoken, and mysterious man and sometimes called him a *tzadik* (pious saint).[89]

It was Ben-Shoshan who first raised the idea of clearing the Temple Mount, but it was Yehuda Etzion who became the operation's chief ideologist and dynamo. This young man—twenty-seven in 1978—was a typical product of Gush Emunim. He himself had not studied in Yeshivat Merkaz Harav, though his rabbi in Yeshivat Allon Shvut was Yoel Ben-Nun, one of the most influential graduates of Merckaz Harav and a founder of Gush Emunim.

In 1978, Etzion discovered a whole new world: the ultranationalist tradition inspired by poet Uri Zvi Greenberg in the 1930s, the tradition of Malchut Yisrael (the Kingdom of Israel).[90] The unique feature of this vision—as developed by Shabtai Ben-Dov—was the notion of *active redemption*. According to Ben-Dov, there was no need to wait for another miracle. All the conditions for concrete redemption were already present. One had merely to act. He spoke about the building of the Third Temple and the coming of a Jewish theocracy on earth, a government by Torah Law, run by a Sanhedrin, the council of the seventy wise men.[91] No one in Gush Emunim had ever spoken in such concrete terms. None dared press the issue.

Students of messianic movements have long noticed that millennarian types are driven to extreme and antinomian acts when the progress toward redemption—which for a while seems at hand—is all of a sudden stopped. They are fully convinced that an exceptional act is needed to calm the Lord's anger, and that such an act will restore the messianic process and ensure its consummation.[92] This psychological mechanism is probably what inspired the Temple Mount plot.

Ben-Shoshan and Etzion, concerned by the apparent reversal of the messianic process, began to meet regularly. Eventually they decided to expand the circle, and brought in Menachem Livni of Kiryat Arba, a major in the army reserves, as well as other trusted friends. All of them immersed themselves in discussions of the Halakha and the Kabala. The whole project had a spiritual and mystical nature. Chaim Ben-David, who attended the meetings from 1978, told his investigators that "the great innovation for me was that this was a 'physical operation' capable of generating a spiritual operation."[93]

Sometime early in 1980 Yehuda Etzion and his friend Menachem Livni called together a group of eight men. This meeting was the first time the Temple Mount operation was spelled out in detail. Etzion presented his new redemption theology in all its grand contours. He told the group that the removal of the Muslim shrine would spark a new light in the nation, which would trigger a major spiritual revolution. He appeared convinced that the operation was absolutely necessary to continue the process of redemption and that it would solve all the problems of the nation at once. His tone and spirit were prophetic and messianic.[94] Later on, when in jail, he published a booklet in which the entire rationale for the operation was fully presented.[95]

Yehuda Etzion was the most dynamic person in the Temple Mount plot. By 1980, his ideology of active redemption was quite distinct from the Gush Emunim ideology, with Shabtai Ben-Dov, not Rabbi Zvi Yehuda Kook, as its main inspiration. Ben-Dov had died in 1979, and on his deathbed he had urged Etzion to do something about the Temple Mount.[96] Under the spell of Ben-Dov, Etzion felt fully capable of carrying out the Temple Mount plan, with no need for a higher rabbinical authority. (His former rabbi, friend, and neighbor from Ofra, Yoel Ben-Nun, was no longer a partner for discussions and consultations; Ben-Nun later referred to Etzion as a Sabatean, a false prophet.[97])

The other members of the group, however, were not as convinced as Etzion. They raised many questions. Some did not believe the job could succeed technically, and others worried about the political and international consequences. Menachem Livni—an engineer and major in the reserves, probably the most balanced member of the group, who emerged as its operational head—agreed with Etzion in principle, but was apprehensive of the immense consequences. Livni's conclusion, accepted by the rest of the group, was that preparations for the blowing up of the Dome of the Rock could proceed, irrespective of the ultimate operational decision. There were so many details to be worked out that the question of a final decision to strike was for the present irrelevant.[98]

May 1980 was a critical month in the evolution of the Machteret. On Friday, May 3, while a group of yeshiva students were returning to Beit Hadassah in Hebron from Sabbath prayer, Arab gunmen opened fire on them at close range. Six students were killed; several others were wounded. The attack, as we have seen, came as the climax of a period of growing anti-Jewish violence in Hebron and throughout Judea and Samaria. The settlers were certain that the attack was masterminded by the Palestinian National Guidance Committee in Judea and Samaria, an alleged PLO organization that Defense Minister Ezer Weizman allowed to operate almost freely.[99] The settlers felt that only a massive retaliation could get the situation under control. After two meetings in Kiryat Arba, attended by the communal rabbis, the settlers decided to act.[100]

Menachem Livni, a Kiryat Arba resident, knew whom to contact—his friend and partner in the planned Temple Mount operation, Yehuda Etzion. Instead of committing a retaliatory mass murder, in the custom of Arab terrorists, the two decided to strike at the top. The cars of five Arab leaders most active in the National Guidance Committee were to be blown up. The plan was to injure these people severely without killing them. The crippled leaders would be living symbols of the consequences of anti-Jewish terrorism.[101]

The terror operation called by the Israeli press the "mayors affair" was only a partial success. Two of the leaders involved, Mayor Bassam Shak'a of Nablus and Mayor Karim Kahlef of Ramalla, were crippled. Two others were saved when demolition teams were unable to get the explosives into their cars. The fifth case ended maiming an Israeli. The Mayor of El Bireh, whose garage was also set to explode, was not at home. A police demolitions expert was called in and mistakenly detonated the explosion; he was seriously wounded and lost his sight.[102]

The "mayors affair" was a side issue for the group, unrelated to the central Temple Mount Plot. But it, and the popular response, apparently boosted the spirits of the plotters. The settlers in Judea and Samaria, most of whom had no idea about the perpetrators of the act, applauded it overwhelmingly. A representative reaction came from Knesset member Rabbi Haim Drukman: "Thus may all of Israel's enemies perish!"[103]

The group resumed preparations for its assault on the Dome of the Rock. Etzion, who masterminded the plan, and Livni, an expert of explosives, studied the lay out of the Temple Mount and the construction of the Dome of the Rock in minute detail for two years. After stealing a huge quantity of explosives from a military camp in the Golan Heights, they worked out a full attack plan. Twenty-eight precision bombs were manufactured, intending to destroy the Dome without causing any damage to its surroundings.

The group hoped to approach the place unnoticed, but were ready to kill the guards if necessary, and bought special Uzi silencers and gas canisters. More than twenty people were to take part in the operation.[104] Since the time for the final evacuation of the Jewish settlements in Siani was approaching rapidly, the operation, intended to prevent the withdrawal, was to take place no later than early 1982.

The underground suffered, however, from one major drawback. None of the individuals involved was an authoritative rabbi. The question of rabbinical authorization had already come up in 1980. Most members of the group would not proceed without the blessing of a recognized rabbi. But all the rabbis approached (how much they were told about the plan is not clear), including Gush Emunim's mentor Rabbi Zvi Yehuda Kook, either refused their blessing or were at best very equivocal. But Livni, who needed rabbinical approval, was left with no doubt. He *did not* have a green light.[105] When the final date of decision arrived in 1982, the only two who were ready to proceed were the originators of the idea, Etzion and Ben-Shoshan. The grand plan was consequently shelved indefinitely.

The postponement of the Temple Mount operation signified a major break in the short history of the underground. It meant, for all practical purposes, the removal of the millennarian part of the plan from the agenda—the aspect that was so important for Ben-Shoshan and Etzion. So when the underground struck again, the two were barely involved.

The deadly operation was an open attack on the Muslim college of Hebron in July 1983, in response to the murder of a yeshiva student; three students were killed and thirty-three wounded. While logistical support was provided by members of the underground and masterminded by Livni, the operation itself was carried out by three men who had not been involved in the 1980 attack on the mayors. The attack followed a growing wave of anti-Jewish violence, and it indicated the growing frustration with the government's inability to defend the settlers. Crucially, it was approved by rabbinical authorities.[106] It was followed by several smaller acts of terrorism.

The emerging outrage of the Hebron settlers was most noticeable in the last major operation of the underground in April 1984, the one meant to be most devastating. There had been a new wave of Arab terrorism, this time in Jerusalem and near Ashkelon. Shaul Nir, who conducted the earlier attack on the Muslim College and considered it a great success, managed to convince the local rabbis that another decisive strike was needed.

Armed with their authority he prevailed over the unsure Livni and made him plan an unprecedentedly brutal act.[107] Five Arab buses full of passengers were to be blown up in revenge for similar attacks on Israeli buses by Palestinian terrorists. The explosions were planned for Friday at 4:30 P.M., at a time and place when no Jews were expected to be on the road. The explosives were placed under the buses' fuel tanks, to cause maximum damage and casualties.

But by this time the Israeli internal security service had finally uncovered the underground. As soon as the wiring was completed, the whole group was arrested, bringing to an end the activities of the Machteret. Ever since the exposure, a fierce debate has raged within Gush Emunim about the legitimacy of the group's acts and its significance.

A key issue throughout is *rabbinical authority*. The confessions and testimonies of the members of the underground do not clarify whether the leading rabbis of Kiryat Arba were involved in the actions of the conspiracy, or if so how much. But they make clear that *only those operations approved by the rabbis took place*.

The first operation, the "mayors affair," was opposed by Rabbi Levinger—but only because he preferred extreme action and recommended an indiscriminate act of mass violence. According to Livni, Rabbi Eliezer Waldman—a prominent Gush Emunim rabbi and since 1981 a Tehiya Knesset member—even volunteered to participate in the operation against the mayors[108] Two other Kiryat Arba rabbis were instrumental in inducing Livni to commit the last two operations, which involved indiscriminate terrorism. Shaul Nir, the man who led the attack on the Muslim College, told his interrogators,

> I would like to add that in the time span of three years, I discussed the issue with four rabbis, all of whom expressed their support for warning operations within the Arab public. . . . I also heard the names of an additional three rabbis who stated their support in different stages of the operation.[109]

The rabbinical involvement in the terror acts that did and did not take place is of crucial importance. It tells us that the radicalization process that finally produced terrorism within Gush Emunim was not marginal but central. It was a by-product of the movement's belief in its own redemptive role and in the necessity of settling Judea and Samaria at all costs. The idealistic people who began in 1968 to settle Judea and Samaria did not go there with violent intentions. None of them expected to become vigilantes, terrorists, or supporters of terrorism. Yet within twelve years the combination of messianic belief and a situation of continual national conflict with a built-in propensity for incremental violence resulted in extralegalism, vigilantism, selective terrorism, and finally, indiscriminate mass terrorism. Had the Jewish Underground not been stopped in 1984, it might have become a Jewish IRA.[110]

The Movement to Halt the Retreat in Sinai

The Jewish Underground provided by far the most radical reaction to the Camp David Accords and was an important step in the formation of the radical right. Nevertheless, these activities had been conducted by a few people in secrecy, though several hundreds of settlers not directly involved probably knew vaguely about the group. Thus it was not until the April 1984 discovery, arrest, and report of the group's activity that it began to play a significant role in shaping the collective consciousness of the radical right.[111]

That role was filled instead by Hatenua Leatzirat Hanesiga Besinai (The Movement to Halt the Retreat in Sinai—MHRS). The movement, whose confrontations with the authorities and the military reached a peak in April 1982, expressed the accumulated outrage and frustration of all the opponents of Camp David.

The depth of the hostility evoked by Menachem Begin's decision to trade the Jewish settlements in Sinai for peace with Egypt was largely due to the special nature of the Israeli settlement of northern Sinai. The Rafiah salient, a strip of thirty miles stretching from El-Arish in the Gaza strip through Rafiah in northern Sinai, was never an important spot in the ideo-theological map of Gush Emunim. None of the movement's members, even those who thought the territory was part of the "Promised Land," considered the area a vital settlement target. No illicit Gush settlement was started there until 1979.

The importance of settling the area was instead stressed by the strategists of the Labor party. Moshe Dayan, Yigal Allon, and Israel Galili, the three most influential ministers of Golda Meir's cabinet, realized after 1967 that Israel needed a security zone in northern Sinai. The idea of settling the Rafiah salient was predicated on the assumption that Israel was likely to reach a settlement with Egypt, and would need a viable territorial wedge between the Gaza Strip, which would remain in Israel's hands, and Sinai, which would be returned to Egyptian hands. In three wars, each time the Egyptian military moved into Gaza in full force, it held a tremendous strategic advantage. A committee of the Meir cabinet had consequently decided in 1969 to settle the area to prevent direct access from Sinai to Gaza. The first *moshav*, Sadot, was established in 1971.[112]

By late 1972, Dayan had prepared a grand development plan for the region. Yamit, a large city with a deep-sea port, was to be built in the Rafiah salient; it would be a center of a development district reaching a population of quarter of a million by the end of the century.[113] Though construction did not start until the Yom Kippur War, Yamit was completed very quickly. The first settlers arrived in early 1975, and within two years the city had a complete municipal infrastructure.

By the late 1970s the Rafiah Salient was a prosperous area by any standards. In addition to the growing city of Yamit, there were nine successful agricultural moshavim, fine weather and fertile soil made agriculture very profitable. The settlers came to the region not because of Eretz Yisrael ideology, but because they recognized the great economic potential of the area and were promised full governmental support.[114] The leaders of the Labor government encouraged a sense of purpose and pioneering spirit in attracting settlers to Yamit. And the government repeatedly reassured the settlers that Israel would never withdraw from northern Siani.

The Likud victory in May 1977 strengthened the conviction of the settlers that their homes were secure. Begin, they were certain, would never surrender even a single square inch of the area—he and his minister of construction visited Yamit on September 29, 1977. Israel's new premier wrote in the city's guest book, "Jerusalem blesses Yamit, which will be built and become the joy of the nation and its pride."[115] On another visit, this time to one of the flourishing moshavim of the area, Begin, promised that when he retired he would settle there to write his memoirs in their company.

All the hopes and expectations came to an abrupt end with the signing of the Camp David Accords on September 17, 1978. The shock was especially painful because only weeks earlier, Begin had declared, "If at Camp David they raise the issue of evacuating settlements in the Rafiah Salient, we shall pack up and go home."[116]

The settlers also felt betrayed by the agreement of Moshe Dayan and Ariel Sharon to the plan to dismantle the settlements in less than four years and to withdraw from the entire region. The settlers viewed Dayan as the founding father of the venture in northern Sinai. Sharon, well known as an arch-maximalist, was thought to be another safeguard against withdrawal: In the early 1970s, as a general on active duty, Sharon had supervised the evacuation of Arab Bedouins from the area to make room for the Jewish settlements.[117] Just prior to Begin's trip to Camp David, Sharon, as Israel's minister of agriculture, had ordered the establishment of several fake outposts all over the area in order to strengthen Jewish claim to the region in the negotiations. Yet despite all this, when Begin telephoned Sharon from Camp David for the approval of his most hawkish lieutenant, Sharon did not fight against the plan; unwilling to risk his political career, he gave Begin the green light.[118] In due course he was to assume command over the forced evacuation of the settlers and the destruction of Yamit.

Most of the settlers' early struggle against the Camp David Accords was conducted within the context of Banai and the Tehiya. But since it was a struggle of people over their homes and occupations, it had a special urgency and desperation. Several protest organizations sprang up, which added to the militancy of the local population. An apologetic visit by Menachem Begin almost ended in bloodshed. The gentlemanly prime minister was booed and called "liar," "crook," "traitor," and "the shame of Israel."[119]

Things got worse with the first step in the withdrawal from the area, the evacuation of the vegetable nursery of Moshav Neot Sinai. Perhaps a thousand farmers and supporters showed up, including a significant Gush Emunim representation. They refused to evacuate the area, causing a severe confrontation with the army. When the military used water hoses, the demonstrators stoned the soldiers, threw burning brands, and sprayed them with poisonous chemicals. Only the appearance of two cabinet ministers, including Yigal Yadin, Begin's deputy premier, with a promise to reconsider the evacuation plan pacified the settlers and ended the violence.[120]

The most significant struggle against the evacuation was conducted not by the feeble and poorly organized settlers of the Yamit area, but by the Movement to Halt the Retreat in Sinai, an organization that brought all the opponents of Camp David to the concrete struggle of the settlers. Although the movement was established only in late 1981, it had its origins in the incidents of Moshav Neot Sinai in 1979 and in the illicit establishment of a new settlement, Atzmona, in the area in that same year.

Atzmona was established by veteran Gush Emunim members just after the March 1979 signing of the Israeli-Egyptian Peace Treaty, in order to provide a living hope for the dispirited settlers of the area and to become the center of the future struggle against the retreat. Begin's government, guilt-ridden and faced with many other forms of resistance, decided to ignore Atzmona and behave as if it did not exist.[121] But Atzmona's settlers were not totally isolated. Yamit had a *Yeshivat Hesder*, headed by Rabbis Jacob and Israel Ariel (Shtieglitz). The two brothers, especially the younger, Israel, were determined to stop the retreat by all means.

Begin's opponents were also busily ignoring reality. The Tehiya leaders—Yuval Ne'eman, Geula Cohen, Hanan Porat, and others—had made the struggle against the Israeli-Egyptian Peace Treaty their main 1981 electoral theme. Utterly convinced of the truth of their message, they believed that they would get enough seats in the Knesset to veto the continuation of the Israeli withdrawal from Sinai.[122] But the 1981 elections proved them wrong. Begin won the elections handily, and the Tehiya got only 2.3 percent of the vote—three Knesset seats.

The Tehiya's failure left only one course of action open, the activation of the unconventional power of Gush Emunim. The MHRS was established a year before the expected evacuation of Yamit. Faced with the accelerated pace of the retreat—which included generous compensation payments to the future evacuees and the establishment of a new settlement area—the activists of Gush Emunim had to devise an effective anti-retreat strategy.

None of them believed they could overcome the Israeli army. The whole idea of the struggle was to create conditions under which the political echelon *would not instruct* the army to evacuate Sinai.[123] Thus, the leaders of the movement came to the conclusion that their job was to make the price of the retreat higher than the price of Israel's noncompliance with the Egyptian-Israeli peace agreement. They were not, however, ready to consider the most obvious means, armed struggle and bloodshed.

Since they were unable to come up with another feasible solution, they chose a typical Gush Emunim strategy that was partly rational and partly mystical. The rational part was to launch an intense public-relations campaign all over the country, to intensify it with huge demonstrations, and to reoccupy all the deserted houses in the Yamit area. The mystical part had to do with the implied belief that if sufficient devotion was demonstrated, God would interfere and stop the retreat. This mélange of rational and mystical can be detected in Hanan Porat's words:

> There is only one way of action: a creation of a balance of terror in Yamit, an acute, big, and credible balance of terror that would force the government to recognize that the uprooting (of settlements) is impossible. Only such recognition can make sure that a civil war is prevented. Choosing, on the other hand, a moderate course is bound to create confrontation. The government, the Knesset, and the public should be made aware of these matters very soon. . . . We have to give the government sufficient time to find a way out of this muddle. If we dedicate ourselves from now on to the cause, with the utmost devotion, there is a chance to win. Total dedication, truly complete commitment. . . .[124]

Porat did not have to tell his friends, all true believers who had in the past also been involved in illegal settlements, that the utmost devotion (*messirut hanefesh*) they were asked to demonstrate was directed not to the Israeli government but to God Himself. Part of the movement's activists who came to the area continued to believe in God's imminent intervention until the last moment.[125] Several more skeptical colleagues of Porat wanted to make sure that if a retreat did take place, it would not occur before the entire nation was traumatized by events in Yamit.[126] They were certain that this limited goal was within their reach.

The Movement to Halt the Retreat in Sinai reached its final form in only six months, from October 1981 to April 1982. The key positions were, not surprisingly, filled by Gush Emunim veterans, individuals like Uri Elitzur, Moshe Merhavia, and Hanan Porat. The movement demonstrated the unique dedication, organizational skills, and fervor shown in all previous Gush Emunim operations. Hundreds of religious settlers from the West Bank moved to the Yamit region. They brought with them their families, rabbis, and yeshivot. Some of the newcomers settled in motels in the city and organized for a long stay. Others moved illicitly into Moshav Talmei Yosef, which had been evacuated earlier by the army, and occupied its houses. In the last stage of the movement's resistance it numbered about 1000 people who managed to penetrate areas closed off by the army and settle in its deserted buildings.[127] Several hundred supporters were also stationed outside the border of the closed area, repeatedly trying to outmaneuver the army and get in.

The style of the struggle followed the traditional methods of Gush Emunim. Armed settlers with *dubonim* (khaki parkas used in the military), sleeping bags, talith and tefilin (religious objects used in prayer), engaged in profound halakhic deliberations late into the night, Torah lessons in temporary yeshivot, and heated polemic speeches. But there was also a new element in the logistical structure. Many of the individuals who came from the West Bank were not just private citizens (as they had been in 1974–1978), demonstrating against an erroneous government. There were now also public officials, heads and employees of government-financed local and regional councils in Judea and Samaria. The costly operation in Yamit was not financed by private donors. Most of the money came directly from public sources, from the budgets of the regional councils allocated by Israel's ministries of education, religion, agriculture, construction, and internal affairs.[128] Resources granted by the World Zionist Organization were also used.

And the resolution to go to Yamit was not made voluntarily by individual Gush members. It was a collective decision taken by Moetzet Yesha, the Emunim-dominated Council of the Settlements of Judea, Samaria, and Gaza.[129] While no one was forced to come to Yamit, the call was sanctioned by the rabbis, the highest authorities of the movement.

The last stage of the struggle took place inside Yamit and some of its surrounding moshavim. The members of the MHRS organized themselves for a siege within the city in an almost military fashion. Large quantities of food were stored, barricades were erected, and section commanders were named. The conduct of religious ceremonies was especially intensified. Ecstatic prayer sessions were constantly held. Radical and millennarian sermons, preached by the movement's rabbis, became the order of the day.[130] The entire Yamit territory was named a "holy land" and the settlers, a "holy public." Everything there became in fact holy: "holy struggle," "holy purpose," and "holy movement."[131]

The fight was not just for Eretz Yisrael, but also for the Torah of Israel and for the people of Israel. The retreat from Sinai and the evacuation of Jewish settlements were considered act of sin, retreats from the course of redemption. People fully expected a miracle to happen. The religious-messianic psychodrama that took place in the last weeks of the struggle pushed to the front the most extreme religious figures, the mystical rabbis. The ecstatic atmosphere rendered even some legitimation to very exceptional expressions made near the end, such as Rabbi Moshe Levinger's warning that suicide might be committed and Rabbi Israel Ariel's call to the soldiers to disobey orders. Israel's two Chief Rabbis, Mordechai Eliyahu and Abraham Shapira, were called to come to Yamit to rule in these cases.[132]

The struggle reached its peak in the last scheduled days of the retreat. The settlers, whose devotion was no operational match to the twenty thousand soldiers confronting them, refused to leave. They were forcefully dragged out. Many continued to pray until the last moment. Others fortified themselves on the roofs of the buildings and would not let the army get near. The military commanders had to devise a special iron cage, moved by gigantic cranes, in order to outmaneuver the intransigent settlers and remove them.

A special protest tactic was introduced by a small number of Rabbi Kahane's followers. As usual, these people were isolated from the other groups at Yamit and did not form an integral part of the MHRS. Nevertheless, they were welcomed, for the MHRS needed as many people in Yamit as possible. But instead of joining the rest of the organized action, Kahane people fortified themselves in one of the city's air-defense shelters. As the final days of the evacuation approached, they locked themselves in the shelter with explosives, ammunition, and cyanide capsules, and threatened to kill themselves if forced to leave. The situation became very tense, since it was not clear how serious the threat was. It was finally defused by Rabbi Kahane himself, in one of his most rewarding performances ever. Fully aware of the plan of his supporters, Kahane had left Israel for a fundraising trip to America. However, following a personal request of the prime minister, he "agreed" to return and talk to his followers. He was flown back from the United States and was taken from Ben-Gurion Airport, by special military helicopter, to Yamit. The entire nation held its breath while Kahane talked to his followers, finally convincing them to surrender. It was the most favorable publicity Kahane ever had in Israel.[133]

When Yamit was demolished by the Israeli army and the area evacuated, on April 28, 1982, the exact date specified in the Camp David Accords, it was patently clear that Menachem Begin's grand peace move had won. It was, however, just as clear that a new Israeli political subculture had come of age, the radical right. The secular and the religious members of the Movement to Halt the Retreat in Sinai staged a symbolic ceremony to enshrine the loss of Sinai. They read Ezekiel's Sermon of the Dry Bones and swore never to forget the "holy" Yamit. And they made a commitment to return one day.[134] No doubt was left as to what would happen if another Israeli retreat was ever to be conducted, with or without majority support. Kahane's 1984 election to the Knesset, the electoral success of the Tehiya party, and the broad expressions of support for the Jewish Underground, all indicated that in the Israel of the 1980s the new radicals were far from isolation. A process that had started in 1967, and greatly intensified in 1978, was reaching its maturation.

The Politics, Institutions, and Culture of Gush Emunim

Gush Emunim: Twenty Years After

Gush Emunim has changed since the 1970s. From a messianic collective of young true believers who thought they could change the world by concentrated spirituality and pioneering devotion, it has become a movement of dozens of settlements, thousands of settlers, with financial assets and material interest. It has added a maturity and skepticism to its early spontaneity and messianic craze.

But Gush Emunim is still a very dynamic force, by far the most viable component of the radical right. It may also be the most effective social movement that has emerged in Israel since 1948. Political scientist Myron Aronoff has rightly characterized Gush Emunim as "a charismatic, messianic, religious, political, revitalization movement" which has become institutionalized.[1] Its dynamism and success have made the movement, which has no formal membership and has never had more than two or three thousand families of full-time devotees, an essential part of the collective identity of the nation and a partner to some of the most critical decisions of its government. It would not be erroneous to suggest that for much of the larger camp of the Israeli nationalist right, Gush Emunim now fulfills the role that the Kibbutz Movement fulfilled for Israel's Labor during its most glorious days—it is the concentrated inspiration and expression of the dreams of many who believe in the vision of the greater Land of Israel, though they take no active part in its actualization.

The unique force and position of Gush Emunim derive from a special combination of common sociocultural roots and experiences, a strongly held theology, an exemplary leadership, and more than twenty years of political and ideological fulfillment and success. People become part of the Gush usually because they *grow up* into it. The long process of socialization often starts at home, and continues through kindergarten, religious primary school, high school yeshiva, Yeshivat Hesder or advanced yeshiva.[2]

There are, of course, other ways to become part of the Gush Emunim milieu, like *Chazara Beteshuva* (religious repentance) or Aliya from another country, but unless the newcomer goes through a very profound Emunist conversion, he or she is likely to remain at the periphery of the Gush and to play a minor role. Today it is rather easy to be a West Bank settler without being a Gush member, and most Israeli residents of Judea and Samaria are not part of the Gush. Even in Gush Emunim settlements it is not always necessary to be part of the movement.

Gush membership usually presupposes a general commitment to the Kookist theology, and either being part of a settlement or working toward it. Membership also usually presupposes a close relationship with one of the rabbis of Gush Emunim settlements or yeshivot, in which the theology of Merkaz Harav is prominent. Most Gush Emunim members come from middle-class Ashkenazi families and are well educated, often graduates of Israel's best universities.[3] Women in the Gush community usually have a secondary education of ulpanot (girls' religious seminaries) and are part and parcel of the spiritual life of the movement. They are accorded a respect that is not granted women in some other Jewish-religious communities.[4]

Most members read *Nekuda*(Point), the Gush-Emunim-oriented magazine of the settlers in Judea, Samaria, and Gaza. Many of them write occasionally for the magazine and react intensely, through letters and otherwise, to events in the movement's and the nation's public life. They also share and write for many local newsletters.

The homogeneity of Gush Emunim and the intense involvement of its members in the movement's operations has sometimes led observers to view the Gush as democratic and egalitarian. But this is in fact far from true. Gush Emunim betrays an elitist ethos both externally and internally. The movement perceives itself as a vanguard, a small missionary order that has to show the way to the entire nation. Internally, the Gush has always been made up of a small and self-selected hard-core leadership and a wide perpiphery. Not only have full democratic procedures never been used but few among its members have ever raised the issue.[5]

The undemocratic character of Gush Emunim derives from the structure of the Kookist school and the tradition of Merkaz Harav. The Kookist system has always had some kabbalistic elements. Thus, as part of his personal inclination for the study of mysticism, Rav Kook Sr. established a mystical messianic school requiring that its followers share unique personal traits and a special mental structure.[6] Most of the future leaders of Gush Emunim were bright students at Merkaz in the late 1960s. They were attached to Rav Kook's son and successor, Rabbi Zvi Yehuda, sharing his political convictions and his psycho-theological state of mind.

They were, in addition, emotionally close to each other, with strong mystical bond. Haim Drukman, Moshe Levinger, Zalman Melamed, Hanan Porat, Eliezer Waldman, Yoel Ben-Nun, Yohanan Fried, and several other graduates of Mekaz Harav, though not the only active leaders of Gush Emunim, have remained the most influential guardians of the movement's spirit, able to mediate between the aging Zvi Yehuda Kook and the entire movement.[7] Undoubtedly things have changed since the 1982 death of the rabbi; Gush Emunim has become institutionalized but the Kookist circle apparently still exists. Though occasionally in conflict on many questions of policy and practice, the members of the mystical circle (and several other activists who had absorbed over the years the Merkaz Harav legacy) still determine the nature, character, and public profile of Gush Emunim.

And Gush Emunim has become an institution. What began in the mid-1970s as a group of penniless dreamers who struggled for a foothold in the West Bank has evolved into an established network with many assets and resources. Only two institutions of the movement bear its official name—the general secretariat of Gush Emunim and Amana, its formal settlement branch. But active members of the movement control much of the regional and municipal infrastructure of the West Bank. Thus the movement's influence, far outweighing its numerical force, is based on hundreds of paid official positions, large development budgets, and decisive influence on the life of nearly one-hundred thousand Israeli settlers in the West Bank and Gaza, most of whom are not members of the Gush.

All these factors—social, cultural, political, and economic—have combined to make Gush Emunim the key component of the Israeli radical right and its most substantial foundation.

The Political Theology of Gush Emunim

Gush Emunim has always been highly ideological, committed to the theology developed by the elder Rav Kook and expounded by his son in countless articles, lectures, and sermons. Since the Six-Day War, the young ideologues of the movement have spoken and written extensively in such anthologies as *Morasha, Artzi,* and *Eretz Nahala,* journals such as *Amudim, Zraim, Zot Ha'aretz,* and since 1980, *Nekuda.*

None of these writings has been comprehensive, but the general outlines of the Gush Emunim belief system are rather clear. Apparently the political events of the last decade have not changed the movement's fundamental ideology. The Camp David Accords, the retreat from Sinai, Israel's failure in Lebanon, the discovery of the Jewish Underground, and recently the *intifada* (the Palestinian uprising in the occupied territories) may have affected the mood of the movement's ideologues and their optimism regarding the imminence of redemption, but they have not prompted any significant theological reinterpretation.

Given the dialectical and paradoxical nature of the Kookist philosophy, this is not surprising. While Rabbi Avraham Itzhak Hacohen Kook undoubtedly built a major intellectual system, his ideo-theology was not based on logical rigor and empirical verification. Instead, elements of faith, secrecy, unearthly intuition, supernatural illumination, mystery, and paradox have always been essential components of his thought.[8] The consequences for present-day Emunist ideology are that almost any empirical situation can be seen to fit the grand scheme, and no fact can confuse or confute the theory. This is the reason that many members of Gush Emunim have found ways to live in peace with the "treason" of Camp David, while others decide to blow up the Dome of the Rock. It also explains why numerous Kookists are eager to fight for more settlements on the barren hills of the West Bank while others remain in Mekaz Harav and get closer to traditional Jewish ultraorthodoxy.[9] The ideo-theory of Gush Emunim may not fully account for the operations of the movement at any particular historical moment, but it is by far the single most important determinant of the movement's actions. Let us look at its key principles.

Redemptions

The element of Kookist theology most significant to Gush Emunim is the proposition that the people of Israel live in the age of redemption—the salvation promised by the Prophets and desperately awaited by persecuted Jews throughout history is finally at hand, a reality of our time. Following Rav Kook and the traditional Halakhic literature, the terms used to denote this great era are *Atchalta D'Geula* (the beginning of redemption), *Ketz Megule* (the uncovered end), and *B'Ikvata D'Meshicha* (in the footsteps of the Messiah). Rav Kook, who died in 1935, needed no Six-Day War to reach his conclusion. He saw signs of redemption in the very rise of the Zionist movement in the late nineteenth century, in the 1917 Balfour Declaration promising the Jews a national home in Palestine, and in the success of the Zionist venture in Palestine—the return of the Jews to their land and their ability to develop it and reap its fruits.[10]

The Zionist movement had been started in large part as a secular reaction to the orthodox Judaism of the Diaspora, so Rav Kook's proposition was revolutionary and unconventional—allotting a most sacred role in the messianic process to secular Jews who did not even believe in the coming of the Messiah. For many rabbis and Halakhic authorities this was a most preposterous and insulting suggestion. Thus Rav Kook, who was otherwise considered a great religious authority, came to be seen by the ultraorthodox as a religious sinner and a serious threat to the continuation of Judaism.

As for Kook himself, he was able to make this proposition because of his kabbalistic and mystical approach, according to which much more is hidden from sight than is seen. The external manifestations we encounter in the world represent only the barest fragment of cosmic existence, and God has his own ways of bringing about redemption, even if those who play a messianic historic role, the secular pioneers, are not fully aware of it.[11] Although it has been said that Rav Kook preferred the young *Halutzim* (Zionist pioneers) to the orthodox who maintained in Eretz Yisrael the old ghetto spirit of the Diaspora, he fell short of sanctifying secular Zionism. He was fully aware of the paradox built into his bold theory and made it clear that he expected the Zionist movement to return, in due time, to the full Judaism of Torah and its observance.[12] But his theology conferred upon secular Zionism a legitimacy it had never before had. Kook was able to bridge over many differences between secular and orthodox Zionists in the pre-state period, a precedent that later helped Gush Emunim in its contacts with secular elements in Israel.

Rav Kook's historical concepts help explain Gush Emunim's comprehension of the present state of affairs. The Six-Day War, in which Judea and Samaria were conquered and Jerusalem reunited, was no chance turn of events but a major step forward in the messianic process that started with the birth of modern Zionism. Gush Emunim's confidence in its cause is derived from its firm conviction that events have verified Rav Kook's grand reading of history, including the stages that took place long after his 1935 death: the 1948 establishment of the State of Israel, the ingathering of the exiles from all corners of earth, the blooming of the desert, and the glorious 1967 military victory. Since the two Rabbi Kooks were so evidently blessed with heavenly illumination and prophecy, there is no reason to doubt the coming of the next stage, full redemption. As Rabbi Haim Drukman has said,

> I could come up with . . . plenty of quotations from authoritative sources, according to which we are living in an era of redemption, but I prefer to observe reality. After two thousand years Jews return to their homeland; the desolate land is being continuously built; there is a unique process of the ingathering of the exiles; we have won independence and sovereignty which we did not have even during the era of the Second Temple. What would you call this reality if not a reality of redemption?[13]

The devastating military, political, and international losses of the Yom Kippur War raised an important question in many Gush Emunim and Kookist circles regarding the precise meaning of the expected redemption and its timing: were the people of Israel to return to the Torah and Mitzvot (observance of religious injunctions) before a full redemption could be effected?

These deliberations brought up the traditional distinction between *Mashiach Ben-Yosef* (Messiah, the Son of Joseph) and *Mashiach Ben-David* (Messiah, the Son of David).[14] According to this distinction, salvation would come through two consecutive stages of redemption, material and spiritual. The first stage, that of Mashiach Ben-Yosef, is manifested in the material achievements of the nation. This is, according to the Kookists, the stage the nation is presently going through—abundant material and political gains, entangled with immense and costly difficulties. But this period is bound to pass and be superseded by Mashiach Ben-David, in whose day all the spiritual barriers to full redemption, including the lack of full repentance on behalf of the Israeli majority, will be removed. "The course of our redemption," wrote Rabbi Zvi Yehuda Kook, "is a gigantic historical fact. What appears to counter this course is nothing but a temporary halt."[15] There is thus no reason either to worry about temporary delays, which are caused by earthly political problems, or to stop participating actively in the evolving messianic age through settlement and positive action.

With redemption at hand and all of Israel's difficulties being only insignificant setbacks, the Gush can afford a paternalistic attitude toward its rivals, particularly Peace Now. According to the Gush, this latter group, which fights the settlement of the West Bank in the name of peace, lives only for the present, not for eternity. The *Achshavistim* ("Now-nicks") have no sense of Jewish history. They are unaware of the full significance of the current era of redemption.

The Sanctity and Integrity of Eretz Yisrael

The second pillar of the ideological temple of Gush Emunim, the belief that the land of Israel in its entirety is holy, an inseparable spiritual part of the people, is also taken from Rav Kook. The concept *Am Yisrael* (the People of Israel) refers not only to the people but also to the territory and the two are inseparable, especially now that the process of redemption has begun. "The entire matter of Eretz Yisrael," says Hanan Porat,

> is a mysterious issue whose basis is . . . a spiritual attachment to matter and soil. . . . If one goes deeply into the understanding of the relation between the body and the soul or of the relationship between man and woman and penetrates the mystery of the unity of matter and spirit [one is able to understand] the love and the appreciation for each part of Eretz Yisrael just as there is value for every limb of the human body. . . . Eretz Yisrael has an element of life in it, and is tied to spirit so that a surrender of any part of it is like giving up a living organ.[16]

It is important to stress that concern for the territory of Eretz Yisrael never dominated Rav Kook's teaching, and that Gush Emunim's great emphasis on the matter emerged only in reaction to the danger of a territorial compromise with the Arabs after 1967. But once raised, the territorial issue engendered countless statements and essays. Eretz Yisrael became part of Gush's "holy trinity"—Eretz Yisrael, the people of Israel, and the Torah of Israel.[17] According to this doctrine it is erroneous to give back territories in order to "save" peoples' lives; the commonsensical notion that human life is more valuable than land, and that Israel should trade territories to prevent future war, is anathema for Gush Emunim. Rabbi Moshe Levinger, for example, tells us that this trinity is "one spiritual entity" and consequently "the aspiration for the completion of the land is also the aspiration for the completion of the people and the aspiration for the completion of the Torah."[18] Full redemption of the people of Israel can only take place in a complete Eretz Yisrael.

The issue of the integrity of Eretz Yisrael had become especially prominent in the Gush Emunim milieu following the ruling of Rabbi Zvi Yehuda Kook that it fell under the injunction of *Yehareg Uval Yaavor* ("be killed rather than sin") and that it involved *Pikuach Nefesh* (mortal danger). Traditionally, the Halakha recognizes three prohibitions for which a Jew must die rather than commit: idolatry, incestuous relations, and the shedding of blood; surrender of Eretz Yisrael territory is not mentioned there. Rabbi Kook's extreme ruling thus prompted a whole interpretive literature to explain and justify it. The major rationale is that, in this age of redemption, giving up Eretz Yisrael territories, is a sin similar to *Avoda Zara* (the worship of other gods).[19] The seriousness with which Gush Emunim took Rabbi Kook's ruling was demonstrated most acutely in the final weeks of the evacuation of Yamit, when Rabbi Moshe Levinger considered an exemplary *Kiddush Hashem* (martyrdom). The issue was addressed by several Gush rabbis in a most scholarly manner,[20] and Levinger's suicide is said to have been prevented only by a special ruling of Israel's two chief rabbis, who were rushed to Yamit.[21]

When Gush ideologues speak about the complete Land of Israel they have in mind not only the post-1967 territory, but the land promised in the Covenant (Genesis 15) as well. This includes the occupied territories—especially Judea and Samaria, the very heart of the historic Israeli nation, and vast territories that belong now to Jordan, Syria, and Iraq.[22]

Nevertheless, it is important to note that there is at present no drive for expansion beyond Western Palestine. The ideologues of Gush Emunim are convinced that, when the time is right, God will see that the nation extends to its promised borders—at which time one is not allowed to let fainthearted-ness dictate the needs of the present or relinquish what has already been achieved. It is a sacred duty to stand firm, to oppose pressures from abroad, to prevent the establishment of any foreign entity within the boundaries of the Land of Israel, and to continue to assist the great process of redemption.

This position was tested during the first month of the 1982 Lebanon War. Several key Gush figures stated publicly that the great achievements of the army were fully consonant with the grand process of Israel's redemption. They pointed out that major areas in southern Lebanon had once belonged to the tribes of Asher and Naftali, and that most of Lebanon was part of the

Promised Land. Despite the protestations of the Begin government that Israel was not interested in territorial expansion, this statement maintained that an annexation of southern Lebanon was legitimate. Responding to a wave of public criticism, Hanan Porat, one of the drafters of the statement, said,

> Even according to the position of the minimalists, southern Lebanon is part of Eretz Yisrael. Not only is it included in the Promise's borders, but also in the territories we are obliged to conquer and settle, the lands of the tribes of Asher and Naftali, which were mostly in present-day southern Lebanon. He who believes in the truth of the Torah and its eternity cannot, at least in principle, discriminate between Judea and Samaria, and southern Lebanon. It makes no difference whether it is convenient for us and close to our conscience. The Providential truth does not change and will never change. And I want to stress that he who does not clearly rely on the foundations of the Godly command regarding the conquest and settlement of Eretz Yisrael is bound, at the end, to disregard not only Israel's north but also to be ready to make concessions even in its very heart.[23]

Porat's excitement over southern Lebanon did not have a large following and most of Gush Emunim's ideologues did not dramatize the issue of the 1985 Israeli withdrawal from Lebanon. Remembering their 1982 experience in northern Sinai and aware of the desire of the general public to leave Lebanon, the Gush remained silent. The failure to stop the retreat in Sinai taught them that fundamentalist politics in Israel can be successful only if backed by a large nonfundamentalist consensus. And in the case of Lebanon they knew they did not have it. The Gush also realized that the opening of a new northern front would greatly weaken the campaign to annex the West Bank. Nevertheless, several Gush activists argued that the Begin government's decision to leave Lebanon was weak, disoriented, and above all, wrong; the problem was not so much the Israeli majority who wanted nothing further to do with Lebanon, but a government that was unable to stick to its principles.[24]

Zionism and Judaism

Gush Emunim has always seen itself as the revitalizer of Zionism. In its 1974 manifesto the Gush said,

> Our aim is to bring about a large movement of reawakening among the Jewish people for the fulfillment of the Zionist vision in its full scope. . . . The sources of the vision are the Jewish tradition and roots, and its ultimate objective is the full redemption of the Jewish people and the entire world.[25]

Gush Emunim obviously feels that historic Zionism died out in the Israel of the 1950s and 1960s, and that Israelis now live in a crisis born of the fatigue that followed the partial implementation of Zionism in the State of

Israel. This crisis has led to the weakening of the pioneering spirit, to an unwillingness to continue the struggle against the pressures of the outside world (especially the Arabs), and to the growth of a materialistic society in which the needs of the individual have superseded the national mission. Gush members want to overcome the present Israeli decadence by restoring the pioneering and sacrificial spirit of the past.

The attempt to reconstruct Zionism is only part of a larger Gush Emunim project: the Judaization of secular Israel. Most Gush leaders are reluctant to admit that secular Zionism has been deficient since its inception and was consequently *bound* to decline. Rav Kook, though impressed by the deeds of secular Zionists, never endorsed secular Zionism. He would have preferred to see a religious movement lead the modern Jewish return to Eretz Yisrael. Since there was no such movement, and since he was moved by the early pioneers, he devised a unique kabbalistic ploy, the *sacrilization of the profane,* that is his religious legitimation of secular and atheist Zionism.[26] Gush Emunim, while formally loyal to Rav Kook's reasoning, does not operate however under his constraints. Its leaders are aware of the great weakness of modern Zionism, as well as of their own power and potential. Thus, aside from a formal approval of secular Zionism for its past achievements, they are critical of most of Israel's present Zionist movements and parties. And Israel's conventional foreign policy, based on considerations of international interests and opinions, often raises their ire.

Gush Emunim's greatest conflict with modern secular Zionism is expressed in its critique of the Zionist theory of normalization. Both Leo Pinsker and Theodore Herzl, the nineteenth-century thinkers who formulated the classical doctrines of political Zionism, argued for "Jewish normalization." They believed that anti-Semitism was a product of the abnormality of Jewish life among the Gentiles and that the existence of a Jewish state, to which all the Jews would immigrate, would eliminate the hatred of the Jews and solve the "Jewish problem." Once Jews had a state of their own, they and the rest of the world would recognize them as normal human beings and their state would function like any other member of the community of nations.[27]

The normalization approach was never popular in Gush Emunim. Rabbi Zvi Yehuda Kook was known for his great hostility to Gentiles, specially Christians. He was responsible for Gush Emunim's suspicion and hostility toward other nations and for its repeated insistence on preserving the "honor" of Israel.[28] Gush Emunim's first manifesto read,

> Any framework or international organization whose resolutions imply the humiliation of the honor of Israel has no right to exist and we consequently do not belong there. We must leave that organization and wait for the day when the honor of Israel would rise again and the truth among the nations will be uncovered.[29]

The normalization theory was utterly rejected after the Yom Kippur War. From a Kookist perspective, the war should not have taken place. The miraculous Six-Day War had, according to these people, shown God's great interest in a quick redemption. If so, the Yom Kippur War implied the opposite. There could be only one explanation for this war: it was the final attempt of the Gentiles to stop the coming redemption of the Jews. It was a struggle against God Himself. Rabbi Yehuda Amital's essay, "The Meaning of the Yom Kippur War," helped shape the thinking of many Gush members in those difficult days:

> The confusion and sense of unease which followed the Yom Kippur War exposed a deep crisis. This is the crisis of the very Zionist idea in the Herzlian thinking . . . Herzl sought to solve the "Jewish Problem" for the Jews and for the nations of the world. . . . When Israel will have his own homeland and state, it will obtain its proper place in the family of nations. No room would remain for anti-Semitism. . . . But now, just as Zionism celebrates its practical victory, its ideological conception is in a total disarray. The Jewish Problem has not been solved and anti-Semitism has not disappeared but has grown worse. . . .
>
> The dreams of normalization have been exposed as hollow. The State of Israel is the only state in the world which faces destruction. . . . The vision of the prophet—"a people that dwells alone and that shall not be reckoned among the nations"—is fulfilled in front of our eyes in the most physical sense. The earthquake people speak about in these days is not a result of the weakening of security or political thinking but a consequence of the failure of the ABC of the Zionist nationalist theory.
>
> But there exists another Zionism, the Zionism of redemption, whose great announcer and interpreter was Rav Kook. . . . This Zionism has not come to solve the Jewish Problem by the establishment of a Jewish state but is used, instead, by the High Providence as a tool in order to move and to advance Israel towards its redemption. Its intrinsic direction is not the normalization of the people of Israel in order to become a nation like all the nations, but to become a holy people, a people of living God, whose basis is in Jerusalem and a king's temple is its center. . . . What is revealed in front of our eyes is the beginning of the fulfillment of the vision of the Prophets regarding the return to Zion. The steps are the Messiah's. And although these are accompanied by pains, the steps are certain and the course clear. . . . It is time Zionism becomes the Zionism of redemption in our consciousness too.[30]

Amital's negation of the very heart of secular Zionsim was one of many indications that the Gush intended to "reawaken" Zionism somewhat more radically than the public had thought. Gush Emunim has been less interested in a new religious-secular synthesis than in a religious transformation of secular Zionism in ways that in fact deny its essence. Gush Emunim is a special kind of religious movement, an orthodox collectivity whose very essence is the paradox, the unresolved tension between the sacred sin and the obsolete religiosity.

Zionist fulfillment stands tainted by the reinvigoration and institutionalization of profanity and sin which go against the living according to the Torah and which are understood as the falsification of the truthful faith. This is a secular victory which is by itself a very frustrating dissonance. At the same time Zionist fulfillment implies a totally contradictory element—the fulfillment of the obligations of the Torah and the actualization of an article of belief, i.e., of a religious peak. In its struggle with this contradiction Kookism reaches an "idealization of secularity," which is understood as a lofty expression of the religion.[31]

The Kookist paradox should not deceive the observer regarding the true nature of Gush Emunim. The repeated references to the movement's strong attachment to secular Zionism are misleading, for they tell only part of the story. The movement should not be seen as a religious offshoot of the secular Zionist movement, but as a very successful religious raid into the heart of secular Israel. Many Gush members, have moved toward Jewish ultraorthodoxy, which supports this assessment. Facing a growing number of blocks on the road to redemption, frustrated Gush members do not join kibbutzim or go to development towns to strengthen the foundations of traditional Zionism, but turn instead to ultraorthodoxy and the Torah, convinced that the Torah, not the Israeli army, will save the nation from its troubles.[32]

The State and the Rule of Law

Kookist theology is distinguished by its great respect for the State of Israel and its institutions, the government, the Knesset, and the army. Gush Emunim's legendary document, the prophetic sermon that Rabbi Zvi Yehuda delivered at Merkaz Harav on Israel's nineteenth birthday, just before the Six-Day War, emphasizes that the State of Israel is holy:

> And against what was said, "Is this the state envisioned by our Prophets?" I say: This is the state the prophets envisioned. Of course, this is not the state in its completion, but our prophets and their successors said that the state is going to be like that: the seed of Abraham, Isaac, and Jacob will settle and establish there a reality of settlement and an independent political government. . . . It has now been nineteen years of development. . . . We are honored to witness the wonders of G–d and His secrets—in construction, agriculture, policy, security in matter and spirit. . . . The real Yisrael is the redeemed Yisrael, the kingdom of Israel and the army of Israel.[33]

According to the rabbi, Israel and its institutions are legitimate not only because they rely on the support of the people of Israel and are duly constituted, but mainly because they represent the will of God. Israel won its independence not because the Zionists mustered the military and political power to beat the Arabs and win international legitimacy but because God wanted it that way. Being constituted by God, the state deserves the Halakhic status of a "Kingdom," and consequently ought to receive the allegiance of all its citizens and the respect of all the present religious authorities.

This definition of the State of Israel is the great theological divide between Gush Emunim and Israel's religious ultraorthodox. The Gush does not approve of either the extremists of Neturei Karta and the Satmar Hasidics, who consider the State of Israel an apostasy and a direct rebellion against God, or the ultraorthodox Agudat Israel, which participates in the conduct of Israel's public affairs but denies Halakhic status to the institutions of "the Zionists." Gush Emunim's principled commitment to the sanctity of the state of Israel was restated strongly by Rabbi Moshe Levinger when the Jerusalem District Court imposed severe punishments upon the members of the Jewish Underground:

> Following the conclusion and the verdict of the underground trial, it is our duty to remember that the State of Israel and all its institutions, just like her sky, land, and fruits, are all holy. . . . The establishment of the State of Israel means a state and all that comes with a state and is related to a state's existence, schools and synagogues and the institutions responsible for the public life of the state, the government, the Knesset, the courts, the police, the security services and even the prisons are all part of the Israeli statism which is being renewed with the help of God. Thus, when we are about to react—and there is room for reaction—to the conclusions and the verdicts, we have to do it from a position of respect for the people, the land, the state and its institutions, especially those that leave us bitter. This is because a deep and truthful commitment to values shows in time of crisis, when it appears that reality looks hard and cruel.[34]

This glorification of the State of Israel explains why, despite the Gush's many confrontations with the government, the police, and the army, there have been relatively few severe incidents and why the movement has rarely been considered in Israel as a seditious or rebellious organization. However, it does not explain the huge number of Gush Emunim's illicit and extralegal operations. What, in practice, does this glorification of the state mean? How does the movement perceive legitimate as opposed to illegitimate political participation?

It is one thing to avow a deep respect for political institutions and quite another to translate this attitude into compliance with the law. In the case of Gush Emunim the gap seems rather broad. There are two keys to the understanding of the intense extralegal behavior of Gush Emunim: one is the difference between the sacredness of the *State* of Israel and of the *Land* of Israel, and the other is Gush Emunim's legal philosophy.

What we might call "the Gush Emunim doctrine of sacredness "suggests that the State of Israel is not as holy as the territory of Israel. The state is never mentioned as part of the "holy trinity"—the Land, the People, the Torah of Israel. Furthermore, unlike the holiness of the trio which is absolute and eternal, the sanctity of the state is relative and conditional. "The land and the state," writes Rabbi Jacob Ariel in *Nekuda,* are two values whose location in the right place in our scale of values is of great importance and of many practical consequences. Which of them comes first, which is preferable to the other, which is the means and which is the end? . . . The land is not a means for the state but the state is a means for the land. The land is the goal and the state is nothing but the means to achieve this goal. . . . Eretz Yisrael is an absolute entity whose essence does not depend on any political factor [and] the virtue of the state of Israel in Eretz Yisrael is its ability to fulfill the obligation of settling Eretz Yisrael with no constraints or limitation. An Israeli state which limits or inhibits the settlement of Israel by its people loses both its virtue and importance, and in the final analysis its moral and legal authority altogether. In the public struggle being waged on this scale of values, which determines the relationship between the land and the state, the very existence of the state, its uniqueness, Jewishness, and destiny are at stake. Those who place the state in its right position in this struggle—as a tool to secure the sovereignty of the people of Israel over its land—are the ones who secure the continuation of its development, growth, expansion, strength and invigoration.[35]

Ariel's argument provides the rationale for Gush Emunim's great confrontation with the Labor government in the mid-1970s over the issue of settling Samaria. Its extension to include the absolute prohibition of surrendering Eretz Yisrael territories justified the 1982 extralegal operations in Sinai. The argument and the operations were backed by Rabbi Zvi Yehuda Kook's rulings that any prohibition of settlement in Eretz Yisrael by the government Israel was null and void, and that the preservation of the integrity of the Holy Land was a sacred obligation, a case of *Yehareg Uval Yaavor* (be killed rather than sin).

But there was another element—*Gush Emunim's disrespect for the rule of civil law.* Gush Emunim, like several other political groups in Israel, has never respected the rule of law as a principle of good government. Most of its leaders have always been hostile to formality and order, and see no virtue in proper procedures or obedience to the law. Pioneering, self-sacrifice, taking risks, and breaking new ground are the qualities they admire in the early Zionist who settled the land without asking permission. Rabbi Yoel Ben-Nun, the most moderate and civil of all Gush Emunim ideologues, once responded to a query about the Gush's respect for the law.

> It is shocking that Yigal (Allon) speaks about the law. When he makes a decision no law bothers him. When he decided that Hebron [the first Jewish settlement in the Park Hotel] had to exist and it needed arms, he saw to it that arms were moved, under the table, from Kfar Etzion to Hebron. Stealing chickens from the henhouse is a norm the Palmach introduced.[36]

Here Ben-Nun linked the illegalism of the Palmach—the paramilitary units of the Labor movement during the British Mandate—with the extralegalism of Gush Emunim. He intended no irony; he was expressing strong conviction that Gush Emunim on the hills of Samaria in the 1970s was just like the young *kibbutzniks* on the hills of the Galilee in the 1920s;

any government of Israel that barred Jewish settlement in Eretz Yisrael was to be equated with the British Mandate government that issued, in 1939, the White Paper barring Jewish settlement and immigration. It was also to be put in the same category of the Zionist authorities in Palestine in the 1920s–1930s, who were reluctant to permit daring settlement operations in remote areas for fear it would hurt the reputation of the movement and create indefensible settlements.[37]

Settlement of Eretz Yisrael territories is, according to Gush Emunim, the most distinguished Zionist and Jewish virtue. Neither law nor any principle of good government can match it.

Gush Emunim's consensus regarding the permissible and the illegitimate was broken following the 1984 discovery of the Jewish Underground. Suddenly it was learned that the extralegalism of several distinguished members of the movement extended to premeditated killing of Arabs. The first reaction seemed to be general shock and disbelief throughout the settler community, but when the dust cleared, there were clearly two ideological camps within Gush Emunim—those "who understood" the underground and those "who refused to understand" it.

The Halakhic issue at stake was whether the underground constituted *Merida Bamalchut* (a revolt against the kingdom). Rabbi Yoel Ben-Nun, who led the attack on the underground, was very resolute:

> The state is the foundation and the government is the authority for conducting war against Israel's enemies. There are no private wars, and no rules of war are applicable for a private individual, neither from a general moral perspective nor from a moral-Halakhic point of view. . . . Every revolt against the kingdom is also a revolt against God.[38]

While Ben-Nun and his camp were extremely candid about their opposition to the operations of the underground, many of the supportive authorities, and those who "understood" its activities, remained silent. The real controversy within Gush Emunim was conducted in bitter closed sessions, and was revealed only in 1986.

The ones who spoke in support of the Underground were rather cautious. Rabbi Israel Ariel, who was to become the spokesperson of the most radical wing of the movement, responded in the same issue of *Nekuda* to Yoel Ben-Nun's charges. He argued that since the government of Israel was never elected directly by the people, as required by the Halakha, but rather indirectly, it did not fulfill the conditions of Jewish law for a fully legitimate kingdom. He further reminded his audience that Rabbi Zvi Yehuda Kook had made a distinction between state and government:

> Rabbi Zvi Yehuda . . . did not define the prime minister as a king, not even as a judge, but as "judgelike." When Prime Minister Rabin made his reprehensible statement that he did not care if we reached Hebron with a Jordanian visa, he criticized him severely and said: "He who does not care about Eretz

Yisrael, Eretz Yisrael does not care about him." Would anybody call Rabbi Zvi Yehuda an opponent of the government's authority? . . . What else do we need than Rabbi Zvi Yehuda's announcement that in the case of Judea and Samaria no concession will be made and that "it will not pass without a war"? This was said in front of the students of the yeshiva and was published in the press. Would anybody dare call Rabbi Zvi Yehuda "a rebel against the kingdom"?[39]

While Gush Emunim's theoretical commitment to the sacredness of the state of Israel has not changed today, its practical commitment has been eroded. The Gush settlers, bitter about the government's inability to defend them against Arab violence on the roads of Judea and Samaria, find it hard to respect the government. Rabbi Zvi Yehuda Kook is gone, and the "post-Kookist" Gush is in no position to keep the old orientation alive. Though there are several successors to Kook's "moderate" legacy, they do not carry his authority. The dominant line in Gush Emunim now seems not to glorify the sacred state, but rather to challenge the government in the name of Eretz Yisrael and its future.

The Palestinian Question, the Arab-Israeli Conflict, and the Fate of the Israeli Arabs

Gush Emunim's position on "the Palestinian Question" is sharp and unequivocal: the problem does not exist and is no more than a vicious ploy by the Arabs, who want to destroy the State of Israel, furthered by leftist Jews who refuse to see the Arabs' true intentions. Eretz Yisrael in its entirety belongs to the Jews by divine command. The Arabs, whoever they are, have no collective right over the land, and the issue, if there is one, is of individuals who must find a way to live under Jewish rule. The universal principle of self-determination—even if it might have some relevance in other places—does not hold in Eretz Yisrael.

The key question, then, is not, What should be done about the Palestinian nation? but rather, What should be the status of Arabs living in Eretz Yisrael in the age of redemption? Gush Emunim's only official answer to the question was formulated in its 1974 manifesto:

> The Arabs of Eretz Yisrael and other alien minorities living there ought to be given the complete private and legal rights every person deserves. These include the right to emigrate, to own property, to free trial and all the other individual civil liberties. These rights cannot be abrogated, except for direct security reasons. The possibility of granting Israeli citizenship to every alien resident who will be ready to assume all the obligations involved (including service in the IDF or a substitute) should be examined. Nevertheless, it is recommended that the emigration of those who are not ready to receive Israeli citizenship for nationalist reasons will be encouraged by propaganda and economic aid.[40]

This vague statement, which was based on the Torah concept of *Ger Toshav* (alien resident), was sufficiently broad and undemanding to encompass various positions on this sensitive issue in the early days of Gush Emunim. When outsiders insisted upon a clearer statement, Gush spokespersons responded with the famous "three alternatives"—choices that should be presented to Israeli Arabs: (a) to acknowledge the legitimacy of the Zionist doctrine (Gush Emunim's version) and thereupon to receive full civil rights, including the right to vote and be elected to the Knesset (and to serve in the army), (b) to honestly obey the laws of the state without formal recognition of Zionism and in return receive the rights of resident aliens (but no political rights), or (c) to emigrate to Arab countries with economic assistance provided by Israel.

As long as contacts between the Gush settlers and the Palestinian Arabs were limited before the 1978 penetration of Samaria and the beginning of the massive settlement of the West Bank, these general statements satisfied the members of the movement; Gush Emunim sincerely hoped that most of the Palestinians would learn to live with the Jews and opt for the *second* alternative. But this hope was not fulfilled, and the growing Jewish-Arab violence has made it increasingly necessary to translate the abstract Halakhic position on the issue to concrete suggestions and policies.

The moral and political sensitivity of the issue has made unanimity impossible; different parties *within* Gush Emunim adhere to three different proposals for the status of non-Jews in Israel: limited rights, no rights, and total war and extermination. While the positions are usually stated as reaction to actual events, each is anchored in an authoritative interpretation of Scripture.

The first, most liberal, position, sticks to the Gush's original "three alternatives." Limiting Arab rights stems from the conviction that the notion of universal human rights is a foreign ideal that, like other European non-Jewish values, has no meaning in the context of the Holy Land. In the Bible, non-Jewish inhabitants of Palestine were accorded the status of resident aliens, enjoying some privileges but never obtaining rights equal to those of the Jews:

> We are obliged to grant the *Ger Toshav* (alien resident) civic rights, and also a decent social respect and an option to buy houses and land in the country. This implies, of course, that he accepts the authority of the state of Israel and agrees to be a loyal and devoted citizen, which includes the seven commandments of Noah's sons—which are the fundamental laws of human morality. . . . It is however clear that we cannot allow the transfer of Eretz Yisrael lands to the Gentiles of other states, who certainly do not qualify as *Gerim Toshavim*.[41]

Note that even the liberal spokespersons of Gush Emunim no longer talk about granting full *political* rights to loyal Arabs, preferring to leave the issue undefined. But at least they recognize that not all Arabs are dangerous and that many deserve to be treated humanely. Most of the leaders of Gush Emunim and most members share this view. But even among them there are shades and variations—some would use very tough measures against seditious and violent Palestinians, while others call for moderation and restraint.

The second position on status of non-Jews amounts to a denial of all rights, since Arabs are hostile to the Jewish rebirth in Eretz Yisrael and always had been. Proponents of this position do not oppose the doctrine of *Ger Toshav,* but they argue that consistent Arab hostility makes it illusory and irrelevant. Their conclusion is very close to the notorious Kahane position of expulsion.

> The Arab hostility towards the Zionist venture has been proven beyond doubt in many decades of bloodshed, and there is no sign of any change in this hostility or for a reduction in its intensity. . . . The idea that maintains that it is possible to settle within areas of dense Arab population, to expropriate its land, to hurt its national feelings and also to obtain its sympathy by quoting old Arab tales, cannot but make one laugh. Once and for all we have got to clarify to ourselves and to explain to the nation that in Eretz Yisrael either the Arabs or the Jews can live, and not the two of them together.[42]

A poll of West Bank rabbis found 64 percent of them favoring this solution.[43]

The most extreme solution, extermination, was expressed in an essay by Rabbi Israel Hess published in the official magazine of Bar-Ilan university students under the title "Genocide: A Commandment of the Torah." Hess likened the Arabs to the biblical Amalekites, who were deservedly annihilated. The Amalekites, according to Hess, were both socially and militarily treacherous and cruel. Their relation to the Jews was like the relation of darkness to light—one of total contradiction. The Arabs, who live today in the land of Israel and who are constantly waging a treacherous terrorist war against the Jews, are direct descendants of the Amalekites, and the correct solution to the problem is extermination.[44]

Hess's position, relatively isolated, has not been repeated by any Gush Emunim authority. But the Amalekite analogy exists in the minds of a Gush Emunim minority and sometimes appears in conversations and on the pages of *Nekuda.* A Kedumim settler, David Rosentzweig, in a small research project found that in the last fifty years several distinguished authorities had used the analogy when speaking of the unending Arab hostility toward the Jews.[45] And Haim Tzuria, a Shavei Shomron settler, wrote in his article "The Right to Hate," that "a hatred of any enemy is not a sick feeling but a natural and healthy one." He continued,

> In each generation we have those who rise up to wipe us out, therefore each generation has its own Amalek. The Amalekism of our generation expresses itself in the extremely deep hatred of the Arabs to our national renaissance in the land of our forefathers.[46]

Gush Emunim is aware of the political sensitivity of its views; its spokes-persons consistently refuse to discuss the future of the Arabs in Judea and Samaria after the "expected" annexation of the West Bank. They say that their mission is to solve not the Arab question but the Jewish problem on the general principles found in the Torah and Halakha; in due time Almighty God will take care of the details in his mysterious way.[47]

The Invisible Realm of Gush Emunim

Though Gush Emunim originated as an extraparliamentary organization often acting extralegally, its leaders always wished for formal recognition by the Israeli authorities. The reasons were both ideological and pragmatic.

On the ideological level, most of the founders were sincerely devoid of political ambitions; they were less interested in the organization than in its calling. They believed that the settlement of Judea and Samaria was the obligation of the government and not of volunteers. In the early years the Gush considered itself as only a temporary structure that would fade away the moment the Israeli government stepped in and legalized the settlement of Judea and Samaria.

On the practical plane, the heads of the Gush wanted legalization, for they knew that they could not change the demographic balance in the West Bank without official backing. They were fully aware that their early squat-ting drives were only beginnings, a symbolic proof that a Jewish settlement in every part of Eretz Israel was possible and legitimate.

Most of these early aspirations have by now been completely fulfilled, perhaps beyond the wildest dreams of the Gush leaders. There have been difficulties and crises of ideology and leadership, but from a political, organi-zational, and economic perspective the Gush has been extremely successful. It is, therefore, not erroneous to speak of the Gush Emunim *invisible realm,* a highly sophisticated political, economic, and cultural network, which dominates the life of nearly 100,000 settlers in Judea, Samaria, and Gaza, controls the yearly distribution of hundreds of millions of dollars, and signifi-cantly influences Israel's decisions. This Gush Emunim conglomerate is "in-visible," since only a few of its institutions are obviously part of Gush Emunim.[48] The activists of the movement have been able to impart their political thinking to many non-Gush people and institutions, and to control several small but highly important communal positions, thereby assuring that they make the critical decisions.

One reason for Gush Emunim's success is that its activists have moved adroitly from spontaneity to organization without losing their flexibility. In terms of organization, the movement has gone through three stages: *sponta-neous single actions, institutionalized licit and illicit drives,* and finally *full official and state-supported operations.* Each new stage has involved more people, bigger resources, greater proximity to the centers of power, and fuller political legitimacy. Though the political and ideological development of Gush Emunim has been marked by crises and setbacks, its economic and administrative organization has been built up slowly and methodically.

The formative years of Gush Emunim, from 1967 to 1974, were the most important. These were the years when each squatting effort erupted with no grand strategy or highly organized backing. The return to Gush Etzion, the occupation of Park Hotel in Hebron, the early operations of Gariin Elon Moreh, and the illicit settlement of Keshet in the Golan Heights all took place with no established procedures. Highly devoted individuals and groups felt that they had to act, with or without official support, and they did so.

But as isolated and unorganized, as the pioneering Emunist squatters were, they did have three institutionalized sources of support: Yeshivat Merkaz Harav, the Bnei Akiva youth movement, and the Land of Israel Movement. None was fully geared to the specific needs of the settlement Gariinim, but they all rendered moral and material assistance.

Merkaz Harav was probably the single most important support, a solid source of manpower and moral backing. According to many sources, Rabbi Zvi Yehuda Kook turned the yeshiva into a settlement command post. The yeshiva students who lived under his spell were unequivocally encouraged to join the new settlements.[49]

Similarly, the Bnei Akiva movement and several of its yeshivot backed the new pioneers. The number who actually moved to the West Bank in the pre-Gush era was very small, but a movement of many thousands stood behind them. Settlement leaders like Hanan Porat and Rabbi Moshe Levinger, who were also persuasive speakers, became the idols of a whole Bnei Akiva generation. They and several other speakers traveled throughout the country, and their message electrified the youth. Most of the Bnei Akiva organization was supportive too,—teachers, heads of yeshivot and branches, and the Bnei Akiva representatives in such influential institutions as the Jewish Agency and the World Zionist Organization.[50]

Although the unorganized new settlers proved themselves skilled politicians, their lack of political organization led them to depend on the elderly activists of the Land of Israel Movement. The settlers were the darlings of the LIM journalists, writers, and politicians. The notables visited the small settlements, wrote about them, spread their message, and legitimized their actions among the secular public. First and foremost among the LIM admirers was Eliezer Livneh, who constantly communicated with their young rabbis and praised their activities in private and public.[51] Former generals, diplomats, bureaucrats, and professors showed their support. Long before the formal establishment of Gush Emunim, its future activists were already entrenched in Israel's public life.

The second stage began in 1974 with the formal establishment of Gush Emunim. Its first manifesto suggested a platform for the political, ideological, and spiritual takeover of the nation, but the operational meaning of the act was much smaller: the routinization of the practice of the first Gariinim and its formalization. No longer was the creation of a settlement Gariinim to be left to the daring imagination of individuals; an established organization was to plan the activities, logistics, and propaganda. Gush Emunim formalized a *Mazkirut* (executive secretariat), *Mate Mivtzai* (an operational command), and *Moetza* (public council).

The Mazkirut was an ordinary executive committee whose job was to oversee policy matters and coordinate daily activities, but the Mate Mivtzai was a unique Gush Emunim structure. Its task was to prepare and carry out Gush Emunim illicit operations, which mostly involved unlicensed squatting. Since these operations meant outmaneuvering the army, the police, and the other West Bank authorities, the Mate recruited men of great skill and ingenuity—reserve officers, practiced hikers familiar with West Bank topography, veteran illegal settlers from the Mandate period, and logistic organizers.[52] Since Gush Emunim has never had a written constitution, the structure and names of these organizations occasionally changed. An extended Mazkirut was later added and professional departments were established for settlement, *Hasbarah* (public relations and education), organization, and finance. A small *Aliya* department was also added later.

The institutionalization of Gush Emunim in the mid-1970s was not a refutation of its earlier spontaneous character. On the contrary, the same Merkaz Harav core group continued to inspire the Gush and control it with no bureaucratic constraints. Neither rules of formal membership nor a constitution was adopted. No general vote was ever taken and no procedures for legitimate or illegitimate Gush Emunim operations were ever written down. The heads of the movement did whatever they thought fit and moved swiftly from one sphere of action to another.[53]

Instead of dealing with hampering procedures, the Gush devoted all its time to operative matters. Thus while constantly launching settlement drives, and jousting and bargaining with the authorities, the movement was also able to invest great energy in building the Gush infrastructure. Gush branches were opened all over the country to broadcast the message of the movement as widely as possible and recruit supporters and future settlers. In hundreds of *Hugei Bait* (small sessions in private homes), Gush people preached the new gospel. Local volunteers not only announced their commitment to settle in the West Bank, but also actively recruited future colleagues. Gush activists penetrated organized groups like synagogue communities, religious PTAs, and Bnei Akiva alumni circles, greatly facilitating their organizational tasks.[54]

This massive operation, which was not widely reported in the press, involved very little expense. A Gush Emunim branch was usually a small apartment with a telephone. A skeleton Gariin was a devoted individual or a small group of friends who would spend all their free time talking to people and future followers. Favorable Bnei Akiva chapters and friendly Yeshivot

Hesder with larger assets and resources were especially good locations for strong Gush branches and Gariinim.[55]

In this second stage, the Gush established a settlement department. While struggling to maintain their few existing strongholds, mostly in military camps in the West Bank, the leaders of Gush Emunim also started to work on an ambitious plan to settle all of Judea and Samaria. Experts in geography, demography, agriculture, and settlement were asked to help develop an operational program; the result was the 1976 Yesh Plan. Though the Yesh Plan was supplanted two years later by Gush Emunim's Master Plan for Settlement in Judea and Samaria, it had established the new Gush Emunim settlement concept. There were to be three types of settlements: villages of a few hundred people, towns of several thousands, and cities with tens of thousands of residents. The main objectives were strategic—to introduce hundreds of thousands of Jews to the area, to occupy all the strategic strongholds in the mountains, and to secure complete control of the main roads. The resettlement of ancient biblical locations was given a lower priority, though was nevertheless considered important.[56]

The third organizational stage of Gush Emunim began in 1977, when the Likud, under Menachem Begin, won the elections. Though Gush Emunim was a small voluntary movement, it had two important psychological assets: nearly ten years of settlement experience and a healthy skepticism about the ability of the government, any government, to provide for the settlement of Eretz Yisrael. Further, Gush Emunim had the will and the means to push through their demands and were sure that God was behind them. Therefore, though a more sympathetic government had come to power, the Gush did not dismantle its settlement department and leave the job of settling the West Bank to the friendly Ministry of Agriculture. Its leaders established, instead, Amana (Covenant) as their official settlement movement and initiated, two years later, a non-Emunim umbrella organization, *Moetzet Yesha* (The Council of the Settlements of Judea, Samaria, and Gaza). These two institutions, accorded full recognition by the new government, became the foundation of Gush Emunim's political and economic power.

The Evolution of Amana

In 1977, though the movement had big plans, it had only three settlements of its own, Ofra, Kedumim, and Mishor Edomim. There was just one certain way of changing this situation—to establish a recognized "settlement movement" with the full backing of Israel's Ministry of Agriculture and the Department of Rural Settlement of the World Zionist Organization(WZO).[57] Likud's official recognition of Amana was not a mere legal act that could be obtained by any individual land developer: recognition meant that Amana's activities were considered essential for the nation, part of state-supported Zionism. In the past, such recognition had been accorded only to pioneering settlement organizations, the kibbutzim and moshavim movements. Therefore it was extremely important for the extralegal zealots of Gush Emunim to become legitimized as partners in this exclusive club.

There was another incentive. Being officially recognized entitled Amana to large state and WZO budgets, as well as to many other benefits such as secure positions for its members in Israel's settlement bureaucracy and a say in decisions of many official circles. It also meant the right to the paid professional assistance of Israel's top settlement experts.

Amana took advantage of all the benefits official recognition implied. It was run by a Hanhala (Directorate) of thirteen people and a large representative council made up of members from all the movement's settlements. The heads of Amana, veterans like Hanan Porat, Uri Elitzur, Uri Ariel, and Moni Ben-Ari realized that the Gush's informal methods were not suitable for a big settlement organization with money and land. They wrote a short constitution for Amana, which, for the first time in the history of Gush Emunim, introduced democratic procedures. According to the constitution every settlement is entitled to two delegates at the Amana council, and the council was made the final authority on all matters within the movement's jurisdiction. The Hanhala and the organization's influential secretary-general are elected by the council.[58]

The establishment of Amana expanded development opportunities for Gush Emunim but led, paradoxically, to the decline of the movement's guiding secretariat. Eager to shed their image of illegal adventurism, the leaders of the Gush sought the status of a fully legitimate Israeli settlers' movement. Once they decided in 1979 not to establish a political party of their own, they saw no need to continue Gush Emunim formally; now Rabbi Levinger could spend more time in Kiryat Arba, Benny Katzover in Elon Moreh, and Hanan Porat in the Knesset.

Amana took over the Gush offices in Jerusalem and guided a massive Gush Emunim settlement drive. In 1978 it submitted an ambitious plan to the government calling for the settlement of 100,000 Jews in the West Bank within ten years. This program underlay the Drobles-Sharon settlement plan that became the official policy of the World Zionist Organization and Israel's Ministry of Agriculture.[59]

With the government settling urban areas close to the Green Line (the pre-1967 border), Amana could concentrate on establishing new ideological settlements in unattractive but strategic spots in Judea and Samaria, usually in areas with heavy Arab populations or far from urban centers. Constantly keeping the settlement of Judea and Samaria on the national agenda, Amana worked diligently to create new Gariinim, attract industries to the new settlements, and train new settlers for jobs that could support them in their new locations. Amana also developed an absorption and immigration section to attract new immigrants to Emunim's future settlements. It has been so successful that potential settler groups not necessarily identified with the ideology of Gush Emunim have occasionally asked to join it.

Amana's major innovation was the *Yishuv Kehilati* (a communal settlement), a concept developed in the 1976 Yesh Plan. Previously, most settlements supported by the government or WZO were based on an egalitarian socialist ideology—either collective (kibbutz) or cooperative (moshav) agrarian-industrial endeavors. But Gush Emunim was never socialist, and most of its members had a middle-class mentality. The conception of redemption that drove them to the West Bank had a nationalist, not socialist, content. The Likud was also far from socialism: kibbutzim and moshavim were identified with its political archrival, the Labor movement.[60]

Furthermore, water and arable land were too scarce on the West Bank for many kibbutzim and moshavim. The *Yishuv Kehilati* overcame these limitations. While insisting on the communal character and shared responsibility of the settlement, it gave its members great economic freedom. Amana settlers own their property individually and are free to leave or sell it.[61] While the old Labor socialist settlements had been encouraged to become self-reliant and self-sufficient, many members of Amana settlements, up to 80 percent, commute to work across the Green Line every day. The only time Amana exercises formal control over individual settlers is in the selection process. Only individuals who identify with the movement's goals, pass sophisticated tests of suitability for communal living, and endure long interviews with psychologists and social workers are admitted.[62]

The Local and Regional Councils

While Amana transformed Gush Emunim, it was the Israeli government that laid the foundations for the movement's invisible realm. On March 20, 1979, six days before the signing of the peace treaty with Egypt, the military government in the West Bank signed Order 783 establishing three regional councils in the area. Two more councils were added later; all five are governed by the regulations governing Israeli regional councils. In March 1981, Order 982 set up five municipal councils in the West Bank. That order largely duplicated the Israeli Municipal Ordinance, so West Bank municipalities, like their Israeli counterparts, can levy taxes, supply municipal services, nominate officers, and employ workers; the West Bank councils also enjoy planning and building-licensing powers.[63] The Israeli settlement areas were declared "planning regions" and the councils were designated "special planning commissions."

These acts of the Begin government were intended to strengthen Jewish control of the area and ensure the permanence of the settlements. But they accomplished an additional and unintended task: for all practical purposes they gave Gush Emunim control of the entire Jewish endeavor in the West Bank. Even though the Gush has never supplied more than 20 percent of the

West Bank settlers, its leaders, by virtue of their experience, public image, and competence, were appointed to key executive positions in most of the new municipalities and regions. Former illegal settlers and candidates for arrest were now state officials with large budgets, powers, and responsibilities. Amana's small staff and budget were supplemented by hundreds of paid official jobs in its control.

By April 1988, there were forty-eight community settlements incorporated in Amana. Its Emunist settlers numbered about 12,000 to 15,000 (about 2500 families). The WZO investments in these communal settlements alone came to $80,000 per family. There were other supporters of Gush Emunim in towns such as Kiryat Arba, Ariel, Efrat, Ma'ale Ephraim, and Ma'ale Adomim. Gush members head five out of the seven regional councils and exert considerable influence in the towns. Great sums of government money have enabled these municipalities and councils to employ large staffs and provide services of every description.

Meron Benvenisti estimates that in 1983 per capita grants to regional councils were $230 in Gush Etzion, $245 in Mate Benyamin, and $357 in Samaria—two or three times as much as grants to regional councils in Israel proper—Mate Yehuda (the region west of Jerusalem adjacent to Mate Benyamin) $86; Sha'ar Hanegev, $126; and Upper Galilee, $97. Grants-in-aid provided more than half the total income of the Jewish local authorities in the West Bank—Elkana and Ariel 52.8 percent; Ma'ale Adomim, 60.8 percent; and Kiryat Arba, 68.8 percent. By contrast, local councils in depressed areas within the Green Line received grants in the following proportions: Rosh Ha'ayin, 44 percent; Or Yehuda, 36.8 percent; Or Akiva, 28.9 percent.[64] These huge sums of state money amount to preferential treatment for the settlers in the West Bank by the Likud coalition and give Gush Emunim leaders a formidable financial and political base.

Building Political and Economic Power

The solidification of the invisible realm of Gush Emunim was completed in 1980 with the creation of the Yesha Council, the representative organization of the Jewish settlements in Judea, Samaria, and Gaza. From its inception the Yesha Council was designated to become the political arm of the Jewish settlers in those areas.[65] It was conceived by Israel Harel, a journalist, who realized in 1979 that the legitimized Jewish settlements created a new and expanded power base for Gush Emunim.

Gush leaders had been underscoring their demand for more land with a long hunger strike, and Harel realized that he was observing a new Israeli geopolitical entity that was different from the rest of the country, with existential interests of its own. Only 20 percent of the settlers were Gush members, so its critics argued that the Gush could not speak in the name of the entire body. Nonetheless, the movement's leaders were convinced that despite their minority status they could maintain political hegemony in the area.

Unlike Amana and the regional and local councils, the Yesha council never had sought official state status. It was a voluntary legal association intended to represent the entire Jewish population of the West Bank and Gaza in Israel's public and political life.[66] Each settlement, whatever its political affiliation or size, elects two representatives to a general council whose job is to formulate the political position of the settlers on relevant national issues. The real power in the council is entrusted to the *Hanhalah*, a directorate made up of the heads of the regional councils of Judea, Samaria and Gaza and several officeholders who sit *ex officio*. Special committees meet regularly to submit recommendations to the general council, on legal and political matters, as well as for security, economic, education, and information issues.

While the Yesha Council has limited its activities to politics, its heads and those of Amana and the most influential regional councils have aided their movement through their power of the official purse. In the last nine years they have set up a myriad of profitable "development corporations" that have helped build the area. While bidding for contracts issued by the councils, the members of the boards of the corporations have been either the heads of the same councils or their neighbors and associates from Amana. Using machinery supplied by public funds, such as buses or heavy mechanical equipment, they have been able to compete rather favorably against private corporations.

Seeing the success of the development companies, Amana cooperated with two regional councils to create a large West Bank corporation that would attract major outside partners. The new venture, SBA, established its own insurance company and took up major projects such as building a science park in Ariel. It also moved into the home-construction market in both the West Bank and Gaza. It plans to establish several subsidiary firms specializing in a variety of industries and investments.[67] The overseers of the new company, major Gush figures, aim for economic independence from the government, so that in case of conflict they could proceed on their own. In a *Nekuda* interview, Dr. Yosef Dreizin, the executive director of SBA, discussed his desire to follow the historic model of the Zionist Labor movement. Starting in the 1920s, it developed an independent Jewish economy in Palestine, which facilitated the struggle against the British and the Arabs, and later became the solid foundation of the Israeli economy.

> We have in front of us the Histadrut's industries without their faults. We told ourselves: let us erect economic institutions in construction, industry and other fields that could become in the proper time an autonomous system. This will assure the continuous development of the area with no relation, or direct relation, to the political system which may become hostile.[68]

Gush Emunim figures continue to dominate the key institutions in the West Bank and Gaza, despite the growing number of the non-Emunist settlers, for the simple reason that the entire settler community benefits from the arrangement. No other group in Israel has recently received so many benefits and allocations. The West Bank leaders have obtained for their constituency the privileged status of all three of the most preferred groups in Israel—*development towns, pioneering settlements,* and *confrontation settlements.* Instead of asking the authorities to create a special category, these leaders have insisted on their inclusion in *all* the existing categories.

This combined status, confirmed by both government and Knesset, makes the settlers eligible for huge subsidies and concessions. It has also made them almost completely immune to financial cutbacks, even in times of severe austerity. Benvenisti has rightly observed, "It is politically impossible to revoke their status, only to change the entire system of Israeli subsidies. The powerful pressure groups which rely on continued preferential treatment would not allow that, even if they are opposed to settlement in the West Bank."[69] Thus, though the majority of the settlers are not religious and probably do not share the messianic beliefs of Gush Emunim, they need the movement's extensive political skills as much as it needs their support. This interdependence is not likely to disappear soon. The main reason that Israelis continue to move to the West Bank, even during the *intifada,* is the unmatched incentives offered to the settlers. Since only the Gush activists can make sure that this situation continues, the movement's decreasing proportion among the population is unlikely to effect its informal political power.

The Cultural Infrastructure of Gush Emunim

A relatively unrecognized, but essential, part of the Gush Emunim invisible realm is its substantial cultural and educational infrastructure, whose development has started long before the legalization of most West Bank operations and the official recognition of Amana.

Yeshivat Merkaz Harav in Jerusalem has always played a crucial role, especially after 1967, when it became the center of a new dynamic movement. Rabbi Zvi Yehuda Kook, its head, achieved national prominence, and its graduates became the most prestigious group in religious Zionism. Almost every talented Bnei Akiva graduate wanted to study in Merkaz, or at least to be taught by its graduates. And because Merkaz Harav aimed to convert the entire nation to the new "Eretz Yisrael Judaism," it has become preeminently a missionary order. Graduates like Haim Drukman and Tzfania Drori had established Merkaz-oriented yeshivot outside of Jerusalem; others have simply taken over existing institutions throughout the country. The first order of business of most Gush Emunim settlements has been to establish a yeshiva. Hard-core Gush Emunim seminaries such as the

Kiryat Arba Yeshiva of Rabbis Eliezer Waldman and Dov Lior have become emulated models.

The nucleus in Jerusalem was expanded immensely. The Yeshiva Gdola, the traditional four-year post-secondary institution, has been joined by a Yeshiva Letzeirim (a Merkaz prep school), a *Kolel* (an advanced seminary for married male students), two research centers, and numerous institutions for young children of the students and staff. A special youth movement called *Ariel*, more pious and devoted to the Land and the Torah than the old Bnei Akiva, was started. A whole Merkaz enclave was created in the Jerusalem neighborhood of Kiryat Moshe, a milieu of total commitment in which hundreds of teachers and students live with thousands of their family members. Merkaz graduates who leave Jerusalem are encouraged to consider the yeshiva their second home and to constantly return for lessons and consultation.[70] Money is apparently no problem, for the school's growing prestige has attracted big donors. And Merkaz enjoys the strong backing of the National Religious Party and financial aid from Israel's Ministry of Religion—a fiefdom of the party.

Two other important Kookist-Emunist institutions have become powerful instruments of culture dissemination, the Noam Schools and Machon Meir. The Noam Schools are selective elementary schools that place great emphasis on transmitting the Eretz Yisrael message to young children. They are considered an elite alternative to the ordinary state religious schools, and are an important socialization agent. Their high quality attracts many non-Emunist parents eager to give their children a first-class education. Many of them later find themselves parents of young Gush settlers.

Machon Meir is a popular adult institution that provides short and informal religious courses. Its branches, which are now spread all over Israel, attract Jews from Israel and abroad, young and old, who want to learn about Jewish religious orthodoxy in an open and pleasant atmosphere. Though few of the thousands of people who take such courses every year stay, repent, and join the formal Kookist course of ordinary yeshiva life, many leave with a feeling for Gush Emunim and the entire Eretz Yisrael theology.

Most of the teachers and administrators in the Noam Schools and Machon Meir are Merkaz Harav graduates and their confidants. These institutions, like the other Merkaz organs, are thus solid economic bastions of the invisible realm.[71] The lives of many thousands of people depend on their success and prosperity. Thus, the Emunist message, in addition to being an article of faith, is also their prime source of funds.

Nowhere does the economic function of the cultural institutions associated with Gush Emunim stand out so clearly as in the movement's infrastructure in the West Bank. Under the Likud administration, the Ministry of Education and Culture was headed by the NRP's Zevulun Hammer. During his first years in office he was an ardent supporter of the Gush. Hammer's ministry established an elaborate educational network in the West Bank in which the religious section was especially promoted. There are such schools in almost every West Bank settlement, even the small ones—136 of them were registered in 1983–84 (70 kindergartens, 35 primary schools, 5 high schools, 10 yeshivot, 14 kolelim, and 2 religious colleges). There were a separate teacher-training network, branches of the Bnei Akiva youth movement, and libraries—all financed by the state.

The West Bank educational system has thus become one of the settlers' main sources of income. Benvenisti has calculated that in the Mateh Binyamin region, a Gush Emunim stronghold, 10 percent of the total labor force (including women) worked in teaching and administration. He showed that the disproportionate state expense per capita on education had become particularly glaring considering the underutilization of the system: "In 1984/5 there were 16 pupils at the Mt. Hebron elementary school; 72 pupils in six elementary classes in Ofra; 80 students in junior high and high schools in Kedumim; and 95 students in grades 7—10 in Kiryat Arba.[72]

A special section of this institutional complex comprises the Eretz Yisrael midrashot. These are short-term learning centers, whose main purpose is to conduct short courses for visiting groups on such subjects as Judaism, Zionism, and the teachings of Rav Kook, as well as on the wildlife and geography of Eretz Yisrael. The midrashot have never been officially denoted as Gush Emunim organs, since they are under the state's Ministry of Education, just like similar institutions within the Green Line. Nevertheless, most of the West Bank midrashot are located in strongholds of Gush Emunim and were established during Zevulun Hammer's administration. The person designated by the Ministry of Education to oversee the midrashot and other institutions was none other than Rabbi Yohanan Fried, a prominent Gush Emunim veteran. Rafael Eitan, the IDF Chief of Staff, had earlier put Fried in charge of the Jewish education program of the IDF.[73]

While the Eretz Yisrael midrashot have not become a major source of income, they do provide many part-time jobs for students on leave from Merkaz and other yeshivas. And since tens of thousands of Israelis pass through these institutions each year, they are one of the most effective education agents of the Gush.[74]

A more serious effort is the growing academic complex of Midrashat Kedumim, or the Judea and Samaria College. Under Gush veteran Zvi Slonim, it seeks to compete with the nation's *secular* colleges and to become, one day, an alternative to the Hebrew University of Jerusalem and other such "leftist" centers. At present, Midrashat Kedumim is an adult-education center, with courses taught by sympathetic professors from Bar-Ilan, Haifa, Tel Aviv, and the Hebrew Universities. Two research institutions are also part of the growing Kedumim conglomerate; their main purpose is to document the settlement project in Judea and Samaria—and to become the Eretz Yisrael counterpart of the famed Van Leer Institute, which is known for its leftist orientation.[75]

Defending the West Bank Settlers

The invisible realm of Gush Emunim has evolved a district security and defense organization. Almost from the beginning of the Israeli occupation there were security problems in the West Bank. Because of anti-Jewish terrorist and guerrilla attacks, the settlements were designated "confrontation settlements"; special military orders authorized their guards to defend them with force. Many Jewish residents of the West Bank are, in fact, soldiers "on extended leave"—mainly religious students combining military service with advanced Talmudic study. In every settlement one settler is appointed "security officer" and receives a salary from the Ministry of Defense or the Israeli police. The result is that the settlers are directly involved in defense and security matters that were originally handled by the army and the military government.

In 1978, as noted in Chapter 3, Israel's chief of staff, General Rafael Eitan, initiated a policy making each settler community in the West Bank responsible for securing the area and defending itself. Hundreds of settlers were transferred from their regular army units to the West Bank, to protect their own settlements and to secure roads and public property. Every settlement was required to have a fixed number of soldiers, including officers. They were to perform their active duty on a part-time basis while leading normal civilian lives.

In addition, regional mobile forces equipped with armored personnel carriers policed the Palestinian population. Large quantities of military equipment, including sophisticated weapons, have been stored in the settlements under the complete control of the local commanders.[76]

Eitan probably saw the regional defense system as the best and cheapest way to secure the settlements against Arab attacks; the concept was familiar from prestate days, when the border settlements and kibbutzim necessarily defended themselves. Nevertheless, one cannot ignore the dangerous potential of a semi-independent armed force should strong disagreement with government policy arise. When the settler community debates its future in the event of major territorial concessions by the government, a minority reportedly favors armed resistance.

This group, though small, appears to be much larger than the isolated group that resisted the army in Yamit in 1982. Several of the Jewish Underground members were ranking officers in the reserves, and one, Yeshua Ben Shoshan, was a captain on active duty. According to unconfirmed but persistent rumors, none of the responsible officers of the Israeli army knows exactly how many arms are stored in the settlements caches, and no one dares check. While there is no doubt of the loyalty of the vast majority of these soldiers to the state of Israel and to the army, the potential existence of a small seditious element should not be disregarded.[77]

Settler violence and vigilantism reached crisis proportions in the summer of 1985. In June, the Israeli government exchanged prisoners with the Syrian-controlled PFLP General Command headed by Ahmed Jibril. Eleven hundred and fifty Arab prisoners were released in exchange for three Israeli soldiers. Six hundred of the freed Palestinians were allowed to return to their homes in Israel and the West Bank. Most of the freed Arabs had been serving sentences 15 to 20 years, but a few had been serving life terms for some of the most abominable terror acts in the preceding twenty years. Since many of the freed terrorists had been responsible for the deaths of their friends and students, the entire settler community was stunned. The Arab sector saw the exchange as a major victory and gave the freed prisoners heroes' welcomes all over the West Bank.

This was too much for the settlers to take—while twenty-five of their men were serving prison terms for defending the settler community against Arab terrorism, the "real" perpetrators of the bloodbath, as they viewed it, were being freed. Waves of armed settlers roamed the West Bank, usually at night, intimidating the local communities and ordering released prisoners to leave the country at once. Backed by the majority of Israelis, they were not stopped for weeks. There were very few acts of outright violence in these raids, but the settlers made it very clear that no one, not even the army and the government, was going to stop them from defending their families and their ministate.[78]

Since 1985 there have been repeated eruptions of settlers vigilantism. If Arabs threw rocks at an Israeli bus in Judea and Samaria—an act that had become quite common in the area even before the *intifada*—local vigilante road guards would respond swiftly and harshly. They used to enter the neighboring Arab village, smash car windows, break into houses, and warn the local residents against collaboration with the saboteurs. A *Washington Post* correspondent quoted a member of such a group: "The army is not doing its job so we are helping them. . . . Arabs are afraid of us. You can see it on their faces. They know we have no problem protecting ourselves. The stick is the best weapon, not the gun. The Arab knows you will think twice before using the gun, but not to smash his face with a stick."[79]

Aspirations for a Legal Autonomy

Gush Emunim's drive for autonomous institutions goes beyond the administrative, economic, cultural, and military areas; there have been signs that some of its authorities are thinking in terms of autonomous legal institutions as well. An early article in *Nekuda,* written by Rabbi Yehuda Shaviv of Yeshivat Har Etzion, suggested that Gush settlements should not follow the typical Israeli court system, but adopt instead a system of rabbinical courts that would rule according to Torah law:

> I was recently told that there is an intention of establishing courts of justice in the settlements of Judea and Samaria . . . I am afraid that if the new system is made by the ordinary lay institutions we are going to have ordinary courts and stand at a danger of getting less than what we bargained for. Have we only come here to revive desolate mountains, placing on them settlements that live by the common norms? It appears to me that many of us came over to establish new framework of life not just in the economic material sense, but also the social spiritual. . . . I think that one of the most impressive creations here may be the revival of the institution of *communal court*. This institution, apart of its legal authority, is bound to become a comprehensive moral-Halakhic authority.[80]

While no action has been taken on the Shaviv proposal, many Gush members would have loved to see Knesset law supplanted by Torah law and Halakha. It was therefore not surprising that in 1985 the regional council of Mateh Binyamin established a rabbinical court to resolve financial issues according to Halakha. As the announcement of the court's establishment explained,

> The revival of the Israeli nation means also the return of the law of Israel and the management of financial issues between a man and his peers according to the Torah and not according to the law imagined by the Gentiles. It appears proper that settlements that are instituted by the Torah should follow this path, for the law is from God.[81]

Given Gush Emunim's evolution in the direction of political, social, and cultural autonomy, it is hard to disagree with the conclusion of Giora Goldberg and Efraim Ben Zadok that an unprecedented process of territorial cleavage between old Israel and the occupied territories has been in the making for quite some time.[82] While it is hard to predict the end result of this process, it is clear that the leading force in this cleavage, Gush Emunim, has placed itself in a position of power and influence unusual for a movement that probably numbers about 15,000. Recently Gush Emunim has begun broadcasting "positive" messages of patriotism and Zionism from a ship in the Mediterranean—a clear sign that the Gush intends to expand its involvement further, and to move into new territories of influence and control.

Leadership and the Conduct of Politics

It is hardly questionable that one of the key elements in the success of Gush Emunim has been its way of conducting politics, an unusual combination of ideological rigidity and tactical flexibility. Never in the Gush's twenty-three years have its leaders and its members budged from their goal of annexing Judea and Samaria to the State of Israel, thereby advancing the process of national redemption. Yet in order to accomplish this goal they have maneuvered in many directions and have employed a variety of tactics. Observers, unfamiliar with the multidimensionality of Gush Emunim as a religious revival movement, a settlement organization, a Zionist collectivity, an interest group, and a West Bank ministate, find it hard to resolve the fundamentalist image of the Gush and its confessional politics with its political pragmatism and sense of timing. But this rich mélange has become the movement's trademark in the nation's politics.[83]

Though Gush Emunim emerged out of Merkaz Harav and was shaped by the homilies and involvement of Rabbi Zvi Yehuda Kook, it appears the old rabbi had little influence on his students' politics. Rabbi Kook was present at many important meetings and was often asked to rule on critical issues. He was also consulted on many matters and was instrumental in major moves like the formation of the Tehiya party. But due to his age, his limited political experience, and his detachment from everyday life, he was in no position to teach politics to his followers. Kook's most intense political adventure, the 1977 attempt to have Rabbi Haim Drukman nominated as the nation's education minister, failed miserably. The rabbi's typical reaction was to refuse to recognize Zevulun Hammer (who had earlier made him believe he would support his choice) as the actual minister, and to insistently refer to Drukman as Israel's real minister of education.[84]

The people who shaped Gush Emunim's unique style were the settler leaders themselves, Rabbi Zvi Yehuda's students, who were less spiritual and more political. What characterizes the public behavior of prominent settlers such as Moshe Levinger, Eliezer Waldman, Hanan Porat, Benny Katzover, Menachem Felix, Uri Elitzur, Uri Ariel, Daniela Weiss, and others is their natural understanding of the rules of Israeli politics—and of the ways to break those rules without getting hurt. The young rabbis of Gush Emunim—Shlomo Aviner, Yehuda Shaviv, the Ariel brothers, Yoel Ben-Nun, Yitzhak Shilat, Menachem Fruman, Eli Sadan, and others—are highly regarded and are consulted on issues involving Halakhic ruling, but they are not the movement's dynamic actors or public spokespersons. What has made the Porats, the Levingers, and the Katzovers so success is an uncommon combination of three elements: a tremendous belief in their heavenly mission, a great expertise in the traditional wheeling and dealing of the National Religious Party, and a Sabra confidence in the efficacy of the *Dugri* behavior (Israeli straightforwardness).

Gush politics were not developed in any theoretical workshop, but only evolved through trial and error. Nevertheless it is possible to see the group's four operational methods, which escalate in intensity as well as involvement and commitment: the creation of *fait accompli;* lobbying within the administrative echelons; lobbying within the top political echelons; and a final resort to extraparliamentary and extralegal politics.

The Creation of Fait Accompli

The veteran members of Gush Emunim had been committing irreversible acts long before they formed the movement and became its leaders. The tactic was used in the first two sorties of the Merkaz Harav alumni into the West Bank, the settlement of Gush Etzion and the penetration of Hebron. So successful were those two initiatives that they have molded the entire operational psychology of the Gush. The two settlement drives, while different in intensity and controversiality, had two features in common: they were conducted *vis-à-vis* an irresolute cabinet and they had the support and blessings of several cabinet members.

The person who has come to symbolize Gush Emunim's method and who has established through these operations a unique pattern of leadership is Rabbi Moshe Levinger, a small, thin, bearded man with a tormented expression and an ascetic aura. Levinger's father used to tell that young Moshe had been a small and weak child who tried to make up for his poor health by his strong will. The father, a distinguished professor of German origins, was very stern and demanding and the son, who was born in Jerusalem in 1935, grew up in a restrained atmosphere and with Prussian discipline.

Levinger studied in the Bnei Akiva yeshiva of Kfar Haroe and later in Yeshivat Hadarom in Rehovot. Following military service in the Nahal (a unit whose soldiers spend time in kibbutzim), he went to Merkaz Harav and became part of the group that was later to establish Gush Emunim. Levinger joined Kibbutz Lavi in 1962 and served four years as its rabbi, meanwhile working as a shepherd. His second rabbinical job, which he assumed sometime before the Six-Day War was at Moshav Nehalim.[85] From both his kibbutz and moshav experience Levinger obtained a deep respect for the Labor settlement movement. He was never attracted by the Likud and always had a warm spot in his heart for the Labor movement, even during Gush Emunim's worst confrontations with the Rabin administration.

The 1967 war, in which he did not participate as a soldier, transformed Levinger at once. "When I visited Hebron," he would later say, "I underwent an internal turmoil that left me restless for days and weeks."[86] He was determined to move to the new territories and was greatly supported by his extraordinary wife, Miriam, an American-born Gush Emunim legend in her own right. Because Miriam opposed the idea of joining Kibbutz Kfar Etzion, Levinger, together with nonreligious individuals like attorney Elyakim Haetzni and poet Aharon Amir, started to organize a group that would move to Hebron. They published ads in the papers and worked on the project between December and April of 1968. Since there was no official support, and the legal status of the occupied territories was still unclear, they decided to act on their own. The group rented the Park Hotel and moved in. Many members of the first group were certain that an evacuation by the military was inevitable, but Levinger was determined to stay. And stay he did.[87]

Levinger's tactic in settling Hebron has remained the classic strategy. It has four stages: (a) a surprise establishment of a temporary presence, ostensibly for worship purposes; (b) a rigid, highly publicized refusal to evacuate on religious grounds, with a generous interest in a "constructive" solution for the alleviation of "unnecessary tensions" with the army; (c) an agreement to compromise and leave provided a small yeshiva is established in the controversial site, or that the rest of the intruders be allowed to stay in a nearby military site; (d) the establishment, a few years later, of a permanent Jewish settlement at the site of the original initiative. From the first arrival of the Levinger team at Hebron's Park Hotel in Passover 1968 and the following establishment of Kiryat Arba, through his own gradual penetration of the Cave of the Patriarchs, the establishment of Keshet on the Golan Heights in 1974, the fight for Sebastia and the Kadum compromise that produced Ellon Moreh in 1977, to the ordeal of Beit Hadassah in Hebron of 1979–1980, the struggle for Tel Rumeida in Hebron and the establishment of a yeshiva at the Tomb of Yosef in Nablus in the mid-1980s, the pattern has always been the same; the stagging of an overnight surprise presence, the creation of new facts, and the rapid use of new political maneuvers to sustain the momentum.

The secret of Levinger's leadership has puzzled many observers. Neither as a person nor an orator has Levinger ever been very attractive. He is well known for his sloppy appearance, his old clothes and dirty shirts. He is also famed for his complete unpredictability. One never knows when "Rav Moishe" will recommend low-key, friendly talks with the other side—the government, the WZO, the army, or the police—since "they are all holy," or when will he erupt like a volcano, clash with soldiers, scream at politicians, hit an Arab girl who had insulted his daughter, or go on a hunger strike in front of an Arab refugee camp. Many Gush Emunim activists admit in private that they have never been able to figure out this man. But all his critics, and their number has been steadily growing, admit that over twenty years after the Park Hotel operation, Levinger is still the single most influential leader of Gush Emunim and the movement's most respected person.[88]

Levinger is a model case of a charismatic leader, a person who wins the loyalty of his followers not through their minds but rather through their hearts and emotions. He is a living example of the greatest Kookist virtue, *mesirut hanefesh* (a complete devotion to the cause). Time and again this man, who could by now have become a high-ranking Knesset member or the head of a prominent yeshiva, returns to his private war on the roads of Judea and Samaria. There were, of course, many cases in which Levinger consulted with his Gush colleagues and coordinated his protests. But most of the time it was Levinger's unpredictable one-man operations, his marches unarmed in the streets and alleys of Hebron, and his complete fearlessness. Even those colleagues who are extremely critical of Levinger are repeatedly impressed by his tenacity and persistence.

No Gush member, including ideological rivals, has ever seen Levinger or his wife put their own personal interests ahead of the cause. The Levingers, who have eleven children, have always lived very modestly. Since their first trip to the Park Hotel, they have moved four times. Always it has been to extend the Jewish presence in Hebron. This has required constant sacrifices and involved great personal inconveniencies. During the fight for Beit Hadassah, which was led by Miriam Levinger, the family was divided for months and lived like gypsies. At the present they live in a poor reconstructed Arab apartment in Hebron without rugs, television, or many other standard electrical appliances.[89] The man who looks like a tormented biblical prophet and lives like a monk can disappear for days, even weeks, without informing his wife or friends. He is involved in an unending Eretz Yisrael crusade, a journey that was started in 1968 and will probably end only at his death.

There is, finally, the fact of Levinger's legendary success. Undoubtedly one of the main sources of Rav Moishe's Emunist seniority is his continuous success. Not only has he led the drives into Hebron against all the odds, but he was also the guiding spirit behind many of the Gush illicit settlements in the 1970s, the loudest singer of *Utzu Etza Vetufar* (a favorite Jewish song about the failure of evil counselors), a source of inspiration and resolve. His absolute certainty about the infallibility of Gush Emunim, his mysterious messianic craze, and his refusal to break under any pressure have empowered the movement immensely in its hardest times.

One of the unspoken rules of Israeli politics is that no one can beat Levinger.[90] In the last twenty years he has confronted all of Israel's key politicians and no one has been able to stop him or defeat his plans. Levi Eshkol, Golda Meir, Moshe Dayan, Menachem Begin, Ezer Weizman, and Ariel Sharon have all learned to take this small man, who rarely has had a formal authority, very seriously. There was only one moment in the long history of Rabbi Levinger in which he appeared defeated. Following the 1984 discovery of the Jewish Underground and some incriminating evidence against him, Levinger was arrested and kept in jail for investigation. But he was freed after only twelve days with no charges pressed. Unofficial reports indicated that Levinger refused to cooperate with his investigators and that the Shin Bet people realized that they had in front of them a "man made of steel."[91] Rabbi Levinger was sentenced in May 1990 to jail for five months for killing an Arab bystander in Hebron. Very few of his followers took the sentence as a defeat. Levinger himself spoke about his "long awaited vacation" while a cheerful Gush Emunim crowd escorted him to prison, singing "Utzu Etza Vetufar."

Lobbying the Administrative Level

The second stage of Gush Emunim's political tactic has been its quiet lobbying of the administrative echelon of Israel's civil service: the many friendly settlement officials in Israel's Ministry of Agriculture, the Rural Settlement Department of the WZO, the military government of the West Bank, the Ministry of Defense, supportive military officers, and numerous other confidants throughout Israel's vast officialdom. The approach of the Gush has consistently been that even under the most hostile administration it is possible to find individuals willing to help, and that it is a great mistake to judge officials by the positions of their political bosses. Consequently, Gush Emunim has never given up on the bureaucracy and over the years has built a pervasive system of second-level support. Of special importance in this network of contacts have been the majority of officials of the "religious" ministries of Israel's government, the ministries of Religion and the Interior (when it was in the hands of the NRP).

During the early years, the Labor supporters of Gush Emunim, veteran kibbutzim and moshavim members who had later created the Ein Vered Circle, were probably the most effective. Being an integral part of the hard-core Labor elite that built the nation, these people had reached positions of power and influence. Excited by the Zionist pioneering spirit of the young zealots, these Ein Vered activists visited the illicit settlements, encouraged the settlers, shared information on the attitudes of the authorities, and provided logistical support in time of need. Some applied consistent pressure on Itzhak Rabin, Shimon Peres, and Israel Galili during the Kadum crisis; some later joined the Tehiya party.[92] The Ein Vered members acted as a group, but dozens of other officials supported the Gush on their own. A prominent supporter of Gush Emunim in the movement's early days was Ariel Sharon, who had served in the mid-1970s as Rabin's defense advisor.

A representative case of the Gush relationship with the executive echelon of Israel's government was its connection with Uri Bar-On, at the time an army colonel in reserves and an assistant to Minister Ariel Sharon. Bar-On, a native of Nahalal, the first moshav in the history of Zionism, was an old settlement hand. Upon the establishment of the Ein Vered circle he joined and participated in several illicit squattings of Gush Emunim. Even as a private moshav member and a retired colonel Bar-On was an influential person. In many cases he served as a go-between, bringing together the illicit settlers of Elon Moreh and government's officials. In others instances he simply represented the settlers.

Following the Likud victory in 1977, Bar-On was asked by Ariel Sharon, Israel's new Minister of Agriculture and the chairman of the cabinet's settlement committee, to become his assistant in charge of settlement. In that capacity Bar-On became Gush Emunim's primary channel of communication with the entire Israeli administration. There was hardly a single relevant Gush issue that Bar-On was not involved in: surveying the areas for new settlement lands, paving new roads in Judea and Samaria, placing the settlements in the proposed locations, channeling budgets, providing professional know-how and moral support, fighting the case of Gush Emunim within the cabinet and other administrative agencies, and dealing with security matters.[93]

For Bar-On, being settlement coordinator was no ordinary job; it was a calling, he spent his days and nights on the job. Whenever the Gush settlers needed him—and they did increasingly as their conflict with the government intensified—he was there, giving advice, providing inside information, and helping out.

Bar-On was a rugged moshavnik from old Labor stock, not a religious person. But his respect and admiration for the young religious members of Gush Emunim was limitless. They represented the Israel he loved and was part of, and regardless of their fundamentalist theology, he believed they deserved everything. Hanan Porat was once told by Bar-On, in a moment of emotional outpouring, that ever since the fall of his son, a battalion commander in the army, he considered the Gush Emunim youngsters to be his sons. Following the legal crisis that led to the removal of Elon Moreh to a different location in Samaria, Bar-On vowed to join the settlement in the future. During the painful 1982 evacuation of Yamit, which was conducted under Sharon, as defense minister, Bar-On was instrumental as the minister's advisor, in preventing bloodshed. Torn between his official job and his identification with the defiant settlers, he did his best to help the latter in information and logistics.[94]

The activists of Gush Emunim have never formally divided political roles among themselves. But some Gush members are better suited for some jobs than for others. Rabbi Levinger, for instance, has never been considered a good lobbyist; those best suited for lobbying are moderate and soft-spoken individuals who would not emphasize the messianic gospel of the movement but concentrate instead on its settlement record and its contribution to the progress of pioneering Zionism. The best lobbyist in the early days of the Gush was Gershon Shafat; the role was later taken up by leaders such as Uri Elitzur and Uri Ariel. And it was natural that it was these people who were to take over the most organized and orderly institution of the movement, Amana.

Gershon Shafat was an exception among the internal circle that led the early movement. He was much older than most of the others and had no Merkaz Harav education. But long ago he had been a member of kibbutz Ein Tzurim, of the original Gush Etzion, destroyed by the Jordanians in 1948. During the British Mandate, he took part in Bnei Akiva's legendary illicit settlement in Biria and was a member of the Hagana. Shafat was among the founders of the new kibbutz Ein Tzurim, reestablished within the Green Line, and over the years earned a reputation as a first-rate economist and organizer. A prominent and respected activist in the Kibbutz Dati (Religious Kibbutz) movement and in the NRP, he had the right contacts and necessary experience to open many doors.

Shafat was involved in many early settlement activities of the pre–Gush Emunim period and became a member of the first secretariat of the movement. While participating in all the heroic events of the Gush and in its illicit squattings, he remained always in the background, negotiating with the army, and talking to people in the Ministry of Defense or in the Prime Minister's bureau.[95]

Shafat's use of pragmatic lobbying and personal contacts has been assumed in the last decade by younger Gush Emunim activists. Uri Elitzur is a case in point. Although Elitzur studied in Merkaz Harav at the right time (just prior to the Six-Day War), he was not one of the founders of the movement. The son of Yehuda Elitzur, a Bar-Ilan Bible professor of pronounced nationalist views, Uri went to the Hebrew University of Jerusalem to study mathematics, married and maintained no contacts with his classmates.

But the struggle of Gariin Elon Moreh and the pictures of the forced evacuations of its members from Sebastia inspired the Elitzurs, and they joined the Gariin. Uri was soon made a member of the Gariin's secretariat and became very active in its operations. Being more pragmatic than some of the members of the Elon Moreh group, Elitzur was skeptical about its chances of success. He consequently decided to opt for certainty and joined Yehuda Etzion and Gariin Ofra, which, unlike Elon Moreh, was quietly approved by the government as a "working group" in Samaria. Elitzur soon joined the settlement department of Gush Emunim and later moved to Amana.

Throughout this time he was involved in the love-hate relationship of the movement with the NRP, and was among those who left the party in 1979 to establish the Tehiya. Elitzur's emotional stability as well as his political and organizational qualities led his colleagues to place him at the head of the Movement to Halt the Retreat in Sinai. He did not disappoint them. His ability to contain the extremist elements within the movement and maintain good contacts with the authorities, especially the army, throughout the dramatic period, won him great respect by friends and foes alike.

It was natural that this methodical and moderate man would become a key person as the Gush evolved into a stable organization. Elitzur became the senior representative of Gush Emunim in Amana and has been constantly involved in the Gush struggles against and within the NRP.[96] Many were surprised in 1987 when he assumed the headship of the *Hasbara* (information and education) department of the NRP, a rather routine second-level party job. There are, however, many indications that Elitzur was placed near the professional heart of the party as part of the long-range strategy of Gush Emunim to take over this old political stronghold from the inside.

Lobbying the Top Political Echelon

The third form of Gush Emunim politics has been its successful lobbying of Israel's top political echelon, the members of the cabinet and the Knesset. Ever since the end of the Six-Day War, it has been clear that the settlement of the West Bank was a political issue of the highest importance. The decisions on settlement were made by Israel's leading cabinet ministers and most respected Knesset members. No substantial settlement in the occupied territories could have taken place without the consent, collaboration, or secret assistance of at least some of these forces. And no one knew it better than the leaders of the emerging Gush Emunim. Their understanding of the *realpolitik* of the Jewish state has produced, over the years, one of Israel's most effective lobbying systems.

In his bitter 1979 memoirs, Itzhak Rabin provides a rare clue to the Gush's shrewd lobbying during his administration. He tells the inside story of the infamous Kadum compromise in which he, the prime minister of Israel, was forced to a major concession by Gush Emunim against his better judgment. Rabin makes it very clear that his minister of defense, Shimon Peres, betrayed him.

The ambitious Peres, who was envious of Rabin and at odds with Yigal Allon, Rabin's minister of foreign affairs, was identified by Gush Emunim as the soft spot of the Labor administration, the crack in the wall of the Allon Plan—Labor's program of controlling the occupied territories by a combination of military strongholds and a few strategic Jewish outposts, without a settlement of densely populated Arab Samaria. They approached him both directly and through their NRP connections, and Peres helped them in many ways, including his unpublicized agreement that Gariin Ofra would live in the Ba'al Hatzor military camp in Samaria as a "workers group." Further, at the critical confrontation with the army in Sebastia in 1975, Peres was very indecisive. The army, called upon to evacuate the illicit squatters, felt it did not have the backing of a determined minister. Prime Minister Rabin sensed it too and was hesitant in forcing a showdown on the issue. Strengthened by the intense pressure of dozens of Emunim supporters from all areas of Israel's life, cabinet ministers, Knesset members, party politicians, high civil servants, rabbis, writers, and even Diaspora leaders, Peres's complacency was assured.[97]

Thus the movement won its most significant victory, permission for Gariin Elon Moreh to stay in Kadum. And though Kadum was a military base and the group had to be registered as a workers squad, the victory was unmistakable: Gush Emunim had forced a showdown with the government and won. The heartland of Eretz Israel was publicly penetrated.

Since 1977, Gush Emunim's lobbying has been somewhat different. The new Likud administration agreed that Judea and Samaria were open for Jewish settlement, and Menachem Begin referred to Gush members as his "darling children," so there was no longer the critical necessity of cultivating the right contacts and explaining the importance of the Jewish presence in the West Bank. There was, however, a constant need to counterbalance outside diplomatic pressures applied on the government to limit or postpone the process. A new Gush Emunim skill was consequently developed, a special way of talking to Prime Minister Begin and of reminding him of his old commitment to Eretz Yisrael. The person most fit for that task was Hanan Porat, always a pleasant, eloquent, and highly persuasive communicator.

Porat tells how he was invited one night to see Menachem Begin. Gush Emunim was pushing for the establishment of twelve new settlements, but there was opposition within the cabinet. Consequently Begin told Porat that the new endeavor could not be approved at that time. But then Begin said,

> You should go ahead, settle on your own and get organized in the field. And then, after the fact it would be easy for me to say "nitzchuni banai. . ." (I was overcome by my children), for nobody could think in his right mind that I, Begin, would remove Jews from Eretz Israel territory.[98]

Gush Emunim's political lobbying reached an advanced stage in the early 1980s when the movement literally entered the Knesset. The process began in 1977 when Rabbi Haim Drukman was elected to the parliament as an NRP no. 2 representative. And it greatly intensified in 1981 with the election of three Tehiya members to the Knesset, including Hanan Porat.

These people took the evacuation of Yamit as a warning regarding Judea and Samaria; bitter as they were in 1982, they knew they had to work with the Likud to strengthen whatever remained of Begin's commitment to "never redivide Eretz Yisrael." The June invasion of Lebanon created the right atmosphere. Not only did it fit Gush Emunim's political instincts, but it totally removed the West Bank from the headlines. Judea and Samaria became completely open for Jewish settlement, and Israel's new Minister of Science and Energy, Yuval Ne'eman, was made the head of the settlement committee of the government.

The years 1982–1984 were the political apex of Gush Emunim. Gush people were everywhere and knew everything. Some of the most confidential state secrets were discussed and debated in Yesha's internal councils, and most of the ministerial doors were open to the settlers. Minister of Defense Ariel Sharon, who was a great friend, was at the peak of his career and his settlement right hand, Uri Bar-On, knew no limits in his efforts on behalf of the settlers.

The return of Labor to partial power in 1984, as an equal partner in the unity government, damaged the influence of Gush Emunim. The Tehiya, despite its relative electoral success with five Knesset members, had to leave the cabinet and the settlement of the West Bank slowed to a crawl. And though the Likud administration had been good to the settlers in Judea and Samaria in the previous four years, it had left the economy of Israel in shambles. Finally by 1984 the Lebanon war was acknowledged as a national disaster. Even the most ideological members of the Likud understood by then that settling the West Bank could not be the first priority of the new administration.

Gush Emunim had to muster all its experience, ingenuity, and skill in facing the new situation. Since 1984 it has translated its resources into especially effective system of political lobbying, in which the Yesha Council played a dominant role. Harel's organization did not make a great difference as long as the Likud-Tehiya coalition was in power and doing "the right thing." But it went into high gear in 1984.

After the elections, the Yesha council created the position of secretary-general, and Otniel Schneler, a son of another member of Bar-Ilan's faculty, got the job. Though Schneler did not change the direction of the organization, he introduced into Yesha's lobbying a new dimension of professional division of labor. Having Israel Harel in charge of the Ofra offices of the organization and *Nekuda,* the settlers' influential magazine, Schneler spent at least three days every week in Jerusalem, meeting sympathetic ministers like Itzhak Shamir, Ariel Sharon, David Levy, and Yosef (Yoske) Shapiro, and less sympathetic ones like Shimon Peres and Itzhak Rabin. Capitalizing on the increasing number of settlers in Yesha (nearly 50,000 by 1984), the growing power of the invisible institutions of Gush Emunim, and the continued readiness of the hard core of Gush Emunim to go to the streets in time of trouble and block the roads in Judea and Samaria, Schneler felt that the old days of begging were gone: "We have become such an influential body that no minister can afford not to see me, not even Itzhak Rabin. Rabin knows that if he wants Judea and Samaria quiet and the settlers off the roads he has to talk to me."

In 1984 Schneler set up the Lobby, an official Knesset caucus that represented Yesha's interests in Israel's legislature, committees, and corridors of power. Likud Knesset member Uzi Landau assumed the chairmanship of the new caucus (the job was later given to Igal Cohen) and he and Schneler ran it from Landau's offices and through its facilities. The Lobby, whose membership peaked in 1987 to nearly 50 Knesset members (out of a total of 120), convened every Monday afternoon to discuss issues on the agenda. During the week, Schneler, the chairman of the Lobby, and a few active members would stay in constant touch in order to act on emergencies and respond to crises.

The Lobby had thus become Yesha's watchdog in the Knesset, a most effective instrument for gaining quick information, securing budgets, and influencing important legislation. The Lobby was instrumental in 1986 in introducing the notorious law that made a meeting between private Israelis and PLO officials illegal. It was the major Knesset force behind the unsuccessful move to enact a special law pardoning the members of the Jewish Underground. And it made it possible for Schneler and his council to approach Israel's politicians and make demands, not in relation to ideology and Zionism, but on the basis of power politics.[99]

One reason that the Lobby had been so effective is the ideological radicalization of the central committees of the Likud and the religious parties. Almost no Knesset member of these parties could afford, in the mid-1980s, not to appear an ardent supporter of Eretz Yisrael. Schneler and other Gush people, the representatives of the Eretz Yisrael purists, thus obtained a considerable political leverage. They could "stain" right-wing Knesset members, portraying them in public as disloyal to Eretz Yisrael.

Schneler himself became the prototype of a new kind of Gush Emunim activist, a backstage political pro who was less identified with the pioneering of the 1970s than with the power politics of the 1980s. When interviewed, Schneler could not hide his satisfaction at his growing influence and the fact that the content of every Knesset secret meeting or cabinet deliberation pertaining to the settlers or the West Bank, however sensitive or confidential, was known to him almost immediately. The practical result is that Gush Emunim, unlike any other voluntary organization in Israel, is in a position to take a stand and apply pressure on the government of Israel even before decisions have been reached. Thus, for example, long before the completion of the sensitive exchange of three captured Israeli soldiers for 1150 Palestinian terrorists in the summer of 1985, the controversial deal was debated in Gush Emunim's internal councils. Only their fear of a possible public condemnation prevented its leaders from making the deal public in order to sabotage it.[100]

Extraparliamentary and Extralegal Politics

Despite its accelerated institutionalization since 1977, Gush Emunim has never renounced its traditional mode of extraparliamentary and illegal action—witness the open conflicts with Menachem Begin over settlements during his early negotiations with President Carter, the Movement to Halt the Retreat in Sinai, and repeated demonstrations over security issues in the West Bank. The most prevalent recent pattern of extralegal action has been the settlers' vigilantism. The *intifada* that began in December 1987, taking politicians and observers alike by surprise, was preceded by slow but incremental intercommunal violence. This has meant since 1981, over 3000 violent attacks—mostly rock-throwing—on Jews and Jewish transportation by Arabs of the West Bank every year. The settlers have responded with a growing number of illicit retaliatory attacks, which involve shooting to kill or wound, smashing windshields of parked Arab cars, burning houses, and beating up passersby.[101]

The most severe incidents before the *intifada* began at the Deheishe refugee camp in 1986, following a serious incident of rock-throwing, and in Kalkiliya in 1987, after the death of a pregnant woman and child caused by a Molotov cocktail. These cases involved raids of armed settlers who refused to obey the orders of Israeli officers to refrain from passing roadblocks or to stop attacking local people. The *intifada* has only increased these trends to a very high frequency. As much as the army has been trying to keep its monopoly over the use of physical force and maintain law and order, many eruptions of settler violence have occurred. Thus in 1988 the image of Gush Emunim was not so different from its 1978 portrait as a movement of true believers who resort to direct and violent action whenever other channels do not get results. The main difference is that ten years have produced a much larger and more sophisticated Gush.

The theoretical basis of direct action is still actively propagated. There are a growing number of private discussions on the right of the settlers for self-defense, and *Nekuda* propounds many of the same extralegal themes of the previous decade. Referring to Labor's hostility toward the settlers and their endeavor, and to the hardships produced by the unity government under Shimon Peres, Benny Katzover, now head of the Samaria regional council, published a major article in *Nekuda* in 1985 under the title "A Return to the Struggle Methods of Sebastia Is Possible." Attacking Labor's hostility, he wrote:

> Today it has to be said loud and clear: this is the plan of the Alignment [a retreat from Judea and Samaria] which is being carried out under our noses. We have to fight it. A return to the struggle methods used in the past is possible, especially in such places as Tel Remeida [near Hebron] and Nablus. Despite all the problems described above, we have to remember that our condition in the field is very encouraging. About 50,000 Jews live in Yesha today and we hope to double this number shortly, [but] only a settlement of tens of thousands of Jews will assure our future and only in this way we can stop the shameful show of a nation which gives up the heart of the heart of its homeland.[102]

While there was little new in Katzover's statement, it did disclose the next objective of the extremist circles of Gush Emunim, the establishment of a Jewish presence in Nablus. Gush Emunim has never given up on the idea of settling Nablus, though it had not made it an operational goal. Even the radical wing of the movement has been aware how central the city is to Palestinian nationalism, and how hostile its 80,000 residents are toward the Jews. And unlike Hebron, nor is it recognized as a "holy" city. But Nablus was a key Biblical city, Shechem, and much of the ethos of Gariin Elon Moreh was built around the return to it.[103]

It was therefore just a question of time before the issue emerged in public. A partial solution to the dilemma of returning to Nablus was found in the early 1980s with the establishment of a small yeshiva at the Tomb of Yosef, a holy place that was reconstructed earlier and maintained by the military authorities. The Likud government allowed the establishment of the yeshiva provided the students would return to their homes in the surrounding settlements every night. But the built-in anarchist element in Gush Emunim was bound to upset this compromise sooner or later. At Nablus it did, in the person of Romam Aldubi.

Aldubi, the son of a prominent Israel sculpturer, had studied several years at the high-school yeshiva of Merkaz Harav. His commitment to the settlement of Nablus emerged while he was on a rooftop in Yamit struggling with the army. His belief was so strong that Romam was ready to take an almost impossible risk, to go alone to the Tomb of Yosef and start a one-man yeshiva on his own. Aldubi's act of supreme *Messirut Hanefesh* eventually attracted more settlers and yeshiva students, and by 1987 there were about fifteen in all.

But the yeshiva was just a means for Aldubi's real aim, the actual settlement of Nablus. Since 1985 he has managed to attract some followers and to form Gariin Shechem, the Nablus nucleus. The students of the yeshiva and the members of the Gariin have become a focus for many illegal acts and confrontations with the military. The incidents usually occurred when the group tried to pray at the tomb site without official permission, or when its members drove through Nablus in order to demonstrate to the local residents their presence. While Gush Emunim has not followed Aldubi to Nablus and Amana did not give him full support, his extraordinary commitment to the place has become a subject for admiration and respect. The neighboring Elon Moreh offered Aldubi an empty flat and full backing. Several Elon Moreh members have become involved in the yeshiva and were later implicated in concealing evidence in two cases of killings of Arab civilians. Aldubi himself has obtained notoriety for his aggressive behavior in the area.[104]

The career of Romam Aldubi was ended abruptly with the widely reported incident at Beita village, in May 1988. The case was also paradigmatic of the behavior of the Gush Emunim settlers during the *intifada*. Aldubi and another settler led a group of Elon Moreh teenagers for a hike of several miles in the area. What they did not take into account was the awakened animosity and rebelliousness of the residents of Beita, a large Arab village on the route. Although the trip took place during an especially tense period, Aldubi and his colleague were determined not to change their original plan. They also did not bother to coordinate the trip with the army.

The result was catastrophic. The group was attacked by local rock-throwers and later surrounded. Aldubi used his gun and killed one of the attackers. The killing enraged hundreds of local Arabs, who forced the isolated group into the center of the village. Aldubi was badly beaten by the victim's family, and in the scuffle he fatally shot, by mistake, a girl of his own group. The youngsters were finally rescued with no additional casualties, but Aldubi's brain was permanently damaged.

The Beita incident triggered an unprecedented wave of furor and rage among the settlers. Hundreds of angry Jewish residents in the area went to the roads and stopped traffic. The villagers of Beita were blamed for conducting a "pogrom," and the entire radical right was in an uproar. Ariel Sharon demanded that the village be destroyed and that the residents who did not rescue the teenagers be deported. Geula Cohen asked for the resignation of General Dan Shomron, Israel's chief of staff, for failing to defend the settlers and for being critical of Aldubi and the settlers.

The entire political machine of Gush Emunim went into full steam and made the Beita incident a disaster of national proportions. The Ministry of

Defense and the army tried to resist the calls for revenge but were only partially successful. The houses of fourteen families, all associated with the attackers of the group, were blown up hastily. Only later it was learned that several of the accused, who were left homeless, were innocent and that one of them had actually rescued several hikers.[105]

The *intifada* and the growing conflict in Israel over the future of the West Bank leaves little doubt that Gush Emunim's settlers will continue to resort to extralegal action and violence. They have already been involved in many violent incidents and are likely, unless the area is dramatically pacified, to intensify these actions. Thus, all four modes of political action are going to continue to be the movement's modus operandi for many years to come.

Crises and Internal Conflicts

One of the most impressive features of Gush Emunim throughout the 1970s was the skill of its leaders and activists to work together without formal rules and codified procedures. The ability of the movement to challenge the Israeli authorities, to carry out massive settlement operations, to switch jobs and roles among its leaders, and to maintain at the same time complete unity was amazing. Much of this harmony was achieved through the unique authority of Rabbi Zvi Yehuda Kook, who though not involved in the daily operations of the movement was recognized by all its activists as their leader, arbitrator, and final court of appeal. Other reasons had to do with the quality of the Gush leaders and their relative disdain for political careers.

But given the troubled situation in the occupied territories and the intense involvement of Gush Emunim in the political life of the nation, it was only a matter of time before the harmony of the movement was disturbed. Three events in particular—the evacuation of Yamit, the war in Lebanon, and the discovery of the Jewish underground—have shaken the foundations of Gush Emunim in the last decade. While the first two were met by a unified leadership, which made it possible to control the damage, the third found the Gush leadership divided. It consequently had a long lasting impact on the movement.

The Impact of Yamit

The evacuation of Yamit and of northern Sinai was a major blow for Gush Emunim. The Gush as a whole stood behind the Movement to Halt the Retreat in Sinai. Its most revered rabbis and charismatic leaders were involved in this great confrontation between mundane politics and *Messirut Hanefesh*. No former collision of the movement with the government of Israel had required so much spiritual energy, skill, and organization. Nevertheless, Sinai was evacuated. A loss of the magnitude of Yamit would have probably been damaging for any fighting social movement, but for Gush Emunim, a religious and mystical collectivity which appealed during the fight to God Almighty Himself, it was especially painful. It is not entirely clear whether the leaders of the movement were themselves certain about their ability to halt the retreat, but there is no question that they believed that to be effective *they had to be convinced,* and behave properly. The MHRS consequently formulated several messages to the Israeli public, but its main promise to its own followers was unequivocal: *Lo tihiye nesiga* (there will be no retreat).[106] Leaders and activists moved into the area and behaved as if no evacuation was ever to take place. Their devoted followers were inspired to conduct their business as usual until the very last moment and to expect a miracle. The miracle did not come.

The completion of the retreat from Sinai left the leaders of Gush Emunim with a critical problem: how to contain the damage caused by the failure of their promise and prevent internal demoralization. The problem required an explanation of the gap between the movement's success in the 1970s and its failure in 1982. Since both cases implied a struggle against the government of Israel in the name of God, there was an urgent need to explain what went wrong in Yamit and why. A series of internal meetings after the retreat were somewhat effective at explaining the disaster, but less effective in terms of demoralization and damage.[107]

Gush Emunim's major lesson from the struggle was that the MHRS failed because, unlike in the 1970s, the Gush did not convey its message to the majority of Israelis. The Gush activists had spoken so much with each other about the impossibility of the retreat that they convinced themselves that no retreat would ever take place.

The problem of the MHRS, according to the Gush self-criticism, was that *it did not see its appeal to the people of Israel as the most crucial factor for a possible success.* Furthermore, it had been wrong to state categorically that no evacuation would ever take place. No Jew is supposed to make specific deterministic predictions regarding the future. *Hakol tzafui vehareshut netuna* (While everything is predetermined, one is free to choose) was the phrase most often quoted. The MHRS was right to struggle against evacuation, but doing the right thing was not enough politically, and it could not guarantee success. No daring move can ever be expected to succeed unless it relies on national consensus and a broad following.[108]

These conclusions were followed by an effort by several of the movement's ideologues to identify positive results of the struggle—clearly an effort to limit the disappointment among the movement's settlers and control the damage to its image. People spoke about the traumatic impact of the struggle on the nation's psyche and of its clear message to the government that any future evacuation of Judea and Samaria would be impossible. Others stressed the educational experience of the struggle and the further crystallization of the Eretz Yisrael camp. Thus Hanan Porat, a major figure in the MHRS, said,

> In the struggle for the rest of Sinai, "the fighting brigade" of the loyalists of Eretz Yisrael and the loyalists of the course of Israel's redemption was acutally established. Never before have we witnessed such devotion, such intensity, such energy and initiative, and also such a magnitude. This human and energetic arsenal is going to have a continuation. . . . We have created a tremendous reawakening in our youth.[109]

But while Porat and the other Gush leaders may have convinced themselves, they were unable to contain the real harm of the event, the decline of the great spirit of Gush Emunim and the consequent thinning of the movement's edges. The fiasco in Sinai was not an isolated failure. The peace with Egypt capped a five-year period that stood in total contrast to the optimistic message of the movement in the 1970s. The retreat from Eretz Yisrael territories that culminated in Yamit made many former supporters of Gush Emunim wonder about the certainty of its promise and the precision of its analysis. Members of Bnei Akiva and students of Yeshivot Hesder, who had become supporters of Gush Emunim and its greatest source of manpower, began in the 1980s to ask hard questions. Many of them were no longer sure of the promise of quick redemption and of the certain course of the movement. Disappointment seems to be at least part of the reason numerous potential Gush supporters returned to traditional Torah studies rather than to pioneering settlements.[110]

The Amital Controversy

Another blow to the integrity of the movement was the public controversy that followed the war in Lebanon. The beginning of the war, a lightning operation that was meant to be short, was warmly welcome by the Gush. More than any other camp in Israel, the movement had a vested interest in the war, which was intended to eliminate the Palestine Liberation Organization, whose claims, large following, and terroristic acts in the West Bank constantly alarmed the settlers. Furthermore, southern Lebanon was an old "Jewish territory"—land that had once belonged to the tribes of Asher and Naftali and was therefore clearly destined to return to the nation.

But the war did not achieve most of its goals. It was partially successful in destroying the bases of the PLO, but the casualty rate was high.[111] When the first and most intense stage of the war was over, several rabbis closely associated with the Gush learned that the death toll among their students, serving in military elite units, was extremely high.

This was the background for the unexpected critique expressed by Rabbi Yehuda Amital, the head of Yeshivat Har Etzion in Allon Shvut. Amital had never been a close member of the inner Kookist circle that established Gush

Emunim. Older than most of the Gush founders, he was a Holocaust survivor who had not grown up under the influence of Rabbi Zvi Yehuda Kook
at Merkaz Harav. But Amital had always considered himself a devoted
student of the elder Rav Kook and his magnum opus, *Orot*. He was, furthermore, highly respected by leading Gush Emunim figures, and was invited in
the late 1960s by Hanan Porat and Rabbi Yohanan Fried to become the
head of Yeshivat Har Zion in Allon Shvut.[112] Amital's book *From the Elevations of the Depths* had, after the Yom Kippur War, become the most
inspiring document of the young Gush Emunim.[113] Rabbi Amital's convincing explanation for the 1973 war was that it was the final attempt of the
Gentiles to stop the inevitable Jewish redemption. Yeshivat Har Zion had
become a major source of new Gush Emunim recruits; several of the movement's founding fathers, including Rabbi Yoel Ben-Nun, had taught there.

Amital had earlier been critical of what he deemed the unnecessary
extremization of the struggle in Yamit; now he questioned the most crucial
component of the Gush belief, the sacrilization of the Land of Israel. He
made it very clear that Gush Emunim's exaggerated attachment to the territorial dimension of the nation's regeneration was, in his opinion, a wrong
interpretation of the Halakha. It laid the moral foundation for a glorification of armed struggle for the land and was bound to lead to unnecessary
wars and to the unecessary loss of Jewish life. Amital said he had no basic
disagreement with Gush Emunim's "holy trinity"—the sacredness of the
People of Israel, the Torah of Israel, and the Land of Israel—but he charged
the movement's ideologues with an *unbalanced focus* on the third. In using
the injunction "*Yehareg uval yaavor*" (be killed rather than sin) about Eretz
Israel, with no qualifications or exceptions, the Gush had gone beyond "the
opinion of the Torah and the spirit of Judaism." It had become a sectarian,
single-issue movement that ignored crucial elements of the Jewish faith.[114]

One of Amital's most alarming acts was to allow himself to be identified
with a moderate group called *Netivot Shalom* (Paths of Peace), an organization most of whose members were moderate religious activists. Amital was,
surprisingly, backed by Zevulun Hammer, Israel's religious Minister of Education. Hammer, an NRP leader, was never an official member of Gush
Emunim, but in the late 1960s and through most of the 1970s had been a
strong Gush supporter.

Amital's harsh public criticisms triggered an intense ideological controversy within Gush Emunim. Even moderate members of the movement such
as Rabbis Ben-Nun and Tzukerman and activists like Hanan Porat became
furious. Amital, a respected insider, was charged with error and faithlessness
to the tradition of Rav Kook, "A fundamental misunderstanding of the
centrality and importance of Eretz Israel during the process of redemption."
"Eretz Israel," the leaders said, "is an organic part of the essential existence
of the people of Israel. And the bond between the people and the land is
similar to the bond between the spirit and the body—'a healthy spirit must

dwell in a healthy body,' and when the body is hurt the spirit suffers and vice versa."[115]

Gush Emunim's contest with Rabbi Yehuda Amital spilled beyond ideology into politics. Though in 1982 and 1983 Amital had no political interests of his own, he was very influential among students of Yeshivot Hesder, in Bnei Akiva circles, and in the Kibbutz Dati movement.[116] His attack contributed to the erosion of Gush support, for it strengthened the skeptics whose excitment about the earlier pioneering of Gush Emunim was now on the wane.[117] Amital's critique was the first attack on this movement by a distinguished Zionist religious authority and a recognized follower of Rav Kook; it had not been prepared for an attack of this magnitude.

The Crisis Over the Jewish Underground

The failure of the Movement to Halt the Retreat in Sinai and the Amital controversy weakened support for Gush Emunim, yet neither created a rift within the Gush's remarkably cohesive leadership. Differences of opinion did, of course, exist and the 1982 death of Rabbi Zvi Yehuda Kook made them more noticeable. But Gush Emunim's founders remained united on almost all major issues.

This happy situation ended abruptly in April 1984 with the discovery of the Jewish Underground. Very few activists of Gush Emunim had been aware of the existence of the group prior to its arrest. The vast majority of the members were so overhelmed and shocked that their first reaction was one of hostile suspicion toward the authorities. They simply refused to believe that anyone in the Gush could be involved in coldblooded terrorism. Thus they argued that the revelations were part of a leftist conspiracy to smear the settler community. A dramatic meeting of the Yesha Council announced that "the council is convinced that the settlers of Judea, Samaria, and Gaza are not involved in this criminal act, and that there exists no subversive organization whose membership come from the arrested settlers."[118]

But when it became clear that there was in fact an organized conspiracy, and that it was made up of prominent members of the movement, Gush Emunim was very confused. The Yesha Council came out with a strong denunciation of the crime. Rabbi Yoel Ben-Nun, a leading Gush moderate, called for collective soul-searching and termed the activities of the underground "a revolt against the kingdom," a criminal act of the first degree. He forcefully argued that the consensus that had led to the establishment of Israel and upon which the state continued to rely was very delicate. Its existence could not be taken for granted, and no one, not even people with pure motivations, were free of the obligation to respect it. The very existence of the state of Israel could be jeopardized by the thinking of the underground.[119]

The public furor over the underground put all of Gush Emunim on the defensive. Its spokepersons, who had argued for years that the Israeli left had unfairly and intentionally portrayed them as violent aggressors were left with no arguments. Not only had the operations of the underground verified many of the accusations leveled against them all along, but in fact dwarfed most of these early charges.

Never before had the public image of the Gush Emunim community been so grossly damaged. The movement that had portrayed itself as the unselfish instrument of the nation was now in moral disarray. It was reduced, in the eyes of numerous observers and many members, to a bunch of terrorists and supporters of terrorism. And unlike the earlier crises, there was no way the movement could unite behind the underground. An internal rift was inevitable.

The conflict over the underground developed oddly. Few Gush leaders would defend the terror group in public. The only prominent rabbi to do so was Israel Ariel, the former head of Yeshivat Yamit, who by 1984 had apparently lost faith in the Gush's ideological stance toward the State of Israel. He argued that the acts of the underground were not necessarily "a treason against the kingdom" because the government of Israel did not have all the attributes of a legitimate kingdom.[120]

Nevertheless, the real problem of the moderates was not Ariel, but a more prominent Gush activist who chose to remain silent—Rabbi Moshe Levinger, by far the most respected and influential leader. There were two problems with Rabbi Levinger: his refusal to publicly denounce the underground and the thick hints that he was personally involved in its organization. The former issue was discussed in public, part of the open debate, but no one spoke freely about his probable complicity, though Levinger's involvement cast a very dark shadow over Gush Emunim. Rabbi Levinger, to be sure, was never named by the state prosecution as a member of the underground. But he spent nearly two weeks in jail under intense interrogation, and the testimony of Menachem Livni, the "commander" of the underground, incriminated him.

By the summer of 1984, when most of the evidence against the group was made public, it was clear to the movement's heads that insofar as the underground had rabbinical authority, Levinger was the man. Several members of the network testified that he participated in the Halakhic deliberations over the Temple Mount operation, of which he disapproved, and that he gave a green light to all the terror operations of the Hebronite group.

Conscientious and moderate Gush leaders like Yoel Ben-Nun and Hanan Porat found it hard to forgive Levinger for his deviation. Rabbi Tzvi Tau, a leading Merkaz Harav authority, was even more furious. He made it clear that he would not speak to Levinger or appear in any public forum with him until he repented and denounced the underground in unequivocal terms.[121]

The most telling reaction of Gush Emunim to the crisis of the underground was to reestablish the movement's secretariat, which had been disbanded in 1979. After that, while the name Gush Emunim had continued to identify the whole sociocultural community, there had been no official body of that name. Without a Gush nerve center there had been no one to speak authoritatively for the entire movement. Amana, which might have filled this role, had instead become a very professional settlement organization. The Yesha Council spoke in the name of both Gush and non-Gush settlements, and carefully steered clear of specific Gush interests and ideological matters. As long as the informal network was cohesive and its leadership united, there had been no need for a special Gush Emunim executive—the leaders continued to meet informally and pull the strings behind Amana and the Yesha Council. But when the crises began to mount, the informality started to malfunction.

One major conclusion of the soul-searching after Yamit was that the MHRS was a poor substitute for the old Gush secretariat. Had it still been there in full force, things might have been different. Therefore many felt Gush Emunim should be "reestablished."[122] Since the death of Rabbi Zvi Yehuda Kook, people felt, the informal movement needed a spiritual authority that could pass judgment on major issues of principle. Since no leader or rabbi had Kook's stature, the role would best be filled by a council.[123] But these early crises hadn't been strong enough to prompt the reorganization of Gush Emunim. There had been much talk but very little action, until the crisis of the underground.

So the Gush Emunim secretariat was revived at the end of 1984. The movement's informal leaders surprisingly resolved that the new secretary-general of the Gush would be Daniela Weiss, a dynamic former activist of Gariin Elon Moreh and a mother of five, who immediately became the darling of the Israeli media. Weiss had a hard job reviving the spiritual credibility of the movement. She presented the whole operation not as an act of crisis management but as an attempt to add a powerful educational instrument to the existing institutions of the invisible realm of Gush Emunim. The revitalized secretariat had to polish the tarnished image of the settlers and open the eyes of all Israelis to the cultural revolution in the West Bank.

Daniela, as everyone called the dynamic new secretary, conducted long sessions with all the movement's founding fathers, intellectuals, and rabbis. Her impressive reconstruction plan called for an active executive of ten people to handle the day-to-day affairs of the movement, and a council of fifty wise men to examine spiritual and educational issues and recommend long-range strategies.[124] An additional, unstated task of the council was to eliminate unrecognized groups like the underground.

There was only one fly in the ointment: the continued shadow of the underground and the pressure of its trial. Simply reconstituting Gush Emunim could not make the underground vanish and instantly heal the bleeding wound. The trial of the terrorists and the plight of the families and friends of the prisoners continued to haunt the entire settler community. They could not ignore the court struggle of the small group who happened to be "the best and the brightest" of Gush Emunim.

And the members of the underground refused to behave like pariahs in isolation. They spoke, wrote, granted interviews, and made it clear that they believed they were acting in the name of the entire settler community. They also argued that under different circumstances other settlers would have done the same.

Their incessant appeals for support and legitimacy increased the confusion in the Gush. The great majority of the leaders and members of the movement could not, in good faith, dissociate themselves from the prisoners. Feelings of affection for the individuals involved, and a growing identification with the cause of "self-defense," led to increasing support.

This was basically the position of the new secretariat of Gush Emunim. It maintained that *Habachurim Hatovim* ("the good fellows") might have committed acts that were repulsive morally and religiously, but that the real culprit was the government, whose blunders drove the members of the group to their desperate acts.[125]

Thus, the secretariat of Gush Emunim became a party effort to have the members of the underground pardoned, lobbying the government, staging demonstrations, conducting vigils, and sponsoring petitions. The media image it projected was not the one sought by Gush Emunim's moderates, an image of an open body that rejects terrorism and violence. It was instead an image of conflict—with the government, with the legal system, and with anyone else who appeared too critical of the underground. Daniela Weiss had surprisingly become Gush Emunim's leading extremist,[126] with a sharp answer to any opponent, shaping a defiant new posture for the entire community.

Not surprisingly, a vocal minority of Emunim veterans was highly disturbed by the posture of the secretariat. Neither Daniela Weiss nor her two mentors, Moshe Levinger of Hebron and Benny Katzover of Elon Moreh, could convince Rabbis Hanan Porat, Yoel Ben-Nun, Itzhak Shilat, Menachem Fruman, and many of their supporters to keep silent. These moderates could not forget the unpublicized fact that the religious authority behind the terrorism was Rabbi Levinger himself. They were greatly disturbed by Gush Emunim's breach of an early confidential agreement not to identify in any way with the underground. They were also critical of the fact that the deliberative council of 50 elders, which was intended to become the supreme authority of the reconstructed Gush, was never convened by the secretariat extremists for fear it would dictate a different course.

Israel Harel, *Nekuda*'s editor and himself a moderate, opened his journal to the two camps. A fierce theoretical debate raged in its pages, focusing on Gush Emunim's position vis-à-vis the government and the state.[127]

Debating the Security of the Settlers

While the theoretical debate about the underground was important, the substantial controversy behind it had to do with the issue of security in the

West Bank. The main message of the underground was that the government of Israel had not provided proper security and that therefore the settlers had the full right to defend themselves.

This message, while categorically opposed by the moderates, was partially endorsed by the hawks. The latter expressed the hope that the final result of the underground affair would be, not the jailing of decent pioneers who acted out of desperation, but a change in the security policy of the government.

However, the policy was not changed, and since 1984 the hawks have increasingly been disappointed. The underground was not immediately pardoned, and Arab violence and terrorism in the West Bank intensified. The release of over a thousand Arab terrorists in exchange for three Israeli soldiers embittered Gush extremists—not only were some of the worst Palestinian murderers, convicted in court, released, but Jewish patriots who acted against these killers were kept in jail. The struggle for the release of the underground and the security of the West Bank assumed a new dimension of urgency. And in this the Gush was supported by the entire radical right, many Knesset members, and a broad public. The early denunciations of the underground were almost forgotten.

The event that triggered the next crisis between the two factions of Gush Emunim took place in April 1987, in the Arab town of Kalkiliya. A settler car driving through the town was firebombed by an Arab terrorist. A young woman, mother of three children and pregnant, was burnt to death. Her husband and two children were badly wounded.

The result was a furious vengeance raid on the town by dozens of settlers, with the active participation of Daniela Weiss. The marauders stormed through the streets, smashed apartment and car windows, and warned the frightened residents that the entire town of Kalkiliya would be held responsible for any further anti-Jewish act that occurred in its vicinity. The military units that rushed to the scene were defied by the angry protesters, and Weiss herself clashed with the soldiers, throwing rocks at them and cursing their officers. This exceptional act made the headlines of all Israel's newspaper and conquered the attention of national TV and radio.[128]

Gush Emunim was once again instantly identified with the use of brutal force and violence. What was most damaging was not the operation in Kalkiliya but the movement's direct clash with young soldiers. These were again the extralegal settlers of the 1970s who refused to obey the nation's authority, the people who forced the army to send to Yamit twenty thousand soldiers and kept them busy for months.

The Kalkiliya incident and its impact on the Israeli public were too much for the moderates to take. They realized that all their writings, arguments, and moral admonitions in the Gush councils were not taken seriously by the operational echelon of the movement. They felt betrayed and sensed that "their" Gush Emunim was being stolen from them.

Assembling all their supporters, they decided to force a showdown. Ben-

Nun, Fruman, and Porat staged a sit-in in the Jerusalem offices of the movement. Together with the moderate heads of Amana, who were extremely alarmed by the impact of the Gush posture on their efforts to attract new settlers, they demanded that Weiss be fired and that a new and representative Gush secretariat be selected. Threatening secession, they demanded that the Gush change its image and try to reach out to the entire Israeli public, not just to its extremists. They argued that the Gush could not afford to become another Kach, and that even the Israeli left was a legitimate partner in the debate.[129]

The coup attempt of the moderates was only partially successful. Moshe Levinger and Benny Katzover, the strongmen behind Daniela Weiss, were not intimidated. They knew they had a solid constituency within the community and that the moderates were not ready to fight it out all the way. They consequently convinced the ten-person secretariat of Gush Emunim, the only formal body of the movement capable of making decisions, that the status quo had to be maintained. Weiss, promising to restrain herself, was able to temporarily keep her job. The large council of the movement was never convened.

Thus while the moderates proved that their voice within the movement could not be silencedd, the radicals made it clear that they were in control. But both sides also came to realize that their mutual interests and shared beliefs were much greater than their disagreements. By 1991 there was still no substitute for the original Gush Emunim, a settlement movement committed to Eretz Yisrael in its entirety and a loyal representative of the mundane interests of many thousands of settlers. Yoel Bun-Nun and Hanan Porat needed Moshe Levinger and Benny Katzover as badly as they were needed by these extremists.

Gush Emunim, the Settler Community, and the *Intifada*

The December 1987 outbreak of the *intifada,* the Palestinian uprising in the West Bank and Gaza, surprised Gush Emunim as much as everyone else. Very few Gush members, all of them veteran settlers in the occupied territories, believed that the native Palestinians were capable of orchestrating a large uprising and of sustaining pressure on the Israeli forces.

The first reaction of the settlers to the *intifada* was that this was nothing new: Arab rioting, mob violence, and rock-throwing had become rather common in the 1980s.[130] Moreover, there was a sense of quiet satisfaction among the settlers and a feeling of relief. The wide scope of the uprising made the entire nation partner to their feeling of precarious security. It gave credence, so they believed, to their perennial demand that the Arab "terrorists" be dealt with harshly.

And the growing identification of many Israeli Arabs with the *intifada,* which was expressed by demonstrations and sabotage inside Israel proper, was, paradoxically, even more gratifying. It was seen as proof of Gush

Emunim's long-held thesis that the Green Line was meaningless and that Eretz Yisrael was indivisible.[131] Gush Emunim consequently instructed all its members to maintain as normal a life as possible, to conduct field trips and hikes as usual, and to let the army and the police worry about the Palestinians. Settler vigilantism was held to a minimum, and Amana continued to advertise new construction sites in its settlements as if nothing special was taking place.

The event that forced Gush Emunim to face the realities of the *intifada* was the Beita incident in May 1988, which we have seen took the lives of a Jewish girl and an Arab teenager, led to an angry confrontation between the settlers and the army, and produced even sharper conflict between politicians of the radical right and the army chief-of-staff.

The conflict did not help the settlers politically. The early public outrage regarding the killing of the young girl from Elon Moreh was soon replaced by an equal outrage toward the settlers who had not bothered to coordinate their field trip with the army, risked the lives of their children for the cause of Eretz Yisrael, and then dared to blame the military and the government for the incident. The image of Gush Emunim was badly tarnished by the unruly behavior of its members and key leaders.

Gush Emunim was painfully reminded that, as in earlier cases, they could not defy the army without a public backlash. Benny Katzover, the key Gush leader involved in the Beita incident, had to retract many of his statements and to recognize that even with the increased violence of the *intifada*, vigilante activity was unacceptable. Katzover and his friends later learned that even a long hunger strike in front of the prime minister's office would not move Mr. Shamir to "crush" the *intifada* or change the instructions given to the army.[132]

By the second year of the uprising, Gush Emunim was no longer able to pretend the *intifada* was only a small nuisance, and signs of anxiety among the settlers became common. A letter of a young woman to Hanan Porat and his wife, published in *Nekuda,* expressed the new anxiety and fatigue of the settlers:

> No longer am I an outside observer. I am *inside.* And the dream and the hope? Where is the great hope of my youthful days?
>
> . . . Do not misread me. I do not have a personal problem, but the reality around me is very troubling; strikes and sickness, a divided and confused political situation, a stormy intifada, low morale, lack of knowledge and resolve, lack of peace . . . . We are trying to build our own private home, but the noise of reality whistles in our ears. We try to find comfort in Rabbi Kook's writings, in the "vision of redemption," but outside there is a dark and threatening fog. . . .
>
> And I ask myself: Have I had this seed of despair in me all along? Has it been corroding my soul and diverting me from seeing all the good there is and enjoying it? Perhaps. And if this is indeed the case, how am I going . . . to face today's events and tomorrow's?
>
> Please answer me![133]

Even if Gush Emunim had been able to face the *intifada* with unity and determination fully solidified, it is most likely that the hardships of the uprising would have made a serious dent in the mental and ideological shield of its members. And indeed, in a revealing book, *Grey Wind,* published in 1990, veteran Gush member Meir Harnoi provided for the first time a somber settler picture of the ordeals of the Palestinian uprising. The *intifada* has made routine transportation in the West Bank and Gaza a hazardous endeavor, changing the entire life of the settler community. It has produced anxiety and fear, especially for the lives of the children traveling every morning to school through hostile Arab villages. Furthermore, it isolated the settlers from most Israelis who stopped traveling to the West Bank and Gaza, and was responsible for bitter conflicts between the settlers and the army. The refusal of the government to suppress the *intifada* by force and the demand of local military commanders that responses to Arab violence on the roads be extremely restrained humiliated the settlers and made them feel defenseless and deserted. And those ready to risk violent response were confronted with very difficult moral dilemmas involving the killing of hostile Arabs for self-defense and revenge.[134]

But the *intifada* came when the Gush was already maimed and politically divided. Its secretariat was hardly functioning and several of its spiritual leaders were at odds with each other. It was just a matter of time before the ideological animosities and personal grudges were exposed.

The first shot in the renewed controversy was fired by Rabbi Yoel Ben-Nun, the main spokesperson of the Gush's moderate wing. For years Ben-Nun has engaged in talks with the Israeli left, trying to reduce ideological tensions. Now he published several articles calling for a "National Conference." Responding to the controversial idea of Israel's Foreign Minister, Shimon Peres, of convening an international conference to initiate a new peace process, Ben-Nun argued that Israel was on the brink of an ideological war, and that the various parties must be brought together before the situation got out of hand. Noting that the enemies of the nation were capitalizing on Israel's internal divisions, Ben-Nun wrote that if the effort of Israel's enemies to divide it succeeded,

> it will not stop at the Green Line and it will leave us with nothing worth fighting for. This is no longer a question as to whether the right or the left wins. A forced victory by either side may rock the entire boat. This is no longer a question of ideology but a matter of survival.[135]

As patriotic and appealing as Ben-Nun's idea was, not one of his Gush Emunim rivals could ignore its political implications: the rabbi was ready to compromise the sacred principles of the Gush in order to reconstruct the badly damaged national consensus. In other essays, Ben-Nun advocated an annexation of only *part* of Judea and Samaria. Echoing a suggestion of Ariel Sharon to immediately annex the territories included in the Allon Plan, and to grant the Palestinians a limited autonomy in the rest of the truncated West

Bank, Rabbi Ben-Nun made it clear that the original dream of Gush Emunim and the extremists of the secular radical right, of an annexation of the entire West Bank to Israel, was no longer politically feasible.

> The majority of the public is for [keeping] Eretz Yisrael but opposes the annexation of 1.5 million Palestinian Arabs, and it is no longer possible to think that you can annex the territory and at the same time deny Israeli citizenship to its inhabitants. And do not live with the illusion that you can expel them. By the time the conditions for the fulfillment of Hae'etzni's plan [of taking over the entire West Bank] exist, we shall have already lost the historical opportunity and will face a retreat to the 1967 borders.[136]

Ben-Nun's determination to take into account the political realities and present historical opportunities of Israel did not prevent him from addressing the theological part of the problem, the question of redemption. He clearly disagreed with the millennarian vision of Gush Emunim's extremists who hoped for an immediate redemption in which all problems would be resolved by God: "He who cannot see any step but a full redemption, followed by peace and complete tranquillity, is impatient. At present we have no completion at hand, neither a complete land nor a complete nation."[137] And in a direct attack on Rabbi Moshe Levinger—who declared that the time had come for Gush Emunim to transform the nation to a new era of redemption, the elevated stage of *Mashiach Ben-David* ("Messiah, the Son of David," an era that supersede the lower stage of Messiah the Son of Yoseph—Ben Nun wrote:

> The announcement regarding the end of the "Mashiach Ben-Yosef" era is dangerous. This proposition guided ... the thought of Yehuda Etzion[the ideologue of the Jewish Underground who wanted to bring about an instant redemption through blowing up the Dome of the Rock]. . . . It is possible to blow things up, and it is possible to go it alone. It is very easy to "kill now" "Mashiach Ben-Yosef"—i.e., Zionism, the State of Israel, and everything that has been achieved in the present generation.[138]

Rabbi Ben-Nun has never been an easy target for the Gush Emunim hard-liners, for he has rarely depended on the organizational network of the movement. But the hawks were able to strike at Moni Ben-Ari, the secretary-general of Amana. Ben-Ari, a secular settler in Kfar Edomim, was never a member of the inner circle of Gush Emunim. Nevertheless over the years he has become an exemplary figure in the movement: a paratrooper commander, a brilliant settlement planner and educator, and a natural leader. Ben-Ari, who was Gush Emunim's major showcase for the settlement cohabitation of religious and secular Jews, has been for years one of the most effective architects of Amana.[139] Although in the 1980s he became increasingly critical of the radicalization of Gush Emunim and its messianic sectarianism, Ben-Ari was the natural candidate for the top job in Amana once its then secretary-general, Uri Ariel, was asked to head the Yesha Council.[140] His 1988 election as the settlement movement's head, the first nomination of a secular Jew to a top Gush Emunim position, was highly publicized. It was paraded as proof of the "openness" of the movement and its "national" character.

But just a year later Ben-Ari was kicked out. While being interviewed for a planned personal profile, Ben-Ari told *Nekuda*'s reporter that he had privately discussed with prime minister Shamir his own peace plan. Like Ben-Nun's idea, it divided the West Bank into "security zones," which were to be immediately annexed to Israel, and territories designated for Palestinian autonomy overseen by Israel.[141] Although Ben-Ari's plan, like Ben-Nun's, was conceptually unacceptable to Israeli moderates and the rest of the world, since it proposed the immediate annexation of two-thirds of Judea and Samaria, Ben-Ari was immediately punished. Having broken the sacred code of the movement's hard-liners, he could not stay in office.

The rift within Gush Emunim widened further in the spring of 1989. After several Gush activists conducted a series of anti-Arab operations and were publicly supported by leading rabbis, Rabbi Yoel Ben-Nun announced that he could no longer remain a member of Gush Emunim. This was the first defection of an original founder of the movement. It could only be seen as a major blow to Gush Emunim, all of whose rhetoric has been focused on the need to unite the nation.

The sequence of events that led to Ben-Nun's secession began in March 1989 with an intense wave of settler vigilantism in the West Bank. What was new about this vigilantism was that it was led by non-ideological settlers of urban centers such as Ariel, Alfei Menashe, and Ma'ale Edomim. After the Beita incident, Gush Emunim reduced its anti-Arab activities to a minimum, but the unorganized urban settlers became steadily more impatient. Palestinian rebels in the West Bank have not limited their *intifada* operations to Gush Emunim settlements and have become a serious threat even on the 'safe' roads between towns.[142]

The killing of several Jews by Arab-thrown Molotov cocktails consequently produced several massive raids into Arab villages and confrontations with the army. This resulted in a growing feeling in Israel that the government and the army were losing control and that a Jewish *counterintifada* was about to produce total anarchy in the occupied territories. Shamir's readiness to hold elections among the Palestinians of the West Bank in order to advance the peace process added to the security misery of the settlers.[143]

At this point, Rabbi Moshe Levinger was charged with killing an Arab bystander in Hebron, and several yeshiva students from the Tomb of Yosef in Nablus were arrested for killing a young girl and destroying property on a raid in the Arab village Kief el-Hares. However, it was not these brutal acts of retribution that triggered the new storm inside Gush Emunim but their theological justification. At his trial, Rabbi Levinger told Judge Hadaiya that it was all a big frame-up. "There must be some order and justice here.

The prosecution submitted 1500 pages about me killing an Arab. *I did not kill an Arab, but I wish I did.*[144] Rabbi Ginzburg, the head of the Tomb of Yosef yeshiva in Nablus, responded to reports of his students' terrorism by saying that there is blood and there is blood and that Jewish blood is not the same as Arab blood. According to Torah injunction, "He who is not a Jew, and throws stones or threaten Jews goes under the rule 'he who comes to kill you, you should kill him first.' "[145] In announcing his departure from Gush Emunim in June 1989, Rabbi Yoel Ben-Nun did not call for the establishment of a new Gush, loyal to the movement's original ideas. He also did not say he was leaving his settlement, Ofra. Instead, he stated that he could no longer live under the same ideological roof with Rabbis Levinger and Ginzburg and the many other Halakhic authorities who were either supportive of their positions or remained silent. The act was thus mostly symbolic and declarative.

While the Levinger—Ben-Nun scuffles have damaged the ideological integrity of Gush Emunim, and tarnished its public image, they have had surprisingly little impact on the organization of the settler community and on Gush Emunim's "Invisible Realm." By the end of 1989 it was clear that the heads of Amana and Yesha Council were successful in controlling the damages of the *intifada* and internal conflicts. The warring sides continued to argue about such issues as the continued decline of the Gush Emunim secretariat,[146] the unnecessary expansion of Jewish presence in Nablus, exemplified by the high-profile ceremony for the introduction of a Torah Scroll to the Tomb of Yoseph yeshiva,[147] and the loud procession that escorted Rabbi Levinger to jail, in May 1990.[148] But the real action took place elsewhere, involving the addition of several thousand new members to the settler community, and its continued socioeconomic growth. The powerful mechanisms of state support to the settlers, set in motion between 1978–1984, and the very able leadership of the heads of the Yesha Council, were apparently strong enough to keep the flow of public budgets and new settlers to Judea, Samaria, and Gaza. By end of 1990 there were in the occupied territories between 90,000 to 100,000 settlers. New idealistic settlers were being absorbed in Gush Emunim settlements, and the newly created Likud coalition promised to build in the West Bank, until the 1992 general elections, 7000 additional housing units, with an absorbing capacity of between 20,000 to 30,000 settlers.[149]

Two developments made this progress possible: the decline of the *intifada* and the crisis of Israel's unity coalition. The *intifada*, which reached its peak at the end of 1988 and the beginning of 1989, has lost in 1990 much of its momentum. After months of confusion and disorientation, the Israeli army had regained the initiative and was able to apply effective measures against Arab rioters. Dramatic world events such as the fall of the Berlin Wall and the democratic revolutions in Eastern Europe removed the Palestinian uprising from the headline news. Relatively poor, largely isolated, and politically unsophisticated, the Palestinians of the West Bank and Gaza had not given up their uprising but were unable to impress the world and push Israel into concessions.

The decline of the *intifada* was among the reasons for the 1990 demise of the Likud-Labor Unity cabinet, a strange coalition that ruled Israel since 1984. It helped eliminate the relative moderation adopted earlier by Itzhak Shamir, Israel's prime minister, vis-à-vis the Palestinians and the PLO, and was instrumental in fomenting a governmental crisis of the first order. The unity coalition was very bad for Gush Emunim. It forced the Likud to compromise its commitment to the settlement of the occupied territories, isolated the radical right, and made the settler community extremely dependent on unfriendly ministers such as Itzhak Rabin (Defense), and Shimon Peres (Treasury). The demise of the Unity Government and the June 1990 success of Itzhak Shamir to form a narrow right-wing coalition were a great relief. Having Labor out, and Yuval Ne'eman, Geula Cohen, and Rafael Eitan inside the government, was about the greatest thing that happened to Gush Emunim since 1982. The future of the Jewish endeavor in the occupied territories, which for a few years looked bleak, seemed again reassured.

6

The Radical Right
in Parliament: The Tehiya
and Its Political Offspring

Making It to the Knesset

While Gush Emunim has provided the pioneering spirit and institutional infrastructure for the radical right, the Tehiya party has represented it in Israel's established politics. In a political system dominated by party politics, the Tehiya fulfills the classical function of a party. It aggregates many of the political interests of the radical right and articulates them in parliament. It also represents these interests in the media and puts them on the nation's public agenda. Just as Gush Emunim has been a success in settling the occupied territories, the Tehiya party has been a parliamentary success story. Although it failed to break the Camp David Accords, it was very effective in crystallizing an anti-peace bloc in Israel. In 1981 the Tehiya won three Knesset seats (out of 120), and made itself an indispensable partner of the Likud government that found itself entangled in Lebanon. As we have seen, the Tehiya's leader, Yuval Ne'eman, became Israel's minister of science and energy and the chairman of the powerful settlement committee of the cabinet.

After the 1984 elections, the Tehiya became Israel's third-largest party, with five Knesset seats. Despite its refusal to join the unity coalition between the Likud and the Labor alignment, its popularity has risen. Since 1984 opinion polls have been giving the Tehiya and its allies the support of between 6 and 8 percent of the voters. The leaders of the party have been successful in bringing under one roof both religious and secular Jews and in presenting to the public a convincing and credible leadership.

At first glance, the Tehiya appears as the parliamentary wing of Gush Emunim. Three of its top six candidates for the twelfth Knesset, Rabbi Eliezer Waldman, Gershon Shafat, and Benny Katzover, are known Gush leaders. None of the public stands taken by Gush Emunim is ever contested by the secular leadership of the party, and no effort is spared to glorify the Gush and back its public struggles.

Nevertheless, significant cultural and social differences exist between the two. Gush Emunim is a homogeneous revitalization movement whose main concern is the settlement of the West Bank. Despite recent ideological controversies, all members of the Gush agree on fundamental principles and live within the same exclusive *Weltanschauung;* they are settlers in the occupied territories and live the struggle for Judea and Samaria twenty-four hours a day. Most of them are in their thirties or forties; only a few of their leaders are older than fifty.

The Tehiya, on the contrary, is an ordinary political party. Only a few of its members, the elected Knesset representatives and several officials, are full-time Tehiya people. The rest are part-time activists, supporters, and voters who have many other concerns in their life. The secular heads of the Tehiya are older than their Gush Emunim colleagues and are rooted in Israel's defense, science, and settlement establishment, or are journalists and business persons.

Until 1987, the Tehiya party was the sole representative of the "constructive" radical right (as opposed to Kach's "destructive" radicalism) in Israel's parliamentary politics. But other parties contested the territory when former Chief of Staff Rafael Eitan known universally as Raful split from the Tehiya, and when the *Moledet* (Homeland) party emerged under General Rehavam Ze'evi.

Eitan, who joined the Tehiya in 1984 with his Tzomet (Crossroads) group, was never too happy with this arrangement. Though he supported most of the Tehiya's political platform, he became increasingly alienated by the religious and quasi-religious style of many of its leaders, particularly of the vociferous Geula Cohen.[1]

The tension reached a crisis in 1987 when both Eitan and Cohen tried to take over the party by placing their supporters in the organization's key positions, causing a showdown in the party's general convention. Yuval Ne'eman, the leader of the Tehiya, decided to prevent what appeared to be a pro-Eitan coup,and Eitan left the party. Soon he reestablished Tzomet and appealed to his natural constituency: the hard-core Labor people, the Northern border settlements, and the former soldiers who had served under his command.

Ne'eman, Cohen, and their colleagues have contained the damage and preserved the party's integrity, but the split was nevertheless costly. Thus, while Tzomet was able to place two representatives in the Twelfth Knesset, the Tehiya representation was reduce to only three seats. But the diminution of the Tehiya did not result in a decline of the parliamentary radical right. On the contrary, the opinion polls before the 1988 election indicated a growing electoral appeal for the message of this camp.

Against this background another radical aspirant, Rehavam Ze'evi (universally known as "Gandhi"), a recognized Israeli reserve general, concluded that there was room for another ultranationalist party. Since 1985 he has been publicly recommending a "transfer"—an agreed-upon removal of all the Arabs of the occupied territories to the neighboring Arab countries. This was the platform of his new party, Moledet. Ze'evi himself was surprised by the results. Following a short, underfinanced, and understaffed campaign, both he and his colleague Professor Yair Sprinzak were elected to the Knesset.[2]

The Tehiya has survived Raful's secession and the start of Moledet, and is by now a permanent presence in national politics, but it has not fulfilled its original high expectations. When the new group was organized in 1979, it was intended to be more than an ordinary Israeli political party. The organization's founders—especially Geula Cohen and Hanan Porat—longed for the establishment of a qualitatively different entity, something that Israel had not seen before, a cohesive secular-religious movement.[3] Inspired by the Kookist theology, the founders expected the new party to overcome the isolated orthodoxy of Gush Emunim and, through a total commitment to a spirited Zionist program, to become a real bridge between religious and secular Jews:

> We have emerged today to lay the foundations for a new movement—the renaissance movement . . . to establish a living movement; not only a party that focuses on parliamentary activity, but a movement that organically brings together ideological and educational action, pioneering initiatives, and political activity that strives toward the leadership of the nation.[4]

The key element of the new movement was to be the *chavurot*, intimate groups intended to revive the old spirit of living Zionism, involvement, and self-sacrifice. The *chavurot* were to demonstrate the bankruptcy of the other Israeli parties. How this was to be accomplished was stated in the Tehiya's first manifesto:

> A living movement does not become flesh and blood through the polls on election day. . . .
> The strength of the Tehiya movement will be fulfilled in its members, activists that daily go out to initiate a permanent partnership in shaping the thinking of the movement and crystallizing its leadership in the nation.
> These members-activists will be cemented in *chavurot*. . . . The living connection with the movement will be based on the living connection within the chavurot themselves, first and foremost.
> Internally, the chavura will develop human relationships of fraternity and daily partnership in carrying the burden. Externally, the chavura will assume the responsibility for the accomplishment of the movement's goals.[5]

But in reality there was never a chance that the notables who gathered in 1979 would really form a fresh and innovative movement. Yuval Ne'eman, the man who first wrote against Camp David, was asked by his friends to be the Tehiya leader, but he was not temperamentally suited to lead a youthful, revitalizing movement. Cool, rational, and aloof, he has always spoken with the voice of reason. Only one issue mattered to him—Israel's security, which he believed had been jeopardized by the 1978 Camp David accords. Only that issue could cause the former president of Tel Aviv University to sacrifice his brilliant academic career.

Similar security-minded reserve officers joined the Tehiya with the same attitude. They were too old for *chavurot* and confessional politics. Other veterans of right-wing politics in their sixties and seventies came out of the Land of Israel Movement. They were devoted to the cause of Eretz Yisrael but were not the young and energetic group the writers of the manifesto envisioned. The same was true of three other groups that became the Tehiya's main pillars: the Ein Vered Circle, Tzomet, and the "Veterans of the Underground."

The Ein Vered Circle, it will be recalled, came together in 1975 to support the illicit settlement efforts of Gush Emunim. All the participants, members of kibbutzim and moshavim, belonged to the Labor Settlement Movement and were opposed to the Allon Plan. Like the surviving LIM activists, they believed in the importance of the settlement of the West Bank, but were less ideological and bitter. They wanted to share their rich settlement experience with the new pioneers of Gush Emunim, who reminded them of their own glorious youthful days. However, being elderly members of prestigious settlement organizations, they were bad candidates for a new youthful political movement. Moreover, by the time Tehiya was formed, Ein Vered was not very active; Gush Emunim, for whose sake its members had rallied during the Labor administration, did not need their services in the Likud era. Nor did they share the emotional anguish of the betrayed former allies of Menachem Begin that led to the establishment of the Tehiya.[6] In 1979, only a few individuals from Ein Vered joined the Tehiya.

The real revival of this group, in the form of Tzomet, took place in 1983 when General Rafael Eitan retired from his military service. Raful, a symbolic figure reminiscent of old Eretz Yisrael, gathered around him veteran Ein Vered members and new Labor Settlement activists who were enraged by the Israeli "defeat" in Lebanon and critical of the performance of the Likud government in economics and social affairs.[7] Mobilized by the leadership of the prestigious general, they established Tzomet and considered running their own ticket in the 1984 elections. They eventually decided to join the Tehiya, but only for political reasons that had nothing to do with *chavurot*.

The "Veterans of the Underground"—old members of the Irgun and Lehi—represented in the Tehiya councils by Geula Cohen, did join the new party for ideological reasons. But many were disappointed Likud activists and had tasted political power. As much as they wanted a "movement" and *chavurot*, a theme promoted by Geula Cohen, they were also anxious to get real power. They did not seriously expect to take over the government, but the Knesset would provide a visible forum from which to speak to the nation, and it was, even for these critics, a prestigious social club. While they did not exclude direct, movement-wide action, they were too old for grass-roots revival operations all over the country.

It thus became obvious that the only people likely to build the Tehiya as a dynamic social movement, and to staff its *chavurot,* were the enthusiastic youngsters of Gush Emunim. But they, of course, already had a movement, organized in small settlements and yeshivot. The whole idea of the *chavurot* was to expand the Gush Emunim experience to the entire nation and have secular Jews organize and function as the Gush youngsters had been doing in the West Bank. But this vision was no more than the wishful thinking of a few dreamers who were so alarmed by the "disaster" of Camp David that they convinced themselves that they could start a new Zionist revolution.

The person who first understood the failure of the Tehiya as a movement of national revival was Hanan Porat, Gush Emunim's most conscientious leader. In 1979 Porat, excited over the emergence of the Tehiya, recommended that the Gush endorse the new movement unequivocally and asked all its members to join. The issue created a serious rift between Porat and the other charismatic leader of Gush Emunim, Rabbi Moshe Levinger, who thought Porat's endorsement naïve and wrong.

By 1983 it was clear that Levinger was right. The disappointed Porat, in an uncommon gesture, gave up his Tehiya Knesset seat and withdrew to his kibbutz. Though Porat did not attack or criticize the Tehiya, his resignation implied an admission that the movement's great dream was gone. What Porat had discovered was that while the party promoted the right ideology and politics, it was unable to bridge the cultural gap between secular and religious Israelis and was not leading the way in establishing a new existential reality.

Furthermore, the Tehiya also had not appealed to the variegated world of the Zionist yeshivot, religious settlements, and Zionist religious education—institutions always dear to Porat. The secular members of the party did not put a high premium on its slogan *Holchim beyahad* ("Going together"—secular and religious), and never considered challenging the prevailing religious status quo, an arrangement that dominated Zionist politics since the 1930s. Nor were they asked to do so by their religious colleagues. They made no collective move in the direction of greater observance or religious repentance. And they did not progress toward a greater "understanding" of the "true Zionism of our time," the Emunist Zionism. Porat consequently explained his resignation by talking about the Tehiya's,

> inability to fly high the flag of the ideals of Torah and faith and of the full return to Jewish life in its utmost depths. There were people within the Tehiya who could personally express these ideals, but the movement as a whole did not have the strength to say it in full force. The lack of such an announcement in the name of G–d is a terrible want in the course of Zionism.[8]

Several of his colleagues shared the idealistic Porat's disappointment that the Tehiya was unable to become an enlarged Gush Emunim. Nevertheless, few joined him in his new political venture with Rabbi Haim Drukman, the establishment of the religious Matzad movement.[9]

In 1983, though, the other Gush leaders involved in the Tehiya were rather pleased with it. They had not entertained as high expectations as Porat and were ready to live with the new arrangement: that the party would support certain religious legislation in the Knesset and that it would always have between 30 and 40 percent religious representation on the party's top candidate list for the Knesset and other official positions. They knew there was no chance the Tehiya would convert its secular activists to orthodox Judaism, and they supported it in line with their longstanding policy of not placing all the Gush's eggs in one basket.[10]

Rabbi Eliezer Waldman and Gershon Shafat remained in the Tehiya, and as Knesset members have continued to exert great influence within its internal councils. Younger Gush Emunim activists like Benny Katzover and Daniela Weiss have joined the party too. They became prominent activists inside its secretariat, and making sure that on policy issues Gush Emunim's views and requirements were constantly represented.

Transferring the Arabs

One of the most controversial terms associated with the Israeli radical right, and the larger periphery of the Tehiya since 1987, has been the concept of *transfer*—a shorthand for the removal of the Palestinians of the occupied territories and their resettlement in the neighboring Arab countries. The concept was first raised in public by Rehavam Ze'evi, a reserve general and well-known Israeli hawk. Ze'evi argued that the old idea of transfer, a legacy of a series of *yishuv* debates in Mandatory Palestine of the 1930s, was relevant to the present situation in the West Bank and Gaza. He maintained that since the West Bank and Gaza were essential for the security of Israel and their million and a half hostile Palestinians were a mortal liability, the local residents had to be transferred out.

When his idea received positive responses from all over the country, he decided to run for the Knesset. For his list he was successful in attracting several disgruntled Tehiya members, such as Zvi Shiloah and Yair Sprinzak. Both of these LIM veterans were bitter over the Tehiya's decision to join the Likud coalition in 1982 and over its "moderate" and "unprincipled" stand on Eretz Yisrael.[11] Shiloach, who had written earlier about the transfer idea in his book, *A Great Land for Great People*,[12] confided that the whole ideology was crystallized during a seminar he conducted in 1985 for several Israeli hard-liners, including Ze'evi.[13] Ze'evi's list, *Moledet* (Homeland), made the transfer concept the sole plank in its platform, even choosing the letter T as its election symbol.

The introduction of *transfer* to the nation's public agenda in 1987 indicates another step in the radicalization of the extreme right. In 1984 the only party that called for the removal of the Arabs was Kach of Rabbi Kahane. At the time, everyone, including most of the radical right, saw Kahane as a racist and considered his opinions beyond the pale. Even those who agreed with Kahane in principle felt it was dangerous to spell out the idea in public; since 1948 it had been inadvisable for Israelis to talk about a transfer. To broach the idea would have implied a willingness to create another "Arab refugee problem"—the single issue most damaging to Israel in the international arena.

But in the mid-1980s the public climate changed dramatically. The organized campaign against Kahane and his racism after 1984 helped solidify the opposition of the center and the left to his ideas, but it had no effect on the growing camp of the radical right. The increasing friction between Jews and Arabs in the West Bank, the *intifada,* and the intense Palestinization of the Israeli Arabs produced an atmosphere in which any radical solution was seen as legitimate.

Rehavam Ze'evi, who voiced the transfer solution, was original in only one respect: he identified the switch in the nation's public opinion before many of his other colleagues. Ze'evi was, for many years, a political pariah. He had been a legendary Palmach fighter, but had earned a bad reputation while serving as the chief of the Central Command of the Israeli army. Repeated press reports portrayed him as a corrupt general who had been using the military for his own pleasure, material interests, and publicity. Others had stressed his brutality and his tendency to threaten opponents with physical force.[14] In the late 1970s he was involved, as a civilian, in a serious scandal. Several of his friends were identified and arrested as the leaders of Israel's organized crime. Ze'evi's name was repeatedly mentioned with those of notorious criminals, and he was involved in a long and damaging libel suit against Israel's most influential daily, *Ha'aretz.* The selection of Ze'evi to direct the Eretz Yisrael Museum in Tel Aviv did not much improve his public image.

Ze'evi's decision to return to public life waving the transfer banner was a comeback attempt. He knew that no party would ever place him high on its Knesset list; his only chance for political power was to go it alone and try something new. In choosing the transfer theme, he took into consideration the fact that Kahane would probably be disqualified in the 1988 elections, which would release many thousands of votes committed to the eviction of the Arabs.

Ze'evi's gamble proved successful. His slogan *"Anachnu-kan, hemsham, veshalom al Yisrael!"* ("We are here, they are there, and peace for Israel!") had a tremendous appeal.[15] The three-month-old Moledet party, which had no experience or money, surprisingly sent two representatives to the Knesset. Joining Ze'evi was the retired professor of chemistry, Yair Sprinzak, the son of Israel's first speaker and a veteran LIM writer. He had let Ze'evi put his name on the list in order to provide Moledet with minimal public respectability, and suddenly found himself in the Knesset at the age of seventy-seven.[16]

The most important difference between Ze'evi's *transfer* and Kahane's *eviction* is that Ze'evi speaks about an "an agreed-upon" transfer while Kahane recommended a forced, one-sided, expulsion of the Arabs. Ze'evi says that the idea of an exchange of population should be presented by Israel as its main demand in any future peace negotiation with the Arabs. He does not expect the local Palestinians to be happy about the transfer, but argues that if the solution is imposed by Israel and the Arab nations as part of a final peace treaty, the moral agony involved would greatly diminish.

Ze'evi is very resentful of the analogies that are made between him and Kahane. He argues that, unlike Kahane's brutal solution, which has no precedent in the history of Zionism, his recommendations are legitimate reformulations of transfer ideas discussed by many respected Zionists since the emergence of the movement. The platform of Moledet is full of quotations from the founders of Israel, as well as from prominent Israeli politicians like the former generals Itzhak Rabin and Mordechai Gur, stating the need to have an Israel free of Arabs.[17]

Ze'evi's strongest point is his repeated reference to the transfer that actually took place in 1948. He quotes many expressions of satisfaction and joy made by Israel's most distinguished leaders regarding the blessing of the Arab flight during and after the 1948 War of Independence. There is a tremendous hypocrisy, Ze'evi argues, in the ferocious accusations of racism and Kahanism leveled against him by many leftist members of kibbutzim whose homes are built on former Arab soil,

> Kahane talks about eviction, we speak about a transfer. An eviction is neither practical nor political. And it is cruel too. The transfer must be the first item in any negotiation with the Arabs, be it a direct negotiation or an international conference. We have to create here a negative magnet that would encourage the Arabs to leave. Moshe Dayan was wrong, in 1967, when he opened the bridges [across the Jordan River]. Had we created a barrier between the local Arabs who had been working in the Arab countries, and their families, they would have taken their families out. There was no need to establish seven universities or to help them develop agriculture. The entire government policy ought to be changed, to establish settlements, to move to the West Bank hundred of thousands of Jews, and to create a situation in which both the Arabs and the Jews will understand that there is no alternative but a separation of powers.[18]

Critics of Moledet argue that since no Arab leader would ever agree to a transfer, its "good" intentions would lead, in practice, to a unilateral eviction of the Arabs. Against such criticisms, which focus on the practical absurdities involved in their plan, Ze'evi and Sprinzak point out that Zionism was never fully realistic in its demands, but many of its "unrealistic" plans were ultimately realized. Wars and unexpected developments have played an important role in the building of modern Israel, and may in the future.

Further, they argue, there are things short of forced eviction that the government of Israel can do to make the transfer a realistic option: stop employing Arabs in Israel's economy, therefore forcing Palestinian workers to seek jobs in Arab countries, as they did before 1967; discourage the development of industry in the West Bank, as King Hussein of Jordan did when he controlled the area; close all West Bank universities and colleges, instead sending the young intelligentsia to the Arab world for education. The entire Israeli policy on the occupied territories has been, according to the Moledet analysis, disastrous. Israel should long since have sponsored the transfer solution. Nevertheless, it is not too late to change Israeli policy on the West Bank, and in any event Israel really has no alternative.[19]

Although the transfer solution has been mostly associated with Ze'evi, others outside the Kahane camp have come to favor it since 1986. Soon after Ze'evi's first statement, Michael Dekel, a Likud Knesset member and Israel's deputy minister of defense, made a similar declaration. Dekel, a confidant of Itzhak Shamir, did not get the endorsement of his leader or of the Likud, and the party line continued to support Camp David. Nevertheless his statement lent the idea great respectability.

Despite the furor among the left about the growing "Kahanism" of the Likud, Dekel did not retract his words. Instead he stated that he really meant *repatriation,* and not transfer, as a solution for both Arab and Jewish refugees. Answering his skeptical critics, he asked, Why should not the Iraqi ruling party, a minority Sunni group in control of a large Shi'ite population, be interested in several hundred thousand West Bank Sunnis? Could not we use the great Iranian Shi'ite threat to Iraq to solve both our and their problems satisfactorily? Or, why shouldn't Jordan, after reaching a peace agreement with Israel, be interested in strengthening its position in the Arab world by having more citizens?[20] Voices within the Likud made it clear that Dekel's solution did not fall on deaf ears.

The idea gained acceptability at the general convention of the Tehiya party, held in Kiryat Arba in 1986. Discussing the new platform of the party, Ne'eman suggested that any peace with the Arabs would require, among other things, the resettlement of all Palestinian refugees, living in camps in the West Bank and Gaza, in the Arab world.[21] To be sure, the Tehiya had always considered Arab emigration from the West Bank and Gaza highly desirable. But in its earlier platforms it had constantly advocated the "three alternatives" plan of Gush Emunim, which offered the option of emigration as only one of three possibilities.

This orientation changed before the elections of 1988. In discussing the demographic problem, the Tehiya did not conceal its opinion that the problem of most Palestinian Arabs could be solved by transfer, just as the problem of millions of Greeks and Turks was resolved in 1923, or the problem of over million French (and Jewish) citizens of Algeria in 1962. A 1988 Tehiya question-and-answer pamphlet reminded the reader that in Israel's war of independence, 600,000 Arabs left the territory of Israel, and a similar number of Jews immigrated from the Arab countries. "Indeed," it continued,

> there is nothing wrong in principle in an agreed-upon population exchange [transfer], as was conducted between Turkey and Greece, in 1923. . . .
> In summation, we are in favor of a demand to settle the 650,000 refugees outside of our borders. Such a demand, which involves the resolution of a humanitarian problem that the world ought to recognize, suits even the moral and impossible norms that the Israeli left and *"yefei hanefesh"* ["the beautiful souls"—Israel's intellectuals] are trying to force upon us.[22]

Thus, the difference between the manifest transfer of Moledet and the "latent" transfer of the Tehiya is that the former recommends the removal of all the Arabs of the occupied territories while the Tehiya only speaks about the refugees. Tzomet, while similarly avoiding the transfer concept, also sees the political expediency of the removal of the Arab population of the refugee camps from the occupied territories. Its 1987 Kiryat Shmone Convention passed a resolution supporting "an exchange of population as a way to terminate violent confrontations and hostile operations."[23] Its platform leaves no doubt that "as a part of every peace agreement, the residents of the refugee camps inside Eretz Yisrael will be rehabilitated *in the Arab countries* and the remaining Jews in the Arab countries will immigrate to Israel."[24]

The Ideological World of the Tehiya and Its Satellites

One of the typical features of the Tehiya and its political offspring is that while they all project a very ideological image, they are devoid of any original thinking. Neither the Tehiya nor Tzomet nor Moledet has within its ranks an innovative political thinker who has written anything of significance on Israeli Zionism in its post-1967 configuration. The Tehiya especially remains what its founding parent, the Land of Israel Movement, always was: a coalition of old Zionist schools. Eliezer Livneh's original theory, which has been disproved by the developments of the 1970s and 1980s, is rarely mentioned, and its leaders, when in need of a fundamental ideology, draw upon the past, upon the pre-1948 Zionist thinking.[25]

The same is true of Tzomet and Moledet. Though Raful is an anti-intellectual who says he does not need "an ideology," the message of his party clearly spells out the traditional presuppositions of the Labor Settlement Movement.[26] Eretz Yisrael can be redeemed only by hard work and down-to-earth pioneers, people who are ready to fight and die for every piece of a cultivated Jewish land. Moledet, the "transfer" party, is very conscious of its need for a legitimizing set of ideas and symbols—so much so that its heads are at pains to prove that their "extremist" solution draws upon the historical luminaries of the Labor movement, Berl Katznelson, Itzhak Tabenkin, and David Ben-Gurion.[27]

A concrete reminder of the ideological roots of the Tehiya's various schools may be found in the party's chamber in the Knesset.[28] The walls bear the portraits of Itzhak Tabenkin, the ideologist of Hakibutz Hameuchad, who believed in the redemption of Eretz Israel through collective agricultural settlement; of Abraham Stern (Yair) the founder of Lehi, who wanted to achieve the same goal through force and military conquest; of Rabbi Avrham Yitzhak Hacohen Kook, the revered founder of Merkaz Harav; and of Vladimir Jabotinsky, who has never agreed to give up the East Bank of the Jordan. None of the present leaders of the Tehiya cares that some of these historical figures were bitter enemies; they are in fact proud of the maximalist alliance they have forged among the old warring ideologues.

Nonetheless, the parliamentary radical rightists have theoretical arguments aplenty and can express themselves in writing. Several write profusely. Dr. Israel Eldad and Geula Cohen have long been writing columns for some of Israel's most respected newspapers. The Tehiya's Elyakim Ha'etzni has at least one long essay in every issue of *Nekuda*. Secular radicals like Moshe Ben-Yosef also write for national newspapers and regularly publish in *Nekuda*. Yuval Ne'eman and Yair Sprinzak are welcomed commentators in many journals and newspapers, and Zvi Shiloah, the former editor of *Zot Ha'aretz*, is also noted for copious writing.

Thus, though the secular radical right has no original philosophy, it definitely has an ideological framework, a distinct cast of mind, and a symbolic system, all of which differ significantly from both the Kookist world of Gush Emunim and the religious thinking of Rabbi Kahane. Needless to say, the Gush Emunim activists who form an essential part of the Tehiya party do not share this ideational world, but they have no problem living with it on a day-to-day basis. What the parliamentary radical right consists of, therefore, is a special blend of secular ultranationalism that is marked by several key themes.

An Unselective Idealization of the Yishuv Experience

All the spokespersons of the parliamentary radical right draw their inspiration from "the old Eretz Yisrael," and confer a great emotional value upon the pre-state struggle of the Zionist pioneers. The attachment is almost completely unselective. It betrays a strong inclination to create a myth, the myth of the yishuv's golden age. The bitter and bloody conflicts between the opposing Zionist schools of the yishuv are ignored; the period is seen as better than the inferior present in all ways.

The thinkers of the present radical right propound a highly critical conception of *Zionist regression.* The crisis of Camp David was only the steepest slide in a much broader process of national degeneration, a continuous failure to live up to the expectations of the classic pioneering Zionism. Modern Israel faces, they feel, a total collapse: in security and foreign policy, in the economy and society, in public morality, and in nationalist-Zionist commitment. There is one source for all these maladies: "a loss of faith in the course of the renaissance . . . and its conversion into a very narrow triangle which starts and ends up with 'I-Here-Now.' "[29] The purpose of the "process of renaissance" was, and is, a full collective revival of the Jewish nation in all its ancient land and a complete return to the nation's spiritual roots. The purpose of the Tehiya is to stop the degeneration and start anew:

> We have come today to establish a new movement—a renaissance movement. . . . It is necessary to start anew and to reconnect to the process of redemption. . . . In the course of the return to Zion, which started in the last generations, solid foundations have been laid for the redemption of Israel: the ingathering of the exiled, building the land and its settlement, the expulsion of the foreign rulers, the establishment of the state and its solidification, freeing Eretz Yisrael territories focused on the reunited Jerusalem, and the emergence of a solid Jewish society which works and lives on its own land."[30]

The Tehiya's first manifesto contains a masterful compromise among the various Zionist traditions of its founders. Modern (secular) Zionism is not mentioned, while the modern "Jewish renaissance" is, in keeping with Gush Emunim's ideas. And while the emphasis on the expulsion of the foreign rulers pays homage to the former members of the Irgun and Lehi, the mentions of settlement and construction refer to the Labor tradition. The Tehiya Manifesto thus is not a Gush Emunim document. It takes into consideration some of the Kookist symbolic sensitivities without giving up its secular ultranationalist content.

A comparative examination of the 1979 Tehiya manifesto and the 1967 proclamation of its parent organization, the Land of Israel Movement, is very revealing. The LIM echoed what seemed to be the peak of Zionism, the 1967 victory of the Six-Day War. If it had any doubts about the general evolution of Zionism, they hardly showed. The LIM consequently had the leisure to be an ideological single-issue movement struggling against a weak camp of Israeli moderates who thought that territories could be traded for peace.

The Tehiya, which shares all the LIM dreams, is in contrast very bitter and critical. Having gone through the hostile Rabin administration of the mid-1970s and the Begin 1978 "betrayal," it feels that the entire Zionist venture is at risk and that desperate action is needed to save it. The Tehiya, therefore, is not a single-issue movement but a political party with a comprehensive vision. The grand myth of pioneering Zionism is adopted as a creed and the challenge is presented not to one specific policy of the present regime but to the thinking of the entire Israeli establishment. The leaders of the Tehiya do not leave a single doubt that their new movement will "strive . . . for the leadership of the country."[31] They imply that all the other political descendants of the Zionist tradition have deserted it and that they are the only ones who can save the nation. Tzomet and Moledet, especially the latter, are not as broad as the Tehiya in their platforms but seem to deliver the same message.[32]

The State of Israel and the Question of Democracy

The writings of the main ideologues and spokespersons of the secular radical right do not reveal any systematic thinking about the role of the state in public life or any conscious attempt to work out a concept of a state that differs from traditional conceptions held by Labor, Revisionist, or General Zionism. This is somewhat surprising, given the intense preoccupation of Gush Emunim and Kach with questions such as the nature of the desired Halakha state. It would seem that the secular ideologues of the radical right intentionally avoid the issue for two main reasons: (a) they do not have a distinct conception of a state that differs from traditional pre-1967 Zionist ideas; (b) to admit this fact would create a major ideological conflict with their religious colleagues.

Thus it appears that despite the affinity between the religious and the secular radical right in Israel and their intense political cooperation, their fundamental ideologies are worlds apart, and are in fact irreconcilable. Even Geula Cohen and Dr. Israel Eldad, the most neoreligious ideologues of the secular radical right, admit privately that they are unwilling to commit themselves to anything close to a Halakha state. Their desired Jewish state would undoubtedly be "more" Jewish than the present State of Israel, respectful of tradition and national-religious symbols. But it would in no way be a theocracy or a state constituted on the laws of the Torah.[33]

The secular radical right's general conception of the "state" is revealed in its statements about Israeli democracy. The secularists are extremely touchy about the charges often leveled against them of being either non-democratic or a threat to Israeli democracy. The public struggle against Rabbi Kahane, which began after his 1984 election to the Knesset, and took the shape of "a defense of democracy" educational campaign in the schools and in the army, greatly alarmed the leaders of this camp.[34] They were right to conclude that although Kahane was viewed as the main threat to Israel's civic order, they too were regarded with great suspicion. The memories of the illicit West Bank settlements of the 1970s, the 1982 struggle in Yamit, the 1984 discovery of the Jewish Underground, and some of the 1985 statements of the Yesha Council regarding the potential illegality of the Peres administration had placed the entire radical right in a very awkward position vis-à-vis the nation's democratic institutions and tradition. As either ideological defenders of these acts or active participants in many of them, they were portrayed by rivals as the key facilitators of the growing support for Kahane.

This pressure has prompted the leaders of the radical right to make its relation to democracy very clear. Earlier ambiguous commitments were replaced by an explicit statement on democracy in the Tehiya's *Identity Card*, the party platform for the 1988 elections:

> The state of Israel is a democratic state. The democratic government in the state of Israel is an inseparable part of the Jewish-Zionist character of the state but is subordinated to its existential interests as a besieged country which has been living in a state of emergency for forty years.
>
> Ignoring this complex uniqueness of the state of Israel damages both the democratic values of the nation and its vital national-existential interests.[35]

The Tehiya leaders, and their colleagues from Moledet and Tzomet, mean what they say. They think of themselves as democrats and their writings rarely betray a desire for any other kind of state. But the democracy they have in mind is "a Zionist democracy," meaning that the "Zionist" commitment to Eretz Yisrael is fundamental. The State of Israel has no formal constitution, but according to these people it clearly has an informal one, which prescribes that the integrity of Eretz Yisrael is superior to the ordinary rule of majority. No parliamentary majority, nor any erroneous interpretation of this majority by the government of the day, may be used to act against this implicit constitution of the land and of the people. No concept of abstract civil rights could ever be superior to the collective right of the nation to its land and to its security. Zionist democracy should defend, according to the spokespersons of this camp, not only democracy but also Zionism. And if the two collide, Zionism takes precedence.

Referring to the much-discussed issue of the need for an Israeli constitution and the role of Israel's Supreme Court of Justice (*Bagatz*) in the public life of the nation, Dr. Israel Eldad elaborates:

> If it is true that a constitution is introduced as a safeguard against dangers, I am ready to join the camp which demands a constitution for Israel; but on one condition, that we agree on the meaning of Israel and the dangers to its existence. For if there is a danger to Israel then it is first and foremost the danger of the elimination of Zionist and Jewish normativity of the state, the danger of the disintegration of its calling, the sense of its existence, the danger of its dissolution into individuals and rights which are made sacred according to an alien reality. . . . And if the Zionist interest—the Judaization of the Land—and the right of the citizen as an individual are to collide, we have to make sure that Zionism prevails in the name of the Zionist democracy. . . . Israel has a court of appeal . . . but above this court, clearly, openly and assuredly there is another court—a Zionist court of appeal."[36]

Clearly, though the secular ultranationalist leaders are not as dubious about democracy as their religious colleagues from Gush Emunim and not

as hostile to it as Rabbi Kahane was, they are nevertheless not great supporters of modern pluralist democracy. The normative world of democracy in
the era of civil and human rights is alien to these people and has, in their
opinion, no relevance whatsoever to the Israeli experience. If it can be
proved that the Arabs of Eretz Yisrael constitute a mortal danger to the
Zionist democracy, their exclusion from the system does not in any way
impair its democratic character. It is important to stress, however, that
unlike Gush Emunim, the ideational and symbolic world of most of these
people is democratic. In the final analysis, the secular ultranationalist camp
in Israel is not revolutionary and does not basically question the prevailing
concept of the state on the nation's system of government.

But the secular radical right feels that the balance between democracy
and Zionism, which has long shifted in the direction of the former, is in
urgent need of correction. This is probably why the three far-right parties
speak so much about education and Zionist socialization. In their view, it is
the young Israelis, the generation of the future, who must place the nation
back on the right track. Although education has long been a cherished theme
of the Tehiya, there is no doubt that Tzomet has stolen its thunder. Rafael
Eitan, who as chief of staff devoted great energy and resources to the education of underprivileged soldiers, has placed the reform of the nation's educational system *above security and settlement.*

> Only Tzomet gives *education* the no. 1 priority. . . . in Tzomet education has
> a broad meaning:
>
> 1. Education means the development of potentialities—the strengthening of
>   the national capacity to do things.
> 2. Education means the development of values—the reinvigoration of the
>   belief in the truth of Zionism.
> 3. Education means the development of consciousness—increasing the
>   awareness of the individual for his rights and duties in the country, and
>   his sense of responsibility and identification with it.
>
> Without an efficient, progressive, and dynamic educational system, the
> nation will not have the *physical and spiritual* ability to face the challenges of
> the future. Without an education we shall have no security, no economic
> progress, and no social welfare.[37]

The Tehiya and Moledet are more emphatic on the need for a nationalist
transformation of the entire educational system. Moledet speaks of "a total
switchover of the school curricula: the Torah of Israel, the history of Israel,
and the study of the homeland will be introduced as first priority, in order to
block the spiritual erosion, the assimilation, and the self-degradation."[38]
The Tehiya stresses the "special effort . . . to strengthen the state—religious
education which operates in a nationalist-Zionist spirit." It further vows to
prefer, in "the financial allocations which go for culture and art, . . . those
institutions and projects which contribute to the espousal of national, social,
Zionist, and Jewish values."[39]

The leaders of the secular radical right are thoroughly conscious of the interdependence of the political and economic systems of Israel. As champions of a cause that could easily alienate Israel from the rest of the world, including the United States, they are aware of the need for the Zionist republic to be as strong and productive as possible. Thus in 1984 the Tehiya concluded that the economy was in such bad shape that the country needed "an emergency economic regime," which would severely limit the free market and open labor bargaining:

> The serious condition of the economy and our growing dependence on foreign aid make it necessary to introduce an emergency economic regime for a period of one to two years through Knesset legislation, and the introduction of a welfare policy that would close the social gap. These measures will be founded on three principles: the struggle for economic independence, which is a condition for political independence; a just distribution of the economic burden among all the public strata; a courageous leadership that will tell the people the truth.[40]

The platform proposed a total freeze on prices, salaries, and taxes. It called for a large reduction in government expenses, mandatory arbitration of labor relations in the essential public services, and strong incentives for exporting industries. It implied a temporary though unstated limitation of many established democratic freedoms. While the Tehiya dropped the theme of the "emergency economic regime" in 1988, Tzomet was still using it. The 1988 Tehiya platform recommended antistrike legislation and mandatory arbitration for the nation's essential services. It called for a drastic cut in the nation's bureaucracy and an incessant war against the black marketeering.[41]

The ultranationalist stand on the Diaspora is consistent with its emphasis on a genuine "Zionist" democracy in which youngsters are brought up largely in order to strengthen and support it. In the last two decades, many Israeli parties have moderated their criticism of Diaspora Jews who do not immigrate to Israel, but the Tehiya, Tzomet, and Moledet emphatically reiterate the classical Zionist principle of the "negation of the Diaspora." The 1984 platform of the Tehiya, still united with Tzomet, stated:

> The only way to preserve the Jewish nation and to secure its culture and spiritual reproduction, is the concentration of the entire nation in Eretz Israel, to which the beginning of its redemption is closely tied. The movement sees in *aliya* [immigration] a national and personal duty and right of every Jew. . . .[42]

There is no question that the parliamentary radical right is oriented toward a strong and centralized state, and views the state of Israel and its institutions as the most important expressions of the nation. It clearly measures individual Israelis and groups by their contribution to the state and the nation, and not vice versa. But the *conceptual* and *constitutional* framework within which this orientation is perceived and expressed is democratic, drawing directly from the traditional Israeli experience. Although the leaders and thinkers of the parliamentary radical right are critical of specific policies of the regime they do not envision a system of government that is different from the present one, and do not hold the existing regime as illegitimate, even partially. Their answer to critics who ask hard questions about the Arabs is that they do not cater to abstract democratic principles and that they are "Zionist democrats" in the old fashion of the founding fathers of the *yishuv*.

National-Military Struggle as a Virtue

The secular leaders of the radical right see great virtue in the military struggles of the nation. Unlike most moderate Israelis, who hope for peace with the Arabs and seek ways to attain it, the Tehiya and its offspring are suspicious of all available "peace solutions," and constantly glorify the military struggles of the nation, past, present, and future.

The grand process of Zionist "renaissance" is not yet complete, so to remain strong and keep Eretz Yisrael in its entirety, the Israelis must be ready to work hard and fight even harder. There is, they believe, nothing exceptional in this attitude. Nations fight for their freedom and their territorial integrity long after they have achieved independence. Patriotic citizens ought to know that the struggle is virtuous. As Ne'eman writes,

> I do not believe that Pinsker and Herzl [the founders of modern Zionism] would have given up their ideas . . . had they thought that the Jewish state would need a violent struggle on its way to independence and that it would constantly have to fight for survival. . . . Had they not known history? Political Zionism had been especially influenced by the European nationalist movements. Can you show me a nationalist movement that did not go through a violent struggle? Or a European nation-state that did not have to fight for its independence? . . . It is strange to think that somebody in the nineteenth century could have thought that we had reached the end of days. It is true that in *Altneuland* [Herzl's novel about the future Jewish state] the Jewish state does not have an army, but Herzl too was able to distinguish between a novel and a reality. . . . And by the way: in the liberal and socialist world they all admire Vietnam. This Vietnam that fought the Japanese two years, then ten years to get its independence [from the French] and then fought the Americans for twenty years, only to make sure that the entire land remained undivided. And what about the Irish who commit suicide for the integrity of Ireland? And this after a hundred years of a war of liberation?[43]

What is interesting in Ne'eman's argument is not the proposition about the need for a continuous struggle so much as the foreign illustrations by which the argument is supported. Unlike his religious partners, who believe in the singularity of the Jewish people, or his secular colleagues who repeatedly base their arguments on the uniqueness of the Jewish historical experience, Ne'eman is prone to use examples of international history, thus aiming to "normalize" the Zionist case. According to his approach, the ideas of the Israeli radical right are not irrational ideas that can be justified only by the Bible; they are *normal* stands that follow many precedents in world history. The purpose of Zionism is, as it had been in the past, to normalize the people of Israel and make it a nation like all others. And because the nation is normal now, it ought to follow other gallant nationalist movements and fight for its own fulfillment with no guilt feelings.

Political determination and military struggle are not, according to Ne'eman, sources of trouble and national weakness and no one can show that peace presupposes automatic prosperity. Israel's greatest recent event was not the peace with Egypt but the Six-Day War. And it was as significant internally as it was important externally.

> There were people who thought that "peace" would attract *aliya*. Nonsense! On the contrary, the victory in the Six-Day War brought the greatest *aliya* awakening and provided us with two hundred thousand Jews from the Soviet Union. A publicized, determined resolution to settle Judea and Samaria would only attract Jews.[44]

Loyal to their belief in the virtue of military struggle, the Tehiya leaders supported the 1982 invasion of Lebanon. Even though it took place only two months after their forced evacuation from Yamit, they were ready to join the Begin-Sharon administration in this endeavor, to help eliminate the PLO and renew the nation's morale and vitality. The widespread opposition to the war was incomprehensible to Geula Cohen:

> I cannot accept this Diasporic view which we find today in all the opponents [of the war]. They are "dying" to die in pogroms only. They would not lift a finger until the enemy comes with a knife. . . . The Diasporic people, even in our terms, are not allowed to do what the entire world is allowed. . . . And the fear of the Gentiles: what would they say? What was Zionism vis-à-vis the Diaspora mentality? It meant that one was taking one's destiny in one's hands.[45]

It may be erroneous to suggest that Geula Cohen refuses to leave behind her glorious Lehi days and her fights in the ranks of the underground. But the theme of an unending struggle, national as well as personal, does appear in almost every statement she makes or interview she grants. Cohen, who has an endless energy for the cause of Eretz Yisrael, believes that the nationalist revolution the Lehi started almost fifty years ago is not yet over, and that the old fight against the British is still going on, in a slightly different guise. A favorite Cohen image is her self-portrait as a young girl in khaki: "I feel as if I have khaki under my dress. I am still at war. Since the time I joined the underground at sixteen, I have not yet returned home."[46]

A Cynical View of a Cynical World

While most of the religious spokespersons of the radical right view the outside world from the orthodox position of "a people that dwells alone," many of its secular thinkers have a different perspective. Being usually better educated and more experienced than their religious counterparts, they know that there have been chapters in modern Zionist history other than the British White Paper, the Holocaust, and the anti-Israel resolutions of the U.N. General Assembly. Their attitude vis-à-vis the community of nations is consequently more informed and sophisticated than that of Gush Emunim or Kach.

The world, according to the secular radical right, is not as much anti-Semitic as it is cynical and full of respect for force and power. Weak nations can expect no allies or friends. Thus Israel's only hope for independence and respect lies in its political determination and military might.

The main exponent of this approach is Yuval Ne'eman, who has spent many years abroad. It is a grave mistake, according to Ne'eman, to rely too heavily on the Americans or to trust their guarantees. The United States, primarily concerned with its own interests, has betrayed such allies as the Shah of Iran and the Taiwanese. The Americans are pushing for peace in the Middle East—a process that involves immense Israeli concessions—not because they wish to help Israel but because they want to help themselves. They have been losing ground in the area and want to consolidate their position through Israel. And any guarantees they give are based on the promises of the worst of Israel's enemies. Ne'eman thinks it utterly naive to accept these guarantees, especially since the guarantors are themselves unstable:

> Senator Moynihan has assessed the time left, before Saudi Arabia goes through the same process as Iran or Lybia did, as two years. *Should we sacrifice the state of Israel for two years of Saudi oil?* . . . We shall desert Eretz Yisrael, we shall give up Samaria and we shall rely on the sincere desire of the Palestinians, the Syrians and the Iraqis for peace. They will withstand temptation and not take advantage of the opportunity to eliminate us through a surprise attack.[47]

In 1980, Ne'eman believed that the West was losing ground very fast. Iran was lost to Khomeini, Afghanistan had been invaded by the Soviets, and Saudi Arabia was on the brink of collapse. The Middle East was undergoing a sweeping wave of anti-Americanism, and Israel, in order to survive, had to be maintained as a "fortified Island."[48]

This belief became stronger when President Sadat was assassinated in 1981. Ne'eman saw the Middle East as an area of wars, genocides, coups d'état, and instability. One therefore had to act not according to wishful thinking, but on the basis of a worst-case analysis. Israel, said Ne'eman, had to jump off the train of Camp David before it was too late, before the Arabs and the Americans made new demands:

> We have read of those who were on the train to Auschwitz and could jump off—but did not, because they felt it was not honorable. This is exactly the conduct of the ruling establishment of Israel—both the government and the main opposition—in their attachment to Camp David. For the American president [Reagan], Camp David is a matter of the democratic past. . . . The Europeans and the Arabs other than Egypt have never accepted Camp David. President Mubarak looks for a way to go back to the bosom of the Arab Nation, but is ready to play Camp David until April 1982. . . . Only in Israel they believe that nothing has changed.[49]

This cynical and power-oriented approach to international relations led the Tehiya leaders in 1981 to develop a special rationale for the need to break Israel's peace treaty with Egypt and the United States. While the immediate objective was to end the retreat in Sinai, the logic of the argument rested on a cynical view of the way nations keep international commitments. Nations respect their international treaties only as long as these are in their immediate interests. Once the interest is gone, the commitment disappears. The United States had, for example, broken SALT II unilaterally because it found it in its best interest to do so. Only then had it tried to prove the case by showing bad faith on behalf of the Russians. It had also broken its commitment to Taiwan not to establish relations with Beijing.

In a cynical world, the argument implies, you act according to your vital interests, not according to your high-school course in civics. The Tehiya leaders believe that Egypt had violated the Camp David Accords enough to justify Israeli withdrawal from them.[50] Further, when the world learns of Israel's resolve to keep its land, it will stand up and applaud.

> After it is done with its yelling, denunciations, and condemnations, the free world will salute an Israel which will be a lot stronger. The world bows to force, and Israel should consequently not be worried with anyone.[51]

According to the secular radical right, the world constantly applies a double standard. The weak are expected to behave differently than the strong and be more moral. Take the outcry against the Israeli approach to terrorism and terrorists. Critics condemn Israel for mistreating Arab terrorists and blocking media coverage of the *intifada*. But, they say, there isn't much condemnation of other nations in the same situation.

The Falklands War, in which Great Britain fought Argentina, is a favorite topic of the radical right. The war won the support of all the free world, though it was conducted in a most brutal way. The media were barred, and British soldiers were instructed to shoot to kill and take no prisoners.

Finding out from the British press about these latter instructions, Eliyahu Amikam, a veteran columnist of the radical right, wrote:

> And now we can answer the disturbing question: what would the world say if Jews would kill prisoners of war in Israel? It would probably say: What can you expect of the killers of God? Haven't they also murdered Christians for the use of their blood in their religious rites? They themselves admit that Gush Emunim kills children for the same purpose. . . . And what would the world say if Jews would not kill prisoners of war? *It would say exactly the same things.*[52]

The cynical world, we are told, is against the Jews because they have always been weak and still seen weak. It will only respect them if they become strong and behave as the mighty do. The Six-Day War proved, according to this position, that Israel was a powerful nation. No development since the war had justified any change in that behavior or posture. When the United States decides to give Israel massive military, economic, and political support, it does it not because of excessive humanism and pity for the just. "Only the fools," writes Yoash Tzidon, Tzomet's second-ranking Knesset member,

> believe that an American support, or other, is given out of humanism and philanthropy. When the United States thought that Israel was a burden [before 1956], it was cautious not to hurt its other interests. When the Jews managed to help themselves, with the assistance of France, at that time in war with Arab nationalism (a support also based solely on common interests), when they defeated the new Soviet weapons in the Sinai campaign and proved their survival power, things changed. . . . Only when the United States discovered that Israel could be of help, only then did it open its purse for the Israelis.

Tzidon, an air-force reserve colonel, was assured by his American military contacts that the United States would continue to support Israel as long as it remained strong and useful.[53]

The Permanent Hostility of the Arabs

While the arguments on the Arabs voiced by the secular radical rightists resemble those of their religious allies, their political analysis is deeper. Most of the ideologues of the Tehiya, Moledet, and Tzomet speak, to be sure, of the Bible as the main text of Eretz Yisrael, but they approach it more from a historical perspective than a theological or religious one: Eretz Yisrael belongs to the Jewish people not because God promised it to Abraham 4000 years ago, but because the nation was shaped by this promise and has remained loyal to it all through history.

The real contribution of the secular thinkers of the radical right to its ideology lies in their very pessimistic analysis of modern Arab-Jewish relations. Much of their tough stand on the Palestinian question derives from their somber understanding of the dynamics of Arab nationalism. The Arabs in and out of Eretz Yisrael are one and the same, and they are out to get the Jews. "The monster," says Ne'eman,

> has many different heads, each pulling in its own direction. Khomeinist mass fanaticism, a subversive military action of the Gadaffi type, the traditional evil of the Syrians, the Iraqi nuclear effort, or the terrorism of the PLO. When Israel is concerned, all of them will act in unison.[54]

The Eretz Yisrael Arabs—"Palestinians" is a phony unhistorical term invented in order to destroy the State of Israel—have always been hostile to the Jewish claim to Eretz Yisrael. They were violent and terroristic long before there was a single Arab refugee or one acre of occupied territory. There is no indication that the establishment of the State of Israel, the Six-Day War, or anything else has changed their mind. They may say they are interested only in having territories occupied in 1967, but they still have the same purpose in mind, the destruction of the State of Israel.

> The Arabs started the violence. We were on the defensive. We sincerely believed that we should conquer land by Keren Kayemet [the Jewish National Fund] and acquire it by labor, with no bloodshed whatsoever. . . . The Arab violence, terrorism, and wars are the Arab response even to the non-occupying, pacifist, humanitarian, kibbutz-sane Zionism. Those who see Kedumim and Ofra [Gush Emunim settlements] as occupied areas should not be surprised to have Ein Hod [an artists' village near Haifa—an Arab site before 1948 and now a center of moderate Israelis] also seen as an occupied area—the more so because those evicted from Ein Hod are living and are suffering.[55]

The outbreak of the *intifada* in 1987 and the growing danger of the establishment of a Palestinian state alarmed the radical right. Its rejection of the repartition of Eretz Yisrael assumed an unprecedented sense of urgency. Likud's call for Palestinian autonomy in the West Bank, based on the Camp David Accords, as a safeguard against a Palestinian state, has become the main target of the radical right. Their total suspicion of the Arabs has best been expressed in the press by Israel Eldad:

> Is it very hard to understand what autonomy would be? . . . The flags of the Palestian victory would be flown sky high, in "our" areas, Nazaret and Um-El Faham, too. An acting government would be established. The Palestinian anthems would be sung too. And what would you do about the education there . . . when they will teach the Palestinian "Charter" as a constitution?[56]

The Tehiya and its political offspring utterly mistrust the long-range intentions of the Arabs. Their policy consequently starts with the presupposition that no Palestinian nation exists. The whole Arab problem is a case of individual residents whose legal situation will have to be clarified once the occupied territories are annexed to Israel. The 1988 Tehiya platform generously promises that the government of Israel "will not force Israeli citizenship upon the Arabs of Judea, Samaria, and Gaza," and says that they will be entitled to the status of "resident aliens," which grants them all the civil rights of Israelis short of the right to vote and be elected to the Knesset. Citizenship will be granted individually and on the basis of certain rational criteria like demography and the preservation of the Jewish nature of society. Israel would, however, "encourage and help emigration" and insist upon the resettlement of all the residents of the refugee camps in the Arab world.[57]

The Tehiya and Tzomet consider Israeli Arabs to be part of the Arab problem. Israeli Arabs would be able to keep their citizenship only if they serve three years of "national service"—similar to the Jewish compulsory three-year military service. They would be entitled to national insurance benefits only if they fulfilled all their civic obligations and demonstrated their loyalty to the state. Those Arabs, however, who collaborated in undermining the security of the state would lose their citizenship and possibly be deported.[58]

In 1988 the platforms of all the parties of the radical right reacted to the *intifada* and proposed ways of crushing it.

The most simplistic approach to the problem is Rafael Eitan's. Raful, who has always believed that military force can solve political problems is certain that the uprising can be brought down in a matter of days. Life in the Arab cities and villages whose youth are participating in the uprising ought to be made unbearable. Roadblocks, curfews, and deportations of all individuals involved would so upset the daily routine of the Arabs that the uprising would end in a few days.[59]

The Tehiya's program is broader and more sophisticated. The strategists of the party, unlike Raful, are fully aware of the political nature of the uprising and its broad grass-roots support. They know it would take a comprehensive campaign to bring it down, and they are honest about its draconian nature. The *intifada,* according to the Tehiya, is nothing less than "the continuation of the Arab wars aimed at the destruction of Israel." It should, consequently, be fought by the harshest measures. Not only should all the rock-throwers be treated like terrorists and be either shot pointblank, deported, or have their houses blown up, but their entire support system ought to be banned.

The Tehiya's plan for crushing the *intifada* speaks of temporarily or permanently shutting down "associations, institutions, organizations, newspapers, propaganda centers, universities, and schools which serve as foci of incitation and sabotage." Mosques that serve as sanctuaries or training centers for saboteurs would be subject to the inspection of the army or the police. Since the *intifada* enjoys the support of at least 90 percent of all the organized institutions of the West Bank and Gaza, the real meaning of this plan is nothing less than the imposition of unlimited martial law on the West Bank and the suspension of all legal procedures that have governed the area for years. Israel's Supreme Court of Justice, which has prevented some deportations, would no longer have that authority; the entire legal system of the occupied territories would instead be managed by the army.[60]

Crushing the *intifada* is not, however, the Tehiya's complete solution of the problem of the West Bank and Gaza. The real answer should be "a Zionist answer." Each violent anti-Israel operation should to be met by establishing a new settlement.

> The Arabs of Judea, Samaria and Gaza, have to understand that the *intifada* should only bring upon them damage and losses. Their conditions would deteriorate, their rights be reduced, and their institutions shut down. The Jewish settlements in Yesha, on the other hand, would flourish and the number of Jews all over Eretz Yisrael would be increased.[61]

The Treason of the Israeli Intellectuals

Every radical right in any country is intensely hostile toward the left, especially its intellectuals: writers, poets, actors, and other artists. The secular radical right in Israel, no exception to that rule, is extremely obsessed by the "trahison des clercs." That animosity reached a peak during the 1988 Palestinian uprising. While the spokespersons of the right saw the *intifada* as a threat to the entire Israeli venture in the occupied territories, the Israeli intelligentsia was vocally critical of the brutal methods used in its suppression. The rightists found the intellectuals' protests extremely damaging. The case of Dr. Mubarak Awad—a Palestinian who opened a "nonviolence" research institute in Jerusalem and was deported by the government for his concealed rebelliousness—became a test case; the right decried the moral support rendered to Awad by numerous Israeli intellectuals:

> There is more than cynicism in the fundamental position . . . of all the "intellectuals"—ours and the world's—who defend Awad in the name of freedom of the spirit and of "research" (the study of non-violence!). He is not violent, does not even preach killing. He "only"calls for rebelliousness, applauds the riots, "only" demands the eviction of the conqueror. . . .
>
> It is impossible . . . [both] to support nonviolence and to brag about the success of the rebellion. The very call for rebelliousness and the recognition of the PLO and its propositions are already violence per se.[62]

The *intifada* created a serious moral crisis in Israel and prompted an unprecedented wave of protests, demonstrations, and symposia—even an international conference on the psychological effects of the uprising. All the participants expressed understanding and empathy with the Arab population. The Arab scholars among them, who reported on the psychological transformation undergone by the rebellious youth, received intense media attention. About that time, two Molotov cocktails were thrown at Tel-Aviv's most crowded shopping mall, the Dizengoff Center, triggering a ferocious article from Eldad:

> The Dizengoff Center is not just an urban center, but a psychological center as well. What has developed there for years, . . . in its coffee shops and theaters, is a cynical now-ness, a negation of all the values of Zionism and, needless to say, of Judaism. . . .
>
> No, it is not the Arab Molotov cocktails thrown there last week that threaten our existence. The spiritual Molotov cocktails which are thrown from this now-center are the danger, the decay, the emptiness—these are the subjects worthy of the psychiatrists' observation.[63]

Responding to the same incident, Geula Cohen spoke of the AIDS plague of the Israeli intelligentsia:

> If there is today a moral crisis at the very foundations of the national home, it is because the spirit of not a few of our creative intelligentsia . . . been infected by a virus of a modern incurable disease: the AIDS disease. . . . The body of a nation also has a natural immunization system of its own, which, if infected and destroyed, leaves the body defenseless against every common disease. . . .
>
> When a human being, flesh and blood, becomes sick with this disease—he knows he is sick, and goes to the hospital. But those whose spirit is infected with this disease do not know that they are sick and proudly walk the streets while saying, "We are healthy! We are healthy!" God should really pity them, but let Him also pity us—because of their damage.[64]

After several 1989 anti-leftist sabotage acts committed by a secret underground called the Sikarikin, M. Ben-Yosef (Hagar), a leading Moledet ideologist, concluded that the intellectual left had been complaining about the right-wing extremists who resorted to violence against it, but was itself, in fact, "the father of violence in social controversy, which includes physical violence. Whatever the right does in this sphere cannot be but an imitation of the other side."[65]

Leadership and Political Style

Despite the Tehiya's original hope of becoming a cohesive movement of revival made up of many spirited *chavurot,* it has mostly remained a political party of a few active leaders and many passive followers. It is incapable of rewarding a large number of supporters with material benefits and unable to compete with the organizational competence of the National Religious Party, though it has tried to attract religious support. Either because of the expense involved in building a sophisticated political machine, or because of its principled rejection of instrumental politics, the Tehiya has remained a skeleton party with very little organization. The same is true of Tzomet and

Moledet, both of which communicate with their followers mostly through newspaper ads and occasional newsletters.

It thus seems that the main political asset of these parties is not their grass-roots activism but the quality of their leaders. Despite their advanced age, the heads of the Tehiya, and Tzomet (the case of Moledet is not yet clear), project the image of true believers, which is rather rare in Israeli politics. They are seen as honest individuals who do what they say and say what they do, solid people who have sacrificed successful careers for the unstable political life of the extreme right. Together with the exemplary leadership of Gush Emunim, they appeal to those Israelis who are scornful of most of the nation's unprincipled politicians and who look for personal example and genuine concern.

The prominence of these leaders and the weakness of their organizations make the politics of the Tehiya, Tzomet, and Moledet very much a summation of the individual styles of their leaders. There is no real substitute in these parties for Geula Cohen, Yuval Ne'eman, Rafael Eitan, or Rehavam Ze'evi. These individuals don't control their movements the way Kahane dominated Kach, but they nevertheless shape their parties almost exclusively. While the Gush Emunim component of the Tehiya follows the Gush style, which has already been explored, the backgrounds of the secular leaders of the radical right and their individual approaches are different. To a great extent, they make up the story of the entire secular ultranationalist camp in Israel.

Grand Strategy and Scientific Radicalism—Yuval Ne'eman

Since launching a new party to oppose Menachem Begin and the Camp David Accords, Professor Yuval Ne'eman has maintained his leadership position within the Tehiya party. This unpolitical professor, whose analytic language has never appealed to the large masses, has been able to accomplish so much as a result of three unique apolitical factors: his unchallenged scientific status, his strong contacts inside Israel's defense establishment, and a personal disinterestedness in power politics. One of Israel's most uncommon politicians, Ne'eman has contributed a unique style of "rational radicalism."

Yuval Ne'eman has been certified a genius since childhood. Born in 1925 in Mandatory Palestine, he studied at the prestigious *Gimnasia Herzeliya,* a Tel Aviv high school that had been the cradle of many members of the nation's elite. Graduating at fifteen, young Ne'eman went to the Technion and earned his engineering degree before the 1948 War of Independence. At the same time he joined the Palmach and was, by the end of the war, a field officer. In 1952 he graduated from the prestigious École Superieure de Guerre and the École d'État-Major in France.

During most of the 1950s Ne'eman served in the Israeli military intelligence, involved in planning and drafting contingency plans for the army. Many Israeli strategists, including David Ben-Gurion and Yigal Allon, believed in those days that the borders of the State of Israel were not finally fixed in 1948 and that an Arab aggression might justify a new Israeli expansion.[66] It was during his intelligence days that Ne'eman adopted his long-range strategic thinking, which emphasized such concepts as "short and defensible borders," "strategic depth" and "warning space."[67]

After concluding his brilliant army career as Israel's military attaché in London, Ne'eman immersed himself in nuclear physics, completing his doctorate at the Imperial College of Science and Technology. In the early 1960s he made his greatest scientific discovery, proving the existence of the subatomic omega-minus particle of the nucleus, at about the same time as the American Murray Gell-Mann, who later won the Nobel Prize, for which Ne'eman was also seriously considered.

Yuval Ne'eman's extraordinary scientific career and his excellent defense connections were instrumental in his appointment as president of the University of Tel-Aviv, which he guided through a period of expansion in the 1970s. Despite his 1979 decision to sacrifice his brilliant career for the radical cause of Eretz Yisrael, Yuval Ne'eman has never renounced his physics. He has always been happy to leave his colleagues in command and either retire to his own laboratory in Israel or take a research vacation abroad.[68] When asked about the relationship between his science and politics, Ne'eman said,

> Anyone who reads my articles on political subjects knows that my security considerations are totally rational. I am ready to prove that they are almost mathematical. But the fundamental assumption and the comprehensive view behind the security considerations is based on a Zionist belief. And Zionism is not a rational thing.[69]

On another occasion he put it differently:

> I am a father and a nationalist Jew who is ready to fight for his people and who spends a great deal of energy on this. But not for a single moment do I forget that in the final analysis we are nothing but fleas on a mediocre planet which goes around one of the ten million suns that exist in one of the ten billion galaxies that we know about in the universe.[70]

Ne'eman's scientific prominence has not been the main reason for his leadership position within the Tehiya, but it has certainly helped. The other leaders, who usually seem rather mystical and emotional, are pleased with this cool rationalist who provides the mathematical proof that they are right.[71]

An important though rather unpublicized source of Yuval Ne'eman's authority within the Tehiya is his close connections with Israel's defense establishment. Ne'eman was involved in the planning and strategic conduct of three of Israel's wars: in 1956 he was engaged in working out the secret alliance of Israel, France, and Great Britain that plotted the downfall of Egypt's Gamal Abd-el Nasser; in 1967 he helped plot the surprise attack on Egypt;[72] and in the 1973 Yom-Kippur War Ne'eman was in Washington as part of the Israeli team that negotiated the American airlift to Israel and the first disengagement agreements with Egypt.[73] In 1974 Shimon Peres, then Israel's minister of defense, asked him to become his special defense aide, a position he resigned in 1976 following his great disappointment with the Rabin cabinet.[74]

His experience in defense and his expertise in nuclear physics have led to Ne'eman's continuous involvement in the Israeli nuclear effort. He has been a member of the secret Israeli Committee for Nuclear Energy since the early 1960s, and was the Ministry of Defense's chief scientist in the late 1960s. Reports indicate that he has never given up this affiliation; it is common knowledge that some of the nation's most confidential secrets have been shared with Ne'eman.[75]

Curiously, when Ne'eman served as Israel's minister of science and energy between 1982 and 1984, his involvement in the settlement of Judea and Samaria was publicized, but his central work in the fields of nuclear energy and space exploration was concealed.[76] And when Israel sent its first reconnaissance satellite into space in November 1988, long after Ne'eman's time in office, he was one of the most important guests at the secret launching site. The Tehiya 1988 election campaign literature stressed that Ne'eman was one of the nation's best scientists and implied that he was also the father of Israel's first venture to space.[77]

The prestige of Yuval Ne'eman as a scientist and military strategist explains part of his success within the Tehiya. The explanation for the other part is his rare lack of interest in political power and prestige. He has almost never been party to power struggles within the Tehiya. Unlike Geula Cohen, Raful, and Gush Emunim, Ne'eman has never had a "camp" of supporters, nor has he tried to build one. He has never monopolized positions of fame and exposure at the expense of his colleagues. When asked once about his relation to politics, Ne'eman admitted,

> I have never been in need of company, in need of people's noise around me. I live well with people but I have no curiosity about them. . . . The occupation in mediation, in debate, in convincing people, is so unpleasant that I ask myself on many occasions—Why the hell do you need this?[78]

Ne'eman's lack of interest in the personal rewards of politics has served him well. Geula Cohen, for instance, the Tehiya second-in-command, wants constant media attention; she has never felt envious of Ne'eman nor has he done anything to remind the Israeli public that he, not Cohen, is the head of the party.

Ne'eman has made it very clear that he is more interested, in principle, in his science than in his politics, and that if he could be certain that his services were no longer needed by the defenders of Eretz Yisrael he would gladly quit. And this has been, perhaps, the reason why his colleagues have not let him do so. Acknowledging that he has not been the inspiring leader the movement needs, they have nevertheless recognized that only a person such as he could keep the party together.

Ne'eman has never been a good Tehiya parliamentary or extraparliamentary activist; he was most effective when he held executive positions. Determined and unreserved, as minister of science and energy (1982–1984), Ne'eman moved every shekel he could get his hands on to Judea and Samaria, and was part of the great settlement breakthrough in the occupied territories. He was also one of the cabinet's most committed ministers to the war in Lebanon and in general the gatekeeper against moderation and compromise. Ne'eman's unique secular imagery may not be representative of the main bulk of the party's supporters on election day, but it has added a special rational flavor to this radical party. It is not surprising that one of the most memorable pieces by this uncommon person was written in Boston:

> These lines are written against the sounds of *Romeo and Juliet* of Prokofiev, performed by the Boston Philharmonic Orchestra. What a rising rhythm! But were we only to try and stop for a single moment, the entire symphony would have lost its meaning. There isn't here a system in equilibrium in the physical classic sense; a melody is a disparative system like the human being. In the man's body the molecules are never constant and the body replaces them dozens of times through life. People eat, breath, excrete, and sweat. All the agents change and nevertheless there is an identical completeness—not forever, till the harmony declines. The mechanisms of waste exchange work worse and worse until the entire system stops—and dies. Zionism is also such a system. If it stops, it will get lost. Its very existence depends on its being a process. The process changes its shape; new actors enter; but the identical completeness is there and living."[79]

Yuval Ne'eman resigned from the Knesset in the beginning of 1990, a year after his reelection. His seat was given to Elyakim Haetzni of Kiryat Arba, a prominent party ideologue who had long been eager to enter the House. Ne'eman said he was not excited about another four years of ineffective opposition to the large Likud-Labor unity coalition, and could do much better in his Tel-Aviv University laboratory. At the same time, he made it clear that this was by no means a political retirement.

The March 1990 crisis between the Likud and Labor, and the consequent formation of a narrow coalition by Itzhak Shamir, returned Yuval Ne'eman to the government. In June he became Israel's minister of science and energy, and a leading member in one of Israel's most hawkish cabinets ever. It was very indicative of the changing world that less than two months after his return to power, this radical rightist was the first Israeli minister to be officially received in the Kremlin by Mikhail Gorbachev, the leader of the Soviet Union.

The Confessional Politics of Geula Cohen

In 1987 Ne'eman was faced with a critical decision. Rafael Eitan and Geula Cohen, who ranked second and third in the Knesset delegation, were headed on an irreversible collision course, and Ne'eman had to take sides, even though there was the very real chance that the decision would split the party and the loser would leave with many followers. Politically and ideologically he was much closer to Eitan and his matter-of-fact Labor Zionism.[80] But as much as he cared for Raful and recognized his broad electoral appeal, Ne'eman supported Cohen, and Raful seceded. Ne'eman recognized that if the Tehiya party and the radical right could be said to have a single "soul" or "spirit," it was Geula Cohen. Ever since her emotional confrontations with Menachem Begin over the peace with Egypt, Cohen had been the most representative symbol of the radical right, an Israeli exemplary Pasionaria.[81] Geula Cohen was the central figure among the circle of people who had created the Tehiya and by far its most talented and effective communicator. Ne'eman could not ignore the fact that by 1987 Cohen had also become the living war goddess of the radical right; there could be no Tehiya without her.

Geula Cohen has never excelled as a theoretician or a cool analyst of political situations. She feels Eretz Yisrael, loves it, and she is absolutely certain the Jews can keep it in its entirety. International constraints, political difficulties, and tactical problems rate very low in her thinking; she believes that vision, strong will, and unshakable determination are enough to achieve all the nation's goals.

Cohen had been on the "Eretz Yisrael barricades" long before her 1978 confrontation with Begin. She had been the most consistent Likud supporter of Gush Emunim. They needed parliamentary backing, and unlike many lukewarm Likud or NRP supporters, Cohen backed them to the hilt; in gratitude they made her a member of their extended secretariat.[82]

Her consistent Knesset attacks on the Rabin administration—over its 1974–1975 disengagement agreements with Egypt and Syria and the failure to settle the occupied territories—prefigured the political emergence of the radical right. Cohen—who declared in 1979, "the Knesset is a battlefront, not a theater; in the battlefront you fight, not dress in your finest clothes. . . . I am not going to let the Knesset conduct festivals when I smell blood"[83]—has most recently turned her confessional politics against the leftist intellectuals and the moderates. Her Knesset speeches, public interviews, *Yediot Achronot* columns, and numerous lectures have all sought to debunk Israeli leftists and the supporters of the *intifada*.[84]

Geula Cohen was born in Tel Aviv in 1926 to a poor Sephardic family. Her mother came from a Moroccan family that had settled in Palestine two generations earlier. Her father was a Yemenite dreamer who believed that the Zionist return to Eretz Yisrael meant redemption and the coming of the Messiah. At the age of five he had walked across hundreds of miles of desert with a group of Yemenite Jews heading for Palestine. Many perished along the road; he survived, became a scholar and student of Kabbalah, and built a large family.[85] When he died at an early age, he left his daughter Geula with a firm belief in the nation's destiny and an irreversible commitment to bring it about. Geula ("redemption" in Hebrew—"My name obliges me to redeem the people of Israel")[86] joined Lehi, an extremist underground that vowed in 1940 to liberate Eretz Yisrael by force. Cohen won fame as the announcer of the Lehi radio station. Her later autobiography, *The Story of a Fighting Women,* was warmly received; even such an old foe as David Ben-Gurion expressed his admiration for her.[87]

In the early 1950s, Geula Cohen was close to Chug Sulam (Ladder Circle) of Dr. Israel Eldad, who preached the expansion of the borders of Eretz Yisrael to Jordan, Syria, and Iraq; she occasionally wrote for its *Sulam* magazine. And when the members of a small ex-Lehi underground, known in public as the Kingdom of Israel Underground, were caught in 1953 and sent to jail, Geula would visit them every week.[88]

Cohen earned a Hebrew University master's degree in Jewish philosophy and the Bible and became a *Ma'ariv* journalist in the mid-1960s. She launched a popular new weekly section, "roundtable," in which she would interview several leading Israeli figures each week. Cohen never hide her political ideas, but in the pragmatic 1960s very few people considered her extremist opinions either relevant or meaningful. Most of her readers did not care about these views as long as Cohen was a good and provocative interviewer. About that time she established the Midrasha Leumit (National Seminary)—a school for the study of the lessons of the underground—at the headquarters of the Herut party in Tel Aviv.

The Six-Day War returned Cohen to history. She was as thrilled as her other Lehi comrades, and her *Ma'ariv* roundtables were full of interviews with the new heroes of Israel, the victorious army generals; her particular favorites were Ezer Weizman and Ariel Sharon. She herself became one of the most effective proponents of the new territorial maximalism.

In 1969 Menachem Begin asked her to represent Herut in the Knesset, where she proved an extraordinary parliamentarian. An ardent feminist, Cohen has taken a very progressive positions on issues such as abortion, equal opportunity, and civil liberties, and has become the spokesperson for the poor and the suffering. She has acquired a high reputation for honesty and personal integrity, and has been in the forefront of many struggles against the excessive privileges of the Knesset members.[89]

A key to the confessional politics of Geula Cohen is her refusal to approach politics in a calculated and amoral way. Instead she views politics in an Aristotelian sense as a virtuous activity. When a journalist asked if she might retire, she responded, "God forbid! I would die. I think that I cannot live without it. The activity for Eretz Yisrael is a vital drug for me."[90] When talking about her only child, she said, "I am very happy that my son, Tzahi, is a student activist in the student union. It is most important for me that he does not sell washers, for example. For me, political activism is the most respectable occupation in the world."[91] In 1988, Tzachi Hanegbi was elected to the Knesset and became Likud's youngest Knesset member.

Cohen's immense devotion to the cause, her love of politics, her journalistic skills, her parliamentary experience, and her penchant for provocation have all produced one of Israel's cleverest parliamentarians. While not always respectful of the rules of parliamentary politics, in the name of Eretz Yisrael, Geula Cohen has turned parliamentary politics into an art. She admits that all her emotional eruptions in the Knesset during the Sadat visit had been planned in advance.[92] She has indeed made full use of the body's formal and informal rules. Her Knesset speeches have always been full of great rhetoric and drama, and she has set a record for being called to order or being expelled from the Hall. As a darling of the Israeli media, Cohen has become one of Israel's best known politicians and a highly effective communicator on behalf of the radical right.

Some of the greatest successes of the radical right, such as the passage of the Jerusalem Law and the Golan Heights Law, were due to Geula Cohen. In 1980, Menachem Begin's solemn commitments to Eretz Yisrael were greater than his political resolve to carry them out; although fully committed to the integrity of Jerusalem, he had nonetheless never introduced a Knesset bill that would fully legalize the temporary 1967 decree that joined the Arab half to the Israeli half. Cohen started to work very carefully *and secretly* on a draft bill that would formalize the unification of the city and declare it the capital of the State of Israel. She came out with a flawless draft bill carefully based on all of Begin's statements, which none of the experts of Israel's Ministry of Justice could reject on legal grounds. Cohen caught Begin and his people off guard and surprised the entire Knesset. Begin could not avoid endorsing the new law, nor could the Labor party. Everyone recognized that the law would damage Isreal's international relations, while being practically meaningless in terms of the daily affairs of the city, but no Israeli politician could publicly oppose it.[93] Cohen repeated her success a year later with the passage of a law annexing the Golan Heights to Israel. This time, though, she agreed to postpone her bill in return for Begin's commitment to pass it six months later. By late 1981, Geula Cohen could take pride in being personally responsible for the extension of the *de jure* jurisdiction of Israel to both Jerusalem and the Golan Heights.[94]

While hardly religious at all, Cohen is something of a millennarian type and a strong believer in the inevitability of redemption. She *knows* that we are living in an age of redemption, which weaklings try to postpone or cancel. And although she denies it, Cohen loves to fight. All her autobiographical writings suggest that Geula Cohen is enamored of the great myth of the Jewish undergrounds of the 1940s—a myth she herself has been so instrumental in fostering:

He who makes history has no time, or heart, for feelings of vengeance, but history itself is known for her sweet vengeance. "A gang of mad men," they once called the Lehi fighters, all those "sane people" whose eyes were wide open to see from here to there—in inches, and from yesterday to today in seconds, sober to see the valley before they had looked upon the mountain. Today, the mad men of that time are written in the books and are studied in the schools as the nation's heroes.

Cohen's attachment to the old undergrounds goes hand in hand with her confessional ultranationalism and conception of struggle. Nations fight because it is in their very nature to fulfill themselves and to believe that that fulfillment is just. One country's justice sometimes fights against another's justice, yet history is written by those who are not only just but strong. The Palestinians who fight Israel and insist upon their self-determination in Palestine may be just, but they happen to be on the wrong side. Thus the trouble with Israelis who support them is not that they are mistaken in recognizing the justice of the Palestinians, but that they do not understand the question of justice. Discussing the Palestinian determination to conquer the entirety of Palestine, Geula Cohen said,

> I would have done exactly like them. I would have fought. . . . I respect them. I have never believed it was possible to buy them off through an improvement of living conditions. This was the position of the Labor party, paternalism and scorn. . . . I know they believe that this is their homeland. I believe, however, that this is my homeland, completely mine. So we have a struggle here. I do not hate the enemy, I fight it. Justice cannot be divided and therefore these is a war here. . . . The issue is struggle, a problem of power and there is a world outside and it wonders who is just. Yossi Sarid [a major spokesman of the Left] and his followers damage the faith that we are just and encourage the conviction that the Arabs are. This is why they do not help to solve the problem. The enemy would never settle for partition and would not take quality of life either.[95]

Following the 1990 formation of a narrow coalition by Itzhak Shamir, Geula Cohen joined the Israeli government as deputy minister in Yuval Ne'eman's ministry. The new job, which did not imply meaningful executive responsibilities, has nevertheless made the first lady of the radical right, for the first time in her life, a member of the nation's top decision-making body.

Elyakim Haetzni and the Paranoid Style of the Radical Right

A major characteristic of the Israeli radical right has always been an intense paranoia, a division of the world into the sons of light (the "loyalists of Eretz Yisrael") and the sons of darkness (all others), and a constant sense of betrayal by the latter. No one has expressed this paranoia better than

Elyakim Haetzni of Kiryat Arba, a lawyer who has recently emerged as the Tehiya's most provocative speaker. Haetzni was the first choice of the party's 1988 convention for the Knesset slot below the incumbents, which indicates that he is popular and cannot be regarded as a mere nuisance. Clearly, the opinions he expresses are acceptable to many activists of the movement, and are not the strange expressions of an isolated individual as his Tehiya enemies would like to believe. Haetzni's full legitimacy within the party was asserted in late 1989 when the party approved of his succession of Yuval Ne'eman as the Tehiya third Knesset member.

Haetzni was born in Germany in 1926 and arrived with his family in Palestine in the late 1930s. Many of his relatives died during World War II, and the Holocaust has played a major role in shaping his consciousness.[96]

Haetzni first achieved fame in Israel in the 1950s as a young leader of Shurat Hamitnadvim (Volunteer's Front), a small civic organization that took on the entire Labor establishment.[97] They charged Amos Ben-Gurion, the prime minister's son and the deputy inspector-general of the Israeli police, with an unethical friendship and support of an Israeli businessman suspected of embezzlement. Ben-Gurion's libel suit became a major political battle, in which the Volunteer Front's leaders found themselves surrounded and isolated by a huge governmental machine and a hostile establishment press. The trial and appeal lasted more than four years and totally exhausted Haetzni and his colleagues. Their 1960 acquittal on most charges was a pyrrhic victory, for they ended up with no money or energy to continue the struggle. Never would the young lawyer forget the far-reaching arms of the Labor organization that rallied to defend the Ben-Gurion name and mystique.

Haetzni, a successful attorney, was one of the first Israelis to respond to the challenge of the 1967 victory. He supported the Levinger group in the call for the resettlement of Hebron and was one of the early secular settlers of Kiryat Arba.[98] He later became highly involved in the Gush Emunim battle for the settlement of Judea and Samaria, and his legal services have always been available for West Bank squatters. Haetzni has also become very active in the local politics of Kiryat Arba and provided the Yesha Council with highly qualified legal advice.

Elyakim Haetzni is the prophet of doom and gloom of the secular radical right. Ever since the "betrayal" of Menachem Begin at Camp David, he has been living a paranoiac life full of suspicions of the entire world. No politician in Israel can, according to Haetzni, be trusted, and the settlers can rely only on themselves. The Labor party and the Left are self-hating Jews who are ready to sell out the entire state in order to please the world. The Likud, even radical ministers like Ariel Sharon, are also unreliable partners. They have betrayed Eretz Yisrael in the past and for the proper political price will do so again.

Haetzni's political paranoia reached a peak in November 1985, when he led the Yesha Council into a direct confrontation with the government. After Prime Minister Shimon Peres conducted a successful round of talks with King Hussein of Jordan, Haetzni sensed betrayal coming up and convinced the council to pass a resolution declaring illegal any act that surrounded Eretz Yisrael territories:

> Any government of Israel which will commit the following crimes . . . we shall deem illegal, just as De Gaulle treated the Vichy government of Marshal Petain, who betrayed the French people. . . . We wish to warn Prime Minister Peres against the severe consequences of the plans that have been published and this is by proving that the division of the Land and Jerusalem will necessarily lead to the division of the nation.[99]

The resolution, which also called for a public protest against the prime minister, created a scandal. Itzhak Zamir, the state attorney general, warned the Yesha Council about the serious legal implications of its threats. The Israeli press came out fiercely against the irresponsible resolution and excoriated the "Yesha State" for its separatism.[100] Embarrassed settlers called for the resignation of the leaders of the Yesha Council, and the council was forced to retract its statement within three days.[101]

But Haetzni did not apologize. In response to an attack by Rabbi Yoel Ben-Nun, the leader of the moderate wing of Gush Emunim (whom he once called "our Hamlet") Eliyakim Haetzni wrote in *Nekuda*.

> It is a duty and a commandment to shout and raise the alarm. . . . He who calls for silence and tranquility, helps to rob Eretz Yisrael from us. To claim that our rejecting the government's and Knesset's authority to withdraw the state of Israel from the Land of Israel alienates us from the people makes no sense. The source of these arguments is a fatigue of some of our leaders, a sense of inferiority, of self-diminution vis-á-vis the left. . . . The people expect to find in us leaders and guides. The lukewarm calming voices, the futile and banal suggestions—to build, to explain, to unite—are the ones that disappoint the nation and drive it to despair. It is necessary to challenge the thesis that the state is holy and that all the decisions of the majority ought to be obeyed at all times.[102]

Haetzni seems to consider the Israeli mass media the key arena for the public struggle over Eretz Yisrael. His talks and lectures are full of references to the news bulletins of the nation's official radio and television. He is especially sensitive to statements and reports he does not like, of which there are plenty. Most of Israel's television reporters are, according to Haetzni, vicious leftists who identify with the enemy and are responsible for the nation's great demoralization. Instead of strengthening the people's resolve, they weaken it by portraying the enemy as human and just, and the Israeli leadership as incompetent. It does not take much to make Haetzni angry and he is especially sweeping in his attacks on political correspondents. Following a television group interview with Shimon Peres, a favorite Haetzni target, he wrote:

> The interviewers begged most of the political questions. But why the surprise? It was long since pointed out by our Elders that a self-imprisoned person can never free himself from jail. For who are the television interviewers if not people who are imprisoned with Peres in the same spiritual and ideological jail of leftist "Peace-Now-niks," of Jordano-Palestinian concepts. . . ?[103]

Haetzni writes easily and often. He is by far the most prolific writer for *Nekuda*. Almost every issue of the magazine carries his paranoiac warnings and gloomy observations, usually in a prophetic, emotional language.

> Let it be written down and remembered: the heads of the "nationalist camp," including the heads of the settlement in Yesha, have neither struggled nor demonstrated against the seemingly destructive tendencies of the last several months. Moreover, they have not even raised the questions, asked for answers, or tried to understand. Future historians will find it hard to understand why at this critical moment was this entire great and glorious camp paralyzed, disoriented, mute? Only the psychologists will be able to answer that.[104]

It is sometimes unclear how Haetzni, until 1990 a private attorney, makes a living. The man is always involved in some kind of public profitless action: demonstrating, petitioning, criticizing, or suing the authorities, usually alone. He is a one-man radical organization. Disappointed with the Yesha Council's "moderation," he established a new organization, *Elisha* (Citizens for Judea, Samaria, and Gaza) and began publishing propaganda leaflets. He also has been constantly filing complaints with the police against Arabs identifying with the PLO and against journalists who have been "siding with the enemy."[105] In a recent booklet, *Israel Broadcasts—A Profile of Political Corruption,* he presented his collection of "biased" quotations of Israel's top journalists, urging readers to call the heads of the Israel Broadcasting Service directly to complain about their employees, and providing the telephone numbers.

Elyakim Haetzni's position in the Tehiya party has been strengthened by the 1988 elections. Haetzni's conspiracy complex has made him very critical of the election strategy chosen by the leaders of the party, which was lukewarm on the Likud and very critical of the Left. Unlike Yuval Ne'eman and Geula Cohen, he refused to trust the Likud and warned again and again that after the elections its leaders would join forces with Labor and betray the settlers. He called for a direct ideological confrontation with Itzhak Shamir and for a fierce struggle over the more ideological voters of the Likud.[106]

The elections verified Haetzni's worst predictions. The Tehiya was outflanked on the right by Moledet of Rehavam Ze'evi, and failed to capture many Likud voters. Its leaders, who expected to send six or seven representatives to the Knesset, gained only three seats. Following a very shifty process of coalition-formation, in the course of which promises made by Shamir that Yuval Ne'eman would have an influential cabinet post and Geula Cohen be made a deputy minister, the Tehiya was left out in the cold. The Likud and Labor formed a grand coalition that ignored almost all the Tehiya's priorities. Yuval Ne'eman was personally insulted by Shamir who told him he could keep their previous agreement "in the museum."

The verification of all of Haetzni's worst-case predictions made him a dominant force within the party's councils. The December 1988 U.S. agreement to talk to the PLO also helped. Never before did Haetzni's paranoia seem more realistic. It was just natural that when Yuval Ne'eman decided to resign from the Knesset, at the beginning of 1990, his seat was given to Haetzni.

The "Dugri" Politics of Rafael Eitan

The Tehiya party was reinforced in 1984 when Rafael ("Raful") Eitan, the supreme commander of the army between 1978 and 1983, joined the party with a group of supporters who called themselves Tzomet (Crossroads). He and his followers, all members of kibbutzim and moshavim, were strong supporters of the Greater Eretz Yisrael idea as well as being critical of all of Israel's established politicians. They believed that the conduct of the nation's public affairs had gone astray and that simple, down-to-earth politics could solve the problems of the country. Without ever mentioning the term, they were the propagators of a new style of Israeli politics, *Dugri Politics,* an economical, straightforward, and unsophisticated public action.[107] As one of Israel's most popular chiefs of staff, Eitan contributed to the Tehiya a special Eretz Yisrael aura which the party had been looking for ever since its 1979 establishment. He also reinforced within it the military element, which had always believed that the Arab problem had to be seen through "the sight of the riffle." A rugged moshavnik, who never gave up his small Tel Adashim farm and his private carpentry shop where he worked in his leisure time, Raful was a legend in his own time.

However, the Tehiya-Tzomet alliance did not work. Following a long conflict with Geula Cohen and other frictions, it was clear that the style of Raful and the Tehiya spirit could not be reconciled.

Journalist Shlomo Genosar observed the huge gap in style and orientation between Raful and all of the other Tehiya heads:

> Raful the secular fellow from the Valley of Jezrael . . . never felt at home with the Waldmans of the Tehiya. Their hobby horses are not his. Their messianic elements have never stuck to his mind. He trusts his two bare hands more than Heaven's miracles. To change the paratrooper beret to a working hat, yes; to a yarmulke, no. . . . Not an ideological matter, just a different style.[108]

The Raful mystique springs from the simplicity and rudeness of this man. Eitan, who fought in all the wars of Israel, always at the front, and has been wounded several times, is notorious for his poor education and farmer-like manners.

His friends from the Israeli paratroopers, a unit he helped build and led in some of its most illustrious battles, prize Raful as a platoon commander, admiring his courage and combative spirit but they never believed he could rise high in the military hierarchy. The IDF, everyone thought, was too complex and sophisticated for the *moshavnik* from Tel Adashim.[109]

But though Raful was never good in military theory and grand strategy, he happened to be the nation's best soldier under fire. Each time IDF analysts reviewed an Israeli war for future lessons, there was no question that Eitan, the field commander and leader, was second to none. Raful was one of the main reasons that Israel did not lose the Golan Heights during the Yom Kippur War. When several of his colleagues died in the Syrian surprise attack, and others collapsed of fatigue or despair, the man refused to break. He fought with everything he had and stopped the Syrians with a broken and dispersed division.[110]

Ezer Weizman, the Likud's first minister of defense, chose Raful in 1978 to become the commander-in-chief, not for his strategy and organization so much as for his leadership and personal example.

For many Israelis, Raful became the model of the farmer-fighter who has never abandoned the ideal of pioneering Zionism, that of a proud, productive and self-sufficient working Jew. Eitan's refusal to change his manners or rustic home in the moshav just added to his great appeal. During his five years as the top commander of the IDF, which included the unsuccessful Lebanon adventure, Eitan's authority and leadership remained unquestioned. Ordinary soldiers admired their chief for his Sabra simplicity, human touch, and *Dugri* manners. Raful, who had given special attention to the military socialization of deprived youth, could occasionally be seen talking with ordinary privates about their personal problems, and sometimes would even invite them to his small moshav farm.[111]

Eitan's public career has been at least as paradoxical as his military career. No one ever thought that this farmer could be a competent legislator, but his 1988 return to the Knesset under the Tzomet banner made him a legitimate part of the political scene. Unlike most Tehiya Knesset representatives, who have easily become members of the "Knesset club" despite their ideological radicalism, Raful has never joined the political clique, nor has he tried to do so. His speeches remain extremely short and unpolished, and the bills he sponsors are always very immature; the pros never take them seriously. Raful returns the compliment by saying that he names the donkeys he raises in his moshav backyard after Knesset members; when he has 120 donkeys, he intends to bring them all to Jerusalem.[112]

Nevertheless, Eitan's service to the nation's public life commands respect. Despite appearances, he has become one of the Knesset's hardest-working members. Typically putting in a fifteen-hour day, he has been deeply involved in the House's committee work and has been, in addition, very loyal to citizens in need of a Knesset ear.

Raful's chemistry with the young has made him the most popular speaker in the nation's high schools. Rarely a week goes by without at least two or three school lectures. The man's simplicity and *Dugri* style are his stock in trade; students love to listen to his quick, unpolished, and brutally honest answers. For most of what Raful says is less important than how he says it. Responding to questions about his suggestions for dealing with the *intifada* and about the similarity between Israel and South Africa in their treatment of their "inferior" peoples, Raful declared:

> If they put up a road block, then I would send ten armored carriers to the place. . . . If they throw rocks on the road, I will close the road from Naballa to Ramalla and let the guy who wants to buy rice in Jenin go there through Jerico and Dimona and Eilat. . . .
>
> As for South Africa: what kind of comparison is this? In South Africa they do not repress the blacks. They just do not let them rule over the White minority. The only similar element is that the blacks want to take over there, just as the Arabs here. It is therefore necessary to make sure here and there that this never happens, but otherwise I do not see the relevance of the case to the situation here.[113]

No ordinary politician, Raful is rarely ready to compromise his principles. When all the Tehiya Knesset members went in 1985 to Arab Hebron in order to demonstrate their support for the squatters of Gush Emunim in direct defiance of army orders, Raful refused to join—never, he said, would any Israeli soldier see him disobeying military orders.[114] One reason Raful was uncomfortable in the Tehiya was his natural disdain for the style of religious politics in Israel. As an old anti-religious Labor settler, Raful was never at ease with the neo-religiosity of the Tehiya. Rav Kook's message on the mystical bond between the religious and the lay defenders of Eretz Yisrael is meaningless to him; Raful's affection for Gush Emunim was always limited to their constructive settlement role. An old story shows how hard it was for the pioneers who settled in the Golan Heights right after the Yom Kippur War to get help from Eitan, then the head of the army's Northern Command. "I'll give you a good settlement spot. Follow me!" Raful is said to have told the members of Gariin Keshet. They drove and drove, and finally found themselves by the beach of Lake Tiberias—well within the old Green Line.[115]

Eitan's open resentment of religious politics in Israel had led him to break ranks with the Tehiya and vote against the controversial amendment to the Law of Return that states that only a person who was born to Jewish mother or was converted to Judaism by an *orthodox* rabbi is a Jew [the who is a Jew amendment], and against the prohibition on the sale of pork.

Raful, a great believer in the moral virtue of the Israeli army, is resentful of Israeli religious politicians for another reason: their support of the wide-spread *hishtamtut* (desertion) of yeshiva students from military service. The right of a selected few yeshiva students not to serve in the Israeli army, and instead to devote all their life to holy studies, had been recognized in Israel since the days of David Ben-Gurion. But in the old days it had been limited to a very few extremely talented individuals. In recent years, however, with the rise of many yeshivot and the growth in the power of their political support-ers, the phenomenon has become widespread. Even such an ultranationalist party as the Tehiya, which presumably would favor army service, has avoided criticizing the practice because of its Gush Emunim connection. But Raful has never stopped criticizing *hishtamtut*. Clearly he was the wrong man for the Tehiya, and in 1988, at loggerheads with Cohen, and with Ne'eman support-ing her, Raful decided to go it alone—and succeeded.

The June 1990 formation of a narrow governing coalition by Itzhak Shamir has resulted in making Rafael Eitan Israel's minister of agriculture. But the joy of becoming a full member of the cabinet, and of getting a top executive job, did not satisfy Raful. his long-time commitment to a sweeping electoral reform in Israel, an idea supported by most Israelis but unattractive to Shamir, made Eitan a potential troublemaker in the new government. Upon assuming office he promised his voters to quit the government if it does not introduce an electoral reform within a few months.

The Parliamentary Radical Right
and the Likud

As significant as the vitality of the parliamentary radical right is, for years its main asset was the weakness and ineptitude of the moderate right. The Likud bloc, which represents about 30 to 35 percent of the Jewish voters, has become a populist party with little creative direction. After Begin retired, its leadership has been constantly engaged in power struggles and mutual smear campaigns. Its constituency has been united more by an anti-Labor sentiment than constructive aspirations. Missing are fresh ideas and an intelligentsia of any significance.

Herut, Likud's main party and ideological center, is incapable of main-taining a daily newspaper of its own, and its three publications, the weekly *Hayarden* (River Jordan), the biweekly *Be'Eretz Israel* (Inside the Land of Israel), and *Ha'Uma* (The Nation), the political-literary magazine of the Revisionist movement, are dull, uninspiring, and full of anachronistic reinter-pretations of Vladimir Jabotinsky. Herut has always suffered from ideologi-cal shallowness, but for years this weakness was hidden by the unique personality of Menachem Begin. The old commander of the Irgun was not only Herut's founding father and political leader but also its living ideologist. In countless speeches and press columns he personified the tradition of Jabotinsky and gave it a relevant interpretation.

There was always a radical element in the world view of Herut, and Begin himself, in his early days, was responsible for its propagation. But there was also the liberal side of Menachem Begin, and after the 1960s it played a growing role in shaping the man's politics. While nationalistic to the bones and extreme in rhetoric, Begin was no longer a radical.[116] Like Jabotinsky, he recognized that beyond the sphere of Jewish aspirations and politics there existed a legitimate world. He never ceased to believe in international law and perceived diplomacy and compromise as viable political concepts. And like Jabotinsky before him, Begin was even ready to admit (as in the Camp David Accords) the legitimacy of the Palestinian claim for national rights.

Today, there is no inheritor of Begin's approach. Not one of his immediate successors in the Likud leadership is capable of preserving the Revisionist tradition, especially its liberal and humanistic side. Although a new cohort is entering the leadership of Herut, "the princes"—people like Benjamin Begin (Menachem's son), Uzi Landau, Roni Milo, Dan Meridor, and Ehud Olmart—and Israel's former ambassador to the U.N., Benjamin Netaniyahu—they find it hard to project moderate nationalism.

The Herut they have to function within is a populist party whose extremist and vocal central committee is a living contradiction to the spirit and style of Jabotinsky and the mature Begin. Its hostility to the left is so intense that to be moderate in criticizing its policies is seen as treachery. Itzhak Shamir, the head of the party, who was skeptical about the agreement with Egypt, may pay lip service to Camp David, but his language is hollow and unconvincing. While he proclaims his complete allegiance to the legacy of Begin, he often speaks in the Eretz Yisrael "dialect" of the Tehiya.

So desolate is the ideological environment of the Likud that these days the only right-wing criticism of the excesses of the radical right comes from several Gush Emunim rabbis and activists nostalgic for the early (relative) moderation and sense of proportion of their movement. (It is ironic that even on this dimension of self-criticism, it is *Nekuda* the journal of the settlers in Judea and Samaria, that sets an example.[117] Their lack of any independent ideological judgment has led all of Begin's successors to an unequivocal, but empty, support ot the Israelization of the West Bank.)

Most prominent among the Likud supporters of the radical right is minister Ariel Sharon, who has always stood for territorial maximalism and the belief that political goals can be achieved by military means. Even in the 1950s, as commander of the Israeli paratroopers, he authorized unnecessary military operations against the civilian Arab population in Jordan. And in 1970, as a general, he was the architect of the aggressive evacuation of the Beduin tribes of the Rafiah Salient in Sinai, to make room for Israeli settlers. Serving under Begin and Dayan, minister of foreign affairs in Begin's first cabinet, the ambitious Sharon restrained himself and supported Camp David, thereby securing his political future. But since Begin and Dayan have left the government, the rhetoric of the radical right has become much more popular than the cold peace with Egypt. Sharon has had no difficulty fitting in with the new radical spirit, a political orientation based less on intellectual convictions than on natural drives. His penchant for militarism and territorial expansion was most clearly demonstrated in the Lebanon War—which was, to a large extent, his private venture.

The difference between the new radicals and Sharon's group lies not in ideology or aspirations but in integrity. Unlike the true believers of the radical right, Sharon and his close associates are power oriented, and are ready to compromise their principles in time of need. They believe it is important to be at the helm while trying to carry out one's plans, rather than merely articulating them from the opposition benches. But the followers of Ariel Sharon and other Likud extremists ignore their compromises and read their statements as a full legitimation for the program of the radical right.[118]

Ariel Sharon, it should be noted, did not grow up in the Revisionist milieu and is in fact, a direct heir of Labor activism and militarism. But noting the strong Likud attraction to military heroism and maximalist politics, he has galvanized it into a substantial power base. Talented, imaginative, and charismatic, Sharon has been able to keep in the Likud many rightists who might have followed the Tehiya, Tzomet, or Moledet, had these "purist" parties had a chance to form the government.

Sharon's ingenuity and radical appeal were most originally expressed in December 1987, when he surprisingly announced that he was moving to the Muslim quarter of Old Jerusalem. The freedom to settle the Old City in its entirety, especially the Muslim areas close to the Temple Mount, has been one of the greatest symbolic demands of the radical right, which all governments of Israel were careful not to encourage. But in practice the area has become increasingly insecure. Several Arab terror acts since the mid-1980s have discouraged Jews from trying to live there, and have even scared most visitors away. Sharon's move to the area was thus a most dramatic and exemplary act, fully consonant with the Greater Eretz Yisrael rhetoric of the Likud. In one stroke Sharon outflanked the radical right, attracted attention, displayed leadership, and proved he was more loyal to Eretz Yisrael than most of his colleagues in the Likud. Sharon may be ideologically inferior to the "pure" radical right, but he probably has more supporters.

The prosperity and growth of the radical right at the expense of the nationalist right came to a temporary halt in 1989. The start of the *intifada* in 1987 and the PLO's 1988 commitment to abide by United Nations Resolutions 242 and 338 have created very uncomfortable conditions for the continued development of this camp. The formation of a moderate unity government in 1989, which neutralized Sharon within the Likud and pushed the Tehiya, Tzomet, and Moledet into a very ineffective political opposition, had added pain to misery. There were in fact many indications that the

Shamir group that controlled the Likud was moderating its position on Eretz Yisrael—not because of a deep ideological conviction but as a result of the internal damage of the *intifada* and American and international pressure. A new political axis, Itzhak Shamir–Itzhak Rabin (minister of defense) seemed to be dominating Israeli politics, leading it in a pragmatic and moderate direction.

The hopes of the Israeli moderates were shattered in the summer of 1990. A long rivalry within the Likud-Labor grand coalition ended up with the dissolution of the unity government and the formation of a narrow right-wing coalition, the first of its kind since the Lebanon war. Yuval Ne'eman and Rafael Eitan were given key ministerial positions, and Geula Cohen was made deputy minister; Rehavam Ze'evi who chose not to become a full government minister nevertheless pledged to support the coalition in the Knesset. The demise of the Shamir–Rabin axis, and the reaffirmation of the Likud's commitment to Eretz Yisrael were not initiated by Itzhak Shamir, but rather forced on him by his party radicals. These radicals were unhappy with the 1989 creation of the unity coalition, which left the parties of the radical right with no power or influence, and abandoned the party's hard line. They consequently decided to form a Knesset caucus that would constantly lobby for the settlements of the occupied territories and fight all attempts for territorial compromise and concessions to the PLO. The new caucus, which was named the "Eretz Yisrael Front" was initiated by Likud Knesset members Michael Eitan and Tzachi Hanegbi, and included all the members from the Tehiya, Tzomet, Moledet, Likud, National Religious Party, and Agudat Israel, who worried that Eretz Yisrael was "in danger."[119] The thirty-one member caucus was backed energetically by the growing settler community (nearly 100,000 by 1990) and its institutions.

As long as Shamir's opponents were led by junior Knesset members, they did not have a chance. But an increasing *political* rift between Prime Minister Shamir and Likud Ministers Levy, Sharon, and Modai has given the Front of Eretz Yisrael a ministerial leadership capable of solidifying a formidable opposition to Shamir within his own party. The new opposition succeeded in containing Shamir's drift to the center and made it impossible for the Labor party to remain in the unity government. Its leaders, especially Ariel Sharon, later became the architects of the June 1990 alliance between the Likud, the Israeli religious bloc, and the radical right. Itzhak Shamir who successfully avoided the same coalition in 1988, was now trapped. The only alternative to such a coalition was his resignation and retirement, for which he was not yet ready. By the summer of 1990 it was clear that the radical right consolidated its position and power in national politics, and that Israel was heading toward a major conflict with the rest of the world.

The successful penetration of the nationalist right by the radical right is a very significant development. It is not yet clear whether there is here a "critical mass" that can prevent a *full* return of the occupied territories to

Arab hands, but it very much looks like it. These days even labor rejects the evacuation of the settlers from the West Bank. The radical right may not be able to keep the entirety of Eretz Yisrael under Israeli control, but it may counter the pressures for a total Jewish "transfer" out of the West Bank and Gaza, creating conditions none of its adversaries thought possible just ten years ago.

Religious Fundamentalism and Political Quasi-Fascism: Kach and the Legacy of Rabbi Meir Kahane

A One-Man Show

By the time of the assassination of Rabbi Kahane in New York City, on November 5, 1990, Kach had come a long way since its establishment fourteen years earlier. Though Rabbi Meir Kahane's party was disqualified in 1988 by Israel's Central Elections Committee from participating in the electoral process, its critics could not dismiss it as an insignificant or ephemeral phenomenon. Rabbi Kahane's dogged persistence, and the growing acceptance of his message, had made Kach a threat not only to the Tehiya and its political offspring but even to the Likud. It was hardly surprising that the appeal to disqualify Kach—on the grounds of its racist and antidemocratic stand—was endorsed by the Likud and tacitly supported by the entire ultranationalist camp. Not only was Kahane feared by Israel's Arabs; he had also become the nightmare of many Israeli Jews.

Kach remains a protest movement *par excellence,* a politically organized right-wing backlash. Gush Emunim and the Tehiya, like Kach, spring at least in part from protest and frustration, but both have always been constructively oriented; their remedies have been settlement in Judea and Samaria, and rejuvenation of pioneering Zionism. The image they have projected has been youth, optimism, success, and self-confidence. In contrast, Kach seems to attract bitter and insecure people who project a sense of failure: failure in the Israeli economy, failure to identify with the nation's symbols of legitimacy, and failure to advance constructive projects in the manner of Gush Emunim and the Tehiya.

Kach's sole attempt to establish a settlement in the West Bank, El-Nakam (Avenging God), in the early 1980s, failed miserably. When asked

211

why, Kahane had two contradictory answers. First, he said, Kach was never given any land, which a settlement needs. But, second, "None of the Gush Emunim settlements really matters, for if the people of Israel repent, all the problems will be solved by God, and if they don't, no settlement will save them from the hatred of the Gentiles and the wrath of God."[1]

The style of Kach is, consequently, negative and even destructive. It projects a bitter anti-establishment image with simplistic catch-all solutions—evict the Arabs from Israel, eliminate "Hellenism" in the Jewish state. Studies of the demographics of the supporters and potential supporters of Kach indicate that the party has become a prime channel for social protest in Israel.[2] Most of the people who favor Kach emotionally, even though they may not actually vote for it, are attracted to the party because its anti-establishment posture appeals to their immense social bitterness and political alienation.

Rabbi Meir Kahane, a well-educated American immigrant, has surprisingly been able to galvanize this sentiment and forge it into political power. Pre-election public opinion polls showed Kahane with the support of between 3 and 5 percent of the general public. A significant part of that support comes from *emotional protesters*, who favor the extremist leader because they identify with his style and anti-establishment rhetoric.[3] This protest is directed not only at Israel's traditional left, but also at the Israeli nationalist right, which has greatly disappointed its supporters since coming to power.[4]

The Kach phenomenon seems to be pure sociopolitical protest. Although Kahane was an educated and sophisticated person who had read and written a great deal, it appears that most of his followers never read his books and are not familiar with his ultimate objectives.[5] Thus we should distinguish between Kahane and his small circle, on the one hand, and the movement he had created, on the other.

It is the small circle of admirers that had kept Kahane going over the years, whether in Israel or the United States. These people, many from the days of the Jewish Defense League, responded enthusiastically to his sermons, joined his occasional conspiracies, listened to his lectures, read his books and press columns, helped him maintain his small Jerusalem center, the Institute of the Jewish Idea, and had recently joined forces to fulfill his dream of establishing his own yeshiva, the Yeshiva of the Jewish idea.[6] Though Kahane's inner circle had never been large, it supported him politically and emotionally. Thus Kahane could argue before his death that even if he was not successful in politics, he at least devoted his life to the Jewish education of youth, wrote weekly columns and books, and made sure that his Jerusalem museum, the Museum of the Future Holocaust—which purported to document plans now in the works for Jewish genocide—functioned properly.

The Kach movement, on the other hand, for years was an organization with very little substance. Only in 1981 did Kach begin to take on some life with the process intensifying in 1983 after the fiasco in Lebanon and the resignation of Begin.[7] But never has Kach been anything but a right-wing backlash mobilized politically.

Following Kahane's election to the Knesset, Kach established offices in Israel's large cities, but the movement still lacks content and organization. The local branches seem good at stimulating protests and street demonstrations, but are extremely poor in terms of routine political operation. With the single exception of the Kiryat Arba group, the local activists of Kach exhibit neither leadership qualities nor political substance.

Rabbi Kahane was the soul and the engine that drove Kach. He was the founding father of the movement, its only ideologue, public speaker, and representative. He ran Kach in a very personal way, raised its funds, signed most of its checks, and made all the important decisions. He even took care of the logistics of his speaking sorties.[8] Kach never had any written forum of its own, and Kahane was the only one who presented its positions to the public. In 1981 Kahane licensed the General Director of the movement to address small sessions of favorably disposed settlers—on the condition that the main message would be a videotape of Rabbi Kahane's own making while in Ramla prison.[9]

True, the party has some formal organs—a secretariat of seven people and a general council of fifty. But the secretariat had been handpicked by Kahane, and could not go against him.[10] And the council's main function was to let local activists participate and feel they counted; no ideological or strategic deliberation has ever been conducted. Activists met only when Kahane visited; In his lifetime no major step in the life of Kach and no media event could go on without him.

The usual local chapter of Kach amounts to several activists who do the groundwork before Kahane's visits, post Kach's posters, and harass demonstrations and meetings of ideological rivals. Most of these activists are lower-middle-class religious Jews who maintain the movement's operations from their homes with little time or energy, except at election time.[11] In contrast, the main chapters—Jerusalem, Tel Aviv, Haifa, and Kiryat Arba— were connected by a sophisticated wireless transmission network that left the rabbi in control twenty-four hours a day.

The only exception to Kahane's total control has been the Kiryat Arba branch of Kach. It is not a spiritual or ideological center of the movement, but the Kach activists there are capable and experienced settlers who initiate many activities on their own. They also actively participate in the public life of Kiryat Arba and Hebron, and take part in many extralegal deeds and vigilante operations. About 15 percent of the Kiryat Arba residents are Kach supporters; it is the only place in Israel where the party representatives succeeded in being voted into the city council and even becoming for a time coalition partners of the mayor.[12]

But even the Kiryat Arba activists regarded Kahane as their spiritual guide. Some have been former American JDL members for whom the rabbi was also a *rebbe,* a religious and personal mentor. Others are people who feel that Gush Emunim has gone soft on the Arabs; on that question they have sometimes been more extreme than Kahane himself.[13]

Kahane's full control was the central fact of this strange political phenomenon. Israel has seen its share of strong individuals who have created and led social and political movements, and its share of ephemeral one-person election lists. But no Israeli movement that had survived had ever been so totally dependent on one person.

The persistence of Rabbi Meir Kahane in his one-man effort was unique, almost inexplicable. He seemed to be driven by a powerful combination of missionary zeal and personal ambition. His long uphill struggle for political power and recognition, and his repeated setbacks, seemed never to have weakened his commitment to his beliefs nor led him to moderate his radical positions in order to attract more people. There were some reports that he was a moody person who disappeared for weeks or months at a time, studying in the yeshiva or simply doing nothing. Former followers testify that he needed constant action and publicity, and became depressed when he did not get attention.[14] But Kahane always returned, and in the 1988 campaign appeared as healthy and vigorous as ever.[15]

Kahane's complete confidence that he was the only representative of the genuine Judaism of our time, his vehement attacks on the entire roster of the nation's leaders, his moral admonitions and verbal whippings, his refusal to moderate his criticisms even though his ideas and tactics were not shared by a single recognized halakhic authority, and his readiness to fight it out alone indicated that he viewed himself as a biblical prophet. Many of his writings start with "My people" or "Listen, Jews" and are filled with prophecies of doom and gloom or with incredible promises.[16]

But Kahane's ambitions went beyond those of the "ordinary" prophet. His penchant for physical violence led him to repeat that he wanted to control the Ministry of Defense, then become the nation's unchallenged ruler. When asked who in Jewish history was his closest model, he responded with a slight hesitation, "I'd say King David. It was said of King David that he studied every night, and in the morning he would wake up and make war."[17]

Whatever religious or psychological interpretation is given to Kahane's personality, it is clear that Kach has been created specifically to fulfill his ideas. Until Kahane's death, the story of Kach was his personal story, an orthodox rabbi, a journalist, a self-styled ideologue, and a street leader. It was the tale of one man's effort to go against the rest of the world and win. Kahane's unexpected assassination destroyed all these dreams. It dealt a huge blow to his close activists, and to the movement in general, and left their future very much in the dark.

Catastrophic Messianism and Fundamentalist Determinism: The Ideo-Theology of Rabbi Kahane

Rabbi Meir Kahane was a prolific writer and an innovative ideologue. Ever since he established the Jewish Defense League in 1968, Kahane had been writing extensively on public matters with twelve books and hundreds of pamphlets and newspaper columns. Unlike the leaders of Gush Emunim, who grew up in a very structured and collective ambiance, and who had a natural constituency with whom to converse, Kahane always operated outside of established organizations, and needed to write about his ideas to convince people of his views.

Kahane's writings are unmistakably the product of a radical mind that blends his orthodox education of the New York Mirrer Yeshiva, his B.A. in political science from Brooklyn College, his law degree from New York Law School, and his master's degree in international affairs from New York University.[18] Though Kahane's thought is not as theologically profound as Rav Kook's, it nevertheless is a cohesive system of religious ideology. This system is marked by basic assumptions drawn from selective and highly tendentious interpretations of the Bible and Halakhic authorities, by derivative propositions of a general political character, and by radical conclusions. The Revisionist influence of Vladimir Jabotinsky is very marked, and Kahane once acknowledged the influence of Dr. Israel Eldad, the right-wing ideologue of the Kingdom of Israel school. Certain emphases in his writing changed over the years, but his cast of mind remained the same.

The most striking element in Kahane's system is his deterministic fundamentalism. No other Zionist religious writer had so insisted on the doctrine of inerrancy—the necessity to read the Bible as a set of rules and live by them.[19] The fundamentalism of Rabbi Kahane is total, direct, and devoid of mystery. So is his style of writing and preaching. Many of his books are more reminiscent of the Christian evangelism of Jimmy Swaggart and Oral Roberts than the teaching of Rav Kook.

Kahane had never admitted that he saw himself as modern Judaism's angry prophet, but the style and passion of his writings communicate the impression most clearly: The people of Israel are living in sin and are about to be punished. Their only hope is repentence, the sooner the better. Sometimes Kahane writes as the prophet thrown into prison (Jeremiah) and at others as the prophet of doom (Ezekiel).

Kahane's God is, of course, the Almighty Himself, but there is no mystery about Him or about His ways of conducting the world. Basically He is a supreme and sovereign warlord who must be totally obeyed. Kahane's God is very human—if His instructions are carefully followed, He is pleased; if they are disregarded, He gets angry. And since Kahane's Bible makes God's specific orders and political recommendations clear and unequivocal, there should be no difficulty obeying Him. There is, furthermore, no question about the punishment that awaits those who do not, for God is *El Nakam Veshiiem* (the Avenging God).

As respectful as the rabbi is of the Bible, he read it as if it were a twentieth-century manual for the conduct of public affairs. When an American journalist once asked about the realism of Kahane's political suggestions, he responded, "My whole system is based on the presupposition that God is stronger than President Reagan."[20] He has no Kookist problems with God's mysterious ways.

> In Jewish history, from time immemorial, and in Jewish history today, that which will be is conditioned on one thing only: "*If you shall walk in My statutes,*" and "*If you shall disdain My statutes.*" . . . The former guarantees peace and tranquillity and bliss and redemption. The latter assures tragedy and catastrophe. There is no escape from this immutable law of creation. But if one does, indeed, walk in the footsteps of his Creator, then the Father of the Jewish people, the All-Mighty, has obligated Himself to give to His children the promised reward. This is the answer, this is the key to the Gate of redemption. One who understands it shall enter it. One who does not is doomed to be scattered as the chaff in the wind and, G—d forbid, to take many of his brothers and sisters with him."[21]

Kahane's fundamentalist reliance on the Bible as the ultimate guide was matched by his equally bold assertion that he, and he alone, possessed the truth. This was indeed strange, for Kahane insisted that he functioned within a very structured and involuntary theology, the Halakha. Since there are thousands of orthodox rabbis and scholars who are entitled, according to the Jewish tradition, to read Halakha and explain it, one would naturally expect Kahane to have referred to at least a few living authorities. But such reference did not exist. While he did not pretend to be an authority on every aspect of Jewish law (although he repeatedly let one know that he was a *Talmid Hacham*—a Jewish scholar—in the full sense of the term), he saw himself as the sole authority on political and national matters.[22]

In 1974, Kahane established his Center of the Jewish Idea to propagate his theories and beliefs. Most of his publications came from the center and left no doubt as to the rabbi's self-evaluation: "Rabbi Meir Kahane, Philosopher! Visionary! Revolutionary! The most exciting, dynamic, *different* Jewish leader . . . the exponent of the Authentic Jewish idea."[23] In his recent *Uncomfortable Questions to Comfortable Jews,* Kahane went a step further. Defending his so-called "Kahanism," which has come under major public attack in Israel since 1984, he argued against his "leftist" critics:

> Let there be no mistake. . . . These are the real fascists, the real killers. They hate and wish to destroy Kahane—but only as a symbol of that which is the target of their ultimate hate. They hate Kahane because they hate Judaism and Jews, and themselves. And there is nothing they will not do in order to wipe out that Kahanism they correctly see as true Judaism.[24]

Kahanism, then, is not just another approach to the conduct of public affairs, it is *the true Judaism,* and Kahane is its prophet, the only legitimate representative of "the authentic Jewish idea" in this generation. Kahane's self-confidence and total conviction in his personal uniqueness and calling were confirmed in private interviews, in which he admitted that he had no respect for the teachings of Rav Kook, and that Gush Emunim made no difference in the world. Rav Shach, the most revered authority of the ultraorthodox Lithuenian yeshivot in Israel is, according to Kahane "enormous Jew," but on political and national matters he is wrong since he still "lives in the Diaspora." There were, according to Kahane's account, several authorities that agreed with him—most noteworthy among them was Rabbi Mordechai Eliyahu, Israel's chief Sepharadi rabbi—but none of them had the courage to stand up publicly and be counted.[25] Thus, there was only one person in this sinful generation who told the truth, Rabbi Meir Kahane. While Kahane's ideo-theology has been expounded in many books and essays, it can usefully be summarized in several key points, as follows.

The Uniqueness of the Jewish People

Kahane's fundamental, insistently repeated axiom is that the Jewish people is unique, singular and holy, the only nation chosen by God:

> The Jewish people is a unique, distinct, and separate people, divinely chosen at Sinai, a religion-nation, transcending the foolishness and danger of shallow secular nationalism that merely divides without raising up. . . . Its chosenness is not a racial or national thing, but based on the chosen mission; i.e., it is a people that was given a sacred law, the Torah, and an immutable destiny to live and uphold the Torah so as to serve as a light unto the nations. . . . All that has happened, happens, and will happen goes according to a divine plan at the center of which stands the Jewish people.[26]

Kahane's "singularity" axiom is not a detached theoretical proposition to which most Jews might possibly agree, but a fundamentalist operational statement. It means that the Jewish nation is different from the rest of the world and is not, and ought not to be, bound by external laws or universal norms. On the contrary, it possesses a complete system of behavior that is exclusively its own, and it owes no respect to the moral or behavioral norms of other philosophies or nations. Universalism, whatever its worth to mankind in general, does not concern the Jewish people. And since the Almighty God of Israel stands behind his people, its unique path is bound to lead to success.

> Let us not forget that we came to Eretz Yisrael in order to establish a Jewish state and not a Western-style state. Jewish values, not ephemeral Western

values, should guide us. Neither liberalism and democracy nor a so-called progressive outlook should determine what is good or bad for us.[27]

Kahane's particular approach extends to the claim that the Jewish nation is "the heart of the heart of the world and the reason for its existence." What matters, consequently, is not what is going on in the world but what is happening to the Jewish people. The rest is nonsense, an unimportant footnote to Jewish history and reality. It follows that *Kahane has no meaningful concept of international relations or international law:* If there exists a sphere of international relations in which the nations of the world interact and have some common ground rules, that reality belongs to a lower level of human action. It cannot, and should not, bind or restrict the State of Israel.

Kahane's Theory of Revenge and the Call for Jewish Isolationism

There is another powerful source for Kahane's hostility to the rest of the world, a most profound animosity toward and mistrust of the *Goyim* (Gentiles). Since time immemorial Jews have expressed antagonism toward the cruel Gentile nations that have persecuted the Jews and murdered them. Kahane was without doubt the most extreme modern representative of this school.[28] Kahane's hostility to the Gentiles is certainly the strongest emotional and psychological theme of his political theology. There is not a single essay or book in which this enmity and thirst for revenge do not surface. Kahane's emotional reaction to the Gentiles is so profound that *they, not the Jews, are paradoxically responsible for the establishment of the State of Israel.* Israel was established, according to Kahane, not because the Zionists (who did not repent!) deserved it, but as a result of the actions of the Gentiles. The perennial humiliation of the Jews by the Gentiles was, according to this strange theory, also a humiliation of God, Who established the State of Israel as His revenge against the Gentiles.

While the revenge theory was only fully developed in the 1980s, it is already noticeable in an essay Kahane wrote after the 1974 terror attack on a school in Kiryat Shmone that took the lives of many children. In that essay, *Hillul Hashem* (the desecration of the name of God), Kahane developed his answer to the Kookist propositions on modern redemption and the origins of the State of Israel:

> The debate about the religious legitimacy of the State of Israel and its place in our history has been conducted within religious circles for a long time. It has focused on the penetrating and real question: How can a religious Jew see the hand of G–d in a state that was established by Jews who not only do not follow the paths of G–d, but reject Him openly or, at best, are passive to His blessed existence? . . . The State of Israel was established not because the Jew deserved it, for the Jew is as he has been before, rejecting G–d, deviating from his paths, and ignoring His Torah. . . . G–d created this state not for the

Jew and not as a reward for his justice and good deeds. It is because He, blessed be His Name, decided that He could no longer take the desecration of his name and the laughter, the disgrace, and the persecution of the people that was named after him, so He ordered the State of Israel to be, which is a total contradiction to the Diaspora.

If the Diaspora, with its humiliations, defeats, persecutions, second-class status of a minority . . . means Hillul Hashem, then a sovereign Jewish state which provides the Jew home, majority status, land of his own, a military of his own, and a victory over the defeated Gentile in the battlefield, *is exactly the opposite,* Kidush Hashem (the sanctification of the name of G–d). It is the reassertion, the proof, the testimony for the existence of G–d and his government.[29]

Thus, Kahane's State of Israel is not a reward for the Jews, but a punishment for the Gentiles! The specific Gentiles may not be the same, but they are always there—the Nazis, the blacks, the Christians, the Russians, and, of course, the Arabs. Kahane's radicalism, passion and commitment seem to be exclusively rooted in this one element, the insatiable urge to beat the *Goy,* to respond in kind for two millennia of vilification of the Jews. However, since he claims to be more than an individual Jew who seeks revenge, and is rather expressing the Halakha opinion and the voice of God, the vengeance the Jews are supposed to take is not simply a personal act, but the revenge of God for the humiliation He suffered through the desecration of His people.

Do you want to know how the Name of G–d is desecrated in the eyes of the mocking and sneering nations? It is when the *Jew,* His people, His chosen, is desecrated! When the *Jew* is beaten, G–d is profaned! When the *Jew* is humiliated, G–d is shamed! When the *Jew* is attacked, it is an assault upon the Name of G–d! . . .

Every pogrom is a desecration of the Name. Every Auschwitz and expulsion and murder and rape of a Jew is the humiliation of G–d. Every time a Jew is beaten by a gentile because he is a Jew, this is the essence of Hillul Hashem! . . .

An end to Exile—that is Kidush Hashem. An end to the shame and beatings and the monuments to our murdered and our martyrized. . . . An end to the Gentile fist upon a Jewish face. . . .

A Jewish fist in the face of an astonished gentile world that had not seen it for two millennia, this is Kidush Hashem. Jewish dominion over the Christian holy places while the Church that sucked our blood vomits its rage and frustration. This is Kidush Hashem. A Jewish Air Force that is better than any other and that forces a Lebanese airliner down so that we can imprison murderers of Jews rather than having to repeat the centuries-old pattern of begging the gentile to do it for us. This is Kidush Hashem. . . . Reading angry editorials about Jewish "aggression" and "violations" rather than flowery eulogies over dead Jewish victims. That is Kidush Hashem.[30]

Kahane's use of the formal Halakhic terminology of *Hillul Hashem,* and *Kidush Hashem* should not mislead the reader. The sanctification of the name of God is not the main objective. What really comes out of these emotional statements is his conviction that the very definition of Jewish freedom implies the ability to humiliate the Gentile. The stronger the Jew is, the more violent and aggressive, the freer he becomes.

Kahane may not have gone as far as Georges Sorel and Frantz Fanon in claiming that violence is a moral force in history or that violence sets one free, but he does share many traits with both, especially Fanon.[31] For what he is proposing is that an independent Jewish state is not enough. Jewish sovereignty solves only the misery of exile. There is another wound that has to be healed, the pain of humiliation, victimization, and genocide. Kahane does not concentrate solely on the Holocaust, though his reaction to the Nazi genocide has always been profound. For him, though, the Holocaust was a natural product of anti-Semitism, one that could develop in any "normal" nation and is still a historical possibility.[32] The Holocaust and the countless pogroms that preceded it have left in the nation's collective psyche an almost irreparable damage, which can be redressed only by a concrete revenge, a physical humiliation of the Gentiles. Therefore Kahane, like Fanon, is not satisfied with a peaceful liberation. A military force that astonishes the world is needed, "a fist in the face of the Gentile."[33]

Kahane rejects the Gentiles for another reason: their non-Jewish poisonous ideas have attracted young Jews since time immemorial, and have led them to believe that these ideologies could solve the problems of the world.

> How we believed all the false prophets and how we drank eagerly from all the poisoned water! How we ran toward all the glittering frauds and away from the strong and eternal Jewish verities! How we believed in Reform and Assimilation and Enlightenment and Cultural Pluralism and Liberalism and Democracy and Socialism and Marxism and Participatory Democracy and Chairman Mao and Comrade Leon (Trotsky) and Rationalism and the inherent decency of man. . . . All of it died in flames of Auschwitz and the mockery of Stalinist trials and the madness of an irrational mob.[34]

Thus the inescapable conclusion is that Jews should finally isolate themselves from the rest of the world. Given the danger of a future holocaust or even of a nonviolent cultural elimination through assimilation, they should all flock to Israel and sever their ties with the hostile world. At stake is the very survival of all Diaspora Jews, and, according to Kahane, time is running out. No nation or diplomatic relations or economic ties will protect them. But the people of Israel are the children of God, and He rather than any *realpolitik* will solve all their problems. The "increasing isolation of the Jewish people is a blessing and not a curse and a sign of the sure coming of the final redemption."[35]

Catastrophic Messianism

Kahane's early JDL message was far more political than religious, with neither messianic philosophy nor millennarian dreams about transforming

Israel into a Halakhic state. But since the Six-Day War, Zionist fundamental-ism and Gush Emunim have introduced to Israel's public discourse a new paradigm that openly embraces messianic language. In this context, a religious-maximalist creed could be taken seriously only if it included a messianic component, and Kahane quickly began to assert that the Jewish nation is living in a messianic era in which it is about to be redeemed. This had eventually become a fundamental tenet for him, an unquestionable presupposition of his whole theory:

> We are all standing . . . at one of the greatest moments of Jewish history. . . . It is as clear as the sunshine that Almighty G–d is ready now to bring us over the final redemption, and that the beginning of the freedom is already work-ing. We envision now the historical moment of redemption.[36]

Though redemption became central to Kahane's political program, the concept is one of the weakest and most artificial parts of his grand theory. Even within his generally simplistic system it sounds mechanical and uncon-vincing. Kahane addresses the issue of redemption as if it is some kind of celebration that may or may not happen tomorrow, according to the behav-ior of the people. Nowhere does this strange and mechanistic approach show more clearly than when Kahane writes that the event might already have taken place had the leaders of the nation done the right thing:

> We stood on the brink of a complete redemption. If we had only had the courage and the faith to keep it! If we had declared about the liberated territories: "These are ours and have just been returned"! If we had officially annexed them to the state of Israel; if we had taken the Gentiles's abomina-tions from the Temple Mount; if we had expelled our haters from the coun-try; if we had made free Jewish settlement all over Eretz Yisrael mandatory— if we had done all these things without considering the reaction of the Goy, without fearing what he says or does, the Messiah would have come through the open door and brought us the redemption.[37]

Even great Jewish authorities are unsure on such mysterious questions as the meaning and shape of the Messiah and the circumstances of his coming, but this does not seem to bother Kahane at all. Nor does he see fit to discuss or debate the most important messianic philosophy of our time, the Kookist theology and its various interpretations. Kahane's Messiah does not need definition or explanation. He is simply to come at the moment, as defined by Kahane, when the Jewish people are ready.

One of the key features of Kahane's messianism is its catastrophic char-acter. There was always an apocalyptic element in his writing, a message of utmost urgency vis-à-vis a possible holocaust. Long before he moved to Israel, Kahane predicted the violent demise of the Diaspora: not only was Soviet Jewry about to die but American Jewry was as well. To avert disaster, Kahane prescribed "a program for Jewish survival."[38] Israel was, in those early days, a secure sanctuary.

But the rabbi's apocalyptic vision apparently followed him to the Holy

Land. In 1973 and 1974 Kahane wrote two essays: *Israel's Eternity and Victory* and *Numbers 23:9,* in which he first developed his catastrophic messianism.[39] The entire theory was based on a verse from Isaiah "In its time, I will hurry it (the redemption)" (Isaiah 60), and on its rabbinical interpretation, "If they, the Jews, merit it, I will hurry it. If they do not merit it, it will come 'in its time' " (Sanhedrin 93). Redemption, then, is an inevitable part of God's plan and will come regardless of what the people of Israel do. What is left to the Jews is the determination of *how and when* redemption takes place.

If they repent, according to Kahane's interpretation, redemption will come quickly and without pain. But if they do not, redemption will come after great troubles, wars, and disasters. The establishment of the State of Israel in 1948 and the victory of 1967 were unmistakable signs of God's desire to "hurry it"—provided the nation was ready to repent. But the Yom Kippur War proved there was a serious problem on the road to salvation. At that point Kahane warned the people of Israel about the disasters in store should they not respond to God's gesture and return to orthodox Judaism.

In 1980 Kahane had plenty of time to reconsider his grand ideo-theology. He was placed without trial for nine months in the Ramla maximum-security prison for planning to blow up the Dome of the Rock on the Temple Mount (one of many such schemes). It was a productive period, for he completed two major books, *Thorns in Your Eyes* and *On Redemption and Faith,* and a highly original essay, *Forty Years.*

The later book's novelty was Kahane's daring conclusion that in 1948, the year Israel obtained its independence, the nation was given a grace period of forty years in which to repent and prepare for God's hurried redemption. But a warning was implied: if no repentence took place, the *inevitable* redemption ("in its time") was to occur, not out of God's grace but out of His fury, and through a tremendous disaster. The miraculous victory in 1967 showed that God was keeping His part of the bargain and that it was now time for the people to fulfill its part. But the nation had not yet repented by 1980, and its time was running out.

> Consider, Jew . . . *if it is true that the forty years began with the rise of the State—how many years are left?*
>
> Too few. So little time to make the great decision that will either bring us the great and glorious redemption, swiftly, majestically, spared the terrible sufferings and needless agonies, or G–d forbid, the madness of choosing the path of unnecessary, needless holocaust, more horrible than anything we have yet endured. . . .
>
> My people; my dear and foolish people! We speak of your life and those of your seed, your children and grandchildren. Choose wisely! Choose life! The Magnificence is yours for the asking. The horror will be yours for the blindness. Choose life, but quickly; there is little time left. *The forty years tick away.*[40]

Since 1980 Kahane had become the prophet of doom and gloom. One might wonder how deeply he believed in his own predictions, and whether they were an article of faith of a prophet in the tradition of Jeremiah, or an expression of a troubled person who knows no one takes his warning seriously. But when he discussed the issue of catastrophe in private interviews, he said that even if he were the prime minister, a catastrophe would still take place if the nation did not repent willingly.[41]

The Sanctity of Eretz Yisrael

Like other Zionist fundamentalists, Kahane is certain that all of Eretz Yisrael is holy, and that the Jews have an inalienable right to every part of it,

> Indeed, there exists a Jewish state, a homeland for the Jewish people sanctified by a divine promise. This is the basis of the Jewish right. It is not a request, an appeal or a proposition. It is a power of right that does not recognize any denial. . . . Eretz Yisrael is the land of the Jewish people and it claims hegemony over all of it. Our claim cannot be appealed. It is as old as the divine promise that was given to the nation's founding fathers.[42]

God's promise to Abraham is thus as valid now as it was 4000 years ago, and the Jewish right "is not only for a sovereign state but for an ownership over the borders of the entire Eretz Yisrael." The fact that Jordan and other Arab countries now occupy part of that is irrelevant, because they are illegal usurpers. According to Kahane, the 1947 Israeli agreement to have a Jewish state in only a small part of the land was a tactical agreement when there was no alternative. "It was neither a concession nor cancellation of the Jewish right to Eretz Yisrael, only an expression of an aspiration for peace and the realization of part of the Jewish claims until the Messiah comes and solves questions and problems."[43] Since the enemies of Israel have repudiated all the agreements they made, the nation has returned by right to Judea and Samaria, and that act is irreversible. Now if the Arabs agree to peace within their present borders, there should not be another war; they may have their Palestine in whatever territories they now hold. "But if they challenge us and force a war upon us, then, God willing, the rest of the Jewish land will be redeemed and returned to its legal owners."[44]

Kahane's general position on the territorial issue is not particularly radical. Surprisingly, he does not call for *Milhemet Mitzva* (an obligatory war) to regain the entire promised land; in this matter he follows the more cautious Halakha authorities. But on the issue of the occupied territories he is as radical as one could be.

According to Kahane's latest interpretation, in 1967 God directed the Six-Day War, so it is a criminal offense not to abide by his command: Jews should be ready to die rather than surrender the Land. *Yehareg Uval Yaavor* (Be killed rather than sin) is the rule that should govern the case. Kahane's position on the territorial question includes both a profound fundamentalist attachment and strong insistence on territorial integrity.

Indeed, he further maintains that Israel's national interests dictate that even occupied territories that were not included in the biblical promise may not be returned to the enemy. Only under the strict conditions that imply unconditional surrender, irrevocable readiness for peace, and recognition of Judaism's religious superiority is negotiation over territory permissible. This places him among the most extreme members of the Greater Israel school.[45]

The Arabs

No political issue occupied and obsessed Rabbi Meir Kahane more than the question of the Arabs in Israel and the occupied territories, even before he moved to Israel. When the JDL embarked on its violent course in late 1969, it demonstrated and protested at the Arab U.N. delegations in New York.[46] After he came to Israel in 1971, the Arabs became Kahane's prime target, both for polemics and for aggressive actions.

Kahane's profound internalization of the age-old suffering of the Jews, and his consequent hostility to the Gentiles had been the most dominant force in his political psychology. And for Kahane, the Arabs were the ultimate Gentiles. The majority of them have never recognized the Zionist venture in Palestine. Their most important leader in Mandatory Palestine, Haj Amin al-Husseini, the Grand Mufti of Jerusalem, conspired with Hitler to participate in the Nazi "final solution," and had been involved in many pogroms against unarmed Jews. Since 1948, the Arabs have been responsible for five wars with the Jews, and have vowed, after each defeat, to destroy Israel. Arab terrorism has been a major factor in the life of modern Israel, and the 1968 PLO Charter incorporated it into a cohesive ideology.

It would be surprising if an obsessed ideologue like Kahane had not made the Arab issue his major stock in trade. Kahane stated his theory in a nutshell by saying that the Arabs are "thorns in our eyes." They are vicious and mortally dangerous, and they ought to be expelled from the Jewish state by any means.

Kahane's theoretical discussion of the Arab problem has two aspects, religious fundamentalism and secular nationalism. Like the writers of Gush Emunim, Kahane addresses two major questions: First, do the Arabs have any collective or individual rights in the state of Israel? Second, what should the government of Israel do about the answer to this question? Most of the Gush leaders visualize several possible solutions, but Kahane—who cited most of the same Halakhic sources—is decisive. His fundamental proposition is that all authoritative Jewish sources make it clear that the Promised Land was given to the chosen people in a specific way. They were not offered a choice, but were commanded to live there and shape *Am Segula* (A special nation) in isolation, with no interference from others:

It is impossible to shape holy, glorious and virtuous people as a minority in the land of another nation, since the culture of the majority is inevitably bound to penetrate, influence, corrupt, tempt, and distort. The Jew is commanded to make a holy nation out of himself, and this is possible only in isolation, free of others' influence. This is the reason why the special Jewish people . . . was given a separate and unique land to live in, in order to create a holy, virtuous society that would become a light unto the Gentiles, to be separated and followed. . . . The land *was taken* from the Gentiles—the Canaanites—in order to make it possible for the Jew to fulfill his calling.[47]

Kahane does not make the usual nationalistic argument—that the land is Jewish property because it belonged to the Jews before they were forced into exile, since they never gave it up willingly. Instead he argues that the land is owned by the Jews because they *expropriated* it in the name of God and his sovereign will—an act that can be repeated today with no remorse, since God's will has not changed.

Consequently, secular legal arguments on the Jewish absolute right to the land are irrelevant. Kahane's God, acting in a very personified way, has seen and understood since time immemorial the problems that might emerge if the issue of the ownership of the land had not been settled clearly. God therefore made it absolutely clear that only one nation had the right to Eretz Yisrael.[48]

Kahane's position is that aliens in general and Arabs in particular have no *a priori* rights in the country whatsoever. Whatever rights they may enjoy depends on the good will of the Jews, the full owners of the country. And these rights are limited at best, for the Halakha instructs that alien residents can never be equal members of the community and enjoy full political rights.

Thus, even Muslims who qualify for some rights can never become full citizens of the state of Israel. A Muslim may remain on the land as an alien resident, pay special taxes, submit to special labor regulations, and swear allegiance to the state. But even then, he will not be able to live in Jerusalem, will occasionally be checked for his loyalty, and in general must be "humble and low."[49]

The Arabs who are not ready to live according to these rules, and thus remain hostile to the Jews, will in Kahane's scheme be treated according to the biblical regulations applied by Joshua Ben-Nun to the ancient Canaanites. Joshua, he reminds us, sent the Canaanites letters offering them three alternatives: leave the land, fight for it and bear the consequences, or peacefully surrender to the Jews and obtain the status of loyal resident alien.[50]

Kahane's fundamentalist approach, a strict twentieth-century application of a three-thousand-year-old biblical ruling, is augmented by a meticulous secular-nationalist analysis. According to Kahane, there is no Palestinian people to deserve the right of self-determination. The real Palestinian question is basically a problem of individual Arabs who live in Eretz Yisrael, who should be treated as individuals. "There are Arabs, those who had lived for years in Eretz Yisrael, and they are part and parcel of the Arab nation.

We respect ànd recognize their existence, but they are not Palestinians, for such national definition had never existed."[51]

Nonetheless, Kahane was aware that there are Arabs who *believe* they are Palestinians and are ready to fight for that conviction, an awareness that made him by far the most pessimistic Israeli ideologue on this issue. Unlike most of the thinkers of the radical right, he believed that even the Israeli Arabs—those who stayed in Israel after 1948 and received full Israeli citizenship—have been "thinking Palestinian" all along. Like the Arabs of the West Bank, they believe they are Palestinian and consequently pose a mortal danger to Israel.

> Not only the Arabs of the liberated territories see themselves as "Palestinian" and believe that the Jews plundered their homeland. Even the Arabs . . . who have received Israeli citizenship since 1948 . . . who enjoy freedom in the Jewish state, think that. . . .
> Let us suppose that the peace had somehow been achieved and that all the "outside" Arabs . . . have recognized Israel. Israel would not be freed of Arab nationalism even then. She will not be freed from the burden of the inside Arab population . . . a large public that is hostile to the Jewish majority and the Jewish state, and wishes to see it destroyed, or at least see its character and national identity changed.[52]

The Israeli Arabs, according to Kahane, are more dangerous than the Arabs of the occupied territories; they enjoy full political rights and can use Israeli law to protect their subversive activities. Though they do not serve in the army and pay very little in taxes, they are entitled to all the benefits of the Israeli welfare system. The "demographic problem"—the danger that the Arabs will eventually outnumber the Jews and take over the state by democratic means—applies to Israeli Arabs as much as to the Arabs of the occupied territories. Israeli Arabs take special advantage of the National Insurance Institute, which encourages large families by giving generous allowances to families with more than three children. Thus, Kahane maintained, they do not have to make war against Israel in order to take over. Since their birth rate is much higher than that of the Jews, all they have to do is produce many children.[53]

Once the Arabs become 30 or 40 percent of the population, they will be in a position to dictate Israeli politics. They will demand greater representation and more power. Since Israel's government has always relied on coalitions in which small partners have had great influence, the Arabs would need only about 25 percent of the Knesset seats to become the major power-broker of Israeli politics. Thus Kahane believed that if the present system of Israeli government is not changed soon, the Jewish state will be destroyed.

> The confrontation will come when the Israeli Arabs become one-fourth or one-third of the nation's population. The riots and civil disobedience will be seen on television screens all over the world. Bombs will explode and dozens

will die in the confrontations between soldiers and Arab citizens. . . . World public opinion will turn against Israel and the American Jews will argue and split. In the Knesset, twenty-five or thirty Arab Knesset members will disturb the sessions, and will demand autonomy and proper representation for the Arabs. Aliya to Israel will practically stop . . . and the rate of emigration, on the other hand, will increase.[54]

With Palestinian extremism within Israel continuing to rise, Kahane argued that his conclusion "they must go" was increasingly true and relevant.

Judaism versus Democracy

Just as Kahane's position on the Arabs became more radical, so did his views of democracy. The rabbi was by far the most vocal enemy of the democratic principle and system of government is present-day Israel. At the beginning of his career in the United States, Kahane had little to say about democracy and concentrated on Jewish self-defense against ethnic hostility. In Israel, however, as his radical solution for the Arab problem crystallized, Kahane had repeatedly been accused of being anti-democratic. He consequently had to clarify his stand on the question of democracy and the rule of law.

His 1977 book *Law and Order in Israel* concerned the controversy over the illicit settlement of Elon Moreh. Here Kahane made clear that he considered democracy an alien, Gentile idea. If a democratically elected Jewish government obeys religious laws and an interpretation of Orthodox authorities, then it is admissible and fine: but if it does not, all its laws, regulations, and policies are unacceptable and false.[55]

Before 1978 Kahane was still optimistic about the ability of the "right" rulers of Israel to encourage the Arabs to leave Eretz Yisrael and to introduce a more intense Jewish culture and education through the democratic process. These changes, he thought, could be accomplished without a fundamental constitutional revolution in Israel. But the 1978 Camp David Accords and the public campaign to silence him after his 1984 election to the Knesset radicalized his position a great deal. The first salvo in his comprehensive attack on liberal democracy in general, and Israeli democracy in particular, was his 1980 attack on Israel's Declaration of Independence, which had become his principle ideological target. In his most recent book, *Uncomfortable Questions to Comfortable Jews,* Kahane gives one of his most forceful theoretical arguments on the fundamental gap between Judaism and liberal democracy.

> The liberal west speaks about the rule of democracy, of the authority of the majority, while Judaism speaks of the Divine truth that is immutable and not subject to the ballot box or to majority error. The liberal west speaks about the absolute equality of all people while Judaism speaks of spiritual *status,* of

the chosenness of the Jew above all other people, of the special and exclusive relationship between G–d and Israel. The liberal west speaks of subjective truth, of no one being able to claim or to know what is absolute truth, while Judaism speaks of objective, eternal truth that is *known,* having been given by G–d at Sinai. . . .

But above all, Judaism differs from liberal and *non-liberal* western values in that the foundation upon which it rests is that of *"the yoke of Heaven,"* the acceptance of G–d's law and values and concepts as truth, without testing them in the fires of one's own knowledge, choice, desires, and acceptance. . . . It is the Almighty who created the world and the word, who created finite and stumbling man, who created justice and decency and mercy and good, and we accept that because of that. It is this Yoke of Heaven, the setting aside of our will before His . . . , that is the fundamental of Judaism.[56]

Kahane's first argument about the epistemological difference between the liberal West and Judaism, is, of course, not new and does not pertain to Judaism alone. Every fundamentalist preacher could probably make the same proposition, just as every devoted Marxist or ideological fascist could. His second argument regarding the complete sovereignty of God and the prohibition on testing His decrees leaves very little to the judgment of the individual believer. The practical conclusion of this *totalistic* (or perhaps totalitarian) Jewish epistemology is that the individual Jew, his family, and his community have no civil rights in the modern sense—a "blasphemous" concept that is meaningless and useless.

The liberal west speaks of tolerance and the obligation to respect all views regardless of their rightness or wrongness, while Judaism demands that the Jew choose truth and the path of right and not tolerate evil in his midst. And so the homosexual, the prostitute, the abortionist, the addict are not permitted the tolerance of living their own lives as they see fit, for Judaism is not a certificate of license, but of obligation. . . . The liberal west categorically negates certain concepts—i.e., vengeance, hate, and violence—almost *a priori,* while Judaism speaks of "a time to love and a time to hate, a time for war and a time for peace," with the need and commandment to love the good and hate the evil, to seek peace but to go to war against the wicked, with vengeance at the proper time, *an obligation* in order to show that there is a Judge and there is justice in the world.[57]

Democracy, so it appears, disturbs Kahane not because of the Arab problem and its danger to the existence of Israel, but because it is totally alien to the Judaism of the Torah. The fact that 3000 years have passed since the laws of the Torah were written does not disturb Kahane at all. He sees the entire experience of liberal democracy, in which Jews have taken a major part in the last two centuries, as meaningless. Only rarely does Kahane admit that Western democracy is preferable to some other systems.[58] The vices of this permissive system—"a state in which all the ugliness and obscenity of animal hedonism and bestial selfishness can be given free rein in order to enslave and then destroy the special Divine image that was given to man"[59]—and the decadence of its society and culture have such a dangerous and corrupting influence on youth that no element of democracy can be good. Kahane's attacks on democracy are full of vitriolic comments and bitter irony:

> Liberal democracy is a sociologist's Garden of Eden, a kind of Paradise Found, of Margaret Meadism. Having discovered that there exists a Pacific island with natives who eat their mothers-in-law, the liberal democrats postulate that there is surely no objective prohibition to eat mothers-in-law, that the failure to eat mothers-in-law is rather a specific cultural aberration of the west, and this holds true of all taboos and prohibitions. Truth, says liberal democracy, is in the mind of the believer and no one has the right to declare that he possesses it and therefore demand the right to impose it on a majority that disagrees or denies it as being truth.[60]

Orthodox Judaism simply can't be assessed according to the norms of liberal humanism and democracy, and this fact lies at the root of Kahane's apparently rude and discriminatory treatment of Arabs. Judaism, in his view, simply does not recognize the Arabs as equal to the Jews and is very specific about their low status and future in the Jewish state. In *Uncomfortable Questions*, Kahane is at pains to prove that the Judaism he writes about is the same Judaism that says to greet the Gentile in the marketplace with *shalom* (peace) and believes that all men are created in the image of God. Opponents argue that Kahane takes from the Bible and Halakha only what suits his warlike theories, and ignores the human and compassionate face of Judaism. Kahane responds that Judaism makes a fundamental distinction between the private and personal sphere of the individual and the national and political sphere.

> The greatest value is peace? Of course. . . . The Jew greets the gentile with peace, and he deals with him with respect and honor and decency in all his private and personal relations with him—but not as a *citizen* of the Jewish state. Not as one who has any *national* say in the Jewish state. And certainly not even "shalom" to an *enemy*.
>
> "All men are made in the image of G–d?" Agreed, embraced wholeheartedly. And what relevancy is that to all of the above? All men are made in the image of G–d, and when they are decent we owe them the basic decency and respect we would owe to any Jew. But again, this is limited to the private and personal sphere. The national sphere—state and people and citizenship and equal political rights in a Jewish state—are not the province of non-Jews. One is obligated to run miles to help a decent gentile in his personal problems but not an inch in the sphere of national equality.[61]

Any "Hellenist" or "Neo-Hellenist" who attacks him is "standing outside the pale of that Judaism which, to his horror, is the 'Kahanism' of his grandparents as far back as Sinai."

The Status of the State and a Jewish State

Kahane's repeated attacks on the norms, politics, and culture of democracy and Israel's democracy in particular, set him apart from most of the rest of the radical right. The Kookist theology, for example, sees the secular state of Israel as the legitimate precursor of the Halakhic Kingdom of Israel; despite the mistakes of its lay leaders, it is holy. God will see to it, in his mysterious ways, that in due time its citizens will repent and it will become fully Jewish. But in the meantime the government is duly constituted and deserves full respect and obedience.

For Kahane though, the holiness of the modern state of Israel does not extend to its lay institutions and leaders. The state is holy because God willed it to be, as an instrument to avenge His desecrated name among the Gentiles. The lay leaders of Israel who do not recognize the greatness of God and refuse to repent are sinners. Their actions, policies, and non-Jewish behavior are blasphemous. Their laws and institutions do not deserve allegiance or obedience.

> I will never accept the "right" of man and state to be ugly and selfish and addicted to evil and animalism. I will never accept a state that insanely sanctifies the concept of "freedom" of pornography and unbridled, illicit, and perverted sex, and murderous abortions, and artistic national suicide, and drugs that ravage the soul and kill the spirit of heaven within the unique child called man. Never. That is not freedom. That is slavery. . . . And the Almighty who took the Jew out of the physical bondage of Egypt never meant to then take him up to his own land to build a state of slavery of the soul and spirit.[62]

Kahane criticized the political culture of Israel for being "Hellenistic" and its leaders for being "Hellenized"—to be fought against just as the Maccabees fought an earlier Hellenized leadership. Kahane's vitriolic attacks on the "Hellenized" and "Gentilized" indicated that this struggle was of even greater importance than the fight against the Arabs, for it involved the very soul of the nation.[63] During the Knesset debate over a bill to bar the production and selling of pork, Kahane told his colleagues that:

> a huge struggle is going on today, much larger than the Jewish-Arab crisis, the struggle between the Jews and the Hellenized. This is the modern phase of an ancient war. . . . The first person killed by the Maccabees was a Jew who wanted to eat pork. And in this hall today a species has found his progeny—the pigs who defend the pork.
> The real obstacle to the salvation of the people of Israel . . . is the presence of one portion of the nation, the haters of Israel. . . . The real struggle is with them, the struggle between the real Jews and the gentilized. . . .

Kahane's ferocious attacks on the "Hellenized" leaders of Israel and on their "Hellenistic" regime, like his battle against democracy, was a continuation of a perennial struggle that started long before the principles of modern democracy were worked out, including the principles of democratic opposition. Thus it is legitimate to use the ancient instruments of political fight with no remorse or hesitation. Although Kahane spoke openly against Jewish civil war, the analogy with the "Hellenized" was very instructive.[65] Judah the Maccabee did not kill only Greeks. He and his Maccabee brothers killed many Jews in the name of God. Given Kahane's fundamentalist convinction that the glorious past can and ought to be relived, his August 1984 column in *The Jewish Press,* in which he advocated the complete elimination of Jewish political leaders whose actions are "consciously aimed at destroying the sacred values of the Jew and the State," was not surprising.[66]

The Political Program of Rabbi Kahane

The operational plan of Rabbi Kahane was directly derived from his fundamental ideology. It called for two transformations in Israel—a change in the status and conditions of the Arabs, and a transfiguration of Israeli Judaism.

His solution to the Arab question was simple and short: "Separation, only separation." It was based on two essential policies: first, a forced expulsion of large numbers of *disloyal* Arabs from the land of Israel; second, a legal derogation of the remaining *loyal* Arabs to second-class residents inside Israel.

Since 1972, Kahane consistently argued that the Arabs must be removed from Israel. But his first plan was a rather "moderate" attempt to entice the Arabs to leave voluntarily.[67]

His 1973 book *The Challenge* laid out his full plan: a trust fund of $20 million, donated by rich Jews, would finance Arab emigration. The people behind the fund were also supposed to look for emigration sites in several countries and make arrangements for a larger operation. Even if there were not many emigrants, they would nevertheless make a difference and set a trend.[68] Israeli Arabs were promised immunity from this operation, and Arabs from the occupied territories, who were ready to swear allegiance to the state, were to receive citizenship after five years of naturalization.

But by 1981 Kahane became much more radical. So had his "separation" program. The government of Israel was now to manage the emigration plan. Israeli Arabs, like the residents of the occupied territories, were now to be encouraged to leave. In *Thorns in Your Eyes,* Kahane talks about emigration either to neighboring Arab countries or to other countries. Willing emigrants would be compensated for their property on the same scale as Arab countries would pay Jews emigrating to Israel, and they would be given job training so they would arrive in their new countries prepared for the job market. But the most important new element in the 1981 plan is that it is no longer voluntary. All those Arabs deemed disloyal by the government of Israel would be forced to leave. Anyone who opposed the order to leave would forfeit the right to an emigration allowance and would later be expelled by force.[69]

The alternative to forced emigration would be a public expression of allegiance to the State of Israel, recognizing the inalienable right of the Jews to Eretz Yisrael in its entirety. But even this commitment would entitle Arabs only to residency rights; participation in national politics would be out of the question. Every young Arab would have to join a national labor brigade for the same period that young Jews serve in the army, followed by similar reserve duty. Within the reorganized Jewish state there would be a strict separation between Jews and Gentiles, and intermarriage or sexual intercourse between a Jew and a Gentile would be a capital crime. Male Arabs who approach Jewish girls would be subject to fifty years in jail.[70]

Alien residency permits would have to be renewed each year, so each resident's loyalty can be carefully and continuously checked. But even Arabs who fulfill all requirements would not be completely secure. The total number of alien residents would be set each year according to the nation's economic and security needs, so even "loyal" Arabs might have to be expelled. Kahane did not foresee a major problem in putting his "separation" plan into effect: the Arabs were so scared of him that at the moment he became Israel's prime minister or minister of defense, most of them will simply leave.[71] Had the 1967 Israeli government been strong and decisive, most of the disloyal Arabs would have left already, as they did in 1948.

As for the Jewish program of his future administration, Kahane was surprisingly moderate. His latest plan, which appeared in *Uncomfortable Questions,* called for "a state of a Jewish totality," which means among other things the new laws on Jewish state education, the sanctification of the Sabbath, and the prohibition of intermarriage. But it also makes a rather unexpected apologetic commitment to parliamentary democracy:

> The pity is—the tragedy is—that most Jews do not believe that Judaism is Divine and therefore do not accept it as the foundation of the state. And so, because of that—but only because any attempt to establish a true Torah state would lead to a bitter civil war among Jews—I would not be prepared to establish a state that would bar elections involving parties that do not accept Torah law as authority. But know that punishment will be forthcoming against a people that refuses to create the kind of society that G–d demands. Tragedy. But we can never create the conditions that will lead to certain civil war among the Jews.[72]

What Kahane does not explain, of course, is why he feels that only the abrogation of democracy would cause a civil war. Would he be willing to give up his plan for the eviction of the Arabs if this issue also becomes a *casus belli* for a significant number of Israelis? And what about the other provocative items in his program, such as the suspension of the traditional Israeli legal order in the case of Arab terrorists? In this statement Kahane refrains from his usual biblical analogies. He doesn't even mention the prophets of Israel—whom elsewhere he cites repeatedly as guides for present action—who were never ready to make such concessions. Kahane may be serious in what he writes in this paragraph, but it is totally inconsistent with everything else he has ever written.

One cannot but suspect that this concession was made with an eye on Israel's Central Elections Committee, which was expected to rule before the 1988 elections whether Kahane's platform conformed with the requirements of democracy. After Kahane's 1984 election to the Knesset, it passed a bill barring racist and anti-democratic parties from participating in the elections. The explanation of Kahane's moderation in his chapter on the Jewish State may have had more to do with the new law than with the rabbi's true intentions.

But there is another possible explanation. Kahane's proposed reforms would not leave much room or freedom for other parties representing secular Jews. For Israel under Kahane would become "a state of Jewish totality." All public schools would be religious, and books and cultural activities would be strictly censored. A total respect for the Sabbath and the rules of Kashrut would be enforced too. Though this may not seem such a radical program, the implied consequences of Kahane's plan would be nothing less than a total transformation of the Israeli society.

Kahane's real program included an entire overhaul of the Israeli legal system, the expulsion of the Arabs, the removal of the Muslim shrines on Temple Mount, the establishment of Jewish anti-terror squads that would punish anti-Semites all over the world, a total rejection of the Christian Mission, and a complete repudiation of any form of Judaism other than orthodoxy. Under such conditions, no secular political party would be able to function.

Political Style: The Dynamics of Quasi-Fascism

We have examined Kahane's thinking to identify his place on the ideological map of the radical right. But only a close examination of Kach's actual *modus operandi,* its imagery, rituals, and identification symbols—can locate it on a general political map. Such an examination suggests that Kach is what might be called a *quasi-fascist movement.* The term quasi-fascist implies a distinct political style (though not the ideology) that was typical of the nonruling fascist movements in Central and Western Europe before World War II, and of neofascist movements today. Fascist movements are characterized by a combination of bitter anti-establishment sentiment, an appeal to insecure working-class and lower-middle-class people, a broad use of extraparliamentary and extralegal action, and a systematic resort to street hooliganism, violence, and occasional terrorism. What distinguishes the quasi-fascist from the fascist movement is basically its ideology. The classical fascist ideology is secular, revolutionary, anti-religious, and anti-liberal.

It aspires to the establishment of a new order, which is anti-democratic, hostile to bourgeois decadent society, and oriented toward physical struggle.[73] A quasi-fascist movement, according to the present definition, does not have all these elements, but it has a strong *behavioral similarity* to the fascist movements.

Kach fits the quasi-fascist model better than any other known model of political action. Though it functions within a democratic system, its politics are conducted outside the rules of the democratic order. It could be argued that before he reached parliament, Kahane had to use fascist tactics to attract attention and remain in the political arena.[74] But since his 1984 election to the Knesset, the political style he forged for many years has not changed. When asked in an interview why he had not changed his rude political manners since entering parliament, in order to gain legitimacy and respectability, Kahane shrugged and said he did not understand the question. "I did what I had to do. I am a man of truth and I do not recognize any other way to tell the truth."[75] The behavior may be counterproductive: many Israelis, who either identify with Kahane's ideology or his political program, would never join Kach precisely because they are deterred by its political style, which is almost unprecedented in Israel's public life.

The practice of Kahane and his followers shows that the quasi-fascist behavior is more than a publicity tactic. It was the second nature of Kahane, and remains the dominant behavior of most of Kach's activists, and of many of their followers. It seems to have four components.

Legitimation and Use of Violence and Terrorism

Ever since the early days of the Jewish Defense League in New York, Kahane emphasized the importance of physical force. One of the pillars of the JDL's ideology was the notion of "Jewish iron." Kahane, it is true, did not invent either the idea or the metaphor: he adopted it from the ideology of Vladimir Jabotinsky. The expression *Barzel Yisrael* (Iron Israel), according to Jabotinsky, meant that in the Diaspora or under foreign rule, Jews were no longer to bow to their oppressors but were to respond to them in kind, with physical force, if necessary. It also meant that the sovereign Jewish state should have a strong army, capable of defending it against all threats.

Kahane was so impressed with the notion of "iron," and the application of physical force for self-defense, that he divided the JDL in America into two groups: the *Chaya* groups and the Scholar groups. *Chaya* in Hebrew means animal, and *Chaya* squads were in charge of the use of violence against the JDL's rivals.[76] When he was brought to trial in New York in 1971, one of the main charges against Kahane was illegal possession of guns, ammunition and explosives. Kahane—who had no hesitation allying himself with the Mafia boss Joseph Colombo, Sr. founder of the fake Italian-American Civil Rights Association[77]—had no problem translating the idea of "Iron Israel" into the actual use of firearms against the enemies of the Jews. Some of his followers—members of the JDL and probably of a *Chaya* squad—planted a bomb in the offices of Sol Hurok, the Jewish impresario who used to bring Russian artists to America. The bomb set the place ablaze and killed a young Jewish secretary who worked for Hurok.[78]

It was the first of a series of terrorist acts that identified the behavior of the JDL and its splinter groups long after Kahane left the United States. Since the mid-1970s, the American JDL has been consistently classed by the FBI as a terrorist organization.

Kahane never denied his penchant for violence, and in his own account of the Jewish Defense League, he devoted a whole chapter to the justification and rationalization of its violence. While making the usual argument that "violence against *evil* is not the same as violence against *good*," and that violence for self-defense is fully legitimate, Kahane reached his famous conclusion that since Jews have been victimized for so long, "Jewish violence in defense of Jewish interest is *never* bad."[79] Jewish violence, according to this theory, is nothing but an extension of Jewish love, *Ahavat Yisrael.*[80]

In Israel, there was no place for further expression of "Jewish iron," because the country had been sovereign since 1948 and Jabotinsky's notion has been realized in the Israel Defense Forces (IDF). But unlike Jabotinsky's recognized successors, Meir Kahane was apparently not satisfied. Though he did not establish *Chaya* teams in Israel, he maintained that if the state was unable or unready to react in kind against those who spill "so much as one drop of Jewish blood," then it was the duty of individual Israelis to do so. Slowly and without developing a full-fledged ideology of terrorism, Kahane took to legitimizing anti-Arab terror, a message his followers fully absorbed and acted upon. One of Kahane's great historical heroes had always been David Raziel, the first commander of the Etzel underground in Palestine in the late 1930s. In 1937 Raziel introduced massive Jewish counterterrorism against the Arabs, opposing the official Zionist policy of *Havlaga* (self-restraint). Raziel's idea—that Arab civilians, even though they are uninvolved, should pay for what was happening to Jewish civilians—has been especially attractive to Kahane.[81] And he never cared to recognize the fact that Raziel's successors, including another hero of his, Menachem Begin, had renounced indiscriminate terrorism by the 1940s and had, since the establishment of the State of Israel, respected the law and trusted in the Israeli army.

In 1974, Kahane first broached the concept of T.N.T. (acronym for *terror neged terror*, i.e., Jewish terrorism against Arab terrorism). In *The Jewish Idea*, he suggested that a "worldwide Jewish anti-terror group" be established. "This group must be organized and aided in *exactly the same way as the terrorists are aided by the Arab governments*. With a totally serious face, the government of Israel must deny any connection with the group, even while allowing the *same* training bases on its soil as the Arab states allow the terrorists."[82] He even recommended using indiscriminate terrorism against the populations of those Arab countries that provide the PLO with financial, political, and military support.[83]

Kahane's espousal of brutal Jewish counterterrorism had not changed much over the years, and in his latest book he vowed to establish, upon assuming the leadership of Israel, special Jewish anti-terror groups that would operate all over the world and help Jews wherever there is trouble, disregarding the local authorities and their laws. Since the government of Israel was not receptive to his notions, Kahane's followers and other individuals inspired by his idea soon started to act on their own. Out of fear of the Israeli police and secret services, they did not try to establish a permanent terror organization, but rather engaged in occasional anti-Arab atrocities, using the symbol of T.N.T.[84]

Kahane's devotees were actively involved in the intensification of the conflict between Jews and Arabs in Hebron in the 1970s. Yossi Dayan, a student of Kahane and later the secretary-general of Kach, has been caught and arrested several times for provoking Arabs in the Cave of the Patriarchs. In an interview he once said, "I have had more trials than the number of stars on the American flag."[85] Before the recent Arab uprising, which changed all the rules of public conduct in the West Bank, it was usually Kahane's followers who acted in response to Arab attacks, although by the middle of the 1980s such pretexts as acting only in reaction to Arab violence seemed decreasingly necessary. Craig Leitner, a Kahane student, described a typical mid-1980s operation:

> One day towards the end of July 1984, I agreed with Mike Gozovsky and Yehuda Richter to operate against the Arabs. We left Kiryat Arba in a hired car, headed towards Jerusalem. . . . That night around 23:00, we went to the Neve Yaakov area. Yehuda was driving. Around midnight, we saw an Arab in his twenties walking along the road. I said, "Let's stop the car." I went out and hit the Arab with my fist on the shoulder. I also kicked him. He escaped into the night. We continued to Hebron and it was decided—I don't remember by whom—to burn Arab cars. We had in our car two plastic bottles containing four and a half liters of gasoline. In Hebron, Yehuda stopped the car. Mike took the gasoline and poured it under several cars, maybe three. After Yehuda set the cars afire, we moved, not waiting to see what would happen. There were dogs around and I was afraid that they would wake up the neighbors, or perhaps bite us and we would get rabies.[86]

Leitner and his friends later fired on an Arab bus, wounding several passengers. When asked for his reaction to their activities, Kahane expressed total approval. He said that he was sorry that they would have to spend years in prison, and added that, in his eyes, they were Maccabees. Later, Kahane placed Yehuda Richter, the main suspect in the operation, as number two on his list for the Knesset. Had Kach won two seats in 1984, Richter would have been released from prison, due to the immunity of Israel's Knesset members. Richter was also known as the commander of the "suicide squad" in the shelter at Yamit. When asked once by a journalist whether he would be willing to instruct his followers not to hit innocent Arabs who happened to be near a terror attack, Kahane responded, "No, I would not. As long as they are here we are lost. I have no way of knowing if this Arab or another is innocent. The real danger is the demographics."[87]

Kach's most aggressive local stronghold has always been Kiryat Arba. Activists such as Yossi Dayan, Eli Haze'ev (who was killed in the 1980 PLO attack on the Yeshiva students by the Beit Hadassah in Hebron), Baruch Marzel, and Shmuel Ben-Yishai have initiated countless violent operations against the local Arabs since the mid-1970s. Unlike Rabbi Levinger and Elyakim Haetzni, who have said all along that they are interested in peaceful coexistence with the native residents, Kach people have never concealed their hope for a massive emigration. The only reason for their relative restraint has been their fear of the army.

In 1986, they established the Committee for the Preservation of Security, whose stated purpose was to patrol the roads in the area against rock-throwers. But during the *intifada,* the committee became a most aggressive vigilante group. Its notorious commander, Shmuel Ben-Yishai, publicly declared that any incident involving harassment of Jewish traffic would make him shoot to kill without warning.

> I do not shoot in the air, I shoot to kill. . . . It is stupid to fire the entire magazine in the air! Only the Jews speak about the "purity of the arms." Just a minute! Listen who is talking about morality: Shamir, the biggest terrorist? Rabin, who killed Jews on Altalena? The Americans, who murdered the Indians?[88]

Kach was violent long before the recent Palestinian uprising. Its entire posture—the yellow shirts with the black clenched fists, the attacks on Arab families within the Green Line who move into Jewish neighborhoods, the chasing of innocent Arab workers for the fun of it, the anti-Arab "victory parades," the attempts to break up leftist meetings in a style reminiscent of the Italian fascists of the 1920s—have all spelled out hooliganism and violence. But the 1988 Palestinian uprising prompted Kach to expand its activities. Kach's recent operations, which have already caused the death of several Arabs, indicate that its main activists are certain that the decisive battle for Eretz Yisrael has already started.

Xenophobia, Social Darwinism, and Racist Symbolism

Kahane's anti-Arab strain has already been discussed. Even as a political stand, it is profoundly radical and exceptional in Israeli terms. Almost no one else came up with such a blunt proposition for mass Arab expulsion and for systematic discrimination against the remaining Arab residents. Kahane's popular publications and speeches, however, reveal an even deeper layer of animosity. They show that Kach, like many movements of the radical right in the United States and Europe, displays a strong xenophobia, with heavy racist overtones.

The racist propaganda of Kach follows the usual racist pattern in its mixture of superiority complex, sexual anxiety, and certain elements of an inferiority complex. Arabs are seen as both inferior and superior—inferior as all the Gentiles are, namely by not being the chosen people of God; superior in numbers, growth rate, and cruelty. They are the incarnation of the ruthless Gentiles who have persecuted the Jew all through history. As early as 1973 Kahane coined the terms *Hebronism* and *the mentality of Hebron*.

> What is the mentality of Hebron? This is the Arab mentality that calls for the annihilation of every Jew living in Israel. This is the reality of that 1929 summer day when men, women, and children were slaughtered and massacred in Hebron's streets, houses, and Jewish stores. When Yeshiva students and their families, Ashkenazim and Sefaradim, were tortured and raped, although they were not Zionists. This is the reality of the disturbances of 1920, 1921, 1936–39, and 1947. "Hebron," in short, is the Arab plan which the Arabs are ready to repeat every day if they just could.[89]

There is a strong duality in Kahane's descriptions of the Arabs. On the one hand, they are proud, determined, and smart people who pursue their national interest, as all nationalists patriots do; their resistance to the hegemony of the Jews is understandable, because under Jewish rule they cannot fulfill themselves and be a free people. But they are also called "dogs," "roaches," "Nazis," and "murderers," as treacherous as snakes and as dangerous as wolves.

Not only are they collectively dangerous, but they have also developed methods to individually defile the purity of the Jewish nation. They date Jewish women, sleep with them, and even want to marry them and take them to their villages. Kahane's leaflets on this issue were blunt, brutal, and highly offensive. Leaflets passed out to non-Israeli Jewish women studying in Israel say, among other things, "You are Jewish—be proud of it! Do not date Arabs!" The leaflets also quoted a lecturer "well versed in the atmosphere of Arab student life" on campus as saying: "I wouldn't say it for all of the mixed [Arab-Jewish] couples on campus, but in some of the cases it is very much a matter of (being) the best way of screwing the Jewish state—to screw a Jewish girl and broadcast the fact as widely as possible."[90]

Kahane intensely used the sexual anxiety of insecure lower-class Israelis, especially in poor areas and development towns. In 1979, Kach members talked about the establishment of "Jewish honor guards," which were to identify Jewish women dating Arabs, to warn them about the consequences, and to intimidate them. In the 1980s, there was no need for honor guards.

Anxious families of girls dating Arabs found their way to Kahane and made him their official protector.

It is not clear whether the number of Arabs dating Jewish women, especially from religious families, has grown, but the sensitivity to the issue certainly has. Several of Kahane's followers have "rescued" Jewish women who had married Arab men and become unhappy with life in the Arab village. Since Jews remain Jewish whatever formal conversion they undergo, and since according to the Halakha the children of a Jewish mother are Jewish, these rescue operations were hailed as a great Jewish *mitzva* (virtuous accomplishment) and were highly publicized among Kahane's potential constituency.[91]

Nowhere had Kahane's brand of Social Darwinism been so clearly demonstrated as in a bill he submitted to the Knesset. The proposed "law to prevent assimilation between Jews and non-Jews, and for the preservation of the sanctity of the people of Israel" would completely separate Jews and non-Jews in Israel: in schools, camps, dormitories, beaches, neighborhoods, and apartment buildings. It would further introduce special anti-assimilation programs to the national school system and completely eliminate all non-Jewish preaching and teaching; violators would be sentenced to five years in prison. The law also bars mixed marriage and dating, and offers especially severe punishment for Gentiles who seduce Jewish women by pretending they are Jews. Likud Knesset member Michael Eitan has compared Kahane's proposed laws to the Nazis' racist Nürmberg Laws.[92]

Kahane, as we have seen, did not accept the charge that he was a racist. His writings and lectures are full of references to the Bible, Maimonides, and other great authorities; that, he felt, exonerated him from the charge. The problem is that *his fundamentalist reading of the Halakha was racist*. Not a single Torah authority, today—prominent rabbis who read the holy sources just as Kahane did and may be just as unhappy with democracy and modern culture—supported his legal initiatives. Not a single one of them—all good Jews who worry a great deal about assimilation—speaks like Kahane, or uses similar slanderous and racist expressions.

A typical Kahane speech went like this:

> The Arabs are cancer, cancer, cancer in the midst of us. But there is not a single man who is willing to stand up and say it. I talk to young Jews who are just out of the army and they do not have jobs. No jobs? There are jobs! The Arabs have jobs! . . . Why? Because the greedy Jewish employer keeps two Arabs for the price of one Jew. An abnormal nation! A nation of suiciders. . . . I am telling you what each of you thinks deep in his heart: there is only one solution, no other, no partial solution: the Arabs out! out! . . . Do not ask me how. . . . Let me become defense minister for two months and you will not have a single cockroach around here! I promise you a *clean* Eretz Yisrael! Give me the power to take care of them! [standing ovations][93]

Kahane's slogan "I say what you think" was undoubtedly one of his most effective racist tactics. He was well aware that he spoke to Jews who, as a persecuted minority, have been traditionally socialized to civility and tolerance. But he also knew that Arab violence and terrorism had given many Israelis second thoughts about this tolerance, and that some feel a conflict between their traditional civility and their drive for revenge. Kahane's racist rhetoric was directed at exactly this conflict. What this licensed rabbi did, in a sense, was to tell people that they should not be ashamed of their most brutal drives because these are both justified and sanctioned by the Halakha. There is no shame or disgrace in the hidden desire to drive out the Arabs, because they are both inferior and vicious.

Propaganda and Smear Campaigns

A typical feature of fascist and quasi-fascist movements is their quick shift from ideology to propaganda and from propaganda to smear campaigns. These tactics are effective with the typical crowd that is attracted to such movements, the scared and insecure, and Kach follows the pattern. One can find some very thoughtful essays by Rabbi Kahane in which he seriously tried to derive his political ideology from the Holy Scripture and distinguished rabbinical exegesis, but he also produced vulgar speeches and leaflets whose contents amount to criminal incitement.

The propaganda style of Kach is immensely different from that of all the other components of the radical right. Gush Emunim, the Tehiya, Tzomet, Moledet, and the cultural radicals have often been as hostile to the Arabs, and as critical of the government as Kahane, but they differed from him on two points of style: their written rhetoric and their verbal rhetoric are one and the same; and they speak to different publics in the same language.

What made Kahane so resemble the propaganda masters of classical fascism was his incredible demagoguery and linguistic opportunism. When Kahane talked to a learned public in a yeshiva or in one of the Gush Emunim settlements, he was the *Talmid Hacham* (Jewish scholar). All his arguments were supported by Torah quotations and Halakhic references. He was composed, spoke at ease, and talked in the learned style of his writings. His political insinuations were exactly in sympathy with those of the audience: the love of Eretz Yisrael, the danger of the PLO, the threat of the leftists. When Kahane was invited to an American campus—in 1988 he spoke at Yale and Princeton—he was again serious, poised, and self-controlled, but then he was also the *theologian,* the Jewish rabbi who speaks to the Gentiles in the divinity school in their own language: dry, logical, learned, and polished. The audience could hardly believe that the rabbi's real pulpit was not the speaker's stand in the faculty club, but the platform in the marketplace.

But it was in the marketplace and in the public square that Kahane got his main support. Kahane's propaganda and smear campaigns had always been marked by extremely bitter anti-establishment rhetoric, by a caustic exposure of "the concealed and vicious, the true," face of the Jewish leadership of his time. There were few leaders of the American Jewish community or Israeli society whom he had not castigated as traitors or Gentile-lovers: the people who "Gentilized" Jewish education in the United States, did not do a single thing to help European Jewry during the Second World War, and were later fearful of the American blacks;[94] the people who harassed the real freedom fighters in Palestine (i.e., members of the Irgun or the Lehi), wrote the fallacious declaration of Israel's independence, and did not drive *all* the Arabs out;[95] the people who are ready now to make territorial concessions—in short, the "gentilized and Hellenized Jews."[96]

One of sociologist Karl Mannheim's most brilliant discussions of the ideological battles of his time had to do with the phenomenon of *unmasking,* or *debunking,* official political ideologies. What Mannheim noticed among both the fascists and the communists of his time was their need to expose the "true" face of the enemy, its "real" class or cultural hidden interests.[97] Kahane's marketplace rhetoric was a perfect example of this "unmasking" phenomenon, and not a single speaker in Israel could match him in his expertise.

Nowhere does Kahane's progression from ideology to propaganda and from propaganda to smear campaign show more clearly than in his treatment of the problem of the oriental Jews in Israel. In 1973 he wrote in *The Challenge,*

> Many people talk about the social gap, but few of them have ever visited a poor neighborhood. Speaking about the social problem, they pay lip service and pacify their conscience in the routine text that the budget is insufficient for both targets: security and the war on poverty. It is depressing to watch people swept by the flood of demagoguery about the misery which airs social and ethnic hatred for the benefit of the political pros. A whole camp of payers of lip service is sitting on a powder keg and fools itself that there will be no fire. The camp of the demagogues heats the powder keg and knowingly plays with the fire.[98]

Kahane understood what was then called "the problem of the ethnic-social gap," and was keenly aware of the explosive potential of the issue. And despite his denunciation of the "payers of lip service," he was not blind to the potential benefits of using the ethnic and social problems of Israel to broaden his political base. When asked in an early 1973 interview about whom he sees as his potential constituency, Kahane responded, "I go to the neighborhoods, to the poor, to the people who have nothing and are not interested in anything, and I offer them action. There is drama here, it is interesting because it opens new vistas for a bitter, frustrated people full of problems."[99]

As early as 1980 Kahane started to address the Sepharadi Jews in Israel, especially the poor from the development towns, arguing that not only had the government done nothing about the Arabs, but it was also *deliberately* discriminating against Sephardim. According to this line of argument, the Ashkenazi government had never done enough for the Sepharadi immigrants, and now its lenient policies toward the Arabs, and the payment of subsidies for large Arab families at a time of serious economic crisis, were about to destroy them. If the Arabs were not constantly subsidized and their tax evasions ignored, Jews could live in prosperity—especially Jews from the weaker economic strata of the population.

Kahane knew his audience. The Sepharadi Jews have indeed suffered from a difficult absorption process, especially during the 1950s, and from cultural discrimination. Not a few of them have developed a genuine anti-Ashkenazi sentiment and a special animosity toward the Labor movement, which dominated the country for many years. But Kahane, an Ashkenazi immigrant from the United States, accentuated their sentiments in a way no one had done before. There was said to be a "conspiracy of the Ashkenazi establishment to help the Arabs instead of the Sepharadi Jews." The Ashkenazi leadership was portrayed as not caring about values like paternalism and chastity. It allowed Arabs into Jewish society and made it possible for Arab youngsters to seduce poor Sepharadi Jewish girls.

Playing on the sensitivities of some in his audience, Kahane went to development towns and poor neighborhoods and told lurid stories. He told the "Yemenites" that during the 1950s, six hundred Yemenite babies were stolen from their mothers in the hospitals, right after their birth, and given to respected Ashkenazi families for adoption. The parents, who had just arrived in Israel, were told that the children died, and had no means to check on the story.[100] The "Iraqis" were told by Kahane, who had spent many months in jail, that Israel's prisons were full of Iraqi criminals. They were then asked in a rhetorical way whether there were Jewish murderers or bank robbers in Iraq. Since the expected answer was generally negative, Kahane's audience was left with no doubt as to the identity of the real criminal: the Ashkenazi establishment, which ruined the traditional family and its morals and drove the young to crime. Kahane was especially effective with the North African immigrants who were reminded that in their native countries—Morocco, Tunisia, Algeria—their daughters never dated Arab boys. But in independent Israel, the dream of generations of suffering Jews, they did so.

What Kahane usually forgot to remind his audience was that the Ashkenazi establishment that many of them hated—the Labor movement, the Histadrut, the kibbutzim—has been out of office since 1977, and that a new establishment had emerged, the Ashkenazi-Sepharadi leadership of the Likud. Since many of these people supported the Likud, the shrewd Kahane rarely mentioned that the real economic disaster of Israel took place under a Likud administration. He also did not mention that the Likud and the religious parties were as responsible as the Labor movement and the "leftists" for the laws that gave the Arab citizens of Israel all national insurance benefits. It was much easier for Kahane to sustain the myth that Labor was still in power and that its manipulative leaders were behind all the miseries and troubles.[101]

The Leader's Principle

When the JDL was established in America in 1968, it was a collective venture of several New York Jews cooperating to found the movement under the inspiration of Meir Kahane. In 1969–1970, though it was already clear that Kahane was the ideologue, the newsmaker, and the leader of the group, he was still nevertheless accountable to several colleagues in the JDL.

In Israel this situation changed. Kach was Kahane's own product. People of some theoretical and practical weight, like Yoel Lerner and Yossi Dayan, who were once part of the movement, were never allowed any leadership roles.[102] And thus, gradually, with no theoretical insistence on the "leader principle," Kahane had become the sole ideologue, the only decision-maker, the key speaker, and the fund-raiser of Kach. He made all public statements, and no major move was ever made without his approval. He inevitably found a reason to discharge any talented member who rose to prominence in Kach.

Since Kahane had never subjected himself to a thorough psychological interview, it is hard to tell what led him to do as he did. But clearly Kahane had always had an insatiable need for publicity and total confidence in his leadership abilities. In America, Kahane never spared a gimmick to make the front page of the *New York Times* or the *Daily News*. His political personality seems to have been shaped by the America of the late 1960s and by pundits like Jerry Rubin, who once said "You can't make a revolution without a color TV."

When he first came to Israel in 1971, Kahane had to *invent* events in order to constantly remain in the news. Since as a new immigrant he did not have credibility to deal with the Arab question, considered a high state-security matter, Kahane came up with very bizarre ideas such as demonstrating against a visit of the President of Nigeria, attacking the claims of the black Jews of Dimona to being fully Jewish, and invading the Finnish embassy in Tel Aviv to confront the diplomatic representatives of the Soviet Union about Soviet Jewry. To counter the notorious Christian organization Jews for Jesus, Kahane invented "Christians for Moses."[103]

Journalist Yair Kotler, who studied some of Kahane's most spectacular activities of the early 1970s, reached the conclusion that many of those events were faked, planned purely for publicity. Kahane's famous 1972 attempt to smuggle arms out of Israel, in order to avenge the blood of the Israeli athletes murdered in Munich by blowing up the Lybian embassy in Brussels, was leaked, according to Kotler, by Kahane himself. Yosef Schneider, who was Kahane's first lieutenant in the 1970s Israeli JDL, told Kotler:

For Kahane the end justifies the means. Everything for Kahane is public relations. He discloses details about plans that are already in the oven, to the authorities, in order not to damage himself and his people, not to have arrests. In this way he reaches his goal: wide publicity for himself and large echo for his deeds.[104]

A rare insight into Kahane's self-perception as an undisputed leader has been provided by Eli Adir, Kach's former director-general. Adir worked for Kahane for only nine months in 1984. Many political observers of Kach believed that Adir was the best thing that had happened to Kahane in a long time, that he offered a rare opportunity to change Kach's illegitimate political image and gain respectability. Adir, a thirty-year-old platoon commander in the Israeli reserves, was exactly what Kahane needed. A graduate of Technion in construction engineering with a master's degree in industrial management, Adir did not project borderline criminality of the usual Kach activist. He was a sabra (a native Israeli), spoke the matter-of-fact language of the new generation of Israeli university graduates, and seemed very accomplished. The fact that a rational and successful engineer like Adir was ready to join forces with Kahane could have had a great effect on many Israelis who would never give the extremist rabbi a second thought.

During his Technion years, Adir had participated in the growing confrontation between Jews and Arabs on the campus, and was once seriously stabbed by an Arab student. Long before Adir joined Kach, he was made a hero by Kahane, who told his story in *Thorns in Your Eyes*. The incident was used by Kahane to illustrate his argument that there was no room for reconciliation between Jews and Arabs.[105]

But just nine months after he joined Kach, becoming the darling of the press, Adir followed Yoseph Schneider, Yoel Lerner, and Yossi Dayan—earlier Kahane lieutenants—by leaving the movement. His account of his premature departure provides the most recent inside evaluation of Kahane's behavior and self-perception:

> According to his understanding, everybody he does not like should be removed in the most brutal way possible. It starts with the Arab question, where the solution is to remove an Arab by force, even to remove an Arab village by force. It continues in the approach to the parliamentary bodies of the left and extends to his closest friends. The whole atmosphere is one of constant struggle, frontal conflict with everything that stands in his way, a constant show of force.
>
> There is never any attempt to talk, to convince. The answer is always, "This is the way I want it." When several members of Kach commented that it is not prudent to call the Arabs "dogs" in public, Kahane responded, "But they are!" This style deters many people. Naturally he surrounds himself with people who need to be told what to do, and he tells them. Thus, it is correct to say that the movement is indeed Kahane, and that there is no Kach without him.[106]

Rabbi Meir Kahane lived in a world of his own, bounded and defined by his own truth, mission, and rules. He no longer even pretended to be equal to others, his movement's members included. A Kach activist who once came to Kahane to discuss with him the nomination of delegates to the party's general convention heard him say, "It's a good thing Kach isn't a democracy. I'm the only one to decide what will and will not be."[107]

From Disqualification to Assassination

Two weeks before the general elections in October 1988, Kach was disqualified from running for the Knesset. The disqualification was the most devastating blow to the political hopes of this movement. The judgment, first pronounced by the Central Elections Committee and later upheld by the Supreme Court, meant that the movement could not run for political office and that its head, Kahane, lost his position as member of parliament. The disqualification drove Kach back to its pre-1984 status, that of a semilegitimate extraparliamentary movement. And it greatly reduced its chances of gaining legitimacy and becoming an influential force in the nation's public life.

The disqualification was expected. The party had first been disqualified by the Central Elections Committee before the 1984 national elections, on the grounds of Kahane's racist platform and his rejection of Israeli democracy. But at the time this act was overruled by the Supreme Court for lack of proper legislation. Though the court agreed with all the arguments of the committee, it ruled that Israel's electoral law had no applicable provision that barred racist or anti-democratic parties from elections.[108]

The ruling was a clear message to the Knesset to amend the electoral law, and Kahane's election to the Knesset in 1984 made this legislation all the more urgent, and in 1985 the amendment was passed. The provision stated that any party whose platform was racist and anti-democratic, and whose behavior involved "incitement to racism," was unqualified to run for the Knesset.[109]

The only one who did not take the new legislation seriously was Rabbi Meir Kahane. He had almost three years to face the new challenge and prepare for it. Surprisingly, he did nothing. Given his long extremist record it is not certain whether he could have met the conditions of the new law, but he certainly made no such effort. Instead of moderating his positions tactically, making a conditional commitment to democracy, and instructing his followers to temporarily reduce their violent profile, Kahane intensified his crusade against the "treacherous Arabs," the "Gentilized" Jews, and their elected and nominated officials. His proposals in the Knesset were extremely racist and his speeches were as vitriolic as ever. Fully convinced of his growing popularity and appeal, Kahane acted and spoke as if nothing could stop him. He ridiculed the Knesset, insulted many of its members, and often called for the dissolution of the duly elected government.[110]

A series of special Knesset resolutions, which greatly limited Kahane's parliamentary immunity and forbade any more of his provocative visits to Arab villages, were disregarded by the militant rabbi. He also disregarded a resolution by Israel's Broadcasting Authority not to cover his activities, which reduced his public impact a great deal.[111] Kahane's visits of the nation's poor neighborhoods and development towns convinced him that the people loved him, and that it was just a matter of time before he would be voted in to full power.

Kahane, who apparently never regarded the law as an effective instrument of government, was somehow certain that God, who brought him to the Knesset, would help keep him there. As late as summer 1988, and against the growing skepticism of his attorneys, he was still optimistic about his chances to run in the coming elections. And when asked why he did not change his image and tactics in order to facilitate his lawyers' job, he said that all his acts were dictated by the Halakha and that there was nothing he could do about it. When further pressed about the other orthodox rabbis in the Knesset, who were also acting in the name of the Halakha, Kahane said they were all wrong.[112]

The disqualification of Kach came, paradoxically, at one of its peaks of popularity. Since his 1984 election, Kahane's appeal had risen and declined several times. But the 1988 outbreak of the *intifada* played right into his hands. Not only was it "good for business," but Kahane could rightly claim that he alone predicted the Palestinian uprising and that it validated all his theories. The unwillingness of the Shamir government to crush the *intifada* infuriated not only the immediate constituency of the radical right but also numerous Likud supporters. Many of these, potential Kahane fans anyway, were further roused by the rabbi's bitter attacks on the "soft" Israeli establishment, which now included Itzhak Shamir. By the summer of 1988, there were several indications that three to five Kach members would be elected to the Knesset; Kahane himself was speaking about seven to ten members. Kach's activists, who were promised by their leader that everything would be all right, were enthusiastic.[113] They worked around the clock, sensing the coming victory.

Kahane's immediate reaction to the disqualification of Kach was surprisingly mild. He seemed almost happy, for once again he was at the center of the nation's attention. Dozens of foreign correspondents showed up in his office. In countless interviews and lectures he unmasked the "real" face of Israeli democracy, which charged him with racism and discrimination but actually undermined its very principles by disenfranchising his supporters. He predicted the near demise of the "Hellenized" Israeli regime and vowed to be there to pick up the pieces.[114]

But the movement itself gave, in contrast, a very poor show. Neither its core activists nor the hundreds of its volunteers were capable of organizing protests and demonstrations. The highly publicized "popular affection" to Kahane was not apparent in the streets. Moreover, the rabbi's call for his supporters not to vote for other parties and to demonstrate against the system by putting white slips in the ballot boxes was poorly attended. Most of Kahane's supporters voted for Moledet or for Shas, the religious party of the Sephardi ultraorthodox.

But in the long run, despite Kahane's occasional remarks about his desire to retire to scholarly life and to his yeshiva, Kahane could never live without politics. It was just a question of time before a new Kahane idea was thrown into Israel's public life, a notion aimed at reviving the Kahanist spirit and Kach's hopes. The idea that arrived was the establishment of the "Independent State of Judea."

The new state was "established" in Jerusalem on January 18, 1989. About fifty delegates (representing settlements in Judea, Samaria, and Gaza) and several hundred observers gathered in Jerusalem's Palaza Hotel to demonstrate their irrevocable commitment to the occupied territories. Reacting to the shift in the position of the PLO vis-à-vis Israel, which resulted in a new American drive for peace, they expressed their determination to create an independent Jewish state, Judea, in any territory evacuated by Israel in the context of a future peace treaty. And to show that the declaration was not an empty gesture, they held a whole ceremony in which a potential state was created with a flag, anthem, elected bodies, and a preliminary constitution.

The founders of the state of Judea pledged full allegiance to the existing state of Israel, its laws, and its agencies, but made it clear that this allegiance would terminate if Eretz Yisrael territories were handed to the Arabs. They vowed to take over any such territory, to defend it by force, and to establish there a fully Halakhic second Jewish state.[115] Rabbi Kahane, who chose to act behind the scenes, was elected honorary president of the new state and its ambassador-at-large to Jewish communities around the world. Michael Ben-Horin, a Golan Heights settler, a veteran of the 1982 struggle in Yamit, and a radical fundamentalist in his own right, was elected to head its seven-person executive committee.[116]

What was new about the executive committee was that its composition was not dictated by Kach. In order to increase the appeal of the new State of Judea, it was advertised as an independent body. Several members of the executive committee, who were elected openly by the entire representative body, were not members of Kach. Ben-Horin himself, though a member of Kach, acted almost independently of Kahane. He invested much time in preparations for the convention and conducted personal meetings in dozens of settlements, in order to convince people that this was an independent venture.

Though Kahane originated the idea of the new state and the whole founding ritual—classic Rabbi Kahane public-relations gimmicks—he was disappointed by the development of the ceremony. Ben-Horin acted too independently, and several delegates to the constituent assembly took seriously the promise that the independent State of Judea would not be a Kach operation. Disagreeing with most of the leaders of Gush Emunim, who were skeptical about the new venture, these delegates thought that the ceremony would send an unequivocal message of determination and resolve to the government and the people of Israel.[117] The last thing they wanted was to join another front organization of Kach.

The result was an unexpected open debate about the prudence of making Kahane the honorary president of the new body. Although he was finally elected, several speakers made it clear that though they believed Kahane's intentions were good, his name was a great liability. Kahane himself, who intended to pontificate graciously over the symbolic event, could not remain silent. He delivered a bitter speech attacking all those who thought they could use the logistics of Kach and its support, but leave its leader out in the cold.[118]

The attempt to make the independent State of Judea independent of Kach as well was doomed to failure. The refusal of all the "legitimate" movements of the radical right to endorse it, and its inability to recruit leading non-Kach activists, made it necessary for Ben-Horin to rely heavily on the resources and manpower of Kach. The only concession he received from Kahane was the rabbi's consent to avoid personal association with the new state, and a permission for Ben-Horin and other activists to speak for it. This led to the movement of the center of the Independent State of Judea to Kiryat Arba, the only place in Israel where Kach members had been able to free themselves from the shadow of Rabbi Kahane and act independently.

Since the beginning of the *intifada,* and especially since the establishment of the Independent State of Judea, Kach's chapter in Kiryat Arba has become the most visible center of anti-Arab vigilantism in Israel, as well as of anti-governmental defiance. The high concentration of extremist settlers including thousands of Kach sympathizers, and the lack of any meaningful Gush Emunim opposition to the radicalism of Kach, have created the critical mass necessary for the takeoff of Kiryat-Arba's Kach. Of particular importance for this development has been the rise of a new breed of Kach activists, young individuals in their twenties or early thirties, most notably Baruch Marzel, Shmuel Ben-Yishai, Noam Federman, Tiran Pollak, and Yekutiel Ben-Ya'acov.

Unlike the elderly Kahane, who no longer participated in violent action, and was carefully avoiding confrontation with the law, his young followers in Kiryat Arba were manifestly violent. They attacked Arab travellers in the open, destroyed Arab property and advertised it, got repeatedly involved in provocative scuffles with the leaders of the Palestinian community in the West Bank, and used every opportunity to harass Jews who maintained a dialogue with the Palestinians. Living in a manifest conflict of legitimacy with the government of Israel, which refuses to crush the *intifada,* these Kach activists have become proud of their countless criminal convictions, and are ready to go to jail. Not only do they appeal to the thousands of settlers in the West Bank, who face Arab violence daily, but also to tens of thousands of Israelis who resent the *intifada,* seeing only its anti-Jewish violent character. And the young activists of Kach carry a symbolic identity card, issued by the Indepedent State of Judea, and tell the rest of the world that the essential infrastructure of the new state is already in existence. Insisting that any territorial concession in the West Bank must be met by violent resistance, they make it clear that they will personally lead the struggle.

In March 1989 the Israeli public was stunned by several acts of high-profile sabotage. A secret organization, which named itself the *Sikarikin,* assumed responsibility for setting ablaze the car of Dan Almagor, a popular Israeli writer and translator, who publicly came out against the army's brutal treatment of the *intifada* and called for direct talks with the PLO. Similar other cases of arson took place at the homes of prominent Israelis who either were involved in direct talks with the PLO or appeared to support legitimizing this organization in Israel. Slanderous graffiti against Prime Minister Shamir were also found.[119] In an anonymous phone call, a representative of the new group told a correspondent of *Erev Shabat* (an ultraorthodox weekly),

> You speak about democracy? There was a Jew here, who wanted to act in a democratic way. What happened to him? He was silenced, and that's it. We are not suckers! Don't frighten me with democracy.[120]

The name of the new organization is significant. The Sikarikin, or Sicarii, were an extreme faction of Jewish Zealots who operated before and during the Great Revolt against the Romans. That bitter struggle led in 70 A.D. to the destruction of the Second Temple in Jerusalem and to the beginning of two millennia of Jewish exile from Eretz Yisrael. The Sikarikin (men of small daggers) conducted a systematic terror campaign against Jewish moderates who were ready to come to terms with the Romans on questions of religious purity. Apart from murdering many Jewish moderates, the original Sikarikin fought the Romans to the bitter end, with the last of their group committing suicide in Massada in 73 A.D.[121]

Although the Sikarikin were later seen by most Halakhic authorities as irresponsible zealots who brought about a destructive civil war, in Jewish collective memory they remain the symbolic defenders of religious and nationalist purity. The small ideological ultranationalist group, *Brit Habirionim* (the Covenant of Thugs), which operated in Palestine in the late 1920s and early 1930s and anticipated the later emergence of Lehi, also referred to itself on occasion as Sikarikin.

While it was not at all clear that Kahane was behind the Sikarikin—and the police assembled circumstantial evidence against Yoel Adler, a strange Jerusalem right-wing loner, accounting for several activities—the group used the language and rhetoric of Kach. There were in fact several reasons to believe that the rabbi himself was involved. In March 1989, Kahane was in big trouble. His movement had lost most of its momentum and the future looked bleak. A decision to form two Kach lists to the 1992 general elections—one official (expected to be disqualified) and the other more moderate—could not relieve the daily malaise and sense of decline. There was a growing pressure to do something of high media visibility and symbolism, so that Kach and its ideas remained in the news. Although Kahane said in a press interview that he thought the acts of the Sikarikin were useless ("Fools, foolishness! What do you get from the burning of the door of Mina Tzemach or Dan Margalit? Who are they at all? Childish!"), their usefulness for sustaining the myth of Kach could not be denied.[122]

Rabbi Meir Kahane was gunned down in New York City on November 5, 1990, while making a speech to a small group of followers. His assassin, an American citizen of Egyptian descent, El-Sayyid al Nosair, apparently acted alone, and was not associated with any known Palestinian terrorist group. Responding emotionally to the growing cycle of Jewish-Arab violence in Israel, he ended the stormy career of Kahane, and may have inadvertently terminated the existence of Kach. Constantly living amid violence and conflicts, Kahane seemed unconcerned about his own fate. He took no special precautions about his personal safety, and made no contingent plans for an orderly succession of leadership in case of his death. Kach, which was always a one-man show, was dealt a mortal blow and appeared as disoriented as ever. Kahane's huge burial ceremony, attended by as many as 20,000 Israeli mourners, was the greatest show of support the slain leader ever had in Israel. And it was full of anti-Arab and anti-leftist violence, well in the spirit of the deceased rabbi. But this seemed to have been a single moment of emotional outpouring, experienced by the entire radical right, not just by Kach supporters. A short time after his assassination it was already clear that Kahane was much more successful in instilling "Kahanism" in Israeli political culture, than in securing the future of Kach.

Beyond Routine Politics: The Cultural Radicals and the Struggle for the Temple Mount

Neither the Gush Nor Kahane

Unlike Gush Emunim, the Tehiya, Tzomet, Moledet, and Kach—all with distinct political identities, organizations, salaried personnel, and legal responsibilities—the fourth component of the radical right is elusive and unorganized. It is made up of radicals who ideologically and politically stand somewhere between Gush Emunim and Rabbi Kahane, but feel uncomfortable with both. They rarely act as a homogeneous group, but share the conviction that only a spiritual revolution could save the nation; thus, we can consider them as a distinct group, the cultural radicals.

Many of the cultural radicals come from the extremist circles of the settler community in Judea, Samaria, and Gaza; others are former Kahane associates, largely in Jerusalem; some come directly from the tradition of the pre-state ultranationalist undergrounds in Palestine. The group also includes several rabbis and laypersons who have independently come to Halakhic conclusions similar to Kahane's.

Their radical approach is thus not a product of a single authoritative school, and it has not been theoretically worked out into a coherent system. It is basically an outcome of a reactionary mood created by the crisis of Camp David, the struggle in Yamit, and the "failure" of the Israeli government to protect the settlers from Arab violence and terrorism; the *intifada* has confirmed them in their convictions. The few cultural radicals who studied in Yeshivat Merkaz Harav are seen as dissenters, graduates who have drawn extreme and incorrect conclusions from the "Kookist" theology.

The common denominators of the cultural radicals are their impatience with Gush Emunim's excessive fidelity to the Israeli government, their disenchantment with the style of Rabbi Kahane, and their rejection of conventional politics. The majority are militant fundamentalists who trust the Sword as much as the Book. They flatly reject unnecessary compromises with the secular government of Israel and emphasize those sacred scriptures that call war against the enemies of the nation obligatory.

The main gap between the cultural radicals and Rabbi Kahane is not in theory but in practice. Most share Kahane's fundamental convictions regarding three critical issues: the need to expel the Arabs from the state of Israel, the rejection of Israeli democracy, and the need to wrest Temple Mount from Muslim control. They are, however, highly critical of Kahane's tactics. They feel he spoke prematurely and too often on events that should take place in ten, twenty, or thirty years, like the forced expulsion of the Arabs or the suppression of the Israeli "traitors"; spelling out such objectives now does more damage than good. Also, they could not tolerate Kahane's personality. They saw him as a violent character and a publicity hound with no sense of teamwork and no patience with the obstacles on the road to redemption. Nor did most of the cultural radicals share Kahane's idiosyncratic anti-establishment sentiment and his sense of alienation from the Israeli body politic; coming from the confident circles of Israel's settlers and ultranationalists, they did not feel excessively bitter nor see their public struggle as a permanent uphill battle.

The cultural radicals are not organized into a coherent front, so it is hard to assess their real power within the radical right or their impact. However, their claim of orthodox purity and their learned interpretations of scriptures do lend them some authority and respectability in the highly ideological radical right. The prestige and fame of several members of this group, especially the rabbis, provide legitimacy for the extreme ideas and plans of many younger followers.

There are indications that the cultural radicals may, in times of crisis, opt for extreme antigovernment action. If such action is sanctioned not just by the successors of Rabbi Kahane but also by other prestigious rabbis, the cultural radicals could become a very important component of any extralegal program. They are thus an essential element of the radical right which cannot be disregarded.

Among the cultural radicals it is possible to identify three groups that interact and overlap: veterans of the Jewish Underground, members of Tzfia, and former associates of Rabbi Meir Kahane.

The "Redemption Movement": Yehuda Etzion and the Theology of Active Redemption

The most concrete expression of the emergence of the cultural radicals has been the discovery of the group named by the press Hamachteret Hayehudit (the Jewish Underground). In reality the group was a clandestine conspiracy of a few dedicated leaders and several hesitant followers, who conducted two major ad hoc terror acts within a period of six years and were caught in the midst of the third. The most spectacular plan of the group, an attack on the Dome of the Rock on the Temple Mount, never became more than an impractical, though well-prepared, plan. The members of the conspiracy never committed themselves to anything formal or considered themselves members of a distinct organization. Their discovery shocked the nation and stunned Gush Emunim—a reaction attributable less to the terror acts committed than to the personal quality of the individuals involved and the novelty of their ideo-theological message.

Their acts of terrorism were not unprecedented in Zionist history. In the 1930s and 1940s, two Jewish undergrounds conducted a very sophisticated terror campaign in Palestine against the Arabs and British. After 1948, though, these movements ceased to exist, and terrorism came to be considered only a barbaric Arab practice. In fact, until 1980, very few Israelis believed that Israeli Jews were capable either morally or politically of being terrorists. When Meir Kahane preached terrorism in the 1970s, he was seen as an "imported" aberration. The few strange followers he assembled were considered marginal, incompetent, and un-Israeli. In fact, up until that time no credible Israeli, members of Gush Emunim included, claimed to be or was associated with planned anti-Arab terrorism. Thus, the Underground shattered the non-terroristic self-perception of the Israelis. It introduced a new dimension of brutality into the life of the nation, and it changed the way many Israelis thought of themselves and their fellow citizens.

While the underground had several active leaders, who had joined for a variety of social and theological reasons, its challenge to the official orientation of Gush Emunim was primarily shaped by the ideas of one person, Yehuda Etzion. Most of the members have "repented" since the 1984 discovery and subsequent imprisonment of the group, and have returned to the bosom of the Gush, but Etzion has not. His prison years have, on the contrary, made him highly critical of the Gush; he has called for its replacement by a more devoted collectivity, *Tnuat Hageula* (the Redemption Movement). The commitment of Etzion to religious revolution in Israel, his critical essays, and his intense correspondence with many people have made him a source of constant ferment and a leading force among the cultural radicals.[1]

Yehuda Etzion was born in Israel in 1951. His father, Avraham Mintz, was a member of the Etzel underground, which operated in the 1940s under the command of Menachem Begin. Mintz settled in Samaria as a member of Gariin Elon Moreh, a true believer in his own right. Etzion thus grew up in a very committed right-wing Zionist home, and from his childhood absorbed nationalist ideas. His native political convictions were first shaped in Yeshivat Kfar Haroe—one of the main schools of the Zionist religious youth movement, Bnei Akiva. Following his military service, he joined Yeshivat Allon Shvut in Gush Etzion (no relation to his name), studying under Rabbis

Yoel Ben-Nun and Yehuda Amital. Etzion belongs to the second generation of Gush Emunim, the youngsters who did not study in Merkaz Harav but absorbed its ideas through the Gush rabbis who had studied under Rabbi Zvi Yehuda Kook. Etzion, who joined the yeshiva after the Six-Day War, was actively involved in the messianic excitement and developments of the time.[2] He was one of the founders of the Gush and took an active role in the saga of Gariin Elon Moreh. In 1976 he led another Gush Emunim gariin to settle Ofra, a Samaria settlement that was to become the ideological and operational center of Gush Emunim.

Until 1978 Etzion was a member of the extended secretariat of Gush Emunim and was highly respected by his peers for his idealism, imaginative activism, and complete *messirut hanefesh*. While unknown publicly, he obtained the reputation of a deeply motivated "doer." His wife, who was interviewed by a *Nekuda* reporter after his arrest, has characterized him in these words:

> He lives on another plane, having a constant sense of supreme mission and broad thinking that is solely directed by the national interest. I know it is hard to believe, but this is the truth. This is the man I live with all the time. This is a person who constantly feels he has a role in the course of redemption and who asks himself every day, "What am I doing for the sake of redemption?"[3]

It is not entirely clear when or how Etzion underwent his ultranationalist conversion. But in the early 1970s this young and dynamic person discovered the writings of two individuals who changed his life: poet Uri Zvi Greenberg and writer Shabtai Ben-Dov.[4] These two writers represented an older ultranationalist tradition, unrelated to the theology of Merkaz Harav.

In the 1930s and 1940s, Greenberg was the inspiration of a generation of nationalists who fought the British in Palestine. Personally not a political man, Greenberg was the Gabriele d'Annunzio of ultranationalist Zionism. His forceful and magnetic poetry reconstructed the ancient myths of the kingdom of David. Greenberg's imagery is full of blood and iron and calls for a forceful conquest of Eretz Yisrael, one that would reconstruct the ancient takeover of the land by Joshua and the great biblical kings.[5] Already in the 1930s it spelled out the demand for a Jewish sovereignty over all the Promised Land, the vast territory that extends from the Euphrates in Iraq to the Nile in Egypt. It was Uri Zvi Greenberg, incessantly invoking the notion of the Kingdom of Israel, who provided spiritual inspiration for Abraham Stern (Yair), the founder and commander of Lehi, and for Dr. Israel Eldad, who has been very instrumental in popularizing the grand theory. Under the long hegemony of pragmatic Labor Zionism, Greenberg's ultranationalism, irrelevant to the political reality of the pre-1967 Israel, lost prestige and influence, though Greenberg himself became a national figure for his poetic achievements.

Etzion's greatest discovery was Shabtai Ben-Dov. Ben-Dov was an obscure figure known only to few friends, a former Lehi member who fought in the 1940s against the British until his capture and exile to Kenya. After Israel's War of Independence, in which he fought as a soldier, Ben-Dov studied law at the Hebrew University of Jerusalem and became a legal advisor in the Ministry of Commerce and Industry. Most of the intellectual energy of this strange man was devoted, however, not to his job but to a diligent study of modern history. Ben-Dov, true to the ultranationalist ideology of Greenberg and Stern, was never content with the territorially truncated State of Israel and with its increasingly materialistic culture. Fascinated by the writings of modern European nationalist thinkers, he searched incessantly for ideas relevant to the situation in Israel. Ben-Dov was especially taken by Lenin and his ideas on the revolutionary avant-garde. This belief, that a small and determined group of people could start a revolution and change history, governed much of his writings.[6]

The Six-Day War transformed Ben-Dov. The man saw his dreams come true.[7] After the miraculous victory, Ben-Dov became very religious and reworked his grand theory. It was time to deliver a glorious message, one that spoke about total national redemption. Ben-Dov's vision was greater and much more ambitious than that of Yeshivat Merkaz Harav: the resurrection of the Kingdom of Israel, the reestablishment of the Sanhedrin (the ancient Supreme Court), and the eventual return of the regal House of David. The center of such a new Israeli polity was bound to be the Temple Mount. And its territory was to encompass the entire Holy Land that God had promised Abraham.[8]

Immediately after the war, Ben-Dov, appealed to Israel's High Court of Justice [Bagatz] questioning the policy of Israel's minister of defense, Moshe Dayan, in permitting the Temple Mount to remain in the hands of the Muslim Waqf—the Arab high religious council of Jerusalem. Ben-Dov argued that the Temple Mount, now in the hands of Israel forever, as the holiest Jewish site, should be returned to Israel to maintain and preserve. It should therefore be administered by Israel's Ministry of Religion and not by the Ministry of Defense. The crux of the matter was Dayan's ruling that the Mount remained an Arab shrine administered by Arabs, which according to Ben-Dov was both illegitimate and illegal. The appeal was rejected by the court on the grounds that it could not interfere in controversial political matters. Nevertheless, Moshe Dayan himself decided to turn one of the gates leading to the Temple Mount into a Jewish site, which opened the area for every visitor. Jewish prayers on the Mount were, however, prohibited, in order not to anger and incite the Arabs.[9]

Yehuda Etzion first learned of Ben-Dov, who happened to be a distant relation, in 1972–73 when he was a yeshiva student in Gush Etzion. But it was not until the late 1970s that Etzion first came to understand and adopt Ben-Dov's ideology. Deeply disappointed by the Camp David Accords, Etzion began desperately to search for a theory that would go beyond the standard theology of Gush Emunim. He was also looking for the act that

could resume the process of redemption that was "brought to a halt" at
Camp David. Etzion found both in Ben-Dov's writings.[10]

In 1979 Ben-Dov was dying, but on his deathbed he encouraged Yehuda
Etzion to destroy the Dome on the Rock, thereby bringing about a new
dynamic of redemption. "If you want to act in a way that would solve all the
problems of the people of Israel," he said, "do this thing!" When Etzion
answered, "But this operation is very hard to accomplish," Ben-Dov replied,
"Hard, but not impossible".[11]

Etzion might not have followed the ideology of Shabtai Ben-Dov had
Camp David not taken place. But in 1978 he started to develop a thorough
intellectual critique of Gush Emunim and the teachings of Rabbi Zvi Yehuda
Kook. Etzion's new theology was written down and published only after he
was sent to prison in 1984, but there is no doubt that this is the thinking that
inspired his activity in the underground. The main thrust of his new theory is
directed against Kook's subservience to the government of Israel. Why, he
asked, did Gush Emunim, which had identified the messianic quality of the
present time, wait for the secular politicians to reach the same conclusion?
He refused to grant full legitimacy to "erroneous" rulers who are committing dangerous mistakes. Attacking the spirit of Merkaz Harav, the fountain-
head of Emunim's theology, he writes that

> the sense of criticism—which is a primary condition for any correction—
> perished here completely. The State of Israel was granted in Merkaz Harav
> an unlimited and independent credit. Its operations—even those that stand
> in contrast to the model of Israel's Torah—are conceived of as "G–d's will"
> or revelation of His grace.[12]

Yeshivat Merkaz Harav, and by implication Gush Emunim, has thus
come to support secular Zionism and all its faults. By concentrating on
settlement only, Gush Emunim no longer thinks in grand terms, nor does it
challenge the ineffectual government of Israel, and according to Etzion therefore fails to do God's will.

What, then, is the alternative? How should the State of Israel be directed?
What course should the misdirected Gush Emunim have taken, if its rabbis
had read the present situation correctly? Following the tradition, which maintains that in the messianic era all statutes of the Torah for the Kingdom of
Israel are binding—as well as the teaching of Ben-Dov and the ultranationalist school of the Kingdom of Israel—Etzion argues emphatically that the
Teken (proper model) of the life of the nation is very clear. This is:

> the proper Kingdom of Israel that we have to establish here between the two
> rivers [the Euphrates and the Nile]. This kingdom will be directed by the
> Supreme Court which is bound to sit on the site chosen by G–d to emit His
> inspiration, a site which will have a Temple, an altar, and a King chosen by
> G–d. All the people of Israel will inherit the land to work and to keep.[13]

Etzion's deviation from the standard theology of Gush Emunim is here quite clear. The present secular State of Israel is not considered sacred, and its acts are not holy. Its leaders are disoriented by their secular democracy and commit one disastrous mistake after another. Further, according to Etzion, it is fully legitimate to portray *now* the outline of the final redemption, which includes a *theocratic government* centered on the Temple Mount and a state that controls, in addition to present-day Israel, the Sinai, Jordan, Syria, and parts of Lebanon and Iraq. Moreover, it is mandatory to strive *now* for the fulfillment of this vision, and Gush Emunim or any other devoted movement should take the lead in the forthcoming struggle.

Why did Etzion focus on the Temple Mount? How did he justify such an incredible operation, more dangerous than any anti-Arab plan ever hatched in Israel since the beginning of Zionism in the nineteenth century? How does the Temple Mount operation fit into Etzion's general theory of redemption? In a short monograph, *The Temple Mount* published in jail, Etzion explained,

> David's property in the Temple Mount is therefore a real and eternal property in the name of all Israel. It was never invalidated and never will it be. No legality, or ownership claim, that is not made in the name of Israel and for the need of rebuilding the Temple, is valid.
>
> The expurgation of the Temple Mount will prepare the hearts for the understanding and further advancing of our full redemption. The purified Mount shall be—if G–d wishes—the hammer and anvil for the future process of promoting the next holy elevation.[14]

The redemption of the nation has come to a halt, according to Etzion, because the Arabs control the Temple Mount. Not until it is purged—which the government should have done—can the grand process be renewed. And since the "horrible state of affairs" is even supported by the government, the task of purging the Temple Mount has fallen to those most devoted and dedicated to Israel's redemption.[15]

But how did Etzion, an intelligent and educated man, believe that Israel could survive the military and political consequences of the destruction of the Dome of the Rock? And how was Israel to conquer Jordan, Syria, parts of Egypt, Iraq, and Lebanon and transform itself, regardless of world opinion, into a Khomeini-like theocracy? Does Etzion consider the constraints of political reality?

In his writings and conversation, Etzion reveals both an otherworldly messianic spirit and a very logical mind; he is a man who talks and thinks in the language of this world but lives in another. His response to the question of political reality is based on the only intellectual explanatory construct possible—a distinction between the *laws of existence,* which dominate the life of ordinary people, and the *laws of destiny,* which dominate the life of the Jewish people once they begin to fulfill their fate in the spirit of the

Torah: "For the Gentiles, life is mainly a *life of existence* while ours is a *life of destiny,* the life of a kingdom of priests and a holy people. We exist in the world in order to actualize destiny." Thus constraints of political reality are relevant only to those who live by the laws of existence.

> Once it adopts the laws of destiny instead of the laws of existence, Israel will no longer be an ordinary state which makes decisions day by day. . . . It will become the kingdom of Israel by its very essence.
> It therefore makes no sense to give the present state any "good advice," regarding its conduct in an isolated "local" situation, in the name of the laws of destiny. This change will take place inevitably, in the immense comprehensive move of the transformation from the state of Israel to the kingdom of Israel.[16]

Operation Temple Mount was to be the trigger that would transform the State of Israel. It was meant to elevate the nation to the status of the Kingdom of Israel, a kingdom of priests capable of actualizing the laws of destiny and changing the nature of the world.

The ideas of Yehuda Etzion won respect within the underground, but were never fully shared by any of his colleagues. Only one other person, the mystical Ben Shoshan, supported the Temple Mount operation to the end. (In fact, Ben Shoshan had a mysterious and Kabbalistic interpretation of the act that was never shared by Etzion or any other member of the group.)[17] And though Etzion, then in his late twenties, was highly respected for his otherworldly dedication and the purity of his motives, he was never ordained as a rabbi or carried any halakhic authority. Even before the group was discovered and Etzion was attacked by Gush Emunim rabbis for his "false messianism," he had a very serious "authority problem." In the highly hierarchical ambiance in which these people operated, he needed to produce an authority that would support his revolution and his rejection of the entire rabbinical establishment of Israel, including Gush Emunim. It was his failure to do so that isolated Etzion within the group and in the end prevented the operation against the Dome of the Rock.[18]

The discovery of the underground lifted Yehuda Etzion from anonymity to fame, making him the center of the resulting storm of controversy within Gush Emunim. Besides being recognized as "the ideologue" of the underground, Etzion gained notoriety for adamantly refusing to apologize for his acts and for challenging the entire rabbinical establishment of Gush Emunim.

Not only was this man responsible for the most dangerous anti-Arab operation ever planned in the history of Zionism, but after his arrest he even publicized it to the nation. After being interrogated by the Shin Bet, Etzion began an intense correspondence with dozens of critics and admirers. Many Gush people wrote to him in fury, demanding an explanation for the disgrace he brought upon the movement. Most focused on the "authority question," asking him to explain his source of authority for risking the nation and damaging the entire settler community.[19] Not a single critic was left unanswered, and his long letters were characterized by their depth and originality. There were admirers too, individuals and rabbis who congratulated Etzion for breaking the taboo regarding the disgrace on the Temple Mount, and who devoured his letters with great excitement.

Etzion gained some legitimacy when *Nekuda* agreed to publish several of his essays. In fact, despite the attacks on him by most of the authorities of the movement, Etzion gained access to the large and attentive readership of *Nekuda*. Even those who disagreed with him completely could not ignore the power of his logic and the originality of his ideas. They were also impressed by his unusual style and his exemplary writing ability. Etzion's ideas and publications, including his *apologia*—the booklet in which he delivered his Temple Mount "sermon," which the court refused to hear—have made him an institution in his own right. Even before he was released from jail he could claim to have several followers and many correspondents.

The Redemption Movement

Though he refused to concede to his critics or apologize for his plan to blow up the Dome of the Rock, Etzion did admit several mistakes. He was erroneous, he said in jail, in believing that a single explosion on the Temple Mount could lift the nation in one blow toward redemption. It was not that the plan was wrong in principle; rather it was premature, since the nation was not ready for it either mentally or spiritually. After 1984, Etzion came to believe that the grand political transformation must be preceded by a cultural revolution, an intense preparation of the hearts of the nation.[20] This is to be begun by the establishment of a small and selected *Tnuat Geula* (Redemption Movement), whose members would act to arouse the new spirit, serving as examples and guides for the next stage of the nation's redemption.[21] Etzion's latest call for the Redemption Movement, and his elaboration on his rejection of the entire order of the State of Israel, were published in late 1988, just before his release from jail, in an essay called "On the Potter's Wheel":

> We have reached a crisis. And out of the very depth of the crisis—out of the pangs of pressure, of the spasms of pain, but also out of happiness and relief—the Redemption Movement is emerging, waking up to be born and begin moving. . . .
> Consecrating our appeal to the truth of the *Rock of Israel*—our readiness to go out in His mission to the people, to dedicate our life to this mission, and to completely devote ourself to it . . . we are planting the seedling of the revival of prophecy in Israel.[22]

Unlike his former colleagues from Gush Emunim, Etzion challenges the foundations of the secular State of Israel and its architects. Neither the

Knesset, the government, nor any other institution of the secular state is sacred. They are "irrelevant system of rules and regulations whose purpose is to organize our daily life with no relation to the Torah of Israel and its heritage, with no interest in the redemption of Israel and with no ability of carrying or serving it." The Knesset, the very expression of Israeli sovereignty, should be replaced by a Sanhedrin, the genuine Jewish Supreme Court.

> We deny the common assumption that the Knesset—the pinnacle of the present regime—deserves this honor. We are starting a major transvaluation, a struggle for a new regime and for the establishment of the Bet Din Gadol (Grand Court); it will lead the nation—and we shall abide by all its rulings—because it will abide by the Kingdom of Heaven and by the yoke of freedom of the Torah of Israel, whose message—the message of G–d written on the Covenant—will be the foundation of the state's constitution here.[23]

Etzion admits that the present rulers of Israel are not illegitimate *usurpers* who exercise control in an illegal way, so they should be obeyed in daily matters. But he argues emphatically that when the government acts against the Torah, it should be opposed. Until the regime is transformed, the righteous should challenge the government and disobey "illegal" orders, even if it means spending time in prison. Further, the righteous must struggle for change together, in the Redemption Movement. Although Etzion's picture of this movement is vague, he seems to see it as *an alternative institution,* a potential source of authority for the nation; it will slowly become "a small Sanhedrin," and in time replace the present state institutions.

> The Redemption Movement has emerged in order to start and lead the journey—educational and practical—from the present state of Israel to the kingdom of Israel. We come to shift and change the heart of the people towards redemption and kingdom—*and thus to change the facts of reality.* We derive our authority from the very movement to change and correct—let us recall, there is a rise here of *a holy spirit.* The more popular we become, the more our nature—which is part and parcel of the nature of the Kingdom of David—becomes recognized, liked, and favored, the more valid we shall be as an authoritative element in the nation; the present regime, which is a stranger to the destiny we are about to fulfill, will, at the same time, erode, be rejected, and disappear.[24]

Although Etzion's 1988 essay does not sound very revolutionary, he in fact makes no commitment to legality and nonviolence. The concluding paragraph seems vaguely threatening. The reader can hardly avoid reading between the lines the long deliberations of the Jewish Underground regarding the operation on the Temple Mount.

> The Redemption Movement is moving now to wake up, navigate and lead the march towards . . . the proper form of national life. During this move we shall have to discuss and decide on each individual step: is it necessary and obligatory . . . or is it prohibited and totally wrong? Or perhaps it is worth-

while but must be postponed. . . . We shall have to take responsibility for our decisions, and when we know for sure that we are able to move in the right direction—and after we have considered, to the best of our ability, the conditions of reality and the expected impact—then that will be the final test: Will it advance the drive of Israel to the deserved life in the light of a king living in Zion?[25]

So far, the real problem of the Redemption Movement has not been Etzion's inability to formulate concrete goals as much as the total lack of candidates to staff the organization and promote it. Etzion was released from jail in January 1989. He celebrated the event by a highly publicized one-man march from the Tel Mond Prison to the Temple Mount. He carried a large banner he had made in jail, which said: "For the Sake of Zion I Shall Not Remain Silent, and for the Sake of Jerusalem I Shall Raise My Voice." Thus he made it clear that his struggle has just begun.

Nevertheless, the first two meetings he held to organize the Redemption Movement—in Jerusalem and the settlement Bracha—have had very little effect. Only about twenty people showed up, and the discussion was very general and unfocused. Thus, while Yehuda Etzion has become a symbol for a new fundamentalist radicalism in Israel, there have been no indications yet that he can translate his ideas into organization and action.[26]

The Tzfia Association and the Radicalism of Rabbi Israel Ariel

Though the April 1984 arrest of Yehuda Etzion and his underground partners brought an end to the secretive part of their activity, it also brought their ideas into the open and made the Machteret part of Israel's public life. The group that assumed the task of presenting the full content of this body of thinking to the public was a small association that called itself Tzfia (Looking Ahead).

Tzfia had grown out of another organization, Laor-Lemaan Achai Vereai (For the sake of my brothers and friends), a solidarity committee formed in Kiryat Arba after the arrest to raise money to defend the suspects and support their families. Laor's leaders insisted that they did not endorse the terrorism of the group, though they could not desert its members, who were neighbors and close friends.

Several rabbis and activists in the new organization felt this kind of support was not sufficient. They believed that the ideas, actions, and individuals involved in the Machteret were right and deserved full support. Eventually this hawkish segment of Laor decided to leave and start an ideological magazine of its own.[27] They felt that the suspects were being deserted, and that none of the publications of Gush Emunim and of the settler community, including *Nekuda*, were ready to give their ideas a fair hearing. "In today's *Nekuda*," said Ephraim Caspi, *Tzfia*'s first publisher, "there is no room for their opinions, or straight talk about the fact that the underground did what the state should have done."[28]

A review of the membership of Tzfia is very telling. The group included most of the hawkish members of the religious radical right with reputations for extreme positions.

The oldest was Rabbi Moshe Halevi Segal, the rabbi who first blew the *Shofar* (ram's horn) in 1931 by the Wailing Wall on the Temple Mount, enraging the British, provoking the Arabs, and officially beginning the modern struggle of the Jews to regain their holiest place. Segal was also a senior member of the Jewish underground during the mandate period, and head of a pre-1948 ultranationalist movement Brit Hahashmonaim (the Covenant of the Hashmonaics), which encouraged its members to join the anti-British operations of Etzel and Lehi.[29] After the 1967 war, Segal was the first Jew to settle old Jerusalem. In 1978 he was a Herut party member who challenged Mehachem Begin immediately after Camp David, calling him a traitor; he then tried to revive his movement to fight the accords.

A much younger member of Tzfia was Rabbi Dov Lior, an immigrant from the Soviet Union, long known for his extreme opinions. A talented graduate of Merkaz Harav, he was a maverick, an independent and unconventional rabbi, and a religious authority in his own right. He and Rabbi Eliezer Waldman are the co-heads of the Kiryat Arba yeshiva, which has produced some very extremist graduates. In 1982 the two rabbis led their entire school to Yamit and played an important role in the Movement to Halt the Retreat in Sinai. The testimonies of the Hebronite section of the underground, which was responsible for the murderous attack on the Islamic College in Hebron and for the wiring of the five Arab buses in the West Bank, showed Lior to be one of the moral authorities of the group.

The organizer and guiding spirit of the Tzfia group is Rabbi Israel Ariel, who studied in Merkaz Harav in the 1960s and was part of the paratrooper unit that conquered the Temple Mount in 1967. "I stood there," he recalled many years later, "in the place where the High Priest would enter [the Temple] once a year, in Yom Kippur, barefoot, after five plunges in the purifying pool. But I was shod, armed, and helmeted. And I said to myself: 'This is how the conquering generation looks.' "[30]

Unlike Hanan Porat and Yoel Ben-Nun, who were also present in the conquest of the Temple Mount, Ariel did not take part in the emerging Gush Emunim. Instead, he chose to join the army and create a new image of a military rabbi, a spiritual guide and a Halakhic instructor who is also a fighter. Ariel served five years as a rabbi in the army's Northern Command and became very fond of the army and of military thinking. In 1975 he left the service and joined his older brother, Rabbi Jacob Ariel, who headed the small yeshiva in Yamit. Long before the establishment of the Movement to Halt the Retreat in Sinai, Ariel was convinced that an exemplary *Messirut Hanefesh* was the only way to stop the retreat. Yamit, he decided, was not to be evacuated and he was there to guarantee it.

Bitter toward the government and its peace policies Ariel joined Kach as its no. 2 candidate for the 10th Knesset (1981). Many of his friends were dumbfounded: how could Ariel, a respected graduate of Merkaz Harav, support the most notorious outcast of Israeli politics? They were answered during the struggle in Yamit: the young rabbi led the most extreme faction of the MHRS, the group that was ready to consider armed resistance. Ariel was convinced that the retreat was a crime against God, the Torah, and the nation, and that it was the obligation of every believer to fight it tooth and nail.[31]

In Yamit, Ariel showed how far he had gone since his days at Merkaz Harav. While Rabbi Zvi Yehuda Kook (who died just before the final evacuation) always insisted that the vanguard should never lose touch with the nation, Ariel did not care. His reading of the Torah and his radical interpretation of Kook's famous injunction, "Yehareg uval ya'vor," made him ready to fight against the treacherous government. And unlike many former members of the MHRS, he has never recanted his conduct in Yamit. Nor would he admit that joining Kahane in 1981 was a mistake.[32]

After the Israeli retreat from Sinai, Ariel moved to the Jewish quarter of Jerusalem and began studying with Rabbi Shlomo Goren, Israel's former chief rabbi. He also started to teach in a yeshiva in the Muslim quarter of Jerusalem, in one of the houses requisitioned from the Arabs. Ariel's recent book, an impressive illustrated study of the biblical borders of Eretz Yisrael, was signed: "Israel Ariel, formerly in Yamit, soon to be rebuilt out of its ruins, now in Jerusalem between the walls facing the Temple."[33]

Tzfia also included two strange Temple Mount devotees, Rabbi David Elboim and Ephraim Caspi. Rabbi Elboim, a Belz Hassid with no connection to the tradition of Merkaz Harav and the messianic craze of Gush Emunim, had long been intrigued by the idea of the return to the Temple Mount and had consequently joined all organizations concerned with it. Since the late 1970s he has been involved in a small family project of weaving the gowns for the Temple's priests. When asked once about the relevance of his project to the present historical reality, Elboim responded, "Did they ask Herzl when the state would be established? I suppose it is a matter of twenty or thirty years."[34]

Ephraim Caspi, the man who took upon himself the task of publishing several of Yehuda Etzion's prison writings as well as the publication of Tzfia, has also been fascinated by the Temple Mount. He built his house facing the sacred site so that he can wake up in the morning and go to sleep at night within view of the holy place. For years he has been involved in the unpublicized operation to purchase and reconstruct old Jewish synagogues in the Muslim quarter of Jerusalem and to buy houses for future yeshiva students.[35]

From its beginning, *Tzfia* magazine has been short of money, and its radicalism has clearly deterred potential contributors. It managed to publish two issues in its first year, 1985, and was then discontinued for nearly three years. Nevertheless, it is impossible not to recognize its innovation and explosive potential. *Tzfia*'s writers have done what its editors vowed to do: break the offical taboo on sensitive issues implied in the concept of redemption. Their radicalism has been especially demonstrated by their opinions on three issues: The status of the Temple Mount, the treatment of the Arabs, and the territory of Eretz Israel.

Tzfia and the Temple Mount

In its first two issues, *Tzfia* surveyed a whole set of problems revealed by the discovery of the underground, but its primary concern has been the situation on the Temple Mount. Tzfia's members did not need young Yehuda Etzion to focus their attention on the holy site; clearly they have been disturbed by the permanent desecration of the place for a long time. The essays on this topic challenged two prevailing approaches to the subject: the belief that the status of the Mount is too sensitive to deal with politically, and the conviction that any change must wait for future generations because of its holy nature.

The political constraints involved in the Temple Mount situation have never posed any serious problems for Jewish fundamentalists, so there is no thoughtful discussion of the political risks involved in an Israeli takeover of the Temple Mount. When *Tzfia* writers do discuss the politics of the holy place, they mainly stress the loss to Israeli national pride engendered by Arab control of the Mount. Though Israel could have taken jurisdiction after the Six-Day War, it was erroneously decided to respect the religious rights of the Muslims and leave them in full control of the area. In return, according to Tzfia, the Muslim Waqf (the highest authority in charge of the Harem-esh-Sherif, the holy area in its entirety), has done everything possible to desecrate the place and humiliate the Jews. This included burying dead all over the mountain in direct contradiction to Jewish law and tradition. The Waqf has also continued building small worship areas on the mount's slopes, further insulting the Israelis by dedicating one to the "martyrs of Sabra and Shatila." And according to alarming reports, the Muslims have been digging in secret under their shrines, in order to destroy the foundations of the old Temple.[36] The State of Israel, according to this perspective, must stop the Muslim desecration of the Temple Mount for reasons of both pride and national sovereignty.

By far the most serious and profound Tzfia challenge on the subject has been its debate with religious opponents of a Jewish return to the Temple Mount. The idea of reviving Jewish worship in the holy place has, since the Six-Day War, been approached by religious authorities with great caution and utmost reverence. Mount Moriah, the Temple Mount, has been the holiest place of the Jews since time immemorial. According to orthodox tradition, the nation was spiritually created by God on this mount and its independence was lost there.

So traumatic was the last destruction, a disaster that sent the Jews into two millennia of exile, that the historic act of the Temple's destruction has assumed a theological meaning. The destruction of the Temple was God's punishment on his people who went astray. Therefore God will decide when they will be forgiven and redeemed. This will be brought about by a messiah, an individual redeemer, in a metahistorical and supernatural act of forgiveness that will involve the rebuilding of the Temple on Mount Moriah. Thus for some ultraorthodox Jews not only the notion of a human-facilitated return to the Temple Mount, but even the idea of participating in the secular State of Israel, is anathema. In fact, the secular Zionist state is seen by them to be a *hillul hashem,* a desecration of the name of God.[37]

While the religious Zionists, and especially the theologians of Gush Emunim, have never shared this conviction, instead seeing in the state of Israel the beginning of the collective arrival of the Messiah, they were very confused and unsure about the Temple Mount. The actual return to the holy mountain and the building of the Third Temple, acts that generations of Jews have cried and prayed for, did not seem possible simply as a result of a military conquest of a secular regime. Instead they felt that a special indication from Heaven was needed.

There was an additional problem, the issue of purification. Several parts of the holy mount are, according to the Torah rules of the Temple, so holy that only purified priests are allowed to walk there. But since the destruction of the Second Temple, the exact location of these places had been lost, and therefore no believer was allowed on the Temple Mount for fear of unintentional desecration of the place.

These uncertainties have led the vast majority of rabbis, including Gush Emunim's mentors, to accept the status quo on the Temple Mount. Rabbi Zvi Yehuda Kook, for example, instructed his students to be patient on the issue of the Temple Mount, stating that it could not be redeemed before the earlier stage of "the building of the Kingdom" had been completed. In 1982 Rabbi Tau, his successor in Yeshivat Merkaz Harav, summarized the official position of the school by the phrase, "The further away we are, the closer we get." What Tau meant was that one does not have to have physical possession of the Temple Mount in order to feel close to the sacred center of the nation. Humility and patience, more than aggressive acts, will bring the people of Israel with the help of God to its complete redemption on the Temple Mount.[38]

This is also the position taken by Rabbi Shlomo Aviner, the head of

Yeshivat Ateret Cohanim (The Crown of the Priests). Aviner's yeshiva, a special annex of Merkaz Harav, was established in Jerusalem in 1978 to commemorate the Temple and to study the rules of the Temple's priests. Several Temple Mount devotees had expected that Aviner, a respected Gush authority, would lead the struggle for the return to the Mount, but he disappointed them. In a special sermon in 1983, "Lo Naale Bahar" (We Shall Not Climb Up the Mountain), he voiced his opinion that there are two separate systems of redemption: redemption that can be advanced by human efforts at the present time and redemption that is in the hands of God. Policy argumentation and recommendations are legitimate, according to Aviner, only in the first case.

> The Temple is part of the coming future, as well as its location. He who wants to touch the Temple Mount, diminishes, reduces, and dwarfs this entire matter, which is beyond our understanding. Only out of the recognition of our shortcomings shall we deserve it. . . .
>
> The more we fear this place, the more we recognize that it is beyond our conception (just as the name of G–d is beyond our conception and we therefore do not express it in writing), the more shall we be part of the Temple's place and be honored to climb up the ladder that is founded in the mundane structure of the state and whose top reaches the sky of the Temple.[39]

Tzfia's challenge to these positions was obvious from the cover of its magazine, which showed a reconstruction of Herod's Temple full of praying Jews. And the message of its various essays stood in total contradiction to Tau's admonition. *Tzfia* writers reason that there is a fundamental flaw in the position of the rabbis of Gush Emunim. If the present State of Israel is sacred and its rise is part of the unfolding messianic age, and if the Six-Day War was a clear sign from Heaven that the process of redemption has reached a very advanced stage, then why should the nation not take control of its holiest site? And isn't the obligation to reconstruct the Temple a direct extension of the obligation to settle Judea and Samaria and return to the old city of Jerusalem? In fact, not only is Gush Emunim's position illogical and false, but leaving the Temple Mount in Arab hands is a punishable sin. "All the disasters of the people of Israel," said Rabbi Dov Lior in an interview in 1985, "took place because the Temple Mount was not redeemed."[40]

The most determined voice in favor of purging the Temple Mount is Rabbi Israel Ariel's. Despite his Merkaz Harav background, Ariel has never been an integral part of Gush Emunim. Somewhere between the time he spent in the Northern Command of the Army and Yamit, he carved out his own rigid fundamentalism, a combination of a mechanistic reading of the holy scriptures regarding Eretz Yisrael and an excited messianism. After the fiasco in Yamit he focused all his attention on the Temple Mount. According to Ariel, the first act of the Israeli government after taking over the holy site in 1967 should have been to tear down the Muslim mosques. But unlike Rabbi Dan Beeri—an underground member and a *Tzfia* writer—who thought that the mosques should have been carefully disassembled in Jerusalem and reassembled elsewhere in the Arab world,[41] Ariel is ruthless:

> it is a shame that we have already sat eighteen years by the mountain and done nothing. About one-third of all the Torah injunctions are related to the small territory of the Temple Mount. It means that in the day we entered the Temple Mount, we, the new landlords were required to clean up the place. The military should have used its demolitions to level the mount. Had it been that way, the spiritual life of the people of Israel would have been revived. . . . With the help of the bulldozers of Sollel Boneh [Israel's largest construction company], which could ruin the mosques in no time, the construction of the Third Temple could have taken place quickly.[42]

Ariel examines the Halakhic aspect of the Temple Mount debate in a comprehensive essay in the second issue of *Tzfia,* which reviews the religious objections to the reconstitution of the Temple at this time. Apart from finding support for his position in Maimonides' conception of redemption, Ariel's most important contribution is his historical analysis of the building of the second Temple in the days of Ezra and Nehemia.

He shows that the reconstruction of the Kingdom of Israel and the Temple were also highly debatable at that time. Only forty thousand Jews lived in Judea, with the vast majority remaining in exile in Babylon. Those that remained in Babylon refused to believe that God had permitted his people to return to Judea and begin the redemption process. This view was corroborated by the fact that no metahistorical messiah existed.

Nevertheless, the devoted returnees realized that as the Temple was the essence of the nation it should be rebuilt, and that this was in fact God's will. Thus, with limited resources they started to build a modest Temple, and in time revived all the Temple's rites and ceremonies, including the animal sacrifices. The new Temple soon became the center of the nation and the focus of its renaissance. Jews from all over the world visited the Temple during the high holidays.[43]

In extrapolating from that time, Ariel saw similar possibilities for the rebuilding of the Temple and a worldwide Jewish renaissance had the government removed the Arabs from the holy mountain in 1967. In a 1985 interview, he stated: "I can see hundreds of thousands of Jews, maybe millions, camping all around these hills, praying, playing, and celebrating the real independence of the nation."[44] Referring to Maimonides' "natural" conception of redemption, which maintains that normal human beings, and not just a metahistorical act, can start the process of redemption, Ariel wrote:

> As against the interpretation that the Temple is the peak of the world and that it is necessary to be competent and "worthy" in order to reach the heavenly plane of its existence—since the Temple is like "another world," "something like the afterworld," etc.—Maimonides refers to an essay . . . which portrays for the reader an opposite situation. The Temple and the worship in it are not something like the peak of the world, a Mount Everest,

but a foundation, a basis . . . one of the pillars upon which the world is established. You remove the pillar and the world may fall apart.[45]

While defending the ideas of Yehuda Etzion on the need to reclaim the Temple Mount, neither Ariel nor any other member of Tzfia expressed in 1985 support for a voluntary operation there. Instead they presented programs for what the government of Israel, as the collective representative of the people of Israel, should be doing. The actual suggestions varied a great deal. The moderates argued for the legitimation of Jewish prayer on the mount in the form of a small synagogue (built in a "safe" corner). Radicals called for imposing complete Jewish sovereignty on the mount with special honor guard, which would ensure that the holy site is fully respected until the nation is ready to build the Third Temple. The extreme position called for active preparations for building the Third Temple. Ariel, by far the most dynamic catalyst in this extreme direction, knew exactly what was to be done.

> The Temple is a concern of this present time. We are obliged to build the Temple just as we are obliged to follow all the commandments of the Torah. It is not that we negate the phenomenon of miracle, but that does not rid us of the obligation to do whatever we have to do. We are working for the Temple-in-the-making just as we did for Zionism-in-the-making. Just as they did not establish a Jewish state right after the first Zionist congress [1896], but built an organization that led to its establishment, so with the building of the Temple . . . [which] is no less visionary than Zionism once was. . . .
>
> You do not build a Temple easily. There are halakhic constraints. There are things that have been forgotten over the years . . . for example the exact location of the site of the altar. In the Talmud . . . there is a description of how the exiles from Babylon found the place. They excavated and exposed the foundations. . . . What will the right situation be? We do not know. It is enough that something will be done on the Temple Mount . . . We know that King Hussein made a mistake when he joined the war [an act that led to the conquest of the Temple Mount]. It may very well be that the next mistake is already in the making.[46]

Asked how would he help the Arabs make the next mistake, one that would trigger a massive Israeli operation to bring about the complete removal of the Muslims from the Temple Mount, Ariel responded:

> BeSiiata Di'Shmaiya [in the help of God]. In order to establish the Temple we need the same system as the Lavi plane, a building of seventeen stories with elevators and offices and huge budgets, contributions, researchers by the dozens, the hundreds, and Halakhic solutions. When we shall build the basic system, the foundations, Heaven will make sure the Arabs make the mistake.[47]

Ariel pushes the logic of Gush Emunim to its ultimate conclusion. If this is indeed an age of redemption, then the conditions are ripe not only for the settlement of Judea and Samaria but also for the settlement of the Temple Mount. The Six-Day War was a link in a long chain of renewal that began with modern Zionism. The process is irreversible and it leads, necessarily, to the building of the Third Temple. If the people of Israel would only do what is possible, God will provide for the rest. And though now may not be the most opportune time for removing the Arabs from the Temple Mount (an excellent opportunity was missed following the 1967 conquest), there is nevertheless no reason to worry. Once all the obligations are met, God will again show his might and provide the necessary opportunity for taking control of Judaism's holiest site.

Tzfia and the Arabs

The reclaiming of the Temple Mount was not the only subject raised by the Jewish Underground and supported by Tzfia. Much of the Gush Emunim criticism of the underground was directed against their conception of self-defense, which they used to justify the killing of violent Arabs. The brutal 1983 attack on the Islamic college in Hebron, in which three students were killed and thirty wounded, and the plan to blow up five buses full of inno-cent Arab civilians, became the grounds for intense condemnation by many movement authorities. Several members of the underground itself, especially Yehuda Etzion, were also outraged by these acts. They were not consulted by the group about these terror acts and felt betrayed.[48]

In contrast, *Tzfia* dissented radically from the general condemnation of terrorist acts. The first issue of the magazine was full of essays, statements, and anonymous letters supporting the entire range of operations of the underground. Readers were referred to traditional injunctions such as 'Haba lehorgecha, hashkem lehorgo" ("If someone comes to kill you, rise early and kill him first"), or "Zechor et asher asa lecha amelek" (Remember what was done unto you by Amalek). Amalek, let us recall, was the most hostile Canaanite tribe during the days of the Exodus and the first settlement of Canaan. It was mischievous, treacherous, and cruel and the Israelites were instructed to eliminate all its men, women, and children.

Elderly Rabbi Moshe Segal used the forum of *Tzfia* to attack a critical essay on the underground by Rabbi Yehuda Shaviv from Yeshivat Alon Shvut. In his essay, "We Have Had Enough of the World's Brotherhood," Segal suggested that Shaviv address his moral outrage to the real murderers, to "the modern successors of Amalek . . . the robbers of our land . . . the people who shed our blood," and not to those devoted individuals who were trying to defend themselves.

> We have tried enough. We had tried to be "a person outside," to be an oil on the wheels of the revolutions of progressive socialism. We preached human-ism and the brotherhood of man. We had made a major contribution to "the great ideals of mankind." What reward have we recieved from the nations of the world? The destruction of six million of our people, the destruction of

Jewish culture in Eastern Europe, which is also now one big prison for millions of our people. Here too, in the renaissance of our nation, we sought and tried "brotherhood of people," bi-nationality and granting privileges to strangers with no obligations. What reward have we recieved?—murders, destruction of property, and a [Palestinian] "Charter" that calls for our elimination in our own land. A rabbi and educator in Israel should preach a departure from the gods of the Gentiles and their fallacious doctrines, a return to the Torah of our forefathers, to the true morality of Judaism, which does not try to please evil people and which teaches "Haba lehorgecha hashkem lehorgo."[49]

In a most provocative article, Rabbi Israel Ariel challenged a Gush Emunim statement that blamed the underground for murder, for violating the command "Thou shalt not kill." Relying on Maimonides and other distinguished Halakhic sources, Ariel maintained that the famous command was never meant to be universal, that only the killing of a Jew qualifies as murder and is punishable accordingly. Killing of a non-Jew is not punishable by society, instead being a matter between God and the killer.[50]

Thus, Gush Emunim's condemnation of the underground is wrong, and the leaders responsible for it have committed a sin of the first degree. They have accused "Jews of Torah and piety" with erroneous and unfounded charges, committing character assassination, which in Jewish sources is sometimes considered equal to actual murder.

Furthermore, Ariel says Gush Emunim is wrong when it claims that the duty to settle Eretz Israel does not allow us to harm Arabs and is not intended to evict the stranger who lives in the land. This, according to Ariel, is a total misinterpretation of the Halakha. The Torah and authorities such as Rashi, Maimonides, and Nachmanides are absolutely clear that a complete conquest of the land cannot be achieved unless all strangers are rooted out. Neither a sale of land nor any other permanent arrangement that would leave the aliens in Eretz Israel is legitimate. Consequently, according to Ariel, "the entire land and every piece of it must return to the eternal ownership of the people of Israel."[51]

The Territorial Borders of Eretz Yisrael

Most of Tzfia's members took positions similar to Meir Kahane's. Though many of them did not like to be associated with Kahane in public, in private they agreed that his Halakhic interpretations were for the most part correct. Some Tzfia members are in fact even more radical and fundamentalist primarily on the issue of the borders of Israel. Thus, while Kahane refused to consider any territorial compromise, he had never advocated expanding beyond the borders of the present State of Israel.[52]

In contrast, Israel Ariel has written a biblical study on the legitimate borders of Israel according to Halakha and tradition, and believes that the

Promised Land that reaches from the Euphrates to the Nile is a reality that can and ought to be actualized today.

> The first and eternal order given to the people of Israel was to reach the borders of the covenant, and it remains an eternal commandment. We should not wait until we are attacked. We have to choose the right moment and start our own attack. It is crystal clear that we have the ability and the power to do so and it is therefore an obligation. The commandment is to attack, to keep the territory and to settle every possible corner of it. In the time of Joshua Ben-Nun the same conditions (of the Israelites being the minority) prevailed, but he did not hesitate. He knew G–d was behind him.[53]

As to the military feasibility of an operation that would pit Israel in a war against Egypt, Syria, Jordan, Lebanon, and Iraq with the expressed purpose of their elimination, Ariel says,

> The command regarding Eretz Israel is *"Yehareg uval yaavor"* ("Be killed rather than sin"). The conquest of the land goes under the same assumption as any other war; in war people get killed. There is a ruling that a war is permitted as long as no more than one-sixth of the nation will be killed. And this was stated in relation to an ordinary war, a fight between neighbors. A war for Eretz Israel does not depend on the number of casualties. The command is *"Ase!"* ("Do it!"), and you may be sure that the number of casualties will thus be minimal. Look at the Six-Day War, for example. Even Rabbi Goren states in his book that casualties cannot invalidate a commandment to fight.[54]

Naturally Ariel was thrilled when Israel invaded Lebanon in 1982. He soon published a monograph, *This Good Mountain and the Lebanon,* that went to great lengths to prove that most of Lebanon is part of the Promised Land. It is mentioned in the Torah as being given to three Israelite tribes, Asher, Naftali, and Zevulun. It was later conquered by David and Solomon, and had a persistent Jewish presence throughout most of history. Therefore, God was behind the Israeli army when it entered Lebanon and He inspired its victory.[55] The command to evacuate Lebanon in 1985 was according to Ariel illegal, since the Torah instructs that one does not retreat if there are other options.[56]

Tzfia 3 and the Assault on Democracy and Civil Rights

At the end of 1988, nearly three years after the second issue of *Tzfia, Tzfia 3* came out. In the new issue, twice as long as the others, the positions of the group have radicalized a great deal. In fact, *Tzfia 3* launched a frontal attack on Israeli democracy and "liberal" Judaism. Many of the learned essays make the late Rabbi Kahane look moderate by comparison, and Gush Emunim positively liberal. *Tzfia 3* is the most extreme document so far produced by the Israeli radical right.

What distinguishes *Tzfia 3* from the earlier volumes is that it no longer needs an "erroneous statement" from Gush Emunim or another "well-intentioned" source as an excuse to reexamine some topics.

This issue is instead a straightforward and comprehensive attempt to examine subjects such as democracy, civil rights, racism, and the status of the aliens in Eretz Yisrael according to the Halakha. The authors do not even try to conceal the true meaning of their conclusions, which amount to an assault on the entire value system of the modern State of Israel. It appears that the authors have long held such positions, but only in 1988 were they confident enough to express them so frankly.

The significance of *Tzfia 3* is, therefore, the readiness of such a learned group of rabbis and thinkers to be so brutally honest about their opposition to the Israeli system, and especially to several "liberal" documents that have been written since 1985 to prove that Judaism does not fundamentally stand in opposition to the values of the modern democratic world. "In the last few years," writes Rabbi David Bar-Haim, a graduate of Yeshivat Merkaz Harav,

> it is possible to recognize a tendancy among several religious circles—a "humanist-universalist" tendency. Many write in favor of the love "for all men that were created in the image of G–d." . . . The obvious purpose of these people is to prove that all men are equal, that a person should not be discriminated against on the basis of his race, and that he who argues against this is nothing but a racist who distorts the words of the Torah in order to make them suit his "terrible" opinions.

After quoting from such religious authorities as Professor Avner Shaki, one of the radical leaders of the NRP, Bar-Haim writes:

> We have before us a very clear proposition: All human beings are equal, Jews and Gentiles. As we shall now see, *this belief stands in total contrast to the Torah of Moses, and is derived from a total ignorance and an assimilation of alien Western values.* It would not even merit comment had not so many people been led astray by it.[57]

Tzfia 3 is the first systematic non-Kahane frontal attack on democracy as a destructive and non-Jewish system of government. Most of the radical right is somewhat apologetic about its negative attitude toward democracy; like the writings of Rabbi Kahane, *Tzfiya 3* is not. Democracy is simply viewed as no good. It stands in direct contradiction to the correct system of government as portrayed in the Halakha, and it is ruining the present State of Israel because it is a foreign system of values. One of the harshest *Tzfia 3* judgments appears in a reprinted 1980 speech made by the late Rabbi Moshe Halevi Segal at the circumcision of Menachem Livni's son, four years before Livni was recognized as the "operative commander" of the *Machteret* and sent to jail:

> All nations should surrender to us, to the King of Israel, to the Messiah of the G–d of Jacob, and should be taught exclusively by us. They must desert their

false beliefs and cultures, and the social systems dangerous for us, to leave this treacherous democracy, which causes Eretz Yisrael to be "Palestine" with an Arab majority, G–d forbid.

We have to do these things as a "legion of the King," but unfortunately this knowledge has not yet penetrated all the ranks of the nation. Here sits the first group that has to fly this flag, for the people of Israel, for the G–d of Israel, for the Torah of Israel, for Eretz Yisrael, against the democracy which confuses the truth and justice, and against all the things imagined by the nations of the world.[58]

A most unexpected attack on democracy is found in an essay by Rabbi Binyamin Tzvielli, the former director of the religious department of Israel Radio and Television. Tzvielli, who previously had not been identified as a right wing radical, wants to see in Israel an ideal Torah state as portrayed by the late Rav Kook. To make his case he cites criticisms of democracy from secular sources such as John Stuart Mill ("the tyranny of the majority"), Oswald Spengler ("the decline of the West") and José Ortega y Gasset ("the revolt of the masses") to show that even great non-Jewish scholars have long identified the maladies of democracy and its potential for decline. Therefore, according to Rabbi Tzvielli, it is just a matter of time before the Israelis discover the uselessness and destructiveness of their democracy. Referring to the post-1984 anxiety about the erosion of democracy in Israel, a response to the election of Rabbi Meir Kahane to the Knesset and to the spread of "Kahanism" among Israeli youth, Tzvielli furiously mocks

the democratic psychosis that has taken control of us for no substantial and visible reason, penetrating even the most hidden corners of our society. This psychosis disturbs the peace of even the most devoted and loyal among us, who have started to check themselves very carefully as to whether or not they are kosher democrats. . . .

Democracy is part of the culture of the West, and together with this culture it goes down, and disappears right before our eyes. . . .

The state of Israel is unfortunately far from the ideal Jewish state [as portrayed by Rav Kook], but even this non-ideal state may open up to a new and original course, it may free itself from the democratic myths and hollow clichés that have brought the entire world, and us too, to this sorry pass.[59]

As extreme as Segal and Tzvielli's hostility to democracy may sound, its radicalism is dwarfed by the essay of Rabbi David Ben-Haim on the misconceived equality between Jews and Gentiles. In a thirty-page study that examines all Halakhic authorities who wrote on the subject, Ben-Haim proves that according to the vast majority, the Torah, when speaking about *Adam* (a human being), never includes Gentiles in this category. He points out that ten recognized Halakhic authorities repeatedly proposed that Gentiles are more beast than human and that they should be treated accordingly; only two authorities recognize non-Jews as full human beings created in the image of God.

What comes out of all this is that according to the prophets, and also according to our sages, the Gentiles are seen as beasts.[60]

For every Jew who accepts the Torah as G-d's expression on Sinai, which is valid and binding all through the generations, it is crystal clear that this [interpretation] cannot be compromised or "amended and improved." . . . It is possible that one may see these injunctions as an expression of racism; another may call it a hatred of the Gentile, whoever he is; but as far as the Jew who adheres to the statements of the Torah of Israel is concerned, this is a reality and a way of life which were set for the people of Israel by G-d.[61]

The central essay of *Tzfia 3* is contributed by Rabbi Israel Ariel, the editor of the volume, who wrote in *Tzfia 2* of the inapplicability of the commandment "thou shalt not kill" to Gentiles. This time he focuses on the status of the *ger toshav* (alien resident) in Eretz Yisrael. Not surprisingly, this essay is the most extreme interpretation of a subject that has been discussed intensely by the religious right since 1967. Gush Emunim's position has been that although the Torah prohibits granting *political* rights to the alien resident—even to those loyal to Israel—there were no Halakhic objections to granting them full *legal* and *personal* rights. Ariel spends ninety pages examining all the Halakhic sources on the issue, and his conclusions are quite ruthless. Thus, even loyal aliens are not allowed to have permanent ownership of any land in Eretz Yisrael.

Ariel also questions the acknowledgment by modern authorities that Muslims are legitimate worshipers of a single God, and are thus entitled to the rights of alien residency. He bases his interpretation on Maimonides who found certain Muslim practices to be pagan. Although he writes in a scholarly manner and eschews policy recommendations, any reader familiar with his very dogmatic fundamentalism is left with no doubt: neither Muslims nor Christians qualify as alien residents; both should be expelled from the Holy Land.[62]

Former Kahane Associates:
The Case of Yoel Lerner

Rabbi Meir Kahane was not known for his ability to keep members in his party or associates in his inner circle. Many former Kach activists have nevertheless remained active in the radical right, some even retaining ties with Kahane—Shimon Rahamim, a manager of a small Jerusalem bank and a former director-general of Kach; Yossi Dayan, a Kiryat Arba activist and also a former Kach director-general; and Eli Adir, an Israeli-born engineer who was drafted by Kahane to replace Dayan and was, by far, Kach's most credible contact with the outside world.[63]

One former Kahane associate still active in the public arena is Avigdor Eskin, a born-again Russian Jew who had been a Kach activist in Kiryat

Arba. Eskin, a well-educated, talented young pianist, joined Kach upon his arrival from Russia in 1979, partly in gratitude for Kahane's aggressive struggle for Soviet Jewry, and partly because he believed that Kahane was the most honest politician in Israel.

Eskin's attitude is typical of many Soviet immigrants who came to Israel in the 1970s, and who are hostile to the Israeli left, believing that it "controls the media and poisons the mind of the nation."[64] They are very clear in their views on Eretz Israel and the Arabs, and tend to see the radical right as their natural milieu. Their Soviet experience makes them extremely bellicose toward the Russians and suspicious of empty talk of peace. They feel strongly that, since Jews suffered so much in the past, they are entitled to all the land conquered in 1967. Further, the plight of the Arabs, who are associated in their minds with the repressive Soviet regime, does not appeal to them.

Nevertheless, many Soviet emigrants quickly became disenchanted with Kahane's rude style and counterproductive politics. This was the case with Eskin, who left with the hope of establishing a new movement, the New Israeli Right. The young Russian émigré, who visited the United States as a speaker on behalf of the struggle of Soviet Jewry, had been influenced by the emerging prestige of the new American right and especially by the Moral Majority of Reverend Jerry Falwell.

Joining forces with Likud Knesset member Michael Kleiner, he tried to get American money to support his anti-Russian and antileftist movement and to initiate a right-wing think tank.[65] The project failed and Eskin dropped out of the public eye, but he has remained constantly involved in radical struggles. There is some indication that he agreed to represent certain South African interests in Israel and to write about Israel for South African newspapers.[66]

The person who has become the leader of the activities of several former Kahane associates, and epitomized the love-hate relationship of these people with Kach's chief, is Yoel Lerner. Lerner, who was born in America and educated there and in South Africa, was one of Kahane's early Israeli recruits. A graduate of MIT in mathematics, he immigrated to Israel in 1960 and studied Hebrew and linguistics at the Hebrew University of Jerusalem. Lerner, another born-again Jew and a gifted linguist and educator, taught mathematics, English, and Hebrew at various religious high schools and formulated his extremist opinions independently. Long before he met Kahane he had reached the conclusion that present-day secular Israel was not to his liking. However, being apolitical by nature, he was not involved in any concrete plans to change the situation.[67]

He found out about the JDL in 1972, and joined Kahane, always more attracted to his fundamentalist opinions than to his politics. Kahane had vowed in those days to devote himself to education. He said his calling was to bring up young Jewish leaders who could start a fundamental reform in

Israel. Lerner supported such ideas and did participate in the violent early JDL opposition against several Christian missionary groups in Israel. He was equally committed to the issue of Soviet Jewry, another one of Kahane's concerns. But Lerner became disillusioned when Kahane decided in 1973 to run for the Knesset, a tacit acceptance of the secular parliamentary system.[68] Kahane's conduct in public during his campaign, his style, his constant pursuit of media attention, and his inability to delegate authority caused Lerner to further distance himself from Kach.

Lerner's relations with Kahane cooled significantly in 1974 when the latter lost the election. The fiasco verified Lerner's conviction that Kahane's electoral aspirations were doomed and that the only way to change Israeli society was through a long process of education, partly through a radical religious youth movement. Thereafter, while he remained a member of Kach, he kept a distance from Kahane and initiated several operations on his own, many of which were illegal. In 1974 he was arrested for attacking several institutions associated with the Christian missionary activities. He was sent to jail and was later released on probation. His operations were all carried out by his young high school students, whom he had indoctrinated.[69]

Lerner was arrested again in 1978, this time charged with having established a subversive organization named Gal (Geula Le-Israel: Redemption for Israel), which had procured arms in order to transform Israel into a Halakha state. Gal could never have developed into a serious operation; it was a fantasy organization of teenagers who called themselves "mosquitoes" and dreamed with their mentor about a cultural and political revolution that would transform Israel.

Lerner was sent to jail for his plan to blow up the Muslim mosques on the Temple Mount in order to impede the Israeli-Egyptian peace process and prevent the evacuation of Sinai. Lerner, hardly a competent underground operator, had been under close surveillance by Israel's secret services since the early 1970s. Thus Gal was exposed before it caused any damage. Lerner's greatest success in Gal was to recruit a second lieutenant in the Israeli army, Amnon Azran, who was one of his former students.[70]

Yoel Lerner has claimed a mysterious relationship in the 1970s with Rabbi Zvi Yehuda Kook; when Lerner told the story in 1984, it caused Gush Emunim great embarrassment. Lerner had never studied in Merkaz Harav, but after his 1974 arrest for his assaults on the Christian Mission, the Halakhic legality of his act was questioned. Acquaintances of Lerner suggested that Rabbi Kook would visit Lerner in jail, listen to his explanation, and then issue a Halakhic verdict. Lerner relates that he had a private session with the old rabbi, who gave his full approval. Kook also told Lerner that if he ever needed support for further anti-Mission operations, he could count on the entire student body of Merkaz Harav.

This version of the meeting was never confirmed by any other source. The people who introduced Lerner to Kook were stunned by Lerner's version, for the rabbi told them that he was completely against illegal acts. But Kook, according to Lerner, rejected an offer to meet the three in order to resolve their differences. He insisted, instead, on his prerogative to talk privately with each party and to say to him whatever he had in mind. Lerner says that he learned from the experience that in delicate matters a rabbi may say different things to different people, and "it matters greatly who they are, how pure and dedicated, and also under what circumstances they do what they do or ask what they ask."

Lerner later consulted with Rabbi Zvi Yehuda occasionally. He says he informed him about the existence of the Gal underground. Lerner insists that he received tacit approval for all of Gal's plans, including the destruction of the the Muslim mosques on the Temple Mount.[71] Lerner is thus convinced that had Yehuda Etzion had direct access to Rabbi Zvi Yehuda Kook, he might have gotten the approval of the highest authority of Gush Emunim for his grand plan of eliminating the Dome of the Rock.[72]

In 1981, again out of prison, Lerner became involved in another feeble new radical entity, the Hashmonaim movement of Rabbi Moshe Segal. This pre-1948 movement, it will be recalled, was revived by its leader in 1978 as a direct response to Camp David. Segal's problem was that most Hashmonaim members, like himself, were elderly, and he was eager to recruit young members.

The idea appealed to Yoel Lerner, with his experience in attracting yeshiva students to such causes, so he started to recruit new members. Very few joined, usually high-school yeshiva students, by swearing allegiance at the Wailing Wall and taking part in sessions that combined a religious approach with fervent ultranationalism. Most new members were familiar with Rabbi Kahane's ideas, but like Lerner, were extremely uncomfortable with his methods. They wanted more substance and less propaganda, and were highly skeptical about the ability to act within the secular framework of Israeli politics.

Among the recruits to the Hashmonaim were a few new older faces. One such was Rabbi Dan Beeri, a French proselyte who was later arrested as a member of the Jewish Underground.[73]

In 1982 Lerner was arrested again—this time for trying to place a bomb by Al-Aksa Mosque, the second Muslim shrine on the Temple Mount. As usual he had two of his students with him. His attempt to convince the court that he became party to the conspiracy only to subvert it from within was rejected and he was sentenced to two years in prison. With their leader in jail, many young members of Hashmonaim dropped out of the movement. Not a few of them became involved in the activities of the legal group called the Temple Mount Faithful.[74]

When Lerner was released form jail at the end of 1984, the climate had become more favorable for ultranationalism. The Jewish Underground and Kach were established facts in Israel's public consciousness, and the attitudes that had made Lerner look like a lunatic a few years earlier were no longer exceptional. This situation encouraged Lerner not only to return to the Hashmonaim, but also to start a new group.

The declared purpose of the new body, Hamosad Lema'an Tora Beisrael-Mati (the Institute for the Torah in Israel), is to promote the restoration of the Sanhedrin—the council of seventy sages that was the Jewish Supreme Court and the final Halakhic authority before the destruction of the Second Temple. Lerner disagrees with Yehuda Etzion and Israel Ariel, who believe that the redemption of the nation can be advanced outside the presently recognized Halakhic institutions either by a self-selected Redemption Movement or by a movement to study and rebuild the Third Temple. His argument is that a cultural revolution in the nation can only take place if the existing Halakhic authorities can be convinced to reestablish the Sanhedrin. Although he is confident about his way, Lerner is fully aware of the difficulties involved: "the idea is very revolutionary and I expect great difficulties in its implementation." Lerner recently sent seventy letters to sympathetic rabbis on the question of the revival of the Sanhedrin, but has received only three positive replies, none of which has been fully supportive.[75]

Apparently disillusioned with his unsuccessful sabotage conspiracies, Yoel Lerner has since 1985 also devoted himself to the idea of applying Jewish law to Israeli reality. For over two years he worked on a draft constitution for the State of Israel that would totally be based on the Halakha and the Jewish legal system, though written in the legal terminology of the twentieth century. Surprisingly, Lerner was almost the first to do so. This anti-establishment rebel, who was once characterized by a judge as a complete anarchist,[76] was very happy to learn that the religious division of Israel's Ministry of Education had found portions of his document worthy of being studied in all the nation's religious high schools. Lerner also started an academic legal magazine, *Takdim* (Precedent), and has been successful in publishing contributions by several of Israel's top theorists of Hebrew law, including those who disagreed with his political ideas.[77] And he has initiated several seminars about the Temple Mount and made attempts, though not very successful, to bring together all the groups that have been involved in the drive to establish a Jewish presence there.[78]

The mature Lerner has a very discursive and logical mind. Unlike his police files and public image, which project him as an unrealistic and adventurous fundamentalist, Lerner is in fact a serious person whose arguments sometimes make more sense than the grand messianic theories of Yehuda Etzion or Rabbi Israel Ariel. What distinguishes Yoel Lerner from all the other cultural radicals, and to some extent even from Gush Emunim, is that he has never been impatient for the coming of the Messiah. "How can I know," asks Lerner, "what the intentions of God are, or His timetable? All I do know is what I myself, a believing Jew, am obliged to do. And I shall do it no matter of what the secular State of Israel says or does."[79]

Lerner ridicules the Movement to Halt the Retreat in Sinai and the people who believed they could persuade God by their prayers to interfere and stop the evacuation. He is equally skeptical of his colleagues who are trying to advance redemption through the Israeli political system. His major criticism of Meir Kahane since 1973 has focused on the rabbi's incessantly vacillating attempts to join, or to demonstrate against, Israel's parliamentary politics. "In my entire life I have participated in only two demonstrations, for I have always considered demonstrations futile. When I felt I had to do something" —commit a violent act— "I simply went ahead and did it."[80] As an "elder statesman" of the fundamentalist right, Lerner was invited to join the executive committee of the Independent State of Judea. He did it willingly, but after several futile meetings decided to resign. Instead of really starting to prepare for the time Israel leaves the West Bank, he later said, "They just kept talking."[81]

The Struggle Over the Temple Mount

The cultural radicals have largely steered clear of the growing politics of the radical right, but there is one issue in which they have made a *political* difference—the issue of the Temple Mount. Since this subject may be the most explosive item on the agenda of the radical right, it can illustrate the significance of this group and its interaction with other components of the radical right.

It would be a mistake to assume that the struggle for the Jewish return to the holy place started only in 1984, when the Jewish Underground was discovered. In fact the campaign began in 1967, right after the Six-Day war, though it was slow gaining momentum and public attention.

The first controversial act on the mount took place immediately following its conquest. Rabbi Shlomo Goren, the chief rabbi of Israel's army, tried at that time to place a sacred Ark—a Torah book and a prayer stand—in the southern corner of the Temple Mount in order to establish an Israeli presence. He also opened a temporary office in one of the Arab buildings there. These acts greatly irritated Moshe Dayan, Israel's minister of defense, who ordered the Ark removed and the office closed.[82]

Dayan decided that the holy place would be left under the control of the Muslim Waqf and that Jews would be allowed to visit it only as tourists, not worshipers. The most vital support for Dayan's decision came from Israel's Chief Rabbinate. This institution, the highest official religious authority in Israel, resolved in July 1967 that Jews were not allowed on the mount for fear that "we shall be faulted, God forbid, in breaking a most severe prohibition regarding the desecration of this holy place."[83] Moshe Dayan, invited in 1977 to become Begin's minister of foreign affairs, made the continuation of this arrangement on the Temple Mount his condition for joining the cabinet.[84]

In a reaction to Dayan's 1967 decision, a group calling itself Ne'emanei Har Habait (the Temple Mount Faithful) was formed first in Jerusalem and then later in Tel Aviv. Its members—never more than a few hundred, including their youth movement—would climb up the mount on every major Jewish holiday in an attempt to pray and demonstrate a presence. The head and most active member of the group since its establishment has been Gershon Solomon, a sixth-generation resident of Jerusalem and a prominent Herut member.[85]

Although many Temple Mount Faithful are religious, the movement's ideology is mainly nationalist and secular. Their key point is that the Temple Mount was not just the religious focus of ancient Israel, but also its public and political center. The Kings' Palace was on the mount, and the Sanhedrin held court there. The program of the Faithful therefore calls upon the government to move Israel's Supreme Court, the Knesset, the President's Mansion, and its own offices to the Temple Mount, and to conduct all official ceremonies there.[86]

The Temple Mount Faithful have never abided by the religious prohibition against visiting the site. They have been extremely unhappy with the Chief Rabbinate's glorification of the Wailing Wall—a small part of the external wall of the ruined Temple—since it symbolizes the destruction of the nation, not its renaissance. It was given by the Muslim rulers of Jerusalem to the defeated and humiliated Jews, who were not allowed to climb up the mount, as a small and remote remnant to cherish. Thus adhering to the Wailing Wall while being in full control of the entire area is a disgrace, a calamity of the first degree, and the resolution of the rabbinate is, in the opinion of the Faithful of the Temple Mount, an anachronistic evasion.

Their criticism has slowly gained support. A meaningful endorsement to the Faithful's position was rendered in the 1976 by Rabbi Shlomo Goren, who had become by that time the chief rabbi of Israel. Goren had secretly visited the mount on several occasions after drafting a very strong Halakhic ruling to permit prayer at certain areas on the mount. However, since Goren kept his study secret because of the opposition of the rabbinical council of the Chief Rabbinate, it could not be used for a long time.[87]

The Temple Mount Faithful differ from most of the radical right in their outstanding legality. Its leaders have always been determined to obey the law and all the instructions of the Jerusalem police. The group's most extreme act of defiance has been passive resistance, and they have never clashed with the police.

One reason for their nonviolent approach has been their desire to influence the general public on this issue. Also, they firmly believe that their activities have a sound legal basis. According to state law, the Holy Places Bill, full freedom of access to all holy sites is guaranteed for every worshiper, so the Faithful are convinced that the defense minister's ruling restricting the Jewish presence on the mount is illegal. In appeals to Israel's Supreme Court, the Faithful have tried to show that the ban on prayer in the holy place has no legal basis, a claim enhanced by the group's reputation for abiding by the law.

The peaceful tactics of the Faithful have gained them the support of Israel's Civil Rights Association, an organization otherwise associated with the Israeli left. And in fact on several occasions the Court has ruled in favor of the movement.[88]

However, forgoing extralegal activities has its drawbacks, specifically ineffectiveness. For years no one took the Faithful very seriously, and most still consider them a small circle of crazies making symbolic gestures with no political consequences, merely a footnote to the real action in Judea and Samaria.

The importance of the Temple Mount issue grew slightly in the early 1970s when a handful of religious individuals got together to reexamine the Halakhic status of the holy site. The group named itself *El Har Hashem* (Towards the Mountain of the Lord) and included Rabbi Yoel Ben-Nun and Uri Elitzur of Gush Emunim. A central member of the circle was Menachem Ben-Yashar, a Bar-Illan University scholar and kibbutz member who had been strongly advocating Jewish prayer on the Temple Mount since 1968.

In a critique of the Rabbinate's ruling published in *Amudim*, Ben-Yashar argued that up until the sixteenth century, Jews prayed on the mount whenever it was politically possible, and had even established a synagogue there. It was only after the sixteenth century, as a result of growing Muslim hostility, that Jews were forbidden to be on the mount and given the Wailing Wall as compensation. Thus the Rabbinate's proposition that since the destruction of the Temple, Jews had not been permitted to pray there was, according to Ben-Yashar, erroneous and baseless.[89]

Though Towards the Mountain of the Lord was not a political or protest group, but rather a study group, its establishment was nevertheless important. It signified a prestigious rabbinical interest in the sensitive issue. The group's final conclusions were not made public, but there are indications that the members of the Jewish Underground knew of the group and drew some inspiration from it.[90]

Even earlier, though, the Temple Mount's potential as a religious battleground was clear. In 1969, an insane messianic Australian, Denis Michael Rohan, who wanted to hasten the second coming of Christ set fire to Al-Aksa Mosque. The act shocked the Arab world. Many thousands of Muslims stormed the place and then surged in old Jerusalem in unprecedented fury and outrage. Several Muslim states issued stern warnings to Israel, and the possibility of a *jihad* (holy war) was raised.[91] It took months to convince the Muslim authorities that the act was not committed by a Jew, and that there was no Jewish conspiracy to take over of the holy place.

Another Muslim riot broke out in 1975 when a Jerusalem judge acquitted several Betar youth charged with disorderly conduct on the Temple Mount and recommended that rules and regulations for Jewish prayer be issued by the ministry of Religion. The riots were brought under control by the Israeli police only after three demonstrators were killed, dozens wounded, and hundreds arrested.[92]

In April 1982, an unstable young Jew, Allen Goodman, opened fire on the guard of the Dome of the Rock. Goodman, a disturbed tourist who had earlier volunteered on a kibbutz, did it "to avenge the blood of several of my friends who were killed by the Arabs."[93] The eruption that ensued resulted in the death of two Arabs and the wounding of nine people, including several Israeli policemen. Goodman, who took over the Dome of the Rock, was captured alive by the police and sentenced to life in prison, despite his plea of insanity. Rabbi Kahane offered him free legal services.[94]

Responding to growing pressure, Israel's Chief Rabbinate quietly set up a committee in 1981 to reexamine the Temple Mount issue. The Rabbinate's committee, made up of Israel's two chief rabbis, and rabbis Dov Lior of Kiryat Arba and Simha Kook of Rehovot (no relation to Rabbi Zvi Yehude Kook), was to study the possibility of establishing a synagogue in one corner of the holy site. The impetus for the reexamination was a report by Rabbi Meir Yehuda Getz, the rabbi in charge of the Wailing Wall. Getz, who aspires to return to the Temple Mount as its rabbi, did not act on his own. He had been approached by the Ministry of Religion, which was responding, in turn, to a new threat by a Tel Aviv lawyer to lay the case before the High Court of Justice.[95] Getz himself created a commotion in that summer, when a secret excavation he had made under the Muslim mosques, in order to reach hidden parts of the ruined Temple, was exposed.[96] Both the Muslim and Jewish authorities became understandably touchy on the subject.

The late 1970s and early 1980s saw several other related developments: the establishment of Yeshivat Ateret Cohanim, the project to weave gowns for the future Temple's high priests, and the publication of a study about the exact location of the ancient Temple. While these developments were not political and did not imply a conflict with the status quo, they did illustrate the increasing preoccupation about the holy site and the expansion of the circle of people interested.

Rabbi Shlomo Aviner started Ateret Cohanim as an extension of Merkaz Harav to teach students the centrality of the place for the nation's salvation, though he did not push for an immediate return to the site. Aviner and his deputy, Rabbi Menachen Fruman, wanted their students to be ready for the day when the Third Temple is rebuilt, teaching all the halakhic rules and regulations of the Order of the Sacrifices of the Temple, which had not been practiced for nearly two thousand years.[97] Rabbi David Elboim has already been mentioned. A Hassidic Jew with no direct relation to the Zionist religious camp, he started the complicated job of weaving the gowns for the high priest according to halakhic law—a project that requires a special expertise and several years of dedicated hard work. His work has been seen by many Temple Mount devotees as step in the direction of the awaited redemption.[98]

In 1983, Rabbi Zalman Koren, a teacher in the Kiryat Arba yeshiva, published a study in the religious magazine *Tehumin,* in which he identified several potential prayer areas on the Temple Mount. Although in a slight disagreement with the conclusions of Rabbi Shlomo Goren, Koren, the author of a book on the subject, followed Goren in arguing that several areas on the Temple Mount could safely be used for Jewish prayer. Koren's conclusion was supported by an official endorsement published in the same volume of *Tehumin* by Rabbi Mordechai Eliyahu, Israel Chief Sepharadi Rabbi.[99]

These developments, though not themselves violent, undoubtedly played an important role in the increasing number of clandestine operations at the Temple Mount in the early 1980s. Among them were the attempt of students of Rabbi Israel Ariel to penetrate the area in order to conduct a special prayer service, and the Lifta group's attempt to blow up the Muslim mosques.

At the end of March 1983 during the Passover holiday, a group of thirty-eight yeshiva students, including ten soldiers on active duty, met at Ariel's home for an evening prayer. The group then proceeded to the southern side of the Temple Mount with the intention of digging under the mount by way of an old tunnel leading to the ancient Western Gate of Hulda. The idea was to reach the remains of the Temple, situated under Al-Aksa Mosque, and to conduct a special Passover prayer there. There were rumors that they planned to occupy the place in the style of Gush Emunim's illicit settlements, in order to negotiate a concession regarding the presence of Jews on the Temple Mount. But the plan failed, since the group was caught on its way to the mount. Nevertheless, the prosecution found it very hard to prove any illegality. The "religious conspiracy" dominated headlines in Israel for several days, but ended in a big fiasco.[100]

The Lifta incident was much more serious. In January 1984 a night guard of the Muslim Waqf on the Temple Mount came upon a load of explosives and grenades in the area, and saw two unidentified figures flee. The event stirred tremendous commotion in Israel. The large quantity of the explosives seemed to imply a sophisticated underground and a well-organized conspiracy. There was a strong reaction from the Muslims, who had been suspicious of the Jews all along.[101]

Everyone was surprised when an intense police investigation revealed that the perpetrators were four strange characters who lived in a cave in the deserted village of Lifta on the northern outskirts of Jerusalem. They had planned to blow up the Al-Aksa Mosque for nationalist and religious reasons, but were extremely confused and unclear about their intentions and beliefs. Combining religious repentance with criminality, drugs, and strange symbolism, they had created a small messianic sect based on spiritual purification and an unmediated relation with God. The head of the group was a known Israeli criminal, who had obtained the explosives; the other three members were unstable and homeless. No rabbi or Halakhic authority was involved. They lived in great poverty, and were known only to the other lunatic individuals who frequented the uninhabited village. Only one member of the group was finally found competent to stand trial; two others were sent to a mental institution. The fourth member of the strange conspiracy was never caught, having escaped abroad.[102]

The main difference between these early attempts and that of the Jewish Underground was the quality of the people involved and the sophistication of their plans. The members of the Underground were among the elite of Gush Emunim, individuals with backgrounds in the military and settlement pioneering. Their strong convictions made it impossible to see them as usual criminals.

And their theories demanded serious examination, especially on the provocative Temple Mount issue; no longer could the rabbis of Gush Emunim bury the subject under a cloud of traditional rabbinical prohibition.[103] No one could maintain equanimity vis-à-vis Yehuda Etzion's burning essays in *Nekuda,* which challenged the entire political approach of the movement and promised a new agenda of active redemption. By 1984 Gush Emunim wasn't just a marginal group. It was a central political and cultural phenomenon whose controversies reverberated throughout Israel's public life. Even moderate Gush members, who opposed illegal operations on the mountain site, were highly critical of the government's failure to stop the desecration of the holy place. The Tehiya, Knesset members of the Likud, and rabbis all over the country were forced to take a stand. The place of the Temple Mount in the nation's life finally became a most dramatic and sensitive public issue.

There are many indications that the explosive situation on the Temple Mount was caused not only by the Jews. Persistent rumors about intense Arab activity have existed since the beginning of the 1980s. Besides the building of many new prayer stands, there seem to have been secret destructive excavations of the old foundations of the Temple. Many believe that the Arabs are trying to erase all remains of the ancient shrine, with the issue reaching the Knesset in May 1982.[104]

The intensification of the Israeli-Palestinian conflict after Camp David has been reflected on the Temple Mount. The Muslim mosques have always filled a major political function for the Palestinian community under occupation, since they were the safest place to voice criticism of the Israelis. This was because the government of Israel could not, for political reasons, punish the Mufti and his people in Jerusalem; sermons that in other places could cause reprimands or arrests were delivered openly from the pulpits of the Temple Mount's mosques.

The 1980s saw first an undeclared war between the PLO and the government of Israel, and then a declared one in Lebanon. Unable to face the

Israelis in the battlefield, the Palestinians turned to other fields, and none was more promising than the Harm-esh-Sherif. The memorial for the "sacred victims" of Sabra and Shatila, established in the area as a prayer stand, was the last but not the least affront to the interested Israelis.[105]

A dramatic moment in the political conflict over the Temple Mount was triggered at the end of 1985 by Knesset member Dov Shilansky (who became Speaker of the House in 1988). Shilansky, an emotional Likud activist and a survivor of the Holocaust, first gained public notoriety in 1952 when he was arrested inside Israel's Foreign Ministry carrying a bomb. The deactivated bomb was a symbolic protest against the Reparations Agreement signed by Israel with the Federal Republic of Germany.[106]

In 1985, Shilansky, then the head of the Knesset's Interior Committee, understood that the issue of the status of the Temple Mount was a political goldmine. His Knesset committee had already studied the allegations of Arab desecrations on the mount, but the committee deliberations had evoked little public interest. Shilansky therefore came up with the notion of visiting the mount to demonstrate an official Jewish presence. The idea was equally appealing to Geula Cohen, who served on the committee and strongly favored the Israelization of the Temple Mount.

What followed was an unforgettably chilling scene: A few Knesset members, heavily protected by police, visited the Temple Mount, triggering a violent Arab protest. The MKs barely escaped with their lives, but the political payoff was enormous. For two days the Temple Mount dominated all the headlines.[107] The television showed unrestrained outbursts of Arab hatred that left even moderate Israelis ill at ease. And the entire Israeli right, not just its radical wing, was outraged by the reaction, feeling that the Arabs "needed to be taught a lesson."

Shilansky's committee conducted several more visits, and the Temple Mount Knesset lobby gained momentum and strength. Geula Cohen incessantly demanded probes of Arab acts on the Temple Mount and of the government's refusal to let Jews pray there.[108]

If the transformation of the Temple Mount from taboo to urgent Knesset topic was the most important *political* success of the cultural radicals, the rabbis' conference on the subject was their most rewarding theological accomplishment. Approximately fifty rabbis met in Jerusalem in August 1986. They ruled that not only were Jews allowed to enter the area, but that it was a religious duty and a sacred obligation.

The most prominent among the members of the conference was Shlomo Goren, Israel's former chief rabbi. Finally presenting in public his 1976 study of the geography of the Temple Mount, which determined that an ordinary Jew could go to most areas of the site, Goren expressed extreme concern about the lack of a Jewish presence on the holy place. It was mandatory, he argued, to establish a Jewish synagogue in one of the remote corners of the mount so that Jews could go to the Temple Mount and pray.

> The present situation indicates deterioration. Leftist Jews agitate against our hold of the Temple Mount. The Arabs would have done nothing had they not been supported by Jews. I care nothing for the Mufti. We are talking about the holiest Jewish place. For them, most of the area is anyhow not sacred. It all depends on the minister of religion. The present minister will do nothing; we know him. I hope that the next minister would have the courage to act properly.[109]

Rabbi Goren was not alone. Rabbi Israel Ariel, the indefatigable fighter for the Temple Mount cause, Rabbi Dov Lior, and many other Tzfia members were also present. The cause they had been struggling for had finally received full legitimacy. And there were signs that the convention did not displease Israel's Prime Minister Itzhak Shamir, an ardent, though low-keyed, nationalist. A person in Shamir's office who declined to be identified told the press, "If the Rabbinate will allow prayer, nobody is going to bar it—certainly not Shamir, who hopes to see the Israeli flag atop the Temple Mount."[110]

The growing demand to place the Temple Mount under Israeli jurisdiction has led to the establishment of two new ventures: Rabbi Israel Ariel's Museum of the Temple and the Movement for the Reestablishment of the Temple.

In keeping with is belief that the government should create a huge research center to study all Halakhic questions involved in the building of the Third Temple, in 1986 Rabbi Israel Ariel opened a small exhibition in the Jewish quarter of Jerusalem. The purpose of the small museum is to demonstrate to the visitor that the Temple can in fact be built today and will include the reestablishment of the religious rites as they were held over two thousand years ago.

The ritual instruments on display have all been produced according to the laws of Halakha. The special guide to the museum points out to visitors the relevant Torah paragraphs and carefully explains how every item was manufactured. Ariel's hope is to turn this little one-room exhibition eventually into a research center that will resolve all the unclear aspects of the reestablishment of the shrine "for the glory of God."[111]

The Movement for the Reestablishment of the Temple was created in 1987 by several religious devotees of the Temple Mount who were unable to work with Gershon Solomon and his Temple Mount Faithful. The idea of the new group was *not* to show the Arabs and the world that the Jews are attached to the holy site, but instead to prove to orthodox Jews that there is a religious legitimation for Israel's control of the Temple Mount and for the reinstatement of prayer there. The movement, which was begun by Rabbi Yosef Elboim (David's uncle), has not staged showy operations, but has instead convinced the police to allow large Jewish groups into the area. It leaders have also been trying to obtain permission to pray there.[112]

The worst eruption on the Temple Mount since its 1967 occupation by Israel took place on October 8, 1990, during the Jewish holiday of Succot. And as expected the cultural radicals were at the eye of the storm. A symbolic march of the Temple Mount Faithful and other devotees toward the holy site, which was barred by the police at the last minute, created extreme apprehension among the Muslim authorities. A call for an Arab rally in defense of Harem-esh-Sherif was responded to enthusiastically by thousands of Moslems. Soon the defensive act turned into offense, when the excited demonstrators started to throw rocks at the Jews praying by the Wailing Wall. Succot usually brings a record number of worshipers to the holy site, and well over ten thousand Jews had to escape the barrage. The unprepared and understaffed police unit on the mount lost control and opened fire, using live ammunition.

The results were catastrophic. Nineteen Palestinian Arabs died instantly and nearly one hundred and fifty were wounded. There was no way for Israel to avoid worldwide condemnation, and an immediate Arab demand for severe U.N. sanctions against Israel. The damaging effects of three years of unresolved *intifada,* as well as of the American need to keep its anti-Iraqi coalition from falling apart, two months after Saddam Hussein's invasion of Kuwait, put the Jewish state in a very awkward international situation.

The 1990 Temple Mount eruption was not a chance turn of events. It was instead the logical culmination of a decade-long process of Jewish-Moslem confrontation on the holy site. The 1987 outbreak of the *intifada* has apparently not stopped the momentum of the Jewish struggle over the Temple Mount, but, on the contrary, has intensified it. Faced with the unexpected Palestinian determination to free themselves from the Israelis, the cultural radicals—like the rest of the radical right—could not avoid the conclusion that the final battle over Eretz Yisrael has begun. There was obviously no better time to demonstrate the Jewish determination to keep the Holiest of Holies forever, and to push for its purification. Thus, while the government of Israel has been trying desperately to prevent conflict over the Temple Mount, fearful of its inflammatory impact on the *intifada,* the cultural radicals intensified their involvement.

An indication of the true intentions of the cultural radicals was provided in April 1989 when a highly symbolic operation on the Temple Mount, the conduct of the Passover Sacrifice, an ancient religious rite, was barely averted. The controversial act involved none other than the three most devoted cultural radicals, Yehuda Etzion, Rabbi Israel Ariel, Yoel Lerner, and a few followers. An operation of even greater symbolic meaning, especially for the anxiety-ridden Moslem authorities of the Harem-esh-Sherif, was conducted few months later—an attempt to lay the foundation stone for the Third Temple. The fact that the Temple Mount Faithful who were responsible for the act did not take it seriously made little difference for the

Arabs. Hard hit by the tribulations of the *intifada*, and the bad news of the huge number of incoming Jewish immigrants from Russia, the common Palestinians were ready to believe anything. An explosion on the Temple Mount thus became almost inevitable.

It is clear that the determination of the cultural radicals to place the Temple Mount in the heart of the struggle for Eretz Yisrael has been very successful. The place is today the most volatile spot in the Middle East, perhaps on Earth. Both Jewish and Arab extremists must know that a single operation in the site can destroy years of slow and careful peace process. And it is likely that some of them will try when the time arrives.[113]

The Radical Right,
Democracy, and Zionism:
Past, Present,
and the Future

The emergence of radical right movements such as Gush Emunim, Kach, and their parliamentary colleagues has generated a major intellectual controversy in Israel. Most of the ideologues of the new camp maintain that they are the genuine representatives of pioneering Zionism and of "Jewish democracy," but many Israelis see them as having contaminated the nation and stained its democratic record. Some critics have even argued that the radical right, and especially its religious fundamentalist wing, represent a major deviation from the Zionist ideological and humanist heritage.[1]

The relationship of the radical right with modern democratic thought and Zionism is not just an academic issue. It is germane to the future of Israel's civic culture and the evolution of its system of government. Is the Israeli radical right anti-democratic? Does it pose a real danger to Israel's system of government? Does its ideology really contradict the "classical" Zionist thought and tradition? Is the radical right likely to remain an influential force in Israeli Zionism?

The Radical Right and Israeli Democracy

Even a cursory survey of the statements of the thinkers and ideologues of the radical right suggests that most of them realize many of their beliefs are incompatible with modern democratic principles, and feel uneasy about it. This sense of latent guilt indicates at least a partial commitment to some democratic ideas and practices. The real question, however, is, What direction is this limited commitment headed? Is it a relic from the past, a dwindling homage to the vanishing pre-1967 Israeli order, or is it an indication of a growing support for democracy? On these questions, the radical right appears to be divided into two camps: the religious-orthodox and the secular.

The Religious-Orthodox Camp

All orthodox religious Jews, irrespective of their political convictions, believe in principle in the future establishment in Israel of a Halakhic state, a Jewish theocracy. Though this state is expected to respect certain democratic principles, its system of government would not be democratic and would be founded on a totally different set of suppositions. Like all theocracies, a halakhic state presupposes the existence of an absolute truth and the ability of competent individuals to discern it and to conduct the affairs of the nation in accordance with it.

The primary purpose of the Jewish theocracy is to glorify God and ensure that His commandments are obeyed. Most orthodox Jews presuppose the Torah to be the existing constitution of the nation and recognize the long tradition of its halakhic interpretation as the standing law of the land. For some it means the division of the future government between a ruling king, a descendant of the House of David, and a Sanhedrin—the supreme court and legislative council composed of seventy sages. Such a government would also give great prominence to the central Temple in Jerusalem and its high priests.[2]

What sets the religious wing of the Israeli radical right apart from other orthodox Jews is not the belief in the desirability of a halakhic state but the insistence on its relevance to the current historical reality. Having defined the present era as the age of heavenly redemption, the major thinkers and theologians of the religious radical right believe that the Israeli polity is likely to be transformed into the desired Jewish theocracy in the near future. Members of the radical right differ, however, as to the nature and the timing of this transformation. Three competing interpretations of these issues disclose better than any other indicator the religious right's degree of support for democracy.

Rabbi Kahane took an extremist position, a version of which is shared by a small minority of the cultural radicals. Kahane's appraoch was ruthlessly logical. It assumed that all the conditions for a full redemption of the nation and its transformation into a "kingdom of priests and holy people" are already present. The nation, and especially its leaders who refuse to recognize the great historical moment, are sinning against God. They are illegitimate usurpers and ought to be revealed and punished.

Democracy, according to Kahane, is a proper system for some Gentiles, especially for Western civilization. Most of the nations of this civilization emerged naturally over a long period of time. They came out of tribes and contractual societies. They eventually reached democracy, and for them there is nothing wrong in this system of government.[3]

The case of the Jews is different, however. The Jewish nation did not evolve naturally out of an obscure tribe. It was chosen by God at a conrete historical moment and was made a nation by a unique constitution, the Torah, a divine and unconditional instrument. To be a Jew, Kahane argued, is to belong to an undemocratic holy community which neither needs legitimation from the free will of its individual members nor seeks it from the community of nations.

Thus, a genuine and believing Jew should now be devoted to only one public cause, the delegitimization of the Israeli regime and the establishment of a real "Jewish" state. Kahane's call for the expulsion of Arabs from the Holy Land and his prescriptions for the harsh treatment of "Hellenized" and "Gentilized" Jews derived from this doctrine. As we have seen, Rabbi Kahane did not care about the world, the Gentiles, or anybody who is not Jewish. If the Jews repent and go back to God, then their redemption will be completed irrespective of anything else that happens in the world.

The majority of the cultural radicals, though they accept many tenets of traditional Kookism, are extremely critical of the acts and policies of the State of Israel; nonetheless, they do not question its legality, and they recognize it as the Kingdom of Israel in the making. This school is distinguished by its conviction that a Jewish halakhic state may be introduced gradually through specifiable concrete actions. Purging the Temple Mount and reconstituting the Sanhedrin are the next steps, and may by themselves raise the nation to the higher level of consciousness necessary for the desired political transformation.

These acts, however, can only be authorized by the state. Interested individual believers may act in that direction, provided they do so in a peaceful way. The people who take this stand are not ideologically rebellious. They believe in evolution and trust God that the right events will take place at the right time without any decisive antigovernment action. On the other hand, they insist that an active human participation in the gradual establishment of a halakhic state is both possible and desirable.

What makes the unrebellious cultural radicals really undemocratic is the fact that their commitment to the present Israeli system is very superficial. Unlike Kahane, they have no grand theories explaining why Western democracy is irrelevant to the Israeli existence, or why the Jews should not worry about the Gentiles, the United States, or anything else in the outside world. They simply assume that the democratic status quo is meaningless and that they do not have to waste time thinking about it. As for the Arab question and the more general issue of the non-Jews in Israel, they are very close to Kahane's position of civil discrimination and eventual eviction.

The main body of Gush Emunim, on the other hand, and especially its moderate wing, is closest to the traditional religious approach that *Hakol tzafui vehareshut netuna* (while everything is predetermined, one is free to choose). This assumes that the grand developments are in the hands of God but in daily affairs and small matters the believer has to decide and be held morally responsible for his decision. This school differs from the traditional non-messianic approach, however, in its belief that the people of Israel now live in the final stages of the age of redemption and that progress toward a halakhic state is inevitable. The only concrete participation is the process of redemption that is recommended now is an active political struggle against territorial concessions and a constant drive to settle the Greater Eretz Yisrael. The moderate position no doubt reflects a theological uncertainty regarding the redemptive intentions of God, and an emotional commitment to the traditional Israeli democracy.

The rabbis and theologians of this school are as orthodox and religiously observant as Kahane and the cultural radicals, but they are not as impatient. They are still grateful to the secular government of Israel for winning the Six-Day War and do not push for a new miracle. They appreciate the success of Gush Emunim as a settlement movement and feel very attached to the existing Israeli society. They are committed to the Kookist sanctification of the present Israeli regime, especially its military. Many of their leaders actively participate in Israeli public affairs and the established system is part of their existential frame of reference.

The result of this dual loyalty—a belief on the one hand in full redemption at the present time, and on the other a commitment to the existing Israeli power structure—is a serious theoretical gap. Most of the thinkers of Gush Emunim sincerely do not know what to say about the political transformation to a Halakhic state. Whenever asked they argue that it is not for them, or for any human agent, to try and expose God's secret plan. He will see to that that all the contradictions are resolved in time, and in the meantime there are plenty of other things to worry about and to do.

This approach to Israeli democracy is characterized by a limited allegiance to the present system of government coupled with an intense involvement in national politics and public affairs. The "moderate" religious radicals are interested in the non-Jewish world and are more humane toward the Arabs than their "radical" colleagues. They are critical of the violence of Kahane's supporters and do not endorse his extremist solutions for the Arab question. The Arabs are not "dogs" or animals, though of course they do not deserve full political rights. Careful distinctions must be drawn, and only the terrorists and their accomplices, (a small minority, according to the moderates), should be chased out of the country. What makes the "burden" of the dual loyalty of the moderates somewhat easier is that the commitment of most Israelis to democracy has never been complete. Even under non-religious and nonmessianic Israeli regimes, the Arabs never enjoyed full equality, and the Israelis have never been fully committed to the rule of law. Under these conditions of imperfect democracy, a dual loyalty to two political courses is not necessarily a liability.

The Secular Camp

The secular camp of the Israeli radical right does not share the religious camp's belief in a Halakhic state, and in fact does not even give it serious consideration. Its neofundamentalism and neotraditionalism, which make the present alliance with the orthodox so amiable and harmonious, seem to be limited to the ultranationalism the two partners share and to their common interest in keeping Eretz Yisrael undivided. Tehiya's idea of *holchim beyahad* (going together) has created a better understanding and working relationship between its secular and religious activists, but it certainly has not changed the fundamental epistemologies of either side.[4] There are many indications that the moment the chances for the establishment of a Jewish theocracy become real, the religious-secular alliance will end. With the exception of the small number of secular activists who have been "born again," only very few share the mystical belief of their religious partners that, as their private consciousness is transformed, in due time, they will become good orthodox Jews.

Almost none of the secular Israeli radicals can, in good conscience, be called fascist in the historical sense of the term. None of them despise the parliamentary system in principle, feel bad about the decadent Israeli bourgeoisie, or wish to do away with the general legal order in favor of some *Führer Prinzip* or even a Zionist dictatorship. Most of the secular radical right is a product of many years of Zionist democracy and the lack of an alternative model.

The real challenge of the secular radical right to Israel's system of government is more mundane and pragmatic. This school refuses to pay homage to democracy as a *universal* principle of good government. It is equally not enthusiastic about the association of democracy with a strict interpretation of the rule of law. The State of Israel was not established, according to the secular radicals, in order to have another democracy under the sun. It was created as a safe home for the Jews. No democracy or abstract democratic principles should be allowed to interfere with the *raison d'être* of the Jewish state—the survival and the well-being of a large and secure Israel.

A very specific issue dominates the thinking of the secular radical right and determines its view of Jewish democracy: the demographic danger the hostile Arabs pose to Israel, the possibility that by the end of the century, the Palestinian Arabs will become the majority within Israel. There is therefore a general consensus among many of them that the Arabs of Judea and Samaria—territories destined to be annexed to Israel—should vote in the Jordanian Parliament in Amman; that is, they should live in the Jewish state but have democratic political rights in Jordan.

A growing number of the activists of this camp go a step further. Not only should the Palestinian Arabs vote in Jordan, but they should also live there. These are the proponents of the idea of "transfer"—a "civilized expulsion"—of these Arabs to Jordan and other Arab countries. The demand that the Israeli Arabs, who already have citizenship, be allowed to keep their rights only if fully loyal and serving in the army is also heard. These propositions and many others are made in the name of the security of Israel and are not perceived by the new radicals as immoral or anti-democratic. A typical cliché of the spokespersons of the secular radical right is that they are not anti-Arab but pro-Jewish.

While the attitude of the secular radical right toward Israeli democracy is much simpler and more cohesive than that of their religious colleagues, it is nevertheless possible to identify two different secular orientations.

Several former Lehi members of the radical right and their followers share a romantic and mystical approach to Israeli government. The main representatives of this school are Dr. Israel Eldad and Knesset member Geula Cohen. The key words of the romantic-mystical approach are "nation," "blood," "Land," "glorious past," "the Kingdom of Israel," "our army," "the traitors," and "the leftists." One can detect in this appraoch some flavor of the romantic Italian Fascism of the 1930s, a longing for a close integral community that sticks together, relies on the power of the sword, and lets no mundane interests divert it from its sacred calling. Its proponents are no longer revolutionary, as they were in the 1940s, but the elements of integral nationalism and traditionalism are still very strong. The pragmatic view of this school regarding Israeli democracy, to which they say they are now committed, is that it can and should be limited whenever there is any real threat to its security. The ultimate constitution of Israel should be Zionism (i.e., the *raison d'état*) and not any abstract legal document that draws on the experience of the Gentiles.

The other secular orientation is a security-minded view of Israeli democracy, mostly represented by former members of the Labor movement (Mapai, Rafi, and Achdut Ha'avoda) and their successors. Many of the proponents of this line are former army officers or individuals who have been close to the security apparatus of Israel. Others are members of kibbutzim and moshavim who believe that the real redemption of Eretz Israel can be achieved only through pioneering settlement, and that a truncated land in which Jews cannot fulfill themselves is a sure recipe for a spiritual destruction.

The general approach of all these activists is unsophisticated and down-to-earth. It stresses the fact that the Israelis face a very ominous enemy, the Arabs, who have never given up on the idea of driving the Jews to the sea. All Arabs, according to this school, are the same, and it is a grave mistake to distinguish between them according to national affiliation or degrees of "moderation." No ideology or ideological considerations are necessary to assure the future of the nation—simply common sense. And common sense dictates that the State of Israel must be strong and that its democracy should be suspended if necessary, or not be fully implemented.

The similarity between this group's view and that of their romantic partners renders their association stronger than their alliance with the religious part of the radical right.

What then is the danger posed by the radical right to Israeli democracy? Is there in fact such danger?

In the short run, probably very little. Since most of the new radicals have neither a clear model of an anti-democratic polity nor concrete plans for an immediate takeover, they do not appeaar to pose a serious threat to the Israeli system of government and are in fact part of the established order. The small radical minority that seriously questions the legitimacy of the state, and does something about it, confronts not only the security agencies of the State of Israel but the harsh criticism of its colleagues.

There are strong indications, however, that the radical right's narrow interpretation of democracy is corroding Israel's political culture over time. Even those radicals who claim to be democrats do not conceal their conviction that democracy is inferior to higher collective norms: the integrity of the land, the supremacy of many religious laws, and the *apriori* superiority of the Jewish citizens of the state to all others. The Van Leer studies and the findings of many other scholars regarding the high percentage of undemocratic attitudes among Israeli youth do not establish a unicausal relation between the erosion of the Israel's democratic culture and the radical right, but the circumstantial evidence is overwhelming. For who else, if not the radical right, is the most prominent agent in present-day Israel of intolerant religious fundamentalism, extralegal operations, and xenophobic behavior? In present-day Israel, very much under the influence of the radical right, discussions turn into debates, debates turn into physical clashes, and anti-terrorism demonstrations become violent raids on innocent Arabs in the streets.

There is no question that the growing extremism in Israeli society has been fueled by Arab radicals, PLO terrorists, and their supporters, and by the Arab opponents of an indpendent and secure Jewish state. The *intifada* has also played an important role in the radicalization of certain Israelis, for it has successfully been portrayed by the radical right as another full-fledged Arab war against the Jews.

But the issue under consideration is not Arab extremism and violence but the impact of the new Jewish radicalism. For the first twenty years of their state, the Israelis were able to cope successfully with the Arab desire to destroy their country with almost no cost to their democratic culture. This no longer appears to be the case. The growth of the radical right and its popularity is a serious indication of the decline of Israeli democracy.

Has the civic opposition to the radical right been more attractive, had the major Israeli parties been a source of democratic inspiration and imitation, things might have been different. But Israel's mainstream leaders are uninspiring. They and their parties are identified with the overpoliticization of the nation, with its huge governmental bureaucracy, and with its faltering economy.

It is therefore no wonder that the radical right, which evokes old themes of pioneering Zionism, is attractive and popular. And it is equally not surprising that in a culture full of catastrophic memories and no tradition of democracy, the argument that pluralist democracy is inconsistent with a state of emergency and a constant war is appealing. The rise and popularity of the radical right is probably the moral and cultural price the nation has started to pay for the continuation of the everlasting conflict with the Arabs.

The Radical Right and Classical Zionism

As much as the present ideological debate is Israel between the right and the left revolves around the question of democracy, it also touches on the issue of Zionism. Most Israelis look at "classical Zionism" with great nostalgia. The ideology and practice of the founding fathers—the leaders and thinkers of the pre-state *yishuv*—are seen as the sources of all that is good in the life of the nation. Israel, according to this mythology, was at its best when it was a small Zionist community, before it actually became the State of Israel.

It is therefore only natural that all the parties to the debate refer to classical Zionism as a major source of political legitimacy and fight over its exclusive inheritance. The intellectual controversy regarding the "Zionist authenticity" of the radical right hinges on two separate questions: Do most of the ideas of the post-1967 radical right derive from "classical" Zionism? Were ideas and orientations similar to the ones held by the present radical right central to the historical drive that created the State of Israel?

The two issues are qualitatively different; one deals with ideological continuity while the other with political centrality of ideas. While the spokespersons for the radical right are correct about the first issue, they are wrong about the second. Since both questions are highly pertinent for a proper assessment of the role of the Israeli radical right in over a hundred years of Zionist history, a short inquiry is in order.

While the radical right appears to be less democratic than many of its spokespersons claim, its "classical" Zionist credentials seem somewhat stronger. Many of its post-1967 ideas and practices originated with several schools that existed in Palestinian Zionism from the 1920s through the 1940s. As we have seen, four "classical" schools were especially influential: the ultranationalist tradition of Uri Zvi Greenberg, Brit Habirionim, and Lehi; the radical legacy of Vladimir Jabotinsky and Betar; the "activist" tradition of the Labor movement; and the messianic teaching of Rav Avraham Itzhak Hacohen Kook.

The ideological connection between the past and the present of the radical right is most demonstrable in the cases of the Tehiya and Tzomet. As we have seen, the secular spokespersons of these parties have not really come out with any "new Zionism." Dr. Israel Eldad, Geula Cohen, Yuval Ne'eman, Ephraim Ben-Haim, Elyakim Haetzni, Rafael Eitan, and other less recognized members in the two parties may be addressing new issues but they speak an old language. The experiences of Brit Habirionim, Betar, Etzel, Lehi, and the Labor activism of the 1930s and 1940s are not cherished by these people as only precious relics of the past, but also as ideological guidelines for the future. The British may have left and the nation liberated, yet most other original goals of Zionism have not been fulfilled. The struggle for Eretz Yisrael is going on most ferociously, and Jews are being killed in their own land. The greater Eretz Yisrael is in need of more defense, more settlement, and more Aliya. Under these conditions there is no reason to fold the old flags; on the contrary, against the complacency of the present generation the flying is as relevant as ever.

Unlike the late Eliezer Livneh who realized that the results of the Six-Day War called for a reformulation of classical Zionism, the ideologues of the Tehiya and Tzomet are very comfortable with the old paradigms. Their formative years have apparently left them with such an imprint that they see no need for change. And it cannot be denied that this orientation is also a source of great strength. If the formula worked in the dark past, there is no reason in the world that it should not work now.

The single ideological difference between the past and the present, that does exist, is the ability of the various schools within the Tehiya and Tzomet to work together practically and intellectually. This was hardly the case in the 1940s. The relationships between the ultranationalist believers of the Kingdom of Israel school, who followed Abraham Stern into Lehi, Jabotinsky's devotees who joined Etzel, and the Labor activists of the Palmach, were very strained. Most of them saw all the others as traitors, and were ready to fight them tooth and nail.

In this respect, a major ideological transformation has indeed taken place, and it mostly involves the Malchut Yisrael ultranationalists and former Betar members. Both admit today that they were wrong about Labor settlement and Labor activism, and that without Labor Zionism not a single goal of classical Zionism could have been achieved. But this admission does not amount to a full rejection of past ideas, only to some reformulation. Thus, the old radical right is much less fascist than in the past, and also much less anti-Labor. But it is as ultranationalist as ever, more anti-Arab, and lives altogether well within the old ideological frameworks.

There is no question that Rehavam Ze'evi's call for a "transfer" has been triggered by the growing appeal of Rabbi Kahane's theories in the 1980s. Yet, the idea of transfer has much deeper Zionist roots. As we have seen, the concept of transfer was first used in the second half of the 1930s, in relation to the plan to partition Palestine. In the 1940s it may not have been a leading Mapai concept, but it was part of the Zionist lexicon of the time. The secret committee that was put together during the War of Independence, by Joseph Weitz, the head of the Jewish National Fund, in order to make sure the

Palestinian refugees did not return, was known as the "transfer commit-tee."[5] Zvi Shiloah, the radical ideologue who reintroduced the idea of trans-fer in his book, *A Great Land for a Great People,* and who reminded Ze'evi of it in the mid-1980s, did not need Rabbi Kahane to learn from. He was a member of the old generation who knew the term firsthand.

A retrospective examination of Zionist prewar policy toward the Pales-tinian Arabs lends considerable support for the claim of the Israeli radical right, especially the leaders of Moledet, that they have not created a new ideology. The argument of the radicals is that those Labor leaders who in the 1930s forcefully opposed the power approach of the right toward the Arabs, and in the 1940s rejected the notion of transfer, were not fully honest, and in any event failed their own test in 1948. Labor activists, they say with some justification, were as brutal toward the Arabs as the right, and if they differed with Jabotinsky, Raziel, Stern, and Begin regarding the methods of anit-Arab struggle, the difference was tactical. The radical right reminds us that although the leaders of Mapai were very careful not to speak in public about transfer, many of them were overjoyed when it actually took place in 1948, and considered it one of the greatest miracles of that war.[6]

Most students of Gush Emunim agree today that Rabbi Zvi Yehuda Kook, the mentor of the movement's founding fathers, significantly deviated from his father's comprehensive religious philosophy; that he "national-ized" it, narrowed it down, and chose to ignore many of its universalistic aspects.[7] But very few argue that Gush Emunim can be separated from the legacy of Merkaz Harav, and from the philosophy of Rav Kook. In fact, not a single critic of Gush Emunim denies that the books of Rabbi Kook, the father, are the primary modern canon of the movement, a source of constant inspiration and interpretation. If Rabbi Avraham Itzhak Hacohen Kook is classical Zionism, and he is, then Gush Emunim is clearly rooted in classical Zionism. Like the political ideas of the Tehiya, Tzomet, and Moledet, the ideology of the messianic movement of the settlers in Judea and Samaria is not new and original. Many of its concepts and much of their substance go back to the days of the yishuv. To argue otherwise is to confuse ideas with social forces and to misrepresent the case. Zionism, it is important to remem-ber, never was a monistic ideological movement nor did it have an "official" version. There were always *several* Zionist schools, and some of them were quite radical.

The only school of the new radical right that has no roots in Zionist history, either in thought or action, is Rabbi Kahane's radicalism. To be sure, even Rabbi Kahane tried over the years to look for ideological legitimation in classical Zionism and repeatedly referred to Vladimir Jabotinsky as his great source of inspiration. Some of his early writings are also full of glorifi-cation of David Raziel and Abraham Stern, the Jewish rebels who did not hesitate to defy the British and the Zionist official leadership and introduce anti-Arab terrorism into Palestine.[8] But a close scrutiny of Kahane's thought clearly shows that he is neither a follower of Jabotinsky nor of Raziel, Stern or the young Begin, and that their names and actions have at most been used as building blocks in the Rabbi's idiosyncratic theology. Kahane was undoubtedly a post-1967 ideologue whose ideas and political solutions were totally alien to all schools of classical Zionism.

While the claim of the radical right for Zionist authenticity cannot be disputed, its other claim, that its ideas were central to the actual creation of the Jewish state, can. The individuals involved may have made great personal sacrifices to what they believed was the struggle for independence, yet their ideas and movements only made a marginal difference. The ultranationalist adherents of the Kingdom of Israel, for example, who are very vocal today, represented in the 1930s a very small minority. They only formed a fringe circle within the Revisionist movement, a group Vladimir Jabotinsky could hardly stand. When they followed Abraham Stern to the Lehi underground, the true believers of the old radical right took an utmost personal risk, but they acted in the name of historically irrelevant ideas. Long after it became clear that the critical battle for Eretz Yisrael would be fought between the Jews and the Arabs, Lehi believed that the Arabs could be made friends, and that the British were the main enemy. The right wing of Lehi, led by Dr. Eldad was very slow on giving up its neo-fascist fascination, and even after the establishment of the Jewish state continued to believe in political terrorism.

But in the 1940s and 1950s Jabotinsky's Betar students were also quite marginal. Following their leader's cessation from mainstream Zionism, they refused to work with the organized yishuv. Convinced that complex political problems could be solved by military means, they invested all their efforts in fighting the British. At the critical decade that preceded independence, they did not participate in pioneering settlements, made a minor contribution to illegal Aliya, were not involved in the great diplomatic struggle for the establishment of the state, and were unprepared militarily to meet the major challenge of the decade, the Arabs. Etzel fighters may have been instrumental in driving the British out of Palestine, yet they took no part in forging the political institutions of the Jewish state in the making, and opposed the 1947 U.N. Partition Resolution, which made the establishment of that state possible.

The only future radicals who played a significant role in the critical 1940s, and who were essential for the establishment of Israel, were Mapai activists, and the followers of Itzhak Tabenkin. But their political and military activism was never ideological, and in the 1940s it was not put at the service of the unruly ideologues of Etzel and Lehi.[9] The labor activists were very carefully controlled by the Labor pragmatists, first among whom was David Ben-Gurion. It is not a coincidence that these activists made up the yishuv's special operation units, which acted against the excesses of the old radical right in time of need.[10]

The Holocaust, the 1948 partition of Palestine, the establishment of a parliamentary democracy in Israel, and the need for unglorious solutions for the problems of a young state, made the ideas of the radical right historically obsolete. In the 1950s and 1960s very few Israelis spoke the language of the greater Eretz Yisrael. It was clear that the few followers of the Kingdom of Yisrael school had no chance in national politics. Former activists of Betar, now Herut party members, had discovered the virtues of parliamentary democracy and consistently moved away from extremist ultranationalism. Parliamentary democracy was in, the radical right was out.

The Radical Right Returns to History

The Six-Day War changed Israel's geopolitical paradigm and cultural ecology. The war produced a major territorial expansion, an act viewed until 1967 as totally unrealistic. And it began and ended in a way that made messianic religious thinking and ultranationalist daydreaming seem credible. The war was first and foremost a glorious event of mythic proportions, involving blood, valor, solidarity, and soil. It could be seen as a heavenly message from God. In one stroke it made the right's traditional grand vision historically relevant. It was therefore only a matter of time before the positive ingredients of Israel's new right-wing radicalism—patriotism, militarism, ultranationalism, territorial expansionism, and neo-religiosity—produced political movements.

But at first there was still one element missing for the consummation of a fully articulated radical right: the negative syndrome—bitterness, alienation, and rejection of pluralist democracy. The great 1967 victory was achieved not by a Jewish Sparta but by an Israeli Athens. The regime that won the war and instantly acquired great fame and prestige was open, democratic, pragmatic, and relatively pluralist. There was consequently no immediate historical urge to challenge the prevailing political system.

This is the reason why the early vision of most of the future radicals, the new territorial maximalists of the Land of Israel Movement and the fundamentalists of Gush Emunim, was relatively open, democratic, and optimistic. This openness and toleration now seem especially conspicuous in relation to the Arabs of the occupied territories. The individual Palestinians of the West Bank were honestly invited to take part in building the new Israeli empire. Most of the members of the Land of Israel Movement agreed with Eliezer Livneh that the Arabs should get full political rights in the Jewish State. And the Kookists of Merkaz Harav offered a very liberal interpretation of the Halakhic concept of alien residency, including the possibility that the fully loyal Palestinians would be made equal citizens of the Jewish polity. Between 1967 and 1973, it would have made no sense to raise questions about the excessive openness of Israel's Declaration of Independence or other social and political norms that had become part of the rather pluralistic Israeli political culture.

The missing ingredients were first apparent after the disappointment of the 1973 Yom Kippur War and the rise of popular resentment toward the Israeli top echelon. They were augmented after the 1978 "betrayal" of Menachem Begin at Camp David.

The main reason the radical right was not fully active before 1978 had to do with the belief that Menachem Begin and his Herut party also completely supported the idea of the greater Eretz Yisrael, since the Herut party was always strong in ultranationalist rhetoric. Menachem Begin had made a career out of emotional and symbolic speeches full of glorification of the land in its entirety, the military, and Jewish tradition. And he also played on the Massada complex—the isolation of Israel and the world's unending anti-Semitism.[11]

But there was another side to Begin, that of the legal politican and statesman, which the future radicals refused to see. Furthermore, nobody expected Egypt's president, Anwar al-Sadat, or any Arab leader for that matter, to come to Jerusalem. Thus, in the mid-1970s Begin criticized the weak cabinet of Itzhak Rabin and supported the illicit settlement drives of Gush Emunim.

The Camp David Accords shattered the illusions of the would-be radicals. Begin's "betrayal" exposed the other side of this man and his politics, his desire for peace and his readiness to sacrifice "unessential" parts of Eretz Yisrael to achieve it. It further revealed the growing pragmatism and parliamentarism of Herut, which since the mid-1950s had been slowly moving to the center.[12] And it showed that some elements of Jabotinsky's famed liberalism and humanism, like his willingness to recognize the humanity of the Arabs and his respect for the law, were not forgotten by his most celebrated successor.

Camp David left a political vacuum in Israel that was filled by the extreme right. This was a group made up of old and young radicals who were distrustful of the Arabs, unable to believe that the world was no longer anti-Semitic, and unwilling to give up the dream of an Israeli empire. The radical right bolstered its image as a realistic party with political facts of life. Sadat was the exception rather than the rule among Arab leaders. No other Arab government publicly expressed its readiness to make peace with Israel. Furthermore the world, with the exception of the United States, was lukewarm toward the Camp David agreement. And whereas Israel had surrendered territory with valuable material resources, it was Sadat, not Begin, who earned the greatest kudos.

The contribution of Gush Emunim to the rise of the radical right and to its public respectability cannot be exaggerated. In addition to the movement's great ideological appeal for Zionist religious Jews and nationalist circles, Gush Emunim in the 1970s touched a very sensitive cord in the Israeli collective psyche, the cherished memory of Zionist settlement and pioneering. Veteran settlement activists, and many others who had come into public life through the model of Zionist pioneering, saw in Gush

Emunim the rebirth of their glorious youth. The Gush youngsters were the "genuine" Israelis, the individuals who had revived the real Zionist ideal of pioneering and national fulfillment in a materialistic and decadent age.

Starting in 1974, they flew the flag of Zionism sky-high, just as the nation was undergoing a very severe post–Yom Kipper trauma and when Zionism was being equated with racism in the United Nations and all over the world. And while all the other components of the radical right were working in order *to block* new opportunities and developments (Camp David, the extension of the peace process, a more complete integration of the Arabs in Israeli society, etc.), the Gush emerged in order to build, to create, and to expand the borders of Zion. Gush Emunim bestowed Zionist legitimacy upon the new radical right which the old ultranationalist school of Uri Zvi Greenberg and Israel Eldad had never had. It made the difference between marginality and centrality. And its genuine pioneering spirit made it possible for the new camp to claim that it was the true inheritor of the most glorious Zionist tradition, that of settlement, self defense, and self-fulfillment.

It is rather risky to speculate what would have happened to the radical right had the Gush not brought the settlement issue to the center stage of Israel's collective consciousness. It appears, however, that although some ultranationalist resistance to the Camp David accords would have been solidified, it would have been extremely weak, probably limited to a few veteran extremists of the right and disappointed military officers. The appeal of Gush Emunim, which has never portrayed itself as an anti-democratic movement, seems to have made it possible for many Israelis to reverse their growing commitment to pluralist democracy and newly adopted values such as tolerance, minority rights, and the rule of law.

The radical right peaked during the great settlement years 1979–1984, which were also the years of the Lebanon War and the growth of Arab-Jewish friction throughout the entire Eretz Yisrael. Reality in those years seemed to be following the scenarios of the radical right, and its analysis appeared as convincing as ever. Although the Camp David Accords were not reversed as the extreme right wished, there was tremendous progress in the fulfillment of the Greater Eretz Yisrael idea.

In 1980, on the initiative of Geula Cohen, Jerusalem was officially annexed to Israel by a Knesset basic law. A similar annexation of the Golan Heights took place less than a year later. The West Bank was opened for massive Jewish settlement, and the possibility of its future annexation looked bright. While the Likud could not be fully trusted, because of the original sin of Camp David and its determined 1982 evacuation of Yamit, there were clear signs in its councils of an important political reconsideration. Determined to undermine the negotiations on the Autonomy Plan in the West Bank, Menachem Begin intentionally stalled on the talks with Egypt, thereby causing Moshe Dayan and Ezer Weizman, the two architects of Camp David, to resign.[13]

The 1981 cabinet had two staunch hawks, Ariel Sharon and Itzhak Shamir, as Israel's ministers of defense and foreign affairs respectively. The assassination of Egypt's president Sadat in November 1981 and the significant "cooling" of the peace with Egypt were perceived by the radical right as very blessed signs. There was, they believed, a serious chance that the Likud was "repenting." In addition to the no-constraints policy regarding the settlement of Judea, Samaria, and Gaza, the government poured large amounts of money into the occupied territories. And it did something even Gush Emunim could not accomplish, initiating a massive, heavily subsided housing and settlement program, thereby making the venture attractive to middle-class Israelis seeking spacious yet affordable housing.

The 1982 Lebanon War strengthened the emerging alliance between the radical right and the radicalizing Likud. The war was the culmination of the growing conflict between Israel and the PLO ministate in Lebanon. It also became the meeting ground between the two camps. Apart from its general superhawkish position on security, the radical right had a special vested interest in the destruction of the growing Palestinian menace in Lebanon. As the Jewish settlement of the West Bank intensified, it became clear to the leading proponents of the Greater Eretz Yisrael that only the PLO could stop continued settlement. By the early 1980s the PLO had been slowly taking root in the West Bank and in leading the anti-Israeli struggle there.[14]

Yuval Ne'eman, the most strategic leader of the radical right, was a strong advocate of a massive Israeli operation in Lebanon long before it actually took place.[15] It was therefore not surprising that the Tehiya party joined the Likud coalition in the summer of 1982, less than three months after its three Knesset members were forcefully evacuated from Yamit. And for many of the religious radicals, the Israeli conquests in southern Lebanon were more than just captured enemy territory. They were old Hebrew lands that had belonged to the tribes of Asher and Naftali, part of the Promised Land.

The Lebanon War, as is clear now, was a great failure, and not the least of its victims was Menachem Begin, the prime minister himself. But the radical right and the settler community benefited from every month of its prolongation. From 1982 to 1985, almost no one paid attention to the creeping annexation of Judea and Samaria. World attention was focused on Lebanon, and little pressure was placed on Israel regarding the settlement in the territories. Bitter about its leftist critics at home and abroad, the besieged Likud moved closer to its natural allies from the right, radicalizing its anti-Arab and anti-left rhetoric. By 1984 there was hardly any difference between the two camps.

The appeal of the radical right to many Israelis was further invigorated between 1979 and 1984 by the intensification of Arab-Jewish friction. The 1978 opening of the West Bank for Jewish settlement, regardless of region and density of local population, soon resulted in many violent exchanges. Since the late 1970s the number of anti-Jewish operations increased dramatically, and while most acts of road-blocking and rock-throwing were hardly reported, several terror operations that involved the killing of Jews were instrumental in dramatizing the "viciousness" of the Palestinians. The argument that the government was not sufficiently determined in its defense of its pioneering emissaries in the West Bank was much heard throughout nationalist circles.

A somewhat different process, which also bolstered the radical right's popularity, was the growing animosity between Israeli Arabs and Jews within the Green Line. Part of this process had to do with the increasing "Palestinization" of the Israeli Arabs in the 1970s, the growing identification with the PLO, and the intensifying resentment toward the Israeli order. Another factor involved shifts in the labor market and the increasing presence in Israel of many workers from the occupied territories.

The incident that opened the new era in Jewish-Arab relations inside Israel proper was the 1976 Land Day. An Arab demonstration against official land confiscations in the lower Galilee turned violent; six demonstrators were killed, and dozens of Arab protesters and Jewish police officers were wounded. Extremist Arab organizations like the Sons of the Village arose, and several Arab student groups fully endorsed the PLO platform.

Perhaps the greatest beneficiary of the new friction was Rabbi Meir Kahane, who had argued all along that the Israeli Arabs were the real "cancer." But the radical right's arguments that Eretz Yisrael was indivisible, and that Israeli Arabs and West Bank Palestinains were all alike, also gained credibility.

The perception of a growing Arab menace was further increased by the brittle economic situation in the early 1980s. The ready availability of cheap Arab labor, mostly from Gaza and the West Bank, begun to play a significant psychological role when the Israeli economy started to suffer from hyperinflation. The readiness of Arabs to work for dismal wages created resentful anxiety among the weakest stratum of Israel's workers, the residents of development towns and urban slums. The problem was not so much one of lack of jobs or unemployment as a question of dignity and self-respect. While wages and salaries in all economic levels were constantly being raised, low-paying jobs did not respond to inflation in the same way. Wages that were never indexed, and the availability of cheap, uncomplaining, and un-unionized Arab labor, made it unnecessary for employers to raise their pay for Jews.[16] This created a growing frustration among poor Jewish workers, who had never previously had any doubt regarding their superiority to the Arabs.

Arab competition in other areas like vegetable and flea markets added oil to the fire, and anti-Arab animosity was further fueled by the ideological rhetoric of the time. In the early 1980s Israel's development towns and urban slums had not only become a hotbed for anti-Arab sentiment but also for anti-left hatred. The leftists and other opponents of the Lebanon War were seen as not being real Israelis. They were traitors, "Arab-lovers," even "PLOers." In 1984, the Tehiya became Israel's third-largest party, Rabbi Meir Kahane was elected to the Knesset, and "Kahanism" became widespread—all indications of the success of the radical right and its growing appeal.

By the mid-1980s the radical right had become a legitimate part of the Israeli political landscape. The 1984 creation of the first unity coalition between the Likud and Labor forced the ideologically committed Yuval Ne'eman, Geula Cohen, and their colleagues to stay in opposition, but it did not reduce their popularity or historical relevancy. There were no indications that the Israeli rule of the occupied territories was nearing its end, and the Eretz Yisrael rhetoric of the Likud was as intense as ever. Israel's economic reforms and the Likud's coalition agreement with Labor had been responsible for a great reduction in budgets for new settlements, but the existing ones grew unhindered. It was therefore no surprise that the radical right did well in the 1988 national elections and that the number of its direct representatives increased from 5 to 7 percent of Knesset members. Had Rabbi Kahane not been disqualified just before the elections, the ultra-nationalists might well have controlled at least 10 percent of the House.[17]

The Radical Right and the *Intifada*: From Shock to Recovery

The *intifada* has dealt the radical right a serious blow. The ideologues and leaders of this camp never credited the Palestinian Arabs with the capacity to conduct a successful and sophisticated anti-Israeli struggle, and to maintain the pressure for a long time. The setback to the right has been as much conceptual and theoretical as it has been practical and concrete. The overall effect of the uprising on Israeli society has been a significant increase in the price it was asked to pay for keeping the West Bank and Gaza. This was a novel development, unattended to earlier. The issue of the desirability of ruling and keeping the occupied territories has been on the nation's public agenda since the Six-Day War. But most of the time it was discussed in ideological terms pertaining to the image of Israel one had in mind.[18]

The *intifada* added to this kind of talk another facet, the very concrete question of immediate costs. Meron Benvenisti has convincingly argued that prior to the Palestinian uprising, the overall cost of keeping the West Bank was very low, and Israel in fact gained economically a great deal from the venture.[19] The loyalists of Eretz Yisrael in general and the radical right in particular have always argued that Israel was benefiting from the occupation, and that given the unavailability of a partner with whom to negotiate a peace, there was no immediate reason to even consider a territorial compromise.

The first two years of the *intifada* eliminated this line of argumentation. The economic, diplomatic, military, and moral cost to Israel of keeping the occupied territories has increased dramatically. By the end of 1989, for example, it was clear to most informed Israelis that one of the main reasons for the nation's economic recession was the Palestinian uprising. Israeli producers and manufacturers lost major portions of the Palestinian market in 1988 and 1989. Their colleagues who had become used to cheap Arab labor could no longer rely on the striking people from the occupied territories, who started to work irregularly.

In 1989 the Israeli army was still pretending that its massive presence in the occupied territories was not hurting its military preparedness for more serious missions and for an overall war with the Arabs, but this was very hard to substantiate. The burden of the uprising was felt at all levels, from the young privates who were very unhappy serving as riot police in the territories, to the chief-of-staff and his generals who were regularly involved in verbal scuffles with politicians of the right.

The reluctance of the government in 1989 to grant the army nearly $200 million for *intifada* expenses did not help the morale of its senior officers. And the tarnished Israeli image abroad produced renewed American pressure to negotiate with the PLO, and forced Jewish diplomats to work double time to defend their nation's deteriorating reputation.

The radical right, acutely aware of the threat the *intifada*—and its costs—posed to its own and Eretz Yisrael's future, issued an unconditional demand that the uprising be crushed. Tehiya's plan was by far the most radical; it called for the use of extreme measures in the West Bank, including the deportation of thousands of Palestinian activists, the dissolution of most civil and professional Arab associations, and the suspension of all ordinary legal procedures. Every act of rock-throwing was to be defined as a terror operation justifying a shoot-to-kill order.[20] Some of the leaders of the Tehiya must have been aware of the disastrous implications of their plan for Israel's image and political future; to have published the plan implied an admission on their part that if the *intifada* continued, Israel might lose Judea, Samaria, and Gaza.

The Israeli radical right received further setbacks from the 1988 Algiers resolutions and the PLO's decision to recognize U.N. Resolution 242, which implied its readiness to live peacefully with Israel and give up terrorism. This move was also unexpected by the radical right, and cast it into great confusion. Palestinian terrorism in general and the PLO in particular have long served the Israeli radical right as its strongest case against compromise. Each time an Arab government or leader either spoke about peace with Israel or made some gestures in that direction, the radicals had a ready answer: "But what about the PLO?" The PLO's animosity toward Israel and the PLO Charter, which calls for the elimination of the "Zionist entity" and its replacement by a Palestinian republic, have always been a prime political justification for proposals to annex the territories to Israel. This was, of course, never the real reason for the desire to keep Eretz Yisrael in its entirety Jewish, but it was by far the most effective argument in secular Israeli politics.

The PLO's recognition of the State of Israel and its promise to live peacefully with the Jews added to the agony of the *intifada*. It produced significant American pressure on Israel for a new peace process, and it left the radical right with a much weaker set of political arguments. The fact that the PLO's declarations have not been very successful in expunging its terroristic image and that the Likud government with Labor support continued its opposition to any negotiations with Arafat may have kept the radical right from total panic, yet the memories of the compromise made at Camp David are still fresh. There is no question that by the beginning of 1989 the radical right was in serious trouble.

A third blow to the radical right was the 1988 national elections and the surprising decision of Itzhak Shamir to opt for a national unity government instead of creating a narrow right-wing coalition. After intense negotiations in which the Likud seemed to be moving to the right, Shamir suddenly changed course and established a broad unity coalition with the Labor party and all religious parties. Had Shamir gone with the religious parties and the radical right instead, thereby fulfilling the hopes of the extremists, he would have been forced to deal harshly with the *intifada* and allow a renewed settlement drive. But the prime minister apparently became convinced that the *intifada* could not be put down easily. He also did not want to depend on the radical right and have Ariel Sharon as minister of defense. He consequently opted for a moderate coalition and made Itzhak Rabin the key minister in the new cabinet.

This slap in the face of the leaders of the radical right, most of whom fully trusted the hawkish Likud, was accentuated by Shamir's personal treatment of professor Yuval Ne'eman. Calling on the prime minister about the broken written agreement between the Likud and the Tehiya, Ne'eman was flatly told by Shamir that he could do with the signed agreement "whatever you please." All the painful memories of Begin's betrayal in Camp David surfaced again. The Likud was an unprincipled, duplicitous political party whose fervent statements about the indivisibility of Eretz Yisrael were hollow.

By mid-1989 it was clear to the radical right, just as it was clear to everybody else in the country, that the major axis in Israeli national politics was the alliance between Itzhak Shamir and Itzhak Rabin. This strange covenant communicated pragmatism, unwillingness to crush the *intifada*, and movement under American pressures. The main product of the new axis was the Rabin-Shamir peace plan, in the context of which the Palestinians of the West Bank were to elect their own representatives to negotiate a permanent solution with Israel.

The radical right saw the Shamir peace initiative as disastrous, a sure recipe for future Jewish concessions in the occupied territories and possibly for a Palestinian State. When Geula Cohen was asked, "What happened to Michael?"—Michael being Shamir's *nom de guerre* during his Lehi underground days—she replied with a bitter smile, "The irony is that the commander of the Irgun [Begin] gave Sinai back, and the commander of Lehi [Shamir] is about to return Judea and Samaria."[21]

The year 1990 brought a new hope to the radical right. The *intifada* had become routine, and the Palestinians of the West Bank had failed to translate the uprising into political gains. The leaders of the radical right were still hostile to Shamir and Rabin, for not "crushing' the *intifada,* but they could not deny the partial success of the government's policy.

The *intifada* changed a great deal. What had been a popular uprising featuring daily demonstrations by hundreds of women, children, and ordinary residents, all over the occupied territories, was now reduced to scattered eruptions of a few dozen rock-throwing kids and to occasional sabotage operations by a small number of masked individuals, organized in small underground cells. Much of the killing took place within the Palestinian community itself—executions of Arab "collaborators," individuals suspected of helping the Israelis.

The *intifada* ceased being news almost completely. Hundreds of the journalists and television crews that had come to Israel to cover the uprising now left for Eastern Europe, the newest scene of world action, and the *intifada*'s impact on world opinion declined. The continuous reports about the brutal execution of collaborators by their own kin damaged the Palestinian cause significantly. It gave some credibility to the Israeli argument that the Palestinians were terrorists all along, and that no fight for freedom was involved.

Thus, as bad to Israel as the Palestinian uprising was in 1988 and 1989, it was hard to disregard its limited achievements in its third year. There was no parity between the massive Israeli power in the occupied territories and the Palestinian potential. As Israel regained control and mobilized its military, political, and economic resources against the uprising, it was clear that the end of the occupation was far away. The conviction of Arab radicals that a Palestinian state was just around the corner had proved false.

And there was the fact that the radical right continued popular among ordinary Israelis. Though developments since the end of 1987 were a setback to this camp, they did not reduce its appeal. Opinion polls conducted since the beginning of the *intifada* have shown a growing radicalization among many Israelis vis-à-vis the Arabs and a disappointment with the "moderate" parties. Street demonstrations following anti-Jewish terror acts have been wild and uncontrollable, and the radical activists of the Likud and NRP have only intensified their ultranationalist rhetoric. In the long run, more Israelis than ever before were ready to consider direct negotiations with the PLO, but there was no immediate expression of these attitudes in the Israeli political arena.[22]

The greatest boost for the damaged morale of the Israeli radical right came from far afield, from the 1989–1990 breakdown of communism in Eastern Europe. Like the rest of the world, Israelis were stunned by the sudden

collapse of the Soviet bloc and the democratization of the countries involved, but they had two specific reasons to be especially overjoyed: most of
the new ruler moved to resume full diplomatic relations with Israel, and the
Soviet Union decided to let its Jews out.

Resumed diplomatic relations, usually accompanied by an apology, involved a great victory for Israelis in general, and the radical right in particular. All the communist countries, but Rumania had broken relations with
Israel in June 1967, following the Six-Day War, in protest of Israel's expanded borders and its "anti-Arab aggression." Resumption of diplomatic
relations with Israel in 1990, in the midst of the *intifada,* could not but be
read by the Israeli radical right as a validation of its argument that a strong
and territorially large Israel was no barrier to peace. The acts of the new
leaders in Eastern Europe were presented as a conclusive proof for the long-
held proposition that Israel's isolation in the world was not the result of the
"return" of the nation to its homeland, but rather an expression of anti-
Semitism, communism, and selfish Gentile politics.

Of even greater meaning was the opening of the gates of the Soviet Union
for Jewish emigration. Most Israelis had long given up hope for a massive
Jewish Aliya from the Soviet Union, but the radical right never did. Whenever confronted with the danger that the Arabs of the enlarged Israel would
soon outnumber the Jews, the radical right would mention Soviet Jewry as a
potential solution. When skeptics said that the age of miracles was past, the
rightists pointed to the unpredictability of modern Jewish history, to God's
mysterious ways of handling the world; the Balfour Declaration, the Holocaust, the 1948 establishment of Israel, and the Six-Day War. Thus, the
massive Soviet Aliya that started in 1989 was seen as a miracle of this
category, a proof that the Kookist philosophy was right all along. To be sure,
there were worrisome political developments—the Arab outcry about Russian immigration, and the American demand that Russian Jews not be settled in the West Bank. But these were nothing compared to God's greatness
and splendor, and the new indication that the process of redemption was
moving ahead in full speed.

The complete recovery of the radical right from the political fallout of
the *intifada* took place in June 1990, when Itzhak Shamir was forced to
form a narrow right-wing coalition, an act he avoided in 1988. The great
political coup, marked by the nomination of Yuval Ne'eman and Rafael
Eitan to full cabinet ministers, and Geula Cohen to deputy minister, was not
made by the radical right, but by Shamir's internal opposition within the
Likud. And yet the major beneficiary seemed to have been the radical right.

There was no question, in 1988, that Itzhak Shamir was trying to tone
down the extremist rhetoric of the Likud, and to move it away from the
radical right. Not only did he opt for a broad unity coalition with the
"leftist" Labor, but he conducted a major reshuffling within his own party,
promoting a whole new generation of pragmatic young leaders to full ministerial positions. In what seemed at the time as a political master stroke,

Shamir also succeeded in isolating the radical wing of his own party, led by Ariel Sharon. But Shamir moved too fast, and too carelessly. In addition to Sharon, he also cornered David Levy, the party's most popular vote-getter, and Itzhak Modai, the ambitious leader of the junior partner, the Liberal party.

What followed was a classical Sharon maneuver, a slow galvanization of internal party opposition, an appeal to the "classical principles" of Herut, and a surprise attack at the right moment. The isolated radical right in parliament, and the lobbyists of the settlers in Judea, Samaria, and Gaza were more than glad to join in. Following a growing critique of Shamir's readiness to talk to the Palestinians, and to go along with Itzhak Rabin's plan for local West Bank election, the prime minister started to back off. Faced with a Likud internal revolt, and unable to secure a clear majority for a quick movement on a modified election plan, Shamir started to stall. A coalition crisis with the Labor party became inevitable.

The March 1990 collapse of the Unity Government greatly damaged Shamir's authority. Though remaining at the helm, he lost much of his power and prestige. The silent revolution he tried make in the party, elevating a whole new generation of young politicians, failed miserably. It took him a record time of three months to form a new coalition, and the result was humiliating. In addition to the inconvenient old-new partners from the radical right, Shamir had to make huge concessions to the small ultraorthodox parties, which also became indispensable for his brittle coalition. And three out of his four senior ministers—Levy in foreign affairs, Modai in finance, and Sharon in construction and immigration—were forced upon him against his better judgment.

In the summer of 1990 it was clear that in order to survive, the new cabinet would have to take excessive ultranationalist positions. And indeed, the settlers in the West Bank could not be happier when the new government authorized the building of a permanent construction for the controversial Tomb of Yosef yeshiva in Nablus. The ceremony that ensued involved a total curfew over nearly one million Palestinians in the West Bank, and a huge Jewish celebration in the middle of Arab Nablus. Itzhak Shamir, who surprisingly had no trouble returning to his former self, the extremist commander of Lehi, made clear in a series of declarations that his government would never negotiate with the PLO, would never give up any liberated territory of Eretz Yisrael, and would not bow to any American pressure in this matter. He succeeded in estranging President Bush, and bringing the U.S.-Israel relationship to an all-time low.

When Saddam Hussein, Iraq's ruler's, invaded Kuwait on August 2, 1990, creating an international crisis of the first order, he inadvertently did a great service to the Israeli radical right. Very much like his previous inadvertent contribution to this camp, the launching in 1980 of the Iran-Iraq War, he now helped divert all world attention from the *intifada* and the West Bank to the Persian Gulf. President Bush and Secretary of State James Baker

III, who were just about to apply heavy pressure on Israel to move the peace process ahead, lost all interest in the area. So did the rest of the world and the media. Even the October fiasco on the Temple Mount, in which nineteen rioting Palestinians were killed by the police, and the violent eruption that followed the assassination of Rabbi Meir Kahane, a month later, did not return the *intifada* and the peace process to the headlines.

The Future of the Radical Right

Given the contrary directions of recent events, the future of the radical right appears uncertain. It seems that as long as the Jewish venture in the West Bank continues, and the cost of holding the occupied territories does not increase dramatically, the radical right is likely to continue as a force in the nation's politics and public life. Its ideas will continue to be highly relevant to national issues. But this is not likely to be the case if most Israeli leaders conclude that Israel has to terminate the occupation in order to survive. As in the period after the 1947 partition of Western Palestine, the Israeli radical right is likely to lose its historical relevance, for it will then be addressing moot questions.

Unlike in 1948, however, the fate of today's radical right depends on the opposition of the Likud, not on the decision of the Labor party. In 1948 Israel was totally dominated by Mapai, and both the radical right and the more moderate nationalist right were politically irrelevant. The current situation is different. The Likud has been dominant in national politics for over a decade, and the rhetoric of "Greater Eretz Yisrael" which it propagates together with the National Religious Party and the radical right is shared by more than 50 percent of the voting public. It is therefore clear that if Likud's commitment to the occupied territories remains intact, the radical right is likely to continue to prosper.

The critical issue seems to be the real pressure applied on Israel by the Palestinians and the world community, and the perception of this pressure by the central Likud camp which concentrates today around Itzhak Shamir, Moshe Arens (defense minister), and their political allies. These people, who are not part of the radical right, are nevertheless ideologically committed to the indivisibility of Eretz Yisrael, though they are too pragmatic to commit national suicide out of loyalty to an anachronistic ideology. As long as they are convinced that Israel can safely keep the West Bank and Gaza, and that there is a wide party support for this position, they will do so—their "peace initiatives" notwithstanding. Under these conditions the Eretz Yisrael purists are likely to grow in popularity and political influence. This development seems to have taken place within the Likud councils since the summer of 1989.

But the situation would be different if Likud's leadership reaches the conclusion that Israel should compromise on the West Bank and Gaza. This would not be easy, for as we have seen the Likud itself is partially made up of right-wing extremists, and Shamir or his successors would have to be sure that their moderate position was backed by the vast majority of the party's activists. However, if that happens, the radical right will be Likud's first victim. Unlike the case of the 1979–1982 evacuation of Sinai, in which the nascent radical right was caught off guard, its activists would be ready for the new situation and the Likud would have to move fast and skillfully to isolate the ultranationalists and neutralize their threat. But if such a scenario is realized, the Israeli radical right stands the chance of returning to its 1948–1967 historical marginality.

The specter of civil war haunts Israel. Will a major territorial compromise in the West Bank, one that will either initiate the establishment of a Palestinian state or open the way to a meaningful Palestinian autonomy cause Israelis to fight each other? Given the deep ideological and political stakes involved, a civil war or major violent conflict cannot be ruled out. The existence of nearly 100,000 settlers in the West Bank and Gaza, with at least 20 percent of them highly ideological devotees of the Greater Eretz Yisrael idea, does not promise a happy evacuation.

It appears, however, that a civil war will become possible only if the territorial compromise is imposed by a Labor-led government representing no more than 55 or 60 percent of Israeli voters. Under such a scenario, Israel would be divided along major ideological lines, the right against the left with all the festering wounds of seventy years of Zionist history opened up. If however, the compromise is initiated by a unity coalition made up of the Likud, Labor, and most other Zionist parties, it could muster the support of 80 to 90 percent of the population and thus isolate the radical right politically and morally.

Given the intensity of their commitment to Eretz Yisrael, the radical right and the settler community would probably put up a massive struggle against the agreement, which would include intense protests, extralegal demonstrations, civil disobedience, street violence, and possibly some Jewish fatalities. But both a civil war and a sophisticated armed revolt against the IDF are highly unlikely. There are many indications that even among the messianic settler community, which is devoted to the land for religious reasons, very few would be ready to go against the army and shoot Israeli soldiers point blank. Over and over, one hears reminders of the bloody Jewish civil war that led to the destruction of the Second Temple and two thousand years of Jewish exile from Eretz Yisrael.[23] Instead, small-scale armed resistance and insurrectionary operations are probable.[24]

Even if it loses its fight for Eretz Yisrael and becomes historically irrelevant, the Israeli radical right is not likely to disappear. It will probably continue to play a significant role in the nation's public life and political culture. Unlike the radical right of the 1930s and 1940s, the post-1967 radical right has had a major impact on the thinking of the entire nation. It has also succeeded politically. In Jewish culture such an influence is very hard to erase, especially if backed by leading politicians, committed ideologues, and talented activists.

It seems highly probable that even if the radical right is pushed to the political margins, it will continue to haunt the nation's collective psyche. Long after Judea and Samaria are gone, bitter people will remain who will dream about a possible "second round," the "right of return," and "transfer." The majority of Gush Emunim, which is likely to undergo a major theological crisis will probably urge patience, bow to the mysteries of redemption, and wait for the next Six-Day War—which will only prove that they were right all along.

Glossary

Achdut Haavodah Socialist Zionist party that split from Mapai party in 1944 under the leadership of Itzhak Tabenkin; joined the Labor party in 1968.

Agudat Yisrael An ultraorthodox political party; opposed to Zionism on theological grounds yet very active in government and legislation.

Aliya (Ascent) the coming of Jews to the Land of Israel for permanent residence; considered a major Zionist virtue.

Amalek The local tribe most ferociously opposed to the Hebrew conquest of biblical Canaan; the people of Israel were ordered to destroy it completely, man, woman, and child.

Amana (Covenant) the professional settlement organization of Gush Emunim.

Ashkenazim Jews of north European and western origins; usually contrasted with "Oriental" Jews, or Sepharadim.

Beit Hadassah (Hadassah House) a large deserted Jewish house in Arab Hebron that was illicitly occupied in 1979 by Jewish settlers, whose stay was later legalized by the government; a controvertial place and the site of many violent acts.

Betar the youth organization of the Revisionist movement; established and inspired by Vladimir Jabotinsky.

Bnei Akiva (Sons of Akiva) Zionist religious youth movement affiliated with the National Religious Party.

Brit Habirionim (Covenant of Thugs) a small ideological radical right group that existed in Palestine between 1928 and 1933.

Brit Hahashmonaim (The Hashmonaics Covenant) a small ultranationalist religious movement established in Jerusalem in the late 1930s by Rabbi Moshe Segal; its members were encouraged to join the undergrounds of Etzel and Lehi.

Canaanites (Hebrews) a small anti-Zionist intellectual circle established in 1940 by poet Yonathan Ratosh; has advocated a complete separation between Israelis and Diaspora Jews and the creation of a large Canaanite federation made of Israelis and other Middle-Eastern minorities.

Dugri Israeli term for simplistic, matter-of-fact, straightforward behavior; originally, an Arabic word.

315

Ein Vered Circle nonreligious members of kibbutzim and moshavim who organized in 1975 to support Gush Emunim; first meeting took place in Moshav Ein Vered.

Elon Moreh Gush Emunim's most famous illicit Gariin which was allowed to settle near Nablus after seven previous evacuations by the army.

Eretz Yisrael Land of Israel.

Etzel (the National Military Organization) also known as Irgun; underground military organization during the British mandate, close to the Revisionist movement; most famous commanders: David Raziel and Menachem Begin.

Gahal (The Herut-Liberal Bloc) a political alliance formed between the two parties before the 1965 national elections.

Gariin (Nucleus) a small group of people, usually young, who intend to establish a new settlement.

Ger Toshav (Alien resident) the Torah term for the non-Jew who is permitted to live in the Land of Israel.

Green Line Israel's pre-1967 international border with Egypt, Jordan, Lebanon, and Syria.

Gush Emunim The Bloc of the Faithful, the messianic movement of the settlers in the West Bank and Gaza.

Hagana (Defense) the underground military organization of the Yishuv during the British mandate.

Hakibbutz Hameuchad a settlement kibbutz movement closely affiliated with the Achdut Haavodah party.

Halakha Jewish religious law.

Halutz (pl. Halutzim) pioneer.

Harem esh Sherif (Noble Sanctuary) the Arab term for the Temple Mount and the site of the Al-Aksa Mosque, and the Dome of the Rock.

Haredim ultraorthodox religious Jews, mostly anti-Zionist.

Herut (Freedom) a right-wing political party established in 1948 by Menachem Begin; was the key party in Gahal, and presently in the Likud.

Hillul Hashem Jewish term for the desecration of the Name of God.

Histadrut the General Federation of Labor in Israel, founded in 1920; the largest labor union, and the largest voluntary organization in Israel.

Intifada Arab term for the Palestinian uprising in the West Bank and Gaza, which started in December 1987.

Judea (originally Yehuda) the southern half of the West Bank; main Arab cities: Hebron and Bethlehem.

Kabbalah Jewish mystical texts; also the practice and tradition of their study.

Kach (Thus! or This is the Way!) Rabbi Kahane's political movement, the Israeli successor of the Jewish Defense League.

Kibbutz (pl. Kibbutzim) a socialist collective commune.

Kibbutz Dati (Religious kibbutz) a religious Zionist kibbutz movement.

Kidush Hashem Jewish term for the sanctification of the Name of God.

Kiryat Arba Jewish city adjacent to Arab Hebron, the largest Jewish settlement in the West Bank.

Knesset Israel's one-chamber parliament.

Kookist School students and followers of the Jewish messianic philosophy of Rabbi Avraham Itzhak Hacohen Kook, and his son Rabbi Zvi Yehuda Kook.

Land of Israel Movement (LIM) an ideological movement established in the summer of 1967 to promote the annexation of the occupied territories to Israel, and to fight all efforts for a territorial compromise.

Lehi (Israel's Freedom Fighters) also known as the Stern Gang; an anti-British terror underground established in 1940 by Abraham (Yair) Stern after a split within Etzel; Itzhak Shamir was Lehi's chief of operations.

Likud (Unity) right-wing political bloc, formed in 1973, of Gahal and smaller groups; dominated by Herut; in control of the Israeli government since 1977.

Machpela the Cave of the Patriarchs in Hebron, the second holiest Jewish site, the traditional burial place of the nation's biblical forefathers.

Machteret (Underground) the Jewish underground of Gush Emunim, uncovered in 1984.

Malchut Yisrael (The Kingdom of Israel) an ultranationalist ideology that draws its inspiration from the biblical Davidic kingdom, and calls for the establishment of the Jewish state in all the territories promised by God to Abraham.

Mapai a socialist Zionist party established in 1930, which dominated Israeli politics for over forty years; changed its name to the Labor Party after its unification with Achdut Haavodah and Rafi.

Merkaz Harav (The Rabbi's Center) a Jerusalem Zionist yeshiva founded by Rabbi Avraham Itzhak Hacohen Kook, subsequently led by his son, Rabbi Zvi Yehuda Kook; the school and source of inspiration of all the founders of Gush Emunim.

Messirut Hanefesh (Ultimate devotion) a major Gush Emunim virtue which implies one's readiness to make immense personal sacrifices.

Mitzva a Religious commandment according to the Halakha.

Moetzet Yesha (Yesha Council) the association of the local councils of the Jewish settlers in Judea, Samaria, and Gaza.

Moledet a radical right political party established in 1987 by General (res.) Rehavam Ze'evi (nicknamed Gandhi); main proponent of the idea of "transfer," an agreed upon eviction of all Arabs of the occupied territories.

Moshav (pl. Moshavim) a cooperative agricultural settlement.

National Religious Party (NRP) Israel's most influential Zionist religious party, and a coalition partner in almost all the nation's governments; known earlier as Mizrahi.

Nekuda (Point) the monthly magazine of the settlers of Judea, Samaria, and Gaza; published by the Yesha council and largely influenced by Gush Emunim.

Palmach The permanent striking force of the Hagana, established in 1941.

Rafi a splinter party of Mapai, established in 1965 by David Ben-Gurion after a major conflict with his successor, Levi Eshkol; reunited with Mapai in 1968.

Revisionism A Zionist right-wing political school, and movement, established by Vladimir Jabotinsky in the 1920s.

Samaria (originally Shomron) the northern half of the West Bank; a densely populated Arab area; main city, Nablus.

Sanhedrin the ancient Jewish Supreme Court, made up of seventy sages; normally located on the Temple Mount, the Sanhedrin ceased to exist three generations after the destruction of the Temple.

Sepharadim Jews whose ancestors lived in Spain and Portugal; usually applied to the Oriental population in Israel, in contradistinction to Ashkenazim.

Shas an ultraorthodox party of Sepharadi Jews established in 1984 by former Chief Rabbi, Ovadiya Yosef; very influential and active in national politics.

Shin Bet Israel's internal secret service.

Sikarikin a small anti-leftist conspiracy group that since 1988 has conducted several sabotage acts against Israelis supportive of talks with the PLO; named after a Jewish messianic terrorist group that operated in the time of the destruction of the Second Temple.

Tehiya (Renaissance) The first radical right political party, established in 1979; tries to bring together secular and religious Jews; most known leaders: professor Yuval Ne'eman and Geula Cohen.

Torah the Pentateuch, broadly referred to as the Jewish religious law.

Transfer a right-wing shorthand for an agreed upon eviction of all Palestinian Arabs from the occupied territories and their resettlement in the Arab world.

Tzfia (Looking Ahead) a fundamentalist group established in the summer of 1984 to promote the ideas of the Jewish Underground; led by Rabbi Israel Ariel, it published three large collections of extremist essays.

Tzomet (Crossroads) a radical right political party established in 1984 by General (res.) Rafael Eitan; merged with the Tehiya in 1984, but split in 1987.

Yamit The main Jewish city in occupied northern Sinai; established in 1975 and evacuated in April 1982 in compliance with the Israeli-Egyptian peace treaty.

Yeshivot Hesder a Zionist yeshiva whose students combine rabbinical studies and military service.

Yishuv the organized Jewish community that lived in Palestine before the 1948 establishment of the State of Israel.

Zahal Israel Defence Forces.

Zot Haaretz (This Is the Land) the journal of the Land of Israel Movement.

Notes

Introduction

1. On Gush Emunim see Gideon Aran, "From Religious Zionism to Zionist Religion: The Roots of Gush Emunim and Its Culture" (Unpublished Doctoral Dissertation, Hebrew University of Jerusalem, 1987); David Newman (ed.), *The Impact of Gush Emunim* (London, Croom Helm, 1985); Zvi Raanan, *Gush Emunim* (Tel Aviv, Sifriyat Poalim, 1980—Hebrew); Danny Rubinstein, *On the Lord's Side: Gush Emunim* (Tel Aviv, Hakibbutz Hameuchad, 1982—Hebrew); Ehud Sprinzak, "Gush Emunim: The Iceberg Model of Political Extremism," *Medina Mimshal Veyehasim Beinleumiim,* No. 17 (Fall 1981—Hebrew); "Gush Emunim: The Politics of Zionist Fundamentalism in Israel" (New York, The American Jewish Committee, 1986); For a recent review of the Gush Emunim literature see Eliezer Don-Yehiya, "Jewish Messianism, Religious Zionism and Israeli Politics: The Impact and Origins of Gush Emunim," *Middle Eastern Studies,* Vol. 23, No. 2 (April 1987).

2. Cf. Yair Kotler, *Heil Kahane* (New York, Adama Books, 1986), Ch. 16; Ehud Sprinzak, "Kach and Kahane: The Emergence of Jewish Quasi-Fascism," in Asher Arian and Michal Shamir (eds.), *The Elections in Israel 1984,* (Tel Aviv, Ramot, 1986), p. 182; Also Aviezer Ravitzki, Ruth Gabizon, Gerald Cromer, and Ehud Sprinzak, *The Ideology of Meir Kahane and His Supporters* (Jerusalem, Van Leer Institute Publications, 1986—Hebrew).

3. Since the summer of 1984 the Jerusalem Van Leer Foundation has conducted three surveys of the political attitudes of Israel's high school generation (15–18 years old). The September 1984 study found that 60% of the respondents thought Arabs did not deserve full equality and 42% were in favor of restricting the political rights of non-Jews. The following survey, conducted in May 1985, showed that 40% agreed with Kahane's opinions and 11% said they were ready to vote for him. A further breakdown of the results indicated exceptionally strong support for Kahane's ideas among the religious youth (59%) and among young people of Oriental origins (50%). The April 1986 survey, which was conducted after an intense anti-Kahane campaign throughout most of the political system, showed a small decline in the support for the rabbi's positions. Only one-third of the respondents thought Kahane's opinions were right and 7.5% said they would vote for him. Fifty percent, however, were still favorable to the idea of restricting the rights of Arabs and 56% opposed equal rights to non-Jews. For a further description of the growth of Israeli

ultranationalism see Charles S. Liebman, "Jewish Ultra Nationalism in Israel: Converging Strands" in William Frankel (ed.), *Survey of Jewish Affairs* (London, Associated Universities Press, 1985).

Chapter 1

1. Cf. Hans Rogger and Eugene Weber (eds.), *The European Right* (London, Weidenfeld & Nicholson, 1965), p. 10; Yaacov Shavit, *Jabotinsky and the Revisionist Movement* (London, Frank Cass, 1988), pp. 352–53.

2. Cf. Ze'ev Sternhel, "Fascist Ideology," in Walter Laqueur, *Fascism: A Reader's Guide* (Berkeley, University of California Press, 1976).

3. Cf. Stanley G. Payne, *Fascism: Comparison and Definition* (Madison, University of Wisconsin Press, 1980), pp. 15–17.

4. Cf. Essays in Daniel Bell (ed.), *The Radical Right* (New York, Doubleday, 1963); Benjamin Epstein and Arnold Forster, *Radical Right: Report on the John Birch Society and Allies* (New York, Random House, 1967); Richard Hofstadter, *The Paranoid Style in American Politics* (New York, Knopf, 1965); Seymour Martin Lipset, "The Radical Right," *British Journal of Sociology*, No. 1 (June 1955). Seymour Martin Lipset and Earl Raab, *The Politics of Unreason* (New York, Harper and Row, 1970). Edward Shils, *The Torment of Secrecy* (Glencoe, Free Press, 1956).

5. Gilbert Abcarian and Sherman M. Stanage, "Alienation and the Radical Right," in James A. Gould and Willis H. Truhit (eds), *Political Ideologies* (New York, Macmillan, 1973).

6. *Ibid.*, p. 180.

7. Cf. Seymour Martin Lipset, "The Sources of the Radical Right," Richard Hofstadter, "The Pseudo-Conservative Revolt" in Daneiel Bell (ed.), *The Radical Right;* Joseph R. Gusfield, *Symbolic Crusade: Status Politics and the American Temperance Movement* (Urbana, The University of Illinois Press, 1963).

8. Cf. Lipset and Raab, *The Politics of Unreason*, pp. 12–24.

9. Cf. Hans Rogger and Eugene Weber (eds.), *The European Right*, p. 12.

10. Cf. Walter Laqueur and Barry Rubin (eds.), *The Israel-Arab Reader* (New York, Penguin Book, 1984), p. 127.

11. On Mapai's hegemony and methods see Yonathan Shapiro, *Democracy in Israel* (Ramat-Gan, Massada, 1977—Hebrew); Peter Medding, *Mapai in Israel: Political Organization and Government in a New Society* (Cambridge, Cambridge University Press, 1972); Myron Aronoff, *Power and Ritual in the Israeli Labor Party* (Assen, Van Gorcum, 1977).

12. Cf. Ian Lustick, *Arabs in the Jewish State* (Austin, University of Texas Press, 1980).

13. Cf. Moshe Negbi, *Above the Law: Constitutional Crisis in Israel* (Tel Aviv, Am Oved, 1987—Hebrew), Ch. 3.

14. For a pre-1967 description of the Israeli political system see Marver H. Bernstein, *The Politics of Israel: The First Decade of Statehood* (Princeton, Princeton University Press, 1957); Leonard Fein, *Israel: Politics and People* (Boston, Little Brown, 1968).

15. On Lehi's 1949 dissolution and failure to integrate into national politics see Pinhas Genosar, *Lehi Revealed* (Ramat Gan, Bar-Illan University, 1985—Hebrew),

pp. 7–37; Joseph Heller, *Lehi: Ideology and Politics 1940–1948* (Jerusalem, Keter, 1989—Hebrew), Ch. 12.

16. On Sharon see Ariel Aharon, *Warrior: An Autobiography* (New York, Simon and Schuster, 1989); Uzi Benziman, *Sharon: An Israeli Caesar* (Tel Aviv, Adam Publishers, 1985—Hebrew).

17. The Eretz Yisrael Knesset Front was established in December 1988, immediately after the formation of the new unity coalition between the Likud and the Alignment (Labor party). It was initiated by Likud Knesset members Michael Eitan and Tzachi Hanegbi who were strongly opposed to this move, which left the parties of the radical right with no power or influence. The Eretz Yisrael Front was made up of all the members of the Tehiya, Tzomet, Moledet, and those from the Likud, National Religious Party, Shas, and Agudat Israel who are fully committed to the territorial integrity of the entire Eretz Yisrael, and who worried before the 1990 crisis of the unity government that the coalition with Labor was likely to jeopardize it. While lobbying for settlements of the West Bank and their organizations, the Front's main aim was an intra-Likud mobilization, to counter whatever erosion might have taken place in the positions of Shamir and the "moderates." Interview with Tzachi Hanegbi, December 29, 1988. Also Haggai Segal, "Going for War, Educational War, and Guidance," *Hadashot,* March 3, 1989.

18. Cf. Robert A Dahl, *A Preface to Democratic Theory* (Chicago, Chicago University Press, 1956), Ch. 4.

19. On the *intifada* see Ze'ev Schiff and Ehud Ya'ari, *The Intifada* (New York, Simon and Schuster, 1990); Arye Shalev, *The Intifada: Causes and Effects* (Tel Aviv, Papirus Publishers, 1990—Hebrew).

20. My estimate is conservative and based on regular opinion polls in Israel that indicate a 8–12% support for the Tehiya, Tzomet, Moledet and Kach, a 10% support for the Sharon Camp and other radicals in the Likud, and an additional 3–5% support for the radical right within such parties as the NRP, Agudat Israel, Shas, and the right-wing fringes of the Labor party.

21. Several scholars have written about the post-1967 change in Israeli culture and the emergence of new powerful nationalist and neo-religious ideological and symbolic frameworks. They have, however, mainly concentrated on Menachem Begin and the Likud. The radical right certainly belongs to the "New Zionism," or to the new Israeli "Civil Religion," yet it has a distinct psycho-ideological territory of its own. On Herut's "New Zionism" as an ideology, culture, civil religion, and symbolic system see Ofira Seliktar, *New Zionism and the Foreign Policy System of Israel* (London, Croom Helm, 1986), Chs. 3–4. See also Charles S. Liebman and Eliezer Don-Yehiya, *Civil Religion in Israel* (Los Angeles, University of California Press, 1983), p. 234; Myron J. Aronoff, "Establishing Authority: The Memorialization of Jabotinsky and the Burial of the Bar-Kochba Bones in Israel Under the Likud" in Myron J. Aronoff (ed.), *The Frailty of Authority* (New Brunswick, Political Anthropology, Vol. V, Transaction Books, 1986).

22. Rabbi Moshe Levinger, "Old Flags Should Not Be Thrown Away," *Nekuda* (Hebrew), No. 97 (March 25, 1986), p. 8.

23. A Kach flier distributed to participants in the official commemoration of the hundredth anniversary of David Ben-Gurion's birth, quoted in Gerald Cromer, "The Debate About Kahanism in Israeli Society 1984–1988," *Occasional Papers of the Harry Frank Guggenheim Foundation,* No. 3, pp. 15–16.

24. Author's interviews with Geula Cohen, August 23, 1985, and with Gershon Solomon, February 14, 1985.

25. For an analysis of the fundamentalism of the Ultra Orthodoxy in Israel in relation to the new Zionist fundamentalism of the radical right see Aviezer Ravitzki, "Messianism, Zionism and the Future of Israel in the Divided Religious Schools in Israel," in Alouph Hareven (ed.), *Towards The 21st Century* (Jerusalem, Van Leer, 1984—Hebrew). See also Menachem Friedman, "Radical Religious Groups in Israel: Conservatism and Innovation," in Menachem Friedman and Emmanuel Sivan (eds.), *Religious Radicalism and Politics in the Middle East* (Albany, State University of New York, 1990).

26. Benny Katzover, "The Gravitation Point," *Nekuda* 27 (April 17, 1981), p. 11.

27. Cf. The main representative of this approach was the late Eliezer Livneh in *Israel and the Crisis of Western Civilization* (Tel Aviv, Schoken, 1972). The same approach dominated for years *Zot Haretz*, the magazine of the Land of Israel Movement, which was later channeled into *Nekuda*. It can presently be detected in the speeches and press columns of Geula Cohen and Dr. Israel Eldad.

28. Cf. Ehud Sprinzak, "Extreme Politics in Israel," *The Jerusalem Quarterly*, No. 15 (Fall 1977) and E. Sprinzak, "Gush Emunim: The Iceberg Model."

29. Cf. *Nekuda* 93 (November 22, 1985).

30. Cf. Avinoam Bar Yosef and Yehoshua Bitzur, "A Prime Minister That Surrenders Parts of Eretz Israel Will Be Considered a Traitor," *Yediot Achronot* (November 8, 1985).

31. Meir Kahane, "The Second Revolution," *The Jewish Press* (October 20, 1978).

32. Cf. Nekuda Editorial and Yehoshua Zohar, "The Retreat From Lebanon: Spiritual Weakness," *Nekuda* 83 (February 1, 1985), pp. 5–7; Also, Tzfia report on the establishment of a Gariin (a settlement nucleus) for a future settlement in Lebanon, *Tzfia* 2 (Spring, 1985), pp. 95–96.

33. Elyakim Haetzni, "A State with No Protection Against Internal Erosion," *Nekuda* 84 (March 1, 1985), p. 22.

34. Cf. Elyakim Haetzni, "The 'Focus' That Was Not Focused," *Nekuda* 97 (March 3, 1986), p. 14.

35. A major effort in this direction is Ian S. Lustick, *For the Land and the Lord: Jewish Fundamentalism in Israel* (New York, Council on Foreign Relations, 1988).

36. For a good analytical examination of the different aspects of the new Israeli ultranationalism see Charles S. Liebman, "Jewish Ultra-Nationalism in Israel: Converging Strands."

Chapter 2

1. Cf. Ya'acov Shavit, *Jabotinsky and the Revisionist Movement* (London, Frank Cass, 1988), Chs. 3–4.

2. *Ibid.*, pp. 149–50.

3. On the negative image of the ancient Birionim in Judaism see Ephraim E. Urbach, *The Sages: Their Concepts and Beliefs* (Jerusalem, Magness Press, 1979), pp. 593–603.

4. Cf. Joseph Heller, *Lehi*, pp. 29–30.

5. *Ibid.*, pp. 24–31.

6. *Ibid.*

7. *Ibid.*, pp. 19–35; For a different version see Joseph Schechtman, *The Life and Times of Vladimir Jabotinsky: Fighter and Prophet* (Silver Springs, Eshel Books, 1986), pp. 434–41.

8. For an impressive, although somewhat ahistorical, attempt to portray Jabotinsky as a classical western liberal see Raphaella Bilski Ben-Hur, *Every Individual Is a King; The Social and Political Thought of Ze'ev (Vladimir) Jabotinsky* (Tel Aviv, Dvir, 1988—Hebrew).

9. Cf. Yonathan Shapiro, *Chosen to Command* (Tel Aviv, Am Oved, 1989—Hebrew), Ch. 1.

10. Cf. Shlomo Avineri, *Varieties of Zionist Thought* (Tel Aviv, Am Oved, 1980—Hebrew), pp. 195–202.

11. Cf. Raphaella Bilsky, *Every Individual Is a King*, Ch. 2.

12. Cf. Yonathan Shapiro, *Chosen to Command*, pp. 20–28.

13. *Ibid.*, Chs. 2–3.

14. Cf. Charles S. Liebman and Eliezer Don-Yehiya, *Civil Religion in Israel* (Berkeley, University of California Press, 1983), pp. 74–76.

15. Cf. Yonathan Shapiro, *Chosen to Command*, pp. 38–49.

16. Cf. Shlomo Avineri, *Varieties of Zionist Thought*, pp. 210–15.

17. Cf. Sasson Sofer, *Begin: An Anatomy of Leadership* (New York, Basil Blackwell, 1988), pp. 19–24; Shapiro, *ibid.*, pp. 66–71.

18. On Stern and Lehi see Joseph Heller, *Lehi*, Ch. 4.

19. Cf. Yaacov Shavit, *Jabotinsky*, pp. 350–57; Yonathan Shapiro, *Democracy in Israel* (Ramat-Gan, Massada, 1977—Hebrew), pp. 131–33. Dan Horowitz and Moshe Lissak, *The Origins of the Israeli Polity* (Tel Aviv, Am Oved, 1977—Hebrew), pp. 321–26.

20. Cf. Charles S. Liebman and Eliezer Don-Yehiya, *Civil Religion in Israel*, pp. 30–36.

21. Yosef Gorny, *The Arab Question and the Jewish Problem* (Tel Aviv, Am Oved, 1985), pp. 323–32.

22. For an exhaustive discussion of the transfer issue see Shabtai Tevet, "The Evolution of the Transfer in Zionist Thinking," *Ha'aretz*, September 23, 25, 1988; Zvi Shiloah, *The Guilt of Jerusalem* (Tel Aviv, Karni, 1989—Hebrew), pp. 246–66.

23. Cf. Shabtai Tevet, *ibid.*, September 25; Yosef Gorny, *The Arab Question and the Jewish Problem*, pp. 333–35.

24. Cf. Yaacov Shavit, *Jabotinsky*, pp. 351–57.

25. Cf. Anita Shapira, *Berl Katznelson: A Biography* (Tel Aviv, Am Oved, 1980—Hebrew), pp. 583–89.

26. Cf. Shabtai Tevet, *David's Passion: The Life of David Ben-Gurion* (Tel Aviv, Schoken, 1987—Hebrew), Vol. 3, pp. 162–64.

27. Cf. Zvi Shiloah, *The Guilt of Jerusalem*, pp. 288–300; Shimon Golan, *Allegiance in the Struggle* (Efaal, Yad Tabenkin, 1988—Hebrew), p. 9.

28. Cf. Yehuda Slutzky, *The History of the Haganah*, Part II, Vol. 2 (Tel Aviv, The Ministry of Defense, 1973—Hebrew), pp. 844–50, Chs. 46–48. See also Shabtai Tevet, *Moshe Dayan* (Tel Aviv, Schoken, 1971—Hebrew), pp. 157–74.

29. This was mostly expressed in the War of Independence during which many

calculated attacks on civilian centers were conducted. See, for example, the battle on Haifa in Benny Morris, *The Birth of the Palestinian Refugee Problem, 1947–1949* (Cambridge, Cambridge University Press), pp. 85–94.

30. Quoted by Benny Morris, *ibid.*, p. 27.

31. *Ibid.*, pp. 134–37.

32. *Ibid.*

33. On the internal reaction to the creation of the Arab refugee problem among Israel's top leaders see Tom Segev, *1949: The First Israelis* (Jerusalem, Domino, 1984—Hebrew), pp. 39–47.

34. Cf. Zvi Shiloah, *The Guilt of Jerusalem*, pp. 249–51.

35. Cf. Eliezer Don-Yehiya, "Jewish Messianism, Religious Zionism and Israeli Politics: The Impact and Origins of Gush Emunim," *Middle Eastern Studies,* Vol. 23, No. 2 (April 1987), pp. 222–25.

36. Cf. Yosef Gorni, *The Arab Question and the Jewish Problem*, pp. 350–52.

37. *Ibid.*, p. 395.

38. Quoted by Gorni, *ibid.*

39. Cf. Yonathan Shapiro, *Chosen to Command*, pp. 47–48.

40. On Raziel, Stern and religion see Nathan Yelin-Mor, *The Fighters for the Freedom of Israel* (Jerusalem, Shikmona, 1974—Hebrew), pp. 60–70.

41. Cf. Moshe Halevi Segal, *Generation to Generation* (Tel Aviv, Ministry of Defense, 1985), p. 128.

42. See, for example, Yonathan Shapiro, *Democracy in Israel;* Dan Horowitz and Moshe Lissak, *The Origins of the Israeli Polity;* Peter Medding, *Mapai in Israel: Political Organization and Government in a New Society* (Cambridge, Cambridge University Press, 1972): Myron Aronoff, *Power and Ritual in the Israeli Labor Party* (Assen, Van Gorcum, 1977).

43. Cf. Yaacov Shavit, *Jabotinsky*, pp. 350–57; Ehud Sprinzak "Altalena, Thirty Years After: Some Political Thoughts," *Medina Mimshal Veyehasim Bein Leumiim*, No. 14, Spring 1979 (Review essay—Hebrew).

44. Cf. Dan Horowitz and Moshe Lissak, *The Origins of the Israeli Polity*, pp. 114–17.

45. Cf. Michael J. Cohen, *Palestine and the Great Powers, 1945–1948* (Princeton, Princeton University Press, 1982), Ch. 10.

46. Cf. Dan Horowitz and Moshe Lissak, *The Origins of the Israeli Polity*, pp. 137–46; Itzhak Galnoor, *Steering the Polity: Communications and Politics in Israel* (Tel Aviv, Am Oved, 1985—Hebrew), pp. 103–12.

47. Cf. Joseph Heller, *Lehi*, pp. 113–35.

48. Cf. Yonathan Shapiro, *Chosen to Command*, p. 77; Sasson Sofer, *Begin*, Ch. 5.

49. On Herut's maximalist program and radical myths see Yonathan Shapiro, *ibid.*, pp. 115–22.

50. Cf. Joseph Heller, *Lehi*, Ch. 12.

51. Cf. *Sulam* Vol. 3, No. 3 (June 1951), p. 32. For a general background on the group see Israel Eldad, *The First Tenth* (Tel Aviv, Hadar, 1975—Hebrew), pp. 385–400; Isser Harel, *The Truth about the Kasztner Murder* (Jerusalem, Edanim, 1985—Hebrew), pp. 47–48.

52. Cf. Isser Harel, *Security and Democracy* (Tel Aviv, Edanim, 1989—Hebrew), Ch. 10.

53. Personal interview with Dr. Eldad, February 28, 1985.

Chapter 3

1. Michael Bar-Zohar, *The Longest Month* (Tel Aviv, Levin Epstein, 1968—Hebrew).

2. For a good description of the 1967 escalation that led to the 1967 war see Walter Laqueur, *The Road to War 1967: The Origins of the Arab-Israeli Conflict* (London, Weidenfeld & Nicolson, 1969).

3. Cf. Nadav Safran, *From War to War: The Arab Israeli Confrontation 1948–1967* (New York, Pegasus, 1969), p. 268.

4. Cf. Abba Eban, *Autobiography* (Tel Aviv, Ma'ariv, 1978—Hebrew), Ch. 13.

5. Cf. Avner Yaniv, *Deterrence Without the Bomb: The Politics of Israeli Strategy* (Lexington, Mass., D. C. Heath, 1986), pp. 113–15.

6. Cf. Bar-Zohar, *The Longest Month*, p. 97; Eitan Haber, *"Today War Will Break Out": The reminiscences of Brig. Gen. Israel Lior, Aid-de Camp to Prime Ministers Levi Eshkol and Golda Meir* (Tel Aviv, Edanim Press, 1987—Hebrew), pp. 174–75; Itzhak Rabin, *A Soldier's Notebook* (The Rabin Memoirs) (Tel Aviv, Ma'ariv Books, 1979—Hebrew), pp. 158–60.

7. Michael Bar-Zohar, *Ben-Gurion: A Political Biography*, Part III (Tel Aviv, Am Oved, 1977—Hebrew), pp. 1588–93; Eitan Haber, *"Today War Will Break Out,"* pp. 177–78.

8. The rumor was apparently true. Cf. Bar Zohar, *The Longest Month*, pp. 153–54; for a vivid literary description of the preparations see Haim Be'er, *The Time of Trimming* (Tel Aviv, Am Oved, 1987—Hebrew), pp. 541–44. On the "Massada Complex" see Jay Y. Gonen, *Psychohistory of Zionism* (New York, Master/Charter, 1975), Ch. 13.

9. The Israeli mood before and after the war has been well preserved in Ruth Bondy, Ohad Zmora, and Raphael Bashan (eds), *Mission Survival: The People of Israel's Story in Their Own Words, from the Threat of Annihilation to Miraculous Victory* (New York, Sabra Books, 1968). See also Amos Elon, *The Israelis: Fathers and Sons* (London, Weidenfeld & Nicolson, 1971), Ch. 1; Jay Y. Gonen "The Israeli Illusion of Omnipotence Following the Six Day War," *Journal of Psychohistory*, No. 6 (1978).

10. On the emergence of the "new Zionism" as an ideology, culture, civil religion, and symbolic system see Ofira Seliktar, *New Zionism and the Foreign Policy System of Israel* (London, Croom Helm, 1986), Chs. 3–5; Charles S. Liebman and Eliezer Don-Yehiya, *Civil Religion in Israel* (Los Angeles, University of California Press, 1983), Ch. 5.

11. *Ha'aretz*, 22 September 1967.

12. For a detailed account of the drafting of the manifesto see Zvi Shiloah, *The Guilt of Jerusalem* (Tel Aviv, Karni, 1989), pp. 43–45.

13. Samuel Katz, a veteran Revisionist, told Yair Sheleg of *Nekuda*, who did a major story on the birth of the LIM, that a year before the Six-Day War he participated in a "public trial" on Etzel (the Irgun underground during the British Mandate—of which he was a leading commander) held in one of Hakibbutz Hameuchad's kibbutzim. Benny Marshak, a prominent Kibbutz ideologist who was later to be an LIM colleague of Katz, was ready to participate in the "trial" under the condition that he not be present in the room when the Revisionists testify and vice versa. See Yair Sheleg, "Once There Was a Movement," *Nekuda*, No. 114 (October 1987), p. 37.

14. Cf. Zvi Shiloah, *The Guilt of Jerusalem*, pp. 48–52; Rael Jean Isaac, *Israel*

Divided: Ideological Politics in the Jewish State (Baltimore, The Johns Hopkins University Press, 1976), pp. 54–56; Yair Sheleg, "Once There Was a Movement," p. 58.

15. *Ibid.*, p. 59.

16. Cf. Dan Miron, "A Document in Israel: A Detailed Analysis of the Ideological, Political, Literary-Cultural Origins of The Land of Israel Movement and its Founding Manifesto: The People, the Text and What Have Happened to Them," *Politica* (Hebrew), Vol. 11, No. 16 (August, 1987), pp. 3–4.

17. Quoted in Howard M. Sachar, *A History of Israel: From the Rise of Zionism to Our Time* (Jerusalem, Steimatzky, 1976), p. 673.

18. Moshe Dayan, *A New Map, Other Relationships* (Tel Aviv, Ma'ariv Books, 1969—Hebrew), p. 173.

19. Cf. Zvi Shiloah, *The Guilt of Jerusalem*, p. 48; Isaac, *Israel Divided*, pp. 49–50.

20. Cf. Yaacov Shavit, *Jabotinsky and the Revisionist Movement 1925–1948* (London, Frank Kass, 1988), pp. 139–61; Joseph Heller, *Lehi: Ideology and Politics 1940–1949* (Jerusalem, Keter, 1989), Ch. 1.

21. Interview with Dr. Israel Eldad, February 28, 1985.

22. *Ibid.*

23. Cf. Joseph Gorni, *The Arab Question and the Jewish Problem* (Tel Aviv, Am Oved Press, 1985—Hebrew), pp. 332–38; Yossi Beilin, *The Price of Unification* (Ramat Gan, Revivim Publishing House, 1985—Hebrew), pp. 205–207.

24. Cf. Itzhak Tabenkin, *Collected Speeches*, Vol. IV (Tel Aviv, Hakibbutz Hameuchad, 1979—Hebrew), pp. 340–50. For Tabenkin's post-1967 expressions see Itzhak Tabenkin, *The Lesson of the Six Days: The Settlement of an Undivided Land* (Tel Aviv, Hakibbutz Hameuchad, 1970—Hebrew).

25. Cf. Amia Lieblich's literary description in *Kibbutz-Makom: Report from an Israeli Kibbutz* (New York, Pantheon Books, 1981), pp. 131–33.

26. Quoted in Yossi Beilin, *The Price of Unification*, p. 26.

27. *Ibid.*, p. 28.

28. Cf. Yair Sheleg, "Once There Was a Movement," p. 60; Dan Miron, "A Document in Israel," p. 6.

29. On the Canaanite ideology and history see Ya'acov Shavit, *From Hebrew to Canaanite* (Jerusalem, The Domino Press, 1984—Hebrew); Yehoshua Porat, *The Life of Uriel Shelah* (Yonathan Ratosh) (Tel Aviv, Machbarot Lesafrut, 1989—Hebrew). On the LIM-Canaanite episode see Isaac, *Israel Divided*, pp. 50–53.

30. Cf. Ehud Sprinzak, "Gush Emunim: The Iceberg Model of Political Extremism," *Medina, Mimshal Veyechasim Beinleumiim* (Hebrew), No. 17 (Fall 1981), pp. 28–29; Gideon Aran, *From Religious Zionism to Zionist Religion: The Origins and Culture of Gush Emunim, A Messianic Movement in Modern Israel* (Unpublished Ph.D. Dissertation, Hebrew University of Jerusalem, 1987—Hebrew), Ch. 3; Danny Rubinstein, *On the Lord's Side: Gush Emunim* (Tel Aviv, Hakibbutz Hameuchad, 1982—Hebrew), Ch. 2. For an analysis of the marked theoretical and political difference between Rabbis Kook, the father and the son, see Eliezer Don-Yehiya, "Jewish Messianism, Religious Zionism and Israeli Politics: The Impact and Origins of Gush Emunim," *Middle Eastern Studies*, Vol. 23, No. 2 (April 1987).

31. Cf. Rabb Zvi Yehuda Hacohen Kook, "This Is the State the Prophets Had Envisioned," quoted in *Nekuda*, No. 86 (April 26, 1985), pp. 6–7.

32. Quoted in S. Daniel, "You First Build on Sand and then Proceed to Sanctify," *Hatzofe,* Iyar 23, 1973.

33. Cf. Rabbi Menachem Kasher, *The Great Era* (Jerusalem, Torah Shlema Institute, 1968—Hebrew); See also Uriel Tal, "Foundations of a Political Messianic Trend in Israel," *The Jerusalem Quarterly,* No. 35 (Spring 1985).

34. Rabbi A. I. Hacohen Kook, *The Ha-Raiah Letters,* Vol. 11 (Jerusalem, The Rav Kook Institute, 1962—Hebrew), pp. 176–77.

35. Cf. Menachem Friedman, *Society and Religion: The Non-Zionist Orthodoxy in Eretz Yisrael, 1918–1936* (Jerusalem, Yad Ben-Zvi, 1978—Hebrew), pp. 92–98. For a comprehensive study of the thought of Rabbi Kook, see Zvi Yaron, *The Teaching of Rav Kook* (Jerusalem, The Jewish Agency of Eretz Yisrael, 1979—Hebrew). See also, Rivka Shatz, "Utopia and Messianism in the teaching of Rav Kook," *Kivunim,* 1, 1978; Gideon Aran, *From Religious Zionism to Zionist Religion,* Ch. 3.

36. Cf. Menachem Friedman, *ibid.,* pp. 103–109.

37. It should be noted however, that Rabbi Kook tried to establish a politico-religious movement, *Degel Yerushalaim* (Jerusalem's Flag), but its purpose was less political than spiritual. Recognizing the tremendous gap between secular Zionism and orthodox Judaism, Kook hoped that the new movement, which would be led by high Halakhic authorities, would help the orthodox maintain their spiritual independence while working at the same time with the Zionists and recognizing their political authority. However, the effort failed miserably. Cf. Yossi Avneri, "Degel Yerushalaim," Mordechai Eliav (ed.), *In the Path of Renewal: Studies in Religious Zionism* 3 (Ramat Gan, Bar-Ilan University, 1985); Menachem Friedman, *Society and Religion,* pp. 102–103; 126–128. Gideon Aran, *From Religious Zionism to Zionist Religion,* pp. 121–123.

38. In his original study of Mercaz Harav under Rabbi Zvi Yehuda Kook, Gideon Aran shows that several typical hypernomian components of the would-be Gush Emunim were already present in Mercaz Harav before the great messianic eruption of 1967, but that the claim to spearhead the nation and the confidence to pursue it through public action were only produced by the unprecedented experience of the Six-Day War. Cf. Gideon Aran, "From Religious Zionism to Zionist Religion—Dissertation," Ch. 3.

39. Cf. Uriel Tal, "Foundations of a Political Messianic Trend in Israel," p. 40. For an interesting distinction between "messianism as a theory, a principle of historical interpretation, and 'messianism' which is also an operative program for political action" see Eliezer Don-Yehiya, "Jewish Messianism, Religious Zionism and Israeli Politics: The Impact and Origins of Gush Emunim," p. 224.

40. Quoted in Yochai Rudik, "The Jewish Underground Between "Gush Emunim" and the "Redemption Movement," *Kivunim* (Hebrew) (Summer, August 1987), p. 88.

41. Cf. Rabbi Shlomo Aviner, "And We Did Not Betray Your Covenant" (Hebrew), *Artzi,* No. 1 (Jerusalem 1982), pp. 38–39.

42. Cf. Yair Sheleg, "Once There Was a Movement," p. 58.

43. Quoted in Danny Rubinstein, *On the Lord's Side,* p. 30.

44. Cf. Eliezer Don-Yehiya, "Stability and Change in a 'Camp Party': The NRP and the Revolution of the Young," *Medina Mimshal Veyehasim BeinLeumiim,* No. 14 (1980), pp. 25–52; Danny Rubinstein, *On the Lord's Side,* pp. 31–37. On the

traditional politics of the NRP see Gary Schiff, *Tradition and Politics: The Religious Parties of Israel* (Detroit, Wayne State Press, 1977), Chs. 6–9.

45. For a description of the resettlement of Gush Etzion cf. Yair Sheleg, "Gush Etzion: This Month Twenty years Ago" in *Nekuda* No. 114 (October 1987), pp. 23–27; Peter Robert Demant, *Ploughshares into Swords: Israeli Settlement Policy in the Occupied Territories, 1967–1977* (Unpublished Ph.D. Dissertation, Submitted to the University of Amsterdam, 1988), pp. 116–117.

46. For the Hebron settlement story see Shabtai Teveth, *The Cursed Blessing* (London, Weidenfeld & Nicolson, 1970), Ch. 28; Haggai Segal, *Dear Brothers* (Jerusalem, Keter Publishing House, 1987—Hebrew), Ch. 2; Peter Demant, *ibid.*, pp. 153–61.

47. On Levinger see, for example, Nahum Barnea, "The Dervish," *Koteret Rashit* (Hebrew), May 16, 1984; Amos Nevo, "Who Are You Rabbi Levinger," *Yediot Achronot,* May, 18, 1984; Yehuda Litani, "The Levinger Sting," *Kol Hair,* July 15, 1983.

48. Cf. Yair Sheleg, "Once There Was a Movement," p. 60.

49. Cf. Danny Rubinstein, *On the Lord's Side*, pp. 65–66.

50. Cf. Ehud Sprinzak, "Gush Emunim: The Iceberg Model," pp. 37–38; Moshe Samet, *The Conflict About the Institutionalization of the Values of Judaism in the State of Israel—Studies in Sociology* (Jerusalem, The Sociology Department of the Hebrew University, 1979—Hebrew), pp. 61–64.

51. Cf. Charles S. Liebman and Eliezer Don-Yehiya, *Civil Religion in Israel* (Berkeley, The University of California Press, 1983), p. 36; Gideon Aran, "From Religious Zionism to Zionist Religion: The Roots of Gush Emunim," in Peter Medding (ed.), *Studies in Contemporary Jewry,* Vol. 11 (1986), p. 119.

52. *Ibid.,* p. 130.

53. On Rabbi Zvi Yehuda Kook's teaching see his *In the Pathways of Israel* (Jerusalem, Menorah, 1968—Hebrew).

54. Gideon Aran, "From Religious Zionism to Zionist Religion," pp. 134–36.

55. Cf. Ehud Sprinzak, "Gush Emunim: The Iceberg Model," pp. 37–39.

56. On Yeshivot Hahesder see Mordechai Bar-Lev, "Traditional and Modern Shades in Yeshiva Educational Institutions in Israel," in Walter Akerman, Arik Karmon, David Zuker, *Education in a Society in the Making* (Jerusalem, the Van-Leer Institute, 1985—Hebrew), pp. 425–35; see also Yair Sheleg, "Yeshivot Hahesder," *Nekuda* No. 86 (April 26, 1985), No. 87 (May 24, 1985).

57. Cf. Ehud Sprinzak, "Kach and Rabbi Meir Kahane: The Emergence of Jewish Quasi-Fascism," *Patterns of Prejudice,* Vol. 19, Nos. 4–5 (1985).

58. Cf. Janet L. Dolgin, *Jewish Identity and the JDL* (Princeton, Princeton University Press, 1977), p. 16.

59. Meir Kahane, *Never Again: A Program for Jewish Survival* (New York, Pyramid Books, 1972).

60. Cf. Robert I. Friedman, *The False Prophet: Rabbi Meir Kahane* (New York, Lawrence Hill Books, 1990), pp. 105–108.

61. *Ibid.,* p. 115.

62. Quoted in Ehud Sprinzak, "Kach and Meir Kahane," p. 2.

63. Cf. Robert I. Friedman, *The False Prophet,* pp. 114–115.

64. Rabbi Meir Kahane, *The Story of the Jewish Defense League* (Radnor, Pa., Chilton Book Co., 1975), pp. 75–76.

65. *Ibid.,* p. 142. Kahane, it should perhaps be noted, was strongly influenced

by the "black revolt" of the time, and by slogans like "Black Power," "Black Is Beautiful," etc.

66. Rabbi Meir Kahane, *Never Again,* pp. 123–50.

67. Rabbi Meir Kahane, *The Story of the Jewish Defense League,* pp. 88–93.

68. *Ibid.,* pp. 99–100.

69. Cf. Howard M. Shachar, *A History of Israel,* pp. 14–15, 38–41.

70. Rabbi Meir Kahane, *Never Again,* pp. 74–101.

71. *Ibid.,* "The Anti-Semites," pp. 72–104.

72. *Ibid.,* "Zionism," pp. 151–74.

73. Cf. Yair Kotler, *Heil Kahane* (Tel Aviv, Modan Books, 1985—Hebrew), pp. 99–102; Robert I. Friedman, *The False Prophet,* pp. 127–28.

74. Cf. Ehud Sprinzak, "Kach and Meir Kahane . . . ," p. 3.

75. Cf. Ehud Sprinzak, *The Origins of the Politics of Delegitimation in Israel, 1967–1972* (Jerusalem, Eshcol Institute, 1973—Hebrew), p. 26.

76. *Ibid.,* p. 26.

77. Cf. Yair Kotler, *Heil Kahane,* pp. 153–60.

78. Cf. Robert I. Friedman, *The False Prophet,* pp. 149–53.

79. Cf. Samuel Katz, *Battleground: Fact and Fantasy in Palestine* (Tel Aviv, Karni, 1972—Hebrew); Moshe Shamir, *My Life with Ishmael* (Tel Aviv, Ma'ariv, 1968—Hebrew); Zvi Shiloah, *A Great Land for a Great People* (Tel Aviv, Ot-Paz publications, 1970).

80. Eliezer Livne, *Israel and the Crisis of Western Civilization* (Tel Aviv, Schoken Publishing House, 1982—Hebrew). The only other intellectual product of an LIM member, in which a serious attempt to reformulate traditional Zionism has been made was Professor Harold Fish's, *The Zionist Revolution: A New Perspective* (London, Weidenfeld & Nicolson, 1978). Most of the book had been written, however, after the Yom Kippur War and reflected an altogether different mood than Livneh's essay. Also, it was written by a religious LIM member who tried to transliterate the messianic ideo-theology of Gush Emunim into rational Zionist argumentation. On Harold Fish's contribution see Ian Lustick, *For the Land and the Lord,* pp. 73–84.

81. Livne, p. 7.

82. *Ibid.,* p. 12.

83. *Ibid.,* p. 14.

84. *Ibid.,* p. 71.

85. *Ibid.,* p. 165.

86. *Ibid.,* pp. 220–22.

87. *Ibid.,* Ch. 11.

88. *Ibid.,* pp. 72–73.

89. *Ibid.,* pp. 117–18; See also Moshe Shamir, *My Life with Ishmael,* pp. 161–64; Samuel Katz, *Battleground,* pp. 241–43.

90. Eliezer Livneh, p. 118.

91. Cf. Rael Jean Isaac, *Israel Divided,* Ch. 4.

92. Cf. Moshe Dayan, *Living with the Bible* (Jerusalem, Edanim Publishers 1978—Hebrew).

93. On Allon's early strategic orientation cf. Avner Yaniv, *Deterrence Without the Bomb: The Politics of Israel's Strategy* (Lexington, Mass., D. C. Heath, 1986) pp. 82, 181–82.

94. Cf. Moshe Dayan, *Milestones,* pp. 553–55; also in Zvi Shiloah, *The Guilt of Jerusalem,* pp. 54–55.

95. Cf. Yerucham Cohen, *The Allon Plan* (Tel Aviv, Hakibbutz Hameuchad, 1973—Hebrew). There are several indications that Allon tried to convince the territorial maximalists that his plan was an instrument to enlist the support of the Israeli moderates to retain at least part of the occupied territories; see Zvi Shiloah, *The Guilt of Jerusalem,* pp. 52–54; Yael Yishai, *Land or Peace: Whither Israel?* (Stanford, Hoover Institution Press, 1987), p. 236 (n.25).

96. On the growing internal tensions within the LIM see Zvi Shiloah, *ibid.,* pp. 61–63; Yair Sheleg, "Once There Was a Movement," pp. 60–61; Rael Jean Isaac, *Israel Divided,* p. 58; Yael Yishai, *ibid.,* pp. 103–105.

97. Cf. Zvi Shiloah, *ibid.,* pp. 64–71; Yair Sheleg, *ibid.;* Yael Yishai, *ibid.,* p. 107.

98. Cf. Howard M. Sachar, *A History of Israel: From the Rise of Zionism to Our Time,* p. 676.

99. Cf. Shlomo Aronson, *Conflict and Bargaining in the Middle East: An Israeli Perspective* (Baltimore, The John Hopkins University Press, 1978), pp. 105–10.

100. Cf. Yossi Beilin, *The Price of Unification,* pp. 244–47.

101. Cf. Meron Benvenisti, *The West Bank Data Project: A Survey of Israel's Policies* (Washington, American Enterprise Institute, 1984), Ch. 5.

102. It is important to note that the movement to the right had involved the loss of many Labor people who were unwilling to completely break with their old principles or ideological commitments. Cf. Zvi Shiloah, *The Guilt of Jerusalem,* pp. 94–104; Yael Yishai, *Land or Peace,* pp. 103–105.

103. Cf. Yair Sheleg, "Once There Was A Movement," p. 61.

104. Cf. Zvi Shiloah, *The Guilt of Jerusalem,* pp. 92–94.

105. Cf. *ibid.,* pp. 106–10; Rael Jean Isaac, *Israel Divided,* pp. 139–42. Also, Haim Yahil, *Vision and Struggle: Selected Writings* (Tel Aviv, Karni, 1977—Hebrew), pp. 42–46.

106. Rabbi Yehuda Amital, *The Elevations from Depts* (Allon Shvut, Yeshivat Ha-Zion Association, 1974—Hebrew), p. 41; See also Uriel Tal, "Foundations of a Political Messianic Trend in Israel," p. 39.

107. Cf. Ehud Sprinzak, "Extreme Politics in Israel," *The Jerusalem Quarterly,* No. 15 (Fall 1977), pp. 40–41.

108. *Ibid.,* pp. 40–43; Howard M. Sachar, *A History of Israel,* Vol. 2 (New York, Oxford University Press, 1987), pp. 3–5. See also Golda Meir's account in her *My Life* (New York, Putnam, 1975), Ch. 14.

109. Cf. Eliezer Livne's bitter essays in his *On the Road to Elon Moreh: Zionism in the Direction of Emunim* (Jerusalem, Gush Emunim Publications, 1976—Hebrew), pp. 101–15; Samuel Katz, *A Diplomatic Victory or Geopolitical Holocaust* (Tel Aviv, LIM Pamphlet, 1974).

110. See, for example, Ephraim Ben-Haim, "Only Settlement Will Stop Munich," *Zot Ha'aretz,* No. 174 (October 15, 1974), p. 2; Zvi Shiloah, "In the Collapse," *Zot Ha'aretz,* No. 184 (August 1, 1975), p. 8. On the LIM special sensitivity to Sinai see Yael Yishai, *Land or Peace,* pp. 108–10.

111. Cf. Eliezer Livne, *On the Road to Elon Moreh,* pp. 130–34, Moshe Shamir, *Facing the Mighty War* (Jerusalem, Shikmona, 1974—Hebrew), pp. 206–12.

112. Cf. Ehud Sprinzak, "Gush Emunim: The Iceberg Model," p. 23; Danny Rubinstein, *On the Lord's Side,* pp. 38–45.

113. Cf. Hava Pinchas-Cohen, "Gush Emunim: Early Days," *Nekuda*, No. 69 (February 3, 1984), pp. 4–11; Danny Rubinstein, *On the Lord's Side*, pp. 46–50; Peter Demant, *Ploughshares into Swords*, pp. 293–95.

114. Cf. Hava Pinchas-Cohen, *ibid.;* Peter Demant, *ibid.*, pp. 304–12.

115. "Gush Emunim: A Movement for the Renewal of Zionist Pioneering" (Hebrew) (Undated Gush Emunim Pamphlet), p. 1.

116. Cf. Ehud Sprinzak, "Gush Emunim: The Iceberg Model," p. 31.

117. For a full account of the Kadum Affair see Peter Robert Demant, *Ploushares into Swords*, pp. 381–435; Danny Rubinstein, *On the Lord's Side*, pp. 65–69.

118. Cf. Ehud Sprinzak, *Every Man Whatsoever Is Right in His Own Eyes: Illegalism in Israeli Society* (Tel Aviv, Sifriyat Poalim, 1986—Hebrew), pp. 124–26.

119. On Rabbi Kook's attitude toward the army see Gideon Aran, *From Religious Zionism to Zionist Religion*, pp. 237–40.

120. Interview with Rabbi Yoel Ben-Nun, February 26, 1978. For some afterthoughts about the LIM scepticism concerning Begin, see Zvi Shiloah, *The Guilt of Jerusalem*, pp. 133–38.

121. Cf. Peter Robert Demant, *Ploughshares into Swords*, p. 348.

122. Meir Kahane, "The Activist Column: Reflections on the Elections," *The Jewish Press* (June 3, 1977), p. 20.

123. Cf. Baruch Kimmerling, *Zionism and Territory: The Socio-Territorial Dimension of Zionist Politics* (Berkeley, Institute of International Studies, University of California, 1983), pp. 170–71.

Chapter 4

1. Gush Emunim declared the Camp David Accords a "national disaster" (interview with Gershon Shafat, July 1, 1979). Geula Cohen spoke about "national suicide" and suggested, for the first time, that the Knesset should block Begin by a vote of no-confidence, *Ma'ariv*, September 19, 1978. See also Danny Rubinstein, *On the Lord's Side*, pp. 149–52; Haggai Segal, *Dear Brothers* (Jerusalem, Keter Publishing House, 1987—Hebrew), pp. 39–43.

2. Interview with Yoel Ben-Nun, April 14, 1980.

3. Interview with Rabbi Meir Kahane, June 12, 1988.

4. Cf. Danny Rubinstein, *On the Lord's Side*, p. 174.

5. Cf. Amos Perlmuter, *The Life and the Times of Menachem Begin* (New York, Doubleday, 1987), pp. 391–95. For a critical description of Begin's growing moderation see Samuel Katz, *Neither Might Nor Glory* (Tel Aviv, Dvir, 1981—Hebrew).

6. Cf. Eitan Haber, Ehud Ya'ari, and Ze'ev Schiff, *The Year of the Dove* (Tel Aviv, Zmora-Bitan-Modan, 1979—Hebrew), pp. 172–73. See also Ezer Weizman, *The Battle for Peace* (Jerusalem, Edanim Publishers, 1981—Hebrew), pp. 57–59. According to Israel Eldad's testimony, in 1975 Menachem Begin told a group of LIM leaders that "Sinai is not Eretz Yisrael and we shall give the Arabs autonomy. Why autonomy? asked the late Haim Yahil and Eliezer Livneh. Begin answered that this was his mentor, Vladimir Jabotinsky's position in the famous 1906 Helsinki Conference," Israel Eldad, "Judea and Samaria on Our Shoulder or Palestine on Our Head," *Ha'aretz*, February 4, 1988.

7. For a discussion of several aspects of the Likud's growing moderation and

the 1977 platform, see Giora Goldberg, "The Struggle for Legitimacy: Herut's Road from Opposition to Power" in Stuart A. Cohen and Eliezer Don-Yehiya, *Conflict and Consensus in Jewish Political Life* (Jerusalem, Bar-Ilan University Press, 1986). Rael Jean Isaac, *Party and Politics in Israel* (New York, Longman, 1981), pp. 149–58. David Nachmias, "The Right-Wing Opposition in Israel," *Political Studies*, Vol. 24, No. 3 (September 1976).

8. Cf. *Ma'ariv*, November 21, 1977.

9. Quoted in *Ma'ariv*, November 22, 1977.

10. Quoted in *Ma'ariv*, December 21, 1977.

11. Cf. Ma'ariv, December, 23, 1977.

12. Interview with Gershon Solomon, February 14, 1985.

13. Cf. Mordechi Bar-On, *Peace Now* (Tel Aviv, Hakibbutz Hameuchad, 1985—Hebrew), pp. 14–21.

14. Cf. *Ma'ariv*, April 26, 1978.

15. Several opponents of *Shalom Achshav* (Peace Now) had established a rival organization in 1978 which they named *Shalom Achzav* (False Peace).

16. Cf. "The Camp David Agreements" in Robert O. Freedman, *Israel in the Begin Era* (New York, Praeger, 1982), p. 227.

17. Cf. *Ma'ariv*, September 23, 1978.

18. Cf. *Ma'ariv*, September 27, 1978.

19. Interview with Gershon Solomon, February 14, 1985.

20. Interview with Geula Cohen, April 5, 1979.

21. Cf. *Ma'ariv*, December 6, 1978.

22. Yuval Ne'eman first demonstrated his disappointment with the peace process with Egypt in 1976, when Israel made territorial concessions and gave back the oil wells in Sinai, in the context of the Interim Agreements with Egypt. The talented scientist submitted his resignation as Peres' senior aid and went public with a very critical article in *Ha'aretz;* see Yuval Ne'eman, *The Policy of Open Eyes* (Ramat Gan, Revivim, 1984—Hebrew), pp. 22–51.

23. Interview with Gershon Shafat, July 1, 1979.

24. Interview with Rabbi Eliezer Waldman, April 6, 1978.

25. Interview with Rabbi Moshe Levinger, April 27, 1980. See also Peter Robert Demant, *Swords into Ploughshares* (Unpublished Ph.D. Dissertation submitted to the University of Amsterdam, 1988), pp. 334–38.

26. Interview with Geula Cohen, April 5, 1979.

27. Interview with Rabbi Eliezer Waldman.

28. Interview with Geula Cohen.

29. *Ibid.* For another account see Zvi Shiloah, *The Guilt of Jerusalem* (Tel Aviv, Karni, 1989), p. 184.

30. Interview with Rabbi Moshe Levinger, April 27, 1980.

31. The "Eighteen Tehiya Principles" were formulated by Abraham Stern (Yair) in 1941, for his newly created Lehi underground. The principles were the key ideological tenets of the movement and remained one of Yair's main legacies to his successors. Cf. Nathan Yelin-Mor, *The Fighters for the Freedom of Israel* (Tel Aviv, Shikmona, 1974—Hebrew), pp. 60–63.

32. Cf. *Kol Koreh* (Tehiya pamphlet, Jerusalem, 1979—Hebrew).

33. Cf. Geula Cohen, "The Jerusalem Law: Without Preliminary Fears," *Ma'ariv*, October 31, 1980.

34. Cf. *Ma'ariv*, March 3, 1982.

35. The early target of the war was the destruction of the PLO bases in Lebanon, but it was later expanded to include the establishment in Lebanon a friendly regime that would make peace with Israel.

36. Cf. *Ma'ariv,* July 31, 1981.

37. See Dr. Israel Eldad discussion in *Nekuda,* No. 46 (August 6, 1982), pp. 11–14.

38. Cf. Ehud Sprinzak, "Kach and Meir Kahane: The Emergence of Jewish Quasi-Fascism," *Patterns of Prejudice,* Vol. 19, No. 3, pp. 3–6. Regarding Kahane's early connections with the FBI, see Robert I. Friedman, *The False Prophet: Rabbi Meir Kahane* (New York, Lawrence Hill Books, 1990), pp. 62–63.

39. Cf. Robert I. Friedman, *The False Prophet,* pp. 240–44. I could not verify Friedman's claim that T.N.T. was actually a terrorist organization established by Kahane. In my opinion, T.N.T. was just a slogan resorted to by several Kahane followers whenever they conducted their sporadic and uncoordinated terror acts.

40. Cf. Yair Kotler, *Heil Kahane,* pp. 26–27; also, Rabbi Meir Kahane, *The Story of the Jewish Defense League* (Radnor, Pa., Chilton Book Co., 1975), p. 91.

41. Interview with Rabbi Kahane, April 18, 1973.

42. Meir Kahane, "The Second Revolution," *The Jewish Press,* October 20, 1978, p. 28.

43. Alex Anski and Yitzhak Ben-Ner, "The State of Kach," *Yediot Achronot Weekly,* January 21, 1981.

44. Rabbi Meir Kahane, *The Challenge: The Chosen Land* (Jerusalem, The Center for Jewish Consciousness, 1973—), Ch. 2.

45. Rabbi Meir Kahane, *Thorns in Your Eyes* (New York, Drucker Publishing Co., 1980—Hebrew), p. 51.

46. For an excellent exposition of Kahane's political ideas see his long interview in Raphael Mergui and Philippe Simonnot, *Israel's Ayatollahs: Meir Kahane and the Far Right in Israel* (London, Saqi Books, 1987), pp. 29–90.

47. Cf. Yair Kotler, *Heil Kahane,* p. 144.

48. Cf. Pinhas Inbari, *Triangle on the Jordan* (Jerusalem, Cana Publishing House, 1982—Hebrew), pp. 80–81.

49. Cf. Uzi Benziman, *Sharon: An Israeli Caesar* (Tel Aviv, Adam Publishers, 1985—Hebrew), pp. 219–30.

50. Cf. David Pollock, "Likud in Power: Divided We Stand," in Robert O. Friedman (ed.), *Israel in the Begin Era* (New York, Praeger, 1982), p. 42.

51. Cf. Teddy Preuss, *Begin—His Regime* (Jerusalem, Keter Publishers, 1984—Hebrew), pp. 66–68.

52. Asher Arian, "Elections 1981: Competitiveness and Polarization," *The Jerusalem Quarterly,* No. 21 (Fall 1981). See also Myron Aronoff, "Political Polarization: Contradictory Interpretations of Israeli Reality," in Steven Heydemann, *The Begin Era* (Boulder, Westview, 1984), pp. 66–71. On the new 1981 Begin rhetoric see Nurit Gretz, "A Few Against the Many: Rhetoric and Structure in the Election Speeches of Menachem Begin," *Siman Kriah,* No. 16–17, 1983.

53. Interview with Kahane, June 12, 1988.

54. Cf. Yuval Arnon-Ohana and Arie Yodfat, *PLO Strategy and Politics* (London, Croom Helm, 1982), Ch. 6.

55. Cf. Nadim Rouhana, "Collective Identity and Arab Voting Patterns," in Asher Arian and Michal Shamir, *The Elections in Israel 1984,* pp. 124–125.

56. Mark A. Tessler, "Israel's Arabs and the Palestinian Problem," *The Middle East Journal,* No. 31, 1977; Eli Reches, *The Arab Village in Israel a Revived Political and National Focus* (Tel Aviv, Shiloah Institute Publications, 1985—Hebrew).

57. Cf. Majid Al-Haj and Avner Yaniv, "Uniformity or Diversity: A Reappraisal of the Voting Behavior of the Arab Minority in Israel," in Asher Arian (ed.), *Elections in Israel 1981* (Tel Aviv, Ramot Publishing Co., 1983), pp. 150–53. It should be noted that in addition to the secular nationalist arousal a strongly anti-Israeli religious revival also took place at that time—cf. Thomas Mayer, *The Muslim Reawakening in Israel* (Givat Haviva, The Institute for Arab Studies, 1988).

58. Rabbi Meir Kahane, *The Challenge,* pp. 39–47.

59. Cf. Gershon Shafir and Yoav Peled, " 'Thorns in Your Eyes': The Socioeconomic Basis of the Kahane Vote," in Asher Arian and Michal Shamir (eds.), *The Elections in Israel 1984,* pp. 203–204. Also, Yoav Peled, "Labor Market Segmentation and Ethnic Conflict: The Social Bases of Right-Wing Politics in Israel" (Paper Presented at the Annual Meeting of the American Political Science Association, Atlanta, September 2, 1989).

60. The bitter debate over the Lebanon war made a significant contribution to the ideological conflict over Eretz Yisrael. Gush Emunim and Tehiya speakers came close to charging the "leftists" with treason. See, for example, Elyakim Ha'etzni, "The Left's Blame," *Nekuda,* No. 55 (February 27, 1983), pp. 6–7. On the growing acceptability of Kahane among the youth and the average Israeli see Charles S. Liebman, "Jewish Ultra-Nationalism in Israel: Converging Strands" in William Frankel (ed.), *Survey of Jewish Affairs* (London, Associated Universities Press, 1985), pp. 42–46.

61. Judith Karp, "Investigation of Suspicions Against Israelis in Judea and Samaria," *A Report of the Follow Up Committee* (Hebrew—Confidential), May 23, 1982.

62. Cf. Ehud Sprinzak, "Kach and Rabbi Meir Kahane," pp. 11–12.

63. Cf. Ehud Sprinzak, "Gush Emunim: The Iceberg Model," pp. 31–32.

64. For a discussion of the early security problems in the West Bank see Shlomo Gazit, *The Stick and the Carrot* (Tel Aviv, Zmora Bitan Publishers, 1985—Hebrew), pp. 282–322.

65. Cf. Moshe Dayan, *Milestones,* pp. 497–504.

66. Cf. Michael Roman, *Jewish Kiryat Arba Versus Arab Hebron* (Jerusalem, The Jerusalem Post Press, 1986), pp. 57–58.

67. Cf. Peter Robert Demant, *Swords into Ploughshares,* pp. 369–71.

68. *Ibid.,* pp. 59–62. See also Danny Rubinstein, *On the Lord's Side,* pp. 96–97.

69. Cf Howard M. Sachar, *A History of Israel,* pp. 171–74.

70. Cf. "A Debate on Beit Hadassah," *Nekuda,* No. 17 (September 30, 1980), pp. 12–13.

71. Cf. Ghazi Falah, "Recent Jewish Colonization in Hebron," in David Newman (ed.), *The Impact of Gush Emunim: Politics and Settlement in the West Bank* (London, Croom Helm, 1985), pp. 252–55.

72. Cf. Meron Benvenisti, *The West Bank Data Project,* p. 42.

73. *Ibid.*

74. In his study of the creation of the Israeli Military Government (MG) of the West Bank, Shlomo Gazit makes it very clear that since its beginning under Moshe Dayan, the Military Government was not attractive to talented military officers and that the individuals who came to serve there were second-rate officers who had no

chance of "making it" in the primary course of the army. See Shlomo Gazit, *The Carrot and the Stick: The Military Government in Judea and Samaria* (Tel Aviv, Zmora-Bitan, 1985—Hebrew), pp. 127–29. There are, however, some indications that a service in the MG became attractive to certain individuals *for ideological reasons* of helping build the Jewish infrastructure of Judea and Samaria. For a supportive expression of this attitude, made by General Danny Mat, a former Coordinator of the Operations in the West Bank, see *Nekuda* No. 38 (January 15, 1982), p. 20.

75. David Weisburd with Vered Vinitzky, "Vigilantism as Rational Social Control: The Case of the Gush Emunim Settlers" in M. Aronoff (ed.), *Cross Currents in Israeli Culture and Politics, Political Anthropology,* Vol. 4 (New Brunswick, Transaction Books, 1984), pp. 80–81.

76. *Ibid.,* p. 82.

77. *Ibid.*

78. *Ibid.*

79. Cf. Pinhas Inbari, *A Triangle on the Jordan,* p. 102.

80. Yehuda Etzion, "I Felt an Obligation to Expurgate Temple Mount," *Nekuda,* No. 88 (June 24, 1985), pp. 24–25.

81. Cf. Richard Maxwell Brown, "The American Vigilante Tradition" in Hugh Graham and Ted R. Gurr (eds.), *Violence in America* (New York, Signet Books, 1969), pp. 144–46; John H. Rozenbaum and C. Sederberg, "Vigilantism: An Analysis of Established Violence," *Comparative Politics,* No. 6, 1974.

82. Cf. Richard Maxwell Brown, "Legal and Behavioral Perspectives on American Vigilantism," *Perspectives in American History,* No. 5 (1971), pp. 95–96.

83. Weisburd and Vinitzky, "Vigilantism as a Rational Social Control," p. 82.

84. Cf. Haggai Segal, *Dear Brothers,* pp. 47–54. The whole section on the Jewish Underground is based on Ehud Sprinzak, "Fundamentalism Terrorism and Democracy: The Case of Gush Emunim Underground," *Occasional Paper,* Woodrow Wilson International Center for Scholars, 1987, Washington D.C. See also Yael Yishai, "The Jewish Terror Organization: Past or Future Danger?, *Conflict,* Vol. 6, No. 4 (1986).

85. Cf. Yehuda Etzion, *Temple Mount* (Jerusalem, Ephraim Caspi, 1985—Hebrew), p. 2.

86. Interview with Etzion (in prison), September 11, 1985.

87. One of the reasons for the relative moderate reaction of the majority of Gush Emunim to the "betrayal" of Camp David was the personal affection of Rabbi Zvi Yehuda Kook for Menachem Begin. Cf. Gideon Aran, *From Religious Zionism to Zionist Religion,* pp. 228–29, 239–40.

88. Menachem Livni, *Interrogation* (Court Documents), May 18, 1984.

89. Cf. Haggai Segal, *Dear Brothers,* p. 53.

90. Etzion told me that until the late 1970s he was only partially aware of the tradition of Malchut Yisrael and it took him several years to become converted to its ideas.

91. Cf. Shabtai Ben-Dov, *Prophesy and Tradition in Redemption* (Tel Aviv, Yair publications, 1979—Hebrew). See also Yehuda Etzion, "From the Laws of Existence to the Laws of Destiny," *Nekuda,* No. 75 (July 6, 1974), pp. 26–27.

92. Cf. David C. Rapoport, "Messianic Sanctions for Terror," *Comparative Politics,* Vol. 20, No. 2 (January, 1988), pp. 200–201.

93. Chaim Ben-David, *Interrogation* (Court Documents), April 30, 1984.

94. Cf. Uri Meir, *Interrogation* (Court Documents), April 30, 1984.

95. Yehuda Etzion, *Temple Mount*, p. 2.

96. Quoted in Haggai Segal, *Dear Brothers*, p. 51.

97. Interview with Yoel Ben-Nun, June 20, 1985.

98. Menachem Livni, *Interrogation*, May 18, 1984.

99. On the activities of the National Guidance Committee and the complexity of the intra Palestinian relationships see Pinhas Inbari, *A Triangle on the Jordan*, Ch. 4.

100. Menachem Livni, *Interrogation*, May 18, 1984.

101. Cf. Haggai Segal, *Dear Brothers*, pp. 77–78.

102. *Ibid.*, pp. 99–100.

103. *Ibid.*, p. 291.

104. Livni, *Interrogation*, May 18, 1984.

105. *Ibid.*

106. Cf. Ehud Sprinzak, "Fundamentalism, Terrorism and Democracy," p. 8.

107. Shaul Nir, *Interrogation* (Court Documents), May 9, 1984.

108. The story was told in great detail by Menachem Livni, the "commander" of the underground, cf. Livni's *Interrogation* (Court Documents), May 18, 1984. It should be mentioned that both Rabbis Levinger and Waldman denied those allegations in their investigations.

109. Shaul Nir, *Interrogation*, May 9, 1984.

110. Nir's and Livni's confessions suggest that the growing post-1983 fatalism brought them to the conclusion that the settlers may occasionally have to resort to terrorism to pacify the Arabs. For some general thoughts regarding the evolution of systematic terrorism within non-terroristic movements and democratic societies see Ehud Sprinzak, "Fundamentalism, Terrorism and Democracy," pp. 22–26.

111. According to my rough estimation between 100 to 200 settlers knew something about the underground and its operations. These included rabbis who were consulted, colleagues who refused to participate, as well as wives, relatives, and friends.

112. Cf. Peter Demant, *Ploughshares into Swords*, pp. 236–38.

113. *Ibid.*, p. 240.

114. *Ibid.*, pp. 476–81; Aliza Weisman, *The Evacuation: The Story of the Uprooting of the Settlements in the Yamit Region* (Beth-El, Beth-El Library, 1990), pp. 17–22.

115. Cf. *Yamiton* (Yamit's local weekly), No. 52 (December 29, 1977); Aliza Weisman, *The Evacuation*, pp. 54–55.

116. Raphael Bashan Interviews Menachem Begin, *Ma'ariv*, September 11, 1978.

117. Cf. Demant, *ibid.*, pp. 238–40.

118. Cf. Uzi Benziman, *Sharon: An Israeli Caesar*, pp. 210–13.

119. *Yediot Achronot*, April 9, 1979.

120. Aliza Weisman, *The Evacuation*, Ch. 6.

121. Cf. Ehud Sprinzak, *Every Man Whatever Is Right in His Own Eyes*, pp. 133–34; See also Aliza Weisman, *The Evacuation*, pp. 46–53.

122. Interview with Geula Cohen, 1980.

123. Cf. Haggai Segal, *Dear Brothers*, p. 124.

124. Quoted in *Nekuda*, No. 72 (April 16, 1984), p. 12.

125. Cf. Haggai Segal, *ibid.*, pp. 121–24.

126. Cf. Gadi Wolfsfeld, "Yamit: Protest and the Media-Research Report," *The*

Jerusalem Quarterly, No. 31 (Spring 1984), p. 138; Gideon Aran, *Eretz Yisrael Between Religion and Politics: The Movement to Halt the Retreat in Sinai and its Lessons* (Jerusalem, The Jerusalem Institute for the Study of Israel, 1985—), pp. 46–48.

127. Cf. Gideon Aran, *ibid.,* p. 22.

128. Gadi Wolfsfeld, "Collective Political Action and Media Strategy: the Case of Yamit," *Journal of Conflict Resolution,* Vol. 28, No. 3 (September 1984), p. 375; Danny Rubinstein, *On the Lord's Side,* p. 171.

129. *Ibid.*

130. Cf. Haggai Segal, *ibid.,* pp. 129–31.

131. Cf. Gideon Aran, *Eretz Yisrael,* pp. 62–67.

132. Cf. Haggai Segal, *ibid.,* p. 131.

133. Cf. Gadi Wolfsfeld, "Yamit: Protest and the Media-Research Report," *The Jerusalem Quarterly,* No. 31 (Spring 1984), pp. 140–41.

134. Cf. Haggai Segal, *Dear Brothers,* p. 135.

Chapter 5

1. Myron J. Aronoff, "The Institutionalization and Cooptation of a Charismatic, Messianic, Religious-Political Revitalization Movement" in David Newman (ed.), *The Impact of Gush Emunim* (London, Croom Helm, 1985).

2. Cf. Ehud Sprinzak, "Gush Emunim: The Iceberg Model of Extreme Politics," *Medina Mimshal Veyehasim Beinleumiim* (Hebrew) No. 17 (Spring 1981), pp. 37–38.

3. Cf. David Weisburd and Elin Waring, "Settlement Motivations in the Gush Emunim Movement: Comparing Bonds of Altruism and Self Interest" in David Newman (ed.), *The Impact of Gush Emunim* (London, Croom-Helm, 1985), pp. 185–86. On American settlers and their relation to Gush Emunim and its values see Chaim I. Waxman, "Political and Social Attitudes of Americans Among the Settlers in the Territories" in David Newman, *ibid.*

4. Cf. Gideon Aran, *From Religious Zionism to Zionist Religion: The Roots of Gush Emunim and Its Culture* (Unpublished Ph.D. dissertation, The Hebrew University of Jerusalem, 1987—Hebrew), pp. 318–22.

5. Interview with Rabbi Yoel Ben-Nun, February 26, 1978.

6. Cf. Gideon Aran, *From Religious Zionism,* Ch. 5.

7. *Ibid.,* pp. 331–34.

8. *Ibid.,* Ch. 5.

9. On the tendency in the direction of ultraorthodoxy see Aran, *ibid.,* pp. 342–45. For an excellent general discussion of the various patterns of extremization within the religious Zionist camp see Charles S. Liebman and Eliezer Don-Yehiya, *Religion and Politics in Israel* (Bloomington, Indiana University Press, 1984), pp. 126–33.

10. Cf. Zvi Yaron, *The Philosophy of Rabbi Kook* (Jerusalem, World Zionist Organization, 1979—Hebrew), pp. 272–78. There is a huge literature on Jewish Messianism. On the relationship of the Gush Emunim messianic idea to Jewish messianism in general see Eliezer Shweid, "Jewish Messianism: Metamorphoses of An Idea" *The Jerusalem Quarterly,* No. 36 (Summer 1985); Chaim I. Waxman,

"Messianism, Zionism and the State of Israel," *Modern Judaism*, Vol. 7, No. 2 (May 1987).

11. Cf. Eliezer Shveid, *The Lonely Jew and His Judaism* (Tel Aviv, Am Oved, 1975—Hebrew), pp. 190–91.

12. Cf. Gideon Aran, *From Religious Zionism*, pp. 158–70.

13. Rabbi Haim Drukman quoted by Aran, *ibid.*, p. 444.

14. Cf. Rabbi Yaacov Filber, "The Third Return To Zion," *Morasha*, No. 5 (June 1983) (Hebrew); Rabbi Shlomo Aviner, "The Killing of Messiah, the Son of Joseph," *Nekuda*, No. 11 (1980), pp. 10–11.

15. Rabbi Zvi Yehuda Kook, "Between the People and His Land," *Artzi* (Hebrew) No. 2 (May 1982), p. 21.

16. Interview with Hanan Porat, July 9, 1976.

17. Cf. Gideon Aran, *From Religious Zionism*, pp. 515–16. It should perhaps be mentioned that the "holy trinity" was not invented by Gush Emunim and had been used before by religious Zionism, but the reference to Eretz Yisrael did not imply necessarily the *whole* of Eretz Yisrael. Gush Emunim only revived the slogan and gave it a post-1967 interpretation.

18. Cf. Rabbi Moshe Levinger, "A Spiritual Diaspora in Eretz Yisrael," *Nekuda*, No. 53 (January 14, 1983), pp. 5–6.

19. Cf. Rabbi Zvi Yehuda Kook, "Between the Nation and its Land," *Artzi*, Vol. 2 (1982), pp. 15–23; Rabbi Yaacov Ariel-Shtieglitz, "The Halakhic Aspects of the Problem of a Retreat from Eretz Yisrael Territories," *Morasha*, Vol. 9 (1975), pp. 43–45; Gideon Aran suggests that the key to the rabbi's ruling, which was made against the background of the first disengagement agreements with Egypt in 1975, had to do with Kook's tremendous hostility to American pressure on Israel to give up territories. Cf. Aran, *From Religious Zionism*, pp. 228–29.

20. Cf. Rabbi Itamar Varhaftig, "No Suicide," *Nekuda*, No. 41 (March 19, 1982), pp. 10–11.

21. Haggai Segal, *Dear Brothers: The Story of The Jewish Underground* (Jerusalem, Keter, 1987—Hebrew), p. 131.

22. Cf. Rabbi Yehuda Shaviv (ed.), *A Land of Settlement: Our Right on Eretz Yisrael* (Jerusalem, The Young Mizrahi Generation, 1977—Hebrew).

23. Interview with Hanan Porat, *Nekuda*, No. 50 (November 12, 1982), pp. 6–7.

24. Cf. Yehoshua Zohar, "The Retreat from Lebanon: Spiritual Weakness—Interview with Rabbi Levinger," *Nekuda*, No. 83 (February 1, 1985), pp. 6–7.

25. "Gush Emunim: A Movement for the Rejuvenation of Zionist Fulfillment" (a Gush Emunim early pamphlet, n.d.—Hebrew), p. 1.

26. Cf. Gideon Aran, *From Religious Zionism*, pp. 402–406.

27. Cf. Amnon Rubinstein, *From Herzl to Gush Emunim and Back* (Tel Aviv, Schocken Publishing House, 1980), Chs. 1–2.

28. Gideon Aran, *From Religious Zionism*, pp. 226–32.

29. "Gush Emunim: A Movement for the Rejuvenation of Zionist Fulfillment," p. 6.

30. Rabbi Yehuda Amital, *The Elevations from Depths* (Allon Shvut, Yeshivat Ha-Zion Association, 1974—Hebrew), pp. 41–43.

31. Gideon Aran, *From Religious Zionism*, p. 402.

32. The process of "blackening" has become a reason for grave concern among Gush Emunim circles. Cf. Dan Be'eri, "Zionism: More Than Ever Before," *Nekuda*, No. 95 (January 21, 1986), pp. 8–10; Avraham Nuriel, "The Ultraorthodoxization

of Religious Zionism," *Nekuda,* No. 105 (December 9, 1986), pp. 18–19; Yosef Ben Shlomo, "Indeed, the Flame of Redemption Burns Deeply in Their Bones," *Nekuda,* No. 110 (May 27, 1987), p. 35. See also Daniel Ben-Simon, "An Alien Fire: Yeshivat Mercaz Harav," *Ha'aretz,* April 4, 1986, pp. 4–6.

33. Rabbi Zvi Yehuda Kook, "This Is the State the Prophets Envisioned," *Nekuda,* No. 86 (April 26, 1985), p. 7.

34. Rabbi Moshe Levinger, "They Are All Holy," *Nekuda,* No. 89 (July 7, 1985), p. 7.

35. Rabbi Yaakov Ariel, "The Land and the State," *Nekuda,* No. 28 (May 15, 1981), p. 3.

36. Interview with Rabbi Yoel Ben-Nun, April 24, 1976.

37. Cf. Ehud Sprinzak, *Every Man Whatsoever Is Right in His Own Eyes: Illegalism in Israeli Society* (Tel Aviv, Sifriyat Poalim, 1986—Hebrew), pp. 124–26.

38. Rabbi Yoel Ben-Nun, "Yes, an Autocrtique," *Nekuda,* No. 73 (May, 25, 1984), pp. 13–14.

39. Rabbi Israel Ariel, "Is It Really a Revolt Against the Kingdom" *Nekuda,* No. 73 (May, 25, 1984), p. 16.

40. "Gush Emunim: A Movement," p. 6.

41. Rabbi Shlomo Aviner, "On the Completion of Eretz Yisrael," *Artzi,* Vol. 1 (1982), pp. 28–34.

42. Yedidiya Segal, "Neither Arabic nor Arabs," *Nekuda,* No. 9 (May 16, 1980), p. 12.

43. Cf. Rabbi Israel Rosen, "Yesha Rabbis: To Encourage Arab Emigration," *Nekuda,* No. 115 (November 1987), p. 37.

44. Cf. Rabbi Israel Hess, "The Genocide Rulling of Torah," *Bat Kol* (the Bar Ilan students' paper), February 26, 1980.

45. Cf. David Rosentzveig, "A Time to Break Conventions," *Nekuda,* No. 75 (July 6, 1984), p. 34.

46. Haim Tzuria, "The Right to Hate," *Nekuda,* No. 15 (August 29, 1980), p. 12.

47. Interview with Daniela Weiss, March 4, 1985.

48. For an early analysis of the invisible realm of Gush Emunim see Ehud Sprinzak, *Gush Emunim: The Politics of Zionist fundamentalism in Israel* (New York, The American Jewish Committee, 1986), pp. 18–22.

49. Cf. Gideon Aran, *From Religious Zionism,* pp. 348–62.

50. This is based on numerous interviews conducted with many former Bnei Akiva activists and a conclusive interview with NRP veteran politician Eliezer Shefer, April 9, 1980.

51. Interview with Yoel Ben-Nun, April 29, 1976. On the relationship between the LIM and the Gush Emunim settlers see Zvi Shiloah, *The Guilt of Jerusalem* (Tel Aviv, Karni, 1989—Hebrew), pp. 58–61, 114–23.

52. Interview with Yoel Ben-Nun, April 29, 1976.

53. Interview with Yoel Ben-Nun, February 26, 1978.

54. Interview with Yoel Ben-Nun, June 30, 1976.

55. Interview with Gershon Shafat, July 1, 1979.

56. Cf. *A Master Plan for the Settlement of Judea and Samaria* (Gush Emunim Publication, 1978).

57. Cf. Danny Rubinstein, *On the Lord's Side: Gush Emunim* (Tel Aviv, Hakibutz Hameuchad, 1982—Hebrew), pp. 60–62.

58. Cf. Ehud Sprinzak, "Gush Emunim: The Iceberg Model," p. 48.

59. Cf. Meron Benvenisti, *The West Bank Data Project: A Survey of Israel's Policies* (Washington, D.C., American Enterprise Institute, 1984), pp. 52–60.

60. Cf. Ehud Sprinzak, "Gush Emunim: The Iceberg Model," p. 31.

61. Cf. David Newman, "Spatial Structures and Ideological Change in the West Bank" in David Newman, *The Impact of Gush Emunim,* pp. 175–81.

62. Interview with Amana activist Yoram Adler, October 10, 1979.

63. Cf. Meron Benvenisti, *The West Bank Data Project,* pp. 39–49.

64. Cf. Meron Benvenisti, *1986 Report: Demographic, Economic, Legal, Social and Political Developments in the West Bank* (Jerusalem, The Jerusalem Post, 1986), pp. 56–57.

65. Cf. Yehuda Litani, "The Mass of Yesha," *Ha'aretz,* December 26, 1980; Israel Harel, "Chosen, Not Self Selected," *Nekuda,* No. 11 (June 27, 1980), p. 7.

66. Interview with Israel Harel, June 20, 1985.

67. Cf. Meron Benvenisti, *1986 Report,* pp. 58–62.

68. "An Interview with Dr. Yosef Dreizin, the Director General of S.B.A.," *Nekuda,* No. 68 (January 13, 1984), pp. 6–7.

69. Meron Benvenisti, *1987 Report: Demographic, Economic, Legal, Social, and Political Developments in the West Bank* (Jerusalem, *The Jerusalem Post,* 1987), p. 63.

70. Cf. Gideon Aran, *From Religious Zionism,* pp. 299–301.

71. *Ibid.,* pp. 302–305.

72. Cf. Meron Benvenisti, *1986 Report,* pp. 54–55.

73. Interview with Rabbi Yohanan Fried, March 1, 1985.

74. Interview with Avi Gisser, Director of *Midrashat Ofra,* June 20, 1985.

75. Yair Sheleg, "Rest and Peace," *Nekuda,* No. 94 (December 20, 1985), p. 7.

76. Meron Benvenisti, *The West Bank Data Project,* p. 41.

77. Ze'ev Schiff, "The Military Potential of the Settlers," *Ha'aretz,* November 15, 1985.

78. Cf. Meron Benvenisti, *1986 Report,* pp. 73–76.

79. Glenn Frankel "Israel and the Palestinians," *The Washington Post,* June 1, 1987, p. A16.

80. Rabbi Yehuda Shaviv, "To Establish Communal Courts," *Nekuda,* No. 25 (March 13, 1981), pp. 4, 15.

81. Cited by Yehuda Litani, "Double-edged Sword," *Ha'aretz,* February 21, 1985.

82. Cf. Giora Goldberg and Ephraim Ben Zadok, "Regionalism and Territorial Cleavage in Formation: Jewish Settlement in the Administrated Territories," *Medina, Mimshal Veyehasim Bein Leumiim,* No. 21 (Spring 1983).

83. Cf. David Newman, "Gush Emunim Between Fundamentalism and Pragmatism," *Jerusalem Quarterly,* No. 39 (1986).

84. One of the conditions for Gush Emunim support for the National Religious Party in the 1977 elections was the choice of Rabbi Haim Drukman as the party's no. 2 representative in the Knesset and his potential nomination as the party's first candidate for the Minister of Education. The Gush leaders and their rabbi were stunned when the party finally gave the position to Zevulun Hammer and the conflict was very bitter. Interview with Rabbi Eliezer Waldman, April 6, 1978.

85. Interview with Rabbi Moshe Levinger, April 27, 1980; See also Nahum Barnea, "The Dervish," *Koteret Rashit* (Hebrew), May, 16, 1984.

86. Quoted in Nahum Barnea, "The Dervish," p. 15.

87. Cf. Haggai Segal, *Dear Brothers*, Ch. 2.

88. I have conducted interviews with Gush members since 1976 and there have always been complaints about Levinger's erratic and unpredictable behavior. But not a single interviewee doubted the greatness of the man and his position as Gush Emunim settler no. 1.

89. Cf. Amos Nevo, "Who Are You Rabbi Levinger," *Yediot Achronot*, May 18, 1984, p. 3; I personally experienced Levinger's modesty when I asked to be granted an interview. Levinger told me not to come to his inconvenient house in Hebron but offered instead to come to my apartment in Jerusalem, which he did.

90. Cf. Yehuda Litani's excellent portrait of Levinger, "The Levinger Sting," *Kol Hair,* July 15, 1983.

91. This is based on unofficial discussions I conducted with some of the Shin Bet investigators of the Gush Emunim underground.

92. Interview with Ephraim Ben-Haim, Tehiya leader and a former Ein Vered activist, May 5, 1985. Cf. Aharon Dolav, "If They Will Remove the Kadum Settlement by Force, We Shall Be There Too," *Yediot Achronot,* March 19, 1976. For a very extensive account of the lobbying activity of Labor veterans with the Rabin government see Peter Robert Demant, *Ploughshares Into Swords* (Unpublished Ph.D. dissertation submitted to the University of Amsterdam, 1988), pp. 343–46, 375–77.

93. Cf. Hanan Porat, *In Search of Anat* (Bet El, Sifriyat Bet El, 1988— Hebrew), pp. 143–52.

94. Interview with Uri Elitzur, June 20, 1985.

95. Interview with Gershon Shafat, July 1, 1979; Cf. Haggai Segal, "Mapainik? It Is Partially True," *Nekuda,* No. 114 (October 1987), pp. 28–31.

96. Cf. Haggai Segal, "A Man for Every Season," *Nekuda,* No. 110 (May 27, 1987), pp. 26–29.

97. Cf. Itzhak Rabin, *Soldier's Notebook,* Vol. 2 (Tel Aviv, Ma'ariv Press, 1979—Hebrew), pp. 549–51. For an excellent detailed account of the Kadum Affair, including the backstage operations and pressures see Peter Robert Demant, *Ploughshares Into Swords,* pp. 381–485.

98. Uri Elitzur "The Story of the Twelve Gariinim," *Nekuda,* No. 51 (December 3, 1981), p. 6. Hanan Porat is reported to have effectively continued his lobbying with Begin's successor, Itzhak Shamir. In 1988, Porat was elected to the 12th Knesset as an NRP representative, and has successfully established close personal relations with the Prime Minister, Cf. Orit Galili, "Tentative Membership," *Ha'aretz,* June 6, 1990.

99. Interview with Otniel Schneler, August 5, 1985; Cf. Yehuda Hazani, "A 'Lobby' for the Glory of God," *Nekuda,* No. 84 (March 1, 1985), pp. 24–25; Yoram Shnir, "The Footsteps of the Budget Cuts Lead to the Alignment," *Nekuda,* No. 85 (April 5, 1985).

100. Interview with Schneler, August 5, 1985. On Schneler's exhibitionist style and operation, see Avinoam Bar Yosef, "A Settler in a Jacusi," *Ma'ariv,* July 19, 1985, pp. 6–7. Schneler was removed from office in 1988 because of his exhibition-

ism, close relationship with Likud politicians, and political ambitions which did not square with the Gush Emunim "apolitical" style.

101. Meron Benvenisti, *1987 Report,* pp. 40–44.

102. Benny Katzover, "A Return to the Struggle Methods of Sebastia Is Possible," *Nekuda,* No. 83 (February 2, 1985), p. 13.

103. Interview with Benny Katzover, June 20, 1985.

104. Cf. Haggai Segal, "An Almond Tree Is Flourishing in Nablus," *Nekuda,* No. 54 (February 2, 1983), pp. 7–9; Bambi Ehrlich, "This Dreamer," *Nekuda,* No. 106 (January 9, 1987), pp. 22–25.

105. Cf. For a description of the Beita incident see *Yediot Achronot,* April 7–14, 1988.

106. Cf. Gideon Aran, *Eretz Yisrael Between Religion and Politics* (Jerusalem, The Jerusalem Institute for the Study of Israel, 1985—Hebrew), p. 68.

107. *Ibid.,* pp. 68–79.

108. Cf. Haggai Segal, *Dear Brothers,* p. 137; Also "Round Table" in *Nekuda,* No. 59 (June 10, 1983), pp. 16–17.

109. Quoted by Gideon Aran, *ibid.,* p. 74.

110. Cf. *ibid.,* p. 70; Dan Be'eri, "Zionism, More than Ever Before," *Nekuda,* No. 95 (January 21, 1986), p. 10.

111. On the Lebanon War see Ze'ev Schiff and Ehud Ya'ari, *A False War* (Tel Aviv, Schocken, 1984—Hebrew); Avner Yaniv, *Dilemmas of Security: Politics, Strategy, and the Israeli Experience in Lebanon* (New York, Oxford University Press, 1987).

112. Interview with Rabbi Yohanan Fried, August 7, 1988.

113. See above pp. 64.

114. Cf. Rabbi Yehuda Amital, "In the Trap of Perfection," *Nekuda,* No. 52 (December 24, 1982), pp. 8–11.

115. Cf. Hanan Porat's response to Amital, *Nekuda,* No. 50 (November 12, 1982), p. 6. For an early comment about the potential internal tensions within Gush Emunim see Janet K. O'dea, "Gush Emunim: Roots and Ambiguities," *Forum,* No. 2, 25, 1976.

116. Rabbi Amital's influence among the moderate wing of the religious Zionists led, in 1988, to the establishment of *Meimad* (Dimension), a new party that competed unsuccessfully with the radicalized NRP in the national elections on the religious vote but attracted large public attention. On Amital's career see Giora Eilon, "A Politician Against His Own Will," *Kol Yerushalaim,* July 22, 1988, pp. 16–17; Amos Nevo, "Rabbi Amital: Another Species," *Yediot Achronot Weekly,* October 7, 1988, pp. 34–35.

117. Interview with Yohanan Ben Ya'acov, Bnei Akiva's Secretary General, January 5, 1985.

118. Quoted in *Yediot Achronot,* April 30, 1984, p. 3.

119. Rabbi Yoel Ben-Nun, "Authority Now," *Nekuda,* No. 88 (June 24, 1985), pp. 18–19.

120. Cf. Rabbi Israel Ariel, "Is It Really a Revolt Against the Kingdom," *Nekuda,* No. 73 (May, 25, 1984).

121. Interview with Rabbi Yohanan Fried, August 7, 1988. In June 1989 Rabbi Tau issued a statement supporting Rabbi Levinger's explanation of an incident in which he killed a Hebron Arab in an act of "self defense" (see below).

122. Cf. "Gush Emunim: A Plan for Renewal and Expansion," *Nekuda*, No. 44 (June 11, 1982), p. 23.

123. Cf. "Gush Emunim Wakes Up," *Nekuda*, No. 84 (March 1, 1985), p. 4; Haim Shibi, "The Secretary General," *Yediot Achronot*, March 1985, pp. 8–10; interview with Daniela Weiss, March 4, 1985.

124. Interview with Weiss, March 4, 1985.

125. Cf. Daniela Weiss, "The Friendship," *Nekuda*, No. 104 (November 7, 1986), pp. 10–11, 31.

126. Daniela Weiss attracted much of the fire of the Gush Emunim moderates when, in addition to being very assertive on the issue of the underground, she came out publicly against the Labor kibbutzim and their contribution to Israel.

127. Cf. Menachem Fruman, "I Am Splitting," *Nekuda*, No. 104 (November 7, 1986), pp. 10–11, 31, and also the editorial of that issue; "Shades" (letters to the editor), p. 4, essays by Amiel Unger, Meir Harnoi, Yona Saiif, Dan Be'eri, all in *Nekuda*, No. 105 (December 9, 1986); Benny Katzover, "There Will Be No Hope for Those Who Divide," *Nekuda*, No. 106 (January 9, 1987), pp. 10–12; essays and letters by Aharon Elern, Avi Wolfish, and Zvi Lando, Ester Azolai, Hana Gofer, Haim Shaham, Bambi Ehrlich, Zipora Luria, Zvi Moses, Menachem Fruman, Itzhak Armoni, Ella and Vitto Weitzman and Daniela Weiss, *Nekuda*, No. 108 (March 13, 1987).

128. Cf. *Ha'aretz* and *Yediot Achronot*, May 8, 1987.

129. Cf. Aviva Shabi, "Ruptures in the Gush," *Yediot Achronot*, May 15, 1987, pp. 4–5. On Amana's moderate position see Uriel Ben-Ami's portrayal of Muni Ben-Ari, the new 1988 Director General of Amana, "With Both Hands on the Ground," *Kol Yerushalaim*, July 29, 1988, pp. 23–24.

130. Cf. The Editor, "A Very Important Contribution"; also Shmuel Lerman, "Business (Almost) As Usual," *Nekuda*, No. 117 (January 15, 1989), pp. 6–11.

131. Cf. "Facing the Storm," essays on the *intifada*, *Nekuda*, No. 119 (March 1988), pp. 42–66.

132. Cf. Nadav Shragai, "The Fear from Right and Left," *Ha'aretz*, February 3, 1989.

133. Cf. Yardena (fictitious name), "Where is the Great Hope?," *Nekuda*, No. 128 (March 17, 1989), p. 16.

134. Meir Har-Noi, *The Grey Time* (Bnei-Brak, Avraham Nave, 1990—Hebrew).

135. Yoel Ben-Nun, "Let Us Start with a National Conference," *Nekuda*, No. 117 (January 15, 1988), p. 20. See also "National Conference—Now," *Yediot Achronot*, January 23, 1989.

136. Yoel Ben-Nun, "It Is High Time for Accounting and Concluding," *Nekuda*, No. 123 (September 1988), p. 29.

137. Yoel Ben-Nun, "Redemption: Not in One Generation Not at One Strike," *Nekuda*, No. 119 (March 1988), p. 13.

138. Yoel Ben-Nun, "It Is High Time for Accounting and Concluding," *Nekuda*, No. 123 (September 1988), p. 29.

139. On Muni Ben-Ari see Uriel Ben-Ami, "With Two Hands in the Ground," *Yerushalaim*, July 29, 1988.

140. Cf. Chava Pinchas-Cohen, "The Black Sheep of Gush Emunim," *Nekuda*, No. 126 (January 6, 1989), pp. 30–37.

141. *Ibid.*, pp. 36–37. See also Nadav Shragai, "Loyal to the End," *Ha'aretz*, January 27, 1989.

142. Cf. Oron Meiri and Alex Fishman, "Not in the Underground," *Hadashot,* February 13, 1988.

143. Cf. Ran Kislev, "A Show of Force, or Despair," *Ha'aretz,* May 29, 1989.

144. Quoted by Eyal Halfon, "His Honor the Judge, the Honorable Rabbi Has Just Arrived," *Hadashot,* May 5, 1989.

145. Quoted in Uri Nir and Nadav Shragai, "Settlers Killed a Girl and Wounded Two in an Arab Village Near Ariel," *Ha'aretz,* May 30, 1989.

146. The inability of the Gush Emunim' secretariat to function properly was demonstrated again in March 1990 when Itzhak Armoni, who was made secretary general just a year earlier, resigned. Armoni, a veteran settler and a Levinger confidant, wanted to open up and democratize the movement, but found out, to his great dismay, that his reform ideas were unacceptable to the rabbi who got him the job. Cf. Nadav Shragai, "The Decline of Gush Emunim Continues," *Ha'aretz,* March 30, 1990.

147. Cf. Report by Nadav Shragai et al., *Ha'aretz,* May 5, 1990.

148. The May 1990 sentencing of Rabbi Levinger to five months in prison, for killing an Arab bystander in Hebron, produced an unprecedented show of rabbinical support. A special convention of over one hundred distinguished rabbis ruled that Levinger's interpretation of self-defense was correct and that he did not break any Jewish law. Then, hundreds of excited supporters came out to escort the fighting rabbi on his way to jail. Cf. Nadav Shragai, "Tacit Salut," *Ha'aretz,* May 17, 1990.

149. Cf. Nadav Shragai, "They Call It Thickening," *Ha'aretz,* June 22, 1990. According to the settler leaders, the number of the Jews in the occupied territories reached 100,000 in November 1990. Cf. Editorial, *Nekuda,* 146, November 1990. There was, however, no explanation for the quantum leap from 85,000, which was the number of settlers living in the area in 1989.

Chapter 6

1. Cf. Bina Barzel, "Raful in A Crossroad," *Yediot Achronot,* November 29, 1987.

2. It cannot be doubted that the emergence of Moledet and the split between the Tehiya and Tzomet, *which came about more out of political than ideological reasons,* have produced some political fragmentation within the parliamentary radical right. But the fragmentation has paradoxically strengthened this camp. The Tehiya, which was the first political party of this camp, may have lost its monopoly over the anti-Camp David vote, but has made the radical right a viable option for many Israelis. And this support is increasing. In 1984 the radical right, including Kach, received 5.25 percent of the vote. In the 1988 elections these parties, without the disqualified Kach, increased their support to 7 percent.

The reason that this political fragmentation did not hurt the larger camp of the extreme right is that none of the radical parties has ever appealed to the entire constituency of this camp: the hard core Labor settlement voters, the religious-Ashkenazim, the religious-Sepharadim, the border settlements, and the urban radicals. Consequently, there were almost no hard feelings among the followers of the larger camp about the disunity of their leaders. The voters simply opted for their preferred candidates. A quick review of the 1988 election results suggests, for example, that while the Tehiya remained strong in Israel's urban centers, it had little appeal in the border towns and settlements in the north. Raful, the nation's chief of staff during the Lebanon War, was highly popular there, just as he was in many kibbutzim and moshavim. Moledet may have made it to the Knesset with one seat even without the disqualification of Kahane, but this act of the Supreme Court had definitely put in the Knesset its no. 2, Professor Sprinzak. There are, furthermore, many indications that the Ashkenazi, old Eretz Yisrael image of the three parties has damaged their appeal among the religious-Sepharadi supporters of the radical right. Many of Kahane's potential votes who come from these echelons have moved in the 1988 elections to the ultra-orthodox parties of Shas and Agudat Israel. Moledet alone, with its outright "transfer" message was able to capitalize on the late disqualification of Kahane and it could have probably done better had Ze'evi placed a religious-oriental Jew as his no. 2. In the final analysis, the distribution of the radical vote all over the country does not leave a doubt that the camp of the radical right had become in 1988 an all-Israeli phenomenon. Cf. Boaz Shapira, "One Parliament Member in Fifty Thousands," *Ha'aretz,* December 2, 1988.

3. Interview with Geula Cohen, April 5, 1979.

4. *Kol Koreh* (Manifesto), (A Tehiya Party Pamphlet, 1979), p. 5.

5. *Ibid.,* p. 24.

6. Interview with Ephraim Ben Haim, May, 5, 1985.

7. Cf. Rafael Eitan and Dov Goldstein, *A Soldier's Story* (Tel Aviv, Ma'ariv Publishers, 1985—Hebrew), pp. 329–30.

8. Haggai Segal, "With Hanan Porat," *Nekuda,* No. 71 (March 23, 1984), p. 5.

9. Following his split with the Tehiya party, Hanan Porat tried to establish a new movement *Orot* (lights), which never took off. He consequently joined Matzad of Rabbi Haim Drukman, who had left the NRP several months earlier. The two then decided to cooperate with the orthodox Poalei Agudat Yisrael of Avraham Verdiger, an old political pro who established Morahsa (Tradition) and ran in 1984 for the 11th Knesset. They succeeded in placing two members in the House, Drukman and Verdiger. However, when the NRP, which both Porat and Drukman had been trying "to reform" all along, promised to change and let Gush Emunim people in at all echelons, they decided to rejoin. They dissolved Morasha and united with their parent party. However, this was not done before they were certain about the NRP's promises and the nomination of Uri Elitzur as the director of the influential information department of the party. The move, which involved many Gush people, proved in 1988 very rewarding. A coalition of veteran NRP hard-liners and Gush Emunim chose Professor Avner Shaki, a well-known Eretz Yisrael radical, as the NRP's first candidate for the Knesset and the party's main speaker. It further placed Hanan Porat third on the list and gave the hard-liners a dominant position within the party. The results of the 1988 elections in the West Bank indicated a strong movement of former Tehiya voters to the NRP.

10. Interviews with Benny Katzover, June 20, 1985; Daniela Weiss, March 4, 1985. On the secular-religious nexus within the Tehiya see Asher Cohen, " 'Going Together'—the Religious-Seculer Relationship in a Mixed Party," in Charles S. Liebman, *To Live Together: Religious and Secular in Israeli Society* (Jerusalem, Keter, 1989).

11. Interview with Professor Yair Sprinzak (the author's uncle), June 10, 1988.

12. Cf. Zvi Shiloach, *A Great Land for a Great People* (Tel Aviv, Ot-Paz Publications, 1970—Hebrew), pp. 85–86.

13. Cf. Giora Eilon, "Crocodile Gandhi," *Kol Yerushalaim,* July, 8, 1988, p. 24.

14. Cf. Alex Fishman, "Gandhi: Loyal But Dangerous," *Hadashot,* November, 18, 1988; Amiram Cohen, "The Infertile Tree," *Al Hamishmar,* November 25, 1988.

15. Cf. *Moledet: The Movement of the Eretz Yisrael Loyalists,* No. 1 (Platform and Explanations, 1988).

16. Sprinzak, who chaired the first meeting of the Knesset as the House's eldest member, created a major storm when he added to his opening remarks a lengthy political speech about Moledet's and his own direct historical relation with the Labor movement. Several leftist members of the House refused to swear allegiance to the Knesset without expressing their bitter dismay with the acting speaker (Sprinzak), who was supposed to swear them in.

17. Cf. *Moledet: The Movement of the Eretz Yisrael Loyalists,* No. 1, p. 4.

18. Quoted in Giora Eilon, "Crocodile Gandhi," *Kol Yerushalaim,* July 8, 1988.

19. Cf. Rehavam Ze'evi, "A Transfer Will Take Place in Eretz Yisrael," in *Moledet: The Movement of the Loyalists of Eretz Yisrael,* No. 1, p. 2.

20. Cf. Yair Sheleg, "Repatriation Not Transfer," *Nekuda,* No. 115 (November 1987), p. 16. Another prominent officeholder who referred in 1987 to the transfer as a reasonable and viable solution was Minister Yosef (Yoske) Shapira of Morasha. Saying that a compensation of $20,000 for an Arab family ready to leave Israel was a reasonable sum, Shapira drew the fire of many moderate Israelis including several of his former colleagues from the NRP.

21. Cf. *Yediot Achronot,* April, 14, 1986; Yuval Ne'eman, however, had written about this kind of solution several times in the past. Cf. Yuval Ne'eman, "Samaria: The Foundation for Israel's Security," a May–June 1980 *Ma'arachot* essay reprinted in Yuval Ne'eman, *The Policy of Open Eyes* (Ramat Gan, Revivim, 1984—Hebrew), p. 169; Lo Kach," *Yediot Achronot,* August, 13, 1985.

22. "Demography? There Is an Answer," *A Tehiya Elections Pamphlet,* 1988.

23. "The Tzomet Resolutions," *A Tzomet Elections Pamphlet,* 1988.

24. "The Platform Principles," *A Tzomet Elections Pamphlet,* 1988.

25. For an elaboration on the concept of fundamental ideology see Martin Seliger, *Ideology and Politics* (London, George Allen & Unwin, 1976), Ch. 4.

26. When interviewed for this study in 1985, and asked about his ideological contribution to the Tehiya, Raful responded: "Nothing!" Several Tehiya Knesset members who were present had to explain to the former general that the question referred to his special approach to public life. He then answered in two sentences. To the best of my knowledge Raful has only rarely written newspaper essays and his autobiography was ghostwritten by Ma'ariv journalist Dov Goldstein.

27. This is a common Moledet theme. Cf. *Moledet: The Movement of the Eretz Yisrael Loyalists,* No. 3 (December 1988), p. 4.

28. I am indebted to Aaron Rosenbaum who drew my attention to this fact several years ago. Cf. Aaron D. Rosenbaum, "The Tehiya as a Permanent Nationalist Phenomenon," in Bernard Reich and Gershon Kieval (eds.), *Israeli National Security Policy: Political Actors and Perspectives* (New York, Greenwood Press, 1988).

29. *Kol Koreh,* p. 7.

30. *Ibid.,* p. 5.

31. *Ibid.*

32. "Follow Me to Tzomet," *A Tzomet Elections Pamphlet,* 1988.

33. Interviews with Geula Cohen, April 5, 1979; Dr. Israel Eldad, April 28, 1985.

34. The 1984 election of Rabbi Meir Kahane to the Knesset and the high rate of youthful support for his positions, especially in the army, alarmed public activists and educators all over the country. It resulted in a massive anti-racist campaign in the nation's school system and the army. Numerous symposia "in defense of democracy" were held all over the country and the anti-democratic threat had achieved great visibility. Cf. Gerald Cromer, "The Debate about Kahanism in Israeli Society," *Occasional Papers of the Harry Frank Guggenheim Foundation*, No. 3, 1988.

35. Cf. "Identity Card," *A Tehiya Election Pamphlet*, 1988.

36. Israel Eldad, "Bagatz—A Supreme Court of Appeal for Zionism," *Ha'aretz*, January 21, 1988.

37. "Education," *A Tzomet Elections Pamphlet*, 1988.

38. *Moledet: The Movement of the Loyalists of Eretz Yisrael*, No. 1, p. 3.

39. "Identity Card," *A Tehiya Elections Pamphlet*, 1988.

40. "Platform," *A Tehiya-Tzomet Elections Pamphlet*, 1984.

41. Cf. Tehiya's "Identity Card."

42. "Platform," *A Tehiya-Tzomet Election Pamphlet*, 1984.

43. Yuval Ne'eman, "Zionism Where?," *Ha'aretz*, September 28, 1981.

44. *Ibid.*

45. Dorit Gefen, "Interview with Geula Cohen," *Al Hamishmar*, July 30, 1982.

46. Sarit Yishai, "Geula Cohen: In Love Just as in Politics I Am Going to the End," *Monitin*, February 1979.

47. Yuval Ne'eman, " 'Saving the Area'—By Israeli Concessions," *Ma'ariv*, February 1, 1980.

48. *Ibid.*

49. Yuval Ne'eman, "To Jump Off the Train," *Ma'ariv*, November 13, 1981.

50. Yuval Ne'eman, *Ma'ariv*, June 26, 1981.

51. Yuval Ne'eman, *Ma'ariv*, June 19, 1981.

52. Eliyahu Amikam, "Funny Things," *Yediot Achronot*, June 27, 1986.

53. Yoash Tzidon, "We Are Being Helped Not Because of Excessive Humanism," *Ha'aretz*, March 3, 1989.

54. Yuval Ne'eman, *Ma'ariv*, October 26, 1981.

55. Israel Eldad, "A Misplaced Analogy," *Ha'aretz*, May, 26, 1988.

56. Israel Eldad, "Judea and Samaria on Our Shoulders or Palestine on Our Heads," *Ha'aretz*, February 4, 1988.

57. "Identity Card," *A Tehiya Elections Pamphlet*, 1988.

58. *Ibid.*; "The Intifada Riots: Causes, Solutions and Lessons," *Tzomet Election Pamphlet No. 13*, 1988.

59. *Ibid.*

60. "To Crush the Intifada," *A Tehiya Elections Pamphlet*, 1988.

61. *Ibid.*

62. Israel Eldad, "Rebel and Play a Make Believe," *Ha'aretz*, May 12, 1988.

63. Dr. Israel Eldad, "A Poison from Dizengoff Center," *Yediot Achronot*, June 17, 1988.

64. Geula Cohen, "Infected Creators," *Yediot Achronot*, February 12, 1988.

65. M. Ben-Yosef (Hagar), "This Is the Weapon of the Left," *Hadashot*, March 24, 1989.

66. Cf. Michael Bar-Zohar, *Ben Gurion,* Vol. 3 (Tel Aviv, Am Oved, 1977—Hebrew) p. 1262; Yossi Beilin, *The Price of Unification* (Ramat Gan, Revivim, 1985—Hebrew), pp. 25–28.

67. This is based on a discussion held with a close Ne'eman watcher, military historian Dr. Meir Pail, October 20, 1988.

68. A 1985 *Al Hamishmar* investigation charged Ne'eman of teaching physics in Houston, Texas, for $50,000 a semester while being formally a Knesset member. Cf. Motti Bassok, *Al Hamishmar,* May 10, 1985. Ne'eman's teaching "expeditions" abroad involved him, in July 1982, in a serious legal problem. Just before he was to join the cabinet, it was discovered that he kept for years an illegal bank account in the United States. The State's Attorney General decided not to press charges and instead fined Ne'eman $5000.

69. Zvi Zinger, "Interview with Yuval Ne'eman," April 22, 1983.

70. Yuval Ne'eman, "Private Domain," *Ma'ariv,* March 13, 1988.

71. Interview with Geula Cohen, August 23, 1985.

72. Cf. Adar Keisari, "Introduction," in Yuval Ne'eman, *The Policy of Open Eyes,* pp. 7–8.

73. Cf. Yuval Ne'eman, *ibid.,* pp. 25–27.

74. Yuval Ne'eman renounced his job with Shimon Peres in February 1976. He then published a lengthy essay in *Ha'aretz* in which he expressed his bitterness about the concessions made by the Israeli cabinet to the Egyptians. Cf. Yuval Ne'eman, "Why Did I Leave the Ministry of Defense," *Ha'aretz,* February 6, 1976.

75. This is based on several informal conversations and also on a meeting the author held with Edward Teller, a noted nuclear physicist, when he visited Israel in May 1983. See also Raphael Mergui and Philippe Simonnot, *Israel's Ayatollahs: Meir Kahane and the Far Right in Israel* (London, Saqi Books, 1987), p. 105.

76. Cf. Amos Ben-Vered, "Interview with Yuval Ne'eman," *Ha'aretz,* June 21, 1982.

77. This was a key theme in the Tehiya 1988 television advertisement.

78. Yuval Ne'eman, "Private Domain," *Ma'ariv,* March 13, 1988.

79. Yuval Ne'eman, "Zionism Where?," *Ha'aretz,* September 28, 1981.

80. When asked, in 1985, about her working relationship with Ne'eman and about his approach to politics, Geula Cohen described him as "a real Mapainik." Interview with Geula Cohen, August 23, 1985.

81. Cohen's image as Israel's *Pasionaria* is suggested by Raphael Mergui and Philippe Simonnot in *Israel's Ayatollahs,* pp. 107–108.

82. Personal interview with Geula Cohen, April 5, 1978.

83. Cf. Avraham Tirosh, "Interview with Geula Cohen," *Ma'ariv,* March, 16, 1979.

84. Tzipi Malchov, "Geula: Extra Hours," *Kol Yerushalaim.*

85. Cf. Interview with Geula Cohen, *Monitin,* February 1979.

86. Quoted in Haya Ben-Yosef, "Interview with Geula Cohen," *Al Hamishmar,* July 20, 1979.

87. Geula Cohen, *Underground Memoirs* (Tel Aviv, Karni Publishers, 1972—Hebrew).

88. Interview with Geula Cohen, April 5, 1979.

89. Cohen has been at the forefront of the fight against the extended privileges of many Knesset members who could until very recently serve as lawyers or private

consultants and hold many other lucrative positions. Cf. Geula Cohen, *Ma'ariv*, March 19, 1981.

90. Menachem Golan, interview with Geula Cohen, *Ma'ariv*, April, 27, 1984.

91. "An Interview with Geula Cohen," *Yediot Achronot*, August 1, 1980.

92. Personal interview with Geula Cohen, August 23, 1985.

93. One of the only public figures who came openly against the Jerusalem Law was Mayor Teddy Kollek who was furious about the damage it caused to the city.

94. Personal interview with Geula Cohen, August 23, 1985.

95. Geula Cohen, "The Nation and the Dwarfs," *Yediot Achronot*, April 15, 1988.

96. Cf. Walter Reich, *Stranger in My House: Jews and Arabs in the West Bank* (New York, Holt, Reinhart and Winston, 1984), pp. 20–21.

97. On Shurat Hamitnadvim see Ehud Sprinzak, *Every Man Whatever Is Right in His Own Eyes: Illegalism in Israeli Society* (Tel Aviv, Sifriyat Poalim, 1986—Hebrew), pp. 84–92.

98. Cf. Haggai Segal, *Dear Brothers* (Jerusalem, Keter Publishing House, 1987—Hebrew) pp. 20–25.

99. Cf. Uriel Ben-Ami, "Helpless in Ofra," *Dvar Hashavua*, November 8, 1985.

100. See, for example, the discussion of the possibility of civil war by prominent Israelis in Haim Shibi, "A Civil War," *Yediot Achronot*, November 25, 1985.

101. Cf. Essays by Rabbis Moshe Levinger, Itzhak Shilat, Moshe Shapira, and Yoel Ben-Nun in *Nekuda*, No. 93 (November 22, 1985).

102. Eliyakim Ha'etzni, "It Is a Duty and Commandment to Yell and Terrify," *Nekuda*, No. 94 (December 20, 1985), p. 22.

103. Eliyakim Ha'etzni, "The 'Focus' That Was Not Focused," *Nekuda*, No. 96 (March 25, 1986), p. 14.

104. Eliyakim Ha'etzni, "Why Do You Keep Silent," *Nekuda*, No. 129 (April 1989), p. 12.

105. Uriel Ben-Ami, "They All Were His Enemies," *Yerushalaim*, November 4, 1988, pp. 24–25.

106. Cf. Eliyakim Ha'etzni, "The Catch of the Likud," *Nekuda*, No. 123 (September 1988).

107. Cf. Rafael Eitan and Dov Goldstein, *A Soldier's Story*, pp. 329–334.

108. Shlomo Genosar, "Raful from the Valley, Geula from the Mountain," *Davar*, November, 20, 1987.

109. This is based on personal recollection of the author of many years of reserve service in the IDF.

110. Cf. Rafael Eitan and Dov Goldstein, *A Soldier's Story*, pp. 127–137.

111. Interview with Raful, June 17, 1985.

112. Bina Barzel, "Raful in a Crossroad," *Yediot Achronot*, November 20, 1987.

113. Quoted in Amikam Rothman, "The World According to Raful: Simple," *Hadashot*, December 25, 1987.

114. Cf. Shlomo Geinosar, "Raful from the Valley, Geula from the Mountain," *Davar*, November, 20, 1987.

115. Cf. "The Lonely Man in the Knesset," *Koteret Rashit*, No. 192 (August 6, 1986), p. 10.

116. Cf. Amos Perlmuter, *The Life and Times of Menachem Begin* (New York, Doubleday, 1987), pp. 391–95.

117. Cf. Rabbi Yehuda Amital, "In the Catch of Completion," *Nekuda* 52 (December 24, 1982); Yoel Ben Nun, "The State of Israel Against Eretz Israel?," *Nekuda* 72 (April 16, 1984); "In Favor of Faith and Security and Against the Panicky Cries," *Nekuda* 85 (April 5, 1985); "Authority—Now," *Nekuda* 88 (June 24, 1985); "The Course of 'The Lights' vs. the Course of Deviance," *Nekuda* 91 (September 15, 1985); "Most of Our Members Do Not Think, in Their Right Mind, of Participating in Disturbances, Certainly Not in Rebellion or Civil War," *Nekuda* 93 (November 22, 1985); Menachem Fruman, "Yesha For Our People," *Nekuda* 88 (June 24, 1985); "I Am Leaving," *Nekuda* 104 (November 7, 1986); "To Conquer the Desire to Disregard," *Nekuda* 108 (March 13, 1987); Itzhak Shilat, "To Return to the Main Course," *Nekuda* 89 (July 26, 1985); "Without Hysteria," *Nekuda* 93 (November 22, 1985); "There Are No Shortcuts," *Nekuda* 95 (January 21, 1986). Some of these opinions have also been expressed in *Nekuda* editorials, written by Israel Harel, the journal's editor.

118. Cf. Uzi Benziman, *Sharon: An Israeli Caesar* (Hebrew) (Tel Aviv, Adam Publishers, 1985), Chs. 12, 13, 14; author's Interview with Sharon, September 3, 1985.

119. Cf. Haggai Segal, "Going for War, Educational War, and Guidance," *Hadashot*, March 3, 1989. Likud Knesset member Tzachi Hanegbi (Geula Cohen's son), admits that not all the members of the Eretz Yisrael Front are active on a daily basis and that basically it is a three-men operation. He argues, however, that there is no ideological difference between the Front and the Likud in general and that on many occasions it can get the support of the majority of the members of Likud. Interview, August 28, 1989.

Chapter 7

1. Author's interview with Kahane, June 7, 1988.

2. Cf. Gershon Shafir and Yoav Peled, "Thorns in Your Eyes: The Socioeconomic Basis of the Kahane Vote," in Asher Arian and Michal Shamir (eds.), *The Elections in Israel 1984* (Tel Aviv, Ramot Publishing Co., 1986). This judgment is also based on my own unsystematic observation of Kach and numerous press reports.

3. Cf. Shafir and Peled, *ibid.*

4. This is based on Kahane's own account which I tend to believe; author's interview with Kahane, June 7, 1988.

5. On June 12, 1988, I joined Kahane for a pre-election speaking tour in the Haifa region. During his three speeches, I spoke to about two dozen excited Kahane followers. Not a single one of them had read Kahane's books or recognized the titles of more than two of them.

6. On Kahane's continued relationships with JDL veterans in America and Israel, and on his fund-raising activities see Robert I. Friedman, *The False Messiah: Rabbi Meir Kahane, From FBI Informant to Knesset Member* (New York, Lawrence Hill Books, 1990). During his last five years Kahane had been successful in raising enough money for the establishment of The Jewish Idea Yeshiva in the Jewish Quarter of the Old City of Jerusalem, of which he became the informal head and religious authority.

7. This is also based on Rabbi Kahane's own account. Kahane, whose personal admiration for Menachem Begin had never fully subsided despite his complete disappointment with his political course, argued that the collapse of Begin opened for him political opportunities that were totally blocked before; author's interview with Kahane, June 12, 1988.

8. During my trip with Kahane from Jerusalem to Haifa, he personally reviewed every logistical detail of the program for that evening and the coming week. He also sat with a road map and constantly instructed his driver regarding the best short-cuts. Kahane's driver and bodyguard told me later that the rabbi was always in full control of every detail.

9. Cf. Nadav Shragai, "The Seeds of the Castor-Oil Plant," *Kol Hair,* February 18, 1983.

10. There are countless testimonies to this fact; see, for example, Lili Galilee, "The Great Dictator," *Ha'aretz,* April 26, 1985.

11. This judgment is based on author's interviews with former Kach activists, Avigdor Eskin (February 13, 1985), and Yoel Lerner (December 27, 1984).

12. Following a successful showing in the municipal elections of July 1985, Kach's representatives in Kiriyat Arba signed a coalition agreement with the Kiriya leader Shalom Vach and with his political partner Elyakim Haetzni. The party's main representative in the municipal council, Rami Zait, argued that Kiriyat Arba's Kach was not different in its orientation from most of the population and that with the exception of a demand to fire the Arab workers of the municipality, Kach was to recommend the continuation of all the existing policies. Cf. Zvi Alush, "In Kiriyat Arba They Say: To Fire the Arabs But Not in the Kach Style," *Yediot Achronot,* July 27, 1985.

13. Cf. Yair Avituv, "All Is Well in the Kasba," *Kol Hair,* August 12, 1988, p. 27.

14. Cf. author's interview with Yoel Lerner, December 27, 1984; Lili Galilee, "The Great Dictator."

15. During my June 12 trip with Kahane, I found him as energetic and forceful as he appeared to me fifteen years earlier, when I first interviewed him in Jerusalem. He had no difficulty conducting three consecutive open meetings and acting vigorously on the speaker's platform. I was told by his close assistants that he had been speaking publicly four times a week ever since his 1984 election to the Knesset. Kahane himself told me that this intense schedule was his response to the general boycott imposed upon him by the entire Israeli media. "If the fools think that they can have Kahane forgotten by not giving him TV time and press coverage, they are dead wrong."

16. Cf. Rabbi Kahane's book, *Listen World, Listen Jew* (Tucson, The Institute of the Jewish Idea, 1978).

17. Author's interview with Kahane, June 7, 1988.

18. For an early comprehensive account of Kahane's past see Michael T. Kaufman's investigative report, "The Complex Past of Meir Kahane," *The New York Times,* January 24, 1971, pp. 1, 51. Cf. Yair Kotler, *Heil Kahane,* pp. 23–32.

19. Kahane, to be sure, did not refer to himself as a "fundamentalist," and did not talk about the "doctrine of inerrancy," which belongs to the conceptual world of American fundamentalism. His close reading of the Bible and of Halakhic authorities and his demand that the entire policy of Israel be conducted in accordance with a literal interpretation of these sources indicated, however, the existence of a pure case

of inerrancy. For the doctrine of inerrancy cf. William Shepard, "Fundamentalism: Christian and Islamic," *Religion*, Vol. 17, 1987, pp. 355–56.

20. Walter Reich, "The Kahane Controversy," *Moment*, Vol. 10, No. 2 (January–February 1985), p. 21.

21. Rabbi Meir Kahane, *Forty Years* (Miami, Institute of the Jewish Idea, 1983), p. 66.

22. Author's interview with Kahane, June 7, 1988.

23. Rabbi Meir Kahane, *Listen World, Listen Jew*, p. 147.

24. Rabbi Meir Kahane, *Uncomfortable Questions for Comfortable Jews* (Secaucus, N.J., Lyle Stuart, 1987), p. 12.

25. Kahane said he did not need a rabbi of his own because he was a rabbi himself and was entitled to his own interpretations. However, he admitted that in Halakhic matters he would often go to Rabbi Eliyahu who, Kahane said, was in full agreement with him on almost everything. He told me that when he published his most theoretical book, *On Faith and Redemption*, he sent copies to many authorities, including the rabbis of Gush Emunim. No one responded but Rabbi Eliyahu, and he agreed with every word. When Kahane asked Eliyahu to endorse him in public the Chief Rabbi said he could not.

26. Rabbi Meir Kahane, *The Jewish Idea* (Jerusalem, Institute of the Jewish Idea, 1974), p. 5.

27. Rabbi Meir Kahane, *The Challenge: The Chosen Land* (Jerusalem, The Center for Jewish Consciousness, 1973—Hebrew), p. 175.

28. On the strong anti-Gentile motive in Kahane's thinking see Aviezer Ravitzky, "The Ideological Side" in Aviezer Ravitzky, Ruth Gabizon, Ehud Sprinzak, and Gerald Cromer, *The Ideology of Meir Kahane and his Supporters* (Jerusalem, The Van Leer Institute, 1986—Hebrew), pp. 3–10.

29. Rabbi Meir Kahane, "Hillul Hashem" (a Kach mimeographed article, n.d.—Hebrew).

30. Rabbi Meir Kahane, *Listen World, Listen Jew*, pp. 121–22.

31. Cf. George Sorel, *Reflections on Violence* (New York, Colliers Books, 1961); Franz Fanon, *The Wretched of the Earth* (New York, Grove Press, 1966).

32. Cf. Gerald Cromer, "The Debate About Kahanism In Israeli Society 1984–1988," p. 35.

33. In his *The Story of the Jewish Defense League* (Radnor, Pa., Chilton Book Co., 1975), Kahane has a special chapter titled "Violence: Is This Any Way for a Nice Jewish Boy To Behave?" in which he provides the rationale for the violence of the American Jewish Defense League. The reader is told that among its other purposes, "Jewish violence is meant to . . . Destroy the Jewish neuroses and fears that contribute so much encouragement to the anti-Semite as well as Jewish belief in his own worthlessness. We want to instill self-respect and self-pride in a Jew who is ashamed of himself for running away," p. 142.

34. Rabbi Meir Kahane, *Listen World, Listen Jew*, p. 128.

35. *Ibid.*, pp. 139–43.

36. Rabbi Meir Kahane, *The Challenge*, pp. 9–10.

37. Rabbi Meir Kahane, *On Faith and Redemption* (Jerusalem, The Institute of the Jewish Idea, 1980—Hebrew), p. 59.

38. Cf. Rabbi Meir Kahane, *Time to Go Home* (Los Angeles, Nash Publishing, 1972); *Never Again, op. cit.*

39. Cf. Rabbi Meir Kahane, *Israel's Eternity and Victory* (Jerusalem, The Insti-

tute of Jewish Idea, 1973—Hebrew); *Numbers 23:9* (Jerusalem, The Institute of Jewish Idea, 1984—Hebrew).

40. Rabbi Meir Kahane, *Forty Years,* pp. 6–7.

41. According to Kahane's deterministic logic, the only condition for complete salvation is a full repentance of the entire nation. His expected takeover of political power could be a big step in the right direction, but since he did not plan to impose a forced repentance on the entire people, it would probably not satisfy God. Consequently, Kahane said, he would try to tell the people about the disaster that awaits them but if they choose not to listen then even he would be unable to save them. Author's interview with Kahane June 12, 1988.

42. Rabbi Meir Kahane, *The Challenge,* pp. 20–21.

43. *Ibid.,* pp. 22–23.

44. *Ibid.,* pp. 23–24.

45. Rabbi Meir Kahane, *On Faith and Redemption,* p. 51.

46. Cf. Rabbi Meir Kahane, *The Story of the Jewish Defense League,* pp. 281–85; Yair Kotler, *Heil Kahane,* pp. 92–93.

47. Rabbi Meir Kahane, *Thorns in Your Eyes* (New York, Druker Publishing, 1981—Hebrew), p. 239.

48. *Ibid.,* p. 242.

49. Cf. *ibid.,* pp. 224–37.

50. Rabbi Meir Kahane, *On Faith and Redemption,* p. 68.

51. Rabbi Meir Kahane, *The Challenge,* p. 21.

52. *Ibid.,* pp. 39–40.

53. "Suppose Arafat decides to leave the war trail. Do you think our problems are solved? Forget it! All he has to do is to tell them to make love not war, and we are done for in no time." This was one of Kahane's rhetorical gimmicks that he used repeatedly in his campaign speeches. I heard him repeat it three times in three places in one evening. Author's trip with Kahane, June 12, 1988.

54. Rabbi Meir Kahane, *Thorns in Your Eyes,* pp. 107–108.

55. Rabbi Meir Kahane, *Law and Order in Israel* (Jerusalem, Kach Movement, 1977—Hebrew), p. 8.

56. Rabbi Meir Kahane, *Uncomfortable Questions for Comfortable Jews,* pp. 159–60.

57. *Ibid.*

58. In *Law and Order in Israel,* Kahane argued that the democratic idea was a very important stage in the natural evolution of the modern western society, but that because the Jewish nation had emerged in an unnatural way, as a result of God's special choice, it was inapplicable to the Jews (pp. 3–5).

59. Rabbi Meir Kahane, *Uncomfortable Questions,* p. 261.

60. *Ibid.,* p. 161.

61. *Ibid.,* p. 173.

62. *Ibid.,* p. 262.

63. For an excellent discussion of Kahane's struggle against Hellenism see Gerald Cromer, "The Debate About Kahanism in Israeli Society 1984–1988," pp. 18–22.

64. *From the Knesset Stand: The Speeches of Rabbi Kahane in the Knesset,* pp. 136–37.

65. I personally raised the question of civil war with Kahane and was told in an unequivocal terms that he was against it and under no circumstances would allow it to happen. Interview with Kahane, June 7, 1988.

66. In his August 31, 1984, column in the *Jewish Press* Kahane wrote about the need to eliminate the leftist leaders of Israel (Yossi Sarid, Shulamit Aloni, and others) who destroy the nation from within, but this was the only time he ever advocated the killing of Jews.

67. Cf. Yair Kotler, *Heil Kahane,* pp. 153–54.

68. Rabbi Meir Kahane, *The Challenge,* pp. 49–57.

69. Rabbi Meir Kahane, *Thorns in Your Eyes,* Ch. 11.

70. See Kahane's draft bill in Yair Kotler, *Heil Kahane,* pp. 412–20.

71. This was another of Kahane's rhetorical gimmicks. His entourage also liked to spread the story (unchecked), that a Tel Aviv wedding ceremony was left with no waiters upon the arrival of Rabbi Kahane. The waiters, who happened to be Arabs, were so scared of the rabbi that they simply ran away.

72. Rabbi Meir Kahane, *Uncomfortable Questions,* p. 265.

73. For a concise presentation of the essential elements of the classical fascist ideology see Ze'ev Sternhel, "Fascist Ideology," in Walter Laqueur, *Fascism: A Reader's Guide* (Berkeley, University of California Press, 1976).

74. In my first Kahane study in 1973, I advanced the hypothesis that Kahane was "a headlines politician," for he desperately needed publicity in order to be recognized. Cf. Ehud Sprinzak, *The Origins of the Politics of Delegitimation 1967–1972* (Jerusalem, Levi Eshkol Institute, 1973—Hebrew), p. 28. Kahane himself gave a somewhat similar explanation for his symbolic violence by saying that the use of violence was helpful in focusing the attention of the Jewish establishment on issues he thought were important. Cf. Rabbi Meir Kahane, "Violence as a Political Logic" in *Writings 5732–5733* (Jerusalem, Jewish Identity Center, 1973), pp. 190–94.

75. Author's interview with Kahane, June 7, 1988.

76. Cf. Rabbi Meir Kahane, *The Story of the Jewish Defense League,* pp. 278–79; Janet L. Dolgin, *Jewish Identity and the JDL* (Princeton, Princeton University Press, 1977), Ch. 3.

77. Cf. Robert I. Friedman, *The False Messiah,* pp. 121–28; for Kahane's own account of this strange association see Rabbi Meir Kahane, *ibid.,* pp. 185–91.

78. Cf. *Ibid.,* pp. 142–43. Kahane never bothered to apologize for the killing of the innocent secretary. Instead he complained in his book on the JDL about the refusal of the Jewish establishment to bail out the three JDL youngsters accused of "Jewish political crime." Rabbi Meir Kahane, *The Story of the Jewish Defense League,* p. 191.

79. *Ibid.,* pp. 141–42.

80. *Ibid.,* pp. 75–80.

81. Cf. Rabbi Meir Kahane, "Hillul Hashem," p. 3; *Listen World, Listen Jew,* pp. 88–89; *From the Knesset Stand,* p. 11.

82. Rabbi Meir Kahane, *The Jewish Idea,* p. 14.

83. Rabbi Meir Kahane, *Hillul Hashem,* p. 3.

84. Since May 1975 the initials T.N.T. had occasionally surfaced following mysterious attacks on Arab institutions in Jerusalem. A small group that called itself T.N.T. was arrested in 1975 after setting two Arab buses on fire. Cf. *Yediot Achronot,* June 18, 1975. Threat letters sent to Arab leaders were also signed by T.N.T. In December 1983 there was another series of sabotage acts in Jerusalem associated with T.N.T. Cf. Yakir Tzur, "Military Background, Expertise in Sabotage and Extremist Ideology," *Kol Hair,* December 16, 1983. See also Robert I. Friedman, *The False Messiah,* pp. 241–42.

85. Quoted in Yair Kotler, *Heil Kahane,* p. 257.

86. Quoted in Nadav Shragai, "Going for the Action," *Ha'aretz,* November 27, 1984.

87. Quoted in Haim Shibi, "Wherever There Is Blood Spilled You Find Kahane," *Yediot Achronot,* August 2, 1985.

88. Yair Avituv, "All Is Well in the Kasba," *Kol Hair,* August 12, 1988.

89. Rabbi Meir Kahane, *The Jewish Idea,* p. 13.

90. Kach's leaflet, n.d.

91. Cf. Yair Kotler, *Heil Kahane,* pp. 16–23.

92. *Ibid.,* pp. 292–96.

93. Quoted in Orit Shohat, "Don't Ask Me How," *Ha'aretz Magazine,* May 31, 1985, p. 5.

94. Cf. Rabbi Meir Kahane, *Never Again* (New York, Pyramid Books, 1971), Ch. 3; *Why Be Jewish* (Miami Beach, Copy Service Inc. 1977), Chs. 6–7.

95. Rabbi Meir Kahane, *Uncomfortable Questions for Comfortable Jews,* Ch. 2.

96. *Ibid.,* Ch. 15.

97. Cf. Karl Mannheim, *Ideology and Utopia* (New York, Harvest Book, n.d.), pp. 265–66.

98. Rabbi Meir Kahane, *The Challenge,* p. 144.

99. Author's interview with Kahane, April 18, 1973.

100. Author's trip with Kahane June, 12, 1988.

101. *Ibid.* Kahane was especially aware of his audience's remaining admiration for Menachem Begin. He consequently never criticized Begin directly, but said something like: "Begin was a great man. It is a pity he got into politics at such an advanced age."

102. Author's interview with Yoel Lerner, December 27, 1984.

103. Author's interview with Kahane, April 18, 1973.

104. Yai Kotler, *Heil Kahane,* p. 141.

105. Rabbi Meir Kahane, *Thorns in Your Eyes,* pp. 88–91.

106. Quoted in Lili Galilee, "The Great Dictator."

107. *Ibid.*

108. Cf. "Moshe Neiman vs. the Chairman of the Central Elections Committee for the 11th Knesset," *Verdicts* Vol. 39, Part II, 1985/1986.

109. Cf. "Amendment to the Fundamental Law: the Knesset," *Law Book,* 1155, 1985, p. 196.

110. Cf. *From the Knesset Stand: The Knesset Speeches of Knesset Member Rabbi Meir Kahane in the 11th Knesset* (Jerusalem, Kach Movement, n.d.).

111. The resolution was challenged by Kahane in the Supreme Court on the ground of the authority's violation of the freedom of speech principle. Kahane won his case but continued to receive very little coverage.

112. Author's interview with Kahane, June 7, 1988.

113. The systematic national polls that were conducted prior to the 1988 elections did not give Kach more than 1.5 to 2% of the vote. But *Hadashot,* the only Israeli newspaper that followed Kach very closely through special street polls it conducted since June 1988, thought that Kach could get as many as 4 to 5%. Cf. Rino Tzror, "Go Fight the Wind," *Hadashot,* October 21, 1988. This was also the impression of Al Hamishmar correspondent Gabi Bashan, who spent several pre-election months as a "volunteer driver" in Kach. Cf. Gabi Bashan, "Give Him the

Power," *Hotam* (Al Hamishmar Weekly), October 28, 1988. This was also my own assessment.

114. This was the theme of several public talks Kahane gave immediately after Kach's disqualification. He repeated it in an interview with me on January 18, 1989, arguing that the government's inability to handle the *intifada* would destroy its authority and bring it down. He further predicted that in the not so far future he would be called upon to save the nation.

115. I personally attended the convention.

116. On the zealous past of Ben-Horin and his complex relations with Gush Emunim and Kahane see Haggai Segal, "The Prophet of the State of Judea," *Hadashot,* January 13, 1980; Uriel Ben-Ami, "What Does He Do for the Nation," *Yerushalaim,* January 13, 1989.

117. Most of the leaders of Gush Emunim were aware of the fact that the Independent State of Judea was launched by Kach. Being always reluctant to cooperate with Kahane and his public relations gimmicks, they dismissed the idea as a farce. Those who addressed the issue substantially, like Rabbi Levinger, argued that no act aimed at reducing the legitimacy of the State of Israel was acceptable to them. Cf. Haggai Segal, "The Prophet of the State of Judea."

118. I interviewed Kahane immediately following the termination of the ceremony. Although he tried to underplay the significance of the debate over his direct association with the new state, it was clear to me that he was determined to dissociate himself from it.

119. Cf. Yiga'al Sarna, "The Sicarii: A New Jewish Underground?," *Yediot Achronot Magazine,* March 24, 1989.

120. Avigdor Eskin, "I Am from the Sikarikin: An Exclusive Interview," *Erev Hadash,* March 31, 1989.

121. Cf. David C. Rapoport, "Terror and the Messiah: An Ancient Experience and Modern Parallels," in David C. Rapoport and Yona Alexander, *The Morality of Terrorism* (New York, Pergamon Press, 1982).

122. Journalist Ronit Vardi who interviewed several Kach members on the Sikarikin, and then spoke to Rabbi Kahane, found a gap in the positions of her interviewees. While Kahane said the acts of the Sikarikin were childish and were laid at the wrong door (the right one being that of the Arabs), there was much excitement among the activists of Kach. Kahane spoke a great deal about his yeshiva and the "future leaders of Israel" that were being brought up there, under his direct supervision. And he reaffirmed his confidence that the nation was about to turn to him. "I know that the future is mine. The nation knows already that the Ma'arach (Labor party) is a dead horse and they are about to reach the same conclusion about the Likud. Then, there will only be Kahane. They are bound to get despaired. The Son of David cannot come until people get despaired." Cf. Ronit Vardi, "Kahane on the Sikarikim: Fools, Stupidity, Stupidity," *Yediot Achronot,* April 21, 1989.

Chapter 8

1. Most of Etzion's theoretical essays have been developed out of the intense correspondence he conducted from his prison cell. Upon his release from jail he had seven large files that included a correspondence with about forty to fifty people. Interview with Yehuda Etzion, February 19, 1989.

2. Interview with Yehuda Etzion, Tel-Mond Prison, September 9, 1985.

3. Hava Pinchas-Cohen, "The Wife of Prisoner No. 2," *Nekuda*, No. 74 (June 21, 1984), p. 12. For a good profile of Etzion see Nadav Shragai, "A Monarchist," *Ha'aretz Weekly,* June 1984.

4. Interview with Yehuda Etzion, Tel Mond Prison, September 11, 1985.

5. Cf. a typical Greenberg poem:

> Your masters taught: a country is bought for money. . . .
> And I say: a country is conquered in blood.
> And only that which is conquered in blood, becomes sacred for the
>   nation,
> the sanctity of blood. . . .
> Your masters taught: the Messiah will arrive in the coming generations
> and Judea will rise without fire or blood.
> She will rise with every tree, with each additional house.
> And I say: If your generation slows down
> and does not push the end with both its hands and feet
> and does not come in fire with a shield of David
> and its horses' knee joints do not show blood—
> then, the Messiah would not come even in a later generation, then
>   Judea will not rise . . .
> And that will be the day when from the River of Egypt to the Euphra-
>   tes
> from the sea to Trans Moav my boys will emerge
> and challenge my enemies to the last battle.
> And the blood will determine: who is the sole ruler here.
>
> (Author's translation)

Uri Tzi Greenberg, "One, One and Not Two," *The Book of the Denunciation and the Belief* (Jerusalem, Sadan Publishers, 1937—Hebrew), pp. 163–64.

6. Cf. Shabtai Ben Dov, "What Is To Be Done," in *Prophesy and Tradition in the Redemption* (Tel Aviv, Yair Publications, 1979—Hebrew), pp. 190–211; interview with Etzion, September 9, 1985; see also Arie Bender and Avinoam Ben Yosef, "The Prophet Shabtai," *The Ma'ariv Weekend,* July 26, 1984.

7. Cf. Shabtai Ben-Dov, *After the Six Day War: From the Six Day Victory On* (Ofra, Hamidrasha Beeretz Binyamin, 1979—Hebrew); Bender and Ben Yosef, "The Prophet Shabtai."

8. Cf. Shabtai Ben Dov, *The Redemption of Israel in the Crisis of the State* (Jerusalem, Hamatmid, 1956).

9. Cf. Bender and Ben-Yosef, "The Prophet Shabtai."

10. Interview with Yehuda Etzion, September 9, 1985.

11. Quoted in Haggai Segal, *Dear Brothers* (Jerusalem, Keter, 1987—Hebrew), p. 51.

12. Yehuda Etzion, "From the Flag of Jerusalem to the Redemption Movement," *Nekuda*, 94 (December 20, 1985), p. 28.

13. *Ibid.,* p. 22.

14. Yehuda Etzion, *The Temple Mount* (Jerusalem, E. Caspi, 1985—Hebrew), p. 2.

15. *Ibid.,* p. 5; see also Etzion's confession no. 27, Court Documents, May 13,

1984; Yehuda Etzion, "I Felt I Had to Prepare an Operation to Expurgate the Temple Mount," *Nekuda*, No. 88 (June 22, 1985).

16. Yehuda Etzion, "From the Laws of Existence to the Laws of Destiny," *Nekuda*, No. 75 (July 6, 1984), p. 26.

17. Cf. Haggai Segal, *Dear Brothers*, pp. 52–54.

18. Interview with Yehuda Etzion, September 11, 1985.

19. *Ibid*.

20. Interview with Yehuda Etzion, September 9, 1985; cf. Yehuda Etzion, "To Fly, At Last, The Flag of Jerusalem," *Nekuda* No. 93 (November 22, 1985).

21. Interview with Yehuda Etzion, February 19, 1989.

22. Yehuda Etzion, "On The Potter's Wheel" in Israel Ariel, Moshe Asher, Yoel Rakovsky, Amishar Segal (eds.), *Tzfia* Vol. 3 (Jerusalem, 1988—Hebrew), pp. 353–55.

23. *Ibid.*, pp. 355–56.

24. *Ibid.*, p. 357.

25. *Ibid.*, p. 359. When I tried to verify my interpretation of the paragraph with Etzion, he said that the Redemption Movement would be sovereign in all its decisions and actions and, unlike the Jewish Underground, would seek no rabbinical approval for even its most extreme operations. Responding to my question about another possible Etzion operation on the Temple Mount, he said that he would never again act alone: "Any operation would have to be first approved by the Redemption Movement." Interview with Yehuda Etzion, February 19, 1989.

26. Etzion says he is determined to establish the Redemption Movement and dedicate his life to this project, no matter how long it takes. The creation of a youth movement and the publication of a journal are his immediate goals. However, being short of money and institutional support he has been unable to reach these immediate goals and instead has spent all his time meeting potential supporters and giving talks. When I pointed out to him his meager success suggested that God perhaps might not approve of his approach, Etzion said that he alone was responsible for the lack of success. This man, whose immense idealism and dedication to the cause has led him to refuse to apologize for his deeds and be eligible for a pardon, and whose family life has greatly suffered from his uphill struggles, is the most devoted individual to a cause I have ever met. Characteristicly, Etzion said, "I feel I am not doing enough. If the Redemption Movement is not taking off it is because of me. I simply should work harder." Interview with Etzion, February 19, 1989.

27. Following this split within Laor, the organization was taken over by Gush Emunim.

28. Interview with Ephraim Caspi, July 16, 1985.

29. On Segal's early activism see David Niv, *Battle for Freedom: The Irgun Zvai Leumi*, Part I (Tel Aviv, Klausner Institute, 1975—Hebrew), pp. 180–82.

30. Ronit Vardi and Roni Shaked, "The Temple Mount: Messiah Now," *Yediot Achronot*, June 5, 1987.

31. Cf. Haggai Segal, *Dear Brothers*, pp. 131–33.

32. Interview with Rabbi Israel Ariel, January 31, 1985. When I asked Ariel, in 1989, to recollect his memories about the struggle in Yamit he responded angrily, saying "A struggle? This was not a struggle. People talked, prayed, demonstrated, made a lot of noise, convinced themselves that they were struggling, but they were not. A struggle takes place when a man is ready to fight for what he believes in, and is

prepared to die for it. This is a real struggle." Interview with Rabbi Ariel, February 27, 1989.

33. Israel Ariel, *Atlas of the Land of Israel: Its Boundaries According to the Sources,* Vol. 1 (Jerusalem, Cana Publishing House, 1988—Hebrew), p. 13.

34. Ronit Vardi and Roni Shaked, "The Temple Mount: Messiah Now."

35. One of the unpublicized dimensions of the Jewish–Muslim conflict in Jerusalem has been the struggle to control the area near the Temple Mount. Two Jewish associations, *Atara Leyoshna* and *Atteret Cohanim,* have been involved in recent years in the secret purchase of property in the Muslim Quarter of Jerusalem in order to create a Jewish presence around the holy place. The operation of both bodies, which have included the identification of old Jewish property in the Muslim Quarter and the purchase of Arab buildings, had been conducted in utmost secrecy for fear that the Arabs sellers involved would be executed by the PLO for treason. It has also been conducted against the official policy of the government of Israel and the City of Jerusalem, which is to prevent unnecessary friction between Jews and Arabs in the Old City. Several synagogues and yeshivas have consequently been established in the Muslim Quarter of Jerusalem. Minister Ariel Sharon also moved to the area in 1987, as a symbolic gesture of his support of the struggle for Old Jerusalem. An even more secret aspect of this struggle has been the involvement of Christian fundamentalists. Several Christian groups and individuals, who believe that the Second Coming of Christ will be preceded by a complete Jewish return to the Temple Mount, have supported for years the Jewish purchase of property in the Old City. A strange alliance of Jewish and Christian fundamentalists has emerged out of these efforts. Cf. David Oren, "Lunatics," *Ha'aretz Magazine,* November 11, 1985; Nadav Shragai, "Judaising the Muslim Quarter," *Ha'aretz,* November 11, 1988; Robert I. Friedman, "Terror On Sacred Ground: The Battle for the Temple Mount," *Mother Jones,* August–September 1987. All these reports have been verified for me by Yoel Lerner. Interview, February 15, 1989.

36. Cf. Moshe Asher, "The Temple Mount Is Turned into a Forest," *Tzfia* I, 1985.

37. On the perspective of the ultraorthodox vis-à-vis the State of Israel and the coming of the Messiah see Aviezer Ravitzky "The Expected and the Possible: Messianism, Zionism, and the Future of Israel as Reflected in the Divided Religious Opinions in Israel," in Alouph Hareven (ed.), *Towards the 21st Century: Targets For Israel* (Jerusalem, Van-Leer, 1984).

38. Cf. Rabbi Shlomo Aviner, "Two Talks with Rabbi Tzvi Tau," in Rabbi Shlomo Aviner (ed.), *Iturei Cohanim* (the journal of Yeshivat Ateret Cohanim), No. 3, 1983.

39. Shlomo Aviner, "We Shall Not Climb Up the Mountain," in *Iturei Cohanim,* No. 3, p. 29.

40. Interview with Rabbi Dov Lior, January 19, 1985.

41. Cf. Rabbi Dan Be'eri, "A Temple and A State," *Tzfia* I, 1985.

42. Interview with Rabbi Israel Ariel, January 31, 1985.

43. Rabbi Israel Ariel, "When Shall the Temple Be Built?," *Tzfia* II, 1985.

44. Interview with Rabbi Israel Ariel, January 31, 1985.

45. Rabbi Israel Ariel, "When Shall the Temple Be Built," p. 61.

46. *Ibid.,* p. 62.

47. Ronit Vardi and Roni Shaked, "The Temple Mount: Messiah Now."

48. Interview with Yehuda Etzion, September 11, 1985.

49. Rabbi Moshe Segal, "We Have Had Enough of the Brotherhood of Mankind," *Tzfia* I, 1985.

50. Rabbi Israel Ariel, "Things as They Really Are," *Tzfia* I, 1985, p. 31.

51. *Ibid.*, pp. 34–36.

52. Interview with Rabbi Kahane, June 7, 1988.

53. Interview with Rabbi Israel Ariel, January 31, 1985.

54. *Ibid.*

55. Rabbi Israel Ariel, *This Good Mountain and the Lebanon* (A Gush Emunim Booklet, 1982—Hebrew), pp. 31–32.

56. Interview with Rabbi Israel Ariel, January 31, 1985; Cf. Ariel's introduction in *Tzfia* II, pp. 6–8.

57. Rabbi David Bar-Haim, "Israel Is Called 'Adam'," in Israel Ariel, Moshe Asher, Yoel Rakovsky, Amishar Segal (eds.), *Tzfia* Vol. 3 (Jerusalem, 1988—Hebrew), p. 45.

58. Rabbi Moshe Segal, "The Land, the People and the Torah," *ibid.*, pp. 121–22.

59. Rabbi Binyamin Tzvielli, "Democracy and Its Corruption vis-à-vis Eternal Judaism," *ibid.*, pp. 105–109.

60. Rabbi David Bar-Haim, "Israel Are Called 'Adam'," *ibid.*, p. 61.

61. *Ibid.*, pp. 72–73.

62. Rabbi Israel Ariel, "Israel: One Nation in the Land," *ibid.*, pp. 218–22.

63. For a detailed description of these activists see Yair Kotler, *Heil Kahane* (Tel Aviv, Modan, 1985—Hebrew), Chs. 20, 28, 29.

64. Interview with Avigdor Eskin, February 13, 1985.

65. Cf. Yair Kotler, *Heil Kahane*, pp. 260–63.

66. Meeting with Avigdor Eskin, October 3, 1988. Given their insensitivity to the issue of racism it is not surprising that several former colleagues of Kahane are highly supportive of South Africa and of the South-African–Israeli connection. According to Yoel Lerner, for example, Israel should try to dissociate itself from the United States and create with South Africa an alliance of independent small states which can help themselves and avoid the pressure of the large powers. Cf. Yoel Lerner, "Israel-Republic of South Africa Relations" (Mimeograph).

67. Cf. Yair Kotler, *Heil Kahane*, Ch. 21.

68. *Ibid.*, pp. 182–84.

69. *Ibid.*, pp. 184–86.

70. Lerner's account of the Gal underground, as he gave it to me in 1989, sounded very strange, ambitious, and fantastic. It could not be confirmed by any other source. According to him, Gal was a serious underground with a real chance of overthrowing the Israeli government. It was first organized in 1975, against the Rabin administration. The weakness of the new government, which triggered the idea of the underground, was expressed in the concessions Israel made to Egypt and Syria in the Interim Agreements and in its inability to boost the nation's low morale nearly three years after the debacle of the Yom Kippur War. The underground existed until the 1978 arrest of Lerner, and supposedly had in its ranks some prominent Israeli officials—whom Lerner refused to identify. According to Lerner, he was more a coordinator than a leader, and had he been arrested just four months later, his services would have no longer been needed and other individuals could have taken over. The operational plan of Gal was to conduct a series of fourteen sabotage

acts, each growing in intensity, at the end of which the government of Israel was expected to collapse. The plan to blow up the mosques on the Temple Mount, for which Lerner was arrested, was supposed to be the thirteenth act in the series. Other acts, which he refused to specify, were to bring about the triggering of massive strikes and the paralyzing of the Israeli economy. Lerner says that public opinion studies conducted for the group, as well as other assessments, gave them a 70 percent probability of success which included their chances of convincing the army and the secret services to follow them. After the election of Menachem Begin, the plan was temporarily suspended to give the new Prime Minister the opportunity to lead the nation in the right direction. But following the Begin-Sadat encounter, preparations were resumed. The plan, Lerner says, was to suspend the Knesset and establish an emergency religious regime in Israel. It was expected to be tested in the polls within two years. Interview with Yoel Lerner, February 15, 1989.

71. *Ibid.;* cf. Nadav Shragai, "Yoel Lerner, The Man Who Established Gal, Tells Its Story," *Ha'aretz,* May 11, 1984.

72. Etzion's reaction to Lerner's proposition, of which I informed him in our meeting, was that during the preparatory stages of the Temple Mount plot he sent Yeshua Ben Shoshan to get the blessing of Rabbi Tzvi Yehuda Kook, and that while Kook did not say "no," his response was very vague. Interview with Yehuda Etzion, February 19, 1989. For a description of the Ben Shoshan-Kook meeting see Haggai Segal, *Dear Brothers,* p. 56.

73. Cf. Yair Kotler, *Heil Kahane,* p. 192.

74. Interview with Yoel Lerner, December 27, 1984.

75. Interview with Yoel Lerner, February 15, 1989.

76. When I told Lerner I thought that deep in his soul he has been anarchist all along, he said he did not think so but that a judge in one of his many trials had once said the same thing about him. Interview with Yoel Lerner, February 1, 1989.

77. Cf. Gidi Frishtic, *Takdim,* Vol. 1, Spring 1988.

78. Interview with Yoel Lerner, February 1, 1989.

79. *Ibid.*

80. *Ibid.*

81. Interview with Yoel Lerner, February 1, 1989.

82. Cf. Moshe Dayan, *Milestones* (Jerusalem, Yediot Achronot edition, 1976—Hebrew), p. 498. Moshe Dayan, it should be mentioned, followed an old Zionist political tradition of not getting involved in the holy Muslim places. Theodor Herzl supported the internationalization of the holy sites. Chaim Weizman was not even interested in the Old City of Jerusalem. And when David Ben-Gurion learned in 1948 about the possibility of a Jewish conquest of the Old City he ordered the commander of Jerusalem to assign a special force to shoot and kill any Jew who tried to rob a holy Muslim or Christian sanctuary. Cf. Amos Elon, "The Builders of the Third Temple," in *A Certain Panic* (Tel Aviv, Am Oved Press, 1988—Hebrew), p. 119.

83. Quoted in Nadav Shragai, "The Mount, the House and the Ghost," *Ha'aretz,* February 3, 1984.

84. *Ibid.*

85. Solomon was educated in Betar, the youth organization of the Revisionist Movement, and served as an officer in the IDF. He was badly wounded during a border clash with the Syrians and has been lame ever since. Following his release from the army he became a member of the Herut directorate. In 1978 he left the

party and was among the founders of the Tehiya. Solomon claims he has a large operation of between 1500 to 2000 people, a magazine, "Towards the Top of the Mountain," and an active youth movement. But there is no indication that more than several dozen participate in most of the Temple Mount activities. Interview with Solomon, February 2, 1985.

86. Bamby Ehrlich, "Construction Workers: An Interview with Gershon Solomon," *Nekuda,* No. 62 (August 13, 1983), pp. 16–17, 21.

87. Rabbi Goren actually wrote his Halakhic ruling in 1976 but refused to publish it for a long time for fear he would stir up an endless controversy and alienate many of his supporters. Only in the mid-1980s was he ready to publicly announce his support for the Temple Mount devotees. Goren's official letter on that matter was sent to Knesset member Dov Shilansky, as a response to a question about the Temple Mount he had addressed to Goren a short time earlier. Cf. Rabbi Shlomo Goren, "The Obligation to Enter the Temple Mount," *Tzfia,* Vol. 3, pp. 5–7.

88. Interview with Gershon Solomon, February 14, 1985.

89. Cf. Menachem Ben Yahsar, "The Temple Mount," *Amudim* 263, January 1968.

90. Interview with Yehuda Etzion, September 9, 1985.

91. For a description of the event see Solomon H. Steckoll, *The Temple Mount* (London, Tom Stacy, 1972), pp. 75–80.

92. Cf. Nadav Shragai, "The Mount, the House and the Spirit."

93. Cf. Report by Asher Kijner, *Ha'aretz,* April 15, 1982.

94. *Ibid.*

95. Cf. David Oren, "Lunatics," *Ha'aretz Weekly,* January 1, 1985.

96. Cf. Ronit Matalon, "It Happens Under The Wailing Wall," *Ha'aretz Weekly,* January 13, 1989.

97. Interview with Rabbi Menachem Fruman, January 15, 1985. It should be noted that while Ateret Kohanim had been established for the special purpose of integrating the study of the Temple rules with the ordinary yeshiva curriculum, similar programs, though of lesser scope, have been adopted by other nationalist yeshivot.

98. Interview with Rabbi Kahane, June 7, 1988.

99. Cf. David Oren, "Lunatics"; Also Rabbi David Elboim, "A King's Palace: and Its Fate," *Tzfia* II.

100. Cf. Report by Asher Kijner, *Ha'aretz,* March 14, 1983.

101. Cf. Gadi Baltiansky, "Terrorism on the Temple Mount," *Kol Yerushalaim,* February 3, 1984.

102. Cf. Nadav Shragai, "The Road From Lifta to the Temple Mount," *Ha'aretz,* March 9, 1984.

103. According to Yehuda Etzion, there was always some Gush Emunim awareness of the anomaly of the Temple Mount. Etzion told me, for example, that the situation on the Temple Mount had attracted his attention already in the early 1970s, when he was a student at Yeshivat Har-Etzion, in Allon Shvut. Both he and his rabbi, Yoel Ben-Nun, were responsible at that time for the production of a famous Temple Mount poster. What was special about the large picture was that the Muslim mosques were erased and their place was taken by a large picture of the Second Temple. This poster was to be found in many Gush Emunim homes in the 1970s. Nevertheless, this symbolic act carried very little substance in the collective consciousness of Gush Emunim, and the issue of the Temple Mount was only dis-

cussed once in the secretariat of the Gush, of which Etzion was a member until 1978. The Temple Mount only reemerged in the Gush thinking, according to Etzion, in Yamit in 1982 when the failure of the Movement to Halt the Retreat in Sinai was apparent. At that time several Gush members discussed the possibility of a violent operation at the holy place. However, this was, according to Etzion, "an instrumental approach. The expurgation of the Temple Mount was not seen as a goal in itself, an essential part of the desired spiritual transformation of the nation, but a means to halt the peace process." Interview with Yehuda Etzion, February 19, 1989.

Following the 1983 discovery of Rabbi Israel Ariel's group and its attempt to penetrate the Temple Mount area, Rabbi Yigal Ariel of Moshav Nov in the Golan Heights, and Israel's brother, published an article about the Temple Mount in *Nekuda*. While not challenging the main Gush Emunim line of leaving the resolution of the Temple Mount anomaly for the future, he strongly attacked the government of Israel. He found no justification for the outrageous situation on the mountain and for the government's respect for the Muslim Waqf. Ariel further suggested a series of steps that could be taken at the present time: an intense study of the Temple's rules to be conducted in and out of Yeshivat Ateret Cohanim, an introduction of the subject to schools and yeshivot, the publication of Rabbi Goren's study of the Temple Mount area, a search for a proper place to establish a synagogue on the mount and to pressure the Minister of Religion to make regulations enabling Jews to pray in certain parts of the holy area. Cf. Rabbi Yigal Ariel, "The Temple Mount as the Property of the Waqf," *Nekuda* No. 58 (May 17, 1983), pp. 18–19.

104. Cf. Moshe Asher, "The Temple Mount Is Turned into a Forest," *Tzfia* I, pp. 17–20.

105. *Ibid.*

106. Cf. Dov Shilansky, *In A Hebrew Prison* (Tel Aviv, Armoni Press, 3rd. edition 1980—Hebrew), pp. 11–31.

107. Cf. *Ha'aretz*, January 17, 1986.

108. The Tehiya party first included the demand to place the Temple Mount under Israeli jurisdiction in its 1988 platform. It vowed, if elected to the government, to stop illegal Muslim building in the area, to cut off the political involvement of the PLO in the religious activities there, and to push for the establishment of a Jewish synagogue in a place permitted by Halakha. However, it stated its commitment to leave the Muslims free access to their mosques. Cf. *Identity Card* (A Tehiya 1988 Election Pamphlet).

109. Quoted in Gadi Baltianski "Is the Temple Mount in Our Hands?," *Yediot Achronot*, August 15, 1986, p. 32.

110. *Ibid.*

111. When I visited the Museum in July 1989, Ariel already had genuine samples of the robes of the Temple's priests and 17 out of the 93 utensils required for the holy service. He has recently started to raise a fund of 1.5 million dollars to create the Temple's Golden *Menora* (candlelight). Also see Itzhak Ya'ari, "A Temple Soon," *Yerushalaim*, April 7, 1988.

112. Interview with Yoel Lerner, February 15, 1989. Cf. Nadav Shragai, "A Study Tour of the Temple Mount," *Ha'aretz*, August 3, 1988.

113. When I asked Yoel Lerner, a highly experienced Temple Mount activist, about a possible sabotage provocation on the Temple Mount as an act of last resort in order to halt an inevitable territorial compromise in the West Bank, he said with a big smile, "at the advice of my lawyer I have not heard your question." He later

admitted he could not rule such an act out, although he had no concrete plans. Interview with Yoel Lerner, February 15, 1989. Yehuda Etzion's response was even milder. He has ruled out such an operation almost completely, saying he no longer believes that a single act could bring the people of Israel closer to redemption. In fact, he said, he was opposed to an instrumental use of the Temple Mount in the service of politics, saying, "The question of redemption is spiritual, not political. Our need is not simply to blow up the Muslim Mosques, but to make the people of Israel spiritually worthy of such a development. I was wrong in 1978 when I believed in such a short cut." But even if such a violent act would become mandatory, Etzion confided it would only be approved by the Redemption Movement. Since this movement has not yet come into being, he said, he will do nothing on his own even at a time of crisis. Interview with Yehuda Etzion, February 19, 1989.

Chapter 9

1. This argument has been especially made in relation to Gush Emunim; cf. Amnon Rubinstein, *From Herzl to Gush Emunim* (Jerusalem, Shoken, 1980— Hebrew), pp. 117–20; Zvi Ra'anan, *Gush Emunim* (Tel Aviv, Sifriyat Poalim, 1980—Hebrew), Ch. 4; Y. Harkabi, *Fateful Decisions* (Tel Aviv, Am Oved, 1986— Hebrew), pp. 205–10.

2. On the dilemmas presented to orthodox Jews by the State of Israel see Zalman Abramov, *Perpetual Dilemma: Jewish Religion in the Jewish State* (Rutherford, N.J., Fairleigh Dickinson Press, 1976); Menachem Friedman, *The State of Israel as a Theological Dilemma*, in Baruch Kimmerling (ed.), *The Israeli State and Society: Boundaries and Frontiers* (Buffalo, SUNY Press, 1989).

3. Rabbi Meir Kahane, *Thorns in Your Eyes* (New York, Druker Publishing Co. 1981—Hebrew), pp. 126–27.

4. Cf. Asher Cohen, " 'Going Together'—the Religious-Seculer Relationship in a Mixed Party," in Charles S. Liebman, *To Live Together: Religious and Secular in Israeli Society* (Jerusalem, Keter, 1990).

5. Cf. Benny Morris, *The Birth of the Palestinian Refugee Problem, 1947– 1949* (Cambridge, Cambridge University Press), pp. 134–37.

6. On the internal reaction to the creation of the Arab refugee problem among Israel's top leaders see Tom Segev, *1949: The First Israelis* (Jerusalem, Domino, 1984—Hebrew), pp. 39–47.

7. On the personality of Rabbi Zvi Yehuda Kook, his relation to his father, and his interpretation of the grand philosophy see Gideon Aran, *From Religious Zionism to Zionist Religion: The Roots of Gush Emunim and Its Culture* (Unpublished Ph.D. dissertation, The Hebrew University of Jerusalem, 1987—Hebrew), Ch. 3.

8. Cf., for example, Rabbi Meir Kahane, *Never Again: A Program for Jewish Survival* (New York, Pyramid Books, 1972), Ch. 8; *Listen World Listen Jew* (Jerusalem, The Institute of the Jewish Idea, 1983), Ch. 8.

9. Cf. Joseph Heller, *Lehi: Ideology and Politics, 1940–1949* (Jerusalem, Keter, 1989), Vol. II.

10. David Ben-Gurion used Palmach units in the two major military conflicts that took place in the 1940s between Etzel and the organized yishuv, the *Saison*, (1944–1945), and the *Altalena Affair* (1948). Cf. Shlomo Nakdimon, *Altalena* (Tel Aviv, Edanim, 1978).

11. Cf. Yonathan Shapiro, *Chosen to Command* (Tel Aviv, Am Oved, 1989) 122–28.

12. Cf. Giora Goldberg, "The Struggle for Legitimacy: Herut's Road from Opposition to Power" in Stuart A. Cohen and Eliezer Don-Yehiya, *Conflict and Consensus in Jewish Political Life* (Jerusalem, Bar-Ilan University Press, 1986—Hebrew); David Nachmias, "The Right-Wing Opposition in Israel," *Political Studies,* Vol. 24, No. 3 (September 1976).

13. Cf. Moshe Dayan, *Shall the Sword Devour Forever?* (Jerusalem, Edanim, 1981—Hebrew), Ch. 17; Ezer Weizman, *The Battle for Peace* (Jerusalem, Edanim, 1981—Hebrew), Ch. 29.

14. Cf. Pinchas Inbari, *Triangle on the Jordan* (Jerusalem, Cana, 1982—Hebrew).

15. Cf. Yuval Ne'eman, "To Conquer Southern Lebanon," *Yediot Achronot,* July 31, 1981.

16. Cf. Yoav Peled, "Labor Market Segmentation and Ethnic Conflicts: The Social Bases of Right Wing Politics in Israel" (paper presented at the Annual Meeting of the American Political Science Association, Atlanta, September 2, 1989). This is also based on my talks with many of Kahane's supporters.

17. This is based on my estimation that Kach was likely to get between three to five seats in the 1988 Knesset. The Tehiya, Moledet, and Tzomet currently have seven seats, and two of the N.R.P representatives, Hanan Porat and Avner Shaki, are radical right by any standards. An addition of the Likud and Shas radicals would have made this number much higher.

18. Cf. Ian Lustick, "The West Bank and Gaza in Israeli Politics," in Steven Heydemann (ed.), *The Begin Era* (Boulder, Westview, 1984).

19. Cf. Meron Bevenisti, private communication with the author.

20. Cf. "To Crush the Intifada," *A Tehiya Elections Pamphlet 1988.*

21. Interview with Geula Cohen, March 27, 1989.

22. Cf. Asher Arian and Raphael Ventura, "Public Opinion in Israel and the Intifada: Changes in Attitudes About Security, 1987–1988," Memo. No. 23, August 1989 (Jaffe Center of Strategic Studies, Tel Aviv University).

23. This assessment is based on dozens of interviews with members of the radical right I conducted in the last five years.

24. I have no knowledge of any conspiratorial plans to violently subvert a possible territorial compromise in the occupied territories. This is therefore a "probabilistic" statement based on my "sociological" expectation that an intense extraparliamentary struggle against a territorial compromise and Israeli evacuation of the West Bank, which is *promised* even by the modrate radicals, would necessarily lead to the extremization of a small number of activists and the introduction of violence. Given the narrow and partial legitimacy accorded by many of the settlers to Israeli democracy, their religious commitment to the greater Eretz Yisrael and the large quantities of firearms they posses, the evolution of at least local violent confrontations seems almost inevitable.

Bibliography

English

Gilbert Abcarian and Sherman M. Stanage, "Alienation and the Radical Right," in James A. Gould and Willis H. Truitt, *Political Ideologies* (New York, Macmillan, 1973).

Zalman Abramov, *Perpetual Dilemma: Jewish Religion in the Jewish State* (Rutherford, N.J., Fairleigh Dickinson Press, 1976).

Majid Al-Haj and Avner Yaniv, "Uniformity or Diversity: A Reappraisal of the Voting Behavior of the Arab Minority in Israel," in Asher Arian (ed.), *Elections in Israel 1981* (Tel Aviv, Ramot Publishing Co., 1983).

Gideon Aran, "From Religious Zionism to Zionist Religion: The Roots of Gush Emunim," in Peter Medding (ed.), *Studies in Contemporary Jewry* (New York, Oxford University Press, 1986) Vol. II.

Asher Arian, *Politics in Israel: The Second Generation,* (Chatam, Chatam House, 1985).

――――, "Elections 1981: Competitiveness and Polarization," *The Jerusalem Quarterly,* No. 21, Fall 1981.

――――(ed.), *Elections in Israel 1981* (Tel Aviv, Ramot Publishing Co., 1983).

Asher Arian and Michal Shamir (eds.), *The Elections in Israel 1984* (Tel Aviv, Ramot, 1986).

Yuval Arnon-Ohana and Arie Yodfat, *PLO Strategy and Politics* (London, Croom Helm, 1982).

Myron Aronoff, *Power and Ritual in the Israeli Labor Party* (Assen, Van Gorcum, 1977).

――――(ed.), *Religion and Politics: Political Anthropology* Vol. 3 (New Brunswick, Transaction Books, 1984).

――――(ed.), *Cross-Currents in Israeli Culture and Politics* (New Brunswick, Transaction Books, 1984).

――――(ed.), *The Frailty of Authority* (New Brunswick, Political Anthropology, Vol. V, Transaction Books, 1986).

――――, "The Institutionalization and Cooptation of a Charismatic, Messianic, Religious-Political Revitalization Movement," in David Newman (ed.), *The Impact of Gush Emunim* (London, Croom Helm, 1985).

————, "Political Polarization: Contradictory Interpretations of Israeli Reality," in Steven Heydemann, *The Begin Era* (Boulder, Westview, 1984).

Shlomo Aronson, *Conflict and Bargaining in the Middle East: An Israeli Perspective* (Baltimore, The John Hopkins University Press, 1978).

Edward E. Azar and Chung-in Moon, "Islamic Revivalist Movements: Patterns, Causes and Prospect," *Journal of East and West Studies*, Vol. XII, No. 1, Spring–Summer 1983.

Robert Bellah and Philip Hammond, *Varieties of Civil Religion* (New York, Harper and Row, 1980).

Marver H. Bernstein, *The Politics of Israel: The First Decade of Statehood* (Princeton, Princeton University Press, 1957).

J. Bowyer Bell, *The Secret Army: The IRA 1916–1974* (Cambridge, MIT University Press, 1974).

————, *Terror Out of Zion: The Irgun, Lehi, Stern and the Palestine Underground* (New York, St. Martin's Press, 1977).

Daniel Bell (ed.), *The Radical Right* (New York, Doubleday, 1963).

Meron Benvenisti, *The West Bank Data Project* (Washington, D.C, American Enterprise Institute, 1984).

————, *1986 Report: Demographic, Economic, Legal, Social and Political Developments in the West Bank* (Jerusalem, The Jerusalem Post Press, 1986).

————, *1987 Report: Demographic, Economic, Legal, Social and Political Developments in the West Bank* (Jerusalem, The Jerusalem Post Press, 1987).

Peter Berger, *Sacred Canopy: Elements of a Sociological Theory of Religion* (New York, Doubleday, 1967).

————, *The Heretical Imperative* (New York, Doubleday, 1980).

M. Billig, *Fascists: A Social Psychological View of the National Front* (London, Harcourt Brace Jovanovich, 1978).

Ruth Bondy, Ohad Zmora, and Raphael Bashan (eds), *Mission Survival: The People of Israel's Story in Their Own Words, from the Threat of Annihilation to Miraculous Victory* (New York, Sabra Books, 1968).

S.G.F. Brandon, *Jesus and the Zealots* (Manchester, Manchester University Press, 1967).

Richard Maxwell Brown, "The American Vigilante Tradition," in Hugh Graham and Ted R. Gurr (eds.), *Violence in America* (New York, Signet Books, 1969).

————, "Legal and Behavioral Perspectives on American Vigilantism," *Perspectives in American History*, No. 5, 1971.

Dan Caspi, A. Diskin, and E. Guttman (eds.), *The Roots of Begin's Success* (London, Croom-Helm, 1984).

Michael J. Cohen, *Palestine and the Great Powers, 1945–1948* (Princeton, Princeton University Press, 1982).

Norman Cohn, *The Pursuit of the Millenium*, rev. ed. (New York, Oxford University Press, 1970).

Gerald Cromer, "The Debate About Kahanism In Israeli Society 1984–1988," *Occasional Papers* (New York, The Harry Frank Guggenheim Foundation, 1988).

Janet Dolgin, *Jewish Identity and the JDL* (Princeton, Princeton University Press, 1977).

Peter Robert Demant, *Ploughshares into Swords: Israeli Settlement Policy in the Occupied Territories, 1967–1977* (Unpublished Ph.D Dissertation, submitted to the University of Amsterdam, 1988).

Eliezer Don-Yehiya, "Jewish Messianism, Religious Zionism and Israeli Politics: The Impact and Origins of Gush Emunim," *Middle Eastern Studies,* Vol. 23, No.2, April 1987.

Mary Douglas, "The Effects of Modernization on Religious Change," *Daedalus,* Vol. III, No.1, Winter 1982.

Harry Eckstein (ed.), *Internal War* (New York, The Free Press of Glencoe, 1964).

Daniel Elazar and Janet Aviad, "Religion and Politics in Israel," in Michael Curtis (ed.), *Religion and Politics in the Middle East* (Westview Press, 1981).

Amos Elon, *The Israelis: Fathers and Sons* (London, Weidenfeld & Nicolson, 1971).

Itzhak Engelhard, "Law and Religion in Israel," *American Journal of Comparative Law,* Vol. 35, No.1, Winter 1987.

Benjamin Epstein and Arnold Forster, *Radical Right: Report on the John Birch Society and Allies* (New York, Random House, 1967).

Eva Etzioni-Halevy with Rina Shapiro, *Political Culture in Israel* (New York, Praeger, 1977).

Ghazi Falah, "Recent Jewish Colonization in Hebron," in David Newman (ed.), *The Impact of Gush Emunim: Politics and Settlement in the West Bank* (London, Croom Helm, 1985).

Franz Fanon, *The Wretched of the Earth* (New York, Grove Press, 1966).

W. R. Farmer, *Macabees, Zealots and Josephus* (New York, Columbia University Press, 1956).

Leonard Fein, *Israel: Politics and People* (Boston, Little Brown, 1968).

Harold Fish, *The Zionist Revolution: A New Perspective* (London, Weidenfeld & Nicolson, 1978).

Robert O. Freedman, *Israel in the Begin Era* (New York, Praeger, 1982).

G. P. Freeman, *Immigrant Labor and Racial Conflict in Industrial Societies: The French and the British Experience, 1945–1975* (Princeton, Princeton University Press, 1979).

Menachem Friedman, "Religious Zealotry in Israeli Society," in S. Poll and E. Krauz (eds.), *On Ethnic and Religious Diversity in Israel* (Tel Aviv, Bar-Ilan University Press, 1975).

——, *The State of Israel as a Theological Dilemma,* in Baruch Kimmerling (ed)., *The Israeli State and Society: Boundaries and Frontiers* (Buffalo, SUNY Press, 1989).

Robert I. Friedman, *The False Prophet: Rabbi Meir Kahane, From FBI Informant to Knesset Member* (New York, Lawrence Hill Books, 1990).

——, "Terror on Sacred Ground: The Battle for the Temple Mount," *Mother Jones,* August–September 1987.

Robert E. Frykenberg, "Revivalism and Fundamentalism: Some Critical Observations with Special Reference to Politics in South Asia," in James W. Bjorkman (ed.), *Fundamentalism, Revivalism and Violence in South Asia* (Riverdale, The Riverdale Co., 1986).

——, "On the Comparative Study of Fundamentalist Movements: An Approach to Conceptual Clarity and Definition" (Unpublished Working Paper, Presented at the Woodrow Wilson Center Seminar, "Religion and Politics," Spring 1986).

Clifford Geertz, *The Interpretation of Cultures* (New York, Basic Books, 1973).

Rene Girard, *Violence and the Sacred* (Baltimore, The John Hopkins University Press, 1977).

Giora Goldberg, "The Struggle for Legitimacy: Herut's Road from Opposition to Power," in Stuart A. Cohen and Eliezer Don-Yehiya, *Conflict and Consensus in Jewish Political Life* (Jerusalem, Bar-Ilan University Press, 1986).

Jay Y. Gonen, *A Psychohistory of Zionism* (New York, Mason/Charter, 1975).

———, "The Israeli Illusion of Omnipotence Following the Six Day War," *Journal of Psychohistory*, No. 6, 1978.

Erik Hoffer, *The True Believer: Thoughts on the Nature of Mass Movements* (New York, Harper and Row, 1951).

Richard Hofstadter, *The Paranoid Style in American Politics* (New York, Knopf, 1965).

C. T. Husbands, "Contemporary, Right-Wing Extremism in Western European Democracies: A Review Article," *European Journal of Political Research* 9, (1981).

Rael Jean Isaac, *Israel Divided* (Baltimore, The John Hopkins University Press, 1976).

———, *Party and Politics in Israel* (New York, Longman, 1981).

Mark Jurgensmeyer, "The Logic of Religious Violence," in David Rapoport (ed.), *Inside Terrorist Organizations* (London, Frank Kass, 1988).

Rabbi Meir Kahane, *Never Again: A Program for Jewish Survival* (New York, Pyramid Books, 1972).

———, *Time to Go Home* (Los Angeles, Nash Publishing, 1972).

———, *Writings 5732–5733* (Jerusalem, Jewish Identity Center, 1973).

———, *The Jewish Idea* (Jerusalem, Institute of the Jewish Idea, 1974).

———, *The Story of the Jewish Defense League* (Radnor, Pa., Chilton Book Company 1975).

———, *Listen World, Listen Jew* (Tucson, The Institute of the Jewish Idea, 1978).

———, *Forty Years* (Miami, Institute of the Jewish Idea, 1983).

———, *Uncomfortable Questions for Comfortable Jews* (Secaucus N.J., Lyle Stuart, 1987).

Jacob Katz, *Out of the Ghetto* (Cambridge, Harvard University Press, 1973).

———, *Tradition and Crisis* (New York, The Free Press, 1961).

Baruch Kimmerling, *Zionism and Territory: The Socio-Territorial Dimension of Zionist Politics* (Berkeley, Institute of International Studies, University of California, 1983).

Hans Kohn, "Messianism," *Encyclopedia of the Social Sciences* (New York, Macmillan, 1935).

Yair Kotler, *Heil Kahane* (New York, Adama Books, 1986).

N. Lamm, "The Ideology of Neturei-Karta: According to the Satmar Version," *Tradition*, Vol. XII, No.1, Fall 1971.

Walter Laqueur, *The Road to War 1967: The Origins of the Arab-Israeli Conflict* (London, Weidenfeld & Nicolson, 1969).

Sam Leheman-Wilzig, "Public Protest Against Central and Local Government in Israel 1950–1979," *Jewish Journal of Sociology*, Vol. XXIX, No.2, December, 1982.

———, "The Israeli Protester," *The Jerusalem Quarterly*, No. 26, Winter 1983.

Charles S. Liebman, "Jewish Ultra-Nationalism in Israel: Converging Strands," in William Frankel (ed.), *Survey of Jewish Affairs* (London, Associated Universities Press, 1985).

Charles Liebman and Eliezar Don Yehiya, *Civil Religion in Israel* (Los Angeles, The University of California Press, 1983).

————, *Politics and Religion in Israel* (Bloomington, The University of Indiana Press, 1984).

Juan J. Linz, *The Breakdown of Democratic Regimes: Crisis, Breakdown and Reequilibrium* (Baltimore, The John Hopkins University Press, 1978).

Ian Lustick, *Arabs in the Jewish State* (Austin, University of Texas Press, 1980).

————, *For the Lord and the Land: Jewish Fundamentalism in Israel* (New York, Council on Foreign Relations, 1988).

————, "The West Bank and Gaza in Israeli Politics," in Steven Heydemann (ed.), *The Begin Era* (Boulder, Westview, 1984).

Ciaran O. Maolain, *The Radical Right: A World Directory* (London, Longman, 1987).

Seymour Martin Lipset, "The Radical Right," *British Journal of Sociology,* No.1, June 1955.

Seymour Martin Lipset and Earl Raab, *The Politics of Unreason* (New York, Harper and Row, 1970).

Peter Medding, *Mapai in Israel: Political Organization and Government in a New Society* (Cambridge, Cambridge University Press, 1972).

Golda Meir, *My Life* (New York, Putnam, 1975).

Raphael Mergui and Philippe Simonnot, *Israel's Ayatollahs: Meir Kahane and the Far Right in Israel* (London, Saqi Books, 1987).

Benny Morris, *The Birth of the Palestinian Refugee Problem, 1947–1949* (Cambridge, Cambridge University Press).

David Nachmias, "The Right-Wing Opposition in Israel," *Political Studies,* Vo.24, No.3 (September 1976).

David Newman (ed.), *The Impact of Gush Emunim* (London, Croom-Helm, 1985).

————, "Gush Emunim Between Fundamentalism and Pragmatism," *Jerusalem Quarterly,* No.39, 1986.

Janet K. O'dea, "Gush Emunim: Roots and Ambiguities," *Forum,* No. 2, 25, 1976.

Stanley G. Payne, *Fascism: Comparison and Definition* (Madison, University of Wisconsin Press, 1980).

Yoav Peled, "Labor Market Segmentation and Ethnic Conflicts: The Social Bases of Right Wing Politics in Israel" (paper presented at the Annual Meeting of the American Political Science Association, Atlanta, September 2, 1989).

Amos Perlmuter, *The Life and Times of Menachem Begin* (New York, Doubleday, 1987).

David Pollock, "Likud in Power: Divided We Stand," in Robert O. Friedman (ed.), *Israel in the Begin Era* (New York, Praeger, 1982).

Marcel Proust, *A la Rechearche du Temps Perdu* (Paris, Gallinard, 1966).

David Rapoport and Yonah Alexander, *The Morality of Terrorism* (New York, Pergamon Press, 1982).

David Rapoport, "Fear and Trembling: Terrorism in Three Religious Traditions," *American Political Science Review,* Vol.78, No.3, 1984.

————, "Messianic Sanctions for Terror," *Comparative Politics,* Vol. 20, No. 2, January 1988.

Walter Reich, "The Kahane Controversy," *Moment,* Vol. 10, No. 2, January–February 1985.

———, *Stranger in My House: Jews and Arabs in the West Bank* (New York, Holt, Reinhart and Winston, 1984).

Hans Rogger and Eugene Weber (eds.), *The European Right* (London, Weidenfeld & Nicholson, 1965).

Michael Roman, *Jewish Kiryat Arba vs. Arab Hebron* (Jerusalem, The Jerusalem Post Press, 1986).

Aaron D. Rosenbaum, "The Tehiya as a Permanent Nationalist Phenomenon," in Bernard Reich and Gershon Kieval (eds.), *Israeli National Security Policy: Political Actors and Perspectives* (New York, Greenwood Press, 1988).

Nadim Rouhana, "Collective Identity and Arab Voting Patterns," in Asher Arian and Michal Shamir, *The Elections in Israel 1984* (Tel Aviv, Ramot, 1986).

John H. Rozenbaum and C. Sederberg, "Vigilantism: An Analysis of Established Violence," *Comparative Politics*, No. 6, 1974.

Howard M. Sachar, *A History of Israel: From the Rise of Zionism to Our Time* (Jerusalem, Steimatzky, 1976).

Nadav Safran, *From War to War: The Arab Israeli Confrontation 1948–1967* (New York, Pegasus, 1969).

Ariel Sharon, *Warrior: An Autobiography* (New York, Simon and Schuster, 1989).

Ya'acov Shavit, *Jabotinsky and the Revisionist Movement* (London, Frank Cass, 1988).

Gary S. Schiff, *Tradition and Politics: The Religious Parties of Israel* (Detroit, Wayne State University Press, 1977).

Edward Shills, *The Torment of Secrecy* (Glencoe, Free Press, 1956).

Joseph Schechtman, *The Life and Times of Vladimir Jabotinsky: Fighter and Prophet* (Silver Springs, Eshel Books, 1986).

Gershon Scholem, *The Messianic Idea in Judaism* (New York, Schoken Books, 1971).

Martin Seliger, *Ideology and Politics* (London, George Allen & Unwin, 1976).

Offira Seliktar, *New Zionism and the Foreign Policy System of Israel* (Carbondale, Southern Illinois University Press, 1986).

Gershon Shafir and Yoav Peled, " 'Thorns in Your Eyes': The Socioeconomic Basis of the Kahane Vote," in Asher Arian and Michal Shamir, *The Elections in Israel 1984* (Tel Aviv, Ramot, 1986).

Michal Shamir and John Sullivan, "The Political Context of Tolerance: The United States and Israel," *American Political Science Review*, Vol. 77, No.4, December 1983.

William Shepard, "Fundamentalism: Christian and Islamic," *Religion*, Vol.17, 1987.

Emmanuel Sivan, *Radical Islam: Medieval Theology and Modern Politics* (New Haven, Yale University Press, 1985).

———, *Religion and Politics in the Middle East* (forthcoming).

Rita J. Simon, *Continuity and Change: A Study of Two Ethnic Communities in Israel* (New York, Cambridge University Press, 1978).

George Sorel, *Reflections on Violence* (New York, Colliers Books, 1961).

Ehud Sprinzak. "Extreme Politics in Israel," *The Jerusalem Quarterly*, No. 15, Fall 1977.

————, "Gush Emunim: The Tip of the Iceberg," *The Jerusalem Quarterly*, No. 21, Fall 1981.

————, "Kach and Rabbi Meir Kahane: The Emergence of Jewish Quasi-Fascism in Israel," in Asher Arian and Michal Shamir (eds.), *The Elections in Israel 1984* (Tel Aviv, Ramot, 1986). Published also in *Patterns of Prejudice* Vol. 19, Nos. 4–5 (1985).

————, *Gush Emunim: The Politics of Zionist Fundamentalism in Israel* (New York, The American Jewish Committee, 1986).

————, "Fundamentalism, Terrorism and Democracy: The Case of Gush Emunim Underground," *Occasional Paper*, Woodrow Wilson International Center for Scholars, 1987, Washington D.C.

————, "From Messianic Pioneering to Vigilante Terrorism: The Case of Gush Emunim Underground," *The Journal of Strategic Studies*, Vol. 10, No. 4, December 1987.

Solomon H. Steckoll, *The Temple Mount* (London, Tom Stacy, 1972).

Zeev Sternhell, *Neither Left Nor Right: The Fascist Ideology in France* (Los Angeles, The University of California Press, 1986).

————, "Fascist Ideology," in Walter Laqueur, *Fascism: A Reader's Guide* (Berkeley, University of California Press, 1976).

Eliezer Shweid, "Jewish Messianism: Metamorphoses of an Idea," *The Jerusalem Quarterly*, No.36, Summer 1985.

Uriel Tal, "The Foundations of a Political Messianic Trend in Israel," *The Jerusalem Quarterly*, No. 35, Spring 1985.

Yonina Talmon, "Millennarism" *International Encyclopedia of the Social Sciences* (New York, Macmillan, 1968).

Mark A. Tessler, "Israel's Arabs and the Palestinian Problem," *The Middle East Journal*, No. 31, 1977.

Shabtai Teveth, *The Cursed Blessing* (London, Weidenfeld & Nicolson, 1970).

Ephraim E. Urbach, *The Sages: Their Concepts and Beliefs* (Jerusalem, Magness Press, 1979).

Michael Walzer, *Just and Unjust Wars* (New York, Basic Books, 1977).

Chaim I. Waxman, "Political and Social Attitudes of Americans Among the Settlers in the Territories," in David Newman (ed.), *The Impact of Gush Emunim*, (London, Croom-Helm, 1985).

————, "Messianism, Zionism and the State of Israel," *Modern Judaism*, Vol. 7, No. 2, May 1987.

David Weisburd and Vered Vinitzky, "Vigilantism as Rational Social Control: The Case of the Gush Emunim Settlers," in M. Aronoff (ed.), *Cross Currents in Israeli Culture and Politics, Political Anthropology*, Vol. 4 (New Brunswick, Transaction Books, 1984).

————and Elin Waring, "Settlement Motivations in the Gush Emunim Movement: Comparing Bonds of Altruism and Self Interest," in David Newman (ed.), *The Impact of Gush Emunim* (London, Croom-Helm, 1985).

R. J. Zvi Werblovsky, "Messiah and Messianic Movements," *The New Encyclopedia Britanica*, Vol. 11 (New York, Encyclopaedia Britannica Inc., 1981).

Gafi Wolfsfeld, "Yamit: Protest and the Media-Research Report," *The Jerusalem Quarterly*, No. 31, Spring 1984.

————, "Collective Political Action and Media Strategy: The Case of Yamit," *Journal of Conflict Resolution*, Vol. 28, No. 3, September 1984.

————, *The Politics of Provocation: Participation and Protest in Israel* (Albany, The State University of New York Press, 1988).

Brian Wilson, *Contemporary Transformations of Religion* (New York, Oxford University Press, 1976).

Robin Wright, *Sacred Rage: The Wrath of Militant Islam* (New York, Linden Press/ Simon and Schuster, 1985).

Avner Yaniv, *Deterrence Without the Bomb: The Politics of Israeli Strategy* (Lexington, Mass., D.C. Heath, 1986).

————, *Dilemmas of Security: Politics, Strategy, and the Israeli Experience in Lebanon* (New York, Oxford University Press, 1987).

Yael Yishai, *Land or Peace: Whither Israel* (Stanford, Hoover Institution Press, 1987).

————, "The Jewish Terror Organization: Past or Future Danger?," *Conflict,* Vol.6, No.4, 1986.

Shimshon Zelniker and Michael Kahan, "Religion and Nascent Cleavage: The Case of Israel's National Religious Party," *Comparative Politics,* 9, October 1976.

Hebrew

Yosef Achimeir and Shmuel Shatzki, *We Are Sikarikin—Documents and Testimonies about Brit Habirionim* (Tel Aviv, Nizanim, 1978).

Walter Akerman, Arik Karmon, and David Zuker, *Education in a Society in the Making* (Jerusalem, the Van-Leer Institute, 1985).

Rabbi Yehuda Amital, *The Elevations from Depts* (Allon Shvut, Yeshivat Ha-Zion Association, 1974).

Gideon Aran, *Eretz Yisrael: Between Politics and Religion* (Jerusalem, The Jerusalem Institute for the Study of Israel, 1985).

————, *From Religious Zionism to Zionist Religion: The Origins and Culture of Gush Emunim* (Unpublished Ph.D Dissertation, Hebrew University of Jerusalem, 1987).

Israel Ariel, *This Good Mountain and the Lebanon* (A Gush Emunim Booklet, 1982).

————, *Atlas of the Land of Israel: Its Boundaries According to the Sources,* Vol. 1 (Jerusalem, Cana Publishing House, 1988).

————, "Things as They Really Are," *Tzfia* I, 1985.

————, "When Shall the Temple Be Built?," *Tzfia* II, 1985.

————, "Introducing Tzfia"; "Israel: One Nation in the Land," in Israel Ariel, Moshe Asher, Yoel Rakovsky, and Amishar Segal (eds.), *Tzfia* Vol.3 (Jerusalem, 1988).

Rabbi Yaacov Ariel-Shtieglitz, "The Halakhic Aspects of the Problem of a Retreat from Eretz Yisrael Territories," *Morasha,* Vol.9, 1975.

Moshe Asher, "The Temple Mount Is Turned into a Forest," *Tzfia* I, 1985.

Rabbi Shlomo Aviner, "And We Did Not Betray Your Covenant," *Artzi,* No.1 (Jerusalem, 1982).

————, "Two Talks with Rabbi Tzvi Tau," in Rabbi Shlomo Aviner (ed.), *Iturei Cohanim* (the journal of Yeshivat Ateret Cohanim), No. 3, 1983.

————, "On the Completion of Eretz Yisrael," *Artzi,* Vol.1, Jerusalem, 1982.

Shlomo Avineri, *Varieties of Zionist Thought* (Tel Aviv, Am Oved, 1980).

Rabbi David Bar-Haim, "Israel Is Called 'Adam'," in Israel Ariel, Moshe Asher, Yoel Rakovsky, and Amishar Segal (eds.), *Tzfia* Vol.3 (Jerusalem, 1988).

Mordechai Bar-Lev, *The Graduates of the Yeshiva High School in Eretz Israel* (Unpublished Ph.D Dissertation, Bar-Ilan University, 1977).

Nahum Barnea, "The Dervish," *Koteret Rashit* (May, 16, 1984).

Mordechi Bar-On, *Peace Now* (Tel Aviv, Hakibbutz Hameuchad, 1985).

Michael Bar-Zohar, *The Longest Month* (Tel Aviv, Levin Epstein, 1968).

———, *Ben-Gurion: A Political Biography* (Tel Aviv, Am Oved, 1976).

Haim Be'er, *The Time of Trimming* (Tel Aviv, Am Oved, 1987).

Uzi Benziman, *Sharon: An Israeli Caesar* (Tel Aviv, Adam Publishers, 1985).

Raphaella Bilski Ben-Hur, *Every Individual Is a King: The Social and Political Thought of Ze'ev (Vladimir) Jabotinsky* (Tel Aviv, Dvir, 1988).

Rabbi Dan Be'eri, "A Temple and a State," *Tzfia* I, 1985.

Yossi Beilin, *The Price of Unification* (Ramat Gan, Revivim Publishing House, 1985).

Shabtai Ben-Dov, *Prophesy and Tradition in Redemption* (Tel Aviv, Yair Publications, 1979).

———, *After the Six Day War: From the Six Day Victory On* (Ofra, Hamidrasha Beeretz Binyamin, 1979).

———, *The Redemption of Israel in the Crisis of the State* (Safad, Hamatmid, 1960).

Menachem Ben Yahsar, "The Temple Mount," *Amudim* 263, January, 1968.

Judith Carp, "Investigation of Suspicions Against Israelis in Judea and Samaria: A Report of the Follow Up Committee (Mimeograph), 1982.

Asher Cohen, "Going Together—the Religious-Seculer Relationship in a Mixed Party," in Charles S. Liebman, *To Live Together: Religious and Secular in Israeli Society* (Keter, forthcoming).

Geula Cohen, *Underground Memoirs* (Tel Aviv, Karni Publishers, 1972).

Yerucham Cohen, *The Allon Plan* (Tel Aviv, Hakibbutz Hameuchad, 1973).

Moshe Dayan, *A New Map, Other Relationships* (Tel-Aviv, Ma'ariv Books, 1969).

———, *Milestones* (Jerusalem, Yediot Achronot edition, 1976).

———, *Living with the Bible* (Jerusalem, Edanim, 1978).

———, *Shall the Sword Devour Forever?* (Jerusalem, Edanim, 1981).

Abba Eban, *Autobiography* (Tel Aviv, Ma'ariv, 1978).

Rafael Eitan and Dov Goldstein, *A Soldier's Story* (Tel Aviv, Ma'ariv Publishers, 1985).

Rabbi David Elboim, "A King's Palace: and Its Fate," *Tzfia* II, 1985.

Israel Eldad, *The First Tenth* (Tel Aviv, Hadar, 1975).

Amos Elon, "The Builders of the Third Temple," in *A Certain Panic* (Tel Aviv, Am Oved Press, 1988).

Yehuda Etzion, *The Temple Mount* (Jerusalem, E. Caspi Publisher, 1985).

———, "On the Potter's Wheel," in Israel Ariel, Moshe Asher, Yoel Rakovksy, and Amishar Segal (eds.), *Tzfia* Vol.3 (Jerusalem, 1988).

Rabbi Yaacov Filber, "The Third Return to Zion," *Morasha*, No.5, June 1983.

Menachem Friedman, *Society and Religion* (Jerusalem, Yad Ben-Zvi, 1977).

———, "The Secular-Religious Relationships Towards the Establishment of the State," in *Issues in the History of the Yishuv and Zionism No.2: The Religious School in Zionism* (Tel Aviv, Am Oved and Tel Aviv University Press, 1983).

Gidi Frishtic, *Takdim*, Vol. 1, Spring 1988.

Ruth Gabizon, Gerald Crumer, Aviezer Ravitsky, and Ehud Sprinzak, *The Ideology of Meir Kahane and His Supporters* (Jerusalem, Van Leer Institute Publications, 1986).

Itzhak Galnoor, *Steering the Polity: Communications and Politics in Israel* (Tel Aviv, Am Oved, 1985).

Shlomo Gazit, *The Stick and the Carrot* (Tel Aviv, Zmora Bitan Publishers, 1985).

Pinhas Genosar, *Lehi Revealed* (Ramat Gan, Bar-Illan University, 1985).

Shimon Golan, *Allegiance in the Struggle* (Efaal, Yad Tabenkin, 1988).

Giora Goldberg and Ephraim Ben Zadok, "Regionalism and Territorial Cleavage in Formation: Jewish Settlement in the Administrated Territories," *Medina, Mimsal Veyahasim Bein Leumiim,* No. 21, Spring 1983.

Rabbi Shlomo Goren, "The Obligation to Enter the Temple Mount," *Tzfia,* Vol. 3, 1988.

Joseph Gorni, *The Arab Question and the Jewish Problem* (Tel Aviv, Am Oved Press, 1985).

Nurit Gretz, "A Few Against the Many: Rhetoric and Structure in the Election Speeches of Menachem Begin," *Siman Kriah,* No. 16–17, April 1983.

Uri Tzi Greenberg, *The Book of the Denunciation and the Belief* (Jerusalem, Sadan Publishers, 1937).

Emmanuel Guttman, "Religion in Israeli Politics: A Uniting or a Dividing Factor?," in Emmanuel Guttman and Moshe Lissak (eds.), *The Israeli Political System* (Tel Aviv, Am Oved Press, 1977).

Eitan Haber, *"Today War Will Break Out": The Reminiscences of Brig. Gen. Israel Lior, Aid-de Camp to Prime Ministers Levi Eskhol and Golda Meir* (Tel Aviv, Edanim Press, 1987).

Isser Harel, *The Truth about the Kasztner Murder* (Jerusalem, Edanim, 1985).

———, *Security and Democracy* (Tel Aviv, Edanim, 1989).

Y. Harkabi, *Fateful Decisions* (Tel Aviv, Am Oved, 1986).

Meir Harnoi, *The Gray Time* (Bnei-Brak Avraham Nave, 1990).

Joseph Heller, *Lehi: Ideology and Politics, 1940–1949* (Jerusalem, Keter, 1989).

Rabbi Israel Hess, "The Genocide Rulling of Torah," *Bat Kol* (the Bar Ilan student paper), February, 26, 1980.

Dan Horowitz and Moshe Lissak, *The Origins of the Israeli Polity* (Tel Aviv, Am Oved, 1977).

Pinchas Inbari, *Triangle on the Jordan* (Jerusalem, Cana, 1982).

Meir Kahane, *Thorns in Your Eyes* (New York, Druker Publishing Co., 1981).

———, *The Challenge: The Chosen Land* (Jerusalem, The Center for Jewish Consciousness, 1973).

———, *Israel's Eternity and Victory* (Jerusalem, The Institute of Jewish Idea, 1973).

———, *Numbers 23:9* (Jerusalem, The Institute of Jewish Idea, 1974).

———, *Law and Order in Israel* (Jerusalem, Kach Movement, 1977).

———, *On Faith and Redemption* (Jerusalem, The Institute of the Jewish Idea, 1980).

———, "Hillul Hashem" (A Kach mimeographed article, n.d).

———, *From the Knesset Stand: The Speeches of Rabbi Kahane in the Knesset* (Jerusalem, Kach Movement, n.d).

Yehoshua Kaniel, "Religion and Community in the World View of the People of the First and Second Aliya," *Shalem,* Vol. 5, 1987.

Rabbi Menachem Kasher, *The Great Era* (Jerusalem, Torah Shlema Institute, 1968).

Jacob Katz, *Halakha and Kabalah* (Jerusalem, The Magnes Press, 1986).

Samuel Katz, *Battleground: Fact and Fantasy in Palestine* (Tel Aviv, Karni, 1972).

———, *A Diplomatic Victory or Geopolitical Holocaust* (Tel Aviv, LIM Pamphlet, 1974).

———, *Neither Might Nor Glory* (Tel Aviv, Dvir, 1981).

Rabbi A. I. Hacohen Kook, *Rav Kook's Letters* (Jerusalem, The Rav Kook Institute, 1962).

Rabbi Zvi Yehuda Kook, *In the Pathways of Israel* (Jerusalem, Menorah, 1968).

———, "Between the People and His Land," *Artzi*, No. 2, May 1982.

Yoel Lerner, "Israel-Republic of South Africa Relations" (Jerusalem, Mimeograph, n.d).

Amia Lieblich, *Kibbutz-Makom: Report from an Israeli Kibbutz* (New York, Pantheon Books, 1981).

Eliezer Livneh, *Israel and the Crisis of Western Civilization* (Tel Aviv, Schoken, 1972).

———, *On the Road to Elon Moreh: Zionism in the Direction of Emunim* (Jerusalem, Gush Emunim Publications, 1976).

Dan Miron, "A Document in Israel: A Detailed Analysis of the Ideological, Political, Literary-Cultural Origins of The Land of Israel Movement and its Founding Manifesto: The People, the Text and What Have Happened to Them," *Politica*, Vol.II, No. 16, August 1987.

Thomas Mayer, *The Muslim Reawakening in Israel* (Givat Haviva, The Institute for Arab Studies, 1988).

Yuval Ne'eman, *The Policy of Open Eyes* (Ramat Gan, Revivim, 1984).

David Niv, *Battle for Freedom: The Irgun Zvai Leumi,* Parts I–V (Tel Aviv, Klausner Institute, 1975).

Hanan Porat, *In Search of Anat* (Bet El, Sifrtiyat Bet El, 1988).

Yehoshua Porat, *The Life of Uriel Shelah* (Yonathan Ratosh) (Tel Aviv, Machbarot Lesafrut, 1989).

Teddy Preuss, *Begin—His Regime* (Jerusalem, Keter Publishers, 1984).

Zvi Raanan, *Gush Emunim* (Tel Aviv, Sifriyat Poalim, 1980).

Itzhak Rabin, *A Soldier's Notebook* (Tel Aviv, Ma'ariv Books, 1979).

Aviezer Ravitzky "The Expected and the Possible: Messianism, Zionism, and the Future of Israel as Reflected in the Divided Religious Opinions in Israel," in Alouph Hareven (ed.), *Towards the 21st Century: Targets For Israel* (Jerusalem, Van-Leer), 1984).

Eli Reches, *The Arab Village in Israel: A Revived Political and National Focus* (Tel Aviv, Shiloah Institute Publications, 1985).

Amnon Rubinstein, *From Herzl to Gush Emunim and Back* (Tel Aviv, Schocken Publishing House, 1980).

Danny Rubinstein, *On the Lord's Side: Gush Emunim* (Tel Aviv, Hakibbutz Hameuchad, 1982).

Yochai Rudik, "The Jewish Underground Between "Gush Emunim" and the "Redemption Movement," *Kivunim* (Summer, August 1987).

Rabbi Yehuda Shaviv (ed.), *A Land of Settlement: Our Right on Eretz Yisrael* (Jerusalem, The Young Mizrahi Generation, 1977).

Haggai Segal, *Dear Brothers* (Jerusalem, Keter, 1987).

Moshe Halevi Segal, *Generation to Generation* (Tel Aviv, Ministry of Defense, 1985).

———, "We Have Had Enough of the Brotherhood of Mankind," *Tzfia* I, 1985.

———, "The Land, the People and the Torah" in Israel Ariel, Moshe Asher, Yoel Rakovsky, and Amishar Segal (eds.), *Tzfia* Vol.3 (Jerusalem, 1988).

Tom Segev, *1949: The First Israelis* (Jerusalem, Domino, 1984).

Ze'ev Schiff and Ehud Ya'ari, *A False War* (Tel Aviv, Schocken, 1984).

Moshe Shamir, *My Life with Ishmael* (Tel Aviv, Ma'ariv, 1968).

———, *Facing the Mighty War* (Jerusalem, Shikmona, 1974).

Anita Shapiro, *Berl Katznelson: A Biography* (Tel Aviv, Am Oved, 1980).

Yonathan Shapiro, *Democracy in Israel* (Ramat-Gan, Massada, 1977).

———, *Chosen to Command: The Road to Power of the Herut Party: A Socio-Political Interpretation* (Tel Aviv, Am Oved, 1989).

Dov Shilansky, *In A Hebrew Prison* (Tel Aviv, Armoni Press, 3rd. ed., 1980).

Zvi Shiloah, *A Great Land for a Great People* (Tel Aviv, Ot-Paz publications, 1970).

———, *The Guilt of Jerusalem* (Tel Aviv, Karni, 1989).

Eliezer Shveid, *The Lonely Jew and His Judaism* (Tel Aviv, Am Oved, 1975).

Yehuda Slutzky, *The History of the Haganah*, Part II, Vol. 2 (Tel Aviv, The Ministry of Defense, 1973).

Sasson Sofer, Begin: *An Anatomy of Leadership* (New York, Basil Blackwell, 1988).

Ehud Sprinzak, *The Emergence of Politics of Delegitimation in Israel 1967–1972* (Jerusalem, Eshkol Institute Publications, 1974).

———, "Altalena, Thirty Years After: Some Political Thoughts," *Medina Mimshal Veyehasim Bein Leumiim*, No. 14, Spring 1979 (Review essay).

———, "Gush Emunim: The Iceberg Model of Political Extremism," *Medina Mimshal Veyehasim Bein Leumiim*, No. 17, Fall 1981.

———, *Every Man Whatsoever Is Right in His Own Eyes: Illegalism in Israeli Society* (Tel Aviv, Sifriyat Poalim, 1986).

Itzhak Tabenkin, *The Lesson of the Six Day War: The Settlement of an Undivided Land* (Tel Aviv, Hakibutz Hameuchad, 1971).

———, *Collected Speeches*, Vol. IV (Tel Aviv, Hakibbutz Hameuchad, 1979).

Shabtai Tevet, *Moshe Dayan* (Tel Aviv, Schoken, 1971).

———, *David's Passion: The Life of David Ben-Gurion* (Tel Aviv, Schoken, 1987).

Rabbi Binyamin Tzvielli, "Democracy and Its Corruption vis-à-vis Eternal Judaism," in Israel Ariel, Moshe Asher, Yoel Rakovsky, and Amishar Segal (eds.), *Tzfia* Vol.3 (Jerusalem, 1988).

Aliza Weisman, *The Evacuation: The Story of the Uprooting of the Settlements in the Yamit Region* (Beth-El, Beth-El Library, 1990).

Ezer Weizmann, *The Battle for Peace* (Jerusalem, Edanim Publishers, 1981).

Haim Yahil, *Vision and Struggle: Selected Writings* (Tel Aviv, Karni, 1977).

Zvi Yaron, *The Teaching of Rav Kook*, 3rd ed. (Jerusalem, The Jewish Agency Press, 1979).

Nathan Yelin-Mor, *The Fighters for the Freedom of Israel* (Tel Aviv, Shikmona, 1974).

Sarit Yishai, "Geula Cohen: In Love Just as in Politics I Am Going to the End," *Monitin*, February 1979.

Hebrew Periodicals

Al Hamishmar
Davar
Ha'aretz
Hadashot
Hair
Hatzofe
Kol Hair
Kol Yerushalaim
Ma'ariv
Nekuda
Yediot Achronot
Yerushalaim
Zot Ha'aretz

Index